EXPERIENCING YOUTH

First-Person Accounts

Second Edition

George W. Goethals
Harvard University

Dennis S. Klos
California School of Professional
Psychology

UNIVERSITY
PRESS OF
AMERICA

LANHAM • NEW YORK • LONDON

Copyright © 1986 by

George W. Goethals and Dennis S. Klos

University Press of America,® Inc.

4720 Boston Way
Lanham, MD 20706

3 Henrietta Street
London WC2E 8LU England

Copyright © 1976, 1970 by Little, Brown and Company, Inc.

Library of Congress Cataloging-in-Publication Data

Goethals, George W.
Experiencing youth.

Originally published: Boston : Little, Brown, c1976.
Bibliography: p.
1. Adolescent psychology—Case studies.   2. College
students—Psychology—Case studies.   I. Klos, Dennis S.
II. Title.
BF724.G58   1986   155.5   86-23370
ISBN 0-8191-5688-4 (pbk. : alk. paper)

To
Robert Winthrop White
Generous Teacher and Valued Friend

preface

Our purpose in this book is primarily to present a series of auto-biographical studies in what may rather loosely be called the psychology of adolescence. By themselves these cases can be illuminating examples of both the uniqueness and the similarity of human experiencing during the late-adolescent and post-adolescent stages of the life cycle. If used along with a textbook, an anthology, or a selection of short paperbacks on young adult development, these first-person accounts serve as subjective, personal data for analysis in the context of theory or empirical studies.

These cases are rich enough to be examined from several perspectives; the reader or instructor can choose his or her own context or approach. The general introduction and short essays before each subsection of this book are suggestive of *one* approach. Our approach is from the perspective of clinical personality theory — drawing on the psychoanalytic, interpersonal, and phenomenological literature on experiencing and development.

The book is divided into three parts: cases dealing with *autonomy*, with *identity*, and with *sexual intimacy*. This division is for emphasis, and in any given case all three themes may be present. Each case within these three parts has its own introduction, which summarizes some of the narrative and identifies one or more psychological issues raised by the case. With the exception of Case 25, the titles are the creation of the authors of this book, not of the case writers.

The cases for the first edition had two sources: students in a course on interpersonal theory and object relations and students in a course on the psychology of adolescence. All but three of the cases were written by undergraduates at one college. For the second edition, fourteen cases were discarded and fifteen new ones were added in order to broaden our sample and to address issues more contemporary to the 1970's. This new edition includes cases by undergraduate students, graduate students, and extension students at five colleges and universities in New England. Using Lloyd Warner's criteria for assessing social-economic status, we conclude that 40 percent of the cases come from persons whose families are from the lower-middle class and 60 percent from the upper-middle class. There is no representation of lower-lower, upper-lower, lower-upper, or upper-upper classes. Eleven percent of the case authors are black and 89 percent are white. In terms of religious background, 14 percent come from Roman Catholic families, 29 percent from Jewish families, and 57 percent from Protestant families.

Besides featuring cases from a wider representation of students and schools, the second edition includes a note on levels of difficulty for the cases; a new essay on the case method as a teaching technique; a different approach to *Identity*, which is organized around sexual, vocational, political, racial, and ethnic aspects of identity; an additional approach to *Sexual Intimacy*, based on Carl Rogers's phenomenological theory of personal growth; and an *Epilogue* that discusses some of the current issues in the field of personality psychology and the study of lives.

The reader should keep in mind what might be called the "ethnographic present" of the cases. It is easy to assume that since these cases were written by young adults, they will deal almost entirely with problems of late adolescence and young adulthood. Naturally, in many of the cases this is true. However, some cases illustrate the reawakening of early childhood conflicts heightened by the experience of adolescence, or a continuing concern with critical experiences at the time of puberty and early adolescence. It is extremely important for the reader to determine for himself the temporal dimension of each case and to question what might have led the protagonist to adopt that particular time sequence. Another factor to keep in mind is that a case is subject to all the influences to which human beings are vulnerable. No case is a full picture. It is a fragment. It is a still life out of a rapidly moving montage. Just as we never can know enough about ourselves, we never can know enough about the characters in a given case. At best, we have to use calculated inference. The theoretical interpretation of the human personality, particularly personality in as mercurial a period of life as adolescence, requires some way of making systematic the intricacies and contradictions of life. In the theoretical essays, the authors attempt to provide a framework for the disparate ideas and experiences revealed in the cases.

This book is the living record of the generation presently experiencing the transition from the world of youth to the world of the adult. It is in every sense ultimately their book. They are speaking for themselves. They speak eloquently and with courage, and they have permitted us to review the most intimate workings of their lives. All names, dates, locations, and occupations have been carefully disguised in order to preserve each case author's privacy.

Level of Difficulty of Psychological Analysis

Students and teachers who used the first edition in courses on youth have remarked that the cases vary in difficulty; for example, a few of the cases are better understood when the reader has a familiarity with some psychological theory or has had some life experience beyond the college years. For any course, the choice and sequence of cases depend on the type of course, the range of experience and academic level of the students, and the instructor's own evaluation of which cases work best given his or her teaching style. The following rating scheme may help the instructor choose a sequence of cases for a particular course:

> **Level 1:** These accounts of interpersonal situations are so close to the lives of the students that no previous course work is required for a thoughtful discussion. Cases 1, 3, 4, 8, 15, 16, 20, 21.
>
> **Level 2:** Some familiarity with developmental psychology would enhance an *interpretation* of the case material, but is not necessary for an interesting *discussion* where students use their own experiences as bases for psychological analysis. Cases 2, 5, 6, 7, 9, 10, 11, 12, 13, 14, 17, 18, 19, 23.
>
> **Level 3:** These cases are rich enough to be discussed by students at different levels of psychological sophistication; but some previous course work on the human life cycle or some life experience beyond the college years is required for a full interpretation of psychodynamics and interpersonal processes. Cases 22, 24, 25, 26.
>
> **Level 4:** Only the last case requires some previous course work in abnormal psychology in addition to a knowledge of developmental theory. Case 27.

Acknowledgments

We are grateful to numerous people who contributed to the preparation of the first edition: to Susan Adelman, David R. Edelstein, Steven Simon, Malcolm O. Slavin, Gregory E. Thomson, and Susan Contratto Weisskopf for their interest, advice, and support; to Kenneth Keniston, Lee Shulman, and Robert Rosenthal for their helpful and critical suggestions at the beginning of this undertaking; to Natalie N. Goethals and Sarah F. Klos for their invaluable comments and substantive contributions at every stage of the manuscript preparation; and to the editorial staff of Little, Brown and Company, especially David W. Lynch for his careful assistance and Alfred L. Browne, III, for his overall support and encouragement.

We are grateful to the following people for their contributions to the second edition: to Charles Ducey, Robert Goldstein, Gerald Mohatt, Stephen Morse, Alice Skinner, Bonnie Spring, and Robert Steele for their help in gathering some of the new case studies; to Peter Merman, Carl D. Smith, and Bernadette Nelson-Shapiro who made helpful and critical comments on our plan for revising the first edition; and to Mylan Jaixen and Elizabeth Morgan of Little, Brown and Company for their many useful suggestions and editorial assistance.

By its very nature, this collection exists because a group of students trusted their teachers. Their willingness to make public a portion of their lives is something that can be acknowledged but never fully or sufficiently.

Our thanks to Robert W. White, to whom this book is dedicated, are difficult, if not impossible, to communicate. Although he did help to review and criticize both preliminary and final forms of the first edition, his contribution is much more profound. For more than twenty-five years, as Professor of Clinical Psychology at Harvard, Robert White guided generations of students with a patience that knew no bounds, with a meticulousness that had no limit, and with a sense of scholarship that few could ever emulate. He was not only a scholar, but an artist of the case; and we hope this small token that we have made to him will speak, too, for the many students whom he has taught and deeply influenced.

contents

autonomy

identity

sexual intimacy

A Guide to Teaching and Learning
with First-Person Accounts

Uses of Case Material

One of the questions most frequently asked the editors of *Experiencing Youth* is, "How do teachers and students use these case studies in their courses?" This introductory essay is an answer to that question based on our own and other instructors' experiences during the last few years.

This case book has been used in courses such as Psychology of Adolescence, Psychology of Adjustment, Personality Theories, Introductory Psychology, Youth and Society, Human Sexuality, Human Development, Interpersonal Relations, Group Dynamics, Psychobiography, Counseling Psychology, Marriage and the Family, and American Character and Social Structure. Some instructors use case studies as data on the psychological functioning or organization of the "whole person" by considering the case writer's beliefs, values, attitudes, needs, interests, aspirations, feelings, fantasies, defenses, or interpersonal style. Other instructors analyze interpersonal relationships, especially between parent and child, siblings, and peer intimates, and within peer groups, or the whole family as a social system. Here the academic task is to identify patterns in the quality and levels of interaction and communication. Still other instructors prefer to address the case material mainly as it relates to a particular developmental issue or social issue such as sexuality, sex role, intimacy, dependency, defensive or coping style, drug use, political activity, generational differences, alienation, or youth culture. Many of the case studies are so rich that they may be approached from all three perspectives. The case studies are used most often in discussion groups of ten to twenty persons, typically formed by sectioning large lecture courses. However, some teachers ask students to read a case study before coming to a lecture so that the instructor can refer to that case when speaking on a particular topic. Those teachers use the case data to illustrate the application of a theoretical concept or the relevance of a generalization based on trends in research results. The instructor's analysis of the case material can be a model for students to emulate or a topic for later discussion. Cases also have been used in conjunction with written assignments; a consideration of case material in terms of certain concepts or research conclusions can be the basis for a short paper or an examination question.

Students typically find case studies interesting and personally relevant, and sometimes have to wrestle back their loaned copy of the book from roommates, friends, and parents. Students need no incentive to read these accounts and will, if asked, proceed straight through the book in one week. However, experience has shown that reading one case after another without intervening discussion and consideration of course concepts leaves the reader with a feeling that case material is disjunctive with academic study. We emphatically recommend that cases be assigned one at a time along with relevant theoretical or research material chosen from a journal, monograph, reader, or textbook. Case material provides an opportunity to test the usefulness of a theory or a set of research conclusions. Trying to apply a concept or generalization to actual data facilitates the student's understanding, recall, and awareness of the proper limits for application. A case typically has so much in it that students appreciate the instructor's providing a context for examining the case.

Since a good case can support several kinds of discussion, teachers with various interests or approaches can use the same case in different ways. In order to understand the potential uses of cases, we asked instructors to give examples of readings they actually assigned along with particular cases. The diversity of approaches to the same case is illustrated by the list of readings that teachers matched with Case 24, "The Magician": Sigmund Freud's "On Narcissism" (1914); Rogers' "To Be That Self Which One Truly Is" in On Becoming a Person (1961); Sullivan's "Early Adolescence" in The Interpersonal Theory of Psychiatry (1953); Laing's "The Inner Self and the Schizoid Condition" in The Divided Self (1965); Jourard's "Healthy Personality and Self-Disclosure" and "The Lethal Aspects of the Male Role" in The Transparent Self (1971); White's "Competence and the Psychosexual Stages of Development" in The Nebraska Symposium on Motivation (1960); Erikson's "The Life Cycle" in Identity: Youth and Crisis (1968); Putney and Putney's "Sexualization" in The Adjusted American (1964); Maslow's "Love in Self-Actualizing People" in Motivation and Personality (1954); Goffman's "The Arts of Impression Management" in The Presentation of Self in Everyday Life (1959); Bugental's The Search for Authenticity (1965); Blos's "Postadolescence" in On Adolescence (1962); Fairbairn's "Schizoid Factors in the Personality" in An Object Relations Theory of Personality (1962); Fullerton's "The Pool of Eligibles" in Survival in Marriage (1972); and chapters from Winch's Mate Selection (1958). After a while, each instructor will discover combinations of concepts and cases which students can respond to and which will work well within the rationale or structure of the course.

Reading a First-Person Account

Often we ask students, "What went on in your mind as you read that case study? Can you recall your thoughts or feelings?" We ask this question to identify personal styles of case reading and to learn why some people seem to get more out of the experience than others do.

On first reading, most people have one or more of the following experiences: being engrossed in the writer's account of his personal world; feeling a persistent urge to pass judgment on what the writer reports; using the first-person account as a stimulus for thinking about one's own "case." A reader who is captivated by the writer's subjective report is likely to say, "I have never known anyone like that — it was fascinating to hear about someone so different from me," or "Until I read that case I never dreamed that someone else had the same kind of family [etc.] as mine." Seeing another person's point of view can be informative or reassuring if the reader is open to listening and learning. With the attitude that *any* case can teach him or her *something* about human experiencing, a reader will find each case a potential psychological adventure.

The second type of reaction to a case, treating it as an opportunity for passing judgment on the case writer, is ultimately less rewarding. People sometimes doubt the sincerity of the case writer and dismiss the case as invalid, incomplete, or biased. Very few people retain this attitude after learning that other readers had a different experience. And a few people limit themselves to using the case as an opportunity to affirm absolutes about morality or normality. They seek an answer to the question, "Is such and such right or wrong, healthy or sick?" We hope that this type of reader will gradually overcome dualistic thinking* by being exposed to persons with pluralistic approaches to interpreting human behavior. It is natural to raise questions about basic values — and college students are particularly eager to consider morality and normality when reading case material. However, distinction must be made between exploring the vicissitudes of a value-laden question and seeking a definitive answer that applies to everyone.

The third tendency, to use the case as a stimulus for thinking about one's own experience, may allow one to develop

* Compare Perry (1970).

self-awareness by focusing attention on his or her personal reaction to parts of the case. A few self-conscious notes on the memories, feelings, thoughts, or fantasies evoked by the reading can be a rich source of personal material for later self-analysis. This exercise is usually extraneous to the academic course, but nevertheless is cherished by some students who do it. As they read, these people might ask, "Do I identify or disidentify with certain persons in the case? Do I have intense reactions or no reaction to hearing about another person's experience? Do I tend to explain, defend, criticize, or dismiss certain points of view? Am I interested in *some* developmental or social issues but not in others? Do I feel some anxiety, depression, anger, sympathy, joy, or elation? Do I reassure myself that I would or could handle a situation better than the case writer does?"

Summarizing the point of view of the case writer or of another person in a case study is a useful exercise after a first reading. Difficulty in summarizing another person's point of view sometimes indicates that the reader is judgmental rather than curious and open to learning from others. By trying to understand the writer's point of view a reader can improve his or her ability to listen, to respect the dignity of another, and to learn about human development or interpersonal relations.

The people who learn the most from a case study typically are good at summarizing points of view and are willing to read the case more than once. On the second reading — this time with a good question in mind — one uses the first-person account as *data* for testing the usefulness of a theory or generalization. The goal of a second reading is to identify passages that can be interpreted in light of the values and assumptions of the reader, or those of a theorist whose work is assigned along with the case. Eventually the reader learns not to accept everything the writer says, but to look for direct or indirect corroboration of the writer's interpretation of his experience. Form can be as important as content; how does the writer present his case — with pride, reluctance, apology, denial, obfuscation? And paying attention to what is *not* said by the case writer or noting a discrepancy between what the case writer thought he said and what you heard can help you to understand the writer's personality. Cases are meant to be personally *and* academically useful.

A good case is a tentative bulletin from the core of one's self. It should be spontaneously disclosed to an assumed receptive audience. A good first reading is an encounter with another's experience and one's response. A good second reading is an analytical exercise in which one forms or tests a generalization from theory or research. The epitome of this personal-scholarly approach to personality and social relations is illustrated by Carl Rogers in *On Becoming a Person* (1961) and by Robert White in *Lives in Progress* (1966). They have listened deeply to their clients and students, have carefully considered the assumptions and perspectives of theorists and empiricists, and have used their own experience as a basis for formulating tentative positions on personal experiencing and interpersonal relationship.

Discussing a First-Person Account

We have asked teachers and students to describe what went on in especially successful or educational group discussions of case material. On the basis of what they said, we conclude that certain *attitudes* of teachers and students facilitate or accompany a good discussion.

Probably the most important attitude that group members can share is openness to learning from each other — even from people very different from oneself. This openness includes the assumption that the instructor is just one source of interpersonal learning. When group members assume that they can benefit from considering diverse points of view, they tend to listen more closely to each speaker, ask a speaker to clarify or restate an ambiguous point, and respond directly to the speaker's idea rather than jump into the conversation with a different point as soon as there is a pause or hesitation. When a variety of opinions is valued, people feel freer to speak and to risk making spontaneous or unconventional comments. If there is pressure for unanimity in interpretation, fewer people speak and those who do tend to be guarded or caught up in sensing "what the teacher wants to hear."

Openness to a variety of points of view, however, should be balanced by a willingness for group members to take stands; it does not mean a belief that "anyone's opinion is as good as anyone else's, since generalization per se ultimately is inappropriate in this uncertain world." Discussions tend to be most lively and educational when individuals think through a question and arrive at a conclusion that is felt with some conviction. The conviction comes from combining one's reason, past experience, and intuitive feeling to form a conclusion that can be presented to the group; that is, conviction is felt when one's thought is in line with one's basic values. The goal is to develop a capacity for judgment, rather than a skill for specious explanation. People tend to listen to others who speak with conviction yet are open to hearing opposing or complementary points of view. This attitude is epitomized by the statement, "I tentatively stand by what I say but I am not going to rigidly hold others to my values or view of the world; I am ready to alter my view if people speak convincingly."*

We have also asked discussion leaders for recommendations about teaching techniques that seem especially suited for case discussion. Each of the following comments was recommended by teachers who regularly use case studies in their courses.

Discussions are more satisfying when the teacher assigns a particular case along with some substantive material from a textbook or monograph. The student is asked either to investigate the strength of some generalizations from research in applying them to specific case data, or to test the usefulness of a theory by trying to explain the case data in terms of that theory. If the assigned textbook material is readily understood by students, they can immediately begin to relate it to the case narrative. However, if students have not quite grasped the concepts, it is better to clarify and explain them before the group tries to discuss the case. And if students tend to reiterate case content or give personal explanations of what happened in a case, the instructor will need to redirect the conversation toward specific data-rich passages and their relation to the other assigned material. Theories or generalizations thus provide a context for discussing a case.

Finding a balance between instructor input and student input to the discussion is important; an instructor-dominated discussion may deprive group members of hearing a variety of points of view, and a student-dominated discussion often lacks focus, addresses tangential issues, or becomes mired in nit-picking debate. It is also important to know how to handle disagreement. Disagreement can be educational, especially when the group can identify the basic assumptions and underlying value differences which characterize each opposing view. However, once this is done, the group should go on to another issue.

The transition from one issue to another can be eased by making periodic summaries of what has been said so far. Summaries facilitate awareness of the direction and scope of the conversation and give group members more than one opportunity to hear good points that were made. It is also useful to change the frame of reference several times in a discussion; for example, the case may be considered subjectively in terms of the point of view of each person in the case, and it may then be objectively studied through application of one or more theories to the situations in the case. The objective discussion can be followed by students' views

* See Perry (1970). This is Perry's concept of commitment within a relativistic world.

on the merit of each theorist's likely interpretation. Or the frame of reference can be switched from explaining what has happened to speculating on what might happen. What personal changes are *likely* in the near future given the developmental path and social situation of a case protagonist, and what changes are desirable, from the reader's point of view?

Some instructors highly recommend having each student write a one-page paper on the case before coming to class and then asking for volunteers to read their statements. Other instructors urge students to form study groups of two or three persons to discuss the case before coming to class; the quality and range of class discussion often is better. Two instructors often ask students to role play various persons in a case in order to investigate the implications of various complementary role relationships. And one instructor occasionally asks students to rate various persons in a case using Leary's Interpersonal Adjective Check List and Edwards' Personal Preference Schedule. The most general and frequent recommendation is to discover what works best with the instructor's teaching style and what best fulfills the student's purpose for taking the course. The most satisfied instructors keep trying different methods and have the courage to keep asking students if they are learning.

Selected Theoretical Concepts

In this book we will study personal histories or fragments of personal histories. These are not, however, fictional abstractions; they are the creative projections, to use Henry Murray's term, of people who are in the midst of one of the most complex periods in their lives. Whatever the feelings, the agonies, the joys, the moments of self-assumed triumphs or tragedies, they are presented as they are, and are what they are, because each of the individuals had a vitally alive and growing body, each a personality in the making, each living in the midst of a particular time in political and social history. Like all of us, they are implicated in their times and culture.

The study of adolescence can never be separated from contextual considerations. If adolescence is one of the most tumultuous moments in an individual's history, it is so because much of the inner and outer world is so salient and so vivid to the individual at this time. Further, the individual is intensely aware of and responsive to what previous moments in his history may have engendered. This is indeed an age in which the "epiphanies" of James Joyce abound.

There are myriad ways of approaching the study of adolescence and as many lines of emphasis. In this book, because we are dealing with personal material for the most part, we restrict our discussion to those materials which we feel have the most use in understanding the clinical picture of the individual. We believe that psychoanalytic psychology, using the term very loosely, is probably the best way for a student to learn about the intricacies of individual development. We do not believe that psychoanalytic theory is necessarily holy writ or that it is, within the behavioral sciences, the best approach to understanding human development generally. But many of its ideas are extremely fruitful in understanding adolescence. Unlike child psychology, which has in the work of Piaget a powerful alternative to the psychoanalytic theory of development, the study of adolescence as yet has no alternative, at least not at the clinical level. The introductions that follow thus treat those theoretical ideas which we think now have the most meaning for understanding what is going on in any individual's life during this most ambiguous period of personal history.

It is important to distinguish between that subject matter which deals with adolescence and that which conforms to a theoretical substratum for understanding the dimensions of individual lives. Thus, we do not deal explicitly in the interpretive material of this book with such classical studies as Hollingshead's *Elmtown's Youth* (1949) or James Coleman's study *The Adolescent Society* (1961). This is in no way to be construed as a pejorative judgment of such work. It is rather that we focus here on those aspects of psychology — including psychoanalytic theory — which are most germane to individual cases. It is an author's responsibility to be clear about his focus, and it is his privilege to be selective. Any book, including this one, is to be seen as a beginning of study rather than an end.

The Study of Adolescence by Not Studying It

It can be argued with a great deal of validity that the best way to study adolescence is to read those representations of it produced in the world of creative writing. Of this there is no doubt. The adolescence of the Roman Catholic boy and girl struggling for autonomy is nowhere more brilliantly portrayed than in James T.

Farrell's *Studs Lonigan* or in the early work of Mary McCarthy, particularly *The Company She Keeps*. *Manchild in the Promised Land* by Claude Brown as well as Richard Wright's *Native Son* with almost physical impact depict the world and the coming of age of the ghetto Negro. Marquand's work depicts with acid brilliance what it was to come of age in the upper strata of New England and New York society, and William Faulkner has depicted in *The Bear* the *rite de passage* which marks the transition between the world of the child-man and the man who possesses his own stable sense of person. If one wishes to become halfway facetious, it can be argued that the best way to teach a course in adolescence is to spend a semester reading *The Confessions of St. Augustine*. Nowhere and at no time have the agonies and poignancies of this time of life been so vividly portrayed. St. Augustine's work is important not only in its substance but also in its suggestion that despite variations in time and place there are certain key problems, certain fundamental tasks involved in reaching maturity. One could go on endlessly. On the level of an epic sweep much could be learned about adolescence by studying the early work of James Joyce and the work of Thomas Mann. On a more subdued and simple level Robert Anderson's *Tea and Sympathy* can be seen not merely as a matter of sexual introduction but even more important as the complex problem of what masculinity is and is not to the adolescent male.

Why then is it not possible to adopt the position analogous to Freud's in his discussion of the feminine psyche and say that the study of adolescence is best left to the poet, one's own experience, and future science, and forget or at least minimize the imperfect state of theoretical and scientific knowledge? Such a position is certainly aesthetically pleasing and spiritually satisfying. Yet, scholarship demands that we organize our knowledge as best we can at any time, sparse as it may be. In times of profound, turbulent social change, times that have revolutions within revolutions, it is well for all of us to follow Kurt Lewin's dictum that the best guide to research — or understanding — is good theory. Yet we find ourselves faced with the fact that there is no one theory of adolescence; there are rather different perspectives, different approaches to this problem which range very widely in their subject matter. One purpose here is to try in a relatively small space to summarize certain contemporary positions concerning adolescence.

One final word of a general nature. Since adolescence itself is somewhat of an ambiguity, creating great difficulties in definition, the literature concerning adolescence falls into two quite different general areas. Some literature pertaining to adolescence is explicitly concerned with the adolescent process of development and these

materials stand in their own right, be these the monumental work
of G. Stanley Hall, written in 1904, or James Coleman's attempt to
understand the social networks of the American high school (1961).
As valuable as these works pertaining explicitly to adolescence are,
another corpus of knowledge is as important though not as readily
available to the person who approaches adolescence. We refer to
various articles which, while not dealing explicitly with adolescence,
are of tremendous value in helping us to understand certain of its
dimensions. Examples might be: Robert White's three concise
discussions of motivation and ego integration (1959, 1960, 1963a),
Theodore Kroeber's incisive work on coping mechanisms (1963),
and Roger Burton and John Whiting's work on father absence
(1961). None of these articles deals directly with adolescence, but
all are vital in attaining any degree of sophisticated understanding.
This essay will guide the reader to both kinds of literature so that
his repertoire for understanding this fascinating era and the cases
which follow may be as sophisticated as possible.

Psychoanalytic Theory and Its Contributions
to the Study of Adolescence

One of the most important theoretical arenas for the study of
adolescence is psychoanalytic theory. Here, possibly more than in
any other place, is the caution mentioned previously necessary; one
must recognize the importance of both explicit and tangential
contribution. For example, while Anna Freud's essay *The Ego and
Mechanisms of Defense* (1946) may be interpreted as a contribution
to ego psychology, it can also be seen as a key work in
understanding adolescence from the psychoanalytic point of view.
Similarly, Freud's remarkable discussion of the "Case of Dora"
(1950) can be interpreted either as a study of the etiology of
hysteria or as the study of the problems of the feminine adolescent.
On the other hand, theorists such as Peter Blos (1962) and Erik
Erikson (1959) in particular discuss adolescence and youth
explicitly from the psychoanalytic point of view.

As Anna Freud (1958) has pointed out, the psychoanalytic
concern with adolescence as a period of development has posed
great difficulty and also aroused great interest. Until recently,
psychoanalytic discussions of adolescence have been few and far
between. Anna Freud points out that following the publication of
her father's work in 1905 a hiatus of seventeen years elapsed before
the historically important works of Ernest Jones (1922), Bernfeld
(1923), and Aichhorn (1925) were published. This was no doubt
because of the conviction in early psychoanalytic circles that early
childhood was the critical period in the formation of personality.

It was not until much later that the central meaning of adolescence became clear from this theoretical standpoint. We must digress into why this conviction came about.

In one of his later essays (1933), Freud observes that from the very beginning of psychoanalytic theory and its construction there was the conviction that neurotic disorder arose because of a conflict between human impulse and the inhibitions that human beings during their socialization set up against these impulses. What impulses are involved and what is the nature of the inhibitions?

For Freud the central motivation in human affairs was sexual. For him, all other motives of whatever kind were derived from transformation of man's basic primary process. But impulse alone is not sufficient. It must be applied and expressed. Freud (1950) first saw in the family romance and its culmination in the Oedipal dilemma the key to human personality, and he proposed a concept that became central in psychoanalytic theory: the meaning of object relationships in the human life cycle. Freud illuminated the fact that society demands that the first object relationships, namely those with parents, be rejected before social learning in the broadest sense of the word can proceed. This tumultuous end of the era of childhood, Freud felt, determined relative health or illness for the rest of an individual's life. Interestingly enough, Freud made his statements on this theoretical formulation most explicit in his discussion of feminine development.

As his work proceeded, Freud (1953) began to realize that the physiology of puberty had meaning in and of itself, and in his remarkable essay on the "Transformations of Puberty" he began to elucidate a line of thinking that is still the heart of the orthodox psychoanalytic interpretation of adolescence. Stated very briefly, this position proposes that at puberty, with the physiological changes that occur, the individual for a time is caught between the two worlds — the old object relationships he had as a young child previous to the Oedipus complex and the new object relationships he wishes to form. There is a kind of psychic agony that continues until adolescence is successfully completed. Anna Freud (1958) so brilliantly expands this point in her work on adolescence, demonstrating that this reorganization of sexuality in its broadest sense is probably the most difficult task in an individual's history and leads him, for a while, to become what Kurt Lewin has called "the marginal man." It is a time when young people's behavior is extremely fluid; they can be one day bohemian, the next ascetic, one day generous to a fault, the next selfish and cruel. All these variations, shifts, and changes are related to the adolescent's attempt to cope with these new and powerful impulses.

One contribution of psychoanalytic theory, particularly the

work of Anna Freud (1958) and that of Blos (1962) later, is to sensitize us to the fact that adolescence is a time not only of ego restructuring but of redefining of sexuality and focusing of genital energies away from the family to one's peer group. Those who adopt this position see adolescence as a time of profound upset and conflict, a time when it is next to impossible to distinguish between normality and pathology, a time of rapid and mercurial shifts and changes. They maintain that such an upset is not only inevitable in human development but necessary for normal personality integration.

The Contribution of Erik Erikson. Gardner Murphy (1950) once observed that a historical review of work in child and developmental psychology would reveal all the controversies in the field of psychology as a whole. Similarly, the work of Erik Erikson should be recognized in its entirety, not only as a departure from and revision of the orthodox psychoanalytic position, but also one of the most penetrating attempts to use psychoanalytic theory in a modified form to understand adolescence. Erikson thus exemplifies a continuation of the general position of Anna Freud but has elaborated radically on her focus on intrapsychic conflict, which so characterizes the orthodox position. From his first major publication in the United States to his work in 1968, Erikson has consistently dealt with conceptions that made psychoanalytic theory understandable to a wide audience. He has also laid the foundation of at least one approach to the study of adolescence.

Erikson sees adolescence or, as he describes it, "the formation of identity," as the culmination not merely of childhood but of all the interactions and syntheses of interactions that an individual has had up to that point in his history. Erikson's definition is both extremely specific and useful in helping us to understand human personality. He defines identity as: "The capacity to see oneself as having continuity and sameness. It is the consistent organization of experience." While Erikson gives great weight to the problems of object choice and its redefinition, he also insists that all interpersonal relationships and the values and norms of a society are as important to the adolescent as what is transpiring within him. Thus Erikson attempts to answer the criticism long directed at psychoanalytic theory that it has ignored social and cultural factors and concentrated exclusively upon inner reality. Every student of adolescence in the contemporary scene should be familiar with *Childhood and Society* and Erikson's work on identity. Since these books have had particular relevancy to the authors of the following cases, acquaintance with Erikson's work is essential to an understanding of this book. Certain ideas within Erikson's theoretical framework will be discussed explicitly.

The first of these is Erikson's insistence upon the fact that identity formation in adolescence is as critical for human personality as are the identifications and role modelings accomplished early in childhood. In fact, Erikson's theory of adolescence rests, as he once stated, upon the fact that identity formation is required when childhood identifications are no longer sufficient for shaping one's behavior and one's place in the world. Erikson states that his own work is as concerned with identity formation as Freud's work was with the conflicts of childhood sexuality. Thus, in a sense, Erikson's work has reoriented psychoanalytic theory toward the world of experience and the consistent organization by the individual of his experience in the world of reality. He has not rejected the necessity for personality restructuring; he has merely put it into a much broader context.

The second most important contribution Erikson has made is the way in which he deals with the fact that the task of a normal adolescent's development *by its nature* is part of the human destiny, but that this normal process is impeded by the demands of modern society. Erikson proposes that part of adolescence should be a time when choice may be deferred and experimentation permitted so that a psychosocial moratorium may be part of the life cycle paralleling the psychosexual moratorium that occurs during the period of latency. Erikson's sensitivity to the difference between identity formation in primitive and modern society does a great deal to put the postulations of the orthodox position into a contemporary perspective.

Finally, Erikson continually stresses the interpersonal aspects of human existence and the fact that human personality can never exist in terms of personal desires but must exist instead in a framework involving some degree of reciprocity. This is particularly true of adolescence, where the identity of the individual in its formation is meaningless unless it is seen by society as something of value and something that society can incorporate.

Erikson's insights into society are so many and varied that it is somewhat dangerous to suggest that these three conceptions are the key to his position, which should be read and pondered in its entirety.

The Theoretical Insights of Harry Stack Sullivan. If Gardner Murphy's comment about controversy applies to Erikson, it applies even more to the work of Harry Stack Sullivan (1940, 1953, 1954, 1962). Since his work began to appear in the 1930s and 1940s,

Sullivan has been seen by some to have made a highly original and creative breakthrough not only in therapeutic technique but also in theoretical restructuring in psychiatry. Others, however, view his work as simply a restatement of the orthodox position with an unfortunate change to a contorted vocabulary. However, all agree that Sullivan has made a number of penetrating observations of major importance. The first of these is his complete break and departure from the instinct theory of motivation, so much a part of orthodox analytic theory. He refuses to see man as an animal with a sophisticated set of instincts and insists instead upon seeing him as a cognitive creature with an extremely complex set of motives which have to do, not with sexuality, but rather with the problem of living in such a way as to minimize anxiety. Closely related to this rejection of the instinctual nature of motivation is Sullivan's postulation of the fact that a characteristic peculiar to the human species, central to its very survival, is the need for interpersonal relationships of varying kinds at different stages of the life cycle. Sullivan is explicit about this point: ". . . it is a rare person who can cut himself off from mediate and immediate relations with others for long spaces of time without undergoing a deterioration in personality." Because these interpersonal relationships go through dramatic changes in focus and kind during adolescence, his discussion of the adolescent era — as he describes it — is many-faceted and highly detailed. Finally, by this detailed treatment Sullivan argued, as did Blos later, that adolescence was a general era in development subdivided into a number of quite different but very critical substages.

The key to this contribution is Sullivan's extremely fascinating and somewhat paradoxical ideas concerning sexuality and its timing in the development of human personality. His ideas, vastly different from the orthodox psychoanalytic point of view, are central to his theory of adolescence. To most psychoanalytic theorists, the sexual instinct is a lifelong primary motivational state, with all other motives secondary processes deriving from it. Infantile sexuality as opposed to adult or genital sexuality is simply a different patterning of the same fundamental and lifelong motive. Sullivan's approach to sexuality is entirely different and its implications for the study of adolescence are profound. First, Sullivan dismisses completely the orthodox explanation of infantile sexuality. He sees instead sexual behavior in young children, particularly the manipulation of the genitals, not so much as a sexual act but one of body curiosity. The parents, with fateful consequences, may interpret this behavior as sexual and become extremely anxious about it. This anxiety in the parents, according to

Sullivan, induces anxiety in the child, creating "primary genital phobia." The critical point here is that Sullivan is concerned about sexual malfunction coming from anxiety rather than from the sexual motive itself. Thus, one major difference between Sullivan and others is his complete and overt rejection of the *era* of infantile sexuality.

However, his major contribution to theoretical discussions of sexuality and, by implication, of gender, lies in his claim that the sexual dynamism erupts in adolescence, causing a great deal of complexity for the young person. This difficulty is not merely, as proposed by others, a need to shift objects but a need in addition to integrate some highly complex motivational systems separate and distinct from sexuality itself.

This begins, from Sullivan's point of view, with the onset of a highly powerful motive just before adolescence, which he calls the "need for intimacy." This need, Sullivan contends, is for a collaborative as opposed to a cooperative relationship with another person. "The preadolescent evolves the practice of *collaboration*, a valid functional activity as a person in a personal situation. This is a great step forward from cooperation — *I* play according to the rules of the game, to preserve *my* prestige and feeling of superiority and merit. When we collaborate, it is a matter of we. The achievement is no longer a personal success; it is a group performance — no more the leader's than the led." (1940, p. 55) He postulates that happy intimate relationships with the opposite sex are predicated upon a period in an individual's history when close relationships with members of the same sex are experienced.

This need for intimacy, a powerful motive in and of itself, is combined with an equally important experience. This, in Sullivan's theory, is the driving force of the experience of loneliness which causes the self-contained individual at this period to step out of the protective shell of his own self-system and make an attempt to initiate intimate relationships with other individuals. This is naturally a threat to the individual's security systems, and thus the formation of intimate relationships is fraught with anxiety and, at times, profound psychological disorder.

These difficulties are related entirely to the establishment of intimacy with members of the same sex. Thus, when what Sullivan calls the "lust dynamism" erupts in early adolescence, the individual is faced with a number of extremely important tasks which create what he terms collisions between dynamisms. Briefly stated, one must at the risk of one's own personal security transfer the intimacy need from members of the same sex to members of the opposite sex; one must integrate the intimacy need itself with the new powerful motive of lust; and finally, one must not let this new and powerful motive drive one to reject or avoid the possibility of intimacy. Thus Sullivan sees the world from preadolescence to late adolescence as a time of complicated revisions of a series of motivational systems rather than merely as the repatterning of systems that have already existed.

Possibly the most significant contribution Sullivan has made in this discussion is his insistence that the patterning of sexual and genital behavior — the lust dynamism — is a separate and distinct system from that relating to intimacy. This contribution is unique, and its implication for a study of adolescence in a time of relative sexual freedom has enormous implications. It is possible, using Sullivan's framework, to see in men and women the capacity of forming an intimate relationship of a collaborative nature without *necessarily* integrating into that relationship the lust dynamism. Conversely, this theoretical framework suggests that young people can integrate a lust dynamism together without necessarily forming a true intimate relationship in a psychiatric sense. Thus, sex and intimacy become multiple motivations as opposed to what others have viewed as a compressed unitary process. Some of the vicissitudes of adolescence can arise from problems of intimacy rather than sex.

How do Sullivan and Erikson differ and how are they alike? This discussion is limited to their concern with adolescence. While there are many points in common, the difference between their theories is important and has to do with sequence. To Erikson intimacy is not possible until identity has been completed. Sullivan, on the other hand, believes that identity itself is impossible until intimacy with members of both sexes has been experienced. Thus, despite the similarity and emphasis upon the interpersonal, there is great dissimilarity in their discussion of the meaning, phasing, and timing of intimacy and of genital sexuality. For Erikson, to be intimate with others one must first know oneself; for Sullivan, the experiencing of intimacy with others leads to the discovery of self.

Many writers, from an artistic and theoretical point of view, have represented for us the ways in which the adolescent can become confused, disorganized, and lost. Sullivan has gone further and forced us to look not only at the many things that can happen during adolescence but at the many reasons why they occur.

The Work of Robert White. Robert White offers an interesting contrast to Erikson and Sullivan for a number of reasons. It was observed earlier that some theoretical contributions are directly and explicitly related to adolescence. No contribution is more in this spirit than that of Erikson. On the other hand, we saw that some contributions, though ancillary to the psychology of adolescence, over time have shown themselves to be extremely valuable by deepening our understanding of adolescence. Such a contribution is that of Robert White.

In a series of monographs that began in 1959, White set out to attack three issues: first, in 1959, he summarized material from both psychology and psychoanalytic sources in terms of their adequacy as a theory of human motivations; second, a year later, he offered a careful and compelling critique of the psychosexual stages of development and the life cycle theory of Erikson which, while devastating, was completely constructive in tone; third, having coped with a reconsideration of libido theory, he went on to discuss the problem of ego structure. It is quite possible to consider White's writing as an academic though extremely sophisticated exercise in psychological theory and leave it at that. To do so, however, is to fail to see the implications of his critique of human motivation and the meanings that this critique has for understanding some of the complexities that may lie behind adolescent acts. Possibly the most explicit meaning that White's work has for the study of adolescence is his suggestion that effectance, competence, and the capacity to organize one's self into effective working patterns are as important to the growing individual as is the organization of gender and the resolution of interpersonal sexuality. "Adolescents today learn how to drive cars. Some of them learn to compete against adult records in sports, occasionally breaking them. Some of them become part of the football, band, and cheerleader complex that plays an important part in community entertainment. Some of them try their hands at building workable radio sets, at scientific exploration, at editing newspapers, at writing stories and verse, at musical and dramatic performances, at political activity. All of this belongs in the sphere of work . . ." (1960). Thus White has broadened and deepened the spectrum of what is involved for the adolescent in terms of his motivations and how this complex of motivations can affect ego synthesis.

The Psychoanalytic Position and the Problem of Values

In this essay we have attempted to highlight certain trends within general psychoanalytic theory that have become highly relevant to thinking about adolescence. In concluding this part of the overview, one dimension, one historical trend in psychoanalytic thinking requires comment.

It is interesting that both psychology and psychiatry over

the years have confronted, in quite different ways, a specific value
question which has many implications. This is the degree to which
any human being is a unique case to be treated as such or whether
any individual is but a representative of a large class of individuals,
all of whom to varying degrees form a cluster or a topology of
characteristics. In the world of psychology, this controversy has
been most cogently posed by the late Gordon Allport (1937, 1961,
1968). However, even an older view of personality theory,
psychoanalytically based, reveals a great deal of ambivalence in
the world of psychiatry and psychology concerning the emphasis
that should be placed upon "personality types" — exemplified
particularly in the work of Jung and Adler — and to what extent each
individual in his own complexity must be treated solely in terms of
his own specific characteristics. Any clinical science such as
psychiatry is going to teach its practitioners to deal with individual
cases against a background of character types and the question here
is one of degree.

We are interested here in a change of emphasis within the
ethos or philosophical structure of psychoanalytic theory. In Freud's
original work this position is most poignantly summarized in
Civilization and Its Discontents (1957). In this work Freud
postulates an evolutionary theory of the individual and society that is
immensely influenced by the thinking of Darwin. Society's evolution
and the maintenance of that evolution, Freud argues, must be
continued even though there will be a casualty rate in neuroticism
and mental illness. In a sense, Freud saw civilization as a "good
value" to be maintained even at the price of individual unhappiness
and frustration. By implication, the individual must learn as part of
his socialization at any point in his life to conform to the norms and
values of society.

This, however, is no longer the situation and this important
shift toward the psychology of the individual, as opposed to learning
how to conform, is relevant to a consideration of present-day
adolescence. Erikson, from the time of writing his preface to
Childhood and Society (1950) to his recent redefinition of the
concept of identity, has continually emphasized that the capacity
and potential for healthy personality development resides in the
individual but that this capacity for healthy growth is continually
impeded and deflected by the demands of a technological society.
Thus Erikson sees man as basically good but living within the midst
of a confused and disorganizing social order. This is a far cry from
Freud's basic notions that man was inherently evil and the task of
civilization was to keep him relatively domesticated. Sullivan, too,
makes a great deal of the fact — almost to the level of a kind of

Rousseauan romanticism — that the so-called "warps" in personality, particularly those which the individual brings into the adolescent era, are brought about primarily by the inhuman demands placed upon individuals as they grow up in modern society. Sullivan feels that the basic cause of mental illness, particularly the "ultimate dropout" of the schizophrenic process, is the fact that human contact is extremely difficult to obtain and maintain in the modern world.

Peter Blos too is extremely sensitive to the way in which social and cultural values varying from nationality to nationality and from culture to culture can complicate adolescence. This newer position in psychoanalytic theory gives justification for the restlessness of youth, which ranges from the drug scene to extreme student militancy and activism. In a sense, it might be said that the adolescent is anticipating the next step in psychoanalytic theory, the refusal of the individual to become involved in or committed to a society that is basically sick. This is a far cry from Freud's early attempt to defend the status quo.

Possibly the most interesting and provocative advance in this aspect of theory is the work of the British object relations school exemplified by the work of W. R. D. Fairbairn (1952) and summarized so well in Harry Guntrip's book, *Schizoid Phenomena, Object Relations and the Self* (1968). In conventional psychoanalytic thinking the emphasis is upon the functioning of the ego, or self, in a state of integration. Growing up is a continual process relating to this integration and the self is seen essentially as a unity. However, even Freud saw the basic importance and implications of the mother-child relationship and its termination in childhood and anticipated, in his conception of the superego, the fact that the ego might be divided against itself (or split). One could conceive of oneself both in terms of "I am" and "what I ought to be." It is these original notions of Freud that Fairbairn and Guntrip elaborate. In these works the hypothesis is advanced that within civilized society the development of the schizoid position is almost inevitable, owing to the relationship predicated between mother and child. This has led those who belong to this school of thought to postulate the idea of the multiple ego and the need during the process of maturation to synthesize these various fragments and splits in the ego process. It is particularly germane that the problems of relationships, particularly interpersonal relationships between young men and young women, are shown to be extremely difficult because of this heritage from "civilized" childhood. Though Fairbairn can be criticized for his rather arcane attempt to relate personality to physical types as did Kretschmer (1925) and Sheldon (1940), his basic concern with the high probability of ego splitting and difficulty in coming to grips with the interpersonal because of demands of modern society is a step beyond the value positions of Erikson, Blos, and Sullivan.

This suggests a corollary value issue common in the work of Fairbairn and Sullivan, but at least suggested in the work of Erikson and made highly explicit in the recent work of Laing. All these theorists in varying degrees come to their pessimistic conclusions about ego synthesis through their own basic alienation from modern society. Although the conception of the split ego historically can be traced to Freud's development of the concept of the superego, and though pessimism was certainly an aspect of Freud's thinking, the reader should be careful in recognizing that the reasons for this pessimism are quite different. Further, it is important to remember that the concept of the ego split and its relationship to pathology — to say nothing of the definition of pathology itself — is a matter of degree rather than of fact. Freud, for example, once observed that only a pervert could perform a sexually perverted act. By this he meant that fixated homosexuality or fetishistic sexual behavior was different from nonfixated, culturally defined deviant behavior. Sullivan eloquently argues that maturity is to be measured by the breadth and depth of different kinds of involvements, which is another way of saying that a very strong ego has the capacity to be split but at the same time integrated. Thus, again, the concept of ego splits must be viewed as a matter of degree. In extreme cases, the split ego can indeed lead to pathology; but in other cases the adult with a repertoire of ego dimensions may be doing precisely what Maslow (1954) has so cogently defined as "self-actualization."

It is not an oversimplification to say that as psychoanalytic theory has progressed, we have become more aware of a paradox. Clinical scientists originally were concerned with the individual and his adjustments to a basically sound society. They continue to be concerned with the individual but show an equal interest in the way in which nonconformity may be the only healthy defense against a society that is basically inimical to proper personality growth.

The Interdisciplinary Contributions of John W. M. Whiting and Talcott Parsons. Though Whiting and Parsons are eminent in the fields of social anthropology and sociology, some of their work has profoundly influenced personality theory in general and the study of adolescence in particular. Both men, despite their clear identification with their respective disciplines, have always advocated an interdisciplinary approach to the study of human behavior. Whiting, a graduate of the Yale Institute of Human Relations in the 1930s, has always been concerned about the making of a synthesis between behavior theory and psychoanalytic concepts. Talcott Parsons, one of the founders of the Department of Social Relations at Harvard in 1946, has consistently been receptive to ideas deriving from personality and psychoanalytic theory. Their work, like that of Robert White, is tangential to the work on adolescence, but some of their papers may have tremendous effect over time upon research. Whereas Whiting and Parsons represent the behavioral scientists influenced by psychoanalytic and personality theory, Erik Erikson, the psychoanalytic thinker, gives great credit to anthropologists and especially to Scudder Mekeel in his foreword to *Childhood and Society.*

Parsons as a theoretical sociologist is primarily concerned with problems of social structure, but one of his most provocative interests has been a series of papers that began in 1942 dealing with the problem of age and sex role in the social structure of contemporary society. In 1955, in collaboration with Robert F. Bales, he published a fascinating interdisciplinary study entitled *Family, Socialization and Interaction Process.* Since writing that book he has published a number of provocative papers on youth and youth culture and, in collaboration with Gerald Platt (1969), he wrote a paper that may have far-reaching effects on our understanding of student culture. For our purposes in this book, what concerns us most is Parsons' attempt to understand role differentiation between men and women at different ages in our society and how this differentiation may lead to quite different modes of interaction with the world, personal and impersonal. He suggests that men, in their role of breadwinners, must face the world in a highly active fashion and be continually oriented toward the tasks that they must accomplish; thus their style is essentially "instrumental." Women, on the other hand, more concerned with the world of children, the home, and the emotions, are involved with skills of, as he calls it, an "expressive" nature. Parsons, thus, through his introduction of the notion of instrumental and expressive styles as characterizing the general behavior of men and women is beginning to lay a foundation for understanding one of the most important aspects of identity formation, that is, the assumption of culturally defined gender roles.*

* For those interested in the general problem of sex differences as well as some extremely sophisticated critiques of various positions, there is no better reference than *The Development of Sex Differences,* edited by Eleanor E. Maccoby (1966).

John W. M. Whiting is generally recognized among behavioral scientists for his contribution to the use of the cross-cultural method, his refinement of field techniques which would lead to more standard ethnographic practice, and his general interest in socialization which goes back to his first publication *Becoming a Kwoma* (1941). However, these are concerns of the professional anthropologist. But since the mid-fifties Whiting has become increasingly interested in theoretical issues that are highly relevant to understanding adolescence, not only in contemporary industrialized society but in so-called primitive society. This interest took as its point of departure a doctoral dissertation written by one of Whiting's students, Albert Anthony. Anthony investigated the reason why adolescence, in some societies, is marked by extremely stressful initiation rites, and why, in other societies, it is a relatively tranquil experience. This dissertation was later revised and its general findings were summarized in an article in Eleanor Maccoby's *Readings in Social Psychology* (1958). In essence, Anthony, in collaboration with Whiting and Richard Kluckhohn (1958), saw the initiation rites of various primitive tribes as being highly functional rather than merely quixotic. The function of the rites he examines is to produce by their power a traumatic effect on the young adolescent and thus correct the cross-sexed identification in males who, as a consequence of social structure, had been brought up in mother-child households. This paper was followed in 1959 by Whiting's highly provocative paper presented at the Nebraska Symposium entitled "Sorcery, Sin and the Super-ego." This paper is a brilliant example of the use of the cross-cultural method and highlights Whiting's preoccupation with interdisciplinary theoretical thinking. What is most important about this paper, however, is the way in which Whiting shows how intricately related gender definition is throughout the life cycle, particularly in the experiences of infancy and early childhood. The implications of this paper were explored further in 1961 by Burton and Whiting in a paper on the absent father and cross-sexed identity. This paper is relevant not only to the study of socialization but very specifically to certain ideas that will be discussed in more detail later pertaining to identity and identity formation.

The importance of both Parsons' and Whiting's work is that it forces us to consider sex role and its determination as a highly complex process affected by many social and structural factors rather than merely being genetically determined.

autonomy

Statements about the need of young people to "stand on their own two feet" or "to be independent" have been part of common parlance and tradition for generations. Erikson, in his penetrating essay on American identity (1950), suggests that this has been particularly true of the expectations of adults for adolescents in our society with its frontier tradition. The very fact that this idea of independence is a normal part of adolescence and gaining it marks the end, may cause us to make oversimplifications about what is involved for the adolescent. It is easy to confuse the idea of *independent* action or behavior with the idea of *autonomous* action in a psychological sense. A young person may appear to be behaving independently yet may not be psychologically autonomous. This distinction is not a semantic quibble. It is to emphasize that while an individual may be performing various forms of independent action from the time he can walk he may not be in any sense an autonomous individual.

Autonomy, for the purposes of this approach to adolescence and the cases that follow, is a highly technical conception which derives from certain basic assumptions of psychoanalytic theory. The separation of the conception of *autonomy* from a consideration of *identity* is an artificial device and is made quite consciously for clarity's sake. Certain key problems pertaining to identity relate to the capacity of the individual to be psychologically autonomous. Until the individual can achieve some degree of psychological independence, it is extremely difficult for him to achieve an identity.

The key to much of Freud's thinking about the development of personality is found in two closely related conceptions: identification and the Oedipus complex. Stated very briefly, Freud proposes that the infant and young child goes through a sexual evolution that culminates in his forming extremely powerful and erotically charged relationships with the parents. The crisis of early development brought about by the process of socialization is that these early object ties must be terminated and in this termination the ego of the individual must defend itself against a profound sense of loss. The defense employed is the process of identification which is, as Freud says, the process by which the one ego (self) becomes like another. This is a simple overview of an extremely complex process. It is important for the discussion at hand that until adolescence the structure of the human personality consists largely of roles and qualities he has imitated and internalized from parents and parent figures. Freud saw this process, though traumatic, as absolutely essential not only for the proper development of personality but for the very survival of society. This troubled time in the individual's history was followed by a relatively calm period when sexual urges were repressed and the child at home and in school could learn the skills, values, and norms that would shape him to take his place in society. The various modifications of this Freudian position are beyond the scope of this essay, as are the controversies about whether the Oedipal dilemma and the defense of identification are universal.* We can assume, however, that in every person's life there is a period when emotional relationships must go through a transition from being parent-oriented to being oriented to people outside the family. In other words, as George Peter Murdock (1949) has suggested, all individuals during their lifetime have two family affiliations with their attendant emotional investments: first, a family of orientation into which one is born; second, a family of procreation into which their own children are born.

The critical issue for the adolescent is how, with a reawakening and intensification of sexual drive following puberty, to reject the old emotional ties with parents and invest emotions outward. Some theorists, particularly Anna Freud (1946), see the whole task of adolescence as this shift from investments in childhood objects to investments in peers and adults outside the family. She further postulates, as Freud did in an earlier essay (1953, orig. 1905), that the problem of rejecting older objects can be an agonizing experience for the adolescent because of the primacy of these original ties. Yet, if the personality is to develop with any degree of regularity, despite the depression and melancholia that may accompany it, this process of parental rejection — what Erikson has called "distantiation" — must be accomplished.

Obviously, this task is anything but easy and the emotional complexities involved are intense. One is torn between loyalty and self-definition. One is caught in a conflict between the familiar and the unknown. In this vortex, one can stabilize a new sense of self and become ready for experience that is new and, though unfamiliar and frightening, consistent with maturity.

---

* We have presented here the so-called "Freudian" or "psychoanalytic" position concerning identification. For alternative interpretations, the reader should consult Kagan (1958) and Kohlberg (1964).

A Psychoanalytic Approach

The work of Sigmund Freud is replete with illustrations of the importance of the child's early years, when he makes deep and critical emotional investments in parental love objects. Anna Freud (1958) acknowledges the importance of early object ties and points out that the onset of puberty — and heightened libido — precipitates the need to defend against regression to old object relationships. In renouncing old object ties the adolescent rejects the former dependent role, rejects the parents as suitable objects of new libidinal investment, and turns toward peers of the opposite sex. This gradual renouncing of old object ties typically is accompanied by upset. Blos (1962) elaborates on this view of autonomy by making distinctions among stages of development from early adolescence through postadolescence.

The adolescent's renouncing of old object ties can be facilitated or hindered by parental attitudes and behavior. Typically it takes a relatively autonomous adult to beget a relatively autonomous adolescent. Autonomy is not simply seized or decided on by the adolescent; relative autonomy is the result of reciprocal parent-adolescent interactions, characterized by mutual sensitivity and adaptation to the other person's feelings. More specifically, we propose three aspects of adequate parental facilitation of adolescent autonomy: (1) that the parent recognizes the adolescent as a separate person in his own right, which implies that independent or competent behavior by the adolescent is gratifying rather than threatening to the parent; (2) that the parent can show genuine care or concern but not overinvolvement, and can give or offer but not impose; and (3) that the parent is able to terminate old ways of relating when they no longer are adequate or appropriate, which implies an openness to change that is so necessary for any ongoing relationship. An idealized attachment or a resentful attachment to parents may result if any of these three aspects of autonomy-facilitation are inadequate.

An overprotective or pampering parent hinders the child's developing competence and independence by preempting his normal exploration and opportunity to learn from success and failure. A parent who anticipates a child's needs and tries to fulfill them or who pampers a child by doing for him what no one else will do later

in life interferes with the development of this aspect of autonomy.*
A "close" and hypercompetent parent begets an understriving and
overdependent adolescent who idealizes the parent. A distant and
demanding, hypercompetent parent tends to hold the child to adult
standards; and a parent with unfulfilled aspirations tends to impose
them on the child or interpret the child's accomplishments as
competitive with the parent's. The latter styles beget an
underachieving adolescent who resents parental interference.

A parent who shows "concern" by being self-depriving and
indulging often encourages obedience and gratitude and discourages
disagreement and differentiation between self and child. Years of
"generosity" and guilt-inducement bind the adolescent to the
parent, perpetuate diffuse ego boundaries between them, and evoke
parental idealization. An unconcerned, depriving, or rejecting parent,
on the other hand, discourages closeness and communicates the
attitude, "Don't cause me any more problems than I already have."
Feelings of deprivation, abandonment, inferiority, or futility often
result, and a resentful attachment to parents may be accompanied
by preoccupation with ideals, a desire to be rescued, an elaborate
fantasy life, hyperindependence of other persons, or attraction to
charismatic persons.

A parent who is open to change will be both willing to rely
less and less on power or authority when attempting to influence the
adolescent and able to appreciate (or at least tolerate) the
adolescent's changing status, goals, and values. The parents must
gradually relinquish authority and appreciate differences in order
for the adolescent to renounce old object ties and create new ways
of relating. One of the repercussions of an idealized attachment is
that the "good child" becomes the oversocialized adolescent,
prematurely committing himself to someone else's values rather
than forming values on the basis of personal experience. And one of
the repercussions of a resentful attachment is a tendency to rebel
— to sever ties, to prolong adolescence in order to avoid becoming
that which parents represent, or to date or marry a person who is
particularly unacceptable to the parents. The issues of authority and
differentiation often underlie disputes about sexuality, drug use,
religious belief, political action, freedom of movement, vocational
choice, and mate selection. Thus, true intimacy, or mature

---

* Adler (1956) makes useful distinctions between the pampered child and the
neglected child; our concepts of the idealized attachment versus the resentful
attachment are an integration of Adler's views with those of Anna Freud
(1958), Peter Blos (1962), and Robert White (1963a).

dependency, between parents and grown-up offspring requires equality, appreciation of differences, capacity for mutual change, and emphasis on shared interests and reciprocal needs.

Unless the other-sex parent is particularly powerful or important, the adolescent's relationship to the same-sex parent probably has more influence on his or her developing autonomy. This view is consistent with Blos's discussion of the phases of adolescence (1962), beginning with "Early Adolescence." Also compatible with psychoanalytic theory is the view that one's relationships with siblings always depends on parental attachment. Not until both siblings achieve a mature interdependency with their parents should the sibling-sibling relationship be considered as an end in itself. A psychoanalytic approach to Cases 1–6 is to consider each case writer's unique process of renouncing old object ties to parents.

Topic One

Loosening an Idealized Attachment to Parents

Case 1 / Getting Even with Mom

Cindy grew up viewing her mother as near-perfect — compassionate, considerate, unselfish, bright, and humble. "Your mother is a saint," Grandmother would say. Disagreement, let alone argument, was a sin. Mother was Cindy's confidante and advisor, urging her to disinvolve herself with each of three boyfriends.

Cindy's life became divided into two lives: that of a lethargic "good girl" at home, with each year bringing additional topics that she couldn't discuss with Mother; and of "someone else" at college, who experienced depression, fatigue, headaches, guilt, tears, and decision-paralysis. The joy from being the "ideal mother-daughter team" gave way to feelings of ambivalence, increasing distance, and confusion about how to interact with Mother.

Cindy wants to be a unique and separate person who can "be herself" without feeling guilty. There has been progress in loosening her idealized attachment, but "getting even," that is, the process of getting *equal*, has just begun.

It's difficult to deal with criticizing a mother you've always be-lieved, been told, been proven is perfect. It hardly leaves any energy to develop oneself except in an exact likeness (remind you of "in the image and likeness of God"?). The self-reprisals are severe: one can't deviate from the likeness without pain, but one also knows that one can never quite measure up to the person — the only way would be to *become* the person — something that cannot be.

One of the very first things I can remember about my mother, now that I've taken the time to dig back, seems to have occurred when I was four or five. My mother was driving, and my grandmother (my mother's mother) and I were sitting in the back seat. Being the oldest, a girl, and I'm sure for many other reasons, I strongly wanted to be like my mother. So, after thinking for a minute about it, I said with all the love and admiration I could muster, "Momma, some day I'm going to get even with you," meaning that I wanted to be just like her, and not realizing the other unfortunate connotations of that phrasing. My mother slammed on the brakes, turned around, and hit me, saying, "I don't ever want you to say anything like that again." Naturally, I started crying. I was stunned because I couldn't understand what I had done to make her so uncharacteristically angry and violent — she spanked us, but never in anger like this. Didn't she want me to be like her? Then I tried to explain to her what I meant — my grandmother understood me, or at least she was comforting me, and maybe finally my mother saw my misunderstanding, but I never thought that she believed me. When questioned about it recently, she had no recollection of it.

Perhaps some biographical data would help. My mother was the fourth child out of five, and the oldest girl. From what my grandmother says, my mother was perfect, and her younger sister was full of life, not that that was bad, but my mother was compassionate, considerate, extremely unselfish, studious, quieter, while my aunt was lively, but headstrong and selfish. My mother always got straight A's (I saw the report cards), won honors and distinctions, was well-liked, but not considered as pretty as my aunt, who was beautiful (I've seen the pictures) and was a head cheerleader. My mother never shared my pride in her accomplishments; my grandmother supplied all the information about my mother. She went to Regis College, was a geology major, played the flute, and after graduation worked as a geologist. She met my father after he'd returned from the service — she had gone to elementary school with him. They married when 26, and my mother worked till she had me, at 29.

When I was three and a half and my sister June six months, my parents and maternal grandparents moved into a large house in South Boston. Previously, we had lived next door to them in Medford. A second sister and final child, Beth, was born a year and a half later. Despite the foreseeable difficulties of having two families live in one house, we never had any arguments — my parents never argued, and as children we weren't allowed to fight. My father had come from a broken home (his father had died when he was two, his mother was an alcoholic, and he lived with various aunts and uncles as a child), joined the Army during the war, came back and finished his college education, and then got married. Our family is the only family he'd ever belonged to, so the tensions which could've arisen from having in-laws around, were lessened by this sense of family. Needless to say he's pretty protective of his daughters.

I can't remember a time when I didn't want to be my mother; both grandparents adored her and praised her, as did my father, and all our friends and neighbors. "She's always thinking of others and never herself. Your mother is a saint," my grandmother would say. I tried to be just as unselfish, and would always give myself the "bad" silverware when I set the table, always inflicting little tests of my "sainthood" and selfishness, and as all Catholic girls do, went through a period of wanting to become a nun. I always thought my mother more religious than my father, though I came to discover that my mother's religion seemed so zealous because she was searching, battling, and trying to resolve some of her doubts. The highest compliment I could ever receive was to be told I'm like my mother, probably even to this day.

Throughout elementary school, in retrospect, it all seems so rosy now. I had neighborhood friends, and we used to play mostly at my house because we had the largest yard on the block, something, my mother said later, that she actively encouraged because she didn't want any of us to suffer being told to "go home." During that time, I remember feeling that my mother and I were "confidantes," and was angered only when I discovered some social disadvantages to being "smart." One day I got very angry and started crying, something I rarely did (I was proud of that for some reason), and kicked the back steps, surprising my mother by telling her that sometimes I wished that I wasn't smart. She seemed genuinely shocked and didn't reprimand me for kicking or taking out my anger on something.

Arguing was a real problem. If we cried or fussed over some disciplinary decision, we were sent into the pantry or the back hall till we were "all smiles" (something my grandmother did to her children), and if we threw something in anger we were spanked. When old enough to muster an argument, it seemed like I could never win. I always felt immediately guilty because I thought I was being ungrateful to be disagreeing with her at all. My mother said she could never argue very well with my father. I'm the only one who wins discussions with him, but with all the men I've had relationships with, I've always been reticent to disagree or argue. "Getting angry" was a sin for confession, and I always blamed my lack of disagreement on my "perception" and "ability to see too many sides to an issue."

Most of my friends were paid for their good marks in school, and I fluctuated between being proud and resentful of not being paid. My parents would say "very good, but you could do better in this subject." They were never too lavish in their praise, something I only consciously admitted (and they admitted, too) last year in a questionnaire used in a psychology course. They said that they had both seen plenty of spoiled children, didn't want theirs to be that way, and decided not to give too much praise, something they say they regret now, but, in practice, haven't altered radically.

Fifth grade was the first time I ever froze in front of my mother. It was Parents' Day in the class and when called upon, I answered everything entirely wrong. I can remember feeling really uncomfortable, embarrassed, and spied-upon, as if I were disappointing my mother in front of everyone. She laughed when we got home, and asked me why was I so nervous, and I can't remember my explanation. All throughout school, when the parents and teachers had conferences, I was sure my mother was holding back either criticism or praise of the teachers. In sixth grade a teacher who held a special class one day a week for brighter children gave my mother the compliment she has most cherished about me: "She's an extremely and unusually compassionate child for her age." I was pleased too, for this was the one virtue most prized in my house.

Junior high brought my mother and me closer together in the midst of all the changes. She tried to bolster my ego when I listed the usual complaints of being fat, ugly, friendless (my complaints haven't changed over the years, except that after coming to college, I now add "stupid"), but throughout junior high my insecurities didn't cut into my academic effectiveness too much.

By then I had started to lean strongly toward literature and away from science. Mother always delighted in buying me at least one book for Christmas and birthdays, as I delight in buying just the perfect book for her now. By that time, too, I had already taken many lessons in several areas of endeavor at my mother's urging, and I was continuing the piano, which my grandmother had started me on at the age of five. At the recitals, despite the fact that I was one of the oldest and, for that reason, one of the best students, I would always hear voices saying how terrible I was while I was playing. My mother never believed this nor explained it.

From elementary school through high school, I occasionally would stay at my cousins' house for a few days (the children of my mother's lively, full-of-fun sister). She didn't seem anything like a mother to me at all. With eight kids, you have to be a little more freewheeling or die. The fights and feuds always amazed me, but in a strange way excited me, too. We always raised a lot of hell, had a wonderful time, and I invariably got reprimanded or spanked when I went home for being fresh and flippant, which meant I was probably trying to bring a little of the other life-style back home with me. It didn't work.

When I took the entrance exam to get into high school, I was typically a bit apprehensive about getting in. When a neighbor expressed the sentiment to my father and me, "Oh, you don't have to worry about Cindy, she'll get in!", which objectively was a pretty safe and true statement, since it was not a difficult school, my father immediately said, "Well, I don't know. We can't say that, she might *not* get accepted. We'll see." At my house conceit and pride seemed to be equated. I was terrifically proud and impressed by both of my parents' accomplishments — my grandparents, relatives, and neighbors were always praising them — yet neither would take any credit or even *mention* things. Rather than list on any informational form "vice-president," my father always made me write "banker." To this day, I always get anxious and say my father works in a bank, much the same as I don't like to say where I go to school, or mention past accomplishments when asked. My parents again have since said that they tried "to instill humility in an exceptionally talented daughter," afraid I'd become conceited. (I shudder as I wrote that, still not sure that I'm not bragging or "sounding off" for the world in an obnoxious way what I've never felt safe to say.) I've always thought that my parents were *too* humble for their own good (or for my good) and that maybe they were suffering the same thing; but my mother said, when questioned, that my father, due to his family life, has always needed only self-pride, and as for her, well, "The delightful thing about middle age is that you no longer care what people think." I often prayed for middle age.

High school now seems to have been more of a trauma than I thought it was. I changed after nine years of public school to a parochial school, and the shock in teaching and discipline techniques was intensified by the fact that I had a very sick (mentally, that is), power-hungry, paranoid nun for virtually all of my classes my freshman year. My mother was my closest confidante — I had girlfriends but my mother and I were "kindred spirits," a closeness that we delighted in. We used to stay up very late together and discuss all sorts of things over a cup of tea. When my father came into the kitchen, I'd often stop talking; we were usually discussing things I wouldn't discuss with him, and I'd feel a little guilty excluding him, but sometimes glad it was "just us girls." Then I'd wonder why there was so much I couldn't discuss with him — why we both felt so uncomfortable. Sometimes I worried he'd be jealous of me monopolizing my mother because it didn't seem to me that she spent time like this with him.

During my high school years I went out with three boys for extended periods of time, and it was always most important to me what she thought of them. The first boy (ah, yes, my first true love) had graduated from high school and I was just entering the ninth grade. He came to my house only once. The rest of our time together was spent as counselors at a day camp. He was entering the service and was having a party at the end of the summer. My mother and I discussed it since I wanted to go but was afraid to. My mother gently agreed with me, said I couldn't go so I'd have an excuse, and suggested that maybe I shouldn't see him anymore, to which I readily agreed.

The next boy was the same age as the first — a recent high school graduate — and I was entering the tenth grade. He was truly obnoxious, my whole family agreed afterwards, and I could sense their dislike early on. At the end of the summer my mother once again suggested that I break up with him, which I gladly did.

The next long romance was my first serious one (senior year in high school) and the first relationship where sexual intimacy went beyond a goodnight kiss. Dan was ill at ease with my mother, which distressed me a good deal, and although my mother thought he was nice, I knew she didn't find him intellectually my equal, something which made me uneasy. On a few occasions, Dan said something to me in the house which my mother didn't like, and I felt torn. My best girlfriend was very jealous of my dating at the time, and my attempts at reconciliation totally alienated Dan and made me constantly torn between boyfriend and best friend.

My mother and I had discussed menstruation, but not intercourse, which I learned about quite accidentally in a baby book, and I was quite shocked and even a bit repulsed. I timidly approached her (seventh grade) and asked her how people mated and she laughed and told me. That was pretty much the last personal reference to sex. We've discussed it abstractly ad nauseam in social terms of birth control, abortion, premarital sex and the damaging psychological effects thereof to girls, male attitudes, etc., and despite that fact that my mother is radical in many areas, and liberal with other people's daughters regarding sex, the message tends to come through rather strong and clear that, as the old joke goes, "The Irish can steal, drink, lie, cheat, and even miss Mass and get away with it, but heaven help them if they enjoy sex or get pregnant out of wedlock." My mother has said several times that she doesn't see why there's so much emphasis on sex — it's not all that important after you're married anyway. My father and I have never discussed the matter. The closest he'll get to sex is to tell us to close the blinds when we're getting dressed, and to tell us to put on a robe over our pajamas and bathing suits.

I felt very badly that there was a part of my life I couldn't discuss with my mother, and equally guilty that she would be horrified and hate me if she knew. Yet, my affection for Dan balanced the dichotomy in my mind. When he broke up with me the following summer, I went into a very bad depression — my mother wouldn't love me if she ever knew what I'd done, and Dan does know and he doesn't love me either. So I must be a very wicked girl. I kept very busy but was very hurt over Dan and anxious about starting college.

My acceptance at the college of my choice was an incredible surprise, and my family was ecstatic, which very quickly settled into our usual silent pride and fear on my part of telling others and thereby incurring bad reactions. After one week at school, Dan came back, and we started going out again, which I don't think my mother approved of. I also continued to see other guys I met at school. We had agreed to date others, and although this did not work out too well, practically or emotionally, it satisfied my mother.

Meanwhile, the part of my life which I couldn't discuss with my mother was enlarging. New experiences which I knew she wouldn't approve of couldn't be told to her because I didn't want to lose her approval. Perhaps most of all, I mourned the loss of perfect knowledge between my mother and me. And in face of such perfection, I always thought it must be *my* fault, and had to cope with the guilt. I went home once a week at least, and usually stayed overnight. After a while the two lives became difficult to reconcile. When I was at home I felt guilty that I wasn't at school, and when at school, responsibilities at home, real and imagined, beckoned. I fell in with two senior guys and got wrapped up in their senior malaise of late hours and little work. They forgot to mention that they were biochem geniuses who didn't need to study, and so I suffered the consequences. And my mother called, and I kept saying not much of anything until she mentioned that she was afraid I was getting drawn into a small little world. Rockets went off when she criticized my first attempt at escaping from home. She said at another time, happy with the pablum I was feeding her, "Oh, I'm so happy for you and I just want you to take advantage of all the wonderful opportunities over there. You may come out and decide to marry a policeman in Malden, but at least it will be your decision and you'll know some of the alternatives." It may as well have been a curse. She was crying with joy, I guess, and I knew I was disappointing her.

My mother occasionally and anxiously mentioned that I never seemed to mention much work. How could I tell her that maybe other students were just as frightened as I, but did not show it? They were hard, brisk, frightening people who would not give an inch for fear of losing their souls. How could I tell her that I stayed up listening to raps on the revolution from my friendly next-door anarchist until 4:00 A.M. and slept all day out of fatigue, world-weariness, and depression only to come alive again at night, long after the last class was over?

The summer was a hard one — but I fit back into the mold fairly easily. Sophomore year would be better she said. It wasn't. Sophomore year was the critical cut against my mother, giving away her prize, my virginity. It's a very funny story in a lot of ways. Though it was not as calculating as all this, a coldly logical bit of my mind was at work somewhere. My counterpart turned out to be foreign, not exceptionally intelligent (I had to feel superior), someone whose tastes were very unlike mine (I attributed it to cultural differences), and someone with whom I would eventually break up. Since pregnancy would probably tear our house asunder, I went on the pill before ever having intercourse, a move I found ironically calculating at the time. Since the gynecologist was on the same floor as the psychiatric social worker I'd seen and was a disapproving older woman, I was terrified that she would come to take me away, and a tug of war would follow between the two doctors.

Our regular night for sleeping together was Saturday night, which meant that I invariably missed Mass, with non-Catholic Bruce. One Sunday afternoon we went to my house for dinner for the first time. I felt like a modern-day Lady Macbeth, afraid everyone could smell the telltale semen.

Our sexual involvement had started in January and by April it was already painfully clear to me that Bruce and I weren't remotely good for one another. After the semester break, I was really run down and sick. Bruce had returned to Switzerland and I went home and slept for a few days straight. I'd started to become dizzy and nauseous, which I attributed to the pill, but which also incapacitated me to the point of not going to classes. Whenever I miss class, I get the feeling of horribly disappointing the teacher, and I find it very difficult to overcome the guilt. I humble myself and return, yet I always seem to find myself in positions where I have to miss a class. Sometimes it is legitimate, but sometimes I think I do it purposely, somehow to show that I'm not a "good girl" or to make someone come after me. Well, I couldn't face going to class discussions and yet the guilt was consuming me.

Bruce didn't understand, so I stopped telling him about such things. Sometimes I slept ten hours a day, twelve hours a day, often when he was staying over so I wouldn't have to make love with him. My parents were worried because, despite the sleep, I always looked ghastly and tired and didn't try to take care of myself. I repeatedly went to the Infirmary for checkups for mono, anemia, leukemia — you name it, I didn't have it. One internist suggested that the symptoms were all of acute depression, but I said I knew why that was, and I wouldn't go back to the social worker I'd seen before.

So instead I started crying. I'd walk around the city and find myself crying all of a sudden, much to the dismay of people I ran into. I was very much afraid of losing my mind. My mother came over to school one Saturday and we had lunch at the park. She told me I looked very pretty, which started the weeping immediately, because I always needed to hear her say that but I never believed her.

I had been getting excruciating headaches which I attributed to tension and anxiety, and I had one then. It was a strangely silent afternoon on my part. I had to be very careful because the temptation to tell her everything was very great. I told her that I always felt worthless, stupid, ugly, fat, a generally rotten selfish person, and now my concern for others, my great "compassion," the one good thing I could say about myself, had been termed "a morbid interest in other people's pathology" by the woman at the Infirmary. Worse than this, why did I care so terribly much about what other people thought about me and why did I always assume their opinion to be much more valid than my own? Where does one find self-confidence or the courage to believe in oneself? And despite what I looked like, why did it matter so terribly much? And above all, why was I still going through the same junior high trauma as a nineteen-year-old; why wasn't I over with it long ago?

My poor mother. What could I expect her to say? She always said the same things, but I never believed them when I had to drag it out of her. She said I wasn't being logical or even using common sense. Didn't I know the facts to be otherwise? She would answer each of my questions and fears and trying to bolster me, say, "Honey, you're too old for this sort of thing," in a worried tone.

I replied, "If I'm still doing it then I can't be too old. I obviously still need it for some reason. Reason doesn't even help. To know a thing is not to believe it."

Then, exhausted, I switched the emphasis and said that Bruce had been bothering me a lot lately. And my mother suggested that maybe I really wanted to break up with him if he was causing me all this grief. With relief I decided that to prolong things would do no good, so I would break up with him. Then my mother — feeling a bit more relieved — dropped me off at the Infirmary so I could get something for my headache.

The doctor there made one of the all-time imbecile remarks. He said, "What are you college girls doing to yourselves here? These years should be the happiest time of your life!" To which I replied, "If *this* is the happiest. . . . The reason it's rough is because we are expected to have such a great time so the middle-aged people won't be disappointed." I took the pills and ran.

I found that whenever I had to take a birth control pill at home I would get tremendous headaches, and so I came to forget to take them home (accidentally on purpose). This summer it became necessary to finish out the cycle while living at home, and I went through extraordinarily elaborate precautions of hiding them. I used to take them on my lunch break at work to avoid the headaches and fears at home.

For the past two summers it has been very noticeable that I have been away from home for the year, and has been increasingly difficult for me to handle. Both summers I've gone away for a week by myself at the end — the first to Nantucket, and last year on an ocean cruise. I think that they were the best times I've ever had in my life. For once, I didn't wake up in the morning with one parent perched on each shoulder. I had no responsibilities except pleasing myself and no one to answer to. I conveniently left all thoughts of my parents on the shore. My father couldn't understand how I could stay by myself for a week. He said, "Don't think that you have to stay there; you can always come home." My mother knew better, since she had helped me to arrange it all and was very glad that I was going.

I can remember how it felt to call her from the island. I didn't call for the first two days or so because I was having too good a time, and I felt that calling would be giving part of it up, part of myself up. For the first time I felt completely on my own, very strong, very alive, and happy. The feeling lasted quite a long time after I returned home too.

The miracle about this sense of freedom and activity can be better understood when contrasted with my normal feeling of paralysis. Over the years I had found out or been told that there were a lot of things I could do pretty well, yet none became a persisting passion, and I rarely found enough energy or pleasure in the occupation to sustain it, unless, that is, I was doing it for someone else. Then it was all worthwhile, and there was no amount of time or effort too great to work for a friend or a loved one. Then and only then did I thoroughly feel satisfied in creating, and only then did the constant nagging fear that "I should be doing something else" leave.

As I grew older, my mother sometimes became alarmed at the lengths to which I went, and she said that sometimes such presents obligate one rather than please one. My mother and I talked about the fact that sometimes in being generous, you may be used by other people, and sometimes you may be acting generously in order to bind someone to you. This bothered me tremendously, and I asked my mother if she ever felt used.

"There are times when I let myself be used by someone because there is some good behind it that I want to accomplish. The other person's intentions aren't as important to me as what's being done. So, in those cases, I'm not really being used — it's a conscious choice on my part."

For some reason I didn't question her about *her* motives for doing good. As usual I just questioned my own, which has resulted in agonizing decisions over my motives and over "how nice to be," when I really don't think kindness or affection should be meted out that way. And when thoughts of my mother occur for some reason, a decision usually results in paralysis, which for all practical purposes is a win for my mother.

This paralysis extends into other areas. My mother is the real handyman at our house and rather than have her teach us or try to learn, we let her do it. It's easier than doing it the wrong way (or at least not her way), than having her laugh and think how stupid you are for not knowing it. For instance, none of us particularly knows how to cook — with both my grandmother (telling my mother what to do) and my mother in the kitchen, there isn't room. I know my mother feels guilty about this, since my grandmother never fails to remind her that she hasn't done her job as a mother, and so it just gets to be a vicious cycle.

Another example, after sewing for Home Ec. in junior high, I bought some material to make something. I decided I didn't like it after a while and so never finished it. The next time I wanted to make something, my mother laughed, brought up this incident and said, "You never even finished that!" Even now, seven years later, she still mentions that. I always feel like if she had some enthusiasm for what I was doing, I'd finish it, but I usually get pessimistic quips from her, and when I get frustrated she turns it around so that it's my fault. If it's not worth it to her, it's not worth it to me.

So, I guess rather than risk being laughed at, or discouraged, I don't attempt anything at home. I don't take criticism very well, she says. As soon as I step into the house, this lethargy settles over me, so that I don't even make it up the stairs to put away my things. I tend to putter around downstairs and sit and talk over tea until the least little thing becomes an effort. My mother always complains about how little she gets done (housework, not community or church work), and how disorganized she is. I guess I follow in her footsteps.

The trouble is that when I am doing something, especially something I enjoy, I always feel guilty and that I should be doing something else, and it usually gets back to what my mother would think I should be doing. If I go to bed early, I should be up late studying. If I sleep late, everyone's ahead of me, and I should have been up at seven. Sometimes, it seems that no matter what I do it's wrong.

I really only started to question my mother last year, after one incident in particular. My high school boyfriend, Dan, was having a New Year's Eve party which my girlfriend and I wanted to attend. We live in South Boston, and he was living in Cambridge in an apartment. The party would probably go very late, and a lot of people were going to stay overnight. It had been more than a year since Dan and I had been romantically involved. I knew the people who were going to be at the party.

My mother said "No." She always said that she tried to say "Yes" as many times as possible, but this time she said "No" to something I had been *certain* she would agree to. I was truly shocked and tried to diplomatically press her for an answer. She was getting more and more agitated, something I had never seen in her before. Finally I said, "OK, Mom, I won't go; let's not discuss that, but tell me why I can't go. I honestly don't see the reason. I know you must have one, and I want to see why I'm so far away from your thinking."

She said that unfortunate things happen when people get drunk, and I assured her that I wasn't going to, nor did I feel anxious about the guys there since I knew them all, and most would be with dates. As for sleeping there, both Sally and I would be there, and we'd be on the couches or sleeping bags. Dan was like a brother to me now, but she couldn't believe that nothing was going to happen. I said, "You have to trust me all year, right? In a coed dorm, where your bedroom is also your living room, right? And I handle things pretty well on my own. When I come home, I expect the same confidence in my judgment. Don't make me regret coming home."

I had beaten my mother in the argument and we both knew it. She teared up and said, "All right, it may be irrational. I can't explain it or defend it, but I don't want you to go. Now please, can't we leave it at that?" We did, although we were both upset. Often I had argued to test her, but never really because I thought she was horribly wrong. Nor had I ever known her to be irrational or this emotional. It was a shallow victory to see her so upset and vulnerable. I didn't like seeing that.

Another similar incident occurred this past summer. I had met a man at the end of last year who had been amazingly kind to me when I needed kindness very badly. While Bruce's kindness turned out to be merely a set of manners, John's kindness was compassion. We became very close in the last month we had together, and although we both knew that no promises could be made for over the summer, despite my usual caution (and/or pessimism), I felt that our bond would last and be strengthened by our letters. John was in Hawaii for the summer on an NSF grant and had invited me to come over if I could. The decision *was* more involved this time, and I had some doubts myself, but my mother's arguments had the same fearful tone and we argued long and hard over it. Again, I didn't get to go, but I did make reservations and was pretty close to going unannounced to my mother for a weekend, until the hijackings started. I could picture myself on the front page of the *Globe,* about to shoot the hijacker, saying, "I'm sorry, but you see my mother doesn't know I'm here."

This portrait has been extremely slanted — all the bad has simply rushed out of me, so that my mother must seem like an ogre. Perhaps this is my attempt to make my mother perfect again, and make amends for all my trespasses against her — that may be, but on a realistic level, I feel the need to show the other side of the relationship.

The strangest thing is that I'm sure my mother has little idea about all of this and would be crushed to know this is the way I feel. We've always considered ourselves to be best friends, the perfect mother and daughter team. Many of my friends have envied this, and in fact, been mystified by it. I have come to find out that she says she's not laughing at me when I think she is, does not find me stupid, etc. In other words, she's not doing it on purpose or consciously. It's just the combination of the two of us, the way I perceive things. I can see this explanation is rapidly turning into an excuse before my very eyes, so I'd better stop.

My description has not been particularly exciting, dramatic, or even traumatic. In fact, I've had difficulty in recalling any specific incidents at all. My problems don't stem from scarring events, I guess, but steady, subtle, life-long treatment and pressures — harder for me to recognize and deal with because I don't know what life is like without them.

I'm beginning to start a life of my own "with a little help from my friends." And it hurts drawing away from my mother. At times, I'm almost overcome, yearning for that time of perfect knowledge between the two of us. As I've been thinking about and writing this paper, I've been finding it very difficult to talk with her at all, something new and sad, and she senses something going on, but for some reason cannot ask me about it. The other night on the phone instead of her usual sign-off to "Talk to you soon" — she said, "Well, talk to me," in a voice with not a little pleading. I'm afraid I'm acting like a demanding child, making demands on a parent and taking it as my due without any gratitude. I don't want to try to "get even" with her, and I hope this distance between us isn't permanent. As soon as I feel like a unique person, unique and separate from her, then those boundaries will be enough, and I can relax the artificial ones. And maybe then, as a friend has said, I can start to feel remorse instead of guilt for what has occurred.

Case 2 / Goodbye, Big Girl

Margi, the youngest of three daughters, had a special relationship with her father, a boy's prep school counselor-in-residence. The aura, mystery, and allure of the "men's world" at the church-school, and the spontaneous romps and games with Father left Margi with an image of him as a "near, touchable god." Margi strove to please her father and felt injured by his candid comparison of her to her sister.

Father's natural comfort with nakedness, during Margi's childhood years, later sharply contrasted with his discomfort with sexuality. The passing of her childhood was followed by the waning of their idyllic father-daughter roles. His "place of distinction" eroded as he became less pleasant to live with and as Margi tried to remedy his unhappiness. His case illustrates the inadequacy of old ways of relating and the necessity for discovering new ones.

Although I'm not sure whether memories are shaped by pictures and stories or vice versa, one of my earliest memories is playing "mousie" under a blanket on the floor. My sisters would play too; they were at best inconsequential, but usually more annoying, for they would get in the way of what I considered Daddy's and my game. I was the mouse and he was the ogre, the cat, the monster-type who would roar and try to catch me. We had to stay in the dark, under the blanket, squealing — the safety zone was in Mummy's world of light and the sofa. I would make as much noise as possible to get more attention than my two other sisters who were older.

Being the youngest I was glad I didn't outgrow games as quickly as they did — I got a bonus by being the smallest, especially in the garbage pail game, where my father would catch us and cross his legs and we'd go head first down through the hole to the floor, being paddled (patted) on our bottoms all the way. I remember thinking that I would soon be too big for that nonsense.

The first time I tied my shoe was on a Sunday when the whole family was going over to school to eat. I wanted to make sure Daddy noticed the accomplishment, though I knew I was annoying him by holding everybody up; I sat there and glowed.

My father is a boy's prep school counselor, which means by virtue of his long vacations and of our on-campus house we, the three girls, saw a great deal of him; he spent a lot of time playing with us, taking us on his walks, talking to us as he gardened, and camping in the summers. However, there was always a specialness to the occasion when he was there, though my mother was the spirit of the event — she was the laughing one, the dancing one. It was as if Mummy were so much a part of the girls' trio, so much a part of the joke which my grandfather had sent to my father — "Trois filles avec la mère font quatres diables pour le père" (three girls with the mother make four devils for the father) — that she never could hold my father's place of distinction. She couldn't give me the special thrill which I got watching my father shave in the morning — he would grimace at me in the mirror, making me part of the production, but I was very aware that there would not be any theatre if he did not grow whiskers. In a similar side-participating manner, I would join in the "wee-wee" routine by holding his penis when he urinated. It seemed like such a wonderful tool, plaything, weapon. In fact, I often wondered why battles were not fought by pissing in the enemy's face, for nothing seemed more fascinating or more repulsive — the very thought sent shivers down my spine.

My mother's and sisters' world seemed a little ordinary compared to the maleness of his world. In the morning he would go meet "the boys" who were all in coats and ties. I'd watch him put his tie on with great reverence. The school bells would call him away. In the evening he would go to chapel to sing with the boys — the chapel with its darkness, and its musty, woody, masculine smell; the walls would shake as all the men sang in their deep voices. It had a whole aura of mystery and allure which was missing in our (Mummy's and my sisters') light and airy church. We did not have the ritual, genuflecting in front of the glowing red light, or the bell tolling at strange places during the service. Even now I hesitate to show visitors the interior of the chapel. When Mummy and we three went with him, we would sit in the balcony, above, apart from all the men.

My father's world seemed unattainable though he himself seemed so near; it was almost as if with a lot of effort, of time, I might be able to touch the core of that male world and have something more than my mother and sisters. I tried to be good in both worlds. I remember a Saturday morning when all my friends were playing outside, below the window where I was washing a big yellow bowl. I felt that I was in charge of the kitchen — of my mother's world — and thought that when my father came home he'd find me there instead of Mummy. I felt in control.

I knew that money often bothered him, for he would be tense with Mummy when she went shopping, so I tended to save my money in order to please him. However, I had to be generous with it to please my mother. The presents I bought were never for myself but rather "to be generous" towards my mother or sisters; they probably were not for Father for he would not have approved. I remember with glee I bought my first — and only — doll. After years of thinking dolls were "silly," "childish" — not for the tomboy I considered myself — I went with my mother when I was eleven and chose the most expensive doll I could find; she warned me that, like most of my other infatuations, I would not play with it, but I persevered as usual, and afterward made sure my father knew of the price. I didn't play with it.

We have a summer house which has no electricity or running water, so we'd wait until it rained to bathe. There was a great amount of enchantment and excitement for me to watch my father out in a thunderstorm stretching toward the rain, naked, in lightning and thunder — yet he was such a near, touchable god. During the days, he would leave, axe and saw in hand, for his trees while we would stay close to the house. He would carry me up the hill in the evenings, pointing out the deer and stars. Mummy would make me walk like the others.

He seemed the strength of our world. When I was six, the family went to Belgium — rather he took us to Belgium. It was unfamiliar, dirty, and frightening, with rabbits and chickens alive in the market. I felt he steered the boat and found us a home. We were walking down the street as a family and I knew Mummy wasn't happy but I stuck with my father, for he'd pull us through. Mummy was just as lost as the children were. My parents were discussing whether to stay another year over there, which he wanted; she didn't. We stayed.

By then I knew that doing well in school pleased him — made him happy with me and brought out the not-often-given praise. The three of us would go off to school in the morning, walking across the city; he would start with us as he went off to his higher, harder university. We had a special game — just the two of us. I would run to the end of the block, one street over, and turn to wave; I was always afraid he wouldn't be there but he always was. At night he would listen to me as I recited poetry that I had learned.

I can remember having no idea what sex was, and I didn't need to explain to myself that my parents slept in the same bed for the same economical reason my sister and I slept together — the same economy which led us all to having baths together, all five of us, or at least with my father. However, their room did seem darker and more mysterious.

In fifth grade my mother told me very vaguely how babies were made. She seemed much more anxious than I thought the whole concept warranted. She said men and women who loved each other slept very close together. I asked her if they were asleep when it all happened; she looked uncomfortable, said no, and left. I pondered the situation, thinking there was something unsolved, and decided Mummy had to stand on her head with her legs open. This certainly didn't sound very loving. I wondered how they could take it seriously — why Mummy wouldn't seem silly, why she would not be embarrassed. I became self-conscious and uncomfortable, the same way I felt when I was gardening with my father without a shirt and Mummy rushed out to give me one, saying I was too big, too old not to wear one — Daddy had not noticed, or rather had not said anything. I was very angry with my mother but embarrassed for not knowing better.

In seventh grade I was invited on an afternoon date by someone whom the class did not approve — he wasn't cool, but I was somewhat intrigued with the idea of dating. I had unsuccessfully tried to hide when my "cool" friends walked by, by leaning down to tie my loafers. When he brought me back home he insisted on walking into my dark house with me (his father who was a priest was waiting in the car). Then he had the incredible nerve to put his arm around me and kiss me on the cheek. There was a mirror behind us and not only could I feel the complete awkwardness of the situation, but I could see it. Four-fifths of me was indignantly furious while one-fifth was pleased I was able to have some boy attracted to me. I certainly did not think of it as sexual. The hall was dark — I left it that way, for it added to the earthshaking event I imagined I had just been through. My father came in as I paced in the semi-darkness saying "ou, ou, ou" — shaking my fists while smiling. I wanted to tell him of my anger — of my conquest. He asked me what was the matter, but didn't pursue the subject whatsoever when I said "nothing." I was burning to tell him of Lonnie's audacity and my attractability — but did not want to risk it. I wanted his concern, anger, interest — any reaction.

At breakfast one day I started to put a second piece of toast in the toaster, and he looked annoyed and said I did not need two. I didn't know whether he cared that I would get fat or whether he was saving money.

I wanted a horse. My mother thought it was too dangerous, too unknown, but my father, in his usual attitude that anything new and adventurous was good for his children's spirits, collaborated with me, and during a football game slid me $200 for my prize of power between the legs. He was an initiating factor but didn't seem to care afterwards. It was my animal, and I was to do all the caring. No one else in the family rode.

I went away to prep school — which was close enough for me to be able to come home and to be friends with the boys (unlike my sisters' schools). On the first telephone call home I cried to my mother and talked about my Latin to my father. He always liked to talk with the friends I brought home. Strangely enough, not until I was returning for my last term did I realize how much my presence nearby had meant to him. In the car, in the dark, he said that that year had probably been one of the happiest in his life with me and my friends home so often. I had thought that we (Dad and I) hadn't been getting along well at all, since I always felt deceived by his not being kind to Mummy and not seeming as happy to see me as I thought he should — or a father should. I persistently asked him how he compared his daughters. He finally said Sal was probably the smartest but did not work as hard as I did. I felt absolutely devastated, for I knew how much he admired intelligence. My fantasies weren't holding up to reality.

Birthdays were especially important, for he'd write a letter especially to me, especially about me. Unlike my mother's letters which were always full of love and light, he seemed to ponder his thoughts and words, remembering the foliage the day I was born as he drove up to the hospital.

The night I was tapped head of the school — in the dark of our chapel — the thrill was in telling my parents. The next day I received a letter-card from my mother with "Love" "Love" "Love" and flowers all over it, while my father's letter (on a scrap of paper in his usual tight manner) said what an honor it was — how no one in the family had had such a position of responsibility. I thought everything would be wonderful when I saw him again, but the usual close-quarter irritation prevailed.

The summer after freshman year at high school, I went on a camping trip with my attractive male cousin and my father. That spring one of my strong feelings was the need to make my father happy, since both he and my mother considered him a sad, gloomy person. Thus I asked him to go camping with me, for he supposedly liked camping and new people. I felt I was the center of the affair and had to keep the conversation going and the two happy: one whole morning we "improved" my vocabulary; it was off to an awkward start for I could not balance the atmosphere. I tended to exclude my father, which of course made things more tense. I knew he was unhappy and it was my fault, but he must seem so miserly and unpleasant in the eyes of my admired cousin. I was to do the cooking on a dollar a person a day, which seemed so generous. At night, Bart and I would go off and talk about different people we had made out with — I made a point of making myself sound experienced; we left Daddy alone and smoked. When he would stop at the places he wanted to see, we'd sit in the car and giggle. At night I did not know how to put the sleeping bags — I slept in between them. We camped next to a lake; I was very embarrassed and uncomfortable when Dad washed his crotch. Neither

Bart nor my father seemed to try to make the situation less tense at all.
Bart read *Catch 22*. I couldn't wait to get home, but I didn't want anyone to know we had had an awful time.

At Dad's recommendation, I applied for a scholarship and
went to Scotland for a year. When I came back he met me at the boat
— I had carried his present of goat's cheese and Armagnac personally
the whole trip. On the first trip alone together I tried to think of things
to talk about and ended up reading him the history papers I'd written,
but stopped since I felt so vulnerable to criticism from him; I never
felt I wrote well and did not like to give him evidence.

My sister had just been married, and I asked him if he ever
thought about them sleeping together (I'm sure the question was put
in a theoretical form). He said he did not think about those things —
that Mummy worried about that sort of thing. In fact, he never has
acknowledged his daughters' sexual lives whatsoever. Both my sister
and I have gone on many trips with men by ourselves, and certainly
my mother knows we have slept with boys, but my father never confronts the obvious. Once at the dinner table when I was home with my
"young man" whom I'd been living with, I asked my father what he
thought about people living together. I pushed the talk closer and
closer to home. I finally asked what he thought of my sister and her
man traveling together for a year in Europe. He said he assumed they
were just friends.

Margi: And what if they slept together?
Dad: Then that would be too bad.
Margi: Would you think less of her?
Dad: I'd be sorry.

Everyone at the table was uncomfortable, but I so wanted a confrontation of the issue.

I feel I can only earn his admiration and love; I do things
that I know will please him even now. I always read my papers to him
(except this one). The high point of last year's academics was the letter he wrote congratulating me for my marks. He said no one in the
family had done so well in a comparable university. But when we got
together, the same old squabbles occurred over ridiculous things. He
must have felt betrayed by my absence when I was needed to work
on the new house this summer, but I was going to be damned if I'd
stick around such an unpleasant person.

The other night I was unhappy and lonely, so I phoned home
to speak with Mummy. Only Daddy was there. He had never shown
much interest in my current affairs, so I felt as if he would be uncomfortable because it was long distance without any apparent reason;
but he talked happily, warming up as the time ticked on. He was
comforting and at the end said "Much love," which Mummy usually

does while he laughs or gets annoyed. Then awkwardly he said, "Goodbye, old girl . . . I mean little girl, I mean big girl."

Topic Two

Resolving a Resentful Attachment to Parents

Case 3 / Something They Had to Do

For years, Jacob Stone wanted to be just like his father, whom he held in awe. He wanted his father's strength but feared his potential for violence. Jacob's preoccupation with comparing his accomplishments to his father's eventually was superseded by his ongoing concern about everyone "playing at being a family." His unsuccessful attempts to unite his bickering parents prompted him to vow to give his life if only his parents would stop fighting. The tension between father and son reached its peak in a dramatic arm-wrestling match.

After his parents' divorce, Jacob purposely "disidentified" with his father and focused attention on capturing every prize at school, playing football violently, and writing romantic poetry. The highlight of a recent visit with his father was accepting a special gift — which his father soon asked him to return. Can Jacob and his father salvage a relationship on mutually acceptable terms? What is to keep Jacob from repeating his father's "mistakes" as husband and parent?

It was my first revelation — that's the only way I can describe it — the feeling of awe and disbelief. I guess I was about four. I was talking to my father; we had just spoken to my grandmother on the phone — he called her his mother. That had never occurred to me before. There was never any conscious recognition that those two people who lived in a warm, radiator-smelling apartment were my father's parents. I had seen the old, oval-shaped and faded photographs of little Samuel hanging on their wall; we even had one at home — a chubby kid with a pompadour sitting on a photographer's pony. But none of this fit in until that one moment when everything fell into place and there I looked at the heavy black mustache sitting in front of me, shaved head glistening, and realized that once *he* was a little boy and he had a mother and father just like I did. I was ecstatic and filled with wonder.

My father saw my disbelief and went through a complete explanation; my mother, too, was once small and was taken care of by her parents. I knew *that* already; it just wasn't the same thing. I like to think of him laughing at this point. I think he was surprised at my question, surprised to find I held him so high, and he was happy. I think he sensed my realization that if he was once like me, then I could become exactly like him. At that point I saw that as a good thing. I saw him as a loving man of incredible strength and tremendous potential for violence. Whenever he got mad, I feared he'd tear down the house. I loved and wanted his strength as much as I feared it. Whenever I saw Yul Brynner in the Genghis Khan type movies, I always thought of him. I can remember one such movie in which Brynner was a mammoth warlord. He had two sons (like my father) who loved, feared, and hated him and his power. In the movie the younger son (I think it was the younger one — my brother is older than I am) challenged his father to a fight. It was one of those really ungraceful, unending battles where nobody stops until one or both can no longer move. I was really excited — the kid seemed to be winning and then the old man reared up, gave a deep laugh and charged, nearly breaking his son in half. That was the end of the fight. My feelings toward it were mixed. It seemed to me that though both were doing all they could to hurt the other, they both loved each other very much. It wasn't that either wanted to harm; *it was something they had to do.* Though I wanted the son to win and though I felt he was right to test his strength against his father's, it seemed right that the kid had lost. The father shouldn't, couldn't be defeated by the son; that wasn't the way it should be — not then.

I had heard a lot of stories about my father. He had worked in his father's garage since he was fourteen; he could drive a truck when he was even younger and could fix an engine after listening to its sound and hearing what was wrong. He had swum two miles without stopping before he was ten years old, was a good fighter and Army lieutenant (that was even better than sergeant), and the first time he met my mother his bathtub was filled with pounds and pounds of spinach he had just bought because it was cheaper that way and spinach is good for you.

He never graduated from high school, though he took a few technical courses at night. He always told me how he had worked since he was young, how his father made him support himself when he was fourteen, and how he wanted me to get a good education and to do whatever I wanted in my life. He seemed both pleased that my life would be "better" than his and a bit resentful that I didn't have to work as hard as he did for the things I got. He would tell me often how hard he had to work and how he always wanted an education. When I was learning Hebrew, I started giving him the lessons as I learned them, but that didn't last too long and I was disappointed in him. I was resolved to working very hard at school, sports, everything, to show him how good I was and how much like him I could be. Everything I did in school made us a little different I guess; we both knew that. He wanted this for me and I did my best to make him proud.

My admiration for him transcended everything. I always wanted to work with my hands on machinery, to drive big trucks, to fix things like he did. I didn't really like spinach but I never lost the image of his bathtub filled with it and up to a few years ago I always ate it — it was good for me and would make me strong — like him.

My family had moved to New Jersey when I was a few months old. For as long as I can remember he had his own equipment and truck repair shop. Someday I knew it would be "Stone and Sons" (and I also knew someday after that it would be "Stone Sons").

When I was nine or so I was at an overnight camp for two weeks. The lake was a mile across — I *had* to swim it both ways without stopping. One day I did and when I went home I told my father about it. He seemed pleased but his reaction was less than what I wanted. Didn't he understand? The whole feat seemed meaningless — he probably did it when he was *seven!* Then I asked him how old he was when he swam two miles without stopping. I don't think he answered that. He understood that it wasn't so much that I was pleased with myself for being such a good swimmer for my age — I was measuring my growth against what I perceived was his own, and on another level, I was competing with him, showing him that I could be everything he ever was.

It seemed as if I had done something wrong. His expression changed and he said very softly that I shouldn't do things just because he had and that I wasn't in a contest with him. I felt awful. I was so sure that I hadn't done it to beat him in anything. He always told me whenever we played any kind of game that he'd never let me win, and that always made me glad. Though I was sure I never could win, it made every little victory seem my own. He always liked to take me to his shop where I'd play mechanic and he seemed to like that. I was sure he'd be just as happy with my swimming feat.

Seeing myself as his favorite, as the one most like him, made me feel good. There were two problems though; first were my feelings that I didn't deserve it and second was my brother's position. He would always help my father out fixing things. He seemed to *really* want to repair things and knew all the names of the different kinds of tools and parts. I thought that some day I really wanted to learn all these things, but I never did much about it. My brother would follow Dad around with the tool kit, and I'd just watch them go by. Yet my father always seemed especially mean to my brother. Whenever he'd hand him the wrong tool, or burr a bolt Dad would call him "louie" (connotation of a lousy worker). This hurt my brother and I didn't want it to happen to me. I felt guilty about the favorite treatment I thought I was getting — my brother deserved it. I did want it though. Even though I hardly ever helped my father, he always described me as being "a good little worker" and my brother as being "lazy." I felt that I looked very much like my father (my brother had my mother's looks) and was so much like him in every other way that I stopped from feeling badly about never really wanting to do all these things. My father acted as if he felt the same way, for he never pressured me to learn to fix things.

When I was about ten my father's business failed. He had been doing well but things got bad and never got going again. I was a little worried about what he was going to do. He told me things were okay and not to worry. I wanted to go out and work; I wanted to help. And I was mad that he had failed — failed me and the dream was all over.

Everyone else was pretty upset and I remember my mother, in some fights about money they had, making some comments about his failure. I was angry about that, angry that she would say that to him, angry to hear in the open that it was his fault, angry at him, and angry at myself for thinking that he had let us down. I saw his own anger at himself and at my mother for reminding him of his failure. I wonder if he saw me as watching him to see what he would do, if he thought I doubted him, and if he knew that I was waiting for him to make a move to right his wrong.

He began selling road building equipment and then after coming out highest on the competitive tests, being accepted, and refusing a high-ranking job in our state, he set up an equipment sales firm of his own. Soon he began doing a lot of traveling out of state. First he was away only a few days a week, but it wasn't long before he was only able to come home on weekends. He'd call every night and say how he missed us all. I'd be especially sure to do well in school each day so I could tell him all the good things that happened.

During this time I asked him quite often why he couldn't work closer to home. He said how he missed us all, how he missed me and wanted to be home more but that there were no new highway projects around, and he had to go where the business was. Whenever I'd ride around in a car and see a road being built near our home, I would wonder about his explanation. It seemed that everywhere I looked there were highway projects. I told him about the construction I'd see, thinking maybe he didn't know about it. I guess it seemed as if I were doubting his sincerity because he would answer, sometimes in a gruff way, explaining again (as if he were very tired of having to go through it) how there really wasn't that much work, how he couldn't help it but that's the way things were.

Gradually the family situation got tight. My father would come home on Friday night. I'd really looked forward to seeing him all week. He'd be there at about six and things would get tense very soon with him and mother bitching. Their fights always seemed trivial to me. Sides would usually start to develop. My brother and mother over here, my father over there trying, I thought, to enlist my aid. I didn't want to stand anywhere because it all seemed so stupid. I'd feel angry at mother for bringing up certain topics and for yelling at him. I knew she was right, though, to ask him the things that angered him so. Meanwhile, my grandmother who had been living with us (at my father's invitation) since her heart attack was just sitting there pretending not to hear the things my father was saying about her.

I felt sorry for my father. He'd been away all week and had come home to see us and was constantly hit with this. I was afraid he wouldn't come home any more and I thought that I probably wouldn't blame him. But still, he seemed as nasty as everyone else; his anger seemed even more frightening and I couldn't understand his attacks on my grandmother. The only sides seemed to be him versus us.

I started going out Friday nights right after dinner. If his plane were late I'd eat before anyone else — just so I could leave and avoid the whole thing. I did nothing about the fighting though I felt I was perhaps the only one who could do anything. My anger increased at everyone, especially myself, for letting the family down. I'd just walk around with a friend, go to the bowling alleys to play pinball, get into fights, drink if we could find anything, try to pick up girls, anything to kill time before I had to go home.

One night we were walking by a house and looked into its brightly lit kitchen. There was a family taking cookies or something out of the oven. The house looked warm and comfortable and happy. At first my friend and I laughed. One of the kids looked familiar; we recognized him as one of the school dinks — white sox, pants up to his chin, etc. For a few minutes I thought how great it was that I could walk around at night and he had to stay home. Then I looked and saw how happy they were and I realized the kid probably liked to stay home. My anger grew and I longed for someone to come up and call me a Kike. I wanted to run home and belt my mother and father for making me go out. Then I thought how it was really all my own fault — I hadn't done anything to help and I ran out whenever we were all there together.

That night when I went to bed I was thinking and half-praying for my grandmother to forgive my father: he really didn't mean what he said. I heard my parent's bed creaking in their room and knew they were screwing. That was good because maybe they talked.

The next day I overheard a conversation between them. My mother seemed about to cry. Except at the funeral I had never seen her cry at all. It scared me and I wondered what my father could have done. From what I heard it seemed as if she had asked him to talk things over and he refused.

A while later I was in bed thinking. It was a weekend so my father was home. I started making a deal; I'll trade my life for peace — if only my parents would stop fighting I'd be happy to die. I said it over and over again until I really thought it would happen. I couldn't sleep and I started shaking and crying and got up and walked down the hall. I told him why I was so upset and asked him to please do something. He told me how I wouldn't die – I believed him and felt relieved, but I still wanted him to do something. All he could say was that he'd try though it was really my mother's problem, not his. I knew he didn't want to say it was all his fault – I didn't think that was it either, but it seemed he didn't want to do anything. It seemed he was feeling really uncomfortable at home. He had to protect himself from assaults everywhere — even in the middle of the night from me.

I believed that perhaps my grandmother's presence was causing the problems. After she died I thought that the source of my father's anger was gone and that things would be straightened out. A day or two after the funeral – my father came home for it – I asked my parents to come with me while I took the dog for a walk. I can remember my anticipation and joy at the thought of this being some kind of turning point. I was doing something to help, I felt I had to.

As soon as we got outside I started my well-rehearsed speech. I said how I thought this would be a good time to work things out. Now that Grandma died we could all forget any problems and stop fighting all the time. My mother put her arm around me. My father kept walking, whistled to the dog, and said only that he had to go out of town in a few days. The dog came and we went inside, going our separate ways.

I thought something good would happen and was proud that I had been the one to get things going. I felt a little bit above them and their fighting; I could see what they could not and I could help them fix things. If all of this really were true, I thought, then it's all up to me.

The next day he took my mother into the living room. He seemed mad or indifferent and growled for me to come in. I sat down and he told Mom to listen to me – I had something to tell her. It would be the two of us against her – I could see it. How could he ask me to do this? I asked him because I thought he could do something and now he was asking, telling me. It was like a game of hot potato but I didn't want to play — it wasn't my game; it was theirs.

I began to think that I couldn't really be like him. I saw him, the person, with anger and hostility — his big car, his fancy clothes, the twirls he was putting on the end of his mustache. Father, the image, was still a warm one, but I figured that was one I must keep quiet; it wasn't real. The dream world was over. The anger grew and at the same time I noticed that I could become surly and moody just like the old man, and I could be mean to my mother and brother just like him, and when I got the chance I really could drink and fight like I knew he could. The situation at home got worse and as things began to polarize a little more, I began to think more consciously about my anger toward him. I really did want to beat him.

Perhaps the biggest turning point came for me toward the end of the summer before ninth grade. (I was fourteen.) I had been at a work camp all summer and was feeling especially virile and omnipotent. I had been elected leader of the village, had lost my virginity, and had become the local seducer (I wondered how many he had had when he was that age), had fooled around with drugs and survived, and had done a lot of forestry and auto repair work (that was the best of all).

It was after dinner and somehow or other my father was going to have an arm-wrestling match with me. I think I was talking about all the big stones we had to haul at camp to build a foundation, and he said something about how strong I thought I was. This was something special, for no one liked this kind of competition and it had always been avoided. My mother protested but we went ahead. The table was cleared; we squared off and locked hands. We both realized that this would be for real. He reminded me that he wouldn't let me win. I knew that. We started. I held off. Our arms stayed perpendicular with no one trying to upset the balance. I pushed then; I was tired of waiting. Nothing happened. He just sat there. Damn him! He isn't trying! I pushed harder and harder and he did the same. I saw his knuckles go white, his face turn red, and the muscles bulge from his huge neck. I thought he'd break my arm in half as soon as he decided to. I wanted to be somewhere else but I knew I had to keep on going. I had to push and I had to win. I pushed and felt him going. I didn't believe it was happening and in my terror I pushed harder, wishing there were coals on his side to burn the silly hairs off his hand. He went down a lot easier than I thought he would. Everyone was quiet. I had won — didn't they see it? My brother and mother left the room. I got up and stared at him. Before I turned to go, he muttered, "You little bastard." I thought how horrible he was, and I didn't leave home that day — this was my territory now, for a little while.

My having to win came out in everything. What bothered me most was that I always did "win" just about whatever I wanted, and I disliked everyone more and more. For if I could win then everyone must be horrible. There was a lot more bitching around the house, some about another woman. I thought that everyone seemed braver in their attacks toward him. Had my "victory" shown fallibility to my mother and brother, not just the two of us? I really wanted my parents to get divorced — I wanted him to stay away. We were all just playing at being a family — couldn't they see? At least a divorce would end the fighting. But they all seemed to hang on as if they couldn't believe it was happening. I just wanted it to end so I wouldn't have to keep on worrying about it.

A few months after the arm wrestle there was another fight on. This was different for it finally seemed as if they were yelling about what I thought I wanted. My mother said how everyone would be happier if he never came home. That stopped him.

"Who thinks that?"

"The kids, ask them."

Christ! He's looking at me. Looking as if I stabbed him in the back, he turned to me with a terrifying expression on his face. Don't ask me please, for your own sake, for my sake. Don't ask me; ask my big brother — what do I know? But I did want him to ask me — wanted to smash him in the face and to see his blood; I wanted to kiss him and tell him I loved him. I screamed back after he called my name.

"Yes, I don't like you coming home when all you do is fight like this!"

I don't know if I said more. I don't remember what happened after that.

Things got worse. One night when he was home on the living room floor, the phone rang very late. There were extensions in all three bedrooms and my mother, brother, and I picked it up to answer at the same time. They said hello, and I kept quiet but stayed on to see who it was. A woman's voice came on "Samuel?" My brother found him, woke him up and when he picked up the phone in the kitchen, I heard everyone else click theirs down. I gently hung up as well. I didn't want to think about it at all and I went to sleep.

My mother and brother seemed in shock. I felt pretty un-moved. I was glad; I thought that something had happened. Besides how could they be so unprepared for it; hadn't they seen it coming for years? I don't see how he could have stayed after that. His home seemed a place where only the labels of relative veiled his real adver-saries. He had suffered the final humiliation with that phone call and there could be no turning back without admitting and apologizing publicly. I couldn't do that and I knew he couldn't either. What made it worse, I was sure, was that I had stabbed him in the back when he needed me most. The fault was clearly mine and I feared being exposed for that.

A few weeks after he had left it was parents' day at our school. My father was going to be in town for a while to "clear up some business" and he wanted to come. My brother and I were to meet him in the morning before my football game. He came to school too late for the games. We then had a very uncomfortable and strained lunch. My mother had wanted to come but left early — afraid she would see him. After lunch we went home (my mother was out). When we got there Dad took me into his room. With tears in his eyes he said how he couldn't live with my mother any more — how things were always bad and now he just knew he couldn't stay. We would still see each other, though, and he'd take care of us. I disagreed with him about everything always being bad. Before his business failed and for a long time after that I always thought of our home as a very happy one. We did many things as a family — went on vacation together, went to the lake almost every Sunday; it seemed that everyone really liked each other. But I did agree that he had to do it, and I cried with him because it was very sad and I felt sorry for both of us. I avoided the rest of the day by seeing a friend. While I was gone he took most of his clothes and some art work from the house. When I came back he was gone (I was relieved), and my mother and brother were fighting. She was angry because my father had come back and taken the prints and statue. There was a lot of emotional strain around. My father was very deceptive and we had to be — that's what the lawyer said we should do and I didn't want to have my loyalty doubted, as I doubted it myself. Everyone was pretty vehement, and I became that way as I saw more and more of what he was doing and saying. Eventually it took three years (I was seventeen) until a divorce came through. He was so deceptive and uncooperative that it ended up with his suing my mother for desertion — no payment of the money for the debts of his she had paid, no alimony — only an agreement to support my brother and me in school. As it turned out he paid none of this.

I didn't see much of my father for those three years. For the first year and a half we'd get together every four months or so — actually only a total of perhaps six times. From then on I didn't see him until this past June, when I went to New York for a few days. The visits were never pleasant — it would always turn out that we'd catch him in lies about his love life or his finances, and often it seemed as if physical, not just verbal and emotional, violence was going to break out.

I denied as much as I could that I was like him. It seemed to me that his big problem was an insensitivity to anyone but himself, and I became very conscious about hurting anyone. At school I felt I had to do well to prove to my mother that I was worth all that she went through to make things good for me in spite of what had happened. I aimed for every prize I could get at the school and was successful in getting many: I got several letters, was Senior Marshall, High Honors — the whole bit. I always wanted my father to know about this for I had to show him I could do it and I wanted him to be proud and I wanted to prove my worth to him. I felt guilty about getting the awards, about my success. I would think that I was fooling everyone — if only they knew what I had done, what I was, they'd laugh.

But I still wanted to see my father. I came to realize that this desire was not really for him — as the person he was at that time, but for some idea of what he was or could be like. It was nice to think of the idyllic relationship that was gone, if it ever had been there. I think that's why he gave up with visiting or trying to communicate at all. The visits were a strain on him, there were too many factors weighing on everything that was said and he was very defensive. Our fights seemed to be like those between him and my mother — avoidable if someone just overlooked a lot of things. I was too hurt, too guilty, and too concerned about betraying my mother and brother to allow things to pass — slurs on my mother, her whole family, my brother, and so on. He was in the same situation and it didn't matter who was right or wrong — there was just too much for it to be smooth and calm.

Two things happened to me — two contradictory things, I guess. While I became very involved in the violence of contact sports, I began writing poetry that came from an entirely different world. I began to see football and lacrosse as releases for a lot of hostility; I knew I needed that and I enjoyed it very much. In football I was moved to the line after my first year. I hated playing defense; you had to make the first move. In offense you knew that the bastard playing opposite you — crouched two feet in front — was going to bring his forearm up to your head if you didn't hit him low, hard, and fast. Wham — helmet toward the crotch, hit, slide in with your shoulder, bring up the arms, push and hope he falls so you can break some ribs. That's what it was and I felt justified in trying to really hurt people.

At the same time I became more serious about writing poetry. The world I created was one of softness, golden clouds, persimmons and love. But there was always in the poetry the fear of never getting to that world and of losing it if it were ever reached. (I called it Willowild after the first poem of that type I wrote.) The poetry was release, a good way to leave. But sometimes Willowild would disappear for poems that came from my nightmares.

I thought all along that if I could be on my own, that if financial and legal matters were all straightened out, I would like to see him, to look at him somewhat objectively and tell him I loved him and it was all right — something I hadn't done since things started getting bad.

I got my father's phone number and called him. We made arrangements to meet in New York. I was away for the summer, as I had been since I was thirteen, and though my mother knew I would be seeing him, I didn't feel terribly guilty about betrayal — or at least I wouldn't let myself feel I did.

The whole trip was idyllic, outwardly. We didn't fight, mainly because we both stayed away from touchy subjects and stopped ourselves from saying many things; his wife was with us all the time anyway and she calmed him down when he got excited. He liked the mustache I had and bought me wax and showed me how to curl it like his — which I did as long as I was there (when I got home I quit using the wax).

In the course of the weekend I found, or sought and found, many similarities between us: in our sense of humor, in the way he treated his new wife — the gruff kidding around like the way I was at times with my girlfriend. I wanted to find these similarities and I did. I accepted his life style — the big car, the plush apartment, the expensive restaurants, even the Bloody Marys for breakfast, though it did bother me. I wasn't surprised by the incongruence of his life with the way he had portrayed it to us — I expected that. It irked me though when he tried to tell me how difficult things really were. I didn't dispute any of it, though. When he tried to rationalize my opulent treatment and so on I just said it didn't matter and we went on to talk of mustache curling and other safe topics.

He had a collection of pocket watches (he didn't use any of them) and he wanted me to have one. There was one that was his favorite — it turned out to be mine as well, oddly enough. It was not as valuable as the rest but was an old railroad watch, big and heavy and made of brass. I figured that like me, he would want to give away his favorite thing to someone he loved. I seemed right in that, for he did let me have it.

I left feeling pretty happy, glad I had gone. Both of us promised to see each other regularly, which neither of us believed would happen. I knew how unreal the whole visit was, but I didn't think about it. I had the watch, another symbol of the image and I was happy.

About a week later I called him and he asked for the watch back. I avoided calling or writing because I feared he'd press me for a date when I would come down again. He didn't do that, only gave me some line about how he liked to switch around with his watches and I could have another one. I didn't bother saying that I knew he never used any of them, etc. I said okay I'll send it to you and the call ended. I really had expected this but I put it out of my mind. I knew he wasn't that much like me; I knew he was selfish and too insensitive to let me have it. But I liked the whole idea of the thing even though I knew it was out of Willowild, and I knew you can't try to have Willowild without getting burned in the end.

I carefully wrapped the watch, insured it and sent it back with a note on the back of the package saying I didn't want another watch, thanking him for letting me have it for as long as he did. I don't think I was trying to be sarcastic. I'm sure he saw it that way — saw me as not understanding anything at all and as being very insensitive and selfish. And I'm sure his anger came as well and that it was directed largely upon himself as mine was.

I haven't heard from him, nor he from me since. That's good because I know what it would be like. The illusion is still there and this paper has brought the intense anger back because it's destroying that illusion a little bit. It's making me see that it is an illusion, and it will be a little while before I can separate the fantasy world from the real one and be able to live with them both. Since I saw him, I've come to grips with my anger. I won't let it spill over on to other people and I don't feel bad about having it. I don't have to prove how sensitive I am — I feel I can react naturally — being neither oversensitive nor overly hostile. I know too that all that's a rationalization for not being able to work things out better.

There's one girl I love. We went out for a few years pretty steadily. She was my Willowild; she received all the love I wanted to give so badly, and she filled the loss I felt. We still see each other and sleep together — though both of us have found other partners. I see her now as a person, though, not as an illusion, and I've found that I love her even more. I can live with the reality of the present situation without having to fantasize. But for a very long time I loved the shit she gave me; I loved the proof of the inevitability of loss.

Case 4 / Wanting Them to Know I Was Growing Up

These are recollections of one girl's preadolescence, eight to ten years ago. The simplicity of life was curtailed with the birth of a younger sibling and the increasingly strained relationship between her parents and older brother. Jan was a good girl and seemingly didn't require as much attention as her adolescent brother or baby brother.

This was the time of putting up with father, wanting mother to initiate the transition to a bra, feeling betrayed by mother, turning to brother, and expecting suddenly to be beautiful.

Jan attributes her feelings of resentment to her mother's psychological absence at the crucial time of her daughter's puberty. The quality of relationship with one's same-sex parent may be especially important at this time of great expectation, social comparison, and role transition.

I am trying to write about the time in my life when I started changing visibly into the person I am now — when I started being aware of patterns of behavior that I still go through now. But my memories of that time, broadly fourth grade through seventh grade, are very fragmented. I remember specific incidents clearly. The labor is to set them in a context.

I remember fourth grade, when I was nine and ten years old, as the time when the simplicity of life was broken. My mother became pregnant again in the fall of that year. Up to then there had been only two children, my brother, who is 18 months older, and I. I think that we all felt that our positions were very fixed; we knew what each of us did within the family, and we knew how we reacted to each other. Then my mother told us that she was going to have a baby, and my brother and I had to react some way to that. My brother, Richard, was very surprised. I told my mother that I'd expected it, since she'd been sick and kept going to the doctor. It seemed that since I was a girl I was supposed to understand that sort of thing.

My mother was thirty-nine and she had a fairly difficult pregnancy. She was sick a great deal and that, I think, was a constant minor embarrassment. My birthday came when she was seven months pregnant. We always took birthdays very seriously in my family and still do. That night she cooked all my favorite food, but then she started feeling sick and went to bed. Daddy set up a card table in their bedroom so we could eat with her, but my mother couldn't eat anything and kept groaning. My father couldn't watch TV with me because he had to take care of Mama, and I was very angry at both of them.

My mother went to the hospital early one Saturday morning, and my father called us later to tell us we had a new brother. I'd wanted the baby to be a girl. It didn't seem fair that now there would be more boys than girls in the family. But my father took us out to dinner that night at a grown-up restaurant and I felt much better. I baked a birthday cake for my new little brother, and my father and brother and I came home after dinner and ate it.

My mother had bought lots of food that was easy to cook so I could make meals while she was in the hospital. One night I was making tuna fish sandwiches for dinner. My father had started hard-boiling some eggs, then he went out in the yard to play baseball with my brother. I mixed tuna fish with mayonnaise and put the hard-boiled eggs on a separate plate. When my father came in he was angry at me because the eggs were supposed to go *in* the tuna fish. I told him I was only ten years old and he was expecting too much of me, and I started crying and ran away. My parents kept telling my older brother and me that even though there was a new baby they still loved us just as much. Privately, we knew they were feeding us some more of that child psychology crap. We knew they still loved us. It was the disruption in our lives that bothered us.

Things seemed different, not only because of the baby. The lady next door had had a baby at approximately the same time. She asked me if I wanted to baby-sit. I thought I was too young but my mother said it was all right. So I spent afternoons walking the baby carriage up and down the street for a nickel an hour. I wanted to help take care of my own little brother, too. I could hold him while he had his bottle, and diaper him, walk him, and help put him to bed at night. My older brother helped sometimes, but he wasn't *expected* to. He was running around with his friends most of the time. We'd always had neighborhood friends together, but about that time he dropped out of the kickball games in the street and started seeing other people he knew from school. Boys would come to our house in the afternoons to see my brother and either they'd go away outside somewhere or they'd shut themselves up in my brother's room. Of course they wouldn't let me play with them. I remember deciding to try a different approach — I would bring them lemonade and cookies and draw the blinds and turn on the lights in the late afternoons the way my mother did, but they just laughed at me.

Life at school was changing, too. We were always proud because we went to the only elementary school in town that let out at 1:00, before lunch. So all through first, second, and third grades the usual way of playing was to invite someone to come home with you for lunch. She or he called his mother to make sure it was all right, and your mother always had extra sandwiches. Then you played until five o'clock, when everyone always had to go home for supper. I don't remember caring particularly about whom I played with. But by fourth grade, I think, people were becoming more separate. I had started Hebrew School in third grade, and that was a major division. Some people had to spend two or three afternoons a week at Hebrew School, and some people didn't. Some people were Jewish and still didn't go to Hebrew School — they were strange and had no place at all. Other divisions began. Mildred had already started developing. When she had to take off her clothes for the fourth grade physical, we all stared at her. There was a rumor that Betsy's mother was an artist and drew naked people and that Phyllis said she had seen them.

I had two best friends. One of them was Kay, who lived down the street. She was tall, thin, blonde, and blue-eyed. She was also Unitarian. We did things together. We went to the playground after-noons after school — she taught me how to go hand over hand on the parallel bars, how to light a match, and how to climb the chain-link fence. There was a quietness and appropriateness to her house that ours never had. Her only sister was three or four years older, her father worked at an insurance company and always came home for supper, her parents had separate bedrooms. They even had a dog, a beautiful black and white collie named Prince. They went to Maine for the summers, while we only went for occasional rides to the beach. Sometimes we would sit in the kitchen and talk to Kay's mother while she cooked. I was Kay's "smart" friend. I would talk on and on to her mother, but I don't think Kay and I talked very much. We went to the library together and read the same horse and dog books.

My other best friend was a girl who had moved to town in third grade, Libby. She lived farther away, and her family was differ-ent, too, though in another way. Her parents were very strict and didn't let her do things like sleep over at other people's houses. But in other ways she seemed much more sophisticated than I. She asked me to go to the movies with her once, and I expected that her mother would pick us up and take us. Instead, her mother dropped us off at the theater and picked us up afterward. I was lucky I'd brought money just in case — usually the mother who took you brought you in and paid for the ticket.

Libby and I talked endlessly. We stayed inside the house and played games. One of our favorite was making up a romance for our fourth grade teacher. Her name was Miss Quinn, and, though she had white hair, she was the only pretty teacher in the school. She read to us frequently from a book called *Richard Halliburton's Book of Marvels*. Richard Halliburton was an adventurer who did things like swimming through the Panama Canal. It was obvious to all of us that Miss Quinn had a good deal of admiration for Richard Halliburton. So Libby and I alternated playing Richard and Kathleen (Miss Quinn's first name). In our most completely worked out scenario, Kathleen was at the top of the Alps (represented by the top landing of our steps) and Richard was painfully climbing the Alps step by step in an at-tempt to reach her.

Libby went to Hebrew School, too, but she was a grade below

me. We could walk there together, but we didn't see each other in class. She was, and is, a very beautiful girl. She sang well (I am tone-deaf) and was good at music. In the fourth grade, she was chosen to play the fourth grade flutophone solo in the spring concert, even though she'd just moved to town. I dressed up for the concert and my family took me to see her, but I was jealous. . . . I suspected she knew things I didn't about getting along in the world.

Fifth Grade. Libby and I were in different classes for the first and only time in all of elementary school, junior high school, and high school. I sat near Bill, Ruth, and Karen. Bill told dirty jokes continuously, and Ruth encouraged him. She wore peasant blouses that she puffed out in points to make it seem as if she had breasts. Karen had just transferred to our elementary school and was the most popular girl in the class. She had long blonde hair and an artificial tooth in the front of her mouth that everyone found fascinating. She lived on top of the hill and she had her own horse. Everyone wanted to be invited to Karen's house to play and ride her horse, but she never asked me. I started feeling that fifth grade society was passing me by. I told my mother and asked her what to do, and she told me. I could invite Karen home with me and she would make sure we had a good time. But I knew that wouldn't work, and I was angry at my mother for being so silly as to suggest it. My mother had convinced me to have my hair, which had been growing since first grade, cut — she said it was always messy and I never took good care of it. I felt robbed, ugly in short hair, and the only girl in the fifth grade who wore glasses. Bill always went around the class room pulling up the skirts of girls in the class. When he pulled up my skirt once he started laughing and said I was wearing boys' underwear. My mother always bought me white cotton underwear and I knew other girls wore underpants that were blue or pink or had flowers on them, but my mother said they were more expensive and impractical.

When I was in the fifth grade, my brother was in seventh grade. He always came home late from junior high school, because he wanted to stay for sports practice, or to fool around with his friends. Then my mother would worry and my father would yell at him. My father didn't consider my brother's reasons for being late legitimate. He thought that my brother should come home right after school and study. I didn't understand it either. I'd always been smart in school and when we started getting homework in the fifth grade, I handed mine in on time and done neatly. My parents expected me to be smart and good in school, and I was. They praised me and were angry at my brother. My brother started making fun of me all the time. I was "fat and ugly and dopey."

We still played together sometimes, but only rarely. One night my parents went out and left us home together to babysit, and we sat up telling each other all the dirty jokes we'd heard in school. It was illicit and pleasant. But most of the time when we were alone together we ended up screaming and hitting each other. My little brother had slept in my parents' room until he was a year old, and I slept in the other big bedroom that had two twin beds, while my older brother had the small bedroom. I kept begging my parents to let my little brother sleep in my room, but they said he couldn't, since I was a girl. Instead, they moved us around so that my two brothers shared the bigger room and I had the smaller one. I missed my old chest of drawers and the white organdy curtains my mother had let me pick out. Libby and I started reading magazines and making up plans to redecorate our rooms. We wanted dressing tables and wall paper with lavender flowers and canopy beds. The only compensation for having my room changed was that I didn't have to sleep with my grandmother anymore when she came to visit. My grandmother went to bed early, and I'd begun to hate having to undress in front of her.

The summer after fifth grade, Libby, my brother, and I all went to the same Jewish camp. Libby is a year younger than I, and I was secretly gratified that she was put in the youngest bunk and I was two bunks ahead of her. But she still fit into camp life much better than I did. She was cute and people made a pet of her. I was very tall for my age, and awkward. My mother had made me get a permanent before I left for camp, so my short hair would stay neat. Instead, it was a frizz over my head all summer, and I felt that my mother had betrayed me again. The other girls in my bunk were already setting their hair at night and worrying about their clothes. I read a lot and helped write our bunk skit. The counselors said I was an ideal camper.

Though we were supposed to be learning how to swim, and sail, and play tennis, we spent most of our time talking about boys. Each male counselor had a group of girls attached to him, who formed his following. I was very unhappy and left out until I became close friends with a girl named Sarah. We found out that we were distant cousins, and that seemed like a miracle and made us even more special friends. She lived somewhere in Ohio, but we'd never met each other before. Like me, she hadn't come to camp with a trunkful of clothes; like me, she was smart in school; and, like me, she was confused by most of what was going on. I don't remember what we talked about. I only remember that we would go into the bathroom at night when we were supposed to be asleep and discuss things endlessly. We held hands sometimes when we walked places.

I rarely saw my brother at camp. The boys' camp and girls'

camp were fairly separate, and he was in the next age group. Occasionally, he would come over to visit me, when we got packages from home. I was overwhelmed by his assurance and social success in the camp world — several girls had crushes on him. He was also somewhat of a rowdy and was almost not invited to come back. I wanted his approval very, very much, but didn't know how to get it. He didn't like my clinging to him, and he didn't like my wanting him to help me with things. He also didn't approve of my dependency on our parents. I adopted a kind of waiting attitude to him — letting him know I loved him and would always want to see him when he could see me.

Sixth Grade. How could so much have happened in one year? My brother's Bar Mitzvah was in October of that year. My parents were giving him a big party and I was allowed to invite one friend to keep me company. I chose Libby. I had expected that we would sit with my parents like children, but Libby seemed to think that we would be guests and sit with my brother's friends. We started talking on the telephone every night, planning what we would do and what we would wear. We made up a secret language. In our community, Bar Mitzvah parties were very important. They were everyone's initiation into . . . something or other. Not adulthood. They were the beginning of the social differentiation that parents emphasized between Jews and non-Jews. You only invited Jewish friends to Bar Mitzvah parties most of the time. Because you didn't want to *marry* someone who wasn't Jewish, and if you never started liking or dating a Gentile, there'd be no problem. Libby told me her mother was going to let her wear a padded bra to the party. I told my mother and cried because I'd be the only girl there without a bust, but my mother told me not to be silly. Once my mother and I bumped into Libby and her mother when we were both being taken shopping. Libby was having a fight with her mother because she wanted to buy shoes with heels on them. I didn't want shoes with heels. I'd never even thought of it. My mother told Libby's mother what a good girl I was and I was embarrassed.

Libby decided she was in love with my brother. I wasn't surprised because I loved my brother, too. I decided I was in love with my brother's best friend from camp, Stuart. That added another dimension to our telephone conversations. We could discuss for hours whether my brother would dance with Libby, and whether Stuart would dance with me. I knew that my brother didn't like Libby particularly, since she was my friend, but that didn't seem to make any difference. At the party, neither of them paid any attention to us, of course.

Soon after that, Libby and I had a fight. She'd started playing with a girl named Linda. Once again, she seemed to be moving into a world I didn't understand. She and Linda both played games I wasn't good at, like softball, and spent a lot of time talking to Linda's older sisters, one of whom was pregnant. Linda was also the second prettiest girl in the sixth grade (next to Karen) and had a boyfriend. I told Libby if she wasn't going to be my best friend I didn't want to be friends at all, and we stopped speaking to each other.

In the meantime, I played with Kay most of the time again. Kay's father had bought a kiln for making ceramics, and we spent most of our time in her basement that winter, making things. When her father was home in the evening, he would come down and help us, teaching us how to apply the glazes. We went ice skating in the afternoons and played with the stilts she'd been given for her birthday. We also decided to try to learn how to do cowboy rope tricks. In the spring, we ran around with all the boys and girls in our neighborhood, most of whom were younger. There was a vacant lot behind my house, and sometimes we played tag there, or sometimes we gathered different kinds of flowers to make magic spells with.

We had dancing class on Wednesday afternoons in the school auditorium. At the beginning of the hour, girls sat on one side of the room and boys on the other. I remember sitting there next to my friends and staring at the line of boys, wondering how I could make one of them come over and ask me to dance, to avoid the embarrassment of being left out. Libby made fun of me one afternoon for wearing knee socks with my black flats and I pushed her because I was so angry. Then I was shocked at what I'd done — girls weren't supposed to hit people. In the springtime one day Libby said hello to me and suddenly we were speaking and friends again. I didn't understand why she'd been allowed to end the fight on her terms, but I was grateful to be back in her good graces.

About that time I decided that I needed to get a bra, since most of the other girls had one. I didn't know how to bring up the subject with my mother. I wanted her to talk to me. Finally I told her that I didn't want to wear undershirts any more. She took me to the store to get a bra. At first I kept forgetting to wear it. When my father was driving me somewhere later that week, I pulled up my jersey in back to show him what I was wearing, and I walked into my brother's room one morning and asked him to hook it for me. I wanted them both to know I was growing up.

What were my parents doing all that time? I felt farther and farther away from them. They fought with my older brother constantly. My older brother didn't want to get good grades in school. He didn't want to go to Hebrew School. He wanted to get Boy Scout merit badges (but my father was never home to help him) and to be on the school basketball team and to hang around after school and smoke stolen cigarettes. When I intervened on my brother's side, my father would say, "Don't you go mixing in now. It's none of your business." He treated my mother the same way, when she tried to temper his anger. And when I took my father's side, as I occasionally did, it made my brother hate me.

My parents were arguing between themselves, too. My father was rarely home, and when he was home he would be tired and hungry and irritated. My mother seemed to regard my father as something to put up with. She was loving and patient and kind and thoughtful until some unkind, unthoughtful, critical thing he said drove her too far, and then she would blow up and they would both scream at each other until my father slammed out of the house. My older brother and I were supposed to have inherited his temper. I began fighting with my father, too, about little things, like not finishing my asparagus or going barefoot in the house. We would scream at each other and sometimes hit each other. Then I'd be sent to my room and eventually my mother would come and comfort me and tell me that the only thing to do when Daddy was in a bad mood was to avoid him. I learned to kiss my father and tell him I loved him, then get out of the room fast when I saw trouble coming. But I resented my mother for not being able to find a better way to deal with my father. She almost never lost her temper with me, but I began picking fights with her, and when she did get angry, reconciliation was always a lengthy process, involving many apologies from me.

I'd always expected to grow up and suddenly be beautiful. It was that way in all the books. But I wasn't beautiful at all. And my mother wasn't any help. Other girls' mothers took them shopping and took them to beauty parlors and told them what to do, I thought. My mother seemed to expect me to figure out for myself what she had never learned. She was pleased when I got good grades, but it seemed that she wanted something more from me, that she never taught me how to do.

Before I left for camp again, the summer after sixth grade, Kay and I went bicycle riding. Afterwards we went to her house and I remember staring into the mirror in her bedroom. I pinched my cheeks to make them look pink, then told her that when you did that your eyes looked brighter, too. It was something Libby had taught me. She wasn't interested. And after I came back from camp that summer and seventh grade began — seventh grade with temple dancing classes and its round of Bar Mitzvah parties and girls starting to wear lipstick and use acne medicine and get excused from gym on certain days of the month — I hardly saw her any more.

Topic Three

Sibling Relationship in the Context of Parental Attachment

Case 5 / If You Had Been a Boy, I Would Have Married You

After the sudden and violent deaths of their parents, Laura, who was eight, and Sue, who was twelve, lived with an aunt and uncle. Part of their "unmeasurable love" for each other has included a constant "deadly measuring": endless comparisons about their appearances, accomplishments, sexuality, personality styles, and timing of development.

They had quite different relationships with their parents and reacted to loss with quite different ways of grieving and coping. Their recent marriages have not altered their pacts, affectionate feelings, and fantasies about each other. Further development of personal autonomy and marital intimacy may hinge on their seeking a less intense attachment and a more contemporary basis for relationship.

Married and living hundreds of miles apart, Sue and I continue our relationship more by our mutually recognized close feelings for one another than by letters or visits. But feeling quite separated from me, she recently wrote:

> I feel an unmeasurable love for you — sometimes "almost more" than for Jack [Sue's husband] — at least that is what he may sense. But it is so different a love — not one that deflects or cancels out the other. He tells me, "Just look, can't you see that it's not reciprocated fully? Everyone can see that." That shakes me — it may be true — but he has admitted that he is terribly jealous — so I will try not to think about intensities of love — at least not now when we must show our husbands that they are most important. Long ago I began to live a more full life by imagining that part of me lives inside my sister, to make use of her experiences in shaping my personal philosophies. The gross side of this leads to a deadly measuring. "More/Less? Better/Worse?" Maturity will ease this I pray. I wasn't so aware of this compulsion before we were married, but it must have been there. I remember I had it only in Hawaiian antique shops [Sue and I traveled to Hawaii together two summers ago] — the conviction that you were the beautiful one, that your taste was better. We used to enjoy a code language full of our own humor. I never felt jealousy when I described my beautiful, intelligent sister — it was above that. "Sister? But you're so *nice* to each

other." Twins people thought us – perhaps sensing the closeness
and mutual dependency, I was always younger if they thought us
just sisters. We remembered Tabby [Tabby was our cat when we
were children], all our Christmases, and that difficult time. [The
"difficult time" refers to the first few years that we lived with our
aunt and uncle.] No one else can ever know these things. You
make my past an immediate, a tangible thing. Without you there
is the danger that Martinville [Martinville is a small town in Vermont where we lived with our mother and father] would seem a
story I heard so many times that it became part of me – but
vaguely, myopically, not analyzed. Dead leaves fallen from once
living trees. Our parents.

I too feel an "unmeasurable love"; Sue is more than my sister. And
Jack is justified in his jealousy, for Ty would feel jealous too if he knew
to what extent I loved Sue. I agree – "It is so different a love – not
one that deflects or cancels out the other." However both Sue and I
feel that husbands can change but sisters are forever – Sue will always
by my only sister and literally my closest relative.

Jack's comment that her love is not reciprocated fully by me
seems more a comment thrown to Sue in jealousy than anything with
truth in it. However, this comment "shakes" Sue and she puzzles over
it. Unsure that Jack speaks out of jealousy, she is yet hesitant to explore the ramifications of his remarks. She "will try not to think about
intensities of love." Sue asked me at one time, more than a year ago,
"Do you think you love Ty more than he loves you?" I said that I
thought that he loved me more. She seemed surprised. Perhaps she felt
she loved me more and loved Jack more than we loved her. Sue feels
she needs others, I believe, more than they need her.

My sister continues in her letter ". . . I will try not to think
about intensities of love – at least not now when we must show our
husbands that they are most important." Sue and I have made conscious efforts to show our husbands that they are most important. This
past summer Ty and I decided to travel through Scandinavia for our
honeymoon. We wrote Sue and Jack, who were living in France, and
asked if they would like to go with us. Surprisingly they said yes, and
we signed them up with the group. Although it meant coming to
Boston from France and returning to Europe in ten days, Jack and
Sue came for our wedding first before the trip. Jack undoubtedly
thought this extravagant; I even would have understood if they did
not want to pay the money for this, but Sue said that she would never
have missed my wedding. She was like a mother wanting to be at her
daughter's wedding.

Although it might seem that Ty and I were doing something
difficult combining our honeymoon with traveling in a group including

Sue and Jack, Ty and I had been going to bed together for two years. It was actually Sue and Jack who had more difficulty. One major problem was their comparison of Ty and me to themselves. This comparison had many aspects, but perhaps the most important one was their evaluation of our sexuality with theirs. Jack had been to bed with a woman only once before his wedding night, and Sue was a virgin at twenty-four when she married him. Jack's one experience had been traumatic, so I've been told, and Sue had "saved" herself for marriage. She told me at one time that she was probably a little too excessive in waiting for her first experience until she was married, and she also had felt some disappointment in Jack.

Sue felt that Ty knew much more about women than Jack. During a conversation not long before our trip, I had told Sue that Ty had had experiences with other girls — he had the aura of a "stud" to Sue and Jack as well. Tanned and wearing T-shirts and shorts, Ty did look the part and I agreed with Sue when she said several times that he was very masculine. She said he had the best legs she had ever seen on a boy. I remember trying to let her get a look at Ty's nude back because I thought it was especially worthy of admiration. I think she finally saw — who couldn't help but see in the small quarters. Ty told me that she had told him he was a very sensual person. There was never any question of who went to bed more often during the trip; it was assumed that we did. Sue had written to me that Jack had been impotent when they first married, and this undercurrent of Ty's sexuality perhaps was continued by Sue's unfulfilled expectations.

Perhaps surprisingly I had felt that I would like to share Ty with Sue. A warm and affectionate man in many ways, Ty, I believe, could give Sue affection in addition to mine. I have never felt jealous when Ty has kissed her hello, and I have actually wanted him to. Perhaps I would not feel this way had I any doubts of Ty's love or felt he was particularly attracted to Sue. One night the spring of my freshman year Sue came to visit me, and Ty, Sue, and I went to Williams for their spring weekend. A friend from our town wanted a date. Ty and I were hoping to be with each other, and there were two double beds in the motel room. However Sue refused to sleep in the same bed as Don. So in our bed we had Ty in the middle and Sue and I on either side. We laughed about the situation for awhile and I felt very happy that night. Sue could see that she was included in my life and that I wanted her to feel loved. I thought of her also as our child.

It may seem strange that Sue stayed a virgin until she was twenty-four, but our aunt and uncle would never have tolerated premarital sex. They are quite Victorian, in fact Aunt May only left Sue a descriptive book about sex and in turn wanted her to explain it to me. By the time Sue talked to me, I actually knew more than she did (which was not much). Not wanting her to think bad of me, I did not tell her of my relationship with Ty until 1½ years after we started having intercourse. Unsuspecting of my sexual experience with Ty, our aunt made sure that Sue stayed with me the night before my wedding so she could tell me what to expect, for Sue had been married six months. We spent most of the night having me answer *her* questions as she rubbed my back. I felt the older sister again that night.

We have always given each other backrubs: probably she has enjoyed them more than I because she requested them much more. When Sue was tense, mother rubbed her and also our aunt did, so to her they are a sign of love and concern. We have felt good that we were sisters and able to do things like give backrubs to each other without the discomfort or embarrassment which usually arises from being too close to a member of the same sex.

Sue has mentioned that in college she was rubbing a girl-friend's feet and another friend was shocked, feeling that she was being slightly perverted. But in Hawaii when we traveled together, we held hands several times as we walked through the street, a custom which the Hawaiian women share with many European women, and it mutually felt good to be able to do this without receiving stares. We both need a great amount of physical contact and affection. Our affection for each other has been transmitted through words, hugs, and kisses whenever we leave each other for a period of time — I think we have a physical attraction for each other although I would say mine is a need for affection more than a sexual one.

Perhaps Sue has slight homosexual leanings, for she has admitted having a strong attraction to a few girls. The girls she has been attracted to have either been mother figures or someone whom she admired physically. Her senior year at college she was dressed as a French noblewoman and danced in a minuet with a girl dressed as a courtier. She told me that this girl looked very handsome in her costume and the two of them kept staring at each other as if they desired one another. Katherine was another girl from college, a mother figure, who weighed about 200 pounds. Sue lived with Katherine and another girl in Philadelphia, where she met Jack, also. Katherine took care of Sue, brushing her hair, hugging her, calling her "my little pixie." Sue told me that Katherine was actually beautiful when naked, having the most magnificent derrière she had ever seen — she was a perfect Rubens. At one time Sue took a photo of Katherine bare-breasted. Their relationship virtually ended with Katherine's jealousy of Jack. Perhaps the "unmeasurable love . . . almost more than for Jack" which she has for me does not have to be "so different a love" than her love for him. Sue needs affection, and separating sex from affection sometimes is a difficult operation.

Sue and I had many pressures on our relationship when we first went to live with our aunt and uncle in Florida after our parents died. The auto accident started the "difficult time" that Sue mentions in her letter to me. Sue was twelve, I was eight, and our difference in age greatly affected the way we each adjusted to our new home. Our only aunt and uncle were ten years older than our parents. Uncle Bill was an engineer working in a distant city during the week, and driving home on the weekends. Aunt May, Sue, and I stayed at home all week, and thus our environment was hardly a typical family one. Our aunt was so much like our mother; our uncle however was distinctly different from our father, and we hardly had time to understand him. He insisted on talking baby talk to us and getting his own way. Understandably he resented our coming to take his wife away from him literally, as well as from his primary place in her thoughts. I desperately wanted a father and tried to do anything to please him. I did not mind his baby talk and endured his idiosyncrasies as long as I felt this would make him love me more. But Sue could not tolerate what she thought was his childish characteristics such as "getting back" at her if she did something he especially disliked; for example, if he thought she shut the door in his face he would slam the door back at her.

I wanted to completely shift my allegiance from my real parents to my aunt and uncle, Mr. and Mrs. Banes. I wrote over and over "L-A-U-R-A B-A-N-E-S," my new name, during that first week, and I was ready to call them mother and father. However I found that I was not able to do these things. How could I be their child and Sue's sister while she still remained a Blake? As she was too old to be able to shift allegiances like me, I finally chose by the covert pressure put on me to remain a Blake. Although once again two years later I tried to call Aunt May "mother," I never was able, for Sue had already won a major battle. She needed me as a strong link to our past childhood.

I can remember an incident when I was three when I felt another intense loyalty to Sue. Our mother had gone to the hospital to have our younger sister, and Sue and I stayed at a woman's house for several days. Sue was playing a game with other children, a fantasy about being locked in a jail with only bread and water to eat. This imaginary situation was a reality to me. I felt Sue was actually locked in jail and I was afraid for her and afraid that she would remain separated from me. I did not want her to be hurt and thus have her leave as our mother had left. Sue symbolized constancy to me then, as she had later when our parents died.

Two opposing forces were pulling me throughout these years, loyalty to my sister, and a desire for a mother and father. These forces seemed incompatible much of the time since as long as I had a sister, I could never really be my aunt and uncle's daughter. I loved her, but I wanted to forget about her and what she represented, our real parents, and life in Martinville. I became uncomfortably silent and would empathize with her during the times my uncle would criticize Sue, but I would also feel a certain pleasure during these occasions for I felt he loved me then. His criticism pointed to a further rise in my relative position to Sue. Sometimes as I grew older I began to meekly defend her, but of course his criticism also became less and less through the years.

After he had been mad at her, Sue would try to get back at him in covert ways such as turning his silverware upside down when she set the table. Joining her in some of her secretive, harmless ways of getting even with Uncle Bill, I would make up rhymes and songs with Sue or hide something that was his. I desperately wanted them to get along, but if they could not, I hoped he would not yell at *me* most of all. Sue was careful to leave me out of the arguments, she has told me. She realized that I was trying hard to love Uncle Bill. Unfortunately one of their most used accusations was, "You don't love your sister — you only love yourself." Sue got particularly upset when they said this because I was one of the only things she felt she loved. I think she worried that I would be turned against her. Together we would talk about our parents and the things we did in Martinville; she felt more peaceful after doing this. My sister drew me into these conversations to tighten our mutual bonds as well as just for reminiscing. We had something together which our aunt and uncle couldn't share. Undoubtedly she felt a responsibility to take care of me, but she was having too much trouble herself to be able to do this.

Everything must have seemed so much easier for me than for her. In many ways she needed me while I wished she were not there. Uncle Bill paid particular attention to me — on the weekends he would always give me rides on his shoulders and we would walk around our lot looking at the flowers and peeking in at Aunt May in the kitchen. They encouraged my having friends and bringing them home with me, never complaining of the long drives to take me to most of their homes. Sue had one very good girlfriend during our first years in Florida, at an age where I could not really understand Sue's problems and be a companion to her for we were struggling with our own particular adjustments. The most puzzling and discouraging thing to me was that Sue seemed rather un-self-sacrificing for not giving in to Uncle Bill in order to avoid conflicts like I did. To her I must have given in too easily, and I must not have had a mind of my own, but I feel she sensed my great need for parental love and knew she could not give it.

I must give some of our background to explain the confession of Sue's "imagining that part of me lives inside my sister, to make use of her experiences in shaping my personal philosophies." Sue was quite introverted and although people liked her, she was hard to approach, I feel. She spent much of her time painting and reading and did not date more than a couple of times until her senior year in high school when she met Fred. In Martinville she had had many boyfriends, even to the point of being called "boy-crazy" by a couple of mothers. Sue did not feel able to cope with relatively intense and demanding relationships when she was in junior high and high school. She had so many problems of her own, not getting along with Uncle Bill, her loneliness for our dead family, and a fear of losing any people she might become close to. I was very different from her — Sue commented that I never wanted to be alone in the house and she was correct.

I wanted to be popular and was elected to many offices in schools. I felt a compulsive need to have everyone like me and would be very bothered if someone did not. Sue was proud of my popularity but later I felt envious of her much less acute need for approval it seemed. She welcomed me into her room to tell her of all the boys who seemed to like me and seemed to enjoy hearing as much as I liked talking about them. One of the boys whom I especially liked and who liked me had a brother in her senior class who was very popular. I think she felt proud that I was able to get along with this type of person to whom she did not feel close. She writes, "I never felt jealousy when I described my beautiful, intelligent sister — it was above that." Her few girlfriends were not in the "popular" group although mine were always among this rather defined class. I wished that I could have been prouder of my sister in this aspect, but I also did not want her to surpass me.

Sue's visits to Cambridge once or twice a year have been another indication of her wanting to share my experiences. We have had perhaps our happiest times together during these periods. I took her to a class seminar at one time, and she was allowed to sit at the table in the group. She was the only one allowed this privilege, I think because people could sense how close we were. If she did not quite seem like a twin, she was like my younger sister who I was showing around the school. Many people took her as such.

One time we stayed in a rooming house in Cambridge that had a rather Victorian sitting room and bedroom. It was like being two matronly spinsters who kept house for each other. Perhaps I should now mention a fantasy which we have shared. It is of being old ladies who live together. We are spinsters, perhaps having suffered tragic love affairs. We would be known as sweet, enjoyable old ladies who would be popular to have for dinner and who would travel. We still believe that we will someday travel together again like we did in

Hawaii, perhaps if we become widows. Since Sue and I both have trust funds giving us $11,000 or so each year, we see this travel as a possibility.

When she writes, I enjoy her telling in detail what her average day is like so I can picture what she is doing; she enjoys receiving the same information. Before Sue was married I envied her rather glamorous life like she has probably envied mine. Living by herself, painting, and totally free, she seemed happy to me, but perhaps her life was less glamorous than empty. However Sue does not seem to get as lonely as I do. She enjoys being alone for long periods to read and think. On our Hawaiian trip she asked me to leave the hotel room one of two times so she might have a day to herself in order to collect her thoughts. She was very apologetic to me when she asked for privacy and seemed to feel guilty.

I have enjoyed her telling of her life in France last year, and before I got married I had a fantasy that Ty would somehow leave me or die so that I would have to come to France and be consoled by Sue. She or even Jack and she would comfort me. She and I would enjoy shopping together and viewing the palaces and art. Sue has mentioned that she sometimes thinks of the money we could use for trips and shopping together and viewing the palaces and art if we did not have to support husbands. I would be much less a burden on her than Jack is in many ways. She not only would not have to support me, she would not have to be the sole one to cook, wash, and clean — she has thought of this a few times too.

Having a part of me living inside her, Sue thinks, leads to "a deadly measuring, More/Less? Better/Worse?" Although we have a very close relationship, we still are siblings and have rivalry. Sue was almost four when I was born. Our parents' first child and a very pretty girl, she was used to receiving attention and having her own way. She remembers feeling proud of me, the new baby, and taking care of me but would call to mother's attention that I had almost no hair nor fingernails. Although I don't remember, Sue admits blaming many of her mistakes on me. One time she broke a vase and told mother that I had done it; I did not understand but told mother that I was sorry. She had a precocious ability to draw and I tried to follow her example, even getting credit in my grade school for having some ability myself although it was nothing more than being able to copy her. I would lose patience with myself in playing games because I was not as good as she was. Sue was jealous of me however because I got to do things sooner than she had been able to do them because she had "broken the way."

After we came to live with our aunt and uncle, I became the more competent one. I was entrusted with the responsibility of getting

Sue up in the morning and was left with the tasks of responsibility. It seemed that I was the older in many ways because I would be on time while Sue was always late. A year and a half ago I decided that Sue and I should go to Hawaii together and left her with arrangements of getting a travel agent since I was having finals. Two weeks before our departure our uncle had to visit her and do the planning himself.

She writes, "I was always younger if they thought us sisters." This observation which many people make must not be based only on outward appearances. Sue has not wanted to grow up, although this feeling became less acute when we began living with Aunt May and Uncle Bill. Her childhood she remembers as her happiest period and remembers vividly when she was eight thinking that when she was old she would wish that she were a child again. Never wanting anything to change, she felt a nebulous fear that nothing good would last. At the beginning of her menses I remember her hysterical crying in the bathroom and my mother and father taking trips in to comfort her.

The "deadly measuring" became noticeable to her after our marriages. Was this because we were now on a much more equal footing? She could no longer be the younger one? We had to prove ourselves as wives and as couples with our husbands? The spring before last, Sue met Jack and fell in love with him; this was not long after Ty and I had decided that we could marry sometime in one or two years. At Sue's wedding last year everyone was surprised at how much Jack and Ty looked alike. Both were the same height and had the same color hair and eyes. We were, in a far-fetched way, twin-couples. The strange phenomenon was that somehow I had the impression that Jack was half-Jewish like Ty was, and I told many people this. To my knowledge people still believe this although Jack is of Polish ancestry. We have hoped that they would be good friends, and it seems that they are compatible. Sue had had many opportunities to marry, but she finally decided that she should marry Jack. Perhaps my impending marriage persuaded her, although I would think she would not recognize this. I felt very depressed when she married. After the ceremony I cried uncontrollably until Sue left Jack against his will and came to comfort me. She said, "Laura, if you had been a boy, you know that I would have married you." Although I was pleased with this confession, it sounded strange.

In school I have always received better grades than she, mostly A's instead of her B's and C's. By doing this I compared myself favorably with my sister, at least in the eyes of my uncle who wanted me to do well. I don't know when Sue told me but I knew by my junior year in high school — when Sue had been tested for her I.Q., that she received a very high score. Called into the counselor's office, she was told that they were expecting her to be achieving a great deal for her

I.Q. was 165. Sue said that she did not know she had received such a high score but that at the time of her testing she knew that she was doing very well. Her I.Q. score has given me complex feelings. First, I don't believe that the test was accurate because we would know if there were a genius in the family, secondly I had been proud of her for just getting the score once, and thirdly I feel that no matter how good my grades in high school might be or how well my college grades compare with hers, she has proven herself by achieving 165 on an I.Q. test. It would seem that she does not ever need to feel worried if people criticize her intelligence. However on our trip Jack treated Sue's opinions as if they were worthless. He kept saying that she was not rational enough and belittled what she said. Ty joined in the criticism somewhat. Sue at one point cried. The men did not criticize me for being irrational. Even with her test score, there seem to be reasons that Sue would feel unsure of herself.

In her letter Sue continues, "You make the past an immediate, tangible thing. Without you there is the danger that Martinville would seem a story heard so many times that it became part of me – but vaguely, myopically, not analyzed. Dead leaves fallen from once living trees. Our parents." This last part of her letter explains more than any other thing why we have such a close relationship. We survived the auto accident together, and we have the uncanny feeling that we will die together. When we went to Hawaii we held each other's hands during take-offs and landings, ready to die with each other. I remember the car accident very vividly. Sue cried continuously before the accident, impervious to our mother's consolations. There did not seem any rational reason for her hysterics, but she said that she knew we were going to crash. Our father continued to drive along the winding and precipitous mountain road and nothing seemed farther away to me than our deaths. I remember distinctly Sue's remark, "Laura won't die: The name of the peak is St. Laurent."

Sue symbolizes stability and continuity. She will always love me, she will always help me. Several Christmases ago we gave each other gold wedding-band rings with engravings inside them. I initiated the idea and told her that if she ever needed me very badly she should send me the ring and I would come under any circumstance. She engraved on the ring she gave me "love and help always." I have no doubt that she would leave Jack to come to me if I really needed her.

But our relationship is not all love, a losing of oneself in the other. As Sue wrote, there is "a deadly measuring" between us. We mutually envy each other. I honestly feel her side of the scales is heavier, but I also feel that I want to be myself and would not change positions with her. I do not believe that Sue does realize how much I envy her, but it would be uncomfortable to tell her.

Jack, Sue, Ty and I split from each other in Scandinavia as we went on separately. When we met with each other again in Belgium, Sue had been chosen by a producer to be the female lead in a travelog to be shown internationally. She and Jack stayed there for three weeks while she made the film. Of course I was envious as well as happy for her, and I know that I could never have been chosen for the part for Sue is prettier. It is best for me to try to forget what I envy; however, I think Sue tries to mentally balance the scales, "Better/Worse? More/Less?" This certainly leads to much unhappiness. I try to understand that we both must work with what we ourselves have and try not to measure ourselves against each other. This comparison with each other was done to us when we were younger by our aunt and uncle and perhaps Jack is now making these comparisons again. Studying for his Ph.D. Jack probably values my applications to graduate schools for next year and shows his approval of this to Sue. He also does not criticize my irrationality as he does Sue's. My sister does not receive enough appreciation from him, and he is expecting her to act like the older sister. Am I more a challenge to her now that we can be compared more on the same level as married, grown women? Sue hopes that "maturity will ease this." Perhaps maturity will also ease our mutual dependency.

When I visited her in Philadelphia, two years ago, Sue said, "Laura, I did not realize how depressed you get." I was surprised that she said this for I had just been through a short but intense period of depression. Perhaps more than anything, I envy her lack or seeming lack of mental depression and frustration. She seems less concerned about achieving and thus has less anxiety when she does not. At times I literally hate myself for not being the way I want to be. I feel she has many more talents than I have — drawing, painting, cooking and decorating, as well as other things which I have mentioned. However, she does not seem to use them. Although I do not feel I am overly motivated, at least I want to accomplish certain things, and perhaps I have done more than she has with my life so far.

Sue is rather like our paternal grandmother who wanted to be a "fine lady." To some extent she identifies herself with this dead grandmother. Nana, who also lived in Martinville was a small, pretty woman. Sue has told me that Nana said that small breasts were the sign of a lady. This smallness is something which Sue shared with Nana, and I certainly do not. Not an active or personally ambitious woman, Nana defined herself in rather Victorian terms; she and her husband did not kiss the last nine years before she died. (Her death occurred six months before our mother, father, and little sister died.)

To everyone in our family, I remarkably resemble our mother. Sue's and my maternal grandmother still cries whenever she first sees me after having been away. Grandmother even screamed one evening when I came to the back door because she thought I was Mother. Fortunately people have tried not to stress this resemblance. Nana and mother had a very difficult relationship. Living in the same small town, they could not help but have disagreements over our father's life and how the household should be run. Our mother kept her emotions very concealed and her bitten fingernails were usually the only sign of her anxiety. However, I have heard from my aunt and sister that one time Nana said one thing too many for Mother to stand. Mother, rushing up to her, put her hands around Nana's neck and began strangling her before she even realized what she was doing. Sue has agreed with me that some of my inner turmoil could be related to that which Mother had.

Sue has also said that she has felt guilty over the way she treated Mother when she was alive. Sue and I both took our father as our favorite, and Sue has memories of hurting remarks she gave to Mother. But she has said that as she grew older, Mother and she began having more things in common, and she imagined that Mother could have been a very good companion to a teenage girl.

Case 6 / Teaching Ourselves to Cackle

At the time of Connie's birth, there already was considerable strain between her mother and older sister, Kim. With the role of "obstreperous daughter" already taken, Connie eased into the complementary position of "less willful daughter." The sisters competed in separate arenas for recognition and affection from Mother. Both Mother and Kim were powerful figures in Connie's childhood. She didn't emerge from the shadow of her older sister until Kim went off to college.

The struggle for interpersonal power, the seeking of gender identity, and the deprivation of affection and acceptance intertwine as themes in Connie's dreams and fantasies. Witches luring their victims with poisoned gifts are both frightening and fascinating; she feels a primordial identification with her fantasied creations.

A strength of this case is Connie's richness of imagery and exposition of her view. But a weakness is that Kim undoubtedly has had very different perceptions and interpretations which the reader would need to consider for a balanced and fuller understanding. Nevertheless, this case provides a unique opportunity to consider a sibling relationship in the context of two mother-daughter relationships.

I'm not at all sure what I would be if Kim hadn't been — and been first. Mother says now that she wasn't ready for Kim; she was herself only 22, had been an only child, and knew little about infants. Apparently, Kim and Mother battled from the start. Kim would howl with hunger and frustration, and Mother, whose current mentor was a rigid advocate of schedules and discipline, would withhold the conciliatory cracker, or not help Kim down from the chair she had precociously climbed. By the time I was born, she had relaxed somewhat, had read Spock at least, and claims that I was a more "accepting" child, less irritable, less willful. At any rate, the relationship between Kim and Mother has always been abysmal. As a small child, Kim never accepted a kiss without turning away, and to this day (she is now 32), their relationship has remained a nightmare of misunderstandings, tension, infliction of will, without a single tender break that I can recall, but that is another story. I tell it only because it is a necessary catalyst to our story, as Mother was a necessary catalyst to my relations with my sister.

My earliest sense of "self" was that I was Kim's little sister. Apparently, I didn't speak until nearly three — she did all the talking for us . . . or maybe I was overwhelmed at having such an articulate big sister. I preferred to operate with minimal sign language. We were often dressed alike — she in red, I in blue. Judging from pictures, it appears that there was affection between us at this early stage; there are pictures of us hugging and squeezing each other. I don't remember ever receiving any physical affection from her . . . these hugs must have stopped when I was three or four. After that, there was some affectionate teasing between us . . . tickling bouts, giggling, but mostly I remember how we opposed each other, not fighting physically, but working out "psychic survival systems" that depended on Destruction through Definition and Possession. It seemed as though we competed for everything — friends (she had the advantage here, being the elder, and thus possessed more status), the affection of a younger sister (too young to enter the rival system, except as pawn), and "qualities." If one of us was one thing, the other could not be so; it was too threatening. Thus, if Kim was good in school, I could not be . . . that territory was staked out. If I could write poetry, she had better not try. She was athletic, I dramatic, and so on. This might have been fine, if we really were so different, but I don't think we were, or had to have been. In many ways, we became what we were in perverse reaction to the definition of self each handed to the other.

I defined her in part just by being BORN — by threatening the love between Kim and Mother that must have been precarious from the start. Kim was old enough and powerful enough (in relation to me) to define me more vocally and vigorously. I remember the nicknames she had for me: "Goon-girl," "Goofus," or just, "Idiot Child." Nothing unusual. But I thought as a child that she was a sort of witch: that if she said something, it became fact. She told me in 8th grade that I would never make it through algebra, and sure enough, I cried the

first night of that bloody subject because I knew I would never understand the meaning of "X" and, sure enough, I had to go to summer
school. "Are any of your friends as dumb as I am?" I once asked her.
(She had to think for a while before she came up with one.) I was
thirteen at the time, the high (low?) point of my "dumb" years. A year
later I asked her if anyone in her class was as flat-chested as I. ("Am I
doomed to be a braless freak or is there some hope that I'll sprout as
late as sixteen?") She really had to think on this one, but couldn't
come up with a soul. I was cursed.

Why the hell I asked her these questions is, in a way, more
shocking than her answer. It has occurred to me that I needed to be
a masochist — so that we would "accept" each other. Yet in our
perverse way, we did love each other, or try to. We crooned little
"hate" songs to each other, taking popular love ditties and giving them
the appropriate deadly twist, "Why do I hate youuuuuuu?" we sang.
I remember teasing Kim (for her I was a sort of witch too, though
Mother was Chief Witch) and when I invoked BADMORNINGWAKE-
LOOSE, (instead of goodnightsleeptight) she couldn't close her eyes
until I'd lifted the curse. Once, to get a real reaction, I bent over and
showed her my ass. . . . It worked; she went screaming from the
room. (It's good to have memories like this . . . for it is too easy to
see myself as passive in our relationship, but I see now that in my
ornery little sister way, I did get back at her.) And I remember one
tender incongruous moment, when Kim told me she had always loved
my face. Did I tell her something equally nice? I don't remember.
Mostly we compared each other in the most idiotic ways . . . whose
voice was higher (mine, that was better) . . . whose hair was darker
. . . (hers, that was better).

Kim claims now that it was obvious that I was loved more,
encouraged more by parents than she was. It's true that I got great
praise when I acted, which is no doubt why I did, at least at first. I
remember Kim's pain when I was in these plays. . . . She could never
bear to hear me complimented or applauded . . . and she herself
maintained a stiff silence, though she did go to these performances.
Even now she turns away if I am embraced or responded to effusively
in her presence. I was aware that I had an easier time with parents
than she had, that they could relax and be more "parental" with me,
but I often felt victimized by Kim and her problems. Once I came
home and announced that I had a lead in the school play, only to be
shushed because Kim was in the room, and would be hurt if she
heard. I don't remember thinking that Mother loved me more than she
did Kim, but she must have given this impression. We have an aunt
whom I met for the first time rather recently. She was unexpectedly
cold to me, but later, when she did warm up, she explained that,

Mother had always boasted about me so that she was sure I would be obnoxious — her sympathies were with the neglected Kim. (She had met Kim several years before she met me. . . . Perhaps this added to the coldness.) To me, Kim never seemed to be neglected, for there was such a barrage of words, of emotion even of a negative sort, going in her direction, while I, the "well-adjusted" one, the middle one, was left to fend. I blamed her as well as my parents for their difficulties. She was wicked and would go to hell (it didn't matter that we were Jewish). In a fit of impotence and disgust, I would sit under the ping-pong table and pray for her soul, as I listened to the battle cries. (My ping-pong table piety period, as my husband later called it.)

Kim and I shared a room from the time I was twelve to the time I was sixteen, and she went to college. What strikes me now is my passivity in an intolerable (and possibly fixable) situation. There was only room for one desk, and it was hers — I studied on the bed (mostly I scratched a bad case of athlete's foot) with no place for books or papers, dumbly resigned to messiness, low grades, and itching feet. One of the reasons I felt so neglected by parents at this time, was that it appeared OK to everyone that I should get barely passing grades. . . . I suppose they were unconsciously relieved that I was not going to compete with Kim for the A's. Our beds were placed head to head in "L" form, so that Kim's long dark hair switched in my face whenever she turned (a super masochist, I) I don't remember ever attempting to move the beds or ask for a part of the desk, or insist on rooming with our little sister, or live in the study. No, it seems I had to suffer. Complaints and criticism were always dealt with bitterly and defensively in our home — so much so that one never thought in terms of positive action; there was either a "scene" or one was mute, but problems were seldom confronted, let alone solved.

Neither of us dated much in high school, yet I had "boyfriends" at this time — guys who would come over informally to see me, as girls would — and I remember consciously basking in the realization that they found me warmer and more responsive than Kim. (Or would she only freeze when I was there?) Once, during the time I was repeating algebra in summer school, Jon called; he had dated Kim once several months before and had called to ask her out again. I remember flirting outrageously . . . she was at camp, and Jon and I ended by being "boyfriend" and "girlfriend" for the rest of my high school career. Kim and I never discussed Jon; later I wondered whether it was a critical incident, following the pattern (from her viewpoint) of my taking away something which might have been hers. From this point of view, the importance of the object taken is immaterial; the fact that there had been no real relationship established between Jon and Kim is less important than my imposing, my stealing. (An unsur-

prising metaphor for our psychic reality was the materially real act of
stealing from each other. I remember our hiding one another's library
books so we would have to pay. When I was older, love letters disappeared from my drawer, but I never could be absolutely sure.)

When Kim left for college, I became "me" in a sense never before possible. Immediately, my grades shot up; I inherited a desk to
work at, my thoughts became more organized and purposive, and —
maybe most important — my dreams were freed from the flailing black
whip. Curiously, no one at home expressed much surprise at the
transformation: the explanation was that I was at last free of math
courses. It took a long time for me to realize I could be intelligent,
that I could ski, that I could do any of the things that Kim had done
well at, and at which I would have been doomed to fail.

Of course this picture of me as total reaction to Kim is simplistic. I had often been perceived as sensitive or intelligent before
Kim left; it was only that she had an uncanny ability to make me
disbelieve what others tried to make me believe. And while I note
my passivity in relation to her, I also see a burgeoning competitive
streak. Perhaps it would be best to say that by crumbling my pedes-
tals, she forced me to stand on my own feet. Away from Kim, I more-
or-less bloomed. Away from parents (and me) Kim seemed to bloom
too; hers was an upward course all the way — she went right according
to the Bright Jewish Girl Schedule. After college she went directly to
grad school, became a lawyer, married an ambitious, scholarly Jewish
man (who resembled me in some features of his personality and tastes),
had a son, became active in Women's Lib, and in general seems happy
(at a cost I'll consider later). My successes have been more inner:
some extremely happy and long-lasting relationships (though not my
marriage), music, a rich fantasy and dream life. But I've no doubt that
Kim had her inner successes too.

For about a ten-year period I rarely saw Kim. Then curiously
(or perhaps not), I ended up living in a building adjacent to hers in
the city — both of us married. She was not jealous of my husband,
both of us were tucked away in quite different spheres, and for the first
time in our lives, we seemed to achieve a stable relationship. We didn't
see too much of each other, and when we did it was as couples. The
basis for whatever closeness we achieved was a shared hostility toward
our parents — mostly Mother. It's true that I was hostile toward
Mother at this point, but I was disgusted at myself for feeding more
grist into the maw of her already over-stuffed mill. Yet I realized that
as long as I joined in Kim's alienation from our parents, she would accept me, and my need for acceptance clearly overcame any reluctance.
By this time Kim had rejected my parents almost totally. (My!) She

barely went to the post office to pick up occasional gifts they would send; she would allow them to visit, but after several hours would inform them that she had work to do, etc. Her attitude was that if people make it too difficult for you to function, you have to lop off those people from your life. (I remember shuddering as I heard her express something that I at least partially agreed with, but would never act upon.) "When will she lop me off?" I remember wondering. Meanwhile, I thought of parents as well-meaning bulls in a psychic china shop — awkward, constantly saying or doing the wrong thing, but obviously trying. I never saw Kim *trying* with my parents.

When my marriage was making death rattles, Kim was close by and played the role of sister-consultant. More consultant than sister, really, but her interest warmed me. The complete rupture (marital) occurred a year later, at which time Kim, her husband, and child were living in England for the summer. Though I wasn't exactly basking in memories of her reflected warmth, I made arrangements to stay with them for a two-week period. I was hungry for family, for inclusion, and wanted badly to see Samuel, my nephew. I thought that perhaps, for the first time, Kim and I would become close. After all, if my position had ever been threatening, it wasn't now, or so I thought. I was husbandless, childless, degree-less, with little idea of where I would go next, or what I would do.

I should have been warned by the sign on the door. It said whoever might visit would not find them in since they had gone away for the week-end. (They had forgotten to take the sign down when they had returned. I was, I guess, "whoever.") For the first day or two (Carl had gone on a brief trip), Kim and I did have some good talks, probing our childhood, discussing old boyfriends. I appreciated the quickness of her mind, the aptness of her suggestions, and realized that we had so much to say to each other. I was mentally patting both of our backs for having overcome such difficult barriers.

But on the second or third day of my visit, the relationship began to deteriorate, slowly at first, and then increasing with furious momentum. Perhaps Carl's return was part of the cause. Did she fear his being attracted to me? Was I being seductive? I had thought not, but perhaps was so unconsciously; or was Kim seeing me that way no matter how I behaved? Money became a metaphor for possessiveness and belonging. Kim told me the first day what proportion of the grocery bill she expected me to pay — whoosh, went any chance on my part to be spontaneous and generous. Since I enjoyed doing the marketing, Kim started leaving pound notes for me ($2.40) with which to do the family shopping. Of course one pound doesn't go far — in four days I had spent the price of my return ticket to London. When I mentioned this, Kim gaily declared that she kept thinking of pound notes as a lot of money, and then (not so gaily) that I was being obnoxious about money. The pattern continued. . . . Paying my way at each museum and tea shop kept me reminded that I was *not* one of the family. (This on top of Carl's receiving a substantial salary for the summer.) By the end of the trip, an almost forgotten little-girl desire to steal overcame me. I ended up taking a ritual envelope from them, and packing it away.

Kim's reactions to me defined those days in England, and I realized with incredulity what much of my childhood had been like. I was "shushed" continually. Nobody consulted me about a trip "we" were planning to take to Scotland — I might as well have been a child, or better, the child of a distant relation. When Samuel broke a glass while I was in the room (Carl also was present), I got a lecture on irresponsibility, and comments concerning the incident continued during my stay: "Curious, he never broke anything before Connie was here," etc. Shit! Incidentally, I think I did become more irresponsible. At any rate, I lost all confidence with Samuel after a few days. I saw Kim react with distaste to my gesturing, to my overly exuberant descriptions of Ireland. (When I praised Ireland, she interpreted the remark as a denigration of England.) It was frightening to see with what rapidity the confidence-building of ten or fifteen years was shattered . . . for both of us, really. As our relationship crumbled, there seemed to be more attempt to show me how close they were as a family. Kim and Carl had always been overtly affectionate, but never so much as now. Samuel was taking his first steps, and there was joy and pride in their parenting. I remember a scene of them seated on the floor, with Samuel between, being gently pushed from one to the other. It looked like a small fortress. Perhaps from my work in theatre, I was excessively conscious of configurations. There would somehow be room for Kim and Carl and Samuel's stroller as we walked, but no room for me, so I would be ahead or behind, studiously taking pictures, or examining an apricot tree, trying not to emphasize my distance. Pictures were another means of exclusion. I took almost a roll of them; they had a camera along too, but never took a picture of me. (I feel petty in recounting all this, but yes, I did feel petty, mean, ungenerous in every way.)

Finally, things exploded. I think it was when I had a mental picture of what driving to Scotland would be like . . . me, packed in the back seat, like Frankie in *Member of the Wedding*. Trouble is, I wasn't a Frankie. It began with what was to be a quiet, dignified little cry in my room, but then I found I couldn't stop. I went for a walk, hoping to pull myself together, and couldn't. I knew I had to deal with Kim, to ask her *why* and *how;* after all, couldn't she see what was happening? And Carl, sensitive, bright, couldn't he see? Finally I returned, still aching and embarrassed, but wanting to talk.

Kim was coldly "objective," frighteningly so. She admitted the truth of my perceptions, that she was aware "that I might feel left out." She asked me why I hadn't objected much earlier to their shows of affection. . . . Hell, could I tell her how humiliating it would be to object to their kissing? She admitted that I caused her to regress, that she lost confidence around *me.* She saw herself becoming accusatory, commanding, petty, and didn't like herself. But she felt unable to stop; my gestures, my intonations caused a visceral reaction that made her irritable. She ended by saying, "If it was love you wanted, why did you come here? There was never any love in our family."

Crazy, but I felt relief when she said that — the sort of sick relief one feels when a relative dying slowly and painfully finally does die. The threat realized . . . this is what it felt to be lopped off. Carl's reaction to all this was one of sympathy and concern for both of us, but ultimately, of course, he was concerned with Kim's psychic well-being. He suggested that perhaps we should be resigned to a screwed-up childhood, that would make any real change in our relationship improbable. I didn't go to Scotland.

And what now. It is easy to say that the burden rests with her, that one cannot, after all, force a relationship. I am not a masochist, or particularly passive; I am not in any meaningful way defined as "Kim's little sister." If she will only have me on these terms, I can't come to know her well, for that definition of self atrophied when she went to college. But damn it . . . I could like Kim. In the course of writing this study, I found myself rereading a few letters we have written each other — one I wrote at thirteen; "I hope we can share problems together this year," and one she wrote me, wishing me a sweet sixteen birthday and promising me a gift. I felt like an archeologist on a dig: "Yes, you see! There *is* evidence of prehistoric affection!" I know our rebuffs to each other now are a sort of dare (Prove you love *me,* even if I seem to be rejecting you). But life is too short for such games and half-truths.

Several more episodes have occurred since the summer in England. Our visits to each other have been guarded, circumscribed, our words pruned. No more attempts at intimacy, at probing the past. I'll not make the mistake of going "for love" again. I would like to be hopeful, but my prognosis is a bit dreary.

For fun, I've included four dreams I've had concerning Kim. Two episodes of dreaming are from a journal I kept in England. The

others were recorded later. I've written them down exactly as I wrote
them when they happened, so if they seem jumbled and cryptic, it's
because they were, and I am.

August 6

Dreams of restriction — victim of past experience, back in Jr.
High, acted quiet, menaced, later — tried to fly, first through tall building with lots of compartments, couldn't find the window out (familiar
dream) later, flying outside, but menaced by intricate system of telephone wires — kept entangling me — kept me from liberation. (I received a letter from Bettina Aptheker in dream, but didn't help.)

August 7

Much attention to flying. I was asked, "How do you fly?" I responded, "The most important thing is confidence, the will to fly. You
start with minor elevations, pressed against walls, hugging the ceiling
— then you leap. (I knew if I was wrong, would fall and kill myself,
but didn't believe I would. Also, idea of becoming a witch so I could
fly better.) Then — wonderful flying sequences — could hear a great
rush of wind — soaring up and down in *open* spaces. Later, sitting in a
class (or something) I was "arrested." Crime was using maiden name —
also "driving carelessly," but this charge was less specific. I laughed at
the arresting officer, but as Connie Gordon was marched off and
booked. I had a great time telling them off, wasn't intimidated, soon
realized it was a mistake. (They realized it too — had thought I was a
young girl, "Karen," from California.) They realized finally I was 29,
had graduated, was "intelligent." I used these facts in my defense.
They had thought I was lying.

In another sequence, I stood up to Kim, who shushed me and
implied that it was my fault that we hadn't gone somewhere in Scotland *she* had wanted to go. Stood up to Kim and arresting officers in
same loud, arrogant tone.

November 13

Another confrontation dream with Kim. She and Carl were
tossing Samuel back and forth between them, while he laughed and
prattled. Then, casually, she turned and informed me that they expected me to babysit for them that evening. I told them sorry — I had
a date. All the while they argued with me, Carl was fondling Kim's
mouth so that I practically couldn't see her lips move. I asked him to
please stop. Around us were "witnesses" who sympathized with me —
I argued quite sensibly that I'd been given no notice and was busy.

Later, went to see Kim alone and said we were going to a jazz place that night and I couldn't possibly babysit. She said it was simply that so and so (another babysitter) was nicer than I am. I said I didn't give a damn — that being the nicest, sweetest person in her eyes didn't matter to me anymore. She was silent. I closed the door and walked away, feeling triumphant.

Early April

Kim and I had a lunch appointment. I took a bus to meet her, but missed the stop. It became hazy and raining. Later I saw her looking small, vulnerable. "But," she said, "you could have taken the bus back after you missed the stop." And I replied, "Yes, but you have been fucking me over all year," but her tears stopped me. I grew small inside and said, "But I don't want revenge. I love you and want your respect."

Several weeks ago, both my mother and father stayed with me at my apartment for a most revealing two days. Some psychological incubus was pressing hard on my chest. . . . There was much I needed to get "off," questions that had to be asked. As closely as possible, I recorded afterward my "transcriptions" of relevant questions and answers:

Me: When did Kim first oppose you?

Mom: Didn't I ever tell you about the Battle Royal? It happened about two weeks or a month before you were born. I was panicky at the idea of having two babies. Well Kim was a pretty grown-up eighteen-month-old kid, in many ways, and she had to realize that this chick had to get out of the nest . . . that she couldn't be Queen anymore. For five days we fought. I told her that her bottle was broken, and I wouldn't go back on my word. She refused to take anything out of the cup. I refused to give her the bottle. I don't think she drank anything for five days, except what she got in her food. She must have gotten a little dehydrated (nervous laugh). I *asked* people, and they all said, "Don't give in to her. Some take longer, some earlier. They all give in eventually. The important thing is not to back down."

Me: What happened after the five days? How did Kim act? [I didn't ask, but was thinking, did Kim mourn for her bottle as a lost object?]

Mom: She started jabbing her finger in and out of her mouth . . . sort of an oral masturbation. Her finger got quite swollen and sore. We had to bandage it up to keep her from hurting herself. [I express surprise.] Oh, that was nothing. When I was a child and sucked my thumb, my thumb and fingers were put in a steel encasement.

Me: Did Kim show hostility when I was born?

Mom: No . . . she didn't show much of anything. Oh, we let her play with you a little, but she never showed emotion. That was why it was so hard to see that there were problems. If she'd only *acted out!* She did start wetting her bed again (had been toilet trained at about a year) but we expected that.

Me: Did she know that you were going to have a baby?

Mom: I assume so.

Me: Did you tell her?"

Mom: I don't think we told her specifically, but she must have known. She was such a smart little girl . . . so sensitive. She took everything much harder than other children. When she got the measles, she wasn't white with red spots like other children . . . she was red with white spots.

Me: Did she watch when you nursed me?

Mom: No. I was afraid she'd be jealous. Daddy would keep her entertained in the living room while I nursed you in the bedroom. Daddy made me feel that nursing was a very private affair — not for the family. I was lonely and miserable in the bedroom.

Me: When do you remember Kim first acting in a hostile way?

Mom: Before she was about seven, Kim never let us know what she was really thinking. But after this time she became more openly hostile to both of us. You had taken some candy from a store, but you were only five — I didn't scold you. I assumed you didn't know better. A little later, Kim was caught stealing some cheap jewelry in the dime store. I was with her and I didn't scold her either. But I knew *she* knew better, and she scolded herself, which was worse. She felt that she had been treated unjustly, that it was all right for *you* to take things, but not *her*. She didn't kiss me goodnight that night. And ever since then she would turn her head away when I came to tuck her in. Do you remember when Kim stole your bank?

Me: Vaguely.

Mom: She had it for a whole year. I knew she had it, but she would deny it, and I had no evidence. Finally, after a year, I gave her closet a thorough cleaning, and sure enough, the bank was wrapped in a towel and stuck way in the back. . . .

Money. The situation in England, the demand that I *pay* continually for everything I get (and then some), and my desire to steal from them — all of this begins to "glister" with new-shed light.

But I was as dedicated a thief as Kim — maybe more so. Our

burglaries were reciprocal: she would take from me and I from her. Or, no, . . . that was a later pattern. The original pattern (also learned from Mother during those two days) was that I would steal money from Kim and use it to buy her a present. Apparently, I often left her little things — packets of trading cards, candy, but with money taken from her. I realize the connection of this early experience with one I had about five years ago. I had had a dream in which I was attracted to Carl. The day after the dream I was grocery shopping and suddenly was overwhelmed with a compulsion to steal something. I stole a vanilla bean. Again pure tokenism . . . I never used it any more than I used the envelope. Once, when I was nine years old, I was caught stealing in a dime store. My stolen object — a Valentine. I find, by the way, that an excellent barometer of my psychic well-being is this temptation to steal. It doesn't seem to matter whether I give in to it or not; the thefts are always token, and I haven't much truck with capitalism anyway. The problem is the invidious temptation when I'm feeling guilty, or neurotic, or threatened by separation.

Gifts. They were a problem in my family, for a gift should be warm and spontaneous (like a good BM, I guess), and ours never were. They were only given on State Occasions — birthdays, Hanukkah, and possibly, as souvenirs from trips. Trip presents are decidedly lesser, as can be seen by a card from a gift I received after my parents' trip to Mexico: "I was going to save this for your birthday, but why wait." Gifts to Kim — at least Mother's and mine — are almost invariably rejected. With Mother, I think this is always true. The only presents she accepts are those she specifically asks for . . . everything else is wrong somehow and is sent back. (The cheek turned away from Mother's poisoned kiss.) And in part, I agree with Kim's perceptions, for Mother has sent her some ugly presents. . . . Certainly, one can read ambivalence in them, if not downright hostility. With me, Kim is only supercritical, implying as she thanks me that the gift for Samuel was *almost* but not quite right. When Samuel was born, I made a stuffed animal for him, virtually baby-proof, which was not given to him on the grounds that he might bite off its firmly sewed on round button eyes and swallow them. (Or was it really on the grounds that, along with polka-dotted arms and legs, I had fashioned a tiny polka-dotted penis for this boy child? You can never be sure with my sister. Maybe this was an adult version of my bending over and exposing myself to her . . . or who knows?) Anyway, Samuel never saw it. The only time I remember receiving presents from Kim, by the way, was during our stable period in the city. Before and after there were none, except a wedding present, and the "required" birthday presents when we were quite young. In England I was told quite bluntly that although my birthday was to be spent there, they weren't in the habit of celebrating such occasions, and I shouldn't expect any special treatment.

Kim has practically stopped giving presents to family on special occasions. She has also practically stopped phoning or writing anyone. She will accept State Visits, if they are short and rather formal. (Even in the city when I lived next door, I was told to always telephone before dropping over.)

Finally — Poison and Witches . . . the most exotic saved for last. When I read Freud on the subject of weaning, how the milk is viewed by the infant as once good — now bad (poisoned), bells began ringing in my head. I remembered a conversation I had several years ago with Kim, during our "let's get Mother" stage. She told me that in kindergarten she used to be afraid to come home for lunch, because she thought the food would be poisoned. Moreover, she feared that Mother and I — left at home — turned into *witches:* the Big Witch and the Little One. *Mon Dieu* . . . how it all fits. I had no idea before this that Kim shared my witch fantasy. I knew that we "defined" each other, but never realized that "fellow witch" was part of the definition. (Though whether Kim saw herself as witch, I don't know.) For both of us, Mother was Chief Witch.

When I was a small child, I was more afraid of witches than anything. . . . Before writing this paper, I had attributed it to watching the Wizard of Oz at too tender an age. . . . Everything else I feared, I feared because of its connection with witches; hence, the dark was fearful because witches might be hiding in it. Even when I was an adolescent, Kim would tease me by asking me — in daylight -- if I believed in witches. No! I DON'T! And then . . . in the night, she would say to the dark: "Connie doesn't believe in witches, she DOESN'T BELIEVE! And I would become fearful, for if the witches knew I didn't *believe* in them, they would seek revenge, and come to claim me. I BELIEVE, I BELIEVE!

Certainly I believed that Kim and Mother still had power over me and that their long hair switching in my face at night (Kim's as she turned in sleep; Mother's as she kissed me goodnight) was Witches' Hair. And I made myself into a sort of witch too. In fact, the first part I played in a school play was the Wicked Witch, who at the end of the play was transformed into the Good Fairy. Good me, bad me. Good Kim, bad Kim. Good Mother, bad Mother. Where other children taught themselves to whistle, we taught ourselves to cackle. My favorite reading was fairy tales, especially Grimm and Andersen. Not surprisingly, my feelings toward witches were more complicated than unalloyed fear. Attraction was perhaps an equal component, for I not only feared and hated my mother and sister, I loved them too, and they me. The witch, with her poisoned gift, was a perfect symbol for all of us. "Take a bite from the pretty red cheek of the apple, my dear," the Witch said to Snow White.

I have had recurring dreams of witches over the years: witches beckoning to me, stirring potions, inviting me to taste, to put my finger into their brew. The dreams are highly sexual and full of mixed fears and attractions. The central question that ran through them was, "Am I a witch or not? Am I to join them or not?" I have thought of these as lesbian fantasies, but in a way, that is an oversimplification. Sister, mother, women — repulsion and attraction, fear of collusion, fear of isolation, incorporation or expulsion, poisoned milk and poisoned apple. What is curious is that most of my really satisfying relationships have been with women — that the primal fear/fascination has not kept me from seeking them as intimates, but rather seems to have energized me, to give me a feeling of relatedness that seems to go beyond the simple fact of shared gender. Perhaps it is that being a witch in my dreams is intimately connected with being a woman . . . not just me, or Kim, or Mother. Our bodies are somehow secretive. . . . We concoct within stews of blood, and issue babies. And we fly — my dreams are full of flying. Ironically, I can be liberated as a witch, as a woman, and fly out of the tangle of fears.

An Interpersonal Approach

Harry Stack Sullivan's theory of interpersonal development rests on the basic assumption that the experience of anxiety is unavoidable, always has an interpersonal context, drastically interferes with need fulfillment, and prompts a person to develop elaborate "security operations" for avoiding or minimizing that experience. By the time a person reaches early adolescence, he has developed (1) a repertory of security operations which work at least "well enough" and (2) a network of personifications of self and others which are partly "accurate" and partly distorted. A personification is a mental organization of one's accumulated experiences while interacting with another person. For each dyadic relationship, a person has a personification of self and a personification of the other person. Personification of self and parents — or self and all "significant others" — are particularly important and elaborate. One's

personification of the "good self" stems from an accumulation of all
the interactions in which needs were fulfilled, whereas one's
personification of the "bad self" stems from an accumulation of all
the interactions in which anxiety was experienced and needs were
frustrated. Personifications become distorted when a person
experiences anxiety. A person raised in a relatively secure
interpersonal environment expends much less energy in anxiety
avoidance, has a larger variety of needs reasonably fulfilled, and has
more accurate and differentiated personifications of self and others
than does a person who has habitually interacted with anxiety-prone
significant others. The more a person relies on security operations
while interacting, the more he resists change, does not learn from
his interpersonal relationships, and tends to be caught up in
self-imposed "restrictions in the freedom of living." Consider the
following analogy, which illustrates some of Sullivan's concepts.

It is appropriate for a young child to wade in shallow water
close to shore while attended by an adult. With increasing age a
series of water skills can be acquired: blowing bubbles, learning to
float and tread water, taking a few strokes in water not over one's
head, and eventually building greater confidence and competence at
coordinating stroking and breathing. Relying on water wings or an
inner tube for navigating on a lake is fun and appropriate for
children but is cumbersome for an adolescent, who should be
progressing to stroking-breathing competence and then to safety
and rescue techniques. But because of fear or inadequate
opportunity, many people do not get beyond the stage of staying
close to shore, and thus they *miss the experience* of swimming to
islands or across the lake. Others do not get beyond the stage of
using an inner tube and, although they could paddle across the lake,
it would take much more effort and could be disastrous if the inner
tube broke. The greater the fear or lack of opportunity, the less likely
it is that a person will progress to a higher level of skill and
enjoyment. Sullivan's concept of restrictions in the freedom of living
is analogous to relying on an inner tube or doing no more than
wading, once a person reaches adolescence or adulthood. A
preoccupation with anxiety-avoidance retards further development
and leaves unchanged the personification of self as a "wader or
paddler." Security operations or swimming skills which worked "well
enough" in childhood often are inadequate in adulthood.*

In his chapter "Late Adolescence" in *The Interpersonal*

---

* People who enter psychotherapy typically complain that they employ "flotil-
las of inner tubes" yet still feel insecure or cut off from free swimming in the
stream of life. An experienced therapist doesn't try to take away the "inner
tubes," but instead works on "elementary strokes and breathing."

Theory of Psychiatry (1953), Sullivan asserts that not until late adolescence do people begin to "manage" moderate levels of anxiety: that is, begin to want to face and overcome their anxiety rather than simply avoid it. The feeling of anxiety tells them that their interpersonal security is threatened and that unless that feeling is *lived with* while new ways of relating or new personifications of self and other are formed, the old ways of relating and the *formerly* adequate personifications will prevail. People update their personifications of self and others by (1) not holding old conceptions of people, but instead trying to recognize more contemporary behavior and efforts to change; and (2) seeking "consensual validation" of one's personifications — that is, testing their accuracy against the points of view of a variety of significant others. Also, by late adolescence, people become more willing to "be themselves" despite the interpersonal risks. Disagreeing with significant others or expressing anger toward them is the kind of "being oneself" that is most often anxiety-arousing. Constructive confrontation is a sophisticated interpersonal skill that is seldom learned because anxiety either interferes with initiating confrontation or causes it to degenerate into an exercise in guilt-inducing or threat-making. Constructive confrontation requires communicating what one wants and feels, trying to understand the other person's point of view, and remaining open to compromise and toleration of differences. Sullivan thought that a willingness to risk anxiety, an openness to learning from others, and an *appreciation* of others' differences indicated self-esteem and social maturity. An interpersonal approach to Cases 7–10 is to consider the ways people in each case avoid anxiety or grow in spite of it.

Topic Four

Updating Personifications of Self and Others

Case 7 / It's Better to Keep the Peace

Alan and his recent bride are uneasy about visiting his parents at home. Alan suspects that his mother is withholding information about Dad's "health problems." When he confronts his mother with his feelings Alan receives no verbal response from her. Later he becomes angry when family members have opinions and values different from his own. He feels he must either suppress his views to keep the peace or vehemently argue and later feel guilty. Alan's personification of himself as a potential counseling psychologist influences his actions and his interpretation of the situation at home.

Alan's mother's old personification of him, as the good boy who seldom disagrees or feels angry, is inconsistent with his now confronting her on the issue of withholding information. Alan, his father, and his sisters tend to relate to each other through Mom — and personifications of each other ultimately involve Mom, a powerful figure in the family.

An interpersonal analysis of this case might address these questions: What sort of a relationship does each person want with other family members? How does each person avoid or reduce anxiety? What changes in familial relationships are likely or desirable in the next few years?

As we came near to Michigan, I began to experience both excitement and a feeling of apprehension at the prospect of our impending visit with my family. Sharon, my wife, and I had not seen my family since their visit to Boston last spring. It was nearly the end of the summer now, and I thought of how much my teen-aged sisters must have grown since I last saw them. I thought too about my father's recent illness.

"I wonder how he will look," I asked myself. "He'll be thin, no doubt." I felt eager to see him and yet strangely apprehensive about it. "Why am I so reticent about our impending visit?" I thought. "Perhaps because I am afraid Dad might have taken a turn for the worse. Maybe Mom didn't tell us all there was . . ." The words that Mom used in her letter to tell us about Dad's illness kept going through my mind — "Nothing physically wrong, nothing physically wrong . . . what does this mean?" I asked myself. Mom was her usual vague self in her letter. All seemed to be well, but was it? Dad sounded OK on the phone when I called after receiving Mom's letter. At least he sounded OK. He sure sounded tired, though, like he hardly had enough energy to talk.

At this point my mind flashed back to my first reading of Mom's letter. She hadn't written for four or five weeks, and I was a little worried as not hearing from Mom usually means that there is something wrong at home. Yet, I thought, all people become irresponsible correspondents in the summer, even mothers. I remember reading the first paragraph of her letter.

"Dad's been ill," Mom wrote, "and has been out of work for five weeks now. But don't worry, as he is under doctor's care and there is nothing *physically* wrong with him — just the pressure of work."

I remembered the feelings that ran through me as I read that first paragraph and the remainder of the letter, each of equal force and each vying for power over the others. I felt a great deal of sympathy for Dad and I despaired at the thought of his being ill. To-gether with sympathy and despair, I felt an intense anger.

"Here I am, twenty-six years old," I remembered saying to my-self, "and Mom doesn't tell me until five weeks later that Dad has taken ill! Does she have no confidence in me? Maybe she is trying to protect me. Protection, yes, that is it."

From past experience I knew that Mom's attitude was to pro-tect her kids, if possible, from any unnecessary hurt. Remembering this, my angry feelings soon subsided. I then remembered how Sharon had reacted to Mom's letter.

"What if he had died?" I remember her saying with character-istic vehemence. "We wouldn't have even known that he was ill!"

I remembered vowing to say something to Mom about this during our August visit. As we drew near to Michigan, I reaffirmed to myself my pledge.

It was nearly ten o'clock when we drove into our driveway. I was quite pleased by our timing, as I had written that we'd be home around ten and here we were right on the nose. I felt good about my-self because, by the use of my little trick to tell the family that we'd be home about two hours later than I anticipated so as not to worry them if detained, I accomplished my task with supreme perfection.

I beeped the horn and heard our family dog begin to bark. Then I saw Brenda, my seventeen-year-old sister, appear on the back porch. By the time Sharon and I got out of the car, everyone had descended from the porch to greet us. It was a kissing and hugging affair. Together with Brenda there was Barb, my closest sibling, three years younger than I, and her husband Tom. Liz, my thirteen-year-old sister, was there too and, of course, Mom and Dad.

When I hugged and kissed Mom, I sensed that same warmth which I had so often felt in her presence. She had a big smile on her face and seemed to have a few tears in her eyes. I thought to myself that she must be so happy to have all of her kids together again.

When I stuck out my hand to shake hands with Dad, he grabbed my hand and pulled me toward him and gave me a big hug, an act uncommon to him as he is not the kind of man who openly dis-plays his feelings. I felt really good about Dad's expression of love. Then a thought crossed my mind:

"I wonder if he thought he'd never see me again?" But I was too excited by the whole occasion to dwell on that question too long, and I turned to see how everybody was. "Hey," I yelled out, "Dad and Tom are wearing mustaches! They look pretty good."

"We thought for sure that you'd come home wearing a beard," Mom replied jokingly.

I kidded back saying, "I'm a clean upstanding fellow."

After everyone had pitched in and helped move our belongings into the house, we all settled in the living room. Barb asked me how my summer's work at the hospital had gone, and I proceeded to give a lengthy account of my responsibilities. As Barb proceeded to ask more questions, I became conscious of the possibility that others might not be interested in the topic. Thus I glanced around the room as I answered some of her questions. It appeared that the women were interested. Dad and Tom were watching a football game on television, so it was hard to tell about them. At one point Dad seemed pensive and, thinking that perhaps he was identifying with some of the patients in the hospital, I answered the questions succinctly. Mom seemed interested in what was being said, as she nodded frequently and appeared to be concentrating on what I was saying. I felt happy to be the center of attention, and I felt that I was a little special in that I had had an experience which no one else in the family had had. I got the feeling by Mom's expressions that she was proud of her son and this made me happy. Although Mom didn't ask any questions, appearing content to let Barb take the lead, she conveyed to me the feeling that she was deeply interested in what I had done.

Sharon and I slept late our first morning home. After breakfast, Mom and I found ourselves alone as everyone else had gone off to do one thing or another. We hadn't really talked about Dad's illness the past night, except of course Dad's telling us that he felt pretty good, as I didn't want to bring it up for fear that Dad might be sensitive about it. No one else really offered much. Yet I was very anxious to hear exactly what had transpired, and I asked Mom to tell me the whole story from beginning to end.

She proceeded to explain to me that she noticed that Dad did not seem to be himself. He was awfully tired at the end of the day, more so than usual. And he wouldn't say much about his work, only that it was going all right and that she shouldn't worry. Well, as Mom said both by word and expression, she *was* worried.

"I had lived with your father for too many years not to know that something was profoundly wrong," she said with a look of anguish on her face and an expression of concern in her eyes. "Finally I couldn't stand it any longer," she said. "Your father kept putting me off so I decided to go to his office at the store. I told him that I was not leaving until he told me what was wrong. Dad said, 'I'll tell you when I get home tonight, I promise.' Well, I agreed to that," Mom went on, "so I left the office. But before I left the store I asked Mike (Dad's assistant and life-long friend of the family) if any salesman had been in yesterday. You see, I noticed that there was extra mileage on the car recently and I asked Dad about it. He said that he had taken a salesman to lunch. Well, Mike said that there was no salesman in yesterday or all that week for that matter."

I nodded, as I listened intently to what Mom was saying, wishing impatiently that she would talk faster.

"When I told Mike what had occurred," Mom went on, "Mike said immediately, 'Alan's a good person, Sarah. I've known him all of my life, and he's a good father and a loyal husband.'"

At this statement, the expression of concern left Mom's face briefly, and she smiled. I returned the smile, as I thought of what a wonderful friend Mike had been over the years, but my smile was only a halfhearted one as I wanted Mom to go on. After this momentary humor, Mom's face turned again to concern and mine with it.

"Your father refused to tell me that night when he got home what was wrong. The next night, as I was worried almost to death, Dad collapsed while trying to climb the front steps after returning from his day's work. Rushing to him I finally found out what was wrong as Dad said: 'I'm having a heart attack. I'm done for!'

"Well," Mom said, "I was pretty sure he wasn't having a heart attack. Having four kids and a husband, I had become pretty astute in the ways of physiology. I consoled your father and called the doctor. He assured me that my diagnosis was correct. After a complete physical checkup, the doctor assured us that there was no physical cause to Dad's collapse. He put him on tranquilizers and told him not to go to work for a month."

"And the car?" I asked in a somber tone.

"Your father had been taking drives in order to get some fresh air because he was having trouble breathing," Mom answered.

As Mom completed recounting for me the sequence of events which led up to the present, I sat there stunned, staring off into space. A host of thoughts and feelings seemed to be tossing around within me. For one thing I felt a great deal of admiration for Mom. She had gone through a lot with Dad, and I was sure that it was only through her help that Dad was able to recover rather quickly from a state of complete exhaustion. I glanced at Mom and shook my head in disbelief and yet profound respect for her. She returned my nod as she began to clear the morning dishes from the table.

"The visitors we had, Alan. You should have seen them, and the calls we got! Your dad is respected by so many people!"

"Oh," I thought to myself, "Dad is so lucky to have a woman this devoted." I was filled with intense love for Mom. For a moment, I compared her love for Dad to all the lack of love between husband and wife that I had read about in the files of patients at the hospital. Then in my mind I made, without forethought, another comparison and this brought tears to my eyes. I thought of Willie Loman in *Death of a Salesman*. "Sure there are some differences," I thought, "Willie was a failure at his job and Dad's a success. Yes, so much of a success that they want him to do two men's jobs," I said to myself, half joking. But somehow I was sure that Dad had contemplated suicide as he went on those rides. My mind pictured Dad driving along, wondering whether or not he should take his life. With that thought a great sadness overcame me.

As *Death of a Salesman* and Dad's experience continued to roll around in my head, I thought of Willie Loman's and Dad's inability to communicate with their wives. "Both men had such devoted wives," I thought, "yet both men were pathetically unable to tell their wives what was bothering them."

Thinking in this vein, I felt caught in a general aura of depression. Within my depression I felt a strong urge to try to overcome this inability to communicate. As I sat there, I became more determined than ever to tell Mom of my disappointment concerning her not telling us until late in the game of Dad's illness.

I proceeded cautiously, reminding myself as I began to be as tactful as possible. "Mom," I said in a low voice, "I was sorry you didn't tell me about Dad until he was getting better. I appreciate your concern to keep me from unnecessary worry, but something serious could have happened. Dad could have died, and we wouldn't have known the difference. Besides, you could have used some help, especially if things had gotten worse." The more I said, the more upset I became and the more I forgot my commitment to be tactful. With a stern voice, I continued:

"We've got to be able to communicate with one another. Unless we do, we'll be no good to one another. In the days ahead things may get worse and we'll have to help each other. But we have to know what's going on first."

Mom had begun to wash the dishes before I began to speak, and she continued at that task throughout my monologue. She never looked at me during the whole thing which indicated to me that she was not at all happy with what I had to say.

Continuing my little speech, my state of depression began to give way to a feeling of anger. "We've got to trust one another," I said in an angry tone.

Mom seemed to feel my anger as she worked more feverishly at washing the dishes, yet she didn't respond verbally to my remarks. I could see some expression of anguish on her face, but I didn't react to it. I merely continued my monologue, emphasizing the same points over again but in a slightly different fashion. Soon thereafter, Dad came into the kitchen. His presence seemed to make the subject inappropriate, and the subject was changed. It was Dad who changed the subject, but I readily went along with it, feeling a sense of relief that a new topic was at hand.

Dad asked in a concerned way how the latter part of the spring semester had gone and said that he was happy that I enjoyed my work at the hospital so much. Then he asked me what my plans were after graduation.

"Well," I replied, "I think I'd like to continue work in the counseling area. As a result of this summer's work, I think I'd like counseling very much and I think that I could become an excellent counselor." The feelings that I had during the previous conversation had left me now, and I felt no dominant feelings.

"These plans will, of course, necessitate more schooling," I went on.

"Where will you apply?" Mom said in a concerned fashion, as she sat down at the breakfast table.

"I'm not sure right now," I replied dispassionately. "I've got to begin to send away for catalogues."

"It would be good," Mom suggested quickly, "if you could go to school either near us or near Barb. That way we could visit both of you during the same trip."

Mom's remarks reminded me that she did not like the idea of my being so far away from home. Barb being in Cincinnati wasn't so bad because it was within a day's journey by car, but Boston was two days away and this seemed miles away to her.

"Oh, I think that I'll be able to find something much closer," I responded optimistically but with little serious thought.

I had no plans for the afternoon other than simply to lie around the house to rest as I was still exhausted from yesterday's travel. Hoping to get some sun, I went out into the yard and plopped down on one of our lounging chairs. Barb and Mom soon joined me, and we began speaking of material success and what constitutes happiness. For the initial part of the conversation, Mom remained a silent, involved listener. Not long into the discussion, I found that Barb and I had diametrically opposing views. I was expressing in what began as a very objective, detached manner my view that all people in this country should have the opportunity within reason to live the kind of life they wanted to live. Everyone, at the very minimum, should have enough food, medical care and a decent education. "This should be true even in Appalachia," I suggested.

Barb put forth the argument that she does not have the right to judge for another what constitutes happiness. "I do not have a right to judge for another person," Barb stated with increasing vehemence, "what is good for them. Who am I to say to someone in Appalachia that they should live in our society and be subject to all the pressures that we're under? How do I know that they are not happier right where they are!"

"Now I have known you for a long time," I thought to myself, "and for as long as I can remember you've been about as selfish as you can be. You and Tom have just purchased a thirty thousand dollar home, and your big problem is determining how you are going to display all of your furniture."

At this point I became more riled and began to state my argument with more force. I cited the recent CBS white paper report on hunger in the United States and asked Barb how she could justify her argument in the face of downright starvation.

At this point we were both riled and anger was apparent on both of our faces. Barb began to shed a tear or two which I was not unaccustomed to during our long relationship. She hung in there though, and I admired her for that.

Then Mom spoke up and, with vehemence equal to ours, made some remark which I immediately interpreted to be one which supported Barb's stand and which furthermore seemed to confuse what was already a confused conversation. This made me mad, and I became more determined to make my point.

"Look," I said, "let's take Jim C. (the son of a college dean) and me and a kid from Appalachia and look at each of us in terms of our opportunity to attain our intellectual potential and thus make us happier people. Now Jim's family is of the upper crust. His great grandfather was a doctor, etc. He goes to Yale because everybody in his family goes to Yale. He gets a good education and he'll probably write a number of books in his lifetime. Now take me. I didn't come from a family that made it a long time ago. Consequently, I went to college in my home town and have been struggling ever since to realize my academic potential. Now take the kid from the Appalachian region. He may be a genius, but he'll never reach his intellectual potential."

I had been looking at Barb during my discourse. Now Mom began to speak, and consequently I looked at her. On her face I saw an expression of anger as I don't remember seeing before.

"If it weren't for all those high-class smart people," she yelled out almost in a state of rage, "we wouldn't have had all those wars that the average person has had to fight!"

With a look of anger on my face and a tone of disgust, I said, "Oh, that's not what I was talking about. I haven't been talking about high-class versus low-class people. I just used that as an example of how everyone doesn't have an equal chance to develop intellectually."

That was my verbal response, but underneath I felt frustrated and hurt. As Mom's statement rolled around in my head, I began to get her point. "You're telling me that my people aren't good enough," I said to myself. "Yes, that's what she thought I meant." With this thought repeating itself in my head, I began to feel pretty lousy that I had said such a thing. Of course, I didn't mean what she took it to mean, but I should have realized that she'd react like that.

The conversation lasted not long thereafter with Barb and me doing the rest of the talking. Barb and I agreed that we more or less meant the same thing; we were simply using different words and arguing from different angles.

After Barb and Mom went into the house, I began to mull over the conversation. "Barb and I are more or less in agreement," I thought, "with an emphasis on the less!" Barb and I had never really gotten along, however, so this argument was not so terribly startling. I felt angry and resentful that people could dream up so many great intellectual arguments to defend their downright selfishness.

With Mom it was a different story. I felt hurt and somewhat angry because she had sided with Barb, and I felt guilty because I must have hurt Mom deeply for otherwise she would not have responded in such a manner. More than anything else, though, I felt a sense of estrangement from her. It was like she and I weren't on the same wavelength anymore, and I didn't like the feeling. At that point I began to experience another emotion that would raise its ugly head again during the course of my "vacation" — despair.

That evening while Mom, Dad and I sat together on the back porch we talked about many things. I asked about all the relatives and how my recently married cousin was doing. Mom related to me in vivid detail how Judy was getting along and how her mother (Mom's closest sister) was relating to her newly married daughter. Mom told me that Judy and her husband had purchased more furniture than they could reasonably afford and that they were just now beginning to realize it. Then I asked a question that had become a subject of controversy the world over. "What," I said, "do you think of the Pope's recent Encyclical in opposition to birth control?"

"Well," Mom replied, "I don't agree with it. It seems to me that people should have a right to decide that sort of thing for themselves," she continued with the high degree of conviction and concern with which she speaks on all religious matters.

"Yes," Dad said concurring, "I think the Church is wrong here."

"I know that our bishop," Mom went on, "fought at the Vatican for a liberalization of this policy, but he was apparently turned down."

"Why don't you do something about it," I queried, "if you disagree with the policy?"

"I can't see that it would do any good," Mom said disparagingly. "The Pope has made his decision."

"But do you agree with it?" I replied.

"No, I don't, but what can I do?" Mom said with a sense of frustration about her.

"You could write a letter of protest to the bishop, or you could get the people in the parish to sign a petition in opposition to the Encyclical and you could send it to Rome," I replied with less emotional detachment than when I first asked Mom and Dad's opinion about the Encyclical.

"I don't think that that will do any good," Mom retorted, not really responding in like kind to my degree of involvement in the issue at hand.

At that point I thought to myself that I should drop the whole issue. Mom and Dad never have been people who would fight for their position on certain social issues, and it seemed foolish to think that they were going to start now. Besides, I'd just get all riled up and no good would come of it. "Better to have peace," I thought.

Sharon and I visited a number of my old friends during the next few days and things were going pretty well. Dad was feeling pretty good, although he would tire quickly. He and I played some short-hole golf together. We would sit and relax between holes in order to rest a bit. We had many pleasant conversations during our games. I made sure he'd win the match so he would not feel as if he were "over the hill" as a result of his illness.

But one afternoon things changed for the worse. Barb, Sharon, and Mom had gone to look at a house that Mom and Dad were thinking of purchasing. I was sitting out on the lawn when they came back, and Sharon joined me while the others went into the house. I asked Sharon if she liked the house. She said that she didn't care for it, too "middle-class" for her. There was little individual identity to it. Then she told me of the conversation that she, Mom, and Barb had had as they toured the house. They were talking about the cost of living, getting established, etc. After a few rather obscure remarks by Mom, Barb said it outright:

"What we are trying to say," Sharon told me that Barb said, trying in vain to say it jokingly, "is that we think that you and Alan are crazy having Alan in school. You both could be working so that you would be building a financial foundation for your life."

Sharon had a look of disgust on her face as she recounted for me what had transpired. I became deeply pensive as she told me what went on, and I looked at the ground. I felt really annoyed at Barb. "One minute," I thought to myself, "she argues that she cannot judge how others ought to live, and then the next minute she applies her goddamned materialism to me, saying that we'd be better off if we too would buy up the world!"

Anger was not the only emotion that I was feeling. Besides being annoyed, I was hurt. Mom had told me in effect that she would like to see me live another kind of life. That hurt. For a moment, I felt as if I were going to cry. I then looked up at Sharon and gave her a halfhearted smile, thinking to myself that at least I have a companion in my struggles. That was important to me, for, at that moment, it seemed to be her and me against the world.

An hour or so later, the family sat down to dinner. To my increasing dismay and frustration, the conversation revolved primarily around buying things, with Mom and Barb taking the leading role. As their conversation proceeded, I sat there unable to say anything as my pensive mood returned. I ate my food in silence and for the most part kept my head lowered. Glancing up occasionally, I saw that Mom seemed to be enjoying herself. She had a smile on her face and in between words with Barb she would make sure everyone had their plate filled. At one point I tried to smile, but I couldn't seem to bring myself to do that. I felt those same feelings I had had when Sharon was telling me about her previous conversation with Barb and Mom begin with steadily increasing force to recur. By the end of the meal I was nearly bursting with emotion. Then, as if desirous of providing me with an opportunity to release my pent-up emotion, Barb said pointedly:

"Well, brother, you've been awfully quiet during this meal! Don't you have anything to say?"

I responded angrily and said in a loud voice, "What I have to say you wouldn't want to hear!" Then I gave her and Mom a look that could have killed, and I got up from the table and stalked out of the dining room.

Going outside, I sat for a while on the lawn to cool off. A strange and frightening sensation overcame me. I felt like those with whom I had dined were not my family; they were just any old people, people who perhaps I didn't know but who chose to sit beside me in the restaurant. Then my mind focused particularly on Mom. It was from Mom that I had felt so much love and acceptance over the years. She was the person to whom I had gone whenever I needed someone to talk to, whether it was for purposes of confiding in someone or perhaps just to test my ideas. We had had such a close relationship through the years, but now somehow everything seemed to be shattering before my eyes. Again I felt alone and hurt, and I despaired.

After the dishes were done Mom joined me on the lawn. She chose to ignore our previous battle and so did I. We made small talk, each seemingly trying to forget our previous conflict. Each of us in the past proved to be people who could let "bygones be bygones," and this occasion proved by superficial appearance to be no exception to the rule.

A few days later Barb and Tom were preparing to leave. They planned to spend a few days with Tom's family before heading back to Cincinnati. As we stood out in the drive, we went through the ritual of saying goodbye. Barb and I gave each other a big hug, neither of us seemingly meaning it. Mom typically shed a few tears, as was commonplace with her when any of her kids were going off for an extended period of time. Needless to say, after all the conflict we'd been through I was delighted to see Barb leave. "Now," I said to myself, "Mom and I can get back on good terms."

My thoughts about my future relationship with Mom turned out to be accurate. My relationship with Mom seemed to pick up directly after Barb's departure. We had a number of good talks about relatives, Dad, and my vocational future.

During the course of one of these conversations, I asked Mom about Liz's illness over the winter.

"She was awfully sick, Alan. Three times during the course of the winter she had strep throat," Mom said with compassion. "I took her to the doctor's office on a regular basis. She was so sick, but during the whole time she was an excellent patient. She painted and sewed and read when possible. When she couldn't read, I read to her. I stayed by her by day, and I got up three or four times during the night to give her medicine and make sure she was all right."

Mom had a very concerned look on her face. It almost seemed as if by recounting to me Liz's illnesses, she was living through them. "That must have really gotten you down," I replied.

"Well, you know when my kids are sick, I'm a nervous wreck. Thank God she pulled out of it. Not until she had nephritis, though."

"What's that?" I asked.

"Infection of the kidneys," Mom replied. "Liz was living on penicillin most of the winter."

Mom hadn't written us about Liz's illnesses until she was progressing quite satisfactorily. I felt no compulsion to tell Mom that she should have informed us, however. Actually, I gave it very little thought. Liz had been a sickly child, so another illness was far from startling. I simply accepted what Mom said and responded with feelings of sympathy for the demanding winter she had spent.

"It wasn't an easy winter for you, was it, Mom?" I asked rhetorically as I sensed by tone of voice and expression a woman standing before me overwrought with the frequency and duration of her child's illness.

At dinner a few days later we got on the subject of politics and the recent riots and assassinations. The conversation was going along fairly well until Mom began presenting her conviction that it is the Communists who are instigating all of the social upheaval. At first I thought that Mom was kidding, but then she went on to expound her theory in a serious tone. The more she talked the angrier I got. What made me even madder was Brenda nodding her head in agreement. She had written me recently of her ideas of the Communists being behind these social conflicts. Finally, with my anger increasing, I blurted out:

"It's not the Communists who are behind what's wrong in this country. It's those fine, upstanding people who love America and who are at the same time bigoted and selfish who are causing our society to fall. Take New Hampshire as an example. My friend there tells me that none of those people flew their flags at half-mast when Martin Luther King was assassinated. The only time they'd do that is if George Wallace were killed! These people aren't Communists — they're fine, upstanding Americans who hate Negroes!"

I had fire in my eyes as I spoke, and much to my dismay I lost my appetite in the process. Mom didn't say a word in rebuttal. She seemed startled when I first began to speak and afterwards appeared falsely passive. Dad had tried to break in before I had finished talking, but I rebuked him. Now that I was finished he made a joke, not realizing the friction between Mom and me. I laughed politely.

The Democratic Convention was on television during that week and Sharon and I stayed up 'til the wee hours of the morning to watch the crucial vote. While I hadn't campaigned formally for McCarthy, I felt myself getting more and more saddened as it became clearer that he was going to lose at the hands of the Humphrey-Daley political machine. I reached a point of disbelief and anger when the cameras focused on students being beaten by the Chicago police for no apparent reason.

When we finally went to bed I found that I couldn't sleep. Thoughts of the Convention rolled around in my head and I thought of Mom and all the conflict we experienced during the last week and a half. Somehow it seemed that both the Democratic Convention and Mom were telling me to go to hell. I lay there for perhaps two hours before going to sleep, during which time I was close to tears at some moments and I felt like I would like to scream at others. I didn't do either.

The rest of the vacation was spent in relative calm. Sharon and I visited with other friends of mine. Mom invited all the relatives over during one evening, and the night was spent in gaiety and fun. It was with fun-filled evenings such as these that the vacation drew to a close.

As we were saying good-bye prior to our departure, I gave Mom a big hug which seemed to me to be more of a perfunctory one than a real one. Noticing that Mom wasn't tearful as is normally the case, I thought momentarily that perhaps she was happy to see me go. I then gave Dad a big hug during which he kissed me on the cheek. I really enjoyed that, and I could sense a feeling of love radiating between Dad and me to a degree I've never experienced before.

Driving back to Boston I thought of the pain of growing up, of cutting the umbilical cord. I felt deeply hurt that the vacation had gone so poorly. I felt guilty for being so aggressive, unsympathetic, and without understanding in my relationship with Mom. I remembered the look in Mom's eyes as she spoke in defiance toward all the high-class people who have made a mess of the world. I chided myself for reacting often exclusively intellectually without being at all responsive to her feelings. Then I became angry with myself. "Here I am contemplating choosing counseling as my life's vocation," I thought, "yet, I was so unresponsive to Mom's feelings. Why?" Soon I gave up trying to discern the underlying causes as I just didn't want to think about it anymore. I was in a somber mood but strangely mixed in was a feeling of happiness. The vacation was over.

The day after we arrived in Boston I wrote a letter to Mom and Dad explaining that I had planned to speak further with them about our lack of communication during Dad's illness, but during the hubbub of the vacation it slipped my mind. I tactfully explained that during a crisis situation both the person to whom the crisis has occurred and those immediately involved in helping the person through the crisis need support. I suggested that we should try to increase our communication with one another so each of us would be in a position to lend a helping hand to all those involved in the crisis situation.

About two weeks later I received a reply from Dad. In his letter he acknowledged full responsibility for not informing us immediately of his illness. He said that he understood how we felt and thanked us for writing. On reading the letter, I thought that I hadn't really been heard, but nevertheless I felt gratified that I had fulfilled what I considered to be my responsibility.

While Dad and the kids kept up our ritual of writing at least one letter per week, I received only one letter in two and a half months from Mom. This is highly irregular for her. I interpreted this to mean that she too was deeply disappointed by our recent inability to relate effectively with one another.

Case 8 / Dad, the Workaholic

Michael describes his father as honest, generous with money, self-denigrating, not in touch with his feelings, well-intentioned, and insensitive to the implications of his actions on others. Father is caught in a work frenzy, in which there is little distinction between work life and family life. Michael feels more like a "loved employee" than a son. His appreciation of his father's good intentions and gradual "understanding" of his father's motivation contrast with his resentment of his father's placing low priority on their relationship and giving only grudging recognition of Michael's accomplishments. Striving to resolve his ambivalent feelings, Michael perseveres in a self-imposed "Like Your Father" campaign.

The tone of "being stuck" permeates the case, even to the last sentence. Michael's personification of self seems to include "someone who seeks 'insight' and avoids confrontation." His personification of father includes "the person who sets the 'ground rules' for our relationship." Relinquishing old images and unsatisfying ways of relating ultimately requires communicating one's feelings and wants and assuming partial responsibility for the direction and quality of relationship.

The day began very typically for that summer after freshman year. Waking at about one in the afternoon, I dressed hurriedly in order to attend my father and mother at a local restaurant for their daily business lunch. My father's office is in our home; my mother is his secretary. If my mother takes time to cook lunch, it is time taken from his work, so we had business lunches and often business dinners. Since my father did not want me to start working (i.e., summer jobs) until I was at least a junior or senior in college, I worked for him by running errands, writing speeches, advising him on personalities, and keeping the household in order while he and my mother were working. Their daily routine started at seven or eight A.M. and lasted until eleven, twelve, one, sometimes two into the next morning. I always opted out of this pell mell at about six o'clock when I could be sure of getting my friends together for cards, swimming, talking, or movies. Fortunately for my mother and for myself, my father was out of town two, three, and four days at a time, back for a similar number of days, then gone. Our family has adjusted itself to this routine since we moved to New Orleans nine years ago.

On this particular day my father was angry at my mother for some dictation errors. He complained and bitched at her all afternoon and for the whole trip to the airport. As chauffeur, I could "concentrate" on driving and was not required to be an unwilling participant. Nonetheless, I always was acutely aware of the tone of my parents' relationship, indeed of all the relationships in my family. Alternately,

I was angry at him for being petty, I was feeling guilty for being angry, and I resented my mother for not standing up for herself more forcefully. She could rise up and calm my father's petulant rage fairly easily. On this occasion, however, I think my father had a legitimate reason to complain, none to bitch. My mother accepted his childlike anger as a motherlike wife, in silence, with full assurance that in a twinkle of a jet exhaust she could drop her pose as a mild mannered suburban housewife and become Supermother, able to soothe angry feelings with a single glance. Then I, almost as mild mannered as she, would instantly metamorphose into the favorite of the family, the home town star, the horror from Harvard, her stellar sidekick, Marvelous Michael.

Nevertheless this fight disturbed me. After graduating from high school, I had driven my mother and sister on our semiannual summer trip across the United States to San Francisco. During the course of that summer I read Dale Carnegie's *How to Win Friends and Influence People* and decided that it would be possible using his techniques to control my ambivalent feelings toward my father and allow my genuine desire to understand and love him to emerge. My efforts to get involved in his work, which occupied 80 percent of his time and attention, were not always rewarded. Driving back from San Francisco, he returned my opening maneuvers, designed to learn what made him so "good" at becoming friendly with his business associates, many of whom we stopped to see on the trip, with vituperative salvos designed to let out all his frustrated fatherly feelings, which he felt unable to express before. At any rate, my "Like Your Father" campaign culminated in a brilliant insight as to why my father should work so damned hard that he treated his family like loved employees. Thus, when we let my father out in front of the airport, he realized his truculence that day had been unfair. He also realized in a thoughtful gaze at my mother that he loved her very much and would miss her while away so much that as usual he would call home each night. I decided to share my previous summer's "brilliant insight" with her to explain this sudden shift.

"You know, Ma, I think I know why Dad gets so wrapped up in his business. He had to accept a lot of responsibility at a young age. [At age twenty-five he traveled in the Mideast with thousands of dollars in cash setting up the Standard Oil supply network after the war.] He is afraid of failing."

My mother, now more normally attired in dragon-proof clothes, replied, "You're right. He is afraid of failing, but not for that reason. You see your father had his confidence badly shaken by the attitudes and successes of his father. He never felt loved or approved of as a boy" (which I knew).

After a short, intense discussion about death, she made me promise to cremate her when she died. She thinks expensive funerals are a tragic waste. Then she continued.

"Your father also was hurt when he came back from Europe after the war and discovered his first wife running around; then his confidence was shattered completely when she left him, taking everything he owned."

Which I did not know, and which in fact no one in my family had known except all my older relatives and my parents. The pain of that first marriage was so great that he had insisted on keeping it secret from his children for twenty-five years. My mother swore me to secrecy. She said Dad would "kill" her for telling me. She asked if I would like to stop for food and talk. Two seconds later I screeched into the parking lot of a place called the Marriott.

After hearing about two miscarriages, a near divorce, and a crazy uncle (all family secrets), I had to reexamine my past attitudes towards my father and his relationship to my mother, two older brothers, and my younger sister. In looking back I see how his parents' influence and his early frustration as a young man translated into his behavior as husband and father. Before my mother's dramatic disclosures I could find no satisfactory answers to explain the ache I felt buried in me, perhaps the same kind of deep hurt he lives with and fights with even today. The best way to describe the etiology of that pain is to divide our relationship into three modes: work, my life without him, and problems communicating feelings.

By general agreement within the family, my father is a workaholic. He works not in order to be successful, not in order to get away from home, and not in order to "do something" for humanity; he works because he must. He is a good, exceptionally honest, likeable, and giving person particularly when he works with clients and associates. He has no hobbies and very few friends outside of business, but he maintains interest in widely divergent fields of business independent of the trade association for petroleum markets that employs him. He spends a great deal of time on the phone and traveling. Everything he earns and owns he gives freely to his family; in fact since his recent financial success he makes it very difficult to refuse his offers of money and things. He feels as if all he can offer his children are his earnings, so that when I declined his gift of an automobile, I felt guilty for having hurt his feelings. Yet the importance of business to him goes far beyond this "unselfish" motive.

On that summer day my mother also told me of a nervous breakdown Dad suffered when he chose to quit his twenty-year-old job at Standard Oil rather than accept another offered to him as part of a consolidation. We moved from New Jersey shortly after to San

Francisco where he loafed and he looked for another job. Six months later he found one in Chicago.

On one of our cross-country trips during this period of frequent moves, we stopped late at night for a visit in Fairfield, North Dakota where he had grown up. He had left Fairfield to attend college in San Francisco; one of the few from a town of three or four thousand to do so. His father had been a very well respected businessman and town politico, who apparently did not have much time for his children. Instead, he delegated responsibility for raising the children to my grandmother. She drove one of my uncles insane; he wandered for ten years after WWII avoiding "aliens" and refusing to contact my grandparents. His father died knowing only that he had been discharged from the service. She produced one fully neurotic daughter, and another survived by leaving home and marrying a psychologist, who convinced me that my grandmother is a sick woman bent on maintaining social appearances and on overcoming the effects of her German immigrant childhood. Standing beside the car that night, urinating on the desolate plains leading into Fairfield, my father commented to me, "You've got to come back to this town with a million dollars tied around your neck." That was one of the few times I have ever heard him talk about his feelings toward his hometown, and one of the few times I remember him talking about his feelings.

Aside from summer vacation/business trips, my family did not normally "play" together. When we were home on weekends or evenings we worked around the house, if my father had the spirit to bludgeon us into it. Otherwise we watched television together. As each of my older brothers was able to drive and to accept more responsibility, my father gave it to them in the form of endless series of errands. After years of disdaining any personal complicity in this work frenzy, I realized that only by becoming an errand boy would I have ground for establishing lines of communication with him. During my high school years I did very well academically, fairly well socially, and extremely well in extracurricular activities like debate. Yet each grade report, each girlfriend, each debate trophy I brought home received stilted praise and sometimes, "Your mother is very proud of you." Each one of my successes exaggerated our differences. He thought so little of his abilities that he presumably thought he could offer very little in the way of advice. My intelligence, my "confidence," and my interests threatened him with further disgrace and I knew it. I hated his work compulsion; he used it as his defense. When he used it to retreat from me, I let him know that I hated it. I was the voice of the opposition. He could not compel me to work as he did my older brother Paul, who is not intelligent and successful. I hated the way he treated me when I did work for him. Given my antipathy, as soon as he felt on solid ground he criticized. I tried consistently to be an expert on anything and everything, using my wits to defend myself and to attack him. I developed a fine reputation as a "know-it-all" and I am an interrupter par excellence. This continued until I started my "Like Your Father" campaign. Then, after a rough period of indoctrination, I accepted his direction and after a time came to enjoy doing his errands well, talking about his business problems and receiving praise, often at the expense of my older brother.

The source of my resentment did not lie solely in Dad's compulsion to work. Rather it more generally stemmed from his absence at important times in my life. Each young child feels alone from time to time. As I was growing up, I learned very early that my parents didn't like talking things over. Dad spent a great deal of his free time while I was young earning a master's degree in business administration. Fairly frequently he was gone for six-week business trips for the company. My mother was around all the time, but she didn't encourage any of us to just talk about our feelings. So, like many children, I did not tell them of my fear and confusion when mysterious authorities intervened in my school and social life, when excruciating shyness frustrated my adjustment to new neighborhoods, or when puberty grabbed me by the pants and threw me over a cliff. I learned self-reliance quickly and depended on my wits to figure things out. When understandably I wasn't a Little League version of Lou Gehrig, I lied about my performance to my family. When I wanted to be a Scout, I mimicked my brothers. When I needed a father for father's nights, my oldest brother Bill, whom I admired greatly would come; if he could not, I attached myself to another family and lied about why my father was absent. My mother and my brother Bill were a great help to me during these times, but I wanted a father like my friends' fathers, and I did not understand why my request should be refused again and again.

Scouting occupied a large part of my early adolescence, and I did succeed in achieving the rank of Eagle as my father had, and as my brother Bill had before me. However, Scouting emphasizes the importance of father-son relationships in particular, and family involvement in general. I felt forced to lie and make excuses for my family and for my father on, may I modestly say, a grand scale. Soon I had no control over my excuse making. I used them everywhere and in patently unbelievable situations.

On the occasion of a fairly important father-son dinner, I decided to test my father's willingness to be my father. Asking two weeks in advance, I collared him into agreeing. I was ecstatic, but worried. The dinner started at seven in the evening and although he would be out of town most of that day, he promised me he would be back in the afternoon, well before it was time to go. Four o'clock, I looked out the windows. Five o'clock, I walked in the street. Six o'clock, I felt empty, but I dressed. Seven o'clock, I was hot with grief and hope. Eight o'clock, nine o'clock, I sat in front of the television seeing nothing, hearing nothing, immobilized with rage. I wanted to hurt him, but when he arrived apologizing profusely about delays, all I could manage were a few chastising and forgiving words. I left. Before I went to bed that night, I approached him in the dining room, his papers spread out on the table. I told him I understood how he had been delayed talking to clients. I tried to hug him goodnight, but he pushed me away in fright yelling, "Boys don't do that." I never asked him again.

Goaded by the example of my friends' fathers and families, I also tried to organize family outings. Of course, I failed. Each one of my siblings moved in radically different directions, and my parents busied themselves with their own problems. My mother was the co-ordination center for these diverse movements. In a sense each of us was tethered to her and only to her. I felt a protective love for my younger sister and a guilty anger toward Paul, whose violent temper and social failings caused constant strife within the family.

Bill went away to college when I was twelve so that when the family moved from Chicago to New Orleans, he quickly became a legend. My father placed Bill's image so high in my mind that every time he came home for vacations I expected his toes and ears to be frostbitten from standing exposed to the elements and to the Gods on his magic mountain. Bill was acting out one of my father's secret ambitions. Bill would be a doctor. I competed vicariously with that image throughout high school.

While my father struggled to establish himself in a new territory, I attached my affection to a variety of father figures. Neighbors, friends' fathers, and teachers did nicely, but none as nicely as my senior year Government teacher and debate coach, James Kent. My bitterness toward my father did not disappear, but my angry moments subsided substantially as Jim's influence became more pronounced. No one who meets him is unaffected. Many in the high school feared his forcefulness, including the principal, but all respected him. I suppose most adolescents have experienced adulation for a teacher, coach, or family friend, but I think I feel especially strongly about Jim. His image and presence still affect me. On the rare occasions when I could have introduced my father to him, it totally escaped me that I had not done so, until Jim asked why when the two men stood twenty feet from each other, I had not. To this day they have not met.

Some important dimensions of my father's personality are best described in contrast to Jim's. Jim is perceptive, quick, sensitive to the emotional assumptions underlying the actions of others. My father has a very difficult time deciphering motives. In fact, he rarely tries to do so except insofar as he asks, "Why do they do this to me?" Jim is very intelligent, pensive, and usually has well reasoned opinions on political and ethical issues. My father accepts the status quo, politically and morally. His opinions reflect social custom, paraphrases of some "authority figure," or the redneck biases of his Southern clients. Dad always calls Jim "Mr. Kent." Jim is prodigiously adept socially, confident, and beautifully articulate. My father succeeds socially when the rationale for the interaction rests in a good humored business mode. He tells wonderful stories and jokes. Otherwise, he vacillates between withdrawing (TV watching) and winning favor with teddy bear childishness. Jim talks easily about his feelings and about sex. Whenever "sensitive" topics are broached, Dad clams up, hangs his head, and shuffles his feet until the conversation shifts to familiar ground. I asked him once why he never talked to me about anything sexual, why I had to learn about it in the streets. He grinned and said, "Well it was more fun that way wasn't it?" Both Jim and my father are perfectionists. When I get advice from Dad, it consists primarily of stock phrases like: "Plough ahead." "Keep plugging." "For God's sake don't be a sap like me." "Go into a profession, so you can be your own boss." He denigrates himself frequently, and has an unbelievable respect for "authority." On the whole, unlike Jim, he is a well-meaning, loving man whose attempts at communication nonetheless almost invariably sound stilted, tentative, and forced. I am impatient with these attempts, compounding his frustration.

My mother's surprise revelations during that summer's super session helped me make sense of a last trait of this peculiar man and of my ambivalent feelings towards him. Since the desertion of his first wife and his subsequent remarriage to my mother, five years younger than himself, my father had become an intensely jealous man, very dependent on my mother's constant attention. Fifteen years ago Dad's persistent (and unfounded) suspicions nearly drove her to divorce him. In fact, the day on which she and her mother were out "talking things over" and making decisions, Dad was at home physically sick with fear and worry. As a boy of seven I crouched behind our big living room sofa while he roamed our house crying, demanding "Where is Judith?", asking me "Where is your mother?" Since I was the only one home with him at the time, I sneaked out from behind my shield long enough to try and reassure him that she would be home soon. He seemed not to hear as he made an impassioned dash for the bathroom. After many similar trips and after at least a gallon of Kaopectate, he retired to his large, dark bedroom.

He saw a psychiatrist to help him with his jealousy, and my

mother stayed with him. He is intensely devoted to her, but he still is extremely dependent on her attention — to the dismay of his children and in-laws. This dependence often took the form of using her as his communications link with the world — i.e., his children and neighbors. We always discussed problems of any kind with her alone or accompanied at a distance by him. My mother became the daily arbiter of our youthful demands. She became an all-wise, all-controlled Supermother because her husband treated her like a mother/wife and because she didn't object to her role. She was hurt when I halfheartedly demanded that she not wash and iron my clothes.

I cannot count the number of times my father poked his head into our den, and being unsuccessful at getting one of his TV-watching children to work on one of his projects, then pleaded, "All right, if you won't do it for me then do it for your mother." Or shortcutting himself, he would see a full trash can, then corner one of us and state with apparent sincerity, "Your mother wants you to take out the garbage." Circuitous communications and duplicitous requests so characterized my father's interaction with me that he infuriated me easily when he made even a legitimate request in this fashion. But his indirectness has its humorous side.

I felt as if my "Like Your Father" campaign payed off in diamonds when he dropped me off at college for freshman year — three times. Each time he came back, sent my brother in the dorm after me, then reminded me of some minor thing. The third run through I hinted that he was making excuses in order to come back. He said, "No, no. It's your mother. She just can't stand to see you go." My mother sat comfortably in the back of the car smiling.

As the strife caused by my brother Paul's school and social problems worsened, I became even more intensely dissatisfied with the way in which my parents had gone about raising a family. Paul sought my parent's love and approval even more desperately than I ever could. He didn't read between the lines. He made the mistake of taking my father literally. Any action which received praise from them he repeated again and again beyond the point of utility, and beyond the point of continued tolerance by my parents, my sister, or myself. If they criticized him, he would bellow, hit the walls, and complain (rightly) about favoritism. My father's "strategy" towards Paul was curiously enough constant criticism, "because if I don't, he won't be prepared for it in the outside world."

Between being hotly critical of my father's attitude and guiltily resentful of Paul's demands, I eventually opted out. At first I sided with my parents, then I sided with my mother who in later years took a more compassionate and coolheaded stand between the combatants. Finally, I rose above the melee completely and would alternately give advice to my beseiged mother or leave the house. These fights embarrassed and angered me, but I suppressed these emotions fiercely.

In fact, as I entered high school, I suppressed all my true feelings while at home. Mostly my Marvelous Michael image filled in my lapses of expressiveness. I remained silent (and superior) thus protecting any vulnerability by being honest. Rarely challenged, I knew everything and had little patience. I paid for this control with acute attacks of anxiety, depression, and self-hatred. Schoolwork seldom followed me home; I spent a lot of evenings in front of the TV or reading while arguments filled the house. I so completely turned off my sensitivity to those around me that often someone trying to get my attention would have to come over and physically shake me after trying unsuccessfully to get it by talking to me from across the room. Sometimes those shields would not suffice, and I would spend hours driving around in the car, walking in the woods or talking to a friend.

The last incident in which I could not suppress my anger toward my father surprised me as much as anyone. Our entire family gathered around the bedside of my father the night before he had lung surgery for what might have been, but was not, cancer. He transferred his business to the hospital, tied up his phone for hours, and spent most of the visiting hours dictating letters to my mother. I didn't approve of him wasting his time on business, but I accepted his need to compensate for real anxiety at that juncture. However, when our last ten minutes together as a family, before we would have to leave, were about to be dedicated to changing a routine doctor's appointment for my sister, I balked. It was nearly ten o'clock at night. Fighting my rage, I quietly walked out of the room and paced down the hallway. Bill followed me and convinced me that I would never forgive myself if my father died on the operating table.

Since Bill had almost died of pneumonia as a teenager, due to an initial reluctance to treat his symptoms, my father had become overreactive to sneezes, cuts, and any other medical ailments. By making a fuss over "objective" problems, he could also safely show his love and competence. I first started having problems with chronic diarrhea when we moved to Chicago. Once every two weeks, and sometimes more often, I would be immobilized by stomach cramps and an ardent desire to hang around the bathroom. This problem continued until I was a senior in high school, when it developed into a more diffused, chronic pain in my abdomen. I felt awkward about the fuss made over medical problems, so I kept my complaints to myself. A physician gave me tranquilizers; a university psychiatrist gave me insight.

Problems of the psyche were beyond the competence of my father. When I called him in the spring of my freshman year at college,

I asked him to drive up and take me home. He quietly and calmly agreed. Four hours later, he called again and suggested that I could fly home for a few days if I wished. I did. Three days later, never having discussed my dissatisfaction with college, my mother discreetly asked me if everything was "all right." She added, "Don't do this again. It scared your father silly."

My relationship with my father has changed substantially over the years. We have both marred it with inconsideratenesss, hurt, anger, and desperation in our desire to come to terms with each other. As I have grown older and have gained insight into his motivations and feelings, we have been able to appreciate good times more often. But we share a legacy of memories which affect us even today. It is fitting that I close this somewhat onesided account by describing the unusual circumstances surrounding my twenty-first birthday. It represents the finest example of our missed love, and for me, it represents (hopefully) my last immersion into the rage of my childhood and into self-pity.

As I neared the end of my year away from college, I got a job as fork-lift driver and part-time carpenter for a large construction project in New Orleans. I had moved out of my house into an apartment, signaling to my parents my determination to become financially and emotionally independent. They did not completely accept the rationale behind my move and were inclined to interpret it as rejection. Since they were busy with their normal summer schedule of cross-country traveling and conventioneering, however, they did not dwell on my absence from home.

Two weeks before my birthday in the middle of the summer, my mother called and invited me to dinner. I accepted the invitation with gratitude; my own cooking is nothing compared to my mother's.

Over dinner my father described his itinerary for the coming month. My sister and mother would be in New Jersey attending the wedding of an old friend. He would meet them there, then fly to Chicago for a business conference with his boss. That conference would end definitely at three o'clock and he would fly to New Orleans for one day to treat me to dinner at the restaurant of my choice. He had already forewarned his boss that he must leave as soon as the conference ended, but he "didn't want him to know why." There would be no slipups.

As soon as he outlined this plan, I was sick. My twenty-first birthday was relatively important to me, but long dormant memories of unkept promises nagged at my innards. Besides, I had already eaten at most of the restaurants in New Orleans with him on our business lunches. And I had a girlfriend with whom I would have been very glad to share a quiet birthday in my apartment (she lived there off and on). Why did he want to make such a commitment? I knew he would bring a gift, but gift-giving in my family has been an awful experience for me. I felt as if *he* felt obligated to come. I did not look forward to the date, but I agreed. There would be slipups.

One week later he confirmed our arrangements, but he added a new twist. The flight he would catch left fifty minutes after the conference ended. He could make the flight if he left immediately. Allowing for any possible delay, he scheduled a backup reservation that would have him arrive in New Orleans in time for a late dinner, but in time. After a complicated series of phone calls to various places in the United States, we settled the arrangements for once and for all.

On the morning of my birthday, I went to work as usual. I started framing a tool shed which I had designed and of which I was very proud. That summer morning was warm with a touch of coolness in the shadows. I hammered happily, completely absorbed in technical problems. At noon I realized it was my birthday. I thought of my impending rendezvous and felt the empty anxiety I reserve for speeches in front of large audiences and for my father.

Sweating under the late afternoon sun, I packed my tools in the back of the old '62 Fairlane I bought for working. She was my first car. Humming country tunes, I drove to my parents' home in an exclusive neighborhood in New Orleans. While there I fixed myself a large glass of iced tea and waited. Not even television could stem my growing conviction. "He will call. Something will go wrong." I waited until 4:30. He called.

"Listen, Michael? I'm at the airport in Chicago. Cummins pulled me over after the meeting and kept me until just a little while ago. That bastard, I had told him two weeks ago I had to leave right away. He just did it to provoke me. But I wouldn't give him the satisfaction of having me beg to leave."

I thought, "To your son's twenty-first birthday?" I said, "That's all right. You'll be on the other flight then?"

"Yes."

We confirmed the arrival time of the other flight, and he asked me to be sure to find a place open and serving at 10:15. I hung up the phone and felt immensely relieved that my fears were being confirmed and that the worst was yet to come. At least there was no uncertainty now.

I drove back to my apartment and climbed into my old fashioned tub which was so small that I washed my torso and my legs in shifts. I cooked up a little grub just to keep my stomach from growling impolitely, then I sat down at my typewriter and wrote a

long overdue letter to a friend writhing in the clutches of the Campus
Crusade for Christ.

Feeling good about that, I dressed in my finest banker's grey,
then proceeded to gas up the car and clean her for inspection. I left
for the airport directly from the gas station in order to arrive at 9:15,
an hour before his plane landed.

Confidently maneuvering in traffic, I pulled into the airport
parking lot on schedule, found a perfect parking spot, then whisked
into the terminal. Locating the gate number, checking and double
checking the accuracy of my information, I went directly to the gate
and planted myself in the seat closest to the disembarking ramp. He
would have to be blind and invisible for us to miss each other.

At 9:45 the airline announced a delay in the flight's arrival.
First they announced 10:30, then 10:45. No matter, we could still make
it to the Chinese restaurant downtown which according to my calcu-
lations was only fifteen minutes away. I would have to stay up much
later than I usually am able. Work began at an obscene hour. My
greatest vice is sleep. But I had granted a stay of retirement for my
girlfriend's benefit and I supposed I could do the same for my own
father. I magnanimously slumped down in my seat and crossed my
outstretched legs.

The plane arrived at 10:45. I craned my neck above the crowd
trying to catch an early glimpse of him. Unlike students who usually
sit in the back of planes and hence come out last, he typically sits
forward and would be off with the second wave of passengers.

He was not in the second wave, nor in the third, nor in any of
the others. As the crew members and tourists with potted plants
straggled through the gate, I contemplated going past them and looking around the plane. After all, what if he had had a heart attack and
was lying under a seat with his eyes open, ignored and left to die
because they all thought he was looking for a dropped penny? But I
scratched that idea as improbable since I knew my father well enough
to know he wouldn't stoop for a dropped penny, it would have to be
at least a dime. Boy Scout's Honor.

Keeping my cool I sauntered over to the flight attendant's desk
and asked when the rest of the passengers on the last flight from
Chicago would disembark. He looked at his watch and with great
solemnity replied, "Fifteen minutes ago, sir."

Losing my cool I was lost in the turmoil of the thousand emotions I have felt for that man in the last twenty-one years. I had known
something would go wrong from the start. My father (and the rest of
my family) are chronically late. But I hadn't considered the possibility
that he could wait at an airport for three hours, then miss a plane. As
I walked down the concourse I wished some mugger would have tried

something funny, I was ready for vengeance. I had switched off my guilt machine (with difficulty) and was giving full rein to anger.

Cruising rapidly toward the upper entrance, I bared my teeth at a girl who looked up at me in passing. I thought, "Maybe he slipped past me. Maybe he arrived when I stupidly read that parking stub. In that case he'll be at the luggage counter. It wouldn't hurt to check." He wasn't at the luggage counter, and I silently cursed myself for such stupidity.

Stomping out the *lower* entrance to the airport terminal (which I wouldn't have done otherwise), I asked myself what possible excuses he could make this time. Suddenly, I stopped dead in my wing tips; I heard him calling my name.

"Michael, where in the hell have you been? I've been waiting here over an hour. I looked all over the airport for you."

"I was at your gate waiting."

"Oh. I didn't think to look there. Your mother always picks me up here at the bus stop." (Boy Scout's Honor.)

"How did you get here?"

"Well, I waited in the airport at Chicago for a while, but I talked to a ticket agent about my problem and we arranged to route me to St. Louis, catch a connection to New Orleans and arrive at ten o'clock."

"I'll be damned."

Sure enough, I was damned. The restaurant was closed so we ate at the hotel across the street. It was a place called the Marriott. There was no room at the bar, so he bullied the *maitre de* into clearing a little table. He was going to buy his son a drink. He is very, very fond of making a big production of such things.

"Dad, I'm kind of tired and I have to get up early, could we skip the drink and just eat?"

"Two gin and tonics, and in rocks glasses, please."

"How was the wedding?"

"I didn't stay for it, but your sister stunned everybody. Say I've got a little something here for you, I thought you might like to have it on your birthday."

"Gee, thanks."

It was another camera. I thought the one I got for Christmas was fine, but this one had a built-in electronic flash, the newest thing. A smaller bag contained a (used to be) ten-cent, pink rubber ball which you can't find anywhere outside of Jersey and which I know for a fact is the only decent ball you can get for playing stickball in the Garner Avenue Elementary School playground. How *he* knew, I will never be able to guess. Boy Scout's Honor.

Dinner was terrible. I was tired. I was choking on my depression and was feeling withdrawn. My father felt like shit, because he could easily see my dissatisfaction with the whole affair. I began feeling guilty about spoiling his treat, so I perked up and asked him about the conference.

Later I drove him home and stayed the night. The next morning he couldn't conveniently arrange a ride back to the airport for his flight out, so I skipped work and drove him.

I couldn't speak to anyone about the encounter for three days. At the end of that time I wrote a letter to my brother, Bill, hoping, but not knowing that he would understand. Exorcists never have it so good, I think.

I am not a bad person. My father is not a bad person. I love him and he loves me and we both love Ma and Bill and Paul and Sis. But I am sure that *both* my father and myself are convinced that we are rotten to the core for not meeting cordially and adaptively for a late night birthday celebration. I hesitate to think about what his father must have been like or what my children might be like. I can reflect on the past without rancor, well, without too much rancor. My mother says he broods these days over how he lost the love and respect of his children. Both of us will undoubtedly resolve to straighten "it" all out next vacation, and as inevitably as in the past, when we do meet, we will smile, share a big handshake and carefully avoid the subject.

Topic Five

Being Oneself Despite the Risks

Case 9 / A Little Depressed, but Nothing to Worry About

In the fall of his sophomore year in college, Will experienced an "all-pervading self-consciousness . . . where there was no *Me* that had its own positive identity and generated its own self-sustaining justification for being." Will's self-consciousness was acute in the classroom, in the dining hall, on dates, in sports; almost any social situation was anxiety-arousing and left him feeling "on trial with no defense." He was most reluctant to take initiative. to accept responsibility for his actions, to express his feelings, and to disagree with other people. When pressed, he acquiesced, choked up, or came to tears.

Will's recollections of several interactions with his father reveal a pattern: spontaneous action or self-assertion by Will often was belittled by his father. Over time, Will exposed fewer and fewer parts of himself to others and lost touch with what he wanted and what he stood for. Underlying his depression was anxiety about "being himself."

In October of my sophomore year in college the bottom dropped out of my life. I've never before been so intensely depressed for such a long period of time.

It hit me while I was bringing a girl back from a date. Her name's Jeannie; I met her at the first mixer of the year. That was a pretty unusual occurrence for me. My whole freshman year I went to mixers and met a total of one girl, whom I took out twice. My history in high school was even worse. The first time I held a girl's hand was in tenth grade, and I never necked with a girl. I guess that qualifies me as pretty horny, but the strange thing was that it was a "forever" horniness. By that, I mean in high school I wasn't radically disturbed by the lack of sex because I never imagined myself as being desirable enough for anyone to enjoy sex with me — it was something wholly unattainable and thus easier to accept.

That attitude changed drastically the summer before my sophomore year. That summer I worked in Maine at a coast resort employing about fifty-five people. We all got to know each other well, and, in a situation that was unique for me, I found I could walk into the dining hall, scan the people and feel able and comfortable to sit and talk with anyone there. Along with this grew the realization that some of the girls there actually liked and respected me, both as a person and as a potential sex partner. I never had intercourse with anyone there, but I advanced to the stage of heavy petting with three and prolonged necking with two more which was nearly comparable to intercourse in my eyes, considering my past lack of experience.

So when I came back to school I felt considerably more competent with girls than before, and this feeling seemed to be justified by the first mixer. I danced with a lot of different girls, and felt comfortable doing it. Sometimes I even talked to girls between dances — unheard of for me. I saw Jeannie early in the evening and danced with her a bit, and then moved off. I saw her again later, so I went over and we smiled at each other, talked and danced for a few minutes, and then mutually decided it was too hot (which mixers always are) and went out for a walk. She's a freshman at Simmons and hadn't seen my college before, so I showed her around. Then we picked up some Cokes and I asked her back to my room.

My God! This was a stunning victory for my psyche. I had actually introduced myself to a girl with a feeling of self-composure, danced with her with a feeling of cool, separated from her with (I thought) graceful tact, reestablished communication with her with mutual sincerity and goodwill, and then taken her for a walk and conversed with her with a feeling of mild wit and self-assurance. And now I was asking her to my room. And she came. This type of thing had happened to me in Maine, but never before at college.

Back at the room, my feelings remained pretty much the same. I put on a record but couldn't figure out how to turn on the amp (it's my roommate's stereo). Jeannie solved this minor disturbance by flicking the power switch to "on," and I laughed. (In my pre-Maine days an occurrence like that would have paralyzed me with embarrassment for the rest of the evening.) We then talked for a while. Jeannie lit a cigarette, which made me feel she was pretty sophisticated, but I didn't panic. I felt that even though I was dealing with what was obviously a pretty cool girl, I was competent and interesting enough for her to respect me. So we talked for a while. It was pretty much the usual getting-acquainted-mixer conversation, but as we talked I didn't feel the overpowering embarrassment which usually compels me to ask meaningless questions without interest and smile inflexibly throughout. Here I was asking the usual questions, but not simply out of embarrassment over what to talk about. I felt, at least partially, a sincere other-directed interest and involvement with another being. I make the "partially" stipulation because there wasn't a total unified sincerity within me. On another level I was still self-consciously wondering about the effect I was making, how well I was playing my *role*. But my self-consciousness was so much smaller than usual that on the whole I was comfortable and relaxed, not afraid of breaks in the conversation, and at ease with my own self-image.

We ended the evening with some necking and I took her back to the mixer. After that I took her out two or three more times, and the dates were all right — nothing spectacular. I never felt any lasting sincere commitment to Jeannie while I was with her, but for the most part I was relaxed and at ease with her on dates, and that was such a step up for me over my pre-summer days of self-consciousness that I was pretty satisfied. Plus Jeannie's a pretty good-looking girl and we necked a lot, which kept me happy.

But something happened on our third or fourth date while we were walking back to Simmons from the subway. I don't think it was the date itself that caused it, because I can't remember anything specifically bad about the date. We were just walking along and suddenly I felt this all-pervading self-consciousness. I was exposed, vulnerable, and worthless, and there was no *Me* that had its own positive identity and generated its own self-sustaining justification for being. Instead, here was this 5'9" slightly balding (but concealed with long hair) large-nosed entity who was on trial and had no defense. There was no positive, unique, and worthy motivating force within me. Jeannie would say something and I would think, "What should I say? Should I say anything? Holy Christ, what am I doing out with a girl? If I can just hold out till I get her to the dorm, I'm safe." Everything I said was a cliché or trivial, all my actions were trite and insincere, and there was no possible reason for anyone else to respect me because *me* as a self-assured, competent being did not exist. That was the beginning of my depression.

I stayed depressed and confused, pretty much without let-up, for the rest of the term. Lots of the time I just sat in my room and stared and thought, and to get to my desk and books or to the living room and people was an incredible distance through my mind. It was much less painful to stay in my room and get stoned or listen to music than to go outside, because outside were activities and people, and both put pressure on me to perform. But how could I perform when I totally lacked any feeling of self-respect. I escaped into apathy. And when you read that word imagine being inside an immense black pillow with the down pressing on your mind, restraining it. And on top of that, you don't want to move anyway, except that all the time you want to move so bad that it hurts.

I was close to only one person on the East Coast, my roommate Tom. By "close" I mean able to associate with most of the time without feeling really anxious. Tom and I had lived in the same freshman dorm. I didn't know much about him besides his name and that he seemed like a pretty cool guy until the spring of freshman year, when he asked me if I wanted to room with him. I felt flattered – I had been planning to room single and didn't much care which house I ended up in – so I said sure and we were friends. We did a lot of stuff together after that – Frisbee, volleyball, and a couple really ritualistic things: every couple weeks we'd go down to his room for a marijuana session that included a set sequence of events – rolling (Tom always rolled because my j's never burned right), his Strobe light, Joe Crocker, The Rolling Stones, Milkshakes, a few sets of hysterical laughter, and then to bed. And every Friday and Saturday night we'd walk around the city for an hour or so looking at girls and generally getting horny. This fall we more or less took up where we had left off – I felt comfortable with Tom most of the time (although sometimes I'd get uptight even with him) and expected him to be the leader in most of our activities (we'd be sitting in the room and he'd say, "Let's go to a movie," so we'd go). I usually didn't suggest what to do, and I acquiesced to Tom's better judgment on things like room furnishings, paint colors, and poster placement.

One incident about the beginning of the year sticks out in my mind. Tom and I were rooming with upperclassmen who are all four-year friends. It was decided that we should jointly furnish our big living room, and everyone would share the cost. So Tom (who knows the stores), me (as Tom's roommate), and Jamie (one of the seniors) drove into town to buy the furniture. I just kind of stood around feeling useless while Tom and Jamie decided what we needed and how much. When we got back with the load and the rest of the guys found out that the bill was over $100, a couple of them got a little pissed. Steve turned to me and said, "Willie, a *hundred* dollars? Jesus, how could you go out there and spend $100?" When he said *you* and meant *me* I suddenly realized what I had done. I had gone with these guys feeling in my own mind that I was simply an underling there to help carry chairs. It never occurred to me that I had an equal share of the responsibility along with Jamie and Tom, or that I could and should take a part in the decision-making and that my opinion might be respected.

Sometimes I wonder why Tom and all my new roommates call me Willie. My name is Will.

After my downfall in October, one of my most painful experiences occurred every day: squash practice. I went out for the squash team in the spring of my freshman year. I went to practice for the intramurals and after a couple weeks asked the coach if I could stay with the team. The competitive season was already over, but he took me on and gave me a lot of lessons to help me catch up. I did leg exercises during the summer, and this fall the coach told me I would play varsity. It scared the hell out of me. I've been in competitive sports all my life — baseball, tennis (I was captain of my high school team) — but I never felt at ease with the other members and in competition I never felt like I should win. So when the coach told me I was on the varsity I didn't feel excited or nervous, I felt total despair — competition was for me a perpetual anguish to be borne because I could never win; it was unthinkable that I could ever ride the wave of self-assured competence of the victor.

This attitude carried over into practice, and I dreaded reporting to the courts every afternoon. Occasionally squash made me feel very proud, but that was only when the coach gave me a lesson and heaped me with paternal praise. When I played the other team members and had to assert, to achieve, to prove myself as an equal, I fell apart. I felt stupid, self-conscious, embarrassed, and in general my thoughts were so fixed on myself that I didn't think about my game. I never flowed into a bout on the wave of creativity you need to analyze and defeat someone else; I entered it thinking, "Jese, it's nice of this guy to play me. I hope I can give him a little competition before he beats me so he doesn't think I'm a complete fool." I didn't look my teammates in the eyes very often, or speak to them unless they said hello first. I always smiled when they talked to me and laughed when they made a joke, but I never made any jokes myself.

In late November, after sitting alone in my room thinking for a couple hours, I gathered all my equipment together and went to tell the coach I was dropping squash. I went early to get there before the rest of the team. I told the coach I had decided to quit. He asked me why. How do you tell someone your whole life is your reason? I said, "Uh, well, I mean, I'm not really sure, coach," and fifteen minutes later I left his office having promised to stick it out.

A strange phenomenon happened to me during this period when I went to eat, not all the time but occasionally. I would walk into the dining hall feeling extremely self-conscious. There would be this vacuum of anxiety in my stomach and I would be scared to look any place except at the ground. The possibility that someone I knew would walk past and push me to the wall about deciding whether or not to have eye contact, whether I should say hello, what would I do or say if he stopped to talk, that possibility was a constant dread. I sat alone if I could. And as I ate, my mind would come to a morbid focus on each little movement I made — how I moved my eyes, the exact way I held my fork and cut my meat, the way my mouth opened and my jaws moved when I chewed. And I would worry, mainly about if the people around me could tell how ridiculously self-conscious and exposed I felt. And after a few bites I just wouldn't be hungry anymore — there would simply be no desire to eat — so I would walk back to my room staring at the ground and think some more.

It was very hard for me to study. When I tried to read I would either lapse into daydreaming or else uncontrollably get bogged down in word-by-word details. I really dreaded papers. I saw them as a challenge to my creative competence and the thought of starting a paper intensified the knot of anxiety that was constantly present someplace below my chest. So I looked for any excuse not to start papers, putting them off until I could say to myself: "There's so little time left that there's no way I can do a good job on this paper, so I might as well just slop anything down and turn it in." That logic usually relaxed me enough to get the paper done.

In high school I was valedictorian. For four years I followed one studying philosophy: study every subject every night. I started on my papers as soon as the assignment was given, always wrote rough drafts, and never asked for extensions. Except once. My junior year I was working on a term paper that a "select" group was doing for American history. Every time I tried to start writing I got discouraged and gave up. I finally broke down and got an extension through the first weekend of Christmas vacation, and most of that weekend I was in a state of despair. I even cried a little. That was the third time in my life I cried as a result of school. The second time was in fifth grade when the teacher praised the girl next to me and then criticized my work. I felt a hopeless sense of failure and cried. The first time was in first grade when the teacher told us to write down our names and I didn't know my last name.

I went home for the Christmas break after seeing a psychiatric social worker and making a shrink appointment for January. I had written my parents that I was seriously considering dropping out, and had received several concerned letters and phone calls as a result. When I got home I had a long talk with my mother about how depressed I was, at the end of which she hugged me and said, "I'm so sorry, Will, I wish I could help you." The hug repulsed me — it was probably the third or maybe fourth time I can ever remember my mother hugging me. With her it's not exactly spontaneous. I've never hugged my father. I've seen them hug each other maybe twice a year — on each other's birthday, at which time a self-conscious kiss usually accompanies the hug.

While I was talking to my mother, the same thing happened that had occurred on my earlier trip to the Student Health Service. Whenever I tried to describe how I felt about my father, I cried. This also usually happens whenever I disagree with something my father says to me. If I try to talk back, disagree verbally, I choke up and feel like the tears are about to come, at which point I acquiesce because what would I answer when he asked, "Why are you crying?"

Until I was in the tenth or eleventh grade, I thought my father was perfect. That is not to say I didn't have disagreements with him, but they were disagreements with an important stipulation: he was always right. It wasn't that he beat me or something until I admitted to him that he was right — he rarely physically punished me. I just always felt that although we might have a difference of opinion, it was ordained that he was in the right, or rather, that I was in the wrong.

Until I was four, I didn't have a father — my mother's husband died before I was born. Then my mother remarried. I don't remember much about my first years with a father. A few incidents stick out in my mind. I remember that once a week my father washed my hair, and I hated it because it always felt to me like he was tearing my scalp apart. I thought he was doing it on purpose and I'd scream at him to take it easy. But he'd hold me in front of the basin and in a kind of smiling tone of voice say, "Now, Will, that doesn't really hurt, does it?" or "Gotta get your hair clean." Sometimes my mother tried to intervene, but never with any results.

When I was in fifth or sixth grade I was sitting at dinner with several guests and relatives. I got into an argument with my father over something and made what I thought was a winning reply. I was standing next to him at the time and impulsively clapped my hand over his mouth while tauntingly saying something like, "That settles that, huh?" He grabbed my wrist and pressured me down to the floor, after which I was sent to my chair to finish dinner in silence.

In seventh grade I shot a robin by mistake. We used to shoot starlings out our back window with a pellet gun to keep them out of the bird feeder. Sometimes my father would let me shoot the gun, but I hardly ever hit anything, and rarely used the gun on my own initiative. Late one afternoon I saw what I thought was a starling in the tree. My father was downstairs, but the gun and I were upstairs. It's important to understand that I looked at the situation from every angle, because I felt vaguely wrong about using the gun without first asking permission (although this had never been prohibited). So I said to myself, "We shoot starlings. There's a starling in the tree. Therefore I *should* shoot it. Dad has never said not to, so therefore I *can* shoot it." So I shot it and went running downstairs yelling, "I got it," right up to my father with a guess-what-I-did-won't-you-be-proud-of-me expression.

"Got what?"

"The starling. In the tree. One shot."

"I didn't see a starling in the tree."

At this point my stomach started to drop. My mother, father and I walked out to the back yard. "There it is," I said. My father took one look and said (angrily), "That's a robin." I went closer. It *was* a robin. At this point my father asked me, "Why did you shoot a *robin?*" That surprised me a little. I didn't know what to reply. I hadn't purposely shot a robin, since I'd thought it was a starling. Yet it seemed pretty clear that I should have known it was a robin.

"I didn't know it was a robin. I was sure it was a starling."

"How could you have been sure it was a starling when it's a robin?" That overpowered me with smallness, so I turned away with an "I'm sorry" and put the bird in the garbage can.

I guess the reason I thought my father was perfect for such a long time is that whenever we do anything together, he always gives advice and I always follow it, so it took me a long time to discover that there is more than one correct way to do everything. When I don't follow his advice, it leaves me feeling anxious, like I've done something wrong in opposing him. I also notice an interesting occurrence when we have disagreements: I stop thinking. As soon as he says, "Why did you . . . ?" or "Why don't you . . . ?" my mind simply shuts down. It either refuses entirely to come up with an adequate defense or else views the reasons with a sudden involuntary attitude of belittlement.

A case in point: when my parents drove me to school at the beginning of freshman year, they came with me to the bank to open a checking account. I brought them with me because I'd never had a checking account before and I felt unsure about the procedure. The clerk left me with a form to sign, and I put down my full three names. My father immediately asked me, "Why did you sign it that way," (with a little laugh). "That means you have to sign all your checks that way. It's much easier just to put down your first and last name."

"I, ah, I don't know. I just thought, well . . ." I couldn't think of a reason. As I think back now, I had signed that way simply because I had never had a checking account before and I thought maybe the bank required a full signature for identification. It didn't occur to me at the time that that was sufficient justification for my action. I would have liked to have looked him in the eye and said (with a faint smile curling my lips), "What the hell difference does it make?" But that didn't occur to me either.

When I went home at Christmas I didn't talk to my father about my problems at school. I think he said to me once, "So you've been having some problems at school?" in a faintly humorous tone. (This is the tone we usually use toward each other. He did sound concerned about me though. And I really don't doubt that he is concerned about me. He's always done a lot of things with me. For example, he's coached all the Little League and Babe Ruth baseball teams I've played on. Also, in my long talks with my mother at Christmas, she mentioned several times how worried my father had been about me in their talks together.) "Oh, I guess I've been a little depressed. Nothing to worry about, though."

I stayed depressed pretty much until the end of the term. I did little course work. One term paper I simply didn't write and didn't answer the postcard my section man sent me about it. I also skipped a class presentation I was supposed to give for English. The thought of getting up in front of the class and giving a talk and then having our section man interrupt and ask a question I couldn't answer petrified me — I always clutch when asked for a quick judgment or analysis. I was sure that I was failing two courses (although I never checked with my section men), and I told my roommate and my mother that I was pretty sure I would drop out and get a job after finals. But once exams were over a lot of the anxiety just disappeared. One thing that really made me feel good was when Jess (one of my roommates) came in, after hearing I was thinking of dropping out, and said he'd be sorry if I left. He also said that he and the other guys had been sort of half-pissed at me all year for never doing anything with them. That made me feel good. So I stuck around college, switched my major to psychology, and ended up writing a case study.

Case 10 / I Tried Everything

Liz's relationship with Steve is continually affected by Steve's relationship with his sister, Claire. Liz's personification of Claire clashes with Steve's personification of his "little sister," and Liz's feelings of anger and frustration with Claire contrast with Steve's complaisance toward her. Liz elaborates on the difficulty of relating to or changing the interaction patterns which Steve, Claire, and their mother have settled into. Steve now has the role of mediating between his mother, sister, and fiancée.

Relationships should mature as persons in a family mature — and relationship maturation includes updating personifications of oneself and others and seeking more contemporary bases for relating. Liz's case attests to her "engagement" to a whole family, not just to a special person. A crucial question is whether Liz will "be herself" despite the anxiety. This means consistently and clearly communicating how she feels and what she wants, hoping that if others do the same, mutual understanding will lead to mutual acceptance.

It's traditional to hate your in-laws; I've jumped the gun and have an ongoing battle with my sister-in-law to be. I feel like a typical case study in female jealousy, and it's a most unpleasant feeling. It all started two years ago. I had only known Steve for a few weeks when he offered to teach me to drive a stick-shift car. As we were driving around, he suggested that we drop in at his house and play with a newly acquired cat. Although I hardly knew the boy, and I knew we would only stay a few minutes, I was very nervous about meeting his mother. I dreaded the feeling of being judged, and I was really relieved to discover that his sister was home. Steve had told me how nice his sister Claire was, but this was the first time I had met her. She was three years younger than we were and did seem quite friendly. I was amazed and relieved that Claire wanted to spend so much time with Seve and me (judging from my own disappearing act as soon as my sisters came into the house with a boy). I felt much more relaxed with Claire than with her mother, so I was glad she stayed. Steve and I stayed much longer than we had expected, and the three of us spent the afternoon playing with the kitten. On the drive home, I remember commenting on how nice it had been to meet his sister.

For the next few weeks I saw Claire occasionally. We would meet for a few minutes at her house. We were always friendly in a polite sort of way. We talked about how horrible her teachers and courses were, or how glad I was that the year was almost over.

One evening I was invited to Steve's to barbeque steaks. His parents had gone out to dinner, so it was only the three of us again. Claire was going on a blind date that night – a date her brother had arranged with the younger brother of a friend of ours. I thought it was incredibly thoughtful that he had thought of getting his sister a date – such consideration was not an everyday thing for him. It was Claire's first blind date, and she was a nervous wreck. She kept coming downstairs to model possible outfits for us to choose from. She was upset that she didn't have just the right earrings and I remember offering her the ones I was wearing and being very shocked with myself as soon as I had done it. The earrings had been a gift from my grandmother and were of antique carved gold and oriental pearls. I certainly had not wanted to lend them to anyone, but somehow I had felt that I had to offer. I was very relieved, however, when Claire turned down the earrings.

I answered the door for her blind date. Since he had only heard a description of Claire, he thought I was she. We do really fit the same description of height, size, and coloring. Steve and I thought the mix-up was pretty funny, since people are always thinking I am much younger than I am. Claire didn't find the situation quite so amusing. She said it was true that I looked younger than my age, about twelve in fact, but we didn't really look alike at all. She finished off her already irritating description with a comment about how no one could ever mix us up if they looked at my hair since it was such a frizzy mess. It is true that Claire has beautiful, long, straight, blonde hair and that mine is far from straight, but I was really taken aback by her hostility. I tried to dismiss it as nervousness about her date, but I was glad to get rid of her for the rest of the evening.

That night marked the beginning of the end – the development of the hair theme. From then on, whenever I saw Claire she always made some comment on the frizzy state of my hair. Even if she said that my hair looked nice, as she did upon occasion, she would always couple it with "not like it usually does." I was annoyed with these unnecessary remarks but knew it was true that my hair acts like a barometer, changing texture with changes in the weather. But I was furious when she began asking if I ever tried combing my hair, especially after I had only finished doing just that. Claire also began fixing her hair whenever I was around and telling me she just didn't know what to do with it; it was so ugly. I would either tell her how wrong she was, begrudgingly giving the compliment she was after, or act as if I hadn't heard her at all.

The school year ended, and I didn't see Steve or Claire for quite a while. It wasn't until the end of the summer that the three of us were together again. Steve and I had just come home from having

spent our summers apart, when he suggested that we go visit his sister
at her camp. He thought it would be a nice drive, and that we could
go swimming in a nearby lake. Claire was ecstatic to see Steve; she
went around introducing him to everyone in sight. I don't think my
name was ever mentioned in these introductions. Steve and I were
both appalled with the camp atmosphere. All the girls could talk
about were the boys they were meeting, and the socials they were
going to, and the bermuda outfits they were wearing. Even more
shocking was that Claire seemed to fit right in. On the way home,
Steve was upset that his sister was wasting her summer after summer
at that ridiculous camp which she insisted on returning to. Again I was
amazed at how thoughtful it was for him to have thought of visiting
her and how real his concern for his family was (very different from
the aloof and independent image he liked to portray). The next summer he did persuade Claire, who would listen to no one except Steve
on this issue, to go someplace else.

The weekend after our visit was unfortunately the official visiting time for the camp. This weekend was also Steve's birthday. The
two of us had planned to celebrate with a champagne banquet at his
house. His parents went to visit Claire, but Steve declined. Although
he had been there just the week before, Claire was "hurt" that he
hadn't come to see her, especially on his birthday. When she heard
that he was doing something with me, she was indignant. I was annoyed that she should begrudge us any time without her, that she
should make me feel that I was stealing away what was hers. I began
to look forward to the fall, to school, and to getting away.

The first Thanksgiving vacation and visiting at Steve's was delightful, except for Claire. Late one night Steve and I were starving,
and decided to defrost a cake. I went upstairs to see if Claire wanted
any and was quite pleased with myself for having thought to include
her, especially since I had noticed that Steve had begun to tell Claire
to "get lost" whenever I was around. On the way downstairs, I felt a
thud between my shoulders and was sure I would be paralyzed for
life. Claire had punched me in the back. She said something about
what business did I have to defrost a cake and gaily skipped into the
kitchen. I was stunned, shocked, and furious. I couldn't understand
why she had done it. I began to talk to Steve about it, and he felt that
Claire was just feeling a little upset. He felt it was hard for her to
adjust to being the only one at home. He said that before we had
started to go out he had always been home with his sister, especially
when his parents went out. Now he was away at school, and when he
was home he was usually with me. Steve was sure that Claire would
get used to it in a little while. I thought he was underestimating the
situation, but I didn't say anything more.

I began to notice some incredible things that were going on, and Claire's reactions began to make a little more sense. She had recently gained a lot of weight and really was bordering on the fat side. Steve, who has one of those fantastic metabolisms that can instantly burn up massive quantities of food, had never paid any attention to weight. He would probably never have noticed any change, except that I had recently taken to obsessive dieting and had starved myself to a very skinny state. Now Steve also became conscious of weight and began pestering Claire about every morsel of cake, candy, or ice cream she put in her mouth. It was a joke to him because he had never had to diet in his life. He told Claire if she didn't stuff herself quite so much, she wouldn't be such "a fat pig," but could be as thin as I was. I was really surprised to hear him but was also pleased that he was both being hard on his sister and at the same time praising me. I thought this might explain the cake incident. My offering food which Steve begrudged her and unknowingly tempting Claire off her diet was too much for her.

I also began to notice how her mother was treating Claire. Claire had suddenly started calling up boys on the telephone just to talk to them. Her mother was really upset although she had always been encouraging her daughter to go out, to talk to boys, to "socialize." I felt that she had really overemphasized the boy issue in bringing up Claire. She was continually saying that Claire might not do well with grades, but she would certainly do well with boys. Whenever Claire came home from a social event her mother's first question would be about the boys she had met. She would jokingly say that boys were the only thing her daughter was interested in.

As long as Claire hadn't been interested in boys, her mother prodded her. Now that Claire really did seem to be interested in boys, her mother panicked. She was no longer the liberal thinker she liked to consider herself, but was more conservative to reactionary. She set out to correct Claire's telephoning by using me as a tool. She said she had never heard me calling Steve, and certainly we had known each other for a long time. She insisted that I would never do such an improper and forward thing. Little did she know that part of why I never did call was that I was afraid she would answer the phone, and I would be trapped in an interminable phone conversation. Although she nagged about the phone calls, she still thought it was cute that Claire pleaded with Steve to wake her up for a 2 A.M. basketball game with six of his friends. I thought it was absurd, and persuaded him not to include her, but I was surprised it took as much persuading as it did.

To compound the issue, both parents started to badger Claire about her grades. She wasn't working and her grades were terrible. They were sure, however, that Claire was just as smart as her brother, if not smarter, and was just reacting to his successes by not working. Since they prided themselves on this psychological insight, they forgot about psychology and began nagging Claire about work. Unfortunately they used me as a tool. They would tell her they were sure my grades were better than that, and how did she ever expect to get into a good school if she didn't start doing better? Claire wouldn't pay any attention to them and insisted on spending her afternoons and evenings on the phone or watching television. It wasn't until Steve began to talk to her that there was any change. She promised that she would try harder and seemed very upset that she was disappointing her brother.

Tension grew between Claire and me. I began to feel very uncomfortable when I was with her. I was sure she was going to say something insulting or else insist that her brother take her some place — just her. I repeatedly tried to rationalize the situation by saying that Claire did only see her brother on vacations, and she was the only one at home the rest of the time. Then I realized that I had also been the only one home when my sister went to college, and I had never pulled the stunts Claire did. I had never arranged to visit old friends on a Saturday night and insisted that the *whole* family go along. I had never told my sister to stay home with me and forget about her boyfriend. I had never spent hour after hour and evening after evening with my sister's friends, monopolizing the conversation with a discussion of my latest book report, nor had I stormed off hysterical (if I were asked to leave) and insisted that my sister leave her friend and come console me for a couple of hours. Claire had made all these demands and seemed to feel justified in them. Try as I might to understand, after a few moments of just thinking about her, I would be fuming. After all they were my vacations too. What right did she have to make me feel so guilty all the time?

Once I was back at school, however, I would invariably feel that I hadn't made enough of an effort. I began suggesting to Steve that he invite Claire to come and visit for a weekend. I insisted that she would like it. She could stay with me, go to classes and go out. Finally he agreed. Although the visit had seemed like such a good idea from a distance, as the date approached, I panicked. I found Claire a room as far away from me as possible and manufactured huge quantities of reading that I simply had to do that weekend. Everything about the visit irritated me. I was annoyed that I *had* to clean up my room to pass inspection (although Steve insisted that I was being ridiculous), and I was annoyed that Steve went to meet his sister at the train station. I felt that she was a big girl and could really take a bus ride by herself. It seemed absurd that Steve should waste his time going to the train when he had just been complaining about all the work he had to do.

The weekend did live up to my wildest expectations. It was positively awful. Once Claire arrived, I felt that all privacy was gone. She was always in my room. Although she probably thought she was being friendly and would have been rude to retreat to her own room, I felt she had purposely decided not to let me have a moment's peace. Although she was always there, she was not very responsive to anything I said or did. She seemed terribly depressed and when we were with her brother, she was always on the verge of tears. My reaction was probably defensive and paranoid, but it seemed valid at the time. I assume she was miserable because I was around, "intruding on her time." This only made me more furious, and the whole thing quickly snowballed into a horror show. The worst blow came to both of us when Steve got sick. Claire and I were really thrown together. I tried but was pretty miserable myself by this time. I took her to classes and introduced her to friends, and felt really imposed upon while I was doing it. Even just studying in the library with her seemed like an invasion of privacy. I was really relieved when Sunday rolled round and Steve came over early to pick up his sister. I stayed upstairs because the old guilt had crept in and made me feel that Steve really hadn't seen much of his sister and because I was glad to have a few moments by myself. About half an hour later I went downstairs to remind them to start out for the train station and was pretty surprised and annoyed to discover they had already left without saying good-bye. There was a thank-you note in my mailbox, but it was in Steve's handwriting, not Claire's. This was the last straw.

When Steve did call me that evening, I ranted and raved about the impoliteness of their abrupt departure, and the injustices of the entire weekend. He explained that his sister had real problems at home. She had been dating a boy named Larry who her parents had never liked since they insisted he was the cause of her bad report cards. Now they had refused to let her see him, although Claire would not tell why. Actually Steve and I had only seen him once, and only for a moment. Although I had often suggested double-dates to Claire, she had always refused and really seemed to be hiding Larry. She refused to see him when Steve was home, so that she could spend more time with her brother. One evening, however, Steve and I had gone to his house and found his mother quite upset. She had unfairly arranged a baby-sitting job for Claire for the night to keep her from seeing Larry, but Claire had arranged for them both to baby sit. Now her mother assured us that they were certainly "sitting and smooching," since that was all they ever did according to her. She insisted that Steve and I drop in on them to wish them a happy new year and check up while we were at it. We felt ridiculous, but we decided that we really did want to meet this boy. I was amazed that a mother could betray her daughter that way, telling me, an outsider to the family, how she didn't trust her own daughter. I was really angry with her for doing it. When we did drop in on Claire, I was delighted to find her playing Scrabble with Larry. He seemed like a perfectly sweet high-school boy. He didn't seem to be anything special, nor did he seem to be the monster that Claire's parents had painted.

Even though I hadn't thought much of Larry, I really did feel sorry for Claire when I heard she could no longer see him. This new information seemed to explain some of her tears and depression. After a few moments, however, I began reconstructing what Claire must have done. I speculated to Steve that she must have been found sleeping with Larry or had been found using drugs. He was quite annoyed by my suggestion, and told me I was being ridiculous. Just because I didn't get along with his sister, he felt there was no reason to condemn. He insisted that she was a child, much too young for either sex or drugs. He thought it was preposterous that I could suggest such a thing for *his little sister.*

I was hurt that he was so defensive for her and that he felt sex and drugs were fine for me, but not for her. I couldn't resist throwing his little dichotomy back at him. When he realized what he had said and had had time to calm down about my conjectures, he began to retract. He said that whatever she did was her business, and that it was her life. I couldn't forget that his first reaction had been to kill the boy who had "defiled" his sister. Gradually he began to accept the idea that I might be right.

When he was home for the next vacation, the household was really a mess. Claire and her parents were constantly fighting. They all wanted advice from Steve and decided to tell him the whole story. Apparently Claire and Larry had been found sleeping together. Her mother panicked. She was hysterical that her little girl could do such a thing. Her father threw Larry out of the house, forbidding him to ever come again. After many fights, Claire had promised not to see him again but naturally was seeing him "on the sly." Unfortunately her parents had arrived home early with some feeble excuse and had again found them in the bedroom. Now they decided to make sure that Claire wouldn't see him and were picking her up straight from school, bringing her right home, and supervising all her activities and friends.

His parents were surprised that Steve wasn't more upset by this news, although he certainly would have been if he had not been adjusting to it for the past few months. Claire, on the other hand, was very pleased. She thought he was "on her side" as she put it. Claire began complaining about her parents to me. At first I was amazed at this show of closeness and tried to tell her she only had another year at home and things would get a lot better. Then I realized that she was confiding and complaining to everybody who walked into the house. In fact, she couldn't shut up about how awful they were being.

Her mother also began to use me as a sounding board. She would say how she just didn't know what to do with that girl. She made no attempt to keep their problems a secret and even asked my parents how they had survived two teen-age girls.

Claire's relationship with her brother also changed at this point. It became far more overtly physical. Claire had always been too intimate with Steve for my taste, but now she became downright sexy. Before, they had had a ritual of "tickling fights" that had carried over from age four, now Claire always seemed to be hanging on to Steve. She never missed an opportunity for a long hello or good-bye kiss. She began to feed him little morsels from her plate. I had no objections to his tasting her food, but I thought he was more than capable of feeding himself. Steve began to tell me stories of how his sister would wake him up in the morning by trying to pull off his covers, or how she had come into the bathroom while he was taking a shower and had thrown cold water on him. I really got upset by these last developments and told Steve I thought their relationship was far too sexy. Again he told me I was absurd and absolutely ridiculous.

I found the situation repulsive and was glad for the approaching summer. Steve and I had been planning to go across the country since the middle of that year but hadn't yet decided whether to go together or to separate. Anyhow, it was to be a summer away from Claire. Claire too, had plans for the summer. She was to go hosteling in Europe and get a much-needed separation from her parents. Right before Steve and I were to go, Claire broke her leg. Her plans for the summer were ruined. Shortly after this, Steve and I left.

This fall Claire was once again scheduled for a weekend visiting ordeal. I hadn't suggested or even encouraged the visit, but this time there was no choice. She had to come for college interviews. Although I wasn't looking forward to her visit, I wasn't terribly hysterical about it. I was sure things would be much better. Steve and I were engaged. I felt that I no longer had to feel that I had no right to be there, no right to keep him from his sister. I was really wrong. Things were worse than ever. This time, however, I really was busy for most of the time that Claire would be visiting so I didn't need to manufacture new long-standing commitments. I didn't see Claire until late Thursday night, when she discovered that her suitcase had been misplaced. She was upset since we had no idea when or if the suitcase would materialize. I calmed her down and told her she could always borrow my clothes for her interview. We went through my closet and found a dress that looked fine. Just as we were going, Steve came charging in with her suitcase. Claire decided, however, that her own things would be too wrinkled to wear and that she should still wear my dress for her interview. I didn't mind that but was surprised when she decided to wear my stockings and my jewelry also, although those things couldn't have been too wrinkled. I was even more surprised when she told me this wasn't the first time she had worn my things. After my last visit, I had left some dresses at her house by mistake, and she had been using them all the time. I didn't say anything about the borrowing but fumed quietly.

As the weekend progressed I thought it was odd that Claire hadn't mentioned the wedding, not one word of congratulations or anything. I realized it was hard for her, but I thought it was ridiculous to act as if Steve and I weren't getting married, and I didn't want Claire to get away with a defense of silence. I asked her to be a bridesmaid, because my parents had insisted I do it to make the break easier for Claire. It was difficult for me to say that I wanted her to do it, because I certainly didn't want her to even come to the wedding. Apparently, it was even harder for her to accept, and she couldn't bring herself to answer yes or no, or say anything other than "oh!"

Once the topic of the wedding was at least mentioned, Claire began asking about our apartment and what kinds of things we were planning on getting. She decided we didn't need anything. No pots, no bed. Claire felt *some* mattresses would be fine for us. She then suggested that we take down all the doors to make more wall space. I was furious and didn't think it was any of her business to decide what we needed or didn't need. I thought the door issue was a real invasion of privacy. But these comments weren't as bad as her dinner table conversation. Then she decided to warn Steve against asking his parents for a big wedding present. She announced to the entire table that "we were pushing it already." When I asked Steve what she had meant by that, if she meant pushing it by getting married, I was amazed that he hadn't even heard the statement.

That evening six of us went downtown. Steve and I were getting along amazingly well in spite of his sister's presence. We were really enjoying ourselves, when suddenly Claire had an accident. As soon as she looked at the cut, which had broken the skin, but hadn't even ripped her stocking, she began moaning and pulling her hair. Everyone else looked at it and was amazed that the cut was so small. We decided to take her to a doctor just to check. After an hour wait at the hospital — a wait through which Claire clung "passionately" to Steve — the doctor said a tetanus shot was essential and a stitch would help her knee heal faster. Now Claire really got hysterical. She screamed about how afraid of shots she was and insisted that she preferred tetanus. Finally the nurse asked if she was three years old and told her she was disturbing the other patients. Claire insisted that Steve stay and hold her hand. I was given the job of holding her coat, which she could easily have put on a chair or hung up. I couldn't help thinking that the accident had been a real fluke. It seemed incredible that Claire's shoe could have slipped off while she was running and landed half a block behind where she fell without the assistance of a kick. It seemed as if it had almost been kicked off. It had all been timed so well — to interrupt a pleasant evening where Claire wasn't the center of attention.

That weekend Steve's parents and my parents descended for a "family togetherness" dinner. Claire was in her prime. She was all over Steve — hugging him, leaning on his shoulder, and pulling his hair throughout the entire meal. She also insisted that she was unable to walk on her cut, although she had done so quite comfortably the night before, just after the accident. She limped around as if the entire right leg right up to the hip had been injured, not her knee. She was completely incapacitated unless her brother was there to assist her. When we walked to the restaurant, Claire walked way ahead with Steve so that I could hardly see them. Any observer would have thought that she was the girlfriend, not me. I was certainly ecstatic to get rid of her, her ailments, and her demands, on Sunday.

The last time I saw Claire was two weeks ago. Steve and I went home for the weekend to do some errands. As soon as I walked in the door, Claire pounced on me and asked me to come look at her dress for the wedding. I assumed that she was going to be a bridesmaid. I assured her that anything she chose would be just fine, but she insisted that I come and look. I thought it was ridiculous to make such a production, and Steve and I had loads of errands we had to do and very little time. I was also annoyed because I hate shopping. Since she insisted, I said I would go. Claire picked me up early the next morning and we went to see the dress. It was incredible — backless, frontless, satin and lace. It was absolutely out of place for a small afternoon wedding. But Claire loved it, and although I felt pretty ridiculous saying it, I told her it was fine as long as she liked it. Although I thought it was one of the most inappropriate choices possible, I was really relieved to see that at least she hadn't chosen a white dress. Then I really wouldn't have known what to do.

Our next stop was to look at my dress, which came from a near-by shop. Strangely enough, Claire lost the car keys. After a frantic search and a phone call to Steve to come pick us up, she discovered the keys in her pocket, a place she never puts them. I never really expected to care about a wedding gown, but I was really surprised when I saw it. It was gorgeous, luxurious, and really "bridey." I thought it was fantastic and said so, but Claire didn't say a word, not even a feeble "how pretty." I was annoyed and amused by her silence. I think that part of the reason I wasn't hysterical was that I had already started this paper and had started to trace the development of our relationship. I found it easier to be at least more tolerant, if not friendly.

When we went back to Claire's house, I never saw such a commotion over a dress. Her mother insisted she try it on right then and there. Claire more than willingly obliged and got undressed and redressed in front of all of us in the living room. Then her mother began talking about the shoes she would need to get and how she would wear her hair. Nobody had asked me anything about my hair or my shoes, and I really thought that Claire was the one who was getting married. I decided that if a fuss over a dress was going to make a separation any easier for Claire it was well worth it. I just wanted to be left out of the trauma for once. Steve and I beat a hasty retreat out the door, and I haven't seen any of his family during the past two weeks.

identity

The subject of identity and identity formation has become in the popular mind almost synonymous with the work of Erik Erikson. Because of this, one of his earlier definitions of what is involved in identity as "the capacity to see one's self as having continuity and sameness and to act accordingly. It is the consistent organization of experience." The utility, the popularization, and the limitations of this concept have been cogently reviewed by him in his book *Identity: Youth and Crisis* (1968). In the preface, he reviews the whole history of this concept as he has employed it from the time it was first used in the Mount Zion Veterans Rehabilitation Clinic during World War II. In reviewing the use of the term over the last twenty years, Erikson makes it clear that identity was a preoccupation long before its current usage and meaning: both William James and Freud were concerned with this idea and he merely followed their lead. Such modesty is typical of Erikson's generosity. However, it obscures to some extent the fact that Erikson's formulation of ego psychology has caused radical rethinking about ego structure among psychoanalytic theorists.

Probably the most important aspect of Erikson's approach to identity is his conviction, originally enunciated in *Childhood and Society* (1950), that owing to historical changes, the study of identity is as crucial for our time as a study of sexuality was for Freud's time. This shift in conceptualization has two important implications: first, revisions in psychosexual theory were required to take into account changing values concerning sex; second, if identity formation reached a crescendo of importance during the adolescent years the study of youth became as important as, if not more important than, the study of childhood.

It is not the intent of this essay to recapitulate Erikson's work. No student of adolescence should fail to read Erikson's complete works or at least his summary statement on identity and youth. However, to repeat, his is one approach to a complex area and, while brilliant and enlightening, can by its persuasion deflect us from considering specific aspects of identity formation in detail. It must be noted that Erikson himself makes it clear that when one is speaking of sexual identity, personal identity, self identity, one is essentially dealing with smaller, more discrete units of a general process that need to be reviewed in their own right.

Quite generally, therefore, when one is using the term "identity," one is speaking of a general concept or a general category in which a number of subcategories or traits are involved for each individual. Speaking on the most general level of abstraction, it can be said that identity consists of assuming some general adult role congruent with the demands of one's society and behaving in a way which is consistent not only with being an adult but also with being an adult male or female. This leads to more specific subquestions concerning occupational and social identity. The subdivisions that can legitimately be created are endless, as Erikson has pointed out. However, during adolescence two critical questions have to be resolved by each individual: What kind of adult am I going to be, what will my role as an adult be in society by virtue of my education and my occupational choice? What advantages or disadvantages does the biological fact of being male or female create for me?

The difficulties attendant upon assuming one's identity differ markedly from society to society, and from social class to social class. In a paper reprinted in 1958, but written in 1930, Margaret Mead points out that adolescence in primitive society is a relatively simple task. This is because, as she puts it, each young person as he grows up in that society knows from the time he can understand the world around him precisely what role expectations he has, and what responsibilities the tradition he represents places upon him. Identity formation becomes difficult, as Mead suggested and as Erikson made explicit, when one lives in a society where, in the final analysis, one is responsible for constructing one's own identity and where social roles are open to be achieved rather than simply ascribed to each individual depending upon his accident of birth and sex. Thus, when we are speaking of identity, we are for the most part speaking of phenomena peculiar to technological society. However, as will be seen, certain aspects of identity and difficulty in identity formation may exist in both primitive and technological society.

Identity formation is one of the two most important processes for any person as he goes from infancy to being an autonomous adult. A closely related process is that of identification, a largely unconscious process by which the younger child internalizes the roles and qualities of the adults who socialize him. In some societies this kind of role learning and this process may be sufficient. However, as Erikson remarked in 1959, in technological societies identity becomes crucial when the process of identification is no longer sufficient or appropriate for one learning how to place oneself in society. While the relation between identification as a process and identity formation as a task of adolescence is beyond the limits of this essay, the reader should be aware that both of these are critical for understanding the development of personality. For those who wish further information about these two processes, a careful reading of Erikson's early paper on the problem of ego identity (1959) will be extremely helpful.

This book attempts to suggest the priorities of contemporary adolescence in the United States. For purposes of general introduction, the most pertinent issues are those dealing with "national character considerations" of adolescence and with sex role and gender conflict. Both these conceptualizations are tangential to the main stream of the study of adolescence, but must be understood.

When we are alluding to what we have called the question of national character in adolescence, we are addressing the question of the way in which adolescence as an experience has been affected not only by the general factor of technological society, but also the way in which the existence of technology has over time affected the context of adolescence in many different and subtle ways. In 1950 David Riesman published *The Lonely Crowd.* In this remarkable work, Riesman and his associates suggested that character types were related to certain complex relationships between population in general, and birth and death rate in particular. They saw societies in three different categories and saw America as representing an example of a society that had gone through all three of these points of transition. In essence, they proposed that there is an intricate relationship between character type and the value priorities that come about as a consequence of the way in which the family is organized in relation to population, and relative birth and death rates. A society, they propose, as it evolves from being relatively simple to technological goes through three stages: a tradition-oriented stage, an "inner directed" stage, and an "other directed" stage. Riesman suggests that American society is going through a transition from a frontier orientation, when being inner directed was critical, to an orientation of being other directed, quite different but required by the demands of an urban, modern society.

We will not debate the merits or demerits of Riesman's theoretical orientation. Several empirical studies have shown that the general phenomena he has described exist. Miller and Swanson in their book *The Changing American Parent* (1958) show that when inner directed families from the country go into the city, they become other directed. While Miller and Swanson use the terms "entrepreneurial" and "bureaucratic" personality types, they are essentially discussing the same ideas that Riesman proposed. The extent to which this change in orientation has affected the total fabric of social relationships is brilliantly portrayed by John Seeley and his associates in their book *Crestwood Heights* (1956). Here Seeley reveals that the relationship that used to exist between the family, the church, and the school has, since the Second World War, gone through a reshuffling of priorities. What all three of these works suggest is that in technological society, to return to our metaphor, identity formation becomes more and more the responsibility of the individual and is synthesized more and more outside the family unit. Seeley goes so far as to suggest, as does Edgar Friedenberg (1959, 1963), that socialization to all intents and purposes is now accomplished by surrogate agents such as the school and that the family has little, if anything, to do with the creation of personality. This is an extreme position and whether or to what degree, as Riesman has pointed out in his preface to *Crestwood Heights*, this particular conclusion can be generalized beyond suburbia is moot. What is not in question is the fact that the context in which adolescence is experienced has not only changed because of historical factors but also because of subtle changes in the most important context for personality development and its nurturance: the family. Rural society was seen as changing, and while these changes seemed to be having a complex effect upon personality development, the quality of this change and its meaning, particularly to younger people, was not brought into focus until relatively recently.

In 1960 Kenneth Keniston wrote a brief and highly provocative essay for *The American Scholar* entitled "Alienation and the Decline of Utopia." In this essay he had certain things to say about young people and their difficulty in relation to their society which in retrospect seem almost prophetic. In essence, Keniston had become concerned about the way in which many young people were finding it impossible to attain a sense of being placed not only in relation to adults in their society but also in relation to its institutions. He saw a growing degree of separateness between youth culture and the rest of society.

In this early essay, Keniston was writing from the point of view of social commentary. However, this was followed up by his searching clinical exposition "Inburn" (1963). His point of departure for his study of Inburn is reminiscent of an early study written by Henry A. Murray "The American Icarus" (1955). Using the case of Grope, Murray sets the personality structure of an individual who among other things is in the midst of a protracted adolescence. Murray's name for his protaganist — Grope — is suggestive of the lack of resolution and incapacity of this individual to integrate sexuality in any mature way beyond the phallic stage of development. Murray, through the use of Grope's creative projections on the Thematic Apperception Test, suggests a typology which might be rather common in American middle-class males. Keniston, in his work on Inburn (and again the protagonist's name in suggestive), presents quite a different typology. One must ask whether this is because of the times in which the two cases were written or because of the differences between two individual clinical subjects. In any event, Grope's scattered attempts at relationships, regardless of how inept, are strivings to live within a society. This is in stark contrast to Inburn's unwillingness and incapacity to make any kind of place for himself or even evince a desire to make a place for himself in a society which he does not want and cannot accept. In Inburn's case, to what degree does he represent the kind of general issue concerning student apathy so carefully and concisely presented by Paul Walters (1961)? In considering identity, however, what is of import in terms of this clinical case is that the identity of being "uncommitted" or being "alienated" may be one possible way for the adolescent to go through what Erikson has called the psychosocial moratorium. The interesting thing about this aspect of Keniston's work is his suggestion of style of adolescence and identity formation and its close relationship to larger social and cultural factors.

Keniston followed this clinical presentation with two empirical studies, *The Uncommitted* (1960) and *The Young Radicals* (1968). These two studies conclude a decade of work which may well set a model for certain approaches to the study of adolescence generally, and the dissection of identity in particular. While Keniston is the first to make clear that he is dealing with an upper-middle-class sample at a prestigious university, there are elements in his work that hark back to certain classical studies of adolescence; yet because of his inclusion of factors pertaining to social change and ideology, his work may have alerted us to aspects of the adolescent experience that previous studies may have overlooked. What is compelling about these studies is that they alert us to the sensitivity of the adolescent style to social events, and in addition, we can see how quickly the *modal* style changes from the uncommitted and the apathetic to the radical and possibly activist and militant. Many have talked about the way in which the moods and styles of the *individual* adolescent shift and change in the process of achieving identity, but few with Keniston's cogency have shown the way that this personal fluidity can be affected by undercurrents of social change.

Earlier an allusion was made to Murray's work. The point of the allusion and its purpose goes beyond the suggestion of his influence upon Keniston's methodolgy. In a paper presented in 1967, Goethals suggested that one of the critical problems facing those who tried to understand adolescence in the contemporary world was the fact that the myth of Daedalus and Icarus, so much a part of the intellectual substructure of Murray's thinking, may no longer be appropriate in efforts to explicate the world of the present-day adolescent. With the present radical shifts in patterns of authority and definitions of autonomy, the myth that probably fits this generation more closely is that initiated by the nuances of Franz Kafka, particularly the world of noncommunication so frighteningly elucidated in *The Castle.*

To shift to another important spectrum, nothing could be less influenced by history and social change than the fact of gender per se. While the definition of what is considered to be appropriately male and female is inescapable by virtue of being human, the ways in which gender identity come about and the factors which influence it are many. The attacks upon the problem will be represented in this discussion by works that are representative of points of view very different in their emphasis and implications.

One of the problems — and in a sense it is a salubrious one — about Erikson's work is that we tend to be persuaded that his exposition of the concept of identity formation is the only one and that the factors he deals with are the only relevant variables. No doubt they are, particularly in a technological society. However, in considering the question of gender, we become aware of the fact that certain other materials may be of great utility in gaining a more rounded sense of what is involved in identity. In the introduction to this volume, the work of John W. M. Whiting was discussed and his explanation of the initiation rite briefly alluded to.To recapitulate, Whiting and his associates (1958) found that male initiation rites were a functional response to the existence of cross-sex identification in males which if permitted to continue into adult life would cause disruption of the social institutions of certain cultures. Bruno Bettelheim, in his book *Symbolic Wounds* (1954), attempts to show that the initiation rite is indeed related to questions of gender, and although his reasoning and speculations are utterly different from Whiting's, both men's works are essential to a consideration of the question of gender. Bettelheim sees initiation rites of either males or females as a symbolic response to the fact that each person has his or her own gender, yet at the same time aspires to some of the characteristics and privileges of the opposite sex. Sexual identity, as Bettelheim see it, always brings with it both a process of acceptance and a degree of envy. The most important theoretical aspect of Bettelheim's work is his insistence that sexual identity in *both sexes* brings with it a degree of envy of the genital capacities of the opposite sex. This is a rigorous rebuttal to much of the writing about feminine psychology and feminine role. Thus, the initiation rite can be seen as a way in which not only is a correction

or an affirmation of identity accomplished, but in addition some
degree of need for complementation by the opposite sex is
recognized.

An entirely different approach to the problem of gender
identity is that proposed in a paper by Burton and Whiting on father
absence (1961). Here Burton and Whiting make a discrimination
between what they call attributed, subjective, and optative identity.
They state their position as follows:

> We would like to define a person's position or positions in the
> status system of this society as his identity. Furthermore, we
> would like to distinguish three kinds of identity: attributed,
> subjective, and optative. *Attributed identity* consists of the statuses
> assigned to a person by other members of his society. *Subjective
> identity* consists of the statuses a person sees himself as occupying.
> And finally, *optative identity* consists of those statuses a person
> wishes he could occupy but from which he is disbarred.

Burton and Whiting's work is important not only for these
operational definitions of different dimensions of identity but for
their review of the way in which these dimensions can be affected by
conditions in the family, particularly by the presence or absence of
one or another of the parents. Thus, if Keniston has sensitized us
to the effect of political and social ideology upon adolescent identity,
Bettelheim and Whiting have alerted us to the way in which gender
definition can indeed be a precarious matter.

No discussion of identity could be complete without some
reference not only to the substance but the implications of Jomo
Kenyatta's ethnography *Facing Mount Kenya* (1962). Despite its
heavy political bias, which at times changes it from an ethnography
to a polemic, Kenyatta's careful review of what it means to come of
age in Kikuyu culture and his commentary concerning the inherent
integrative capacities of that particular socialization in contrast to
our own, leads one to reconsider a question that has been kept in
the forefront: Do the difficulties in adolescence stem from the
inherently evil aspects of technological society? More important,
in considering Kenyatta's work, one is brought face to face with the
question raised by such anthropologists as Margaret Mead and Ruth
Benedict: Does adolescence exist at all or is it merely a cultural
invention? Kenyatta's work, however, is important for still another
reason in that it suggests a third possible path to identity and
maturity, different from Erikson's notion of the moratorium or
Whiting's elaboration of the initiation rite. This is that many may
attain maturity through a complex set of reciprocities between
generations which carefully and scrupulously age grade the

individual into his proper status at any given time, be he a man or a woman.

As Allen Wheelis has suggested in his book *The Quest for Identity* (1958), the search is never easy and the inner and outer world of the adolescent is in a constantly changing and shifting frame of reference. This highly selective overview points to certain key works that may help us to understand the final step that must be taken before maturity, as a consequence of identity formation, can be assumed.

A Psychosocial Approach

When Erikson applies his concept of identity to *specific* examples of human experiencing, he usually discusses a person's capacity for vocational commitment and sometimes discusses a person's satisfaction with his sexuality (that is, his gender, sexual relationships, and gender role). And the psychological literature reflects this preoccupation with the vocational and sexual aspects of identity, giving less emphasis to the political, racial, and ethnic (religious or national) aspects. The next ten cases are arranged topically to put equal emphasis on each of the five aspects of identity. One can apply Erikson's psychosocial stage theory to these cases by considering each personal account in terms of the normative crises of trust versus mistrust, autonomy versus shame and doubt, initiative versus guilt, industry versus inferiority, identity versus identity confusion.

Another psychosocial approach — not inconsistent with Erikson's — is to consider four areas of identity-seeking: to what extent has the person developed mutually satisfying relationships with (1) family members; (2) friends; (3) employer, coworkers, and recipients of one's product or service; and (4) the community at large? The question of mutually satisfying relationships with family members is identical to the issue of autonomy discussed in the introductions to cases in the first section of this book. Mutually satisfying relationships with peers include not only sexual intimacy, discussed in the introductions to cases in the third section of this book, but also nonsexual friendship. The quality of relationship with employer, coworkers, and recipients of one's product or service indicates a person's vocational competence, commitment, and satisfaction. And, finally, a person's relationship to the community at large refers to the relevance of one's politics, race, and ethnicity to personal development and happiness. For some persons, their politics, race, religion, or nationality is the focal point of identity-seeking. A psychosocial approach to Cases 11–20 is to consider each case writer's progress in these four areas of identity-seeking.

Topic Six

Sexuality and Identity

Case 11 / Appreciating the Woman in Me

At the midpoint of her senior year, Paula recounts the experiences and concerns that are relevant to her developing sense of sexual identity: physical appearance, body awareness and satisfaction, menstruation, masturbation, premarital intercourse, birth control, pregnancy, abortion, bisexuality, sex role stereotypes and myths, women's liberation, sexual counseling, women friends, men friends, dating games and same-sex competition, dependency and commitment in marriage, family and/or career, and her ongoing relationships with both parents. Greater sexual freedom, knowledge of sexuality, and awareness of the political aspects of sex role socialization have made it easier for Paula to question basic assumptions and to do what feels natural. She strives to maintain some control over her development and to fully experience her womanly potential.

Being a woman at Bowdoin College has been a bizarre experience. I was in the first class of freshman women, and we were in the great minority. By now, my senior year, the ratio has improved. For four years, then, I have been living in a basically male environment and I am sure that this has caused me to react more strongly toward women's issues than might otherwise have been necessary.

My college experience has been in direct opposition to my high school years, which were spent in an all girls' private day school in the West. The women at that school were, by and large, from wealthy, waspy families, and were not in the least interested in academics. A good number of them are, rather predictably, married now and attend weekly Junior League and Garden Club meetings. I dislike the roles they have chosen for themselves, since there is no sign of any kind of independence (nor was there in high school when just those women who are now married were in very tight, exclusive cliques). I never really fit in with my peers in high school. I was interested in my studies, I found my family (three sisters) to be a good deal more interesting than most of the girls in my class and certainly more interesting than any of the boys I came in contact (i.e., talked) with.

My home environment was drastically different from that of most of my peers. For one thing, I got along with my parents — not just superficially either — we actually communicated. For another, being Jewish (reform as we were) meant that there was not even a *chance* for my mother to get caught up in Junior League, club-oriented activities (Jews were excluded), even if she were so inclined. As it turned out, after doing extensive social work my mother decided to enter business school. Her pursuing a professional career has had a marked effect on me. Because of her example, I have never considered any life-style for myself except one in which I have a fulfilling career. My mother went through her business school experience before it was accepted for women, surprisingly within the last seven years, and she faced prejudice every step of the way. There was one professor in particular who felt that women had no place in business school, and the few women in his classes received consistently lower grades than the men. After she graduated and began looking for a job, companies told her they didn't want to hire a woman because her home would always come before her work, and they were interested in "serious businessmen." Intellectually, I could relate to her problems, but I couldn't really empathize because I wasn't experiencing any prejudice to my sex then.

One thing I have noticed in my mother and my father since their careers are so terribly important to them is that they are both very selfish. My mother, in particular, gives us less and less of her time. I don't feel that she has found the happy medium between her job and her family. When I am home over vacations, I almost never see her. And she does not rearrange her schedule for me. I feel that I come second to her job more and more. I am closer to my mother than are any of my other sisters, because we share the same humor and are very similar. She confides in me things that she doesn't confide in my siblings. Since I have always been the "special daughter" I have a lot of trouble adjusting to the lack of energy she puts into our relationship.

This has led me to question whether I can ever expect to have a family and a full-time career. There are only so many hours in the day, and I have only so much energy. Is it possible to combine both? I'm not sure that I even want a family at this point, but my mother's inability to deal with the family adequately has made me wonder whether a career would have to be at the expense of the family.

I did feel a great deal of hurt in my high school years in regard to my looks. I have brown hair and brown eyes, and I couldn't accept my rather "Jewish look" because the criteria for attractiveness in my school were blonde hair, blue eyes, and ski-jump noses. To this day, I resent women who look this way, since they represent all the frustration of feeling ugly and left out that I felt in high school. It has taken me years of getting compliments from men (women's compliments didn't seem to help) to finally accept my own personal beauty. Even at the beginning, when men complimented me, I thought they were blind, or had some ulterior motive (whatever that meant!).

And this desire to be pretty tore me up, too, because I wanted to think that my physical appearance didn't matter to me, that my mind was all-important. But I know how concerned *I* am with men's physical appearance — certain things attract me while others do not — so they must care too, and I *do* want to feel good about my body and my physical appearance, not only because it affects how others (usually men) feel about me, but because it affects how I feel about myself. To put it rather simply, I feel better when I look better (or vice versa?). In any case, mental and physical attitudes about myself seem to go hand in hand.

Another reason it has taken me such a long time to accept myself physically is that two very weight-conscious women are my mother and her mother. My grandmother is the hardest to deal with. Whenever I (or any of my sisters) go home and visit her, her first comment is always "You've gained/lost weight." Or, "I don't like your hair that way," etc. Physical appearance is paramount to her and she will not hesitate to tell me exactly how she thinks I look, which could be helpful if I cared to hear about it, but when I'm trying to get away from seeing people (including myself) based on what's on the outside, it doesn't help to hear this kind of evaluation constantly. My mother has always been worried about her weight also. (Both of these women are quite slim and attractive, by the way.) She became addicted to diet pills many years ago because of her unhealthy desire to be thin.

Now I am extremely irritated by weight-conscious women. I find America's Madison Avenue view of the "sexy" woman skinny and unappealing. The whole thing makes me very angry because I see beautiful, full, voluptuous women trying to make themselves look like someone else, which is not only irritating, but unhealthy. I have fought this tendency in myself, too. Lately, I've been very satisfied with my body, even though I do not fit the example set by leggy, skinny, flat-chested women.

I never fully explored my sexuality until I came to college because I had not met many men in high school whom I considered to be bright and attractive. But, I arrived at college and whammo! I didn't know which way to turn. I had a series of short-lived, shallow relationships with me usually calling it quits because someone new had caught my fancy. It is with rather great embarrassment that I relate this part of my life. I was fickle, I was flirtatious, I had a damn good time, but I played "the game." By this I mean that I was a cute flirt in the worst sense. I played little games to attract attention from men who interested me. I didn't let my intellect show, I didn't like being alone to think, and I displayed generally thoughtless behavior. I did not have any close female friends my freshman year. I excluded them because they couldn't flatter me, and I never realized how much I might have had in common with other women — things that men would never share.

I didn't have intercourse until my junior year, when I was twenty. The event was not a big deal for me since I was definitely ready for it, and had worked through any unsubstantiated feelings of guilt about sex by then. My mother had always told me that pre-marital sex was wrong. I realized that I simply did not agree with her. For a long time, however, I did everything but have intercourse. I decided that was absurd and consciously began rejecting my mother's values. One of my younger sisters had intercourse before me or Lynne, and after the initial shock, Mom began to get used to the idea. Now that all her daughters have "gone to the dogs" Mom accepts pre-marital sex. Her morals have done a complete turn-around in the last three years.

By the time I was twenty I had heard that sex was no great shakes. When I was younger, I used to feel that if I found out I had some dread disease and only had six months to live, I would have sex, no matter what Mom thought! I viewed intercourse as something one should never die without experiencing. I was never sure why — whether that was because it was orgasmic, the perfect union, or whatever else the literature I read offered me. But with each suc-ceeding year, more and more of my female friends said sex was *not* earth-shaking and was no big deal after all the noise we'd heard from our parents and everyone else.

Masturbation was always orgasmic. I can remember mastur-bating as far back as my childhood memories go. I was never chastised for it, and my sister and I gave it a pet name, the "wiggly-squirm!" My mother told me years later that she didn't even know how to mastur-bate until she saw us. Somehow, I became socialized and reserved masturbating for the privacy of my bedroom. Mom never told me to stop masturbating in the living room — I really don't remember where I got the idea that this was something that wasn't done in public.

I got my menstrual period on June 24 when I was 13. I'll never forget the date! My main reaction was "Godammit, what a pain in the ass (?) to have to worry about this bloody mess every month!" My mother told me it was wonderful, but still called it "the curse." A few years later I began to enjoy my period because it reminded me that I was a woman and my body was working; and recently my period has come to represent the joy of no worry about pregnancy for another month.

The only problem with intercourse was that of birth control. I was irritated by the lack of safe, easily used alternatives presented to me by the college gynecologist who assured me that what I really wanted was the pill. I was further angered by the fact that I had to spend ten minutes explaining to him why I was not willing to go on the pill because of the hormonal changes involved. I didn't particularly like the idea of having the estrogen convince my body it was pregnant and inhibit ovulation. I wanted to ovulate and have normal periods! How do you explain that to a male doctor? With great reluctance, he fitted me for a diaphragm.

I used it every time, and never missed. I became pregnant over that summer; I knew even when my period was two days late because my body felt different. My breasts were incredibly tender and I threw up in the morning; I had classic first-month pregnancy symptoms. I never described my condition to myself as pregnancy — something had gone wrong and I had to have a little operation to fix it. I never saw myself as carrying a potential child, because as far as I was concerned I wasn't; I didn't want to be, and it was a mistake that I was pregnant. That condition was never meant to be. I was not pleased to find out how incredibly fertile I was. (That sperm had to travel through a ton of contraceptive cream and past a diaphragm — I must be ridiculously fertile and the sperm must be ridiculously gutsy.) I was angry. I didn't deserve to be pregnant—I had been careful. I was scared too, of being in a condition I wanted violently not to be in. I remember worrying that the liberalized abortion laws would be reversed the day before my abortion and I would have to travel to Europe or do it myself and bleed to death. There was *no* way I would have continued that pregnancy. No matter what the consequences.

I am so strongly in favor of abortion that it is one of those issues I cannot even argue about. There aren't two sides to me. Just thinking of all the women who have died or led miserable lives because of such opinions as the Right to Lifers hold makes me foam at the mouth.

I am always surprised when I hear about women who didn't know they were pregnant until they had been pregnant for over three months! Irregularity is one thing, but the changes your body goes through is another. I had a discussion with a woman who is a professor. She appalled me by saying she was pregnant and didn't realize it for three months! She shocked me again by saying that she couldn't understand the usefulness of female gynecologists or counselors! "Women need only a doctor with good expertise and technical abilities. What purpose would it serve for women to talk to someone who has been through the same thing? None. I don't like going to female gynecologists because I am afraid that they are lesbians." My God, and what about male gynecologists who might be lechers! This was a young professional woman talking. Makes me kind of wonder who the women's liberation movement is reaching.

There was never any question about having an abortion, and my parents were extremely supportive. My lover, Peter, was at my side, but he was no help. It suddenly struck me that he could help financially and he could be supportive, but I had to experience the pain and trauma all by myself. I was completely alone — women must experience some things by themselves with no one on whom they can place part of the burden. It is our pain, alone. Men can hold our hands, help us pay, but we will always be the ones with the first-hand experience.

This episode was further complicated by the fact that my father was seeking a high position in the American Medical Association and abortion was one of the big issues. He was in favor of it, and the Right to Life sympathizers would not give him their support. Members of Right to Life happened to be picketing outside my doctor's office on the day of the abortion, and I had to cross through their lines to get into the office! Luckily, they didn't know who I was because I've no doubt (based on some of their previous tactics) that they would have loved to smear me and my father all over the AMA press. My father lost his bid for office but later tried again, switching his stand on abortion in order to offend fewer AMA members. He got the position.

This was definitely a turning point for me. I suddenly wanted to be with other women, to share feelings and frustrations. I had begun to have close female friends during my sophomore and junior years, and I was slowly realizing that there is a quality to a same-sex relationship that can never be found with a member of the opposite sex. It was similar to the realization I had at about the same time that my relationship with my three sisters was something very special that would never be quite the same with other women. We had known each other all our lives, we had argued, fought, giggled until our stomachs hurt, used our very personal knowledge of each other to be vindictive in the most destructive ways, and then cried afterwards and loved each other all the more. We understood the nonverbal communication of every gesture or facial expression and we could see through each other's rationalizations quickly.

My sisters are very special to me. I am twenty-one, and I have one older sister, and two younger sisters. Because of the influence of my mother and the importance of education stressed by our family, we are all career-oriented and also opposed to marriage on theoretical grounds — some of us more vehemently than others.

When I was young, I had fantasies that there existed, somewhere out there, the "right" man for me and I had only to meet him and marry him and my life would be fulfilled. Mom helped this little fairytale along by telling me how wonderful it would be when I was married. (She's changed her tune since then.) During my early high school years I was terribly worried that no man in his right mind would ever want to marry me. My mother made a bet with me. She said, "If you are not married by the time you are twenty-one it's because *you* don't want to be. If I'm wrong, I'll give you $100." Small compensation for misery! She was right — I've been proposed to, and I've *no* desire to get married.

My sisters and I are only now beginning to realize how much we respect each other as women — women who enjoy their solitude and independence and do not depend on men for their happiness. Certainly none of us would say we have reached this ideal (but I think we would all agree that it is indeed an ideal); however my sisters are closer to it than almost any of my female peers. I have great respect for them.

My father is not a father. He is a nice man who lives in our house, treats patients, and climbs the AMA ladder by running for various offices. He is not affectionate with us and admittedly feels uneasy around women. Ironic that he had four daughters! He seems pleased about my mother's career, but he clearly resents her not being home more and the realization that her life in no way revolves around him. He is willing to admit that his life doesn't revolve around her either, but he has a double standard and wants a woman to be at home waiting for him when he comes in exhausted from work. Mom just doesn't fit the bill. I have watched them grow apart and distant and I no longer see how anyone can ever say to another, no matter at what point in their lives, "We will be able to grow together, until death do us part." Someone's growth is going to be hindered by what often turns out to be an unequal symbiotic relationship, and it is usually the woman's.

My mother has been my strongest influence. I have felt hurt and disappointed by my father's lack of ability or desire to relate to me as his daughter and not just as a woman who by some freak chance happens to share his house. Over last Christmas vacation I talked to my mother about Dad. I asked, "What does Dad really think of his kids?" She answered with a question: "Well, how do you think he feels about you?" I said, in the most negative way possible so that Mom would surely dispute it, "He probably sees us as women who live here, whom he enjoys talking to but doesn't desire any closer relationship with and who seem to be trying to tie him down economically and emotionally. He really doesn't want a family, and even though he has one now, he would love to wish us all away." My mother said, "Yes, that's about right. That is how he feels."

Hearing that was really no shock, since those were the feelings I had been getting from my father all my life, but it was a serious disappointment to have it confirmed — no room for hope, or doubt, anymore. I have been consciously looking for a friendly, loving, physical father figure in my friends' papas. In a few cases, I have found satisfactory substitutes. One man in particular, Joseph, has been very fatherly toward me in the few times I've been to his house. His daughter is a college friend of mine. Joseph hugs me when I see him and makes me feel important to him by asking me how I'm doing and giving advice — he cares about me and shows it. I don't think there's anything sexual in my relations with these older men; I just want affection from a male of that generation, since I have never had any before.

My relationships with women have greatly improved over the past three years. When I was a sophomore in college, I lived in a house with seven freshwomen and I served as an advisor, which basically meant being able to tell the students how to get to the library. But the year turned out to be more difficult than any of us expected, because Linda, one of the freshwomen, became very ill with Parkinson's disease. I found myself dealing with potential death for the first time, although in this case death was not anywhere in the foreseeable future. I grew very close to Linda, not only because crises can bring two people together but also because she was bright, perceptive, sensitive, and funny. We loved each other, and she was the first woman I ever became really close to. We shared everything — her fears about her disease, our common disgust at the ineptness of one of the Deans at this school, our confused relationships with men — everything. I realized how much I could give and take from a relationship with another woman. We could openly discuss our feelings about intercourse (which neither of us had had), and masturbation, and we were also physically close; not in an arousing sexual way but in a comfortable manner with no tension.

Linda and I have grown apart over the past few years. Her closest friend now is her lover, Scott, and I don't presently have a "closest friend." I have been hurt by the gap in our friendship and I have become extremely critical of her as well as of many women who have disappointed me. Linda has taken to wearing a different color fingernail polish every day (everything from blue to glitter) and although I know her well enough to realize that she finds it funny, it still disgusts me — fingernail polish represents the whole make-up painted face syndrome that so many women are part of. The main reason that I am so critical of other women is because I recognize habits or tendencies in them that I have in myself, like altering my physical appearance for someone else, and I intensely dislike that.

I am *very* hard on women. If I see any sort of "get the guy" flirtatious behavior I get annoyed because I do the same thing sometimes and hate myself for it. I am especially wary of women who have no same-sex friends. I see myself freshman year as needing reinforcement from men but not women. Since I now understand how special a same-sex relationship can be, I am irritated by women my age who haven't discovered it yet and are still at the stage I find so embarrassing for myself in retrospect. The other night, I was at a restaurant with two male friends of mine, and a woman I lived with freshman year came in. Anne has always represented to me what I despise in women. She is unbelievably flirtatious and uses her body (by posturing) to say "Look at my breasts, look at my body. Am I tempting you? I'm trying to." I feel that I must be very careful when I make such assessments because it is hard to know how much is jealousy (Anne's act is extremely successful and she is very sexy) and how much is real disgust. There I sat in the restaurant, and she waltzed in. She called out "Hi, Dan" to one of the men I was with, looking right through me. I even said "Hi, Anne" but she didn't even hear me. This seemingly trivial exchange said to me that Anne did not view women as worthy of her attention. I recognize exactly what is going on since I've been there myself, and I despise it. Another aspect of Anne's behavior that annoys me is that her posturing is an act; it is not natural. She had to learn to move her body in that way. I dance, and have therefore concentrated on body movement and body language (nonverbal communication) a great deal. I appreciate what Anne is doing, and, again, I do it myself and dislike myself when I do.

I don't consider myself competitive with other women — I don't try to outdo them — but I am put off when I sense that a woman is brighter than I am intellectually. I have spent a good portion of my time in the classroom just sitting there feeling insecure. I hear articulate women as well as men speak, and I clam up. In my freshman English 101 class, I was surrounded by Exeter types who used big words that I had to look up when I returned to the privacy of my room. I had to memorize what I was going to say before I raised my hand, only to find that not only was my mouth malfunctioning, but my memory system had disappeared! I have learned to relax in the classroom, but I'm still bothered more by bright women than men.

Probably the brightest woman I know is my older sister Lynne, who graduated Phi Beta Kappa in mathematics from Oberlin College in three years. She is going on to get her Ph.D. In high school, I was jealous of her brilliance. But I now realize that we have our own unique special qualities and I no longer envy her brains.

One very fortunate thing that happened to me this year was that I found something I am good at, which I enjoy, and which helps women. Because of my abortion experience, I decided to do what I could to see that other women didn't have to feel as alone and miserable as I did. I discovered sexual counseling at the student health services where I now work once a week doing pregnancy testing (the test is so simple that there is no reason every woman can't do it herself!), contraception and abortion counseling, and referral. It is very scary to be a counselor; what right have I to help another woman decide what to do with her body? I am slowly learning methods of giving information without being directive, which is very important. The client must make decisions herself and she must not be allowed to rely on her counselor for answers. Certainly, she should be given support and encouragement, but being told what to do is a different story.

Discovering sexual counseling is a great event in my life because it is the first time I can say, with no rationalizations that I can see, that I have found a potential career that I really want. I had been worried about what the hell I would do after graduation — I invented careers that I knew were not right for me. I have been a student all my life — that is virtually all I have ever known. Leaving the security of academia is a frightening but exciting thought. I look forward to meeting men and women with different backgrounds, who have chosen the academic route to get them where they are. I feel straightjacketed at Bowdoin, as though I know everyone and every potential relationship. There is no sense of mystery for me here anymore. Even though I do not actually know everyone, what is important is that I *feel* I do; I feel that I have reached a dead end. It is time to move on, as they say.

I still have that wonder for romance and mystery that one reads about in *Wuthering Heights*. I am not cynical (or perhaps realistic) enough yet to rule it out. I am a romantic at heart, and hopefully will always be moved by walks with a lover in the light of the full moon, or listening together to an Isaac mass.

I am pleased by the prospect of the unknown, the unpredictable and spontaneous. In *Fear of Flying* Erica Jong describes the "zipless fuck" as one type of completely spontaneous sexual experience. The "zipless fuck" is a fascinating concept that I have been playing with throughout my years of sexual consciousness. The term, according to Erica Jong's definition as tempered by me, means a relationship where feelings are not involved, where activities of the mind in no way hinder or affect a physical relationship. I have found this to be nearly impossible to pull off. I am not sure at this point whether or not I think the concept itself represents an ideal or can never truly exist and is just a momentary delusion.

I have had one official (we had intercourse) one-night stand, with a fellow I met a few months ago. He is a carpenter in the area and he is very attractive. We spent the evening together at Bowdoin. I liked the idea of seeing him because he had absolutely nothing to do with the college, and after four years of Bowdoin, Bowdoin, Bowdoin it was a pleasure. The sexual experience was satisfying but we couldn't relate to each other very well mentally. (I have been careful lately to try to appear tolerant — I no longer say, "He is mindless; he is thick," but I say, "We don't know how to relate to each other and it is both of our problems." Of course, I only half believe that, but it sounds tolerant.) I asked him to leave at about one in the morning. I really wanted him OUT! I was extremely angry at myself, because I realized that I was lowering my standards for men. I would never spend time with women who have personalities like some of the men I hang around with. It's as though there is an added stigma to being male. It reminds me of an attraction I had for a professor two years ago that was based a good deal on the aura attached to his being a professor. He was nowhere near as mature or wise as many of my peers, but he was older and was a professor. So I put up with him.

The professor, John, was very physically attractive and knew a good deal about music, which further interested me. He was in the process of breaking up with his fiancée of three years and was looking for some cute, fun companionship. I was young, naive, and looking for an older, wiser someone to sweep me off my feet. For all of his intelligence, John was not wise (by this I mean not able to be thoughtful, perceptive, farsighted or use good sense — "wise" is very hard to define). I became disillusioned with him, and he with me, I suppose because I wouldn't go home with him.

Ever since then the mystique associated with being a professor has worn off and I am almost (not there yet!) as critical of men and male professors as I am of women. By this I mean my "standards" for men and women are reaching a common ground. If a man is not intellectually interesting to me, I can admit it and realize that it bothers me, rather than make excuses and lower my standards because he is male, or a professor, or a musician, or an artist (those are some of the items that create an added attraction for me). I would like to operate less critically, but I am always making value judgments, subconsciously. (I can feel them — they are there — so why ignore them?)

At any rate, the one-night stand was totally unsatisfactory in retrospect. Such experiences make me feel that perhaps I cannot tolerate "zipless fucks" and that I need a satisfactory mental relationship as well. The problem is, then, that once the mind gets involved, so do feelings and emotions. I begin to enjoy someone's company (a man's or a woman's), I begin to want to see him or her more often, I begin to care, and I become more and more vulnerable to being hurt as my emotional investment increases. There is a great difference between a relationship with a man and a woman. I can be hurt by women as well as men, but it's a different thing. Men can hurt me by making me feel unattractive (I hate the thought that this is so!). Women cannot, because my relationships with women thus far have usually not been sexual, and no judgments are made on this dimension.

There is a stigma that has been ground into me from Day 1 (by TV, by magazines, and subtly from home) that one should strive for a good relationship with a man; women are secondary. I feel this pressure, and it also explains why I had only male friends my freshman year. I am changing in this respect, but still I feel more full with a man than a woman most of the time. I get so angry at myself for feeling that way! It's hard when I feel one way intellectually but another way emotionally. It tears me apart, and I don't respect myself. I wonder if anyone ever gets to the point of complete harmony between what they intellectually and emotionally desire.

Every human has their own sexuality, and I think it is important to allow myself to relate to others sexually, and not repress this inherent part of every character. This includes relating to women sexually. Until I found a woman sexually attractive, I could not empathize with bisexuality. I never, however, thought that it was a disease. When I was 15 or 16 I worked in a professional theatre at home where many of the participants were gay. It never bothered me except that in the case of some of the men I was sorry that I would never be considered as a lover. But I felt separated from that experience because I had never been attracted to a woman. I had never personalized bisexuality. Then, two summers ago, I spent five weeks at a rigorous dance program. A woman my age, Julia, became a close friend of mine. She was a dancer from New York and was one of the most beautiful dancers I had ever seen. She was also quite bright, and played the oboe as did I. She was bisexual and a very physical person — she exuded sexuality in a subtle way. It seemed as though she were not even aware of how sexual she was. I was attracted to her. She was the first woman for whom I had the same kind of sexual feelings that I have for men. When I was around her I felt that same fullness described earlier that I usually feel only around men. I never acted on my attraction; I never even discussed it with her. But I thought about it a great deal, because I realized that I could no longer take the easy path of ruling out bisexuality.

Ever since that summer, I have allowed myself to be more open to women's sexuality — not just their attractiveness in an objective sense, but how attracted I am to them. Last year a woman named Tina came to visit a friend of mine who lived across the hall. Tina was black and had a son. She came into my room quite a bit, which surprised me. She had brought a camera with her and took mostly pictures of me. One night she was in my room and asked, "Would you like a backrub?" I replied, "Sure." She rubbed my back and then asked me if I'd rub hers. I did and she turned over and started to hug me. She said, "Well, do you see what I'm into? How about you?" I maintained my cool on the outside all the while thinking "I've had these theories that everyone is basically bisexual. I think I'm bisexual. Here's your chance, kiddo." So we started necking. I found it very erotic probably mostly because it was so new and taboo. But someone knocked on the door, and it ended. Suddenly, I felt sick. I wanted to leave the situation and pretend it had never happened. The sight of Tina repulsed me. The sight of her son and his toy gun repulsed me. Tina couldn't understand why I kept insisting that I didn't want to see her again. Here is a letter I found under my door the next morning.

Hello Paula,

It's about 15 minutes since you've gone and my mind is whirling out of control as it has all night. I spent most of the dark hours awake contemplating what some of your thoughts might have been.

I, too, had a lot of thinking to do but on a different subject. My question was of what would you be denying yourself? My answer is that only you would know. My selfish motivation is I can offer you joy, inner peace, and fulfillment.

If I may be allowed to analyze myself for a moment you are exactly what I need at this point in time. When I saw you this morning I wanted to persuade you to stay. There's that selfishness again. But, I really don't want to label it selfish. I want to call it selfish because last night I believe that I became a part of you. I believe that during the relaxation exercise we became one in mind and in soul. Your responsiveness warm and gentle, not intense and frantic. You trusted me and I'm so very gratified that you did. I did not get into the personal thing that brought me to visit with Cynthia and hence to meet and acquire a love for you. I'll not go into detail with you until later when you let me know what you are really feeling and when you have your head together.

I hope that mentally and emotionally I offer you a peace that you have not yet found. I want to please and appease you and as a result satisfy myself. I feel at this point I can be very right for you and you've got me anytime you want me.

Last night was the best and most peaceful rest I've had in months. There was not much sleeping on my part but I felt free. I felt that I've followed through on what I want and it's great, you're great! I've decided to stay another day great person. I'm going to allow you to read this letter and think on the contents. I'll be around to talk with you later. Until then . . .

Je t'aime
Tina

I avoided my room like the plague! After she and her son left, I felt as relieved and free as I ever have in my life. Her son left his toy gun behind, and to this day the sight of any such similar toy upsets me. For a while, seeing black women of Tina's build upset me too.

Tina left Bowdoin and returned to Baltimore. She wrote me love letters. I felt physically sick by any kind of remembrance of her and what we did. I still haven't ruled out exploring female sexual relationships but I've certainly drawn back from ever placing myself in such a position for a while. When other women eye me in a sexual way, I leave the room. I can't handle it yet.

I have never spoken of this experience before. Memories of it have plagued me, but bisexuality is still a taboo topic at Bowdoin and I wasn't prepared to deal with the flak and misunderstanding that I would receive by being honest about it. Also, I don't think I was able to deal with it myself and had to repress it until recently.

A great source of irritation for me has been the lack of body awareness that is quite prevalent on this campus. Bodies are often held rigidly and unnaturally and I can literally see the tension of the person through his body postures. I am rather loose and relaxed usually, and I am quite physical with my friends. I tend to touch the people I am talking to, greet friends by hugging them or reaching for their hands. I have trouble relaxing with those who cannot accept such touching. I am always angered when I hear through the incredibly efficient grapevine around here that I am considered to be teasing men by my physicality. This is a particularly annoying theory because it fails to take into account the fact that I am as physical with women as I am with men. Of course, I've had problems there, too. When I was a senior in high school my older sister Lynne came to visit me at school during her vacation from college. We held hands as we walked down the halls of the school. I was later told that the girls in my class were gossiping that we were probably lesbians!

Another source of irritation having to do with my physicality is the lack of understanding on the part of the men I've had sexual relations with concerning the anatomy of the female body, Apparently, almost none of these bright, well-read men have every heard of "The Myth of the Vaginal Orgasm" or of the clitoris. It is difficult to be open about what feels good and what doesn't. Men have it easy because intercourse seems to work rather well for them and they don't have to explain what feels good to be satisfied. When I first started sleeping with Peter, he used to come and then fall asleep, with no desire to find out how I was feeling. This angered and frustrated me so much that I almost broke up with him. (Sex can really affect a relationship!) But we talked about it and Peter never did that again.

I find that I have trouble relaxing physically during sexual encounters because my mind is quite active. I am often so busy thinking "Does he like my body?"; "Will I be satisfied this time?"; and more that I miss the possibility for arousal by being so uptight.

I am also really angered when men share no concern for birth control. Peter had slept with another woman before me, and he told me that they hadn't used *any* contraception. I was livid! She was the one who would pay for it. How dare *he* not consider birth control? How dare *she* not consider birth control? I am amazed at the ignorance and stupidity displayed by my supposedly brilliant friends who have read Dante and can criticize Nietzsche but don't think about possible pregnancy. (How ironic that I was so careful and got pregnant, and Peter's first lover used nothing and did not!) The fellow I had the one-night stand with never asked me about birth control or suggested we think about it. I was on the pill, but his lack of concern really angered me.

Last week the sexual counseling service held a meeting to which the whole school was invited to discuss birth control methods, abortion, and anything else that might come up. I know for a fact, because of my counseling experience, that Bowdoin students as a whole are not well-acquainted with these issues. The following people attended the meeting: the two women who organized it, me, a female dean, a female professor, and one premed male. Of course, there was also a Bergman flick at the same time, but really!

I have strongly revolted against the traditional female roles. For a long time I refused to go near a kitchen, needle and thread, or iron. As a result, I cook much less than most of my more liberated male friends. I am now willing to spend an afternoon in the kitchen and I sometimes even enjoy it despite myself.

I get furious when I see women who had adopted stereotyped female behavior. If I meet my friends' mothers, and they are housewives who cater to their husbands' and childrens' needs, I am disappointed and I think less of them. I am often told that they are happy, so why should I worry? If they haven't been given a chance to know anything else, who can blame them? Television ads tell women to stay in the kitchen or the laundry room so that they'll never be embarrassed by "ring-around-the-collar" or lousy coffee. Who will help them see their way out of the kitchen door when American society tries to keep it locked?

Along with my aversion to household duties goes my desire to have a career. I almost feel that it is an obligation since I am a free woman with no ties to hubby, kids, or kitchen. I feel a lot of pressure to not only go out and get a job, but to get a prestigious job. Sexual counseling doesn't really qualify as prestigious, but it is worthwhile and I won't have to snicker when I tell people what I'm doing like I would if I were going into insurance sales. I can justify such a job to myself and others.

Probably the single most important dilemma I'm facing now is the question of dependence versus independence, of how to be a whole person alone, of how to enjoy my solitude without knowing I will be with someone in the foreseeable future: of being self-satisfied and not needing someone else. The question is whether needing or desiring someone else is necessarily a bad thing, whether independence and dependence can go hand in hand and are not mutually exclusive.

Because of my reaction against any female roles, I revolt against depending on a man for any kind of fulfillment. This is another example of a theory that works well intellectually, but in practice — forget it! I almost always have a crush or a relationship. Rarely do I have no interest in any man, and when I don't I'm usually going through a depression at the same time.

I feel fuller and richer when I am in a relationship. Even my periods of solitude are more enjoyable when I know that I will be with someone special in a few hours. I am definitely more content. When I was seeing Peter, I was happier than I can remember being for so long a time. But our relationship stagnated after about nine months; neither of us was growing and we were quite dependent. It was easier to be with each other than to explore new relationships. I was completely losing my independence; we consulted each other before we did anything. We were a "couple" in the worst sense of the word.

Whenever I become seriously interested in someone, I begin to make future plans for us in my head, even if only to attend a function together in the next week. I have trouble taking things day by day with no commitment involved. I fell for a new transfer student, David (this sounds like something out of *Seventeen Magazine!*), last semester and we began seeing each other. But, he wasn't willing to tie himself down in any way to me. He was able to take things day by day. I was furious at myself for not being able to operate that way, but it tore me apart. I needed reassurance and I didn't get it. The "cons" of our dyad began to outweigh the "pros" for me, so I ended the relationship. That was a tragedy because we had so much to offer one another, but I couldn't handle it his way. And neither of us wanted to compromise. Intellectually, I wanted to (although I'm not really sure of even that, now), but emotionally I could not.

But is there anything wrong with desiring commitment? If it allows both people to attempt more openness and honesty because it reduces their vulnerability, then perhaps not. It is hard to find relationships where both members have similar expectations. One person usually wants more commitment and time invested in the dyad than the other. This leads to confusion and hurt, particularly if neither expresses their feelings. I have been on both sides of the fence, where I was both depended on and depending on in an unequal manner.

I would love to believe that I could be happy alone, without a man. I will always need other people, but I wish I didn't have this constant urge to find a romantic relationship. Even though I do believe that I can learn about myself through others, I don't like the feeling that I depend on such a relationship with a male. Pure independence at this point is an impossibility for me. I've yet to decide if I ever really want it.

Case 12 / Relating to Persons as Persons

Before coming to college, Scott had learned "the male role . . . like an actor learns his lines." His sister had coached him on how to act on a date, and he could "perform" when necessary. At college he became less willing to confine his actions and thoughts in ways that felt unnatural or unpleasant. He could not accept the role or the image of the "beer-drinking, virgin-fucking, muscleman" aspired to by many of his dormitory peers. He particularly wanted to avoid treating persons as *objects* by labeling, stereotyping, and judging. He wanted to stop thinking in terms of "the male role" and "the female role."

An influential factor in his seeing women as persons was Scott's close relationship during adolescence with his mother and sisters; his father died before Scott reached puberty. Other relationships during the college years have also been influential, although at times joyful and at times frustrating. His rejection of the traditional male role was easier than his gradual adoption of more natural and satisfying ways of relating to persons as persons.

Before I moved off campus last year, I was living in a college dorm that prided itself on its members' "masculinity." It had the reputation of being a big party house and of having the most virile men. The house voted not to go coed in the following year on the grounds that its intramural sports teams would suffer, that its parties couldn't last as late, and that the guys probably wouldn't be able to play their stereos very loud if women were living in the house. As social functions, the house parties seemed to be more competitive drinking bouts than anything else. Dates were shuttled in on weekends, it seemed, just because it was important to have a date or so you could boast (or better, admit it nonchalantly) about a good lay or just because the other guys would kid you about not having a woman. There was a general, idealized conception of the beer-drinking, virgin-fucking, muscle man that I just couldn't get into. It has always seemed an act.

I remember coming into one of the parties and seeing three of "the guys" chugging beer. Their dates were standing, admiring their feats, sipping their wine, giggling at the end of each round. After every few rounds, the guys took turns arm wrestling. The same thing would happen the next night, and the next weekend, and the next weekend after that. At first I felt disgusted, embarrassed almost. But thinking about it later I guess I realized that that was their life-style: fine. It was clear to me that I did not want that to be a part of my life-style. I moved off campus largely because I didn't want to live in a dorm with men who were into what I perceived as the basic male trip of entertainer, competitor, and strongman. I didn't want to be anything close to that.

Many times, also, I remember sitting in the dining hall listening to the conversation at the next table. Once it concerned some of the sophomore women (the first class that was entirely coed) who were coming out of the serving line:

"Wow, look at her boobs."

"Hey, girlie!"

"Boy, would I like to get my hands on that red hair — a clatch of red hair."

"Who wants to lay bets that I'll sleep with her next? What a doll!" Perhaps it is because I have felt what it is to be seen as an object, but, for whatever reasons, I am often uneasy looking at others as only objects. Though these remarks are commonplace and easily ignored and though most of the time I was indifferent to them, at times I felt an incredible, irrational revulsion — an overwhelming wish to leave that place, to get out, to get away. I didn't hate any individual men — or any of the women who invited and obviously really enjoyed the comments — but I did hate the atmosphere that bred what I felt was a stereotypic and narrow conception of persons in general.

One time I was talking with a woman, Polly, about another woman, Alison, who was a close friend of mine and whom I often went to see at another college. Alison had been here the year before and had lived in the same dorm as Polly and had gotten into a relationship with a friend of Polly's, Joe. The relationship between Joe and Alison broke up at one point, for many complex reasons, but the process of breaking up went through the gossip grapevine with the result that Joe came out as the "rejected man" and Alison as the "manipulative female." Because I knew Alison I had heard what her feelings were about it; to me it seemed that the relationship had broken up, like most relationships in my experience, from a combination of miscommunications, misunderstandings, hang-ups, and confused feelings. In any case, it didn't seem that either of the labels were adequate ones. So Polly stopped me in the hall one day and said, "Are you still seeing Alison? Do you know what a castrating bitch she is? She is a manipulative female and she is going to screw you when she can." I wanted to yell at her and say, "You don't understand. It's not that simple. Nothing is that simple. Don't judge people like that. You can't pin labels like that."

I didn't say anything back to Polly, but her words, besides making me angry, made we want to leave the school. Everyone, including me too, seemed more and more to be pegging, labeling, stereotyping, judging others, without any attempt at seeing things from another person's point of view or without any understanding of the complexity of relationships. I didn't want to be in an environment that was so full of gossip, labels, reputations, and venom. I wanted to get out. It was too smothering to stay.

It is not only women that most of the men at this college see as objects, but homosexuals are seen in the same way. I remember freshman year coming to this school (all men at the time) and being amazed that no one *ever* mentioned homosexuality, except in reference to "fags." The few times I brought the subject up, no one responded. Having come from New York City where homosexuality is a way of life, having had a number of teachers in my high school who were gay, having lived around it for so long, I never thought of the topic as "something you don't talk about." I didn't understand why it was such a taboo subject here. For me it was an issue and I wanted to talk about it with others, but there didn't seem to be anyone else who wanted to talk about it openly or even very privately. I realize now that though I might have wanted to talk about it, I was hesitant, too, to bring it up very often.

One of the reasons homosexuality was an issue for me was because I had to deal with it in high school. When I was a senior, I used to have long talks with one male friend about what "love" is (the basic adolescent talk) and about the whole range of physical and emotional feelings that went along with whatever we decided love was. At one point he said, with a very definite intensity and seriousness, "Scott, I'm really in love with your body. I want to sleep with you. I want to touch you."

At first I didn't reply because I didn't know what to say. Though I had been approached many times on the street by gay males looking for a pickup and had gotten used to saying no in that situation, this invitation was very different. I knew Tom well, had felt a lot of warm feelings toward him, but had not felt the physical attraction that he was obviously feeling toward me. So I replied honestly, "I don't feel that way toward you." I realized later that he felt rejected and hurt; it took us a while to repair the relationship, though I think we both felt closer to each other in a different way when we finally did.

I learned a great deal about my feelings toward men from that experience: how strong the taboos are in me against touching other men, how my body feels uncomfortable when it is close to another man, my realization that many men are sensitive in many ways in which they are not "supposed" to be, how ambivalent I really was in my interest in getting to know other men fully.

For a psychology class this past year, a marriage counselor came to one of the class discussions. The class focused on the issue of how two people could both have a career and raise a family. It seemed to me that most of the men in the class had never seriously considered the possibility that they might have to sacrifice part of their career and that they might have to take care of the home if they intended to have a family. I guess in terms of my future role as a male, and if I ever enter any sort of a marriage with a woman, I intend to split in some equal fashion the responsibility for supporting a family and for the care-taking that is necessary. It doesn't bother me that I don't want to be that traditional "provider." But during the class, many men felt uncomfortable abdicating their role as "provider," just as many women, it seemed, didn't feel like they were going to have to support a family. In any case, I left the class tired of talking about the male role and the female role — we were all talking about stereotyped ways that people act and we were not dealing with individuals at all. I remember feeling that I wanted to stop talking about my male role and get on with the process of relating to persons as persons, not as men or women.

One of the major influences on my development in general, and on the development of my perceptions of femininity and masculinity in particular, was the situation in my family at my father's death when I was ten years old. Besides my mother, there were my two sisters (six and eight years older than I), my grandmother, and my grandmother's companion. I also had had a "Nanny" who had come to entertain me until I left for school. Throughout my childhood, I was surrounded by women, at least within my family, and when my father died they all became concerned that I didn't have a male figure to look up to. Out of this concern came efforts to teach me all the appropriate role behaviors that they thought I should have.

Often my mother and I would go out to dinner with some family friends and she would give me the money to pay for the dinner and say, "Here, the man is supposed to pay." At one point, I think in the seventh grade, I was going to meet a girl at a movie, but when my mother found out, she said, "But you're supposed to pick her up at her house."

"She can walk to the theater as well as I can," I said.

"But the male is supposed to call for her at her house — and besides, your father would have insisted on it."

"OK, OK, I'll pick her up at her house," I said.

One of my sisters, who was attending college in the South, would come home on vacations and explain to me what the proper conduct of a man should be on a date: to entertain the girl ("always have a couple of good stories"), to keep the conversation light ("girls like to laugh a lot, anyway"), to open doors for her ("girls get offended if you don't"), to walk so that I was on the outside ("girls really appreciate that"), to be sure and call for her on time ("but it's OK if they're a little late"), to pay for everything ("girls are pretty helpless").

I listened to all these instructions and learned them, but it seemed clear to me that these were the things I, as a male, was *supposed* to do. I saw in my own family that women could do all these things as easily as men could. I learned all the appropriate male role behaviors, but I learned them like an actor learns his lines — I could use them when the social situation demanded that I use them and I could put them away when I didn't need them. Perhaps that is why I have always seen the traditional sex roles as great acts.

Also I don't think I ever identified with my father, in any sense of that word. I inherited many of his values and attitudes, but that was because they were passed on to me second-hand by what my mother and my sisters told me he was like. I have very few memories of him and many of them are negative. He was fifty-one when I was born, and so when I was growing up he was too old to play with me very much. He was heavy; when he picked me up, his head seemed huge and his beard was incredibly irritating. I never wanted to be like my father.

It wasn't until a few years after his death that I began to get any sense of who my father had been and to make sense of some incidents I vaguely remembered. At one dinner, when I was about eight, I remember him saying something loud and angry that made both of my sisters burst into tears, get up, and leave the table. It was mystifying to me, except that I knew he had hurt them. But when they left, it seemed that I should do the same, and so I got up and left, too. He had yelled so loud that something must have been very wrong. But apparently he was authoritarian, in the full sense of that word, and would not stand to be contradicted. Maybe he had been contradicted that night, but all I remember is being scared and sorry for my sisters. In any case, in high school when I was thinking about these things, it became clear that had my father not died when he did, my own adolescence would have been very different and much more turbulent.

I remember watching my mother change a lot, too, after my

father's death. When he died, she had to stop being only a wife and had to become a professional woman, while not abdicating her role as a mother. Because she was conscious of this problem, I became conscious of it as well. I remember at one point early in high school when I was complaining at length (and somewhat naively) about the difficulty in choosing a career; she remarked, "Has it ever occurred to you how difficult it has been trying to be a good mother to you and your sisters and also trying to earn enough to support this family?" It was then that I began to think much more about how all those requirements for "Mother" often make it difficult to be "Provider" too.

I was also fortunate to stay close to my sisters for six or seven years after my father's death, during my adolescence. I saw my sister (the one who went to the Southern college) come back and live in New York, in the West Village. Having been inculcated with all the Southern values and the South's conception of the charming, demure, brainless female, she experienced a great deal of confusion as she came in contact with the people living in the Village. She started rejecting all the crap she had been taught not only at college but years before by my father (who was very traditionally Southern himself). She started sleeping around, working in bars, doing everything that ladies weren't supposed to do. When, at one point, she was at home for a weekend, she asked me if I still liked her even though she was promiscuous. That surprised me and so I said, "Yes, I still like you."

"But women aren't supposed to do that," she said.

"Well, why are you doing it?" I asked.

"Because I want to get back at all those people who told me not to, and because I like it, and because I'm learning a lot."

I remember the incident because she said it so intensely, it seemed even then that there was this great war going on in her head. So, I guess I learned through her some of the frustration that many women feel as they work against a double standard and of the difficulty many have in rejecting the values pinned on them.

The other sister had her first abortion before it was legal in New York. She talked to me about it: "Do you know what it is like to look down and see between your legs this little blob that could have been your child?" The father of the child wasn't present at the abortion. I remember sensing the intense bitterness she had toward him, and toward herself also. She was crying and I remember being awed at her pain and her feelings of anger.

That's why I don't like seeing women as many men see them: as "dolls" and "girlies" and "red clatches." I guess I believe that there is usually a lot more to a person than that.

Another experience that has greatly influenced my conception of myself as a male has been a relationship with Paul, a man seven years older than I. We got to know each other during my senior year in high school and we worked together that summer and the one following on a Big Brother project in Harlem. We became increasingly close to each other, and when he said he was going to stop work for a year or so and live in Italy, I decided to take a year off from school and go with him.

It's important to know what Paul is like: he is honest with himself and others; his ability to be open and acceptant of others is by far the greatest I have experienced or seen; he is a very good counselor because he is perceptive, aware, sensitive, empathetic, understanding. Everyone who knows him likes him a great deal. He has a multitude of friends and many close friends.

That Paul liked me as much as he did, that he was willing to spend so much time with me always amazed me. In any case, in the months we traveled together and during the time we lived in Italy, we became closer than I had ever been to anyone. We started sleeping together when we were traveling and eventually, right at the end of my stay in Italy, we had some very intense sexual relations. It's hard to explain the feeling I had when I was sleeping with him, a feeling that persisted for a long time. It was a confused mixture of guilt, abhorrence, tenderness, and care.

During those six months, I was more confused than I had ever been before. Intellectually I had worked out, partly as a result of my relation with Tom in high school, my feelings toward homosexuality. But emotionally I was incredibly ambivalent. I knew that I wanted to relate as fully as possible to Paul, but I could hardly even relax and simply touch him. For so long all those old barriers against touching males were getting in the way. At the same time that I was dealing with my ambivalent feelings about relating to a man sexually, I was also trying to deal with all the rest of the positive and negative parts of an intimate relationship (of course, the two aren't very separate but that was how I was seeing the situation then). One problem I had was knowing whether it was my over-learned inhibitions or whether it was simply basic feelings for Paul as a person that made it almost impossible for me to feel comfortable with him. He said he loved me, but I couldn't for a long time say that back to him — I just didn't know.

Another issue for me was the feeling that I needed to relate intimately with a woman too. I had never before been involved with anyone, male or female, to the extent that I was with Paul. While I never worried about becoming "gay" (because that too implies to me just another set of behaviors, another act), I did feel I needed to have an intimate relationship with a woman, or at least with someone else, so I could get a perspective on my relationship with Paul.

At so many points in the relationship I felt incredibly dominated by Paul: explicitly dominated because he knew what he wanted and where he wanted to go, and so naturally we went to those places and did those things; and implicitly dominated because I started becoming Paul. I was picking up his mannerisms, laughing like him, coming to want the same things from life that he did. Even when I could pinpoint the differences between him and me, it was I who was different *from* him. For me he was the ideal, so much so at times that the only thing I could do was reject him entirely. Bouncing between wanting to be like him and wanting nothing to do with him, I eventually came to a much better sense of myself. I realized that in the end I *had* to define myself in my own terms, if I wasn't going to become some poor imitation of Paul or anyone else either.

By the time I left Italy, I felt much less confused about my physical and emotional relationship with Paul. I had come to the point where I could sleep with him without much guilt or shame or fear. We were able to deal with things in the relationship that were beyond the physical hang-ups. I left because I felt that I had to do the things I wanted to do, even though in some ways I also wanted to be with someone with whom I had grown and changed and who had been largely responsible for that growth and change.

So now I guess I feel somewhat less ambivalent about relating to males sexually and emotionally than I did a few years ago. I haven't had a love relationship with a male since I got back from Italy, in part because I've felt the pressures in a small town and a conservative college against homosexual relations; the stigma that most persons would attach would not allow me to do the things I wanted to do here. Also there have been few men with whom I have wanted to explore the possibility of an emotional and physical relation; and they, I suspect, did not feel that way toward me. For the most part, though, I know I have felt that inevitable hesitancy to begin any intimate relationship with any person, male or female.

One of the relationships that has been most important to me recently has been my friendship with Murray, my roommate. While it is difficult for us to talk about "us" and while we rarely mention homosexuality and rarely show any emotion for each other, there is an unstated, but very strong, bond that I think we both feel. With Murray, I am very comfortable most of the time because I feel that he knows most of my inconsistencies, blindnesses, and hang-ups and is relatively acceptant of them. We get along well, I think, because we are both able to tolerate each other's idiosyncracies, rather than seeking to change them. We are both willing to listen when the other needs to talk. We don't attach great importance to one action but rather are tuned in to a general mood over a space of time. We share things like cooking, shopping, and cleaning without worrying about our "roles."

They are simply things that have to be done to live relatively comfortably; and rather than sticking them on one person, we both do them.

We are content with our friendship as it stands, and we will both feel a great loss after graduation when we split up. But I'm beginning to realize that there is a price to be paid for that contentment: the relationship doesn't seem to be moving anywhere, doesn't seem to be "progressing." Perhaps without the physical dimension, relationships don't move anywhere — I don't know if that's true. But I do know that having lived with Murray for about two years, I have learned a lot just about friendship and what it means to relate to someone very closely but without the highs and lows that sexual intimacy can bring.

But let me try and explain what it has been like for me to relate intellectually, emotionally, and physically with a woman. I met Alison during one summer, soon after I had returned from Italy, and during the time she was breaking up with an old boyfriend. One of the issues she was dealing with then was whether or not she could be on her own and still be happy. She had always had a "boyfriend" and was searching for a greater sense of autonomy and freedom from what she felt was an unhealthy need. For a while our relationship was a friendly brother-sister one. We talked fairly objectively about what we were thinking and about everything except our feelings for each other.

As my attraction toward her grew, I was really confused about what my role in the relationship should be. I wanted to express a very real affection and an increasing attraction on many levels. But I was hesitant to move the relationship to that point. I didn't want to be that next "boyfriend" that cut down on her freedom and cramped her autonomy. I didn't want it for her, and I sure didn't want a "girlfriend" that was clingingly dependent on me.

So for a while, though neither of us wanted to do so, we both kept the relationship fairly superficial, fearing what we both perceived as a fatal commitment to that traditional boyfriend/girlfriend relationship that neither of us wanted anyway. Eventually, just from the amount of time we spent together, our mutual attraction became obvious and the relationship became much deeper very quickly. But then, when we started sleeping together at nights, we seemed to set up an elaborate, unspoken agreement not to see each other very much during the day, to give each other plenty of time to him/herself, to be careful not to make any demands.

The same pattern continued when we left for our respective schools at the end of the summer: we were always considerate of the other person's time, always "understanding" when the other person couldn't make it. By December, the relationship collapsed from too much freedom. We hadn't moved anyplace since the end of the summer. And since our colleges were about two hours away, at best we saw each other three days every two weeks. The distance, the pressures of school on both of us, our own inability to say, "This is what I am feeling. What are you feeling?" made communication more and more difficult. Finally, it broke down, quietly but completely over Christmas vacation.

It took me a long time to recover from the pain of what I perceived as rejection and to make sense of what had happened. I saw finally how I had denied many feelings simply because I was reacting against a stereotyped role. Because I didn't want to be seen by her as the basic male, I rarely showed any angry feelings that I had toward her, generally refused to make demands sexually, listened patiently without showing any jealousy when she talked about some of her relations to other men. I had not been very honest to my feelings, and I later saw that all my "nonaction" was interpreted by her as indifference or dislike.

My whole point in explaining all this is to illustrate how I felt I got caught between the traditional male role and the determination to reject it. It seems to me now much better to listen to both my feelings of aggressiveness and passivity when each comes, to be jealous if that's the way I feel, to make demands when I feel them, to react honestly to the demands from the other, and to listen for all these things coming from the other person also.

In any case, during the spring vacation following that Christmas when we had fallen apart, I felt together enough in my own mind to go see Alison and simply explain why I had acted the way I did, and that I still felt a great deal of love for her. I was able to be open and relatively honest as I talked to her then, and she was able to reply honestly, too. After dinner, I left feeling much better and we were both somewhat hopeful: we would both be in the same town again the coming summer and perhaps we would be able to become close again. Though we were both determined still to be tentative about showing our feelings, we were both also willing to risk expressing them much more than we had done before.

I think Alison and I have come much closer to sharing those attitudes, behaviors, and feelings that are usually reserved for one sex. When we make love, it seems fairly fluid in terms of who is the active initiator and who is more passive; it seems, at the best times, that neither of us worries about who is playing what role. When we go places, we usually communicate where we both want to go or what we both want to do. We ask each other questions about our bodies, our perceptions, our fantasies — subjects we tended to avoid or touched only superficially at the beginning of our relationship.

At one point this past summer, she questioned me about Paul

and my feelings for him. As I talked, there was much confusion, much care, some negative feeling. My thoughts came out in a rush and, I suspect like most people do after a significant self-disclosure, I felt exhausted, weak, and very vulnerable. I was glad when Alison touched me and held me for a while. All my pretensions to strength and calm and self-assurance — all those acts — were gone, but she was still willing to accept me. It felt good to be held and comforted by her then.

Right at the end of the summer, Alison went through a great deal of doubt and uncertainty about the fall and her plans for working abroad this year. She wanted to do it in some ways but was scared of not being able to make new friends and of being alone and of not having the security of an institution like college. I think that was one time when I was able to touch and reassure her, and that felt good too.

When I was writing this study, at times I was angry about letting people in on me. Often I felt that I didn't want others to know what I am like, I guess out of a fear that with all the mystery gone, there won't be much left but some hollow shell. The most difficult decision I had to make with myself was just how honest I was going to be. Because it has been my experience that I grow the most when I am most honest with myself and with important others, I decided to try to be very honest. I felt I had to pay a price for that honesty — during the writing, many unresolved, residual feelings came tumbling out and I found it difficult to do academic and intellectual work and to deal with these residual feelings at the same time. As a result I felt pressured and hassled. But I'm glad now that I wrote it, glad that I resolved some of those forgotten feelings. I learned more about myself. I found more pieces in the puzzle of why I am the way I am.

Topic Seven

Vocation and Identity

Case 13 / Getting in Touch with What I Want

It is February of his senior year, and Mike has not submitted any applications for graduate work or employment. For years his parents have urged him to pursue professional goals diligently and avoid being sidetracked by idle activity or involvement with a girlfriend. Although he has done well in college and probably could enter medical school or another graduate program, he feels "no compulsion to aimlessly squander my youth and vitality perched behind a cluttered desk, peering down a test tube." He has tried not to be like other premeds: professional students who did not have time for relaxation, self-exploration, or involvement with friends — beyond easing the pain of postponed gratification by drinking too much and masquerading at parties. After years of considerable parental pressure, he is unsure of what *he* really wants. He will deliberately take some time to think through his ambivalence toward professionalism and to discover his own solution to the problem of finding a personally satisfying vocation.

It is often stated by respected authorities on the plight of modern man that, whether or not we are aware of it, we are all being controlled and manipulated by large, impersonal, bureaucratic organizations that have the power to make most of the important decisions about our lives. On the other hand, it has been argued that, in the attempt to cope with the ever-increasing complexity and pace of living, one of our greatest dilemmas is the overwhelming number of decisions with which we are constantly confronted. This is surely an interesting topic for speculation; however, in my own case, I can't really say that, until recently, I have ever been overly preoccupied with the whole issue of making decisions. They aren't terribly enjoyable for me, and I make them only when it is absolutely necessary, which usually means that the consequences of not doing so would constitute a threat to the peaceful state of suspended animation in which I much prefer to remain. Whether they are trivial, routine choices, like deciding what flavor ice cream to order, or more important ones, such as choosing a college or a career, my tendency is almost always to avoid committing myself as long as I possibly can and eventually make the decision primarily on the basis of my immediate inclination. I suppose that's not an ideal way of going about things.

Maybe part of the explanation for my apathetic approach is that I am so accustomed to having decisions made for me by my parents. After all, up to this point, my life has been pretty well structured and mapped out in advance; all the choices and answers have been presupposed. It is only now, halfway through my sixteenth consecutive year of academic training, or whatever you want to call it, that I must face the uncertainty of not knowing what is in store for me in the years ahead. There is a sense in which I welcome this situation as an opportunity for a new sort of freedom, a lack of responsibility that I have never previously experienced. However, there also are many times when I am deeply frightened and desperately worried about my future.

The main force that keeps me from becoming what is usually called a dropout or a derelict is, most likely, the strong bond that exists between my parents and myself. You see, I'm basically an introverted and alienated sort of person who possesses both the desire and the potential for just getting lost for a while or for retreating to a quiet, inward, sleepy existence. But my parents are there in the background, with so much of their lives invested in me, and I know that they would be heartbroken if I were to become an idle wanderer, a "lazy bum" who couldn't take the pressure. Also, I'm honest enough with myself to realize that this role would not be wholly satisfying for me, either, for I do feel certain obligations to my fellow men and retain a tenuous, paradoxical commitment to conventional values. So the process in which I am presently engaged consists mainly of enjoying a very intense and time-consuming relationship with a girl, spending some time with friends, doing a little reading, seeking solitude and a chance for self-exploration, and simply trying to recognize and appreciate all the experiences that are a part of my daily existence. This kind of an approach is certainly not wrong in itself; indeed, it appears to be, in many respects, a very nice way to live. Nevertheless, there exists a lingering sense of restlessness and insecurity and an awareness that my style of living also serves the purpose of an aesthetic — it enables me to avoid a long and careful consideration of the course that the rest of my life should take. My problem is that, when I do reflect seriously upon my future, feelings of emptiness and despair often arise.

It's not that there are no desirable options open for me or that certain possibilities no longer exist. In fact, most people who know me only superficially consider my life history to be a model of success, in the conventional sense of the word. In high school, I made sure that I always received good grades, was involved in many different clubs and activities, managed to get elected president of my class one year, was given the "most athletic" designation in my senior yearbook, and so on. It all forms a very pretty picture, but there always was a vague uneasiness and dissatisfaction with myself. At the moment, I am in the process of completing my senior year at one of those private, elite New England colleges that each year turns out an assortment of budding young businessmen and prospective professionals. My academic record is better than most and, from the information that I have been able to gather, it seems that I would have a reasonable chance of gaining admission to medical school or to a graduate school in psychology or education. However, the thought of immediately jumping into any of these things is nauseating to me. It is now the beginning of February, and I have submitted no applications to anybody for anything. The way I look at it, I've been working reluctantly and hard, either in school or in summer jobs, for longer than I care to remember, and it's time for a rest. Or would it be more honest to say that I feel a bit confused and scared when I consider the possibility of plunging into something new and challenging?

I guess it's understandable that my parents worry so much about me and that so many of their hopes and dreams are wrapped up in my life. My father has spent his last twenty-five years as a director of training for a well-known local corporation. His work involves teaching courses in such areas as computer science and accounting to employees who are seeking new skills. In the meantime, my mother has assumed the role of the devoted housewife and mother of two children. It's not a terribly stimulating or satisfying existence for either of them, although they would never admit it to themselves or anyone else. My dad fills up much of his leisure time with a variety of part-time jobs, while my mother spends her days ironing clothes, housecleaning, playing bridge, preparing meals, and so on. The rest of their time is devoted to such things as puttering around the yard, canoe trips down the river, sitting in front of the television, and occasional socializing.

My parents have always considered their children's future to be the first priority, one of the principal reasons for the family's existence. If it were necessary, my father would gladly put all the money that he is able to save towards financing our education. In fact, I suspect that he would rather invest his money in the futures of his sons than to use it for such things as traveling with my mother. Kevin and I are certainly very fortunate in having parents who are so eager to give us their help; nevertheless, I feel considerable indebtedness, resentment, and guilt because of the fact that my father is working to the point of exhaustion in order to send us both to expensive schools. What is more, if I do not continue my ascent toward success and social respectability, they will be greatly disappointed and may feel that all the hard work was for nothing. It upsets me that my parents, who are both in their mid-fifties, prefer to continue sacrificing for Kevin and me, although they now have the freedom of no longer having us at home and the time to do a lot of things that they have been putting off for many years. Am I an irritable, ungrateful kid who doesn't know how lucky he is, or am I at least partially correct in suspecting that my parents have lost much of their capacity to enjoy their lives without gaining meaning through the lives of their children? I'm not sure, and my ambivalence with regard to this issue is extremely keen and troubling.

I suppose that the idea of becoming a doctor first occurred to me back at the age of nine or ten. I had never been a particularly healthy child and, during the fourth grade, gradually began to lose my appetite and strength until Mom and Dad decided that something was definitely wrong. The doctors at the local hospital had absolutely no success in determining what my difficulty was; eventually, they called in a psychiatrist to see if he could be of any help. I can remember him sitting there on the edge of my bed with a container full of water and colored beads that he would rotate in his hands, first one way and then the other, asking me what I saw. Apparently, I was old enough to realize who he was and what he was doing, because I recall either thinking or telling him that he was wasting his time and that there was nothing wrong with my head. At the time, I suspected that someone had gotten the notion that something might be troubling me because of the fact that, for the last few years, I had been having a strange, recurring nightmare which remains vivid in my memory to this day, although I find it nearly impossible to describe adequately. Nothing really happened in the dream — there was only a big, soft, round form, and all of a sudden everything would get rough, ugly, and distorted. It was pure terror. My parents tell me that I would jump wildly out of bed and run screaming around the house. Nothing could bring me out of it; holding me, talking to me, warm milk, and cold showers had no effect upon me. Finally I would emerge from the horrible dream on my own. Now that I am older, every once in a while it will start coming on again, but I always manage to wake myself before the terror siezes me. I've often wondered what would happen if I were to allow myself to experience the entire dream once more.

In any event, after having wasted away from over a hundred pounds down to around sixty, the decision was made to transfer me to a well-equipped and better staffed hospital in a city that was one hundred miles or so from home. After countless pills, x-rays, blood tests, and injections, they made their diagnosis; apparently I was one of the youngest cases of Addison's disease on record anywhere in the country. More than once, I was put on display in a huge lecture hall filled with doctors and interns as a rare example of an unusual phenomenon.

The experience in the hospital, which lasted about a month, made many lasting impressions upon me and was certainly a contributing factor with regard to my interest in medicine. To put it simply, I was fascinated by the shiny, clean, intricate machinery, the plastic tubes running in and out of my body, the forty or fifty needle marks that were visible on my right arm alone, the funny colored pills that were constantly being forced down my throat. And I remember the calm, assuring voices of the doctors as they tried to explain the nature of my problem and told me that I would soon be able to lead a long and healthy life, provided that I was careful about a few things.

So I grew up with the idea in the back of my mind that I would probably like to be a doctor some day; beyond that, I didn't give the issue of my future occupation a whole lot of thought. It just seemed like a logical thing to do — math and science were easy for me, as well as being the most enjoyable of all my subjects. In high school, the whole matter was subordinated to the more immediate concerns of my studies, athletics, extracurricular activities, and friendships. Choosing a career would just have to take care of itself. Even the task of deciding upon a college was somewhat of a chore for me; my parents had to drag me around to look at schools and were undoubtedly more excited about the whole affair than I was. When it was time to apply, I simply chose the three schools that happened to come to mind and filled out the forms. To be frank, the main reasons for my final choice were that the two or three people that I met when visiting the place were nice to me, it was a beautiful day, and the tennis courts were impressive.

Well, as I mentioned before, by the time I had graduated from high school, it must have seemed to most people as if I were well on my way to becoming a successful, well-to-do professional of some sort. It appeared that I should have every reason to be happy, confident, and self-satisfied; however, such a description is far from accurate. The inexplicable sense of dissatisfaction and uneasiness that had been with me for as long as I could remember was, at this time, magnified by a very sad and disturbing experience. Sandy and I had been seeing each other for three or four months by the time that graduation had come around, and my parents were literally frantic and absolutely against the whole thing. This sort of situation was not at all unexpected in my family; there were very few girls who ever met with my parents' approval during either of their sons' high school dating. My parents' attitude was a source of tremendous anxiety and unhappiness for me — Sandy was the first girl with whom I had been involved for any appreciable amount of time. Naturally, she was aware of and very sensitive to the hostility on the part of my mom and dad; when we tried to discuss the problem, Sandy would often end up in tears. My parents were often nearly impossible to deal with and refused to acknowledge the girl's good qualities or the positive effects that the relationship was having upon me. Among all the fears, suspicions, and doubts that they harbored was their insistence that I would not be able to leave Sandy and go away to school to pursue my career goals. I would surely end up being tied down to her and a family and would never have the opportunity to realize my potential. Although I could understand their concern, I knew perfectly well that this would never be the case and told them so. While Sandy and I cared very much for each other, there were some very real differences between us, and I secretly looked forward to the opportunity to bow out gracefully, retreat to a college that was hundreds of miles away from home, and let the entire affair gradually fade away into the past. But my mother and father were adamant in their refusal to consider my side of the picture. We had never been overly communicative; now our talks always seemed to lead nowhere, and all sorts of agonizing incidents became increasingly common. One evening in June, Sandy and I felt like being together and decided to see a movie and then possibly get something to eat at her house. After dinner I asked my father if the car would be available.

"Where are you planning to go," was the response.

"Sandy and I were planning to go see a movie and probably do something afterwards," I replied in a steady voice, trying my best not to reveal my anxiety. He lit a cigarette and stared out the window, and I braced myself for another confrontation. By this time, my mother had appeared in the doorway.

"Michael," he answered, after a tense silence, "you've got to stop seeing that girl as much as you do. You're with her every minute of the day and it can't possibly lead to anything good. It's going to be time for you to go away to school pretty soon and there's just no way that you're going to be able to do it. That girl's never had such a good thing in her life, and she's doing everything she can to tie you down to her."

We had been through the same argument many times before — she was a parasite and unworthy of someone like me — and I knew that attempting to reason with them would only make things worse. Besides, I was angry, disgusted, and afraid that I would start yelling or crying or who knows what. And I hated the way that they never mentioned her name, always calling her "that girl." So I just stood there and gazed at the floor. At this point, my mother must have felt that it was time for her to join in. I remember her words distinctly.

"She's no good, Michael. She's from bad stock and she's just plain no good. Why can't you see that?"

That did it — it really killed me to hear her say that. Sandy's father was a construction worker and her mother worked nights as a waitress, and that wasn't good enough for me.

"Oh, Christ," I screamed, with tears in my eyes, "just shut your lousy mouth. Why the hell do you always think I'm going to marry her or something. I know she's not perfect and you shouldn't think that I'm never going to look at anyone else. I can't think of anything I'd rather do than be away from you and her and this whole mess!"

"Are you in love with her, Michael?" came my father's stern reply, as he turned away and lit another cigarette.

"Well, I guess . . . no . . . I don't know!" I managed to answer in a trembling voice. Everything in the room began to fade away until I was hardly aware of where I was or what was going on. My father was talking again, but there was a loud buzz inside my head and I couldn't begin to hear what he was saying.

"All right," I heard myself saying in a voice that sounded distant and alien, "I don't want to hear it. Goodbye." I stumbled out the door.

The rest of the summer was ruined by a series of similar confrontations. There was nowhere to turn, and something within me began to grow cold and hard. It slowly became easier to return home late at night and see my parents with desperate, searching expressions on their faces or hear my mother crying in her bedroom. It goes without saying that my relationship with Sandy suffered as well.

The experience remains painfully alive in my memory and has helped to form a barrier to any sort of communication between my parents and myself concerning my subsequent relationships with girls. My current approach is to either offer no information at all or carefully select my words so that nothing of importance is revealed.

Among the many reasons that my parents objected to my relationship with Sandy was the fact that they were scared to death that she would influence me to abandon my occupational goals or cause me to be unable to make the adjustment of leaving home and going to college. Despite my assurances that this would never occur, they had no doubt that they were right in feeling the way that they did. "You just don't know," they would say. "We've seen it happen before."

Even if their fears were justified, there seemed to be something wrong with the idea that one must push aside his feelings, abandon meaningful relationships with others, and postpone the fulfillment of personal needs that are so important for an individual's growth and development. My parents' viewpoint was that such aspects of life were of secondary importance in relation to some nebulous career plans, to an orthodox ideal of success sometime in the distant future. Why couldn't they let our relationship run its natural course and leave Sandy and me alone to handle it in our own way?

After having completed my first year at college, it had become evident that the sacrifice of personal relationships, time for self-reflection, and enjoyment of the here-and-now was seen by many people as a necessary and accepted requirement for academic excellence and a ticket to social approval and respect. It was not long before I had come into contact with the professional student, the individual who saw college solely as a stepping-stone in the climb upward into the social hierarchy. People couldn't afford to take the time for relaxation, self-exploration, or involvement with others. At college, I found that the learning experience only began with the courses in cell biology, social anthropology, or art history. We also were given training in common methods of accepting and submitting to the institutional pressure to become an economically productive, achievement-oriented, goal-directed member of the establishment. We were expected to learn how to postpone many forms of gratification, to ease the pain of existence with alcohol, to masquerade at cocktail parties, and to successfully avoid becoming real persons.

The absurdity of the situation, however, was not immediately apparent to me. As an antidote to all of my suffering during the previous few months and to the insecurity that I felt in my new surroundings, I, too, fell into the role of the typical industrious, self-denying college student, immersing myself in my schoolwork and playing on the tennis team. Needless to say, the combination of a tough premedical schedule and tennis every afternoon put great demands on my time, and my involvement with other students outside of these contexts was minimal. But that was the way I wanted things to be, in order to forget about home and make my escape from Sandy a bit easier to bear. (Toward the end of the summer, I had explained to her that it was time for us to go our separate ways, and we were in the process of trying our best to make the transition to being "just friends.") In addition, I felt a strong compulsion to prove to my parents that they were wrong in fearing my inability to make a satisfactory adjustment to life away from home. Because I thought that the measure of my adjustment would be seen largely in terms of my academic success, I purposefully kept busy in order to get good grades. As is the case for so many Americans, the process of continually working and striving also enabled me to avoid the uncertainty and vulnerability that accompanies self-reflection and openness with others.

In retrospect, the first semester appears as a huge blur, a hectic and confused time in which there was frequently the bizarre sensation of being someone other than myself, a detached and disinterested observer of my own actions and experience. In the process of hurrying so determinedly past myself, my health began to suffer. I began to lose weight and to fail, night after night, to get the eight or nine hours of sleep that are necessary for me to remain active and healthy; this is something that a person with Addison's disease should be especially careful never to do. When it came time for final exams, I was physically and mentally exhausted and soon became ill. I arrived home for Christmas vacation in somewhat of a mess.

It was during the second semester that there arose my first serious doubts about becoming a doctor. My premedical courses were intensely competitive, and many, though by no means all, of my classmates were people who did not make particularly enjoyable company. And yet, at the same time, I saw myself becoming more and more like them. Something in the back of my mind told me that, not only would my undergraduate years consist of unending competition and hard work in the characteristic premed fashion, but my life at medical school and as a doctor would be a perpetuation of the same theme. My health continued to be poor, and I began to wonder if the duties, obligations, and burdens of being a doctor would be too demanding on my time and energy.

Toward the end of the second semester, the old and familiar feelings of restlessness and worthlessness returned with far greater magnitude than ever before. There was no particular incident that triggered my sudden and extreme depression, but it settled upon me with terrible swiftness. Part of my trouble was undoubtedly the loneliness that had resulted from my self-imposed estrangement from others; hence, I made an effort to get to know some people a little better. One person in particular, a guy named Peter, stands out in my memory as an especially valuable and helpful friend. However, in attempting to create some friendships with other people, I was rather surprised and disillusioned, and was forced to change some of my conceptions about the qualities that are important in people. My expectation was that the kind of person who was admitted to a highly selective school would be more intelligent, more personable, and less prone to the pettiness and phoniness that went on in high school. Nothing could have been farther from the truth; indeed, many of the people whom I came to know were most adept at using their intellects to devise considerably more subtle, ingenious, and malicious ways to hurt others and still be able to live with themselves. Rituals of disparagement of just about anybody who happened to be a little different or threatening was one of the favorite pastimes of many of my acquaintances. To this day, I have never experienced the sense of comaraderie and belongingness that once existed among my circle of friends at home.

In any event, life was pretty unfulfilling during those days, and a group of us got into the habit of sitting around, drinking beer, and complaining about how this college was the armpit of the world. We all acted as if the institution were the sole cause of our problems; none of us were too eager to entertain the notion that a major source of our difficulties might lie within ourselves.

Summer finally came along and provided me with a much needed opportunity to step back and gather my thoughts, for it had been a very chaotic and discouraging year. A friend of mine found me some work with a local landscaper; it was a good change of pace, and the long, hard days that were spent working outside under the hot sun were invigorating and refreshing. I was also able to land a job in a restaurant and worked there a few nights each week to pick up some extra cash, so that I could help my father as much as possible with the college bills. As the summer wore on and I gained a different perspective on my first year at college, the bad memories gradually faded away, and college didn't seem like such a bad place any more. After all, the premedical courses weren't really too hard, if only I would relax, stop worrying about them so much, and go about my studying wholeheartedly. Although my faith in myself and other people had been somewhat shaken, there still was hope, and there actually were a lot of good people to know, if I were to take the time to seek them out and gain their trust.

During the summer, I also considered more seriously the possibility of psychology as a good field to explore. Even though my two freshman psychology courses had been exceedingly dry and had offered me very little insight into human nature, it seemed that there had to be some interesting courses offered, if only they could be found. By the time that September had arrived, my plans were to continue in the premedical program and also take some more psychology which, I thought, might offer a good alternative to my plans to become a doctor. There was a feeling of renewed self-confidence, but it was not long before I was back in the same old rut again.

It might be worthwhile to reflect a moment on my emerging interest in psychology. It's hard to say what made me think that psychology might be a good direction in which to proceed. Probably the main sources of my motivation was to gain a clearer understanding of myself, to discover a more effective way in which to deal with my difficulties in living and to, hopefully, undergo other sorts of personal growth. Perhaps psychology would lend more meaning to that obscure conglomeration of my dreams, fantasies, images, and memories. It might offer me a framework in which to become more aware of my experience, from which there could evolve a sense of purpose and direction. Along with these more personal incentives, I felt compelled to be of some help to other persons and to direct my efforts toward a future society that would embody my fundamental values; if medicine were not the answer for me, perhaps psychology would be.

Another noteworthy consideration was my curiosity about my friends and acquaintances, who certainly constituted a wide spectrum of types. They ranged from drug addicts and alcoholics to teetotalers, straight-laced, conventional people to small-time student radicals, from morons to intellectuals. What was it that made these people so diverse and unique, and what did they all share as members of the human race? Why was I able to appreciate and find something in common with them all, when many of them were completely unable to get along with one another?

A disturbing and perplexing experience that surely contributed to my interest in psychology was my friendship with Tim, who moved to my hometown during my junior year in high school. Tim was a smart, witty, likeable guy and was one of the few friends with whom I had ever had serious and intelligent conversations; most of our other friends were not prone to thinking too much about things. Our friendship developed quickly and easily, and we began to spend a lot of time together, either in athletics, playing cards with friends or with his parents, or just cruising around and talking.

Tim also introduced me to drinking. My approach to that issue was very cautious and conservative, and I rarely drank heavily. But Tim sure did. Week after week he would let the pressure build up until Friday night and then go out and get smashed. As time passed, Tim started to drink more heavily and eventually began fooling around with marijuana. My reaction was to be relatively unconcerned; most of our friends were already using drugs, and it was no longer any trouble for me to accept. However, by senior year in high school our relationship had begun to deteriorate. Tim was beginning to gobble anything he could get a hold of, including speed and acid, and was spending his time with a very different bunch of people, the kind of people that I had always thought had very little to offer. As it became increasingly difficult to talk to him, I realized that Tim was not using drugs as a form of recreation or as a means of exploring his mind; instead, he was trying to kill the pain somehow, a pain that must have been deep and powerful.

By the time that I had become fully aware of the harm that Tim was doing to himself, we had drifted worlds apart, and the possibility of communication between us seemed no longer to exist. Our friendship had ended, and I felt empty, bewildered, and more than slightly guilty that I hadn't made more of an effort to get through to him. My friends and I felt helpless as we watched him change before our eyes into someone who we no longer knew. To this day, I am at a loss to explain why Tim's involvement with drugs was so self-destructive.

When I went back to college for my sophomore year, my outlook had become considerably more positive. It was going to be a good semester, and I was not going to make the same mistakes that were made the year before. My optimistic attitude was short-lived, however; by the end of October, I was dejected and fatigued, and was soon hit by a severe virus. Fall tennis had been going well up to that time, but the demands that it placed on me were too great to handle. My initial illness led to a succession of colds and fevers that never ended until spring, when warm weather and sunshine returned. I decided not to play on the tennis squad, and I nearly gave up on my studies, passing my time relaxing with friends, daydreaming, and sleeping. Looking back, it seems incredible that my grades did not suffer, for there were times when I neglected my work almost completely; many of the books that had been assigned were never opened. Probably a little luck here and there had a good deal to do with it.

My negative outlook was accompanied by more serious doubts about my future. The prospect of four years of medical school after college was enough to make me sick. My psychology courses continued to be generally unenlightening until the second semester, when a professor who taught part of a course on psychopathology and psychotherapy was able to arouse my interest. I also did some volunteer work with a group of retarded children; the work was fun and rewarding, but there was no question in my mind that I didn't want to spend the rest of my life doing something like that.

When spring vacation arrived, I had convinced myself that my best move would be to take a year off from school, do some traveling, sooner or later find a job, and attempt to discover some sense of direction before resuming my studies. I was in a miserable state of mind, and college life seemed nearly unbearable.

My parents quickly put an end to those dreams, however. My mother's reaction was not too much of a surprise. "Go ahead and quit if you want to," she said. "There's not much we can do about it." Her words knocked the wind out of me for a while. When I finally regained the courage to discuss the matter with my father, he seemed quite receptive to the idea, until he realized that I was considering the possibility of doing it myself. So I gave up and went back to school to finish up the year.

My summer was basically a repetition of the previous one. When it came time to return to school, confusion and discouragement about my future remained, and I certainly did not look forward to hitting the books again. My single goal was to make it through the year in one piece.

For a number of reasons, junior year was not so bad, after all; new friends, more leisure time, and a course in personality theories that was genuinely stimulating and illuminating all contributed to make it an enjoyable fall. Up to that time, most of my contact with psychology had been with the strictly empirical, experimental approach, which was a bit difficult to stomach. At last, I was introduced to a more humanistic outlook that was refreshing and sorely needed. Maybe there was a place for me in psychology after all. The entire question of becoming a doctor started to become less important; I had taken most of the required courses and the option remained open for me.

The remainder of the year was a much happier time. Even my annual winter sickness didn't seem nearly as frustrating or defeating. Although I wasn't spending a lot of time studying, my grades improved, and everything seemed fine. I felt strong and healthy and got into the habit of running several miles every day to stay in shape. I picked up a secondhand guitar and began teaching myself a few chords. Worrying about the future was a needless obsession and a waste of time.

Soon it was summer again, and I found a job painting a house and continued to work as a busboy at the restaurant. Although I was aware that it would have been much wiser to line up a job that was related to my interests in medicine or psychology, there was absolutely nothing available at home. And anyway, I looked forward to a tough, physical, outdoor job. Before I knew it, another summer had passed without my having made any noticeable progress in getting in touch with my feelings about my future occupational role.

This fall, I was faced with the dilemma of deciding between taking my last required premedical course or doing some independent work in psychology. I was quite certain that I would have neither the time nor the stamina to do both. After much deliberation, my first move was to abandon my plans to do a thesis in psychology; although I had been initially enthusiastic about the prospect of doing research, all my doubts and reservations about the future combined to make me think that a thesis would be more of a burden than a pleasure. Later that week, my premedical advisor informed me that my academic record was good enough so that, even if I were to wait and finish my premedical requirements in summer school, my chances for admission to medical school would still be good. If my plans were any more concrete by the beginning of second semester, I could take some more of the recommended courses at that time. He also told me that the chemistry course that I was considering taking was already oversubscribed, although, as a senior, I had a reasonable chance of being admitted. To make a long story short, in my typical lazy, impulsive, and uninspired fashion, I backed out of both the chemistry course and the thesis, signed up for a few courses, and just said the hell with it. I just wanted to graduate, that's all.

Well, second semester of senior year is now upon me. It's hard to say exactly how much progress, if any, I have made in determining the best direction in which to proceed. Nevertheless, I've gone through a lot of changes. Four years ago, I was basically a naive and unsuspecting teenager who planned to go to a well-respected college and study hard to be a doctor for all the right reasons, including the money. At present, I have serious reservations about becoming any type of a professional at all. As far as I can gather, the life of a professional involves a great deal of personal sacrifice, a high degree of enthusiasm and devotion, a willingness to tolerate isolation and loneliness, and a tremendous amount of money. It's not clear that I qualify along any of these dimensions. Such a commitment would be desirable only if I were still able to work out an adequate life-style for fulfilling my personal needs and for enabling me to perform a useful role in helping others. Most of all, I refuse to give my father the encumbrance of financing another four years of school; any further education will have to be supported by my own funds.

I often ask myself whether the whole issue of work is as important as we make it out to be. Many Americans identify themselves so entirely with their occupational roles that they no longer have any idea who they really are. They are so totally immersed in their work and derive such a tremendous portion of their feelings of self-esteem and personal worth from their position in the occupational hierarchy that their values and priorities have been sadly distorted. As a result, they are alienated from themselves and estranged from others. I have witnessed this process on a smaller scale here at college, where countless potentially interesting individuals lose themselves in their studies and come to see their value as persons largely in terms of their grades. These same people appear to be headed, like projectiles, out into the world of graduate school or business, never stopping to examine their motives or question the meaning and utility of what they are doing.

One afternoon during Christmas vacation, while out on the golf course, I expressed similar thoughts to my brother and a friend named Ron. Their reaction was accompanied by laughter and ridicule.

"You've got to have some competition," my brother said. "You just can't sit around and do nothing all your life." Kevin is a year younger than I, goes to Dartmouth, and is nearly positive that he will end up in medical school.

Ron joined him in a voice that sounded almost fanatically self-confident. "Wait till you get out in the real world, Mike. You'll change your mind about a few things. Your problem is that college is so far away from reality that you'll never know how things really are until you get out there."

They had missed my point, and their words made me very angry. What was the use of arguing with them? Now, I am the first to admit that my college is, in many respects, an isolated intellectual enclave, and I don't deny that there are many new experiences awaiting me after graduation. However, I never have liked that expression — the "real world." A given place is just as real as any other and, provided that one is sufficiently aware, he will have the capacity to perceive the inherent possibilities and necessary limitations of his condition and to proceed to act in what he believes to be the best possible manner. What Ron meant by the "real world" was the competitive rat race, and there is certainly nothing more artificial and inflated than that situation. Ron is currently in his first year at business school and is absolutely miserable; he had just finished a lengthy monologue about the place which had prompted me to bring up the subject of Americans' attitudes toward work. Still, he claims that he has no doubts whatsoever, that the time that he is spending there is worth all the sacrifices that he is being forced to make.

Then again, I must admit that there may be an element of truth in what Ron said, for it cannot be denied that one can become stagnated in an isolated community and, hence, be unable to gain access to possibilities that exist elsewhere. Also, it would be very unrealistic and shortsighted to act as if I will never have the responsibility of supporting a family.

My latest aggravation is that I am continually focusing on the drawbacks of each of my alternatives, rather than considering their positive aspects. The thought of high school teaching or counseling brings to mind all of the hypocrisy and dissension that existed among the faculty at my school. The prospect of teaching at the college level is not offensive to my sensibilities, but neither does it particularly excite me, and I fear that I might be seduced into a passive, tame, reclusive existence. Neither do I want to become a high-powered, ulcerated businessman. Medicine is another question mark; I think only of the tremendous amount of further study that would be needed, my lack of stamina and need for large amounts of unstructured leisure time, and the astonishingly high percentage of doctors who must prescribe tranquilizers and amphetamines for themselves in order to get along. The idea of clinical psychology does appeal to me, but I am not at all confident of my ability to handle the intense personal involvement that would be required. Moreover, an effective therapist must be a fairly well-integrated person who has the ability to successfully resolve his own problems. This is surely not a fair description of my present condition; indeed, the process of writing this personal account has made me more acutely aware of my own anxieties, inconsistencies, and inadequacies.

On the other hand, I do feel that, in the last year or so, I have made considerable progress in my development as a person along lines other than that of my occupational identity. I am considerably more aware of my own feelings, beliefs, values, and assumptions, and I am becoming more sensitive and responsive to the needs of others and more knowledgeable and concerned about the nature of the oppression and corruption that exists in our society. Despite having taken a rather formidable battering in the last few years, my sense of self-esteem seems to be reemerging in a more solid and substantial form. Perhaps the firmer identity that I am trying to achieve is a necessary perquisite for deciding what my future occupation will be. In any event, I have decided not to make a commitment until I am sincerely excited and confident about my plans. The struggle with alternatives must come now, not in a middle-age crisis of identity. But is that the right attitude to take? It could also be argued that I should throw myself into something new and see what happens; maybe that is the best way to decide what to do.

With respect to decisions, I am somewhat of a coward; the responsibility of making them is frightening, for every decision is a renunciation and a relinquishment of several possibilities in favor of one. The frustrating paradox that I am forced to accept and enter into is precisely this: if I choose to become a doctor, I will wonder if my talents and abilities would have been better suited for education or clinical psychology — yet, if I choose to become a psychologist, I will regret that I did not go to medical school, instead. I feel like the donkey that starved to death because he was unable to choose between two equally distant bundles of hay. At least, however, I have the consolation of having resisted the pressure to become the donkey that forever pursues the unobtainable carrot.

At any rate, I am learning to be more tolerant of my inevitable ambiguities, restlessness, and inner contradictions. If I can always manage to accept and appreciate the humor in the absurd elements of my life, I will be able to put up with just about anything else. At the moment, I feel no particular compulsion to aimlessly squander my youth and vitality perched behind a cluttered desk, peering down a test tube, or buried beneath a pile of books. Perhaps whatever I choose to do with my time will be the right decision, simply because it will be an expression of where I am as a person at that instant in my life.

Sometimes, when I notice so many of my friends filling out applications and signing up for interviews, I experience uncomfortable misgivings about myself. It's always satisfying to talk to people who are in a similar position to my own. This afternoon, while out walking around to get some fresh air, I ran into a friend whom I hadn't seen in quite some time. The conversation rambled on for almost an hour, whereupon he hit me with the big question, the one that I must have answered a thousand times in the last few months.

"What have you got planned for next year?"

"Oh, not too much," I answered guiltily. "In fact, I really don't have anything planned at all. That's the way I want it for a while. Sometimes it can get a little scary, though."

"Yeah," he said. "They say that a lot of people panic when it finally dawns on them that they haven't got anything lined up to do."

"Well, I get that feeling every once in a while," I admitted. "What about yourself?"

"Oh, same thing," he said. "No big plans. It sounds awful good to me."

"Any thoughts about getting a job?" I asked.

"No way!" he replied with a big smile and a happy voice. "Not a serious job, anyway. I'll probably just wander around, read a few books, maybe head south with the birds next winter. It gets awful cold up here."

He seemed so calm and self-assured as he stood there, and it made me feel a little better about myself.

"You don't look too worried about the whole thing," I remarked.

"What's the use in worrying," he said. "The world's not going to come to an end just because of me."

Everyone has expressed such a thought at some time in his life; this time, however, the words made a profound impression upon me. While I still readily acknowledge my own insignificance, I have no choice but to admit that, in the course of my everyday experience, I tend to take this tiny life of mine much, much too seriously. Maybe it would be more accurate to say that I am often much too concerned with trivialities and diversions that lead nowhere and sadly neglectful of those aspects of my life that are of genuine and lasting significance. At any rate, I am trying, in my own clumsy but well-meaning way, to move toward becoming a whole person, even though it may often appear that I am doing little more than standing still.

Case 14 / The Best of Both Worlds

"Either you want money and power, a specific career, or a certain life-style." Susan thinks she wants a certain life-style, yet she is seriously considering a career in law or psychology. She works part-time as a bartender to working-class patrons. And although her parents and friends disapprove of her taking that job, Susan enjoys interaction with people very different from those at college and at home. Susan's mother enjoys her work outside the home, but Father blames the "bad marriage" on his wife's part-time homemaking and urges Susan to be a full-time housewife *or* an unmarried career woman. Susan wants a family and a career and doubts whether they are compatible — unless her eventual husband wants to do one-half of the childrearing and encourages her career.

I don't think I'll ever know what I'm going to do until it actually comes time to do it. Up to the moment that I accept a job, or write the final letter to a graduate school, I will have doubts. This decision will be so much more important than earlier ones (everybody *knew* I was going on to college, and I am still convinced that the college an individual ends up at is purely a matter of chance) because now the moratorium (was it really?) is over and it's time to face the real world. Even hiding in graduate school is a commitment because whichever school — or field — I decide on will pretty much determine the rest of my career life.

The occupational decision is only secondary. I guess with the "good" liberal arts undergraduate education I have I could get into almost any field after further graduate work. Recently at a colloquium on job opportunities in business fields, I realized that what one of the speakers said was deeply true of myself. "When you're looking for a job, you first have to make a decision between three things. Either you want money and power, or a specific career, or a certain life-style." One thing I suddenly realized — perhaps the only thing I'm really sure of — is that I want a certain life-style. I know I want to be happy and I don't need money for that. But I do need a career — something I can feel proud of, that I am competent in, that I can do besides being a housewife. Not that I feel there's anything wrong with taking care of a house — but I'd get so restless. The life-style I want probably is not in a city, but is somewhere with scenery so when I'm feeling down I can see something beautiful without driving for miles. Somewhere calm and slow. There aren't many places, but there must be a few. And when I realize this I see how much harder my search for a career must be. You either have to find where you want to live — and take whatever job you can get — or try to pursue a career that might lead (with occasional difficulty, I'm sure) to that type of life-style. There's always a chance I'll never find it. But I know that's what I must look for. A very close friend said to me once, "I know what you want, Susan: a beautiful big white house on a hill . . . [money and power!] and you can get it too, but when you get it I think you'll be very unhappy; and then it will be too late." He was right, and that's why this decision is so important to me. I've always wanted to have enough — more than enough — money to be happy (but money doesn't buy happiness), and I'm so afraid I'll lose sight of myself and end up with money instead, which is the wrong thing.

I'm a psychology major. I originally wanted to go to grad school for a Ph.D. in clinical psychology. That's one option. Or work for a while. Or (my latest idea) go to law school. And in the next year before I do finally have to decide, I'm sure I'll come up with two or three (at least) more options. (Isn't it funny how lawyers and psychologists both get paid at least $35 an hour?) Psychology is what I enjoy now — learning about people, trying to understand people, hoping eventually I can put that knowledge to use. I think I'd enjoy being in the situation of a psychologist, ideally. But there are always constraints: graduate work is necessary and schools are very, very selective, and after graduation with a second degree (a second time, another moratorium?) there is still the problem of finding a satisfying job in a market already glutted with psychologists. Or else law. "Everybody

and their brother is going to law school today," said a fellow student
in one of my classes today. I don't know much about law but I'm
intrigued by it — always have been. Must be the part of me that for
two years was convinced I was going to be a math major. Law requires
logic, with facts to back up any statements, and if you get enough
facts — and are convincing — you know you are right. There's certainly
a lot of human psychology involved in understanding how people may
react to you as well as being an understanding, sympathetic listener
for those who come to you. (It seems to me that many people who see
lawyers do have problems on their minds.) I've heard of programs
offering a law degree combined with a psych or social work degree in
three years; sounds like a good compromise for me. I'd ideally like to
find a way of using both interests. *If* law is right for me. That worries
me since I've never taken any courses that would give me any indication
of what law school is like. Next semester I will; I'll delay a final decision
until then. But what I'd really like to do — if I ever get through all this
school — is to work free. Well, not really free because I guess you can't
do that nowadays. To be paid on a sliding scale or be salaried by a
larger program, not to have to charge clients. Lately I've seen so many
people who could use legal help but don't have the money or don't
know where to go. You can't do anything without a lawyer — life is so
complicated — but even if you aren't able to pay, everyone should still
have access to one. Just for advice. Legal Aid has a program now I'd
be interested in — federally funded — but with my luck I'm sure if and
when I ever get through grad school the program would be defunct.
Besides, my mother always wanted one of her children to be a lawyer.

One thing about these last two ideas, I know I won't be wasting my education. I've come so far, with so much money involved
(there it is — money again — always creeps in!). Three years at a boarding school, plus four at one of the most expensive colleges in the
country . . . if you add it up it seems like a fortune already. Invested
in me — I can't imagine. I guess it's another burden on me. I would
feel like I betrayed a trust or let someone down if I don't go on, although I try not to think about it. Financial motivations *will not* be
satisfactory. Most of the money was my mother's — I frequently try to
reassure myself that that is not my reason for wanting to go to law
school. Or any graduate school, for that matter, because I know she
does not want me to stop my education after college.

But I keep wondering whether graduate school is really the
best thing for me. I'd love to get out of school and have a normal
forty-hour workweek with the rest of my time relatively free (instead
of the seventy-odd hours, at least, I put in going to school, between
studying and working). One experience I've had has prompted most
of my thinking, and like any worthwhile experience, it seems to have

created more doubts and uncertainties than resolved any questions. I started last summer as a part-time (weekend) bartender at The Red Boot. Less than fifteen minutes from the center of campus, the world of the bar is more like 5000 miles away. I've met — and become close to — many people who have a very different way of life. Most of them didn't go to college and probably never even thought of it. They're the electricians, plumbers, policemen, and construction workers. But they're happy. Not all of them, to be sure, but some of them are. Enough to make me realize it's not just luck, there is something in that different life. Slowly, I've been drawn into it. At first it was a way of getting away from the college, but then it became more important than an escape. A different side of me emerged — certainly not the girl in the back of the class who doesn't say much but who everybody knew always made good grades (most people's reputations precede them).

It's a freer and easier way of life — and more honest. I guess that is what intrigues me the most — openness and honesty that I have rarely found in the upper-upper-middle-class elite society I've lived most of my life in. I feel now I'm living two lives, and I wouldn't ever give up this new one for the old. This is the reason I wonder so much whether college and graduate school is the right way to find what I want. I've come to know another way of life and I've seen that it can work. It's funny — the few other students who know me here and know where I work seem to disapprove. I think my parents do too, even though they may not realize how much time I spend in that bar. (Especially my mother, who I've always felt was pushing her children upward — that great American dream of upward mobility.) I am not supposed to get involved and actually spend my leisure time there but should just work and observe and think how different I am from them. But I couldn't and I can't. I'm very emotionally involved and besides, I'm more comfortable there than anywhere else. This life seems so very real — as my life in the ivory towers of academia has often seemed so unreal.

I want part of this for my life too. I don't feel I could ever deny my education — that is too much a part of me — and that is the part of me that may go to graduate school and end up in a professional career. But I don't want to lose what I've known of this honest life. I guess I want the best of both worlds. I know this is a terribly idealistic and often impossible goal, but that seems to be where I'm headed. Two lives: a professional life, and my own life — I need to find a profession, or a place in that profession, that will allow me to make the life I want the way I want.

Finding the career that allows for this crazy combination makes it hard in the first place. But I'm a woman, and that poses even

more problems. Despite the women's liberation movement there still
are biases in businesses. Some may hire their quota of women but I
still feel I do not have as good a chance of finding that good job —
I am not sure which job but know it must be somewhere — because I
know a man with my qualifications will be hired first. My mother is
working and she has run up against discrimination — not overt, but
there — many times. She recently tried to get a credit card in her name
and found that for a married woman that is virtually impossible. Even
though she's opened accounts and paid all the bills, there is no record,
since it is all in her husband's name. After so many years of working
and paying bills, she has to establish credit — start all over — to get as
simple a thing as a credit card.

But for some reason I'm not too bothered by most of this.
Maybe I've been sheltered in liberal environments for too long. I just
see the problems I'll have as a woman in the same way as the difficulties in finding the right job for me — as a challenge. I sometimes
surprise myself feeling that I do have enough self-confidence to know
that I can overcome most barriers other people set up in front of me.
They all are barriers of society and of certain professions, set by the
conventional American way of life. But just as my decisions concerning
the way I want to live my life are so much more important than the
decision on a particular career, my decisions concerning myself as a
woman are much more important than these barriers I may worry
about, which come about from the way others see me as a woman.
One of the greatest conflicts in my mind — it's been there for years —
stems from the fact that I know I want to get married and have
children. Oh, I went through a year in high school when both my
roommate and I decided the best thing for both of us was never to
get married. I believed myself — for a little while. I was at a girls'
school, and since then I've found I enjoy male companionship too
much to never marry. My own selfish desire to conceive life, to have
a child, is even stronger. I wonder if in another society I would raise
children without their father. I might, but in our society it would be
too unfair to the child. Despite what some feminists say, we still
haven't changed that much. I want to get married, to make a good
home, and to raise a beautiful family. But yet I've been carefully explaining all my reasons for wanting a career. "Oh, there's the rub!" —
was it Shakespeare who wrote that? The conflicts anyone feels who
wants two equally appealing and equally opposing goals. How do you
compromise? Or should you compromise, to be fair to what you want
to do? No matter how happy or content I might be with a marriage, I
know it would not be fair to myself and the marriage to give up any
idea of a career.

I remember a conversation a very long time ago with my father. Probably driving me to the airport — he always used to — we weren't that close, then, but he always gave me bits and pieces of his thoughts on life. "Susan, one of the problems between your mother and I is her working. Now, I've never discouraged her from working part-time. But that house! What a mess! She should stay home and take care of the house and you children. You can't try to do two things at once, Susan. A woman should be either a wife and mother, or a career woman. That's a decision you'll have to make some day." I sat in the car and murmured some form of assent (I didn't talk too much then — just thought a lot). I thought how I certainly could never marry a man like my father — he's too rigid and conservative — and how glad I was times have changed and even though I would probably have to make a decision, sometime, it might not have to be between two dichotomous opposites. I should have many more options and I think I do. No, I would never marry anyone who would ever tell me what my father said to me that night. He must be someone who will accept — not accept, but encourage — my career. Who will understand that a career means I would not do *all* the housework, cook, clean, etc. We both would. He might even help with the child. I know that now some men do a lot of child-rearing. Some children grow up with a father instead of a mother. I don't — can't — believe a man would ever want to do that for me. I know I would want at least fifty percent of the responsibilities. Maybe it would be ideal to find a husband to take the other half — but somehow I don't think it's possible. At times I surprise myself with my self-confidence, and at times I feel so very insecure.

But if I think about it for very long, I may find such a husband is necessary. Because I've lived through a marriage that tried to survive with a woman combining a career and a home, and with a man sometimes encouraging but silently disapproving — and that marriage failed a long time ago. My parents should have been separated and divorced ten years ago, but they're just getting around to it now. Maybe that's why I remember so vividly that conversation with my father — because my mother has been working for six or seven or eight years; I'm not exactly sure how long. Sometimes part-time, sometimes full-time. But she loves her work. She gets so much pleasure and satisfaction out of it. I watch her and I know I'll never be satisfied without a career of my own. In many ways I'm very like my mother — sometimes too alike and that may be why we don't always get along too well, but we feel the same way about this. And the marriage — well, I think if my mother had realized when she got married that she did want to work and told her future husband this and worked part of it out before the marriage and before the children, it might have made a difference. That is certainly far from being the only problem my parents' marriage has had, but it has not been minor, and I want to make as few mistakes as I have to.

So what am I going to do? Again I want the best of both worlds — marriage and career — must I compromise or can I even find it all? I can't ever decide now — I won't even try to. I've learned many times over that you can't plan your life for yourself. You can give it helpful pushes and prods in one direction or another, but things never seem to work out exactly as you've planned. I know when I have children I may work part-time, no more. Maybe I will not work at all. Should I finish school, get a job — the right one — establish myself, and then have children? I'd be thirty by then. I guess ideally I've always thought I'd have children before then. The time is going so strangely fast. Or I could reverse it and have children and then work. There are so many options. But I guess finding a husband will be as much — probably more — work than finding that one career. (What a thing for a woman to say — "find a husband"!) That's something I'm going to leave alone and let happen. I couldn't ever plan when that man may walk into my life. But I'll think a lot and look into all the options I'd ever be comfortable with — know what I want, decide which career — so when the time comes, maybe I'll know it and be more sure of what I'm doing. "Life is a bitch" — many of my customers tell me that, or if they don't tell me I can see it in their faces. I will probably never have everything going "just right," so if I can make for myself what I can (my career), try to be prepared, and at least go in with the deck stacked in my favor, maybe I'll come out even or with luck, a little bit ahead. That's all I'm asking for.

Epilogue

When I was writing part of this, a friend came up to me and asked me what I was doing. I said, "Well, writing a case study about how I do want a career but know I want to get married and have children too." He gave me a funny look, got up, and hurried away. A minute later, he came back — "You didn't really scare me *that* much, I had to talk to someone. . . ." When I think real hard, I scare myself. But it's so necessary — you're not ever going to get what you want unless you find out what it is first. I had to go very deep, down to thoughts that frightened me. I found many, many doubts, but some relief and comfort too. I must be on my way. And this particular time — two weeks maybe, while I have been writing — has been one of the hardest and most confusing times of my life. You see, someone has asked me to marry him, and it's the first time anyone ever said that to me. It may be scary — my thoughts, and my life — but I know how very real it all is. I have never thought I'd know what I wanted before I sort of stumbled onto it. I've learned, at least, that that doesn't happen for me.

Topic Eight
Politics and Identity

Case 15 / Waking People Up

One of Carol's first political learnings was that materialism and the American work ethic do not make people happy. She vowed to avoid that trap. Later, her high school experience of witnessing a conservative and uncreative administration do little to ease interracial and interethnic tensions left her very critical of hypocrisy, submission to authority, and lack of humane concern for others. She developed an attitude of antiviolence which included not only rejection of war but also objection to the violence of football and of slaughter of animals for food.

At college, students are not only politically dead, but do not even read the newspapers. Students tend to shy away from her when they notice the intensity of her feelings about injustice, apathy, and violence. She has sought out other political students for companionship and the pursuit of shared goals. She is concerned about being a political person — working for change — yet not alienating people by being too critical or solely political.

Not until this past year have I called myself political, although I've been interested in topics of a political nature to some extent since I was in elementary school. Not surprisingly, the first object of my criticism was the school system, although initially I had no thought whatsoever of trying to change it. In fact it wasn't until I was in high school that I tried to specify what it meant to be a political person: to be involved in the political process, usually in government. By last year I felt this definition was inadequate, since many people considered me political, but I was not in government. So I redefined a political person as one who is concerned with and usually is intentionally working for desired change; this work can function on many levels — personal, social, institutional — but normally one works at more than one at the same time. A political person critically analyzes the past and present, and, where feasible, tries to implement his desired changes for the future.

My first important experience in which I stepped outside my native environment and then viewed it critically occurred when I was nine. My family and I spent a year in a small village in Belgium. There I discovered that a car was a luxury, three dresses and skirts comprised a wardrobe, meat was eaten no more than two or three times a week, and one TV sufficed beautifully for the entire village. What surprised me though was that these people were comfortable and happy! This discovery led me to wonder: "Why are Americans so caught up in their materialistic, success-oriented, 'bigger is better' syndrome? After all, think of all the time I'd have to enjoy myself, be happy, if I don't spend all my time making money when I grow up! Yeah, OK, I'm not going to let myself get caught up in that trap. And maybe I'll be able to persuade somebody else too. . . ."

Such were my thoughts when I returned to the United States. I suspect, though, that my experience simply brought to the surface objections I would have voiced sooner or later anyway, because my family, particularly my mother, had the same antimaterialistic inclinations. Also at that time student activism at Columbia was beginning to arouse my parents' interest. Night after night, my father, a middle-of-the-road Republican, and my mother, a *New York Times* Democrat, would discuss politics at the dinner table, usually sympathizing — if only intellectually — with the left-wing students. I listened attentively, well enough anyway to unconsciously parrot my mother's views in the classroom.

If I mimicked my mother in the classroom, I also first thought independently there too. One of my most memorable early disillusioning experiences with the school system occurred the day John F. Kennedy was assassinated. After solemnly announcing the news, our teacher told us to put our heads down on our desks in mourning and respect for the terrible loss of our great President. I obediently lowered my head, but after a moment's reflection, I defiantly raised my head and surveyed the room to find thirty fully obedient classmates. I said to myself: "Why do they have their heads on their desks? Do they care about Kennedy? Do they even know who he was? I bet they don't. I bet they're just putting their heads down to obey the teacher. I bet most of them aren't thinking about Kennedy at all. Maybe some of them aren't thinking, period." Silently, somewhat bitterly, I laughed. "My God, why don't you think for yourselves?" I screamed silently.

From then on I gradually became more aware and critical of blind obedience, submission to authority, and hypocrisy. These critical views were often reinforced by my mother, since she always stressed honesty and independent thinking. With time she became the one sounding board I could always depend on for my ideas and political views. My father, on the other hand, never showed much interest in discussing such matters with me; so the distance between us gradually increased in inverse proportion to my deepening relationship with my mother.

Day after day I would rush home from school with a new idea or some news to share with my mother. While she prepared dinner, we would discuss it. She took my opinions and criticisms very seriously, expecting me to present them and defend them persuasively. Often we got so emotionally involved in these talks that they lapsed into verbal sparring matches, each of us furiously trying to convince the other. The only idea we took for granted was that ideas and opinions were important.

By the time I was finishing eighth grade, my mother had become so disgusted with the stagnant public schools (I agreed with her) that she transferred me to a private girls' school. There, although I found my classmates friendly and my classes somewhat more demanding, I grew to dislike the institution's exclusiveness, snobbery, and inflated sense of self-worth. These objections, when coupled with my opinion that it lacked diversity and a direct link with the problems of the outside world, made me decide to reimmerse myself in the turmoil of the public school system for my last two years of high school.

These two years were probably the most influential in sharpening my political consciousness, for I felt that the school exhibited most of the problems plaguing the city as a whole. I was bombarded daily with incidents and situations which I intensely disliked and desired to change, but felt I was impotent to do so. I felt the overall situation was almost beyond hope: the students hated each other; the administration was so uncreative it "solved" problems with increasingly authoritarian reprisals which gave rise to more rebellious students, who, in turn, made the administration even more repressive, thus completing the vicious circle. The teachers were too concerned about keeping their jobs and ensuring their own safety to take any risks.

Although a myriad of problems engulfed the school, the most fundamental one was hatred, primarily interracial and interethnic, but also between students and the administration, and between students and teachers. Yet nobody DID anything. Sometimes I had a great desire to climb on top of the cafeteria with a bullhorn and dramatically scream, "Hey, LISTEN! We're all hurting each other insidiously and unnecessarily. Nobody can look anybody else straight in the eye for fear of seeing naked hatred. Let's face up to each other, to our problems, and see if something can be done." But something always prevented me — perhaps I sensed the futility of the gesture, perhaps I feared that the situation would become uncontrollable if somebody took the lid off, and perhaps I was simply unwilling to risk myself, to take on more than I could handle. So I remained silent, always almost despairing, but never letting myself do so. Deep down I believed that everybody was basically good and loving, and that maybe if we were honest with ourselves and admitted our fears and insecurities, things would improve. But I simply could not tap that source — it was buried much too deeply under our callousness.

The only way I survived was by thinking as little as possible about the bad aspects. Eventually my senses became so numbed I could hardly distinguish between bad situations and horrendous ones. One day some "friends" of a student who was "high" persuaded him to undress in the middle of the football field at lunchtime. Later that afternoon, when the student was straight enough to be ashamed, he quickly ended his problems with the finality of a bullet through his head. And we students simply shrugged, spiritlessly, impassively. When the art building burned down one night, we hardly believed the official story that placed the blame on an unhappy army deserter. We just assumed it was another act of student vandalism. In the end it didn't matter who was right, what mattered was that we didn't believe the authorities.

My cynicism drained me of all but one strong desire — to GRADUATE. To be DONE. To GET OUT. I got "senioritis" second semester junior year and counted the months, weeks, and finally days from then on. Of course, my half-rebellious nature demanded that I make a few half-hearted attempts to break out of my passivity. I remember once getting so fed up with studying *The Oxbow Incident, Jubilee,* and grammar for most of the year that I pleaded for more interesting books and even offered to pay for an entire class set. The response: a supplemental reading list. I felt like throttling the teacher until I realized that either she simply did not understand my desperation, or she was even more brainwashed than I.

To say that I was inactive is not to say that I was indifferent. I cared, I cared deeply, but I felt I could not engage myself in a quixotic battle against the arrayed forces of racism, hatred, violence, poverty, oppression, stupidity, and a host of other forces. If anything, my passivity deepened my political sense, for I realized that just as there is a time and a place for action, there is a time when action is totally futile.

In fact the only stand upon which I stood firm was against violence. I remember denouncing football, on the grounds that it is violent, in my speech class which had nearly a dozen football jocks in it. How they derided me! They could tolerate me as an antiwar freak, but not as one who was against FOOTBALL. Yet the very fact that they reacted strongly pleased me because it showed that I had started them thinking. I had challenged them, and now they were responding forcefully.

It wasn't until I started to write the speech that I was to give at graduation that I broke through some of my cynicism, apathy, and sense of futility. In reviewing my entire education, I suspected that I had been overly negative and cynical — maybe there had been positive signs in the school system which I had simply ignored. This glimmer of optimism I developed in my speech. Although I never mentioned politics directly, I pointed in that direction, saying, "Do SOMETHING. We've been mauled, molded like clay, treated like objects, but now maybe we have a chance to do something ourselves. We've got to make a commitment, assert ourselves."

Thus I set off to college optimistic that in my new environment I could implement some changes, and prepared to become directly involved in political activities. I was shocked and bewildered to find the college — on the surface anyway — politically dead. Not only did people not want to talk about politics, they didn't even read the newspaper! Suddenly the phrase "ivory tower" assumed an entirely new meaning — here were people living in their own little world, a world so constricted they either would not or could not care to understand the problems outside of it. At least in my high school everybody acknowledged the existence of the problems whether they desired to solve them or not.

I remember vividly the day I heard about the assassination of Marcus Foster, the Superintendent of the Oakland Public Schools. Although I knew next to nothing about Oakland other than its racial diversity and tensions — I vaguely thought of it as an overgrown Newark — I could identify with its problems and imagined the possible political repercussions of the tragedy. Feeling strongly about the news, I spread the word to my friends while they were eating lunch: "Did you hear that Marcus Foster, the Superintendent of the Oakland Public Schools has been killed! I'm really shocked. This is AWFUL, especially since he was black." My friends, surprised by my outburst, politely chimed: "Oh, I'm sorry." . . . "That's too bad." . . . "What a shame." . . . and then calmly continued their conversation and meal. "But," I persisted, "this is REALLY TERRIBLE. What's going to happen? I wonder whether it was a black or a white who killed him. How are the blacks going to react?" Again the lunchers raised their blank, uncomprehending faces, our eyes meeting momentarily but shying away as soon as they noticed the intensity of my feelings. I simply was unable to convey my sense of tragedy, reach any mutual understanding. I began to worry: "Am I strange to care so much about a school system? Was my friends' failure to understand proof of the inadequacy of my communication skills? Did they simply not care, or could they not understand? Am I really just more political than most people?"

This last question led me to deliberately seek out the "political" students. Not long afterwards I joined a newly formed group of people who were committed to nonviolent social change and to community, which involved mutual reinforcement and challenging. To complement my theoretical commitments I also became involved in such visible political activities as organizational work for the UFW grape and lettuce boycott, campaign work for a congressman, and publicity work to arouse public opinion to end aid to Thieu.

Actually these particular activities turned out to be less important than my political friends who were willing to discuss political questions for hours on end. It was at this time that I broadened my definition of a political person to one who is interested in change: for the first time I examined my entire outlook and my own life-style. I realized that my ability to integrate my ideas and goals into my life-style was much harder and more important than my ability to win a debate, write a letter to the editor, or organize activities. In looking at myself rather than at others, I also realized how much I still embodied the American materialistic, success-oriented ethic.

One of the outward manifestations of my effort to change myself was my decision to become a vegetarian. I simply said to myself: "I consume too much food, particularly meat, and then often throw away even more. In becoming a vegetarian I am disciplining myself to adopt a cheaper, simpler, more ecologically sound, and most likely morally preferable diet." Somewhat to my surprise, I found that I preferred my new eating style, for not only did I no longer eat meat, I was now more conscious of all the foods that I ate. However soon I found myself in a dilemma: when I go home for Christmas vacation should I upset my family by announcing my vegetarianism, or should I compromise myself for two weeks? For my father, eating meat at dinner was practically a sacred ritual — would he be insulted or threatened by my action? Finally I decided not to rock the boat and to quietly eat meat during the vacation.

In fact it wasn't until the following Christmas that I decided to stick to my vegetarianism, although I had hinted at my inclinations from time to time in the interim. During the entire trip home at the beginning of the vacation I was extremely nervous and mentally rehearsed my little speech on vegetarianism dozens of times. Somewhat to my surprise and much to my relief, a couple of hours after being home my mother said flatly to me, "Carol, are you eating meat these days?"

Suddenly I breathed a deep sigh of relief and gulped quickly, "No, Mom, I'm not."

"Oh, OK. I'm not surprised, but I'm not going to prepare you any special meals."

"Oh, OK."

And that was that, thank God, as far as my mother was concerned. She casually mentioned it to my father, who grunted, and passed the word on to my grandmother. She was dumbfounded and spoke of it to ALL her friends: "My granddaughter is on this CRAZY vegetarian diet these days. What an absurd thing to do. Maybe it won't last long. Kids are pretty crazy these days, aren't they?" And her friends are people who all nod assentingly. But it was my overweight uncle who reacted most vehemently. Putting his arm around my shoulder he expansively but aggressively said to me: "Now, Carol, listen. I'm going to stop this crazy diet of yours right now. I have an idea! How would you like to have a New York steak at the Four Seasons?"

I smiled, "No, thanks."

"Or how about going to the Mont d'Or?"

"I'm afraid not."

"Listen, I'll take you out to Trader Vic's. We'll have a marvelous time. Delicious food."

"Thanks anyway."

He continued to list all the fancy New York restaurants until he realized I wouldn't waver.

I was embarrassed, amused, pleased, and surprised by his reaction. Although I was taken aback by its intensity, I actually enjoyed disturbing his complacency. I am sure he has flipped through articles on vegetarianism appearing in the Sunday magazine section of the newspaper many times, or even skimmed an article or two about a few silly people worrying about overconsumption, but I was probably the first person to confront him with the idea on a personal level. I literally brought the idea home to him, and, judging from his aggressive response, he took me seriously.

To me this is what politics is all about: getting people to think critically about themselves and others in such a way that they become willing to change. Consequently I place just as much emphasis, maybe more, on ideas underlying institutions and actions than their manifestations, although choosing the particular angle from which to solve a given problem depends upon the situation. Regardless of the specific actions I become involved in, I always try to reach a mutual understanding and to guard against my own complacency and sense of self-righteousness.

I foresee politics in my future, probably as my future. Yet when people ask me whether I like politics I often equivocate. At

times I love it — I enjoy waking people up. At other times I fear it —
I don't want to alienate my apolitical friends by being too critical or
solely political. Yet ultimately I am political because I think it is right
to care — being political is not so much a matter of leading the life I
enjoy as living the life I believe in.

Case 16 / Working Within the System

Ken grew up with the idea that "one must justify his existence . . . by
creating something ennobling or somewhat worthwhile." His sense of
mission and political awareness arise from his Irish Catholic background,
his identification with the style and goals of President Kennedy and family,
and his interaction with his father, a social worker with a sensitivity to
personal tragedy and injustice. Ken's religious beliefs and actions have
evolved into an "eclectic Christianity" which regards the Berrigans, Father
Drinan, and Cesar Chavez as models for emulation.

At college, Ken has played within the rules and been rewarded; he has
worked diligently and has had to "adjust, modify some views, keep silent
on some things . . . and temper some of the passion." He sees his college
as a citadel of privilege and feels ambivalent about being there. His faith
in the system rests on the hope that institutions will be designed for people
and that justice will prevail — in the long run.

More than one political pundit has doubtless characterized my
contemporaries as rather apolitical, unwitting heirs to the legacy of
the sixties. We are not really children of that decade, however. Some
of us brushed the fringe with somewhat precocious political activity,
absenting ourselves from an occasional afternoon of high school classes
to attend a moratorium day demonstration, gauging more than basking
in the approaching autumn of the "movement."

But my political identity does not fully embrace the trends and
passions of the last decade; I have enjoyed *Blowin' in the Wind, Ohio,*
and *Where Have All the Flowers Gone?* for some time now, but they
are really my older brothers' and cousins' songs and memories. I
missed by a year, perhaps two, the sense of moral imperative and half-
naive expectation that made raising the clenched fist more important
than sitting for LSATs. I am caught in the breach between passionate
idealism that seemed to diminish like the echoes of dissident shouts,
and the cool, even self-centered diffidence which pervades my campus
and my associates' dining hall conversations today. Being trapped in
the wake of what many analysts suggest has been a minor social revolution inevitably produces a degree of confusion and ambivalence;
and, to borrow from the travel agents' slogan, getting here has been
"twice the fun."

In a most elemental sense, my first recallable moment of political awareness must have been that unseasonably warm late fall afternoon in a parochial school's third-grade classroom when Mother Superior, voice muffled by tears, broadcast over the public address system that President Kennedy had been shot in Dallas. The long-term effects of this might overshadow any immediate significance the tragedy held for me that day. But for the moment it is not misrepresentation to say that, from the first, my political being was affected, if not molded, by Camelot and Kennedy.

I suppose many of my age would admit to close identification with some link in the Kennedy line, perhaps attributing our seemingly universal tendency toward "liberalism" to the progressive democratic polity they espoused. And I mean to include myself in that number — but there is more to my affinity with the Kennedys than mere absorption of a political tendency.

I have lived all my life seven miles north of Boston; my family is predominantly Irish Catholic and exhibits much twentieth-century Yankee tradition and ethos. These factors, among other things, spelled esteem for the vigorous John Kennedy, admiration of his elegant family, and reverance for his oft-cited courage and integrity. When the dinner table conversations at family gatherings turned to mine and my brothers' futures, the word "senator" was underscored. Not just senator, however; but vigorous, diligent, tall, smiling senator was the role model, if not the holy grail. (Some of my family still optimistically await my inauguration.) Wit and eloquence were a part of the package also — we were forever encouraged to speak our minds, even at a young age, on political matters, regardless of the fecklessness or triviality of our comments. It was the habit of debate, of striding forward, which was meant as lesson. Small wonder that I still today retain something of the Kennedy mystique, dampened as it was by the waters off Chappaquidick.

So in an admittedly feeble reflection of the Kennedy–Harvard–touch-football mode, my earlier days were spent in diligent pursuit of the athletic and the academic, quite apolitical in the sense I would employ today.

That I was a grand little materialist in junior high school, maintaining my own paper route, sometimes with friends at employ, was a source of pride to my family and myself. Indeed, all the promises that work builds character are not vacuous; but if the development of such "American" virtues as thrift, industry, responsibility to clients, etc., was one result, there were more subtle, often unnoticed by-products of the experience of which only in retrospect can I estimate the significance.

Part of my paper route covered a few houses which were the

closest things to a "slum" that I'd ever reach out and touch in my comfortable, middle-income suburb. Several elderly clients and more than one mother with a plethora of small children seemed to scrape change together to meet my $.60 invoice every week. I was always struck by the condition of the interior of their homes, largely that many were considerably inferior to mine. Increasingly I would be impressed by elderly customers, both poor and more comfortable, who in their aloneness would anticipate my coming and hasten to engage me in conversation. My sensitivity at the time was certainly less than overwhelming, but occasional inklings about the pathos of it all would disrupt the otherwise comfortable and uncomplicated current of my existence.

The course of development of my then nascent political self was significantly determined by familial influences, perhaps most profoundly by the attitudes and actions of my father, a man who exhibits a remarkable dichotomy between his liberal sentiments about personal and interactional issues and his political attitudes.

So much of the substance of my father's life suggests that he be conservative politically — everything from his old-school Irish Catholic background to his prolonged involvement with the military, which included World War II veteran status. Long ago he was taught the irreconcilable polarity of communism and Catholicism, of "leftist" and "the American way of life." A flag on the seat of a young person's pants provokes his swift and indignant indictment; and "subversive" and "outside agitator" spice his vocabulary. But you have to juxtapose this outlook with the reality of his everyday, which is essentially his life as a social worker and, if you will allow for an admittedly biased evaluation, a very compassionate and dedicated one. Since his job requires in general a great deal of activity in the criminal court and much interaction with youthful and adult offenders, my father has developed an acute sensitivity to the plight of the violator and has formulated some remarkable insights as to why people break the law. Repeatedly he underscores the background of the accused and the convicted: the broken home, the alcoholic father, the destitute household, the unsated hunger for affection and interest which so often are antecedent to the crime. More often the tone of his narration is of a brokenhearted man (perhaps occasionally angry), one sensing the tragedy and injustice of it all and haunted by the spectre of his powerlessness to somehow divert the onrushing current. What he can do he does, but his most effective response to the procession of human misery is finally an emotional and personal micro-response. He has recognized and grappled with some basic inadequacies and injustices existing in this society, but he has never pursued the seemingly logical and larger implications of his observations: he has never seriously questioned the basic economic and political choices and institutions which might share in the culpability for the human tragedy he confronts every day.

This sort of conservative-liberal dichotomy in my father has had some interesting effects on my emerging political person. Most profoundly, his involvement with and interest in the materially deprived or environmentally disadvantaged has influenced me in a very similar direction. His overriding concern for the underdog, his grief at the misfortune of so many, have left to me a legacy of compassion and a sense of justice. Moreover, his sentiments are perhaps at the origin of any desires I have had to change structures or attitudes or institutions. Much of my political awareness today I might explain by harkening back to themes dominant in the man's life. At the very least his experience would awaken and foster a consciousness about the poor and a concern for what might be broadly (and rather academically) termed human development, and in this manner have important implications for my political person.

Unlike a small minority of my immediate contemporaries or the larger segment of students five years ago, I cannot trace my political development in high school by recounting the list of demonstrations attended or by scheduling the occasions upon which I stuffed envelopes for liberal politicians' campaigns; there was an evolutionary process transpiring, but it did not manifest itself in overt or specific political activity. Consequently, an accurate and economic representation of my political development is difficult to achieve. Perhaps the best I can do is to relate a couple of particularly salient incidents and then speculate briefly on one or two emerging trends in my political personality.

If I had to capture in one word what I was all about in high school, I would seize upon the word "achiever." Intensely goal-oriented, academic, athletic, and social success topped my list of priorities. And all seemed to be integrated under the one umbrella-like end of gathering credentials for admission to a prestigious Eastern liberal arts ivory tower. Yet into what should appear as a predominantly apolitical existence, an occasional and memorable wedge would be driven. Immediately comes to mind the night in my senior year when I listened to Cesar Chavez and fellow migrant farmworkers in the basement of a Catholic church in Boston. The nature and extent of the injustices they had suffered disturbed me deeply, and has since prompted me to participate actively in their cause. But a sense of indignation was not the only dimension to my reaction that evening. The most impressive and memorable characteristic about that group of migrants, some of whom had traveled many days to launch the 1973 boycott in the New England area, was the unbridled joy you sensed in their singing and laughter, the flood of strength which welled up from their sense of community. These were the denied and the forsaken who had come to believe in and insist upon their dignity; in their singing and their passion, their courage and their joy, they were more free than I or perhaps many of the other community liberals who assembled that evening to hear the charismatic Chavez. And so began to stir misgivings and new perspectives on this highly charged, competitive, well-defined, and constrained mode of existence I so eagerly pursued and was so quickly adopting.

Another event which I view as somewhat crucial in my political development was the occasion of a visit to a friend's elderly and alcoholic aunt who resided in one of the more thoughtlessly constructed and thoroughly neglected housing projects in my area. When I passed the point of tolerating the heat and squalor of the woman's hovel (an economy-motivated and deficient frame, which included a flat, and what must have been uninsulated, roof, which acted like a magnifying glass for the July sun's rays), I waded into a group of small children out in the public, concrete covered "yard." One of my friends produced a tattered football and we had everyone passing and kicking, even the little girls. Then came time for some conversation — about family, school, and the like. Many were alienated by the delapidated and unpromising school which we had passed on our way into the project, and all seemed to be able to claim at least five or six brothers and sisters. Among the tattered dresses and smudged faces there was some confusion about "daddies," though one little girl was confident enough to caution us that if her father saw us talking to his kids, he'd probably "beat us up." Sociologists' data was suddenly looking better and better. To say that I left the project that day with a sense of mission would be to overstate the case, but my interests in poverty and related issues were enriched and widened.

Alongside of this rather sporadic nurturing of certain social concerns there developed a couple of more-or-less intellectual aspects of my political being and personality: an interest in feminist issues and a growing awareness of my own sexism and the seemingly inherent chauvinism of American society; and a still ongoing attempt to reconcile and synthesize some of my basic religious and moral principles with my political philosophy and actions.

The feminist issue is crucial to my development for a couple of reasons. Most fundamental about the problem of sexism for me are the questions of social and personal justice involved: the intellectual and psychological etiolation of so many people, the discrimination against half the population of the society, the implicit denial of dignity and self-fulfillment which our culturally and socially conditioned attitudes have so often and effectively accomplished, and finally and ironically, the degradation of our humanity which afflicts both the victim and the chauvinist. On the practical level, perhaps I can best illustrate my sentiments by recalling that the most satisfying personal relationships I have had with women have been and are those with "liberated" women, i.e., people who have struggled for a sense of their personhood and worth, who insist on their dignity as people, who have at least tried to transcend the awful parameters we as a society have established, within which people must confine themselves.

But beyond the basic question of justice which has interested me, the feminist issue adds to my perspective on this society and country — for if it is anything, the question of women's rights is a profoundly political one. The question has given me some slight notion about the nature of institutions in a society and about how they can be instruments for the perpetuation of inequality and injustice. When I began to sense the reinforcing and supportive relationships between societal attitudes, economic motives, and political decisions (and I may have sensed this first with an appraisal of the situation of women in these United States), I just may have crossed some threshold in my political development. In any case, I have been led to question certain social institutions (such as twentieth-century American marriage), the reasons for their existence, and the matrix of legalistic and cultural values which necessitate their perpetuation. These kinds of considerations of course can, and I believe should, be made with regard to a wide spectrum of political questions; indeed, much of my intellectual activity during three college semesters has centered upon grasping these interrelationships and opening to examination the possibility of alternatives — whether that be in the field of interpersonal relations, economic arrangements, or political values. It is almost by definition an ongoing process — one that I am still very much immersed in.

The entrance of certain religious conceptions and ideals has added to the scope and increased the passion with which I pursue these considerations. Out of what seems to be the inevitable lapsed Catholic-agnostic state of the middle-to-late teens, I have emerged with a fairly utilitarian and basic set of religious principles which have significant bearing on my social and political self.

Over the past two years I have been evolving an "eclectic Christianity," attempting to discard the traditional and conservative conceptions of church and religion. I am dissatisfied with an institution which would so pervert the separation of church and state as to excuse the hierarchy and congregation from taking political and moral stances on questions of justice. If what is told to us about this man Christ is half-true, then I am fairly convinced he did not mean for us to sit in comfortable suburban churches singing psalms of sweet refinement while the disenfranchised, the alienated, and the desperate are forsaken and unaided. The church I grew up in was more concerned with what happened in your bedroom than how you conduct yourself at the town meeting which voted to exclude, via snob zoning laws, low-income housing from your comfortable suburb. If I am to embrace the Catholic Church, it must be Philip Berrigan's, not the archdiocese of New York and Terence Cardinal Cooke who support the war avidly and lobby successfully to defeat gay rights legislation.

With regard to much of the theology and outlook of the "establishment" church, I wonder if the Marxists are all that far from being correct in their analysis. Religious institutions can and indeed have been used to placate the angry and oppressed, to require submission and encourage meekness, to help perpetuate structures and institutions of unjust nature.

But I am hopeful for the potential of the religious for morally grounded political activism; there are certainly many important manifestations evident of the synthesis of the political and the religious: the Berrigans, the Drinans, Chavez; there are even some remarkably "radical" pronouncements about social and economic justice emanating from Rome these days. We are yet, however, far from adjudging the gospel as a political manifesto. For me personally you cannot abstract noble sentiments about love and brother/sisterhood from issues of economic exploitation, discrimination, unequal access to institutions of law, and denial of the right of self-determination. And such is at least the general outline of my integration of the religious with my political values.

Where does all this leave me, a student ensconced in a country club–like, elitist, and isolated four-year college?

Leading the life of the university student, I enjoy the luxury of nearly unrestrained mental activity, not only because of the highly intellectual environment, but because I am largely free of concern with the material aspects of the business of living: I have food, shelter, and the necessities of life, plus — a social situation which is characterized by the liberty to experiment with different life-styles and values. Although I am not terribly wealthy myself, I still live amidst affluence, and my life has all its trappings. I have access to the social and occupational credentials of a degree from a prestigious college and all the attendant contacts which this will provide. The environment within which I operate has been characterized by nearly all observers as apolitical, and many of my fellow students exhibit a remarkably conservative political and social outlook. And those who are liberal are essentially conservative in that liberalism. From a practical standpoint this is really quite understandable — we here are the comfortable, and it is a quite rational response to wish to secure the longevity of our good fortune.

In this milieu I enjoy my daily life and am rather excited by many of the things which I learn; it is extremely pleasant to avail oneself of squash courts, swimming pools, lectures, the symphony, cocktail parties, and even the awesomely beautiful natural surroundings. The scenario is idyllic, the existence seductive.

As you might imagine, amidst the clutter of expensive sportscars, corporation presidents' daughters, politicians' sons, and uppercrust values, what I perceive as my political values force me into a fairly awkward position, producing an occasional trauma and more frequent lesser misgivings. I have had to adjust, modify some views, keep silent some things I could have said, and temper some of the passion it would have been, if nothing else, healthy to unleash. I have my reasons. I tell myself frequently that it is because I have come to love as people so many who are of different backgrounds and persuasions here. I have resolved that I must make my peace with the political sterility around me (just as the archconservative politician's son must reconcile himself to the universal liberalism he confronts) to fully appreciate the talented personalities, the rich intellectual life, and the exciting social and cultural possibilities which surround me. And if internally I might preserve the integrity of my value position, then this will be fine.

But there is the haunting self-doubt, the real possibility of erosion, attrition, of co-optation. And sometimes I can sense it happening. By finding my way to this privileged academic milieu, the spectre of affluence and comfort is more within my grasp than it ever was for my parents; this looms appealing and somewhat justifiable. Given the set of ideals and concerns I have outlined, it is finally disturbing. But there is more to the contradiction between my present environment and my identity than this tension.

Somewhere along the line of my experience, I was imbued with the idea that one must justify his existence; I guess the words "meaningful" and "relevant" enter here. It is something like an urge to create — create something ennobling or somehow worthwhile. The convictions and principles I embrace ask certain things of me in this vein. In my most lucid moments, they most profoundly confront me with what is the central paradox of my every day in this citadel of privilege.

If indeed I am concerned for the poor, the "huddled masses yearning to be free," what is my presence here contributing to the accomplishment of that justice which I advocate? Yes, I attend meetings, write an occasional article for the school paper, maybe change a mind or two once in a while. But I must be haunted with the knowl-

edge that I am comfortable while others are in misery; that I am nour-
ished while others starve; that I am growing while others are dying.
The contradictions mount, along with my insistence that I really do
care, that at least I am conscious of the problem and the inequality,
and that my awareness is commendable — all rationalizations which
pale before the realities of injustice and ineluctably destroyed human
potential.

And so I cling to the half-naive justification that the education
and experience may endow me with the insight, the reasoning, and the
determination to act effectively on my convictions, bringing attention
to the questions which sear conscience and demand response. And I
pray that I will not be compromised or rendered ineffectual. But
sometimes it frightens me to realize how much I may already have
conceded.

The problem with this is that it necessarily implies a faith in
that linguistic artifact from the sixties, "working within the system."
This is convenient, if not appropriate for me; I was weaned on the
vision and possibility of young liberal statesmen, I have played by
the rules thus far and have been rewarded by the system for doing
so, and now lately I have witnessed a resident's cronies convicted. But
the doubt persists. The suspicion grows that so many institutions are
unwilling, even incapable, of responding to human needs and moral
imperatives. I'm not sure at this point how many more times I will
hear officials advocate a tightening of the poor's belts as a solution to
inflationary woes, before my "faith in the system" disintegrates.

For now the confidence is tenuous, but viable. Were it to van-
ish tomorrow, I do not believe I would walk out of this dormitory and
this privileged milieu. I probably would pass my copy of *Comrade
George* amongst friends, find another meeting to attend, hold someone
very closely, and write my congressman.

Topic Nine

Race and Identity

Case 17 / Rather Be Somewhere Else

Keith felt little transition between living at home and coming to college;
it was as if he "had been snatched up and thrown into a completely alien
land." The culture shock of being a black person at a predominantly white

college was accompanied by the frustration of a 4.5:1 ratio of black males to black females. In addition to culture shock and an unnatural social situation, Keith had to cope with the death of his father.

At first Keith tended to ignore white people and walk away from tense or awkward situations, but he and other black students realized the necessity of having a voice in the affairs of the campus, especially if they affected black people. Although Keith is now more likely to speak up rather than walk away from an issue, and although he and black students in general are active in campus organizations, Keith asserts that there has not been adjustment, assimilation, or true integration; the community of black students is a psychological enclave within the college.

Viewing my experiences at college in retrospect, numerous thoughts stick out in my mind. Many of them pleasant, too many of them unpleasant.

In some way or another I've concluded that almost all the unpleasant ones can be either directly or indirectly related to my being black. I haven't always felt this way, or perhaps a better explanation is that I haven't always been aware of the fact that being in the situation I am, an urban black, in a small predominantly white rural college town, can cause and complicate many problems.

My freshman year at college was indeed a period for adjustment. Yet I feel that somehow it was too rushed and not an easy time in my life at all.

My older sister was a student at the same college and was somewhat of a cushion during my initial period of uncertainty.

When I drove into the freshman quad, with my sister and her boyfriend, I immediately experienced a feeling that was completely novel to me. Even now it's hard to describe exactly how I felt. I was extremely uneasy and apprehensive about being here. I think that I was actually afraid. I am sure some of the feelings I had were similar to the reaction that all freshmen experience, being away from home for the first time. I can't attribute everything I felt, though, to simply being in a new place. It was being in a situation that was extremely new to me in more than just the environment. There was a certain amount of inauthenticity that I immediately felt toward this new place. None of the things I saw were familiar to me and at that point I realized that I had very little to fall back on. The things I perceived weren't real to me. In no way did it resemble my home and in no way could I ever really make it my home. It was the contrast between what I was accustomed to and what I was presently faced with that caused me to feel the way I did. There were no transitions between my home and coming to this new place, and I felt as if I had been snatched up and thrown into a completely alien land.

Being surrounded by nothing but whites with an occasional black face in the crowd, left me feeling completely out of place. I remember looking around for a familiar face, knowing that I'd never find one. I must have looked like a small lost child.

When I went inside to see my room, one of my roommates was already there, and we exchanged forced smiles and hellos. He appeared to be in more trauma than myself. When I returned to the car my sister asked me how did I like it and I lied and told her it was fine. She must have sensed that I was lying or uncomfortable or something, and said she'd return as soon as she unpacked. I wanted to beg her not to leave me, but I knew I couldn't. I had always been a very independent person at home, and it was strange or a strange feeling to actually need someone. To complicate matters, I wasn't really that close to my sister, because she had been away in prep school and college for the past five years.

I eventually overcame my extreme feeling of being alienated. As I met more black people I began to feel more comfortable. However, even now, my senior year, I sometimes experience a tinge of the alienation and fear, when I am in a situation where I am surrounded by whites. I guess all the initial feelings of uncertainty and instability could be called culture shock.

During a rap session with some freshmen this year, some seniors including myself tried to explain the concept "culture shock." For each of us it meant something slightly different, but for all of us it was a result of being in a place where values, economic and social status, and interpersonal behavior all differed from what we were accustomed to.

I distinctly remember telling them that for me it was an initial shock and didn't persist for an indefinite amount of time, at least not in any extreme fashion. I said that I compensated for the shock by ignoring and overlooking most of the white people I saw. The easiest thing to do was not to acknowledge their existence. I said that I wasn't afraid to deal with white folks, but that I chose not to when it wasn't necessary. Of course, many situations would arise when it would be necessary, and at those times I would deal with whites in a manner I felt was appropriate to the situation. Over time though, I've changed my attitude about how I should or shouldn't relate to whites. I am not as reluctant to speak up and say what I think, whereas my freshman and sophomore years I was more inclined to display a gesture of disgust and merely shake my head and walk away. Sometimes I still deal with whites that way but not as much. Often in those earlier days I would sometimes just make a nasty comment and let the conversation end there, e.g., "That's a fucked-up racist attitude."

I remember one encounter I had with a fella on the soccer team. I immediately disliked him because he always used the term "you people," and like a lot of whites, because of little exposure to blacks (other than the boob tube), thought that blacks were the carefree, senuous darkies of old. Now I understand that many of the things that white people think aren't their fault, merely because of lack of exposure. The only black people they probably knew were Rochester and Beulah. Anyway this fella came up to me one day at soccer practice, while I was loosening up and said, "You know, Keith, I really would like to get to know you people much better." I said, "Oh really," and he said, "Yeah, I would but I find it hard to talk to you people. Everytime I try, no one really seems interested." At first I laughed, something I often do when I am offended. Then I told him, "Well man, it's like this, a lot of us really would rather be somewhere else but we don't have a choice. We know it's something we have to do. And unfortunately this college happens to be somewhat more generous with their financial aid than most places. We have to eat with you, go to class with you, sleep in the same dorms, and use the same bathrooms, and sometimes we just get tired of you and want to be left alone; do you understand"? When I finished talking I got up and walked away and that was the end of the conversation.

For a while I was the only black person on the soccer team, and often the team members would ask me questions about blacks, especially if there was a racial issue in the air. When the black students took over the grill and presented the grievances they wanted dealt with, i.e., increasing the number of black faculty and forming a black dorm, one of the guys asked me why did they do it. I snapped back, "because they were hungry." Sometimes I'll try to explain if the person I am talking to is reasonably sincere in his inquiry. But when I feel that a person just wants to know what the niggers are doing for his own selfish reasons, I become defensive immediately.

I guess I am reluctant to surrender information because of how easily it becomes distorted and misused. The college newspaper has a history of distorting and slanting the information given to them by the Black Student Union. No matter what we tell them they always manage to misconstrue what we've said. So the BSU established the policy of not saying anything unless we can be guaranteed that the information will be unaltered — reprinted *verbatim*.

White people really seem to misunderstand what blacks say, or at least they give the impression of misunderstanding. Take for instance this situation that occurred about a month ago. There is a white guy on campus in my class who I thought was rather down to earth. He was in my dorm freshman year and since then we've maintained fairly consistent contacts. Sometimes we go to the local bar and have a few drinks or go to my room or his room. He's maintained the same type of relationship with several of my good black friends too.

Well about a month ago, he attended a dinner with several of the trustees and gave the impression of being the authority on blacks and black/white relationships at the college. He completely gave the trustees the wrong impression of black student attitudes here. He made it seem like we were the same old happy-go-lucky, carefree negroes. Supposedly he had remarked that, "Oh, yes, the blacks are quite happy here — they're really beginning to integrate into the campus life." To a certain extent what he said was absolutely true; blacks had begun to integrate into the campus life — at least the activities and organizations. It has become apparent to many of us that the only way to ensure that we were represented fairly was to do it ourselves. Our involvement in the college organizations was not out of an overall concern for the well-being of the campus, but for ourselves. This doesn't necessarily mean that we are happy or overjoyed about being here, only that we realize the necessity of having a voice in the affairs of the campus, especially if they affect black people.

So in some cases, my reluctance to communicate freely has been reinforced by the actions of some of my so-called white friends.

I guess being at college has taught me a lot about people, both black and white. There are a number of black people that I've become equally suspicious of as whites. I know that there are always people you distrust, but in some instances the black people I was forced to distrust were supposedly my good friends.

This institution perpetuates an extreme competitiveness, many times outside of the purely academic realm. In the face of competition, some of my good friends have completely overlooked our friendship. There was one incident in particular where a certain brother tried to incriminate me as a shady character, that is, my interest in women was purely physical. What had obviously happened was that we were interested in the same sister, and he was willing to use any means possible to eliminate me as a competitor. At the time I was a freshman and not particularly concerned about my image being damaged by rumors and gossip. The incident did however make me realize something very important. What I realized was that the situation we were in, more than anything else, had caused this brother to act the way he did.

My freshman year was the first one of coeducation at college. At the time there were about sixteen black females and seventy black males. In a situation where the ratio was that imbalanced, one's friendships often fell victim to his physical needs. I had little trouble securing female companions, but most males found themselves traveling to other colleges in search of black women. Too often this "road-tripping" extended past the weekends, and many brothers suffered academically. The lack of black females really created an air of distrust among the males. I can't help but to place much of the blame on the administration. I refuse to believe that they were ignorant of the type of problems this situation would cause. What's even worse is that the black women on this campus were constantly being pursued. I could be guaranteed of finding at least several other brothers when I went to visit a sister. At the time I wasn't perceptive enough nor particularly concerned with the enormous amount of pressure this was putting on the women. It appeared that few of the brothers were aware of or cared about it either. Coupled with the academic pressures and the problems related to just being freshmen, it's surprising how many women did survive.

Another awkward situation created by a shortage of black females was interracial relationships. Most of the relationships were between black males and white females. As a matter of fact all of the interracial couples, my first two years at least, were known through the grapevine.

Almost all of the brothers who had developed relationships with white women, mostly on a physical basis, preferred to keep it quiet. To openly interact with a white woman other than in casual fashion was a direct conflict with being black. It was admission to the stigma that all black males secretly desire white flesh.

I understood the racial implications behind maintaining such a relationship even before I came to college. I haven't, nor do I ever intend to participate in such a relationship. I don't condemn interracial relationships. I just don't partake in them. I feel enough pressures without adding that extra burden. Besides, I've always found color in people a much more attractive quality. Several of my good friends have had secret sexual relationships with white women and have at times encouraged me to pursue several white females that they knew were interested in me. I always declined and thought it much healthier to maintain a relationship where I could display my feelings without fear of being ostracized by my peers.

I imagine that's the only rumor about me that I've never been concerned about dispersing. I know that it's a well-circulated rumor because a certain white female once made a remark about my not "crossing the line."

This certain white female is presently engaged to a black alum. She has always been interested in black men, at least since I've been acquainted with her. Anyway, her roommate usually types my papers. One evening we were sitting around drinking coffee while she corrected one of my papers. We were talking about the upcoming Christmas holiday, and they were considering having a small party before everyone went home. During the course of the conversation this certain white female said she hoped that she didn't get too high, because she was extremely vulnerable and could be easily seduced. Then she said, "Well, Keith, if you're around I won't have to worry, 'cause everyone knows that you'd never cross the line." All I could do was laugh, and deep inside I was rather glad that everyone knew.

I've been approached in several other fashions, some not as subtle as the one mentioned. I shy away from aggressive women, black and white. I figure, well if they act that way toward me, then they probably act in a similar fashion around a lot of other fellas and I'd rather not get involved. This is a small community and a lot of private business often becomes public among blacks and whites.

My sophomore year was the period I experienced a great deal of change. I had to face up to a lot of conflicts and problems I neglected freshman year, if I were to remain in college. I had to overcome a recklessness I exhibited freshman year and begin to take my academics more seriously. My recklessness freshman year can be directly attributed to the death of my father. My father died my second month in college and a partial reaction was a development of a kind of apathy. I became extremely reckless and my academics suffered tremendously. So my sophomore year was a mending of old undesirable ways. I lived in a dorm with about sixteen other black males and we were on an isolated end of the campus. We got to know each other very well as a result and I am sure that having a somewhat familiar peer group made my task of correcting my ways easier. They were familiar in that they resembled many of the fellas I associated with in high school and the constant interacting with them in our own social environment was a direct reinforcement I needed. My sophomore year ended on a very good note and I moved on to junior year with few complications.

I guess, in terms of academic success, my sophomore year was the turning point. I ended up with a B— average sophomore year while taking two extra courses to make up for my deficiencies freshman year. Since then my grades have been B— or better.

The problem still remained of being in a completely alien environment though. Although my mother was aware of the new environment I was entering, she had failed to make me understand the impact it would have upon me. She knew how independent I was and was more concerned with impressing upon me the importance of doing well academically. I guess she assumed that I would manage socially, in spite of the differences. I guess I have managed, but only with a great deal of difficulty. When I say "manage" I really want to specify that this in no way implies a social adjustment or assimilation. It implies just what it says, I managed.

So a great deal of social pressure still exists in spite of my academic success. I guess that strange feeling I first had in the freshman quad should have told me something then — but it didn't until recently — and it is that although I'd eventually adjust to college academically, I would never be able to adjust beyond academics or overcome the social pressures as long as I was in this situation.

Case 18 / The Important Things Didn't Happen in Class

Nicole was recruited from an all-black high school in Detroit. She was told that there would be a few adjustment problems at the small liberal arts college in New England, but that the educational quality of the school would make up for those problems. On arrival at the predominantly white school she felt that she was viewing "an ocean of salt with a few specks of pepper." The "few adjustment problems" included coping with social class differences, with an unnatural ratio of black men to black women, with teachers who had difficulty interacting with anyone but conventional middle-class students, with other black students who urged uniformity of thought and action, and with the political and economic realities of running an Upward Bound program in the community. As she is about to graduate, Nicole feels "as though for the past four years I've been in a state of suspension and now it's time to start doing things again." She is applying to law schools with the intention of eventually doing something beneficial for herself and others.

I remember being somewhat afraid when I entered college in the fall of 1971. I wasn't quite sure of what I was afraid. I was afraid of new things, new people, and I suppose a new sense of freedom. Funny thing . . . this fear had not been felt when I came up for pre-freshman weekend. I was glad to be so far away from my father. I really hadn't expected him to let me visit that weekend since my upbringing had been the most sheltered of shelters. The day after he said that I could come, he borrowed $185.00 from me to pay the mortgage on his house. I'd had a job since I entered high school and my savings account contained enough for such emergencies, and for everything else I needed, since I really had to rely on my own devices for money.

I remember helping my father out on prior occasions when we lived in South Carolina. I was born in Aiken, South Carolina (there are nine of us in all). My father was a cashier in one of the local chain stores; my mother never worked because she was sheltered just as

much as we were, if not more so. We lived in the white neighborhood and were bussed all the way across town to "our" school. "Our"
school contained grades one through twelve while the other school was
divided into grammar, junior high, and high schools. My older sister
Valerie, after reaching high school, attended the same school as I did
even though there was a high school just across the street from our
house. When they had football games, we could have sat on the front
porch and watched but my father always warned us that when the
white kids were using the football field, we were to stay inside the
house. It didn't really matter because he made us stay in the house
most of the time anyway. We didn't have very many friends over because somehow my father always thought the house wasn't presentable
enough. He always wore white shirts to work. The other folks in town
always looked up to him because he was the highest paid black man
in town, making $80 per week. We were the brightest children in the
school we attended. Having the last name Alexis was enough to make
one teacher's pet. My first cousin, born out of wedlock, bore the last
name Alexis and used to pretend that he was our brother. My older
brother would find great pleasure in telling everyone that Raymond
was our cousin and not our brother.

When I was thirteen, my father got into a little trouble, trouble
that meant consequences for all of us. He came home one day and got
the gun. My mother asked where he was going. She held the baby and
he started to play with the baby, saying that he was going to kill a
snake. I remember his exact words: "I'm going to kill me a snake
buddy." He left the house and did not return. At about midnight a
friend of my father's came by and told my mother that my father was
in jail under a $1000 bond for drunken driving and illegal possession
of a weapon. To make matters worse he had threatened a white man
with the gun. We were all afraid because conflict with white people in
that little town always proved to be overwhelmingly distressing. Once
before, some students at my school had marched through the little
town for desegregation of the schools and the parents of the leaders of
the march had lost their jobs while other parents were threatened
with the same loss. The day following the march the KKK arrived and
held a rally in the town square, and that was the end of the marches.

I had gotten my first job that summer, baby-sitting. I only had
the job because the woman had talked to my father and told him that
all I had to do was to watch her two small school-age children and I
wouldn't be cleaning and washing dishes. My father had said that we
would starve before he saw any of us working in a white woman's
kitchen. When my father got into trouble, I was sure I'd lose my job
but my employer never even mentioned it. She or her husband continued to pick me up in the afternoons to watch the kids. My father

went to court and was fined $1000 plus eighteen months' probation. My mother said he was probably placed on probation because the town did not want the responsibility of taking care of nine children. My father refused to go back to work because he said that now they had him under their thumb and he wouldn't take it. He would tell me to go to the store and get cigarettes; when I asked him for money he would tell me to use my money. I was really afraid because school was gonna start in a couple of weeks (late August) and we didn't have school clothes — actually we barely had food. Relatives gave us all the food we had. Moreover, I didn't want to face the kids at school, whom I hadn't seen all summer, or my teachers. My father would be labeled a troublemaker and that would make us the center for taunting at school. About a week before school was to start, my father's probation officer gave him permission to leave South Carolina and go to Detroit where we had relatives. (Coincidentally the probation officer's last name was the same as my last name — Alexis. He's white of course.) My father left us in the country with a distant cousin, and he and my mother and the two youngest children went to Detroit. He sent for us about three days before the schools opened there.

At that time we lived with an aunt. The grammar school I was to attend had just been integrated. I remembered the problems in Greensborough, North Carolina when the schools had been integrated. Little children were beaten and parents lost their jobs. I was scared, because although I had lived in a white neighborhood in South Carolina, all the things I remembered were negative. When we went to the store they sent their dogs after us. There was even a man who would chase us all the way home in his car, and yell, "Nigger, you goddamned niggers, get on home."

My fear was not unfounded because the white kids would chase us home everyday. We didn't have transfers so we were all placed in the lowest tracks in the school. In my own class, the students resented my answering questions that they couldn't answer. I had always thought that white kids were infinitely brighter than black kids, so I got a bit of pleasure out of knowing that in fact I knew quite a few things that they didn't know. Overall I hated the school because at recess time there wasn't anyone; I was the only black person in the eighth grade and our recess was at a different time from the other grades.

My father finally had saved enough money to rent an apartment of our own and we moved to the heart of the black ghetto in Detroit. The new school was all black but I encountered some rather strange things there also. When I transferred from the first school, they had placed me in the next highest track. Academically, my experience was a repeat of my sixth-grade experience in South Carolina. I graduated number two in the class but not before being taunted because I spoke "proper," as they called it. By the time the year was over, however, I had new friends. My all-black high school was just across the parking lot from the elementary school. My high school experience was riddled with demonstrations and protests which I took part in because they were fun (none of them being really worthwhile causes) and they also meant no classes. There was no chance of reprisal against me or any of my family because the numbers were so large, and anyway Detroit was such a big place that such threats couldn't be very effective. My father never knew that I'd taken part in them however, because his comments about the situation were always negative.

I had always wanted to go to college, but my father's attitude had made me want to go more than ever. As a young woman in high school, I had none of the privileges that others my age had. I wasn't allowed to attend school functions unless I was in them and in most cases I wasn't allowed to be in them. I wasn't allowed company as other young ladies were, and judging from my older sister's experience, I'd never be allowed any as long as I resided in his house. I wasn't allowed many female friends either, since they had to meet a certain color standard (fair-skinned) set by my father. He wanted me to be a teacher and attend State University as my sister had done. I told him that there were already too many teachers, and at any rate I didn't want to be a teacher. I wanted to be a lawyer. Actually I wanted to get as far away from home as possible so as to have a legitimate excuse for being there very infrequently. My counselors thought that I should go east to school and I agreed wholeheartedly.

One morning, a monitor came in and informed my English teacher that eight students were wanted in the counseling office, myself included. When we arrived, there was a white man who looked rather frightened and a black guy. They were introduced as William Minser and John Wilson from a small liberal arts college in New England. By the time we arrived, Mr. Minser, after reviewing our transcripts, had informed the counselor that he could only look seriously at two students, myself and Avis Fanning. We were numbers one and two in the class respectively. We all remained, and Mr. Minser and John proceeded to tell us about Berkshire College. Berkshire College was becoming coeducational the year we would enter. There were pictures showing black students lying on the grass in front of Talbot Hall and behind Maywell House. The pictures were very beautiful and the people in them looked very happy. It was small and picturesque and reminded me of the small town in South Carolina. I had really loved the town with its mountains, pecan trees, peach trees, plum trees, that bore pink, yellow, and white flowers in the spring and summer. The pictures of New England town had the same kinds of flowering trees. John informed us that with some hard work we would make it through Berkshire College with relative ease. He told us of the Afro-American Society which sponsored social and cultural events for black students to make things more bearable since there were so few blacks on campus. We were told that there would be a few adjustment problems but that given the educational quality of the school it would be well worth it.

After they had gone, my counselor pulled out the college catalogue and told us about Berkshire College. It was all-male, in the most competitive category of colleges, and had about 1000 students. I wanted to go to a small college because I didn't feel that I'd be able to perform in a big university setting. I didn't get along well with all the concrete and skyscrapers in Detroit and besides New England town was in New England over nine hundred miles away. I couldn't get much further away from home than that.

When Avis and I came to visit Berkshire College, the weekend didn't start out very promising. It was raining and muddy and the New England town we were seeing was nothing at all like the pictures we had been shown. I looked at Avis and she looked at me and we said almost simultaneously, "I don't think I like this place." The next day the sun came out and things looked better. After meeting most of the black students here at the time I began to enjoy myself. There was a big party in the center (Afro Am) and I really began to enjoy the weekend. Prior to visiting Berkshire College, I had received a telegram from Trinity College advising me of the amount of scholarship they would provide. They were providing a full ride for the first year at least. No one bothered to interview me while I was here (we were just watched, I was told later, to discern any adverse reaction), but I did speak with one of the Deans and "quite by accident" (on purpose) mentioned my telegram from Trinity and showed it to him. I was accepted at Berkshire and scholarship announcements were made concurrently. Despite the fact that the cost of attending Berkshire was approximately 200 dollars less than Trinity, the college offered me 100 dollars more in the total package with only 150 dollars of loan for the entire year. Trinity's loan had been about 400 dollars. Well that was it. Berkshire made the best offer in terms of money. I had visited and liked the place. I had never seen Trinity but I knew it was bigger, plus Berkshire was rated higher in the circle of colleges.

During the summer, prior to coming to Berkshire, the conflicts between my father and me continued to mount. I could offer no protest against his house rules since it was simply unheard of as well as unprecedented. I could talk to my mother about it, and though she

sympathized completely she couldn't do anything about it. At the time
I had a job as a driver training assistant. I could work for twelve hours
per day or not work for any hours and still be paid because I always
did whatever paper work had to be done. I usually stayed at work the
entire twelve hours because it was the only time I had away from
home. My father knew that I didn't always work, however. One Saturday morning, I started out for work and my father asked where I was
going. I said I was going to work. He told me that there was plenty of
work to do around the house and to stay home. It just so happened
that on this particular day I had to schedule classes for the next two
weeks. This would be a full day's (12 hours) work since the driver
education facility was a trailer outside of the school and the only way
to contact people was by telephone. I would also have to relocate
people who had failed previous classes and reschedule them for the
next session. It had to be done on Saturday because people were either
in summer school or held jobs during the week. If I didn't do it, the
director would have to do it, since no one else had bothered to learn
how to. The director was a Japanese guy whom I had adopted as my
second father because he always looked out for me. He had taught
me to sign his name and anything that came through I could sign . . .
including passes for myself when I had been in school. I had my own
key to the trailer, and he trusted me completely. I was responsible for
signing and submitting time sheets for the driver education instructors
and even making out the time sheet for my boss. Around the trailer the
instructors called me "Boss Lady" and still do when I go back to visit.
Sometimes the director didn't come in because I was there and no
one would ever know he wasn't there since if asked I said he was out
to lunch or out in traffic with students.

My boss called that day to tell me I was needed for scheduling. My father told him that I wasn't coming in. I was so angry I didn't
know what to do. This very job had supported me all through high
school because my father's priority was not his kids. It's true that we
were poor, but some of the things we didn't have we could have had. I
often thought that he only cared about us as income tax deductions.

At age sixteen I graduated from the chore of dishwashing. My
sisters had inherited the job. Well, I washed dishes for three meals
that day, following my father's orders. He told me to go into the
basement, roll up the carpeting, and mop the floor. I was furious but
knew that I couldn't say anything. When he went to work on Monday
I went to work also. That morning he told me to be in the house at five
o'clock from now on or find someplace else to live. When I went to
work the next day I asked my boss about a place to live. He told me I
should ask Tony, the other assistant. Tony said he had two older sis-

ters who shared an apartment and he'd ask them about it. In the meantime I could stay at his place. He lived about four blocks from my
parents. He loaned me his car and I went home and packed. My
mother told me to keep in touch and let her know how I was doing.
"Take care of yourself and go to school in September. I love you,
Nicole." I took my things to my friend's apartment and returned to
work. I moved to my friend's sisters' apartment two days later. When
I am in Detroit I still live with one of the sisters and her two children.
Needless to say, my chief motive for attending Berkshire College had
disappeared. Tony's sisters were four and six years older than myself;
we got along swell, and absolutely nothing was required of me. I
couldn't pay them rent, so when I wasn't working I attempted to clean,
wash dishes, anything, but they wouldn't hear of it. The older sister
got up at five every morning and got the kids off to school, then returned to bed. The younger sister would get up when I did to go to
work. They were really nice, and I couldn't believe it. Neither of them
had completed high school, and when I mentioned not going to school
they would not hear that either. We went shopping for a trunk and
clothes, and in September I was off to Berkshire College.

When I got to New England town it was beautiful, but there
was something quite different from pre-freshman weekend. Everywhere I looked, there were white people. When I had been here before all I saw were black people. I knew that the school was very
much predominantly white but somehow I thought that I would only
see black folks. The freshman quad was filled with white students and
their parents running back and forth. The only black students I saw
were the three who had arrived in the cab with me from the airport.
Then a sister ran out of the entry I was to live in and offered to help
Avis and myself with our bags. She had a very strange (almost white)
accent and kept asking if we had met all of these people I had never
heard of before. I responded to her rather coldly, I suppose, so she
grabbed the bags and ran upstairs. Avis and I had both asked for
singles so as to avoid rooming with any white girls and had asked for
each other as roommates if that wasn't possible. They gave us singles
adjacent to each other. When we got upstairs and Kathy had gone, we
both broke into hysterical laughter.

When we went to dinner that night there were two long tables
completely filled with black people. All the black folks on campus had
congregated in the freshman quad. I didn't feel comfortable because
even though all the folks at the table were black, they were strangers.
Avis and I leaned on each other pretty heavily at that time. There
were also a lot more fellows than there were women so that the
women were more or less forced to talk. I couldn't force myself to be

very vocal because I had never been very outgoing. That night four or five of the fellows came by and because I didn't know how to talk to men, my responses were very cold and sharp. It didn't take them long to get the message and they left. That night the freshmen were introduced to the Afro-Am society and what a riotous introduction it was. Without going into detailed exposé we were essentially told that we were either *Black* or we weren't. We were told of the racism on this campus and to stand up for our rights. Most of the whites hadn't really encountered black folks or ghetto blacks anyway and wouldn't know how to respond if you decided that you wanted some of everything that Berkshire College had to offer. We were warned about Chriswell house and the Snowden Hall areas as being "redneck" territory. And for certain of us who were frightened or easily intimidated, there were members of the Afro-Am who would be intimidators for the rest of the year.

Well this was Berkshire College. Fortunately for us, most of the freshmen were from all black inner-city schools, and the general personality of the upperclassmen was like home and quite welcomed in the mist of what was beginning to look like an ocean of salt with a few specks of pepper.

There were only sixteen black women and approximately seventy black men. My impression was that most of the women had come here with that thought in mind. The funny thing was that I had never considered the ratio of men to women and consequently had no intention of trying to capitalize on the situation. And besides, I never seemed to see seventy men since I only counted the ones who were potentially attractive.

The women began to play on the ratio but forgot one important variable — or perhaps not one — Smith, Holyoke, Vassar, and Wellesley. There were numerous parties where women from these schools were imported and the Berkshire women were simply ignored. During the week, the Berkshire women were clamored for but once the weekend began, so did the roadtripping. A particular resentment for Smith began to develop. I found it quite amusing, because I didn't feel that I had lost anything in the shuffle.

Classes were another experience. In most classes I was the only black person, and the experience was rather awkward. I remember Government 101 in particular. There were three black students in the class, Brenda, Barton, and myself. I hated this particular class with a passion. All of the white students ran off at the mouth, saying nothing important, as if the only thing they knew how to do was talk. We had been advised that Strauser just loved niggers and it began to show almost immediately. His questions were always a paragraph long and contained so many fifteen-letter words that one needed a dictionary to decipher the questions. Whenever he said anything about blacks, the eyes of the class would immediately turn in our direction since we sat near each other. He also had the terrible habit of putting us on the spot whenever he brought up anything even remotely related to blacks. I began to stare out of the window for the entire class period everyday, because I just didn't want to hear the nothing that the other students took pages of notes on every day.

The assignment for one particular day was the book, *The Greening of America*. When I began reading the book, it sounded so much like the class discussions that I put it down after five pages. In class the next day, he began to ask questions of various students in an effort to get a description of three levels of consciousness contained in the book. As usual, people began to talk a lot of bullshit. He told us to take out a sheet of paper and define them. Well I obviously couldn't so I wrote that they didn't mean anything to me since there was no clear-cut definition and as far as I was concerned the book was useless since it was based upon the three levels of consciousness as a premise. He collected the papers and read them. Then he said, "Miss Alexis, I believe your definition is the best one here." I'm not sure what the moral of the story is.

My final paper for his course, however, was an expression of the disgust I was beginning to feel for Berkshire College. I completely ignored the topic and wrote about "a semester of Government 101." I got a C— on the paper but I got the disgust off my chest. I was becoming more and more frustrated because I didn't know how to study, I had never studied, and I just didn't know how to. I was even more frustrated when I received my grades because somehow I had managed to get three B's and one C and I hadn't done any work. I knew I wasn't performing anywhere near where I thought I should be able to, yet I received the highest average of the freshmen black women.

Well, I was the first person to leave here for Christmas vacation. I spent part of the next semester happily away from Berkshire College at a free school in Boston headed by a black man who was a former Berkshire graduate. The school was beautiful, and the people were beautiful, and coming back to Berkshire wasn't something that I looked forward to. Second semester was horrible. I had been labelled a cold sister . . . well to be more specific, a bitch. I wasn't getting along very well with the other women because we just didn't have the same things to talk about. The majority of the women seemed very much interested in competing with each other in terms of men. At the end of the semester, all I could think about was Detroit, the beach, and the good times I was gonna have. I was the first person to leave at the end of the semester.

At the end of the year six of us had gotten together to room for sophomore year. The quad consisted of Avis, Denise, Pamela, and Nicole and the double had Lisa and Kathy. I think we picked the best possible team. The year was rather uneventful. By now we were quite accustomed to the white girls who came into the bathroom and stared. "Wow, that looks really wonderful, fantastic. How do you do that?"

"Oh, there's nothing to it. My hair behaves like this quite naturally. If it did anything else, I'd start to ask questions."

First semester I got my second D, and since I'd never seen D's before I figured it was about time to do something different. By second semester I was about as adjusted to Berkshire as I would ever be. It was also this semester that I had my first contact with one of the new black professors. The upperclassmen who had taken him the first semester were really impressed but also just a little bit frightened. If *they* were afraid, that meant that *we* surely would be; but a bunch of us mustered enough courage to take his course: The Economics of Being Black. I was already very hesitant, and the first few days of class only enhanced my fear. He called all of the black students by their first names and referred to the three solitary white students out of about forty as "Mr." and "Miss." He demanded clear and precise answers to questions and had no bones about telling a student that he didn't know what he was talking about. The first time he called on me, I wa so scared that I bungled the whole thing. I think he realized what had happened because he let me slide. Then came the mid-term, the equivalent of a twenty-page paper with five days in which to complete it. We were encouraged to work together to discuss the issues raised and then write our own exams separately. It took him approximately two weeks to return the papers. When he did he placed the grade distribution on the board and announced the names of persons who had received A's or B+'s. I was shocked to no end when I learned that I had received an A—.

Two of my roommates were making plans to exchange during our junior year to Howard University, and things were beginning to look pretty lonely for me for the upcoming year. We had all developed a really close relationship because the black women in the freshman class were rather ridiculous. At the beginning of that year, the sophomore black women had organized a sort of orientation meeting with them. Unfortunately there had been several upperclassmen at Berkshire during the summer programs for the freshmen before they entered. Therefore, the incoming freshmen had already been oriented in a negative fashion toward our entire class, both men and women. We had thought the meeting to be a good idea because during the latter part of our second semester freshman year, the tension had become so high that we all got together and screamed at each other. It was very beneficial because everyone found out how other people felt about them and their actions. At that time we decided that whenever we saw someone obviously screwing up, we'd pull their coat and tell them what we thought about it. She might not agree but at least somebody else's opinion would be known. The freshmen women did not take our efforts very kindly. Their reply was that just because we had really made a mess of things our freshman year, it did not mean that they would follow suit. They felt that they could adequately deal with the men, the academics, and the social environment at Berkshire without any help. The irony was that they were less well equipped to deal with Berkshire than we had been, and we had made mistakes and felt that we would probably make more mistakes. It's true that they should have been better equipped academically than we were, having come from better schools, but in other areas they were lacking, since most of them came from sheltered homes or middle-income families and knew very little about racism, and there was necessarily a tension because the blacks who were already here were from a different background. Quite frankly, however, their reaction was not a surprise.

By the end of the semester the new black women (the majority) found themselves doing terribly academically, and their social lives were very chaotic. The black men began to approach us and asked us to talk to a few of them about the way they carried themselves. I wasn't willing to approach any of them because I felt that it would be taken negatively. I sensed that any attempt at talking with them would be unappreciated and taken as something else. At this time, I began to hear various rumors about the freshmen women being afraid of me. I supposed this to be due to the fact that while I wouldn't approach anyone concerning their affairs, social or otherwise, I had no qualms about speaking exactly what was on my mind in their presence even if it happened to concern one of them. As second semester opened I began to think about the coming year. Avis and Denise would be exchanging to Howard University in September, and Kathy was trying to go to Amherst for the first semester of our junior year. Increasingly I began to think about living arrangements for the next year. Having white roommates was simply out of the question, and just as much out of the question was living with the freshman black women. I didn't feel particularly comfortable with them because there was a distinct difference in values, expectations, and reactions to many things. Quite frankly, I felt that making it academically would be somewhat hindered by the problems of adjustment to our obvious differences if we were thrown into a very close living situation.

Lisa Allen and I had become rather close toward the end of the semester. We could talk to each other about mutually important things. We didn't agree on everything, but our disagreements were handled with ease. She, too, was looking for living arrangements for the coming year. She came to me one day and asked if I'd like to live off campus the next year. I said, "Sure." She stated that I was the only woman on campus that she could live with and get along with. The only problem was going to be whether or not I could obtain permission from the Dean's Office. She was number one on the list but since I had never thought seriously of moving off campus, I had never signed up. We talked to one of the deans and he said the circumstances were unusual and therefore arrangements could be made. Lisa was the only black junior woman who would return the next year as a senior; therefore, her roommate would necessarily be an underclassman. He moved my name from the bottom of the waiting list to the top.

Junior year I formed the closest relationship to anyone I've ever had, not only at Berkshire but anywhere. Lisa and I became extremely close. She cared about what I thought, and many times, even though she had reservations about what I was feeling, she never attacked but asked questions, her questions making me question in turn and generally causing me to at least reevaluate those feelings. We talked hours on end about Berkshire and what was happening to us and everyone else here. I didn't like Berkshire because it placed me in a state of, I guess, being nowhere. The academics of Berkshire seemed so unreal, the people seemed unreal, and increasingly it became harder to identify with other black students since it seemed the college was doing some grand experiment in coming up with the perfect black Berkshire student. I didn't identify with any black student who felt comfortable here because it implied being comfortable in other places also. I can't be comfortable because I know where I came from and am going back to, and the black people in the world out there, the real world, are terribly uncomfortable.

In October of my junior year I had my first real contact with the New England town Upward Bound Program. Lisa had attended an Upward Bound board meeting where they were discussing one of the young women in the program. She was living with a family in the town and was doing terribly because she couldn't adjust to living with the family and living in New England town. Lisa suggested that she could live with us since we had an off-campus apartment and there was plenty of room. She wanted to consult me, but she was reasonably sure that it was okay. The Board had to get permission from National Upward Bound since Upward Bound students had never lived with college students. National Upward Bound said yes on the condition that we were black. Laurie came to live with us on trial two days later.

Problems developed because, while she was only sixteen we

didn't feel that we had to be strictly motherly types. We wanted to make it a threesome. At first things were okay. Soon, however, Laurie wanted to be left alone completely to do whatever she felt like doing at any given time. When she first came to live with us she would tell us voluntarily where she was going when she went out. There came a time however when she didn't volunteer it and openly resented our asking. She reiterated that we were not her mother and therefore didn't tell her what to do. To complicate matters, Laurie had a medical problem. She had to wear corrective lenses which she refused to wear. One night after numerous other occasions I was having a talk with her about wearing the lenses. She told me it was none of our business; she knew she was supposed to wear them and she would when she got ready to. At that point I blew my stack because the lenses were for her own good not mine, and quite frankly I didn't appreciate her particular response because she lived in our apartment – free of obligation. The Upward Bound Program gave us $60 a month $20 of which went to Laurie in the form of a five-dollar weekly allowance. She was completely selfish. Everything that belonged to her she kept in the corner of the room which she shared with Lisa. She refused to take part in household chores. We went to the Board with the lens problem. The president sent Laurie a message by us. "Either wear the lenses or she would find her another place to live because part of our responsibility was to see that she wore them."

What angered me most was the more we tried to help the more she threw it in our faces. It reminded me of ultra-liberal whites and the shit they put up with in terms of some blacks, which does more harm than good, because of guilt feelings. I had no guilt feeling about Laurie since I came from a rough background myself. In the spring, because of financial difficulties, it was decided to make the Upward Bound House in which all the male students resided, coeducational. I applied for the position of female counselor. Numerous other black women stated that they wanted to apply for the position but, as things will have it, they foolishly did not apply because they felt that inevitably I would get the position.

Lisa graduated, but our friendship remains intact.

In August of my senior year I arrived at the Upward Bound House, which was a total disaster. The remodeling to be completed over the summer was nowhere near completion. I changed into my jeans and began work. The students began to arrive two days later. The program was in financial trouble and community trouble. The students were not performing, and the viability of the program was being questioned. This year we do or die. The five adults in the house had to tighten things up. We constructed rules and discussed them with the President of the Board and the Chairman of the Personnel Committee. They were satisfactory. There were five students returning who knew what a good time they had had the previous year. There would be two new students. We expected protest and it's exactly what we got. In the beginning they tried everything and got punished for it. I heard things reiterated about our not being their parents. There's a fallacy in that argument, however, since we are their legal guardians while they reside here. There being five adults in the house, two white and three black, gave them another tactic. Why not play the counselors off against the resident couple. Needless to say, part of our responsibility became that of educating the resident family concerning what black children will try to do to them. By mid-semester this became very tiresome and irritating. It was taking too much of our time from our studies and there was hardly time to do anything except baby-sit the Upward Bound students who were really playing games anyway. Important things like reminding them New England town wasn't real were being neglected in lieu of the games they wanted to play. It's hard to explain my disappointment in terms of the things they were forcing me to do instead. It's a difficult task to talk to three young ladies about being a woman and what may or may not be happening to them in New England town when they feel that they already know everything that I could possibly tell them. It makes me think of why relationships with the underclassmen are so difficult. I wonder if I'm superiority oriented. I don't think so because I'm willing to listen, at least, and more to anyone who has something to say. I don't start out with the premise, "She doesn't know anything more than I do," particularly since everyone has different experiences that teach them different things.

Living in the house has had repercussions in other areas. My interaction with other students on campus is very limited since most of my time is spent at the house. I still hear the rumor that the other women on campus are afraid of me. It's getting so that I'm not really terribly concerned because for the most part, all they know about me is my name, and I think it would be awful to be so easily intimidated.

I'll be glad to get out of here in June. There are very few people here that I'll miss and I'm sure the opposite is true. I don't feel that I've gotten very much out of college. The most important things didn't happen in class. I feel as though for the past four years I've been in a state of suspension and now it's time to start doing things again.

Hopefully I'll be going to law school next year and the reason is no longer my father. I want to do something beneficial for myself and for others at the same time.

Topic Ten

Ethnicity and Identity

Case 19 / We Were from Different Worlds

Deborah wants to be loved and be in love. When she is with Peter, she is not certain how she feels. When their relationship is carried on by letter, she realizes her difficulty in distinguishing illusion from reality. Her discomfort with sexual relations results in their being best friends. Strain in the relationship leads to her telling Peter that although she feels love for him, it is apparent that their life styles are incompatible. Deborah's life style has evolved from her New York Jewish background, while Peter's life style derives from his Waspish Philadelphia society. "Though we were together, we were not always *with* one another."

Harvard Square, Park Street, South Station . . . "All aboard for New York!" I was on my weekly journey home, leaving Cambridge and its super-sophistication behind. Kathy and I boarded the train and forged through the aisles jammed with beer can–laden soldiers.

"Oh, there's a guy from my music section," I said, smiling at him down the aisle. He returned the smile hesitantly, looking puzzled.

Kathy and I chatted, trying to kill time as best we could until we got to New York, basis of comfort and love. About half an hour later, Peter came over to introduce himself:

"I'm Peter Shaw. I gather you girls are from Cambridge, but I'm afraid I don't recognize you."

"We're in the same Music I section."

"Oh, that," he chuckled, "I rarely get there and when I do, I'm only half awake. It's so elementary."

"Oh, really, I don't find it that way. In fact, I find it quite difficult."

I was glad when he and Kathy began to exchange tales about European musicians and recital halls (they had both lived there for several years) since his haughty super-sophistication was precisely what wearied me about Cambridge and what I was trying to escape. I was happy to retreat into my own world, until Peter mentioned that he was en route to St. Thomas, Virgin Islands, and I chimed in with romantic tales of St. John and how that was really where he ought to go. He listened seriously, asked me fliply if I wanted to come along and then called his pals over to tell them what I had said. The three had decided last night over Scotch that they would take off the next morning. I was very much fascinated by their impulsiveness and the offhanded way in which they treated their decision implied to me that they must do things like this all the time.

At Westchester Kathy got off and Peter took her seat. As his friends disappeared into the next car, I dreaded the thought that I would have to make conversation with him for the remainder of the trip. Kathy seemed to do all right, but I wasn't interested in him and he certainly wouldn't be interested in anything I had to say. While he talked at me, I more or less tuned out, trying to maintain a reasonably attentive expression.

"When will we get to N.Y. so I can get rid of this character?"

As he persisted in conversation, I began to think that there was something intriguing about him. "He must be a member of a society family: coming from Philadelphia, living in Europe for years, wearing a fancy suit, a pink shirt, and a Thai silk tie, having enough money to take off for St. Thomas on a lark. He was a 'gentleman' through and through, certainly not my type of man!"

As we talked, an extremely precocious boy of about ten sauntered over to us and sat himself down on the arm of Peter's seat.

"Are you two in love?" he asked point-blank. Peter and I looked at each other and burst out laughing.

"What do you mean by that?" Peter asked.

"You know, do you like to kiss, are you engaged, planning to get married, that sort of thing? I was watching the two of you from back of the car and thought you must be."

I certainly didn't know how to respond and waited to take a cue from Peter, who nonchalantly told him we were not engaged, but that we had known each other a long while and were friends. For the rest of the trip we made believe we were boyfriend and girlfriend, creating all sorts of fantasies about where we came from, how we had met and so forth. I was embarrassed by the whole situation, but Peter seemed so much in command that I let him run the show, chiming in only occasionally to verify a story.

As we pulled into Grand Central Station, I felt greatly relieved. We bid the boy good-bye, Peter helped me to the platform with my suitcase and, wishing him a good trip, I took off as soon as I could. When we parted I never expected to see Peter again, nor did I want to, for though I was intrigued by his theatricality, it was obvious that we were from different worlds. After all, I was a suburban Jewish girl and, though I hadn't thought of it in those terms before, this meant certain things to me. Some were merely superficial: my friends and I almost never wore suits and dresses, but instead jeans and turtlenecks, shirts, and sweaters. We didn't date (or at least we never called it dating) but rather went to concerts and films in groups of twos, threes, and fours. Our relationships, whether between males and females or between members of the same sex, were rather intimate: we discussed personal problems about our parents, growing up, past and present relationships with boyfriends and girlfriends, and we shared and criticized each other's poetry and fiction.

What was most important was how informal and at ease we all were with one another since so much was understood; we knew each other's backgrounds, home situations, and the ideals and expectations they held for us. We used the same slang and parodied the same aspects of our upbringing.

Peter on the other hand, was dressed in a suit and tie. As we ate our sandwiches, I picked mine up with both hands and took a generous bite. I was starving! Peter waited quite a while before unwrapping his and, even then, ate it slowly, with reserve. In comparison I felt like an ill-mannered country hick.

Peter spoke articulately of his tutors in Europe and how "Mother" had done this and "Brother John" had done that. I was feeling pretty depressed so that maintaining a stiff conversation was almost more than I could stand and probably (though I never thought in these terms at the time — I had so strongly objected to the supposition of a "Jewish culture" or a "Jewish way of acting") had I met a nice guy from my "neck of the woods," I would have ended up pouring out my heart to him. With Peter, however, I could only feel relief as the train pulled into the station.

This was a feeling which persisted to some extent throughout our relationship. I often longed to be "at home," not to have to explain my terms, my background. I wanted Peter to understand intuitively, and although, of course, he couldn't, I still did not want to explain. Instead I kept wishing, without great expectations.

When Peter called me up a week later, I was extremely surprised, not only that he had called at all, but also because he asked me out for two dates at once. I accepted almost unthinkingly. After all, I was rarely asked out and, besides, I thought it would be fun to see a new side of Cambridge with no strings attached. I felt that he, too, was not asking *me* out (he hadn't even noticed me in music class), but that he just wanted a date and the novelty of our episode on the train had made him think of me as he flipped through his "little black book." I went next door to tell Kathy what had happened and to ask if he had called her first, since it seemed that Peter hit it off with Kathy much better than with me.

"No, he didn't."

I went out many times that spring with Peter and his friends. We would go to a show and dinner and when he brought me back there was no talk of a next time. I might see him two days later or not for two weeks. I supposed he thought me a nice decoration for his arm. I usually just sat and listened to the conversation he and his pals were having, not expecting to be included for I had nothing to add. In fact, I often could not even understand what they were saying. The whole thing seemed reasonable; it was a fair exchange – I was getting around and he had a reliable date. The only thing that baffled me was what he saw in me at all. I figured that with his great experience, he must have all sorts of girls he could call up. But why worry about it? It was nice while it lasted.

One day, however, things began to take a different cast. Peter asked me to come over for a drink one afternoon and when I arrived there was not a room full of people as always, but just Peter, not wearing a suit, but in jeans and shirtsleeves. The glamour and superficialities of our former encounters had been stripped away and there we were, the two of us. I did not quite know how to react and waited for Peter to take the lead. We sat and talked and then Peter, putting on a Dionne Warwick record, asked if I'd like to dance. I was embarrassed by the situation, beginning to feel that perhaps all that had gone before was a prelude to what Peter really wanted: to get to know *me*.

As the dancing turned into a "make-out session," I wondered if this meant more to Peter than it did to me. I did not want to be there, but then again I felt sheepish about refusing him since it would seem that I had been using him as a "theatre ticket" all this time. But when he asked if I wanted to go to bed with him, I was finally able to say it was against my policy. Peter was furious:

"What do you think I am? . . . a big Teddy bear?" he asked. I didn't know what to answer but I did know that I would soon have to level with him, that though I enjoyed being with him, there was no future for us, for we were far too different. I had not really been using him, for I had not suspected he felt anything for me.

Knowing that I would not be able to face him honestly, I resolved to write a note and to give it to him at the end of our next music section. Not more than two hours after I had given it to him, my buzzer rang; Peter had come to talk to me. We went for a long walk, through parts of Cambridge I had never seen (that was one of the things I liked about Peter, he always found an inventive twist on things), as I explained that I wasn't to be relied upon, that I wasn't capable of responsibility at the present. I really wanted to say that nothing could ever work out between *us*, but sitting there, facing him, I could not be quite that honest.

"That's all right," he told me. "I've just been hurt by a girl from Wellesley and I'm not ready for another commitment. I just like you, that's all."

"I'm glad to hear it."

I was both relieved and distressed, relieved that I could continue to see Peter with no strings attached, but distressed that I hadn't been honest, that Peter might hope for a change in my feelings. I'm afraid I could not quite accept the ease with which he had received what I said. And what's more, I was becoming less certain that I understood my own feelings. I guess I wanted my declaration to be a little more upsetting to Peter. I wanted him to want me, to say, "Well, if that is how you feel, we'd better call it quits." Had he done so, I probably could not have consented.

One night Peter dropped by to say that there was a possibility of his going away for a week since he had been commissioned to drive a car to Florida. If I didn't hear from him, that was why. I wondered why he bothered to tell me this. Often I would not hear from him for a week and would think nothing of it. In fact, reliability had never been a feature of our relationship. To my surprise I found myself wishing that he would not go, thinking of how much I would miss him, if nothing more than knowing he was in the same city. Not having heard from him for two weeks, I finally phoned. For two days I could not reach him, which made me almost frantic. I began to feel that he had no right to keep me hanging on, that though we had agreed we had no responsibility to each other, I *did* want to know where he was. And obviously he wanted me to take interest since he had come to tell me he was leaving. What was he trying to do? Get me hooked and then drop the line?

After a few days, Peter called and I politely inquired about his trip. What I really wanted to say was more like, "Where the hell have you been?" but, instead I listened to an hour's worth of tales, waiting for him to ask to see me. When we hung up, there had been no invitation. I had no one to blame but myself, I reasoned, for I had set the no responsibility precedent.

We did not see each other again until exam period a few weeks later when Peter and I studied music with two of my girlfriends and their boyfriends. Somehow being with these two couples put a pressure on Peter and me. There was a sense of warmth, of my belonging to him and him to me that had not been present before. It was nice to know he was there, but still I distrusted my own feelings: "Wasn't it just that I liked having somebody? After all, my friends all had boyfriends. Was it merely the idea of being in love that attracted me and not Peter himself? Did I even know him?"

The night of our exam a party was given by one of my girlfriends to which five couples were invited. Again Peter and I found ourselves among people who were either engaged or involved seriously and we, far less involved than the others, were coupled off as well. We were all folk-singing, each girl sitting on "her man's" lap. Anticipating a lengthy separation, a few of the couples disappeared, at intervals, into the garden, presumably to make love. I was happy to be there with Peter, to have a "mate," but I hoped he wouldn't suggest that we go to the garden, for though I wouldn't want to go, I probably would consent.

I was fond of Peter, there was no doubt of that, but I could not feel comfortable with him. In this crowd of people, as with most of my friends, he was a misfit. He couldn't quite handle himself in an informal situation like this one and responded by dominating discussions, by saying things he obviously didn't believe or hadn't thought through and couldn't support. Not wanting to watch his making a fool of himself, I would begin a side conversation or help with the serving.

I knew that my friends did not dislike him; they even thought he was good-looking and charming, to which I agreed. Nevertheless there was constant strain. But despite these feelings I was coming to the point of not wanting to question myself about how real this all was. The year was ending, I was leaving for Peru and somehow responsibility seemed less important. I would not initiate anything with Peter, but felt fewer compunctions about responding to any warmth he might show me.

After the party Peter suggested that we spend the night on the banks of the Charles. Liking the novelty of the idea, but not wanting to be asked to sleep with him, I informed Peter that I had my period. He said that he understood, so we went, blanket in hand, to the Charles. We talked most of the night about my project for the summer and then about his plans which, strangely enough, I had heard almost nothing about. "Was it that Peter had never spoken of them or that I hadn't been listening?" I could not remember.

As daylight broke we returned to my dorm to pack my things since I was leaving Cambridge that afternoon. I loved having someone take care of me, wanting to do even the most mundane things with me. I watched Peter affectionately as he took over, systematically ordering the cartons, directing me to pack sweaters in this one and blouses in that one.

But as the hour of my mother's arrival approached, I felt I wanted Peter to leave. I knew I could not casually introduce him to my mother as a "friend." He would be cast in the role of a "boyfriend." My parents had always teased me this way. The pain of my ninth grade graduation dance stood out especially clearly; in order to avoid the teasing I anticipated from my parents, I had found it necessary to go to a friend's house to get dressed and to have my date pick me up. In more recent years the teasing had died down since I did not, in fact, have a boyfriend; my friends, male and female, were buddies.

But as I envisioned the cross-examination my mother would give me in the car on the way home, I wished Peter would leave. Introducing him to my mother also somehow made our relationship seem more serious than it was. It was not that I did not introduce most of my friends to my parents, but that Peter seemed to take the prospect of meeting my mother much more seriously than I did. For him it was difficult to talk about parents, brothers, sisters, for they were very definitely part of one's personal life, something one shared only with very special people. Hoping to convey my discomfort I dropped casual hints, but Peter insisted upon staying and seeing the work through to its finish.

The luncheon we had together before leaving was not as uncomfortable as I had expected it to be. Peter and my mother exchanged pleasantries, Peter being especially charming and my mother being properly impressed. I could tell she liked him very much and the questioning that followed later was exactly what I anticipated. "What a charming fellow! What do you think of him? Do you expect to be seeing him much?"

A few hours later as we drove off campus and I looked back at Peter, I was sure he was not the society glamour boy I had once imagined, but what *was* he? I had broken down my image of him, but didn't have one with which to replace it. There was something between us, but it was very uncertain.

Dear Peter,

I had really hoped to hear from you. I know you are busy, but even a short letter would be received with joy. This summer isn't at all what I anticipated. The project is not at all well-defined and our field leader is a number one bastard. . . .

Dear Deborah,

I'm sorry I haven't written sooner, but I'm not much of a correspondent. The summer scene here is quite a delightful change from the tedium of classes. Last night I sat over dinner for two hours and then went to see Sidney Poitier's new film. Speaking of entertainment, I am enclosing a listing of the Boston University Celebrity Series for next year and would like to know what your recommendations are. Stick with me, kid, and you'll be wearing diamonds!

Dear Peter,

I was so glad to hear from you. Things here remain the same. I'm not sure that I'll make it through the summer, but at least the other students on the project are fine people or else I'd go crazy. As for the B.U. Series, my favorites would be Bream, the Juilliard String Quartet, and Rostropovich. . . .

Dear Deborah,

Cambridge is not the same without you. The problems with your field leader really upset me. You had so looked forward to the summer and it seems unfair that it should not turn out for you. I tried phoning you the other night but could not discover the right channel. . . .

Dear Peter,

I so enjoy receiving your letters. It is rare these days to find someone who actually takes the time to hear what you have to say and then responds to it. I would have loved to hear from you, but I might as well tell you that the phones in this town are few; we, unfortunately, are not the proud possessors of such a luxury item.

Dear Deborah,

I only wish I could be in Peru with you. It sounds as if the countryside is magnificent. Who knows? Maybe I'll strike it rich early in the summer and arrive on your doorstep one of these mornings. Then we can both mount our burros and ride away. P.S. I have a surprise waiting for you in Cambridge. After all the machinations with roommates, I have decided to opt out, and there may just be a pad on Putnam Ave. which I can call my very own.

For weeks I dreamed about how wonderful it would be if Peter did show up on my doorstep. The unhappier I became, the lengthier and warmer my letters grew. As Peter repeatedly responded with reassurance and suggestions, I began to believe I was in love with him. I actually felt it was the thought of Peter that kept me above ground. When his letters came, I ravenously scanned them for references to me and to us. Those sections in which he spoke merely of himself or his work did not interest me nearly as much. In talking with other students on the project, I depicted our relationship as extremely intimate. I could no longer distinguish between what had been a reality and what was the creation of correspondence and fantasy.

But what did this all mean to Peter? I had made it clear to him that I needed him, and he did not seem to find my needs too demanding. Perhaps he, too, was falling in love. But I was enamored of the idea of being in love and did not want to question whether Peter's statements reflected his real feeling or whether they came as easily to him and reflected as little genuineness as his answers to the little boy on the train of five months ago. If I pressed him, it would seem that I was serious, and if I found that he were serious, demands I did not want to face would be placed upon me.

In some ways our agreement of non-involvement persisted for me. "Stick with me kid and you'll be wearing diamonds!" What did that mean? And that "pad"? It would be nice to have a friend with an apartment, but why was it mentioned in such an enigmatic way, as if it were to be partially mine? I thought about these things but felt embarrassed about bringing them up with Peter, for they would be too direct and would imply responsibility, something we had agreed was not to be part of our relationship. I wished he would force a discussion of them, but maybe he felt less pressed if he could bring things up without my commenting on them. That way he could air his fantasies and, since I did not react to them, he need not feel I took them seriously.

Nor could I ask these questions when I returned to Cambridge that fall. "Peter was my boyfriend and I was his girlfriend." Exactly what that meant to us, we did not explore. He would invite me to stay at his apartment one night and on the pretext that it was too cold or rainy, it would turn into two or three nights a week. We met every day, usually for lunch or dinner. While I studied at night, he met a friend for a drink, and then we would meet for midnight coffee. But though we were together, we were not always *with* one another.

"Peter, why don't you join us for dinner?" a boy called out from the other side of the dining hall.

"Deborah, this is Jim Thompson and . . ."

"Mary Jackson."

"Hi."

"How's your brother, Peter? I never see him this year."

"He's great. As frantically busy as ever. He hangs around a lot with Jennings and Benson, playing rock, making the scene."

"What about Martin, what's he doing?"

"I don't know. He seems to have phased out of the gang. No one sees him much anymore. . . . And you, what are you planning to do next year?"

"I'm advanced placement, so I get to bask in the University sun one more year."

"That's right, I sure wish I could say the same."

"Are you going CO or turning in your draft card?"

"Nope, that not for me. I've applied for Navy OCS and am waiting for the word."

"Are you serious? My God, man, you're ten years behind the times. But you always were on the conservative side."

"We can't all be rebels, Jim."

"But how do you justify getting mixed up in those horror shows?"

"I don't know, I actually don't think it will be so bad. There's something to be said for learning about leadership. Besides, I'm only twenty and it's not easy to make it in the big bad world of business until you've ripened a bit."

"Are you actually going into business? You really are leading the straight and narrow these days. I mean, of all the mercenary things you can do, that's just the worst. Besides being selfish, it's damn boring."

"Do you live in this dorm?" I asked Mary.

"Yes."

"I used to live here last year, but I escaped as soon as I could."

"Where do you live now?"

"In the new dorm, those singles are a dream."

"By the way, how has the operation been going?" Peter asked.

"Not too badly. It's not the way it used to be in the good old days, but we're doing fine."

"What's the oper—?" I tried to break in.

"I heard about an incident earlier this year which made the whole business sound really shaky. Is that a fact, Jim?"

"Yeah, Mike got himself in a real tight spot and we didn't expect to see him come through it. We thought the Man had him for sure, but things have died down since."

"Peter, I'd think we'd better be going soon or we'll be late," I said nudging him.

"Yeah, soon. We're going to the opera at Lang Hall tonight. Well, I'm glad to hear it's not as serious as it sounded. Maybe I'll join you sometime."

"I really think we'd better leave."

"Okay. It was nice seeing you Jim and . . . ?"

"Mary."

"Yeah. Nice meeting you."

"Yeah."

"See you around."

We left the dining room in complete silence. Peter looked calm and happy, but I was fuming and kept on walking at a rapid pace. Down Garden Street, through the Square and on to Lang Hall. Peter looked at me a few times quizzically but did not press me further. That made me all the more furious. He knew I was angry. He was just being stubborn and would not ask me what the matter was. I forced a smile to those I knew as we found our seats. All through the opera, not one word was uttered. Each time Peter found something funny, he looked at me smiling, but I fixed my gaze on the stage, so incensed that I could barely hear the opera.

"Do you want to go to the cast party?" Peter asked as he helped me on with my coat.

"So I can stand by your side looking pretty and listening to your enigmatic conversation? No thanks. You go ahead. I'm going back to the dorm. I can't take it anymore."

We were now heading for Peter's apartment. "Now just wait a minute. It's not my job to pump conversation out of you. You're a big girl."

"How the hell am I supposed to enter into a conversation when I can't even tell what you are talking about?" I was glad when we reached Peter's apartment because I could tell I was about to explode.

"Ask questions, that's all," he said calmly, as he shut the door.

"Obviously it wasn't as simple as that. What's her name, Mary, seemed friendly enough and she wasn't having an easy time of it either. I did start to ask what the operation was and you cut me right off."

"You know the reason for that, young lady. It's a drug operation and I couldn't exactly announce it publicly."

"WELL then, don't talk about it at the dinner table, or at least say to me 'I'll tell you later.' For God's sake, you make me feel like a non-human china doll while you sit there not even acknowledging my presence. I bet if I had walked away quietly, you wouldn't have noticed. Meanwhile you're talking to a guy who couldn't mean much to you since I stay at your apartment several times a week and have never heard his name. Here I'm supposed to know you well, and I hear you speaking jive talk which I've never heard before and don't understand. It was like I was with another person, a stranger. And this isn't the first time it's happened, but it was the worst, since even the way he was treating you, his rotten sarcasm, didn't make you think twice about alienating me. All I know," I began to scream and cry at the same time, "is I won't take this anymore."

Slamming the door, I ran out. When Peter caught me and brought me back into his apartment, I was relieved.

"You can go if you like, but I want a few things understood. In part, I'm sorry. I didn't realize how much this upset you. But you *do* contribute to it. Judging from past experience, when we go out for dinner or drinks, I no longer expect that you will participate in the conversation. I used to hope that you would, but I no longer do."

"Peter, I'm not a businesswoman or a stockholder and never will be. And that's what you always seem to talk about."

"But you can ask questions. Anything. You *are* an interesting person and people would like to learn about you, if you'll give them a chance."

"But I'm also a shy person and you've got to help me. You're right, I'm not easy to talk to, but . . ."

"Let's work on it together, eh love?" he said, holding me close to him. I smiled for the first time that evening, feeling Peter's warmth again, remembering how good he was to me and feeling relieved that this problem of long standing had finally been brought out into the open.

"You know, I think next year will be really exciting. What I'd really like to do is take off, make that trip around the world I've always dreamed of: new sights, new people every day. I guess eventually I'll have to go back to school, but right now freedom looks good. It's a strange feeling to be flipping through the catalogue for the eighth and last time. It's like a last fling," Peter went on oblivious to the tears that were rolling down my cheeks.

"Of course the room was candlelit. That was why he, who was always so sensitive to my feeling, hadn't noticed," I thought. But it was not until he felt my tears on the pillow that he realized I was crying.

"What's wrong?" Peter looked at me, startled.

"I don't know. It's just, kind of, that I don't seem to fit into your plans for next year, none of which I've heard before and none of which have anything to do with me or which I have any right to. It's like listening to a stranger, only I'm in bed with him."

A strange smile passed over Peter's face. "You mean, you mean," he said hesitatingly, "you want to . . . ? I never realized that you had any desire to think of a future with me."

"What does he mean?" I thought. Here I have been living at his apartment a good part of the time. Haven't my actions communicated anything to him? I was always there — reliable, faithful Deborah doing things for him, putting down her own projects to give him a hand. I almost never went out with another boy, and when I did I was always sure to let him know who it was. It was clear that I was Peter's girl.

But maybe he was being genuine. We never had discussed the future. I, for one, had been afraid; not knowing my own feelings, I had waited for Peter to broach the subject. But he never had.

Whereas I had expected my statement to make Peter uneasy, he seemed overjoyed, as if I had bestowed the most precious gift upon him. I, too, felt overjoyed, for in the past I had been able to voice feelings of discontent, but never positive feelings. "Of course," I had thought, "my actions must convey my love and affection." I felt so full, looking at Peter in the candlelight, knowing, at last, that he knew how I felt.

But why was it always this way? Peter helping me, Peter listening to my problems? It was true that I was attracted to him, in part, because he seemed to be stable and "well put together," but I had never before known anyone who so rarely showed a need to talk about himself, to lose control. It was not that he was unemotional, for with him at times I experienced more warmth than I had ever known.

My initial impression was that he had no problems, but, with time, I became more skeptical; he must be just as crazy as the rest of us, but he doesn't want to talk to me about personal matters. Perhaps he considers it unmanly to open up or perhaps it just isn't part of his "culture." It doesn't seem as if he has any closer friends than me, so this must be his style.

But then, why does he spend endless hours listening to me pour out my heart? He must derive some satisfaction from doing so. His sympathy and suggestions are so wonderful; they show me that he has deep feelings and that he must share some of my problems or he wouldn't be able to empathize so well. But it is selfish for me to burden myself upon him if he cannot share his feelings with me.

"God, Deborah, you're wonderful," Peter was calling to thank me for the box of cookies I had left on his desk. I often baked things and left them in his apartment as a surprise.

"That's okay, I thought you could use them in this time of need. How's the old thesis coming today?"

"Not too well. I don't know what's wrong with me. I just don't have enough time anymore to do even a mediocre job and it's getting me down."

"Look, you've got to work with the time you have, so don't set yourself an impossible task."

Peter seemed like a sad little boy, and I felt he was asking for my help.

"Is there anything I can do, Peter?"

"I appreciate your offering, but you've got your own papers to do. Don't worry about me."

"If there is some way I can help, I'd be glad to. Just let me know."

"If you really mean it, you could help me by transcribing some of the tapes I've got. But it's such an awful job."

"I'm glad to help you. Just don't keep apologizing. I'll be over in about half an hour, after dinner. Okay?"

"Deborah . . ."

"What, Peter?"

"I love you. I don't know what I'd do without you. I can't wait until this is all over, so we can live the good life again."

It was many tape transcriptions and much proofreading later

that I finally got back to the dorm. I felt so badly for Peter that I could not possibly have left even though I resented having to stay. But then again, this was my way of expressing myself to Peter.

Sometimes the ease with which he could say "I love" made me embarrassed and frightened. I *did* want to hear it, but when I tried to respond, I felt myself all choked up. "What is wrong with me? Why can't I say something as simple as 'I love you'? Is it my shyness?" Maybe I was still afraid of demanding anything from Peter, and though my actions must convey my feelings to him, a verbal declaration of love would be of another magnitude.

But there was something else; I was not really certain that I *did* love him. "What is love anyway? I don't know, so maybe this is it." I felt responsibility to Peter; I was his best friend, and were it not for me, he told me, he would hold everything inside. One night he christened me his "safety valve." Yet my inability to express warmth to him disturbed me terribly. I was happy when things like his thesis, with which I could help in a self-sacrificing manner, came along.

And I needed him, too, for his warmth and understanding were things I could not do without and which enabled me to carry on even day to day affairs. Yet, that one question continued to plague me: "Why can't I say 'I love you'?"

In September, at the beginning of the next school term Peter left for his parents' home in Europe for what was to be a three-week stay. Yet there was a finality in the parting:

"Deborah, when I go, I don't want you to feel that you are tied to me. I think you should see other people, if you'd like, for you haven't done enough of that. I may have to go into the Army when I return, I don't know, and I don't want you to depend upon me."

I was gripped by fear as I heard these words. I was going to be all alone as Peter went off to Europe. "But, how wise and selfless he was being. He did not really want me to go out with other people. It was only that his love for me prevented him from being selfish and expecting utter fidelity. And I would have to be mature about it all. He had a lot on his mind, the draft was enough for anyone, and I had to help him by not being demanding. I would go out with other people, as he suggested, but Peter would be back before I knew it."

Dear Deborah,

I regret that our separation had to be as sad as it was. But I felt and still do feel that it was for the best. I have great faith in you. Many times you have shown what a strong person you are, and I know you will have no difficulty in making new friends this year.

Last night my mother came up to my garret room and found me weeping. I think she knew what was eating me, but, in her usually tactful manner, she did not press me for an explanation. Instead, she said she knew how difficult it was to be separated, since she and Dad had broken up after their engagement. [What does he mean by separation? "Broken up"? What is he trying to tell me? This is not quite how I had pictured our separation. He is probably just speaking metaphorically.]

Dear Peter,

I was so glad to hear from you. Though the first two weeks were miserable (every time I bumped into someone you and I know, I could feel the tears running down my face), it is not quite as bad as I anticipated now. You have given me a strength which does not leave me when you do.

But still you had better come back for two reasons. First, I miss you. Second, I got troubles. Saturday night I went over to Bob's for dinner. I hadn't seen him for months and, you know how everyone is especially friendly at the beginning of the year, so when I saw him on the street, I gave him a big hello. We cooked a lovely dinner (by the way, he asks how you are and afterwards I expected we'd go to a movie or something. Well, Bob starts with the "What do you want to do?" routine, making it clear he didn't want to do anything. Next thing I know he comes over and starts to embrace me. I was really shocked! We had just been speaking of you! So, babes, you'd better come back and rescue me from the wilds of Cambridge.

Dear Deborah,

Tonight as I sat at the hotel I was thinking how wonderful it would be if you were here. But there will be many more trips to Europe, together. . . . I spent eight hours today in rehearsal for the ball to be given next month. I have been chosen as escort for a friend of the family's daughter. The pomp and circumstance of the whole affair is something not to be missed. I will send you photos when they are ready.

As you have probably guessed, it now looks as if I will be here a bit longer than planned. Dad has come up with a great job for me, one which it would be foolish to miss, especially since the Army will probably grab me up once I get to Cambridge. So I rejoice that things are better in Cambridge. I will have to leave you to its wilds a bit longer.

I had a feeling that the finality of his farewell meant more than three weeks' separation. He *was* trying to make it easier for me, but somehow I feel deceived, as if his parents somehow have more sway over him than I do and as if, though I'm important to him, my feelings or views are not taken into account when he makes decisions. I can't understand this, for I am certain that he loves me.

Dear Peter,

    I can hardly believe that you have decided to stay longer. I know criticism of your parents makes you defensive, but at the risk of doing so, it seems to me that you are playing in dangerous territory. The Army is not going to care about your good business experience, but only that you are romping around Europe 1-A. Maybe I am being selfish because I love you and want you home again, but I think there is truth in what I say.

    In a way you were right about a separation being good for both of us. Now that you are gone, I spend hours reviewing our relationship and it seems that there are so many things we haven't shared and haven't been honest about. I cannot wait until we are together again, for I feel more relaxed generally and know that I will be able to give more of myself to you, as I've always wanted to. For some reason I have always felt restrained, but now, having spent more time with other people and feeling more at ease with myself, I see a whole new world out there which I hope we can share when you return.

Dear Deborah,

    Your letters make me so happy. Somehow, even being so far apart, I do not feel lonely, but instead full, knowing that you exist and that I love you. It is this feeling which enables me to derive joy from my everyday life. Often I feel a terrible aching and want to hop the next plane across the ocean, but I know that this period is valuable for both of us.

    I have been negotiating with the American Embassy to get the inside story on the draft situation. They have been recommending that I look into the prospect of enrolling at the University here for this year. I have mixed feelings about this plan, since it would be a blow-out academically but might enable me to continue my job which is probably the most valuable option open to me at present. There is no need to say more until I've got all the information.

I can't believe it. First he writes how much he loves me and how important I am to him, and then I fade from the picture as he decides how to spend the year. It is as if he borrows strength and confidence from our relationship, but as if I, in reality, am superfluous to him. He needs assurance of my love and support in order to do things which have nothing to do with me, things which are not discussed with or even known to me.

    "Deborah, a long distance call."

    "Hello?"

    "Hello, Deborah? This is Peter."

    "Peter? My God! Where are you?"

    "Over here. Listen, what are you doing this Saturday night?"

"Hold on a minute, what are you talking about? You mean you're coming back?"

"I thought I'd surprise you, but I couldn't hold out. Well, will you go out with me?"

"Well, I don't know, let's see. I think I can swing it, you moron."

"Okay, I don't want to make it long."

"God, I can't believe it."

"Until then, love."

"Oh, Peter, I'm so happy. I don't know what to say. Good-bye. See you Saturday."

The great day had finally come. "But why the fear? It must just be the excitement." I was glad to have Don come along to the airport, for though I couldn't understand why, I was very apprehensive about seeing Peter again.

"Where is he? The last one off the plane as usual. Oh! there he is!"

He ran up to the glass, blowing kisses through it. And I wanted to return his adoring look, but I couldn't. The man I loved had returned after ten weeks. "Why could I feel nothing but fear?" I suddenly felt constricted and confined; I would have to be Peter's girl. My glorious freedom was about to be taken away.

Peter partially detected my feeling and, when he asked if something were the matter, I promptly replied that I was tired. I was too guilt-ridden to tell him I didn't feel the great passion I had expected. And yet the fact that I had been able to tell him I love him had assured me that I truly did love him and that he was the man for me. It was a rude shock to find that words and letters are far different from realities at times.

The next few weeks I tried desperately to recover my old feelings. I wanted to be in love, what was wrong with me? Peter came over every night for dinner after which I excused myself, saying I had to study. He would leave hesitantly, wanting to, but not quite able to, believe me. Yet he never said a word, but instead looked at me dejectedly.

The demands of the situation were becoming unbearable. I was certain that "love" was not what I felt for Peter. Responsibility, yes, but not love. And now, more than ever before, he needed me:

"Deborah, I have never felt so strongly about you before. When I came back from Europe you had grown. And I hope that will be the last of our separate trips, for we are growing together as well as growing up . . . and we shall see."

That was just the problem. I had grown, realizing that the world Peter and I ensconced ourselves in was not big enough for me. I was very fond of him, he really was my best friend, but our relationship could never lead to marriage and after two years, it was too late to procrastinate further. If only he would share my feelings, it would be so much easier. "How could I have begged him to come back from Europe?" I felt so guilty.

It was not until I developed a crush on a boy I had met in the library that I was able to believe I knew my own feelings. I could not possibly be in love with Peter and I could not deceive him anymore. I resigned to break the news after my last exam. When Peter met me outside the exam room to take me to lunch, he looked as if he knew what was coming. As we seated ourselves at the table we exchanged a painful glance, our lips began to quiver and tears streamed down our faces.

"Peter, this makes me so sad. I don't know how to begin."

"It's over, isn't it? I've known it for a while but was trying not to believe it, until I had to."

"Yes, Peter, it is."

"When did you begin to feel this way?"

"The moment you got off the plane. I didn't want to believe it either. I've tried not to these past few weeks, but the old feeling isn't there. It's not that I don't love you, Peter, but it's so apparent that the life-styles we envision are not at all compatible. And the longer we go on, the more impossible it will be to agree to separation."

"You are right, Deborah. Your intuitions are always so good. That's one of the things I love about you. But I will miss you terribly. It's a strange thing to say, but I almost wish you weren't a girl, because we're really each other's best friends. It's more than losing a girlfriend, it's losing my best friend, my only friend. I just can't face the prospect of living without you."

"Me, too, Peter."

"Deborah, can I see you from time to time?"

"If you like, Peter, but it might be difficult. It's probably better that we don't, at least for a while."

"If you ever want to call, please do. And if you change your mind, I'll always be there. Good-bye, sweetheart. It's been beautiful."

"Good-bye, Peter."

Case 20 / Part of Me Just Wasn't Being Expressed

Paul considers his problems at home to be intellectual rather than emotional ones. He cannot remember either of his parents ever admitting that he was right. His lack of questioning his father's "omniscience" is contrasted with his continual questioning of his mother and of people at school and church.

In order to assess his level of development, Paul compares himself to the fictional Stephen Dedalus, with whom he shares an Irish Catholic background. On first reading *A Portrait of the Artist as a Young Man* Paul disidentifies with Stephen, but a second reading four years later becomes an intense experience involving the issue of freeing oneself from the bonds of one's family, church, and ethnic group.

When I first read James Joyce's *Portrait of the Artist as a Young Man,* I was a senior at an elite suburban public high school. I was a good student, maintaining an even B average, and an athlete, lettering in two varsity sports. Academically, my only outstanding characteristic was my enrollment in an honors English course, and although I retained my usual B average, I had definite doubts about whether I belonged in the course. I was in it primarily because my father, an administrator at the school, felt it would better my chances of admission to whatever colleges I wished to attend. Although my record in sophomore English was not at all exceptional (B's), I was admitted to the honors course at the beginning of my junior year.

I have no doubts now that I could have compiled a much better scholastic record in high school than I actually did, but I just didn't care to make the effort that is required of excellence. My father's presence at school was the major motivational factor in what desire I had to do well in the classroom, and this was based primarily on my father's intimacy with all my teachers and coaches, with the implicit threat of paternal intervention if I didn't do well. Without belaboring this point, it will suffice to note that I took many of the potentially most stimulating courses the high school offered, yet was rarely motivated to do any more than I had to, or to look at my studies as anything more meaningful than required exercises. There was little or no pressure on me from my parents to get A's or anything of the kind, because they did not want to put excessive pressure on me in my schoolwork, as so many parents are reputed to do nowadays. The net result, however, was a "hands off" policy as long as I maintained some sort of academic respectability, which was not at all a difficult task. In the long run, this was probably beneficial, for it allowed me to find my own motivation to learn, but it certainly helped waste my high school years in terms of intellectual growth.

The other side of my life, the social aspect, related most specifically to my activities around the school. I played two sports, soccer and baseball, at the varsity level, and did enough other things around school (choir, newspaper) to win a service award during my senior year. For my parents, this was sufficient, and they never encouraged me to do any more, i.e., date. This was what I felt my major problem to be, a lack of confidence in a heterosexual one-to-one situation, and so I did not date nearly as much as most of my friends. My mother, to be sure, did ask me every now and then why I dated as little as I did, but she always seemed satisfied with the reply that I didn't see any reason why I should spend a lot of time with someone I wasn't really interested in. But, at bottom, I had the feeling she was just as glad I had no particular romantic interest, for it meant I had no personal interests that drew me away from the home. With my father at the high school, everything else I did was part of the public domain.

This caused one other small problem, a nagging doubt that all of my successes were somehow related to my father. Even in situations where he could not possibly have helped me in any way (e.g., during an athletic contest), the fact that he was there and that he knew my teachers, coaches, and advisors better than I did managed to tinge my accomplishments with the vague sense that I might not have done as well if he hadn't been around. This in no way reflected upon my feelings for him, for I love him very much, and did then, as well. But I yearned for the day when I'd do something he had to be told about by *me*, instead of by someone who'd been there, who knew him better than he knew me.

Religion was not really an autonomous factor in my life at this time, being more of an extension of parental control than a separate set of demands. In terms of specific background very little presents itself, for I really did not spend too much of my time thinking about God, or the Roman Catholic Church. Perhaps it would be sufficient to note the one outstanding difference between the religion of my parents and myself. This was our respective conceptions of God; they thought He was omniscient, omnipotent, omnipresent, and all of that, and I wasn't sure what He was, but I didn't think He'd ever done anything outstanding for me. This issue was most evident after I'd made a remarkable recovery from encephalitis, which was naturally attributed to God. My only reaction was to ask why, if He'd cured me, nobody blamed Him for making me sick in the first place? After all, there seemed no more logical reason to assume He'd cured me, than that He'd made me sick. Relief being what it was, my little heresy got very little attention, and it all blew over.

As for *Portrait* itself, my initial reactions to the book were, as usual, minimal. I was bewildered at times by the depth of Joyce's imagery, the intricacy of his prose, and the individuality of Dedalus' childhood. I was typically tardy in completing my assignments, and only did them once, making no extra effort to fathom the book's far-from-clear meanings. My major problem was that I could not "identify" with Stephen Dedalus in the literary jargon, which I felt excused my lack of interest, and therefore did not take him very seriously.

The reasons for my lack of interest in Dedalus were not hard to discover. He was not the sort of boy I had ever admired – he was not in any sense an athlete, nor did he have any desire to be one. This is not to say that athletic ability was the only trait I admired in men, but I was proud of my own talents at sports, more so than I was of any other attribute. I immediately typed Stephen as an egghead, uninterested in anything that couldn't be solved by sheer force of intellect.

Further, Stephen went to an all-boys school, and this didn't relate to what I thought was my own biggest personal problem. As I've said, I didn't date very much, even though I knew I was well-liked by all the girls at school. Had I been removed from all daily contacts with girls my own age, I think my anxieties would have been accented all the more. As it was, I took some solace in the fact that there were several girls at school with whom I was very friendly, in a very safe, social way. I just did not feel that Stephen's situation would have been any improvement on my own and might have increased my anxieties.

So, at the outset I wasn't concerned with *Portrait* in any sense other than that of an English assignment. I had no desire to be an "artist," due largely to a rather limited, conventional conception of the term. More importantly, I had little liking for Stephen Dedalus himself and just did not feel he had very much to offer me.

This feeling continued until about the midpoint of the novel. Then, primarily because of our in-class discussions of the book (as opposed to my reading of it), I realized that Joyce did have something for me, after all. In these discussions, it was emphasized that Dedalus in his quest for self-definition had chosen to pursue a career as an artist, and that to succeed he had to liberate himself from those elements of his past that limited his capacity to think and to create. These were, primarily, his ties to his family, to his country, and to his religion. I began to see each of these as a set of demands on Stephen, as separate but interlocking identities for the young man that served only to narrow him, his actions, his perspectives, and the avenues of development open to him. Each of them presented him with a rather specific set of expectations, capable of stifling his personality and his creativity, if he allowed them to.

At this point, the main thrust of my thoughts was highly personal and was primarily negative. My interpretation of *Portrait* catalyzed a vague sense of frustration I had not articulated until this time. I began to be aware of my own lack of self-definition, although I certainly could not have phrased it as well at the time. I began to see that my life was being lived for me in terms of others' expectations. Most particularly the demands were my parents', but Dedalus' example made me aware of the demands of the Church, which were tightly interwoven with those of my family. At any rate, I began to think a little, and the results were refreshing.

I turned back to the book and really began to try to analyze Stephen, although I did this in terms that related more specifically to myself than to Stephen. The implication that Stephen was not "one of the guys" continued to trouble me. This became very important, because I wanted to be accepted in this way, and yet I began to have a vested interest of sorts in identifying myself with Stephen. I was not able to understand Stephen's ability to abstract himself from the group and either observe them as though he was not there physically or just ignore them. As I have said, I had no idea of myself as an artist, so I could not put this ability of Stephen's in the context of his own personality. I tried, rather, to fit it in with my own and could not do it. This bothered me throughout the rest of the book.

Stephen's family life seemed more relevant to me. Again, I was a bit put off by his willingness to observe and accept his distance from his family, but I identified quite strongly with his parents' demands and expectations (indeed, I very probably magnified them). However, given what I understood as his need to rise above his family, I couldn't understand his ability to accept minor irritations like his father's preachments about never poaching on a fellow and always associating with gentlemen. This sort of innocuous advice was the sort of thing I contested at every turn, gaining for myself quite a reputation as a pretty belligerent debater. I let no idea go unquestioned and could not understand why one of Stephen's radical views let so much irrelevant advice be foisted off on him.

Yet, in a larger sense I was conscious of no great need to throw off any parental "yoke," although I had set my mind on living away at college. My father was the dominant parent, the one whose presence seemed most oppressive, but I admired him very much and objected to his omniscience, not his values or his personality. The main point is that, try as I did, I could not really relate Stephen's family to my own. His father was more a familiar life-style than an everyday presence. His father seemed almost comically outdated, and I could not imagine him presenting Stephen the problems that I felt my father presented me.

All this notwithstanding, my familial problems were far more intellectual than emotional. I felt very secure at home and a bit afraid of Stephen's situation at boarding school. Although I felt living away from home was the sort of situation I badly needed, I was a little apprehensive at the thought, surrounded by people I hardly knew. Home was a nice, safe place to live affording even the luxury of resenting that I lived there after all.

An argument I had with my mother during this period comes to mind in relation to my thoughts about *Portrait*. There had been a provocative (and rather insulting) column in the school newspaper (of which I was an editor) about college admissions officers. While I felt the article was extreme in its criticism and actually pretty ridiculous, I felt the student who had written it had the right to say what he wanted. My mother disagreed and asserted (eventually, very loudly) that I was as responsible as he for having defended nothing more than his right to say it. Finally, she cursed me (something she did not do very often) loudly and irrationally, and I left the house in tears. I hadn't stormed out or screamed a reply as I left (is this my guilty conscience?) but had only wanted to walk for a while and vent my frustrations to myself. Ten or fifteen minutes later my father came driving down the street and called me over to the car. He wasn't angry, which wasn't surprising, but he asked me to come home with him and apologize to my mother. He said he thought I was right and that my mother shouldn't have gotten as mad as she had, but that she was still my mother, so I should apologize. I did to end the whole thing and because it was a lot harder to fight with my father than my mother. He was much more reasonable, and that was an appeal I was far more susceptible to.

I'd been thinking of Joyce on that walk, though, and the passage we'd read in class that afternoon. It was the scene on the beach when Stephen became aware of his spiritual father, the "fabulous artificer," Dedalus. As he lay on the beach, he felt this spirit lift out of him, out of the world of physical reality. I felt it was the physical world I resented, a world where it didn't matter if you were right, when you argued with your mother. I felt that motherhood was fine and that you should love your mother, and all that, but that motherhood didn't mean a damned thing when it came to an intellectual debate. Intellect was the weapon I used against my parents, but it never really worked. I can't remember either one of them ever admitting I was right; my father always said, "Could be," when there was nothing left to say, and my mother accused me of being too stubborn to admit I was ever wrong. At any rate, my intellect was my bulwark against my parents, but it wasn't a very strong one. I wanted from Joyce the way to a life of pure reason where I could meet others (my parents, especially) on even terms, the victor to be chosen by right, not familial might. In Joyce I sought a spiritual guide and ally.

In sum, Joyce never did for me what I wanted him to do. I could not equate his parents with mine, for they did not seem to be as great a force in Dedalus' life as mine were in my life. I had a hint, but that was all. I didn't know what to do with it, or where to go from there.

Religion was another story entirely. Joyce (Dedalus) was from an intensely Roman Catholic background, and so was I. He had considered entering the priesthood, and so had I. And, to varying degrees we had both rebelled at our common faith, although his religion was on a much higher theological plane than was mine. He had to recant a "heresy"; I'd had to leave a high school Christian doctrine class because I constantly quarreled with my teacher. The history of my "heresy" is fairly inconclusive, but it is nevertheless instructive.

I was a high school senior (this took place just prior to reading *Portrait*), and the year's work in Sunday school was to be preparation for a Christian adulthood or something like that. We talked about marriage on a pretty mundane level and higher education, which precipitated my first confrontation. The instructor told us that it was a real privilege to go to college and that we had to make studying our "vocation." Once we got out of college, we had to repay some kind of great debt we owed society for letting us go to college. I guess I just resented the implication that I owed somebody something for having been born intelligent, and I told him so. At any rate, this was only a prelude to a major confrontation that got me "kicked upstairs" to teach the eighth grade.

The issue was military service, and the approved line was that it was something every man owed his country. I was no pacifist and was reasonably patriotic, but I asked only why one's duty to one's country had to be fulfilled in the Army. The reply was something about a "military obligation," and I countered by asking why the obligation had to be military. I wasn't even questioning the need for an army, or anything nearly that drastic, or even a general obligation of service to one's country. To clarify the issue, I asked why, if a man was a better teacher than a soldier, he couldn't fulfill his "obligation" by teaching for the requisite two years. It seemed clear to me that the man was more valuable doing what he did best, as long as that was still in an area that directly benefitted his country. The reply to this was an angry, "What do you think, that you're better than I am? I did my time, and you'll do yours, too!" The time was clearly ripe to move on to other topics, and we did. The next week the priest in charge of religious classes asked me if I'd like to teach an eighth-grade boys' class. I accepted, pleased that he thought me intelligent enough to assume the role of a teacher and that he thought I was better off in front of a class of my own than in my former twelfth-grade class.

However, the feeling of irrelevance that had plagued me in the twelfth-grade class was still present as I began to teach. The material was highly structured, and I felt really smothered by it. Since I was completely uninspired by the material, I very often ran out of material halfway through the class and let the boys leave early after a half-hearted attempt at a discussion. This lasted only about six weeks, until I was stricken with encephalitis and spent four weeks in the hospital and four more at home recuperating. But there was a real feeling of relief at not having to teach any more, since it hadn't been the least bit stimulating. The class and the Church seemed pretty irrelevant to me.

So, in the area of religion there seemed to me to be greater congruences between myself and Dedalus. Although the depths of our questions varied widely, we both questioned the validity of doctrines the Church was unprepared to defend in any but the most traditional terms. However, I recognized that Stephen's attitude was curiously devoted to the Church, for he tried to explore it as intimately as he could. I, on the other hand, was much more interested in getting around it somehow, in ignoring it, rather than in coming to terms with it. An example here is an assignment I had for class relating to *Portrait*. I had to analyze Joyce's use of Saints Michael and Gabriel as symbols and the implications of this use. I did the assignment, in a completely uninspired manner, researching the lives of the saints and trying to figure out what they had to do with the plot. I haven't the vaguest idea of what I found and very probably couldn't have remembered two weeks after the assignment was done. The assignment meant nothing to me beyond its immediate relevance to the text. I had no particular interest in Joyce's use of symbols, since I never planned to do any serious writing, and less interest in the saints themselves. Like the Church itself, they were assignments to be done because they were assigned, not because of any possible value to me.

The one reference to the Church in *Portrait* that seemed very familiar to me was the sermons on hell by Father Arnall during Stephen's retreat. This sort of hell-fire and brimstone approach to Catholicism seemed all too typical to me and was the major factor in what aversion I had to the Catholic concept of sin. Hell was just viable enough to be vaguely unnerving at times, so the horrors of Father Arnall's sermons were sort of a highly literary anthology of everything I thought barely possible if I were adjudged a sinner.

Stephen's reaction to the sermons, though extreme, was therefore comprehensible, for I too was periodically remorseful and fearful for my immortal soul. Usually, these fits of piety and purity resulted from having been discovered at something "sinful" (taking a candy bar in a grocery store when I was eight, or having a couple of issues of *Playboy* when I was in junior high). On these occasions I vowed firmly to reform my entire life and usually kept the vows strictly for at least two weeks. So, although I felt Stephen, as usual, had been a little extreme in his reactions, I understood them in principle.

My basic feeling about the Church, though, seemed much like Stephen's. He felt his Church restrictive; I felt the same. He felt devotion to Church doctrine too exclusive; I felt the doctrine itself was too narrow and rather sterile. He felt there was too much emphasis on what happened if you were "evil"; this was the only aspect of the

Church that meant anything to me. Stephen felt a very real need to free himself from the bonds of the Church; I felt it was pretty irrelevant and something I could just as well do without.

National background was the one aspect of the triad I could not identify with at all. Our work in English class constantly emphasized the need for Joyce to free himself from the bonds of family, church, and state, and I understood the need for the first two. The third was just beyond my grasp. I felt it must have had something to do with a lack of understanding on my part for the peculiarities of Irish life at the time, or of the Irish rebellion, or something of that sort. I was highly interested in and motivated by American politics and had not extended my dissatisfaction with particular individuals or policies to a rejection of our society or culture as a whole. I never really tried to come to terms with Stephen's rejection of Irish nationalism and wrote it off to some sort of indigenous Irish parochialism. I assumed that Stephen shared my own mystification at the Irish way of life. I was satisfied to ignore this aspect of Stephen's spiritual renewal, never trying to find any wider application of his discontent. *I* was satisfied, and that was enough to kill any urge to confront Stephen on his own terms.

My strongest sense at this first reading of the book was one of stifled humanity, felt in very personal terms. I sensed (or wished) that there was something of myself that could not be realized as long as I continued to function in ways that were determined for me by people and institutions alien to myself. This wasn't articulated at the time, primarily because there was as yet no driving need to do so. I was still functioning well, within these limits, and felt generally satisfied doing so. When clashes arose, I dealt with them as isolated phenomena with no great feeling of general discontent. *Portrait* gave me for the first time a sense of oppression, a sense that part of me just wasn't being expressed, because others wouldn't let it be expressed. For the first time, there was a sense that I could find my own "identity," defined only by my own self, and that to accomplish this I had to free myself from artificial strictures. I wanted to grow in ways that were my own in directions that were natural to me. I must emphasize here that this was only an amorphous yearning. I had no ideas about becoming an artist like Stephen Dedalus and never really took him as a sort of "spiritual father" as Stephen took Dedalus. I just felt there was a person within me capable of better things than I had hitherto envisioned for myself, and I felt I could only do these things if I became "myself." To do this, I felt I had to free myself from the demands of my family, of my church, and though I really didn't understand it, my country. I didn't know how, and I had only the vaguest hint of why, but I felt it was something I had to do.

Four Years Later

My second reading of A Portrait of the Artist as a Young Man was a very intense experience, this intensity alone being enough to differentiate it from my first perusal of the book. The second time around, I looked for Joyce's symbolism wherever it appeared important, tried to look at Stephen Dedalus as a real human being, and above all tried to come to terms with Stephen without forcing him to be myself. In fact, this is what struck me the most after reading the book a second time, that I had really tried to confront Stephen on his own terms and that the mere act of confrontation helped me to understand him far better than I had before. The second reading of the book was very much an exercise in self-definition along the lines of the sort of thing I wanted to do when I first read the book. I hadn't done it the first time, because I really did not understand what it was I had to do. This new attitude made the character of Stephen much more understandable, and at the same time, helped me understand myself and my reasons for wanting to read the book a second time and put my impressions on paper.

Until the second reading, I never grasped the real import of Stephen's obsession with his social environment, for it seemed antithetical to his need to divorce himself from it. I see now that he could not really raise himself out of his social world until he fully understood it and could use it to serve his ends instead of being used by it to serve no particular end. I see now that I can only use Portrait if I fully understand it or if I can at least put it into a context where I can observe it and use what is relevant to me while remaining aware of what seems irrelevant. This is a marked change in my attitude, but it does seem to be characteristic of my development in other areas in the past four years.

My life has changed in the past four years, and although this is perhaps not significant in and of itself, the changes have been on the whole quite gratifying. I feel now as though I am in control of my life, that the directions I have taken in the past two years, particularly, are my own, and that I have to a significant degree freed myself from my former subservience to my family, my church, and my society. The fact that I still retain ties to all three after times of real personal turmoil about each of them indicates to me that I have reestablished my former relationships on terms more conducive to my own development and on terms more specifically related to my own personal needs. While the particular histories of the three areas in my personal development are understandably divergent in specific terms, they are alike in that in each area I underwent a period of heightened awareness (in which I became more fully aware of what each meant to me), followed by a period of rejection (in which I resisted all attempts to force me into any particular behavior pattern), and lastly, a period of renewal (in which I reestablished the relationships on a new and significantly different level). Furthermore, within this configuration, I confronted some of the other problems that had bothered me in high school and made definite progress in these areas.

The most important of these has been that of my family, which should not be surprising, since it was clearly the area in the most need of some realignment. The change began when I moved away to college, and I began to have a sense of my own life in which my parents could not possibly have participated. My new friends were my own, the teams I played on were coached by my coaches, not my father's friends, and my dates were my own. I suppose most college freshmen have a feeling of freedom, but I still felt that mine was greater than most, for I felt mine as more than just a freedom to do. I felt a real freedom to *be*, to change the person I had been, to become other things I mightn't have been free to become were I still living at home. My parents reacted in a subdued manner, but it was nevertheless evident that they were fearful of the changes. The most obvious incident between us came as a result of the beginnings of a relationship with the girl I am going to marry next August, Elaine.

We met at the end of the fall semester of freshman year and dated sporadically for about three months. My parents were interested, but this was understandable, for they were interested in everything I did at school, so nothing came of their interest until Elaine and I began to get more serious about each other, dating every week and spending great amounts of time on the telephone. My parents' interest escalated to concern and eventually became a thinly veiled attempt to break us up. In the name of my emotional and academic stability, they urged that I not get so involved with Elaine that I could not adjust to losing her, if that were ever to happen. My reply was that I could hardly hope to give myself to the relationship if I was always conscious of the need to keep my emotional distance from her and that if one made fear of the unhappy consequences the sole determinant of one's actions, one likely would never do anything meaningful or worthwhile. I became very aware of the need to build a family of my own, for this seemed to me a way to autonomy. Elaine was someone I could call my own, someone I had won all by myself, and I determined that our relationship wouldn't collapse because of anything I was lacking. I shouldn't overdo this, because I certainly wasn't the perfect, selfless person, but I did make a real commitment to the relationship, and I know this helped keep us together for a long while until she was as sure as I that she wanted to commit herself to me.

Our relationship has been continuous from the time we first met and has grown in many ways all the while. For a time, though, it seemed that as our relationship grew, my relationship with my parents disintegrated. They became less than satisfied with me (in some cases justifiably, in others, with little real cause), and I really began to resent their efforts to keep our relations on their former smooth keel. If I didn't call them a couple of times a week, they called me, and I really began to be bothered by their incessant intrusions. When they realized that they could not change my feelings about Elaine, they began to work on the specter of her mother, admittedly not an easy person to get along with. They held up my younger sister, Marge, now a junior at college, as the implicit example of filial devotion, and this really bothered me. For the better part of two years, my relationship with my parents was strained at best and outwardly hostile at worst.

It has only been within the past six months or so that this situation has improved markedly. Since our official engagement, Elaine and I have, both individually and as a couple, been accepted by my parents. They have been much more willing to treat us as adults with desires and values of our own, and we have reciprocated to a very great degree. For my part, I have felt a new confidence, the kind that allows me to accede to their wishes with no fear of being overwhelmed by them. This feeling of real control over myself and my own destiny is in no small part attributable to my relationship with Elaine, for the experience of being loved by one with no reason to love me has filled a void I only became aware of after it was filled. The most important factor for me has been that this new emotional constellation has been of my own making, that I am part of it because I helped create it, and that it exists because I sustain it. This in no way diminishes Elaine's emotional commitment, for it only means that without a commitment by either of us, it could not exist. This new emotional constellation is mine, for it could not exist without me. The older constellation, the family of my parents, existed because they committed themselves, and my participation was determined by my birth. In it, I gave and I received, but I could not have the underlying satisfaction of knowing that it existed because of me. Rather, I existed because of it.

My personal renewal has extended to other areas, all postdating the beginning of my relationship with Elaine. For the first time, I have become interested in intellectual pursuits and have perceived them as really relevant to my life. As I became aware that I was in fact in control of my life, I turned to my academic work with a vigor I could not have imagined in high school. It set my sights on a career in education, where I felt I could do something valuable for myself, for others, and for society as a whole. This has given me another sort of overview of various specific aspects of my life (schoolwork, personal relationships, and political values) and has given me a general unity of purpose that I hadn't thought possible four years before. At the risk of overusing the phrase, my marital and career plans have given my life a real sense of coherence in terms of my personal needs and values. It all has begun to seem "of a piece" now, and I no longer feel beset by internal conflict about where I may be going psychologically, emotionally, or intellectually.

Again, I feel I must draw back a bit, so as not to overstate the case, in my satisfaction at these developments. Within these general configurations, I am still unsure of many things. In education, I am unsure of whether I will work on the secondary level devoting myself to the process of education, or on the college level dealing more intimately with a particular field of scholarship. In emotional terms I realize that my "family" has only begun and that my relationship with Elaine will grow and change in ways I can hardly anticipate now.

sexual intimacy

The capacity for gratifying and relatively guilt-free sexual expression with a member of the opposite sex is easy to state as a goal but extremely difficult to achieve. The degree to which the so-called sexual revolution has clarified our values, norms, and behaviors in this intricate area of living is questionable. Many people at the present time understand neither the revolution nor the behavior it suggests.

In his preface to *Patterns of Child Rearing* (1957), Robert Sears observes that prescriptions about child training, be these pontifications by pediatricians or dictums of sound common sense, had, as of the 1930s and 1940s, little support in terms of empirical research. Sears refers to Wolfenstein's review (1953) of the way the patternings of socialization recommended by the medical profession through the United States Public Health Service were capricious and arbitrary, and founded on no more than the style of medical practice at a particular time. This was no doubt because child training was seen as something sacred and beyond investigation which rested solely with beliefs and practices of individual parents.

Similarly, until the publication of Kinsey's work (Kinsey, Pomeroy, and Martin, 1948, 1953) there was no satisfactory empirical work on sexual behavior. Both Hamilton (1929) and Terman (1938) contributed substantial studies which included excellent data on factors pertaining to sexual adjustment in marriage, and Henry's work on sexual deviance (1941) gave a clinical picture of the range of sexual activity to be found in American men and women. But Kinsey's two-volume work was the first large-scale study of sexual behavior per se.

The implications of Kinsey's studies are still being argued and debated. To be facetious, many who read his volumes in the fifties were relieved to find that they were not as deviant as they thought. Others claimed that to reveal such findings to the public was to corrupt their morals. The most important aspect of Kinsey's study, as far as we are concerned, is that it was the first clear presentation of data that suggested the hiatus that exists between the official norms of society and the actual behavior of a supposedly representative sample of men and women. This hiatus between the covert and overt culture was no doubt contributed to by a variety of factors: the change in the status of women after the First World War, the legitimization of sexual enjoyment as a goal of marriage in and of itself quite separate from procreation, and the development in the 1920s and 1930s of relatively certain and aesthetically acceptable forms of contraception.

The liberalization of opinion in regard to nonmarital sex stems from a different source. Organized religion has begun to have a far more liberal and less fire-and-brimstone attitude toward nonmarital sex; some of the most respected clergymen and theologians have suggested that sexual relationships should depend on relative moral values as opposed to absolutes. Possibly the most explicit statement of this is in Joseph Fletcher's works on situational ethics (1966) and the remarkable paper by Heron (1963).

It might be assumed that within this relatively liberal atmosphere the *utopia of genitality* would be more easily achieved. However, in the estimate of these authors, we still remain, in the words of Sullivan (1940), "the most sex-ridden people on the face of the earth," and the key to this situation is what Blos (1962) has referred to as the American tendency to *uniformism*. We seem to have replaced the conformity of Victorianism with the conformity of sexual freedom, and clinical data suggest that young people are as unhappy psychologically with their so-called new freedom as their parents were with the restrictions of a rigid code.

In order to understand what is involved in attaining integrated heterosexual intimacy and why it is difficult even in a period of history when not only liberty but even — to some — license in sexual matters abounds, a number of different kinds of research have to be brought into a preliminary synthesis. These investigations range from highly complex work in physiology to attitude studies. All are important and all can help to understand the complexity of the problem which young men and women face.

It might be remarked that sex is very simple and love very complicated. To be highly speculative for a moment, one reason that young people (particularly middle- and upper-class) have such a difficult time in our society in understanding and coping with sex, comes from a paradox in the American ethos. The United States, to a degree that is probably without parallel anywhere else in the world, brought together the traditions of romantic, even sentimental, love with a harsh Calvinistic outlook. This combination of traditions led to the conclusion that sexual indulgence was tantamount to love and vice versa. This is certainly a laudable ideal. But in actuality it led to a series of unrealistic beliefs concerning the meaning of sex and the meaning of love-intimacy.

It is also a paradox that in a society noted for rugged individualism a characteristic of the adolescent experience in the United States quite distinct, for example, from that of Europe is, as we have mentioned before, a high degree of "uniformism," as Blos observed (1962). Thus, the adolescent peer group places unparalleled pressure of group standards upon its members. There is a supposition that at a particular period of time every individual male or female is ready for the same kinds of experiences. This

assumption has no relation whatever to the physiological facts of the
matter, to say nothing of affective and emotional variations owing to
differences in gender. Tanner's definitive work on the physiological
aspects of adolescence (1962) suggests revision of some earlier
conceptions. We use the word "puberty," for example, to encompass
not only the onset of menstruation in the female and the capacity for
ejaculation in the male, but also the emergence of secondary sexual
characteristics. In a sense this is an accurate understanding;
puberty does bring with it a number of different phenomena lumped
under the general phrase "secondary sexual characteristics." But
two assumptions are made which have caused a great deal of trouble
both for adults and adolescents. The first is that the physiological
changes of puberty occur in all people at the same time. Nothing
could be further from the truth. Although as Tanner has
demonstrated, possibly because of better diet, the modal age of the
onset of menstruation has probably dropped from approximately
twelve years to ten and a half, we must recognize that in any given
representative sample the age of onset of menstruation can
range from eight to eighteen. The psychological and emotional
impact of being "too early" or "too late" cannot be underestimated.
The other misleading assumption is that the appearance of pubic
or axillary hair and the beginning of breast development assure
menstruation or spermatogenesis. The various kinds of
development actually may occur years apart in the same person.
Finding oneself apparently ready in some ways and not in others is
another possible source of profound emotional concern and
confusion. Little is understood about the wide variation in the
timing of puberty and its asymmetrical nature.

On an individual level the most difficult aspect of
adolescent sexuality is understanding the profound differences in
timing and orientation that sexuality has for the two sexes. Kinsey
was, of course, the first to show that sexual outlet — the most
simplistic measure of sexuality — had a very different pattern in the
life of the typical male and female. Typically, males began to
experience high frequency of outlet in their teens while females were
quiescent. Females tended to increase their sexual outlet as they
matured during their twenties and thirties, showing a steady
increase in sexual activity after puberty. Males, on the other hand,
show a sudden increase in sexual activity after puberty and
then — according to Kinsey's data — show a decline throughout life
starting in the twenties. Thus, the orientation of the typical man and
woman toward sexual tension is quite different during adolescence
and young adulthood.

One of the most relevant studies in any careful scrutiny of adolescence is Winston Ehrmann's fine study of dating behavior (1959). Here Ehrmann adds an extremely important dimension to Kinsey's basic data. He reveals, most tellingly, that the general orientation of men and women toward male-female relationships differs not only in quality but in kind and focus. Females, for example, see sexual intimacy as a consummatory act following a relatively long period of affectional and intimate mutual knowledge. Males, conversely, in many instances want sexual gratification first and, following, may or may not form an affectional intimate relationship with their partner. Moreover, Ehrmann's data clearly reveal that sexual activity in the male is affected by the so-called double standard. Phenomenologically, this represents Sullivan's (1953) comment about the tendency of the American male to separate females into "good" and "bad" girls. To some extent even in our relatively relaxed environment men tend to be intimate with (or marry) those women who will not have sexual relations with them and to discard or have ephemeral relationships with those who will form a sexual partnership. It may be that the old adage that men tend to marry the women they cannot rape and rape the women they cannot marry still applies in our supposedly sophisticated age. Possibly for reasons that have been suggested previously, the typical American adolescent, particularly in the college population, seems to be, to use its own metaphor, unbelievably "hung up" on sexual matters.

Possibly the most illustrative works in this connection are the publications of Christiansen and Carpenter (Christiansen, 1960; Christiansen and Carpenter, 1962). In contrasting a Danish community, an American mountain town, and an American Midwest town, they found the following: that the Danes, though extremely liberal in their attitudes toward sexual freedom, felt completely relaxed about whether they ever behaved in a manner consistent with this liberal point of view. Further, the Dane typically restricted sexual intimacy to intended spouse or "steady." Thus, while the attitude structure was liberal, the behavior itself was relatively circumspect. In the mountain community there was consensus and acceptance of extremely Calvinistic standards. Here, as in the Danish sample, there was little conflict between the attitude and the actual behavior. In the Midwest community, on the other hand, the American conflict was most apparent. Those who had not involved themselves in sexual relationships reported feeling inadequate and "out of it"; those who had indulged in sexual activity had done so, not with zest, but with guilt and ambivalence.

The degree to which this conflict is representative of American adolescence generally is of course open to question, and study after study underscores the significance of individual variation. While some are in conflict and profoundly miserable about their experience with sexuality, others make a relatively easy transition. However, there is a high probability that adolescent sexual experience is not a very happy episode in these human beings' histories. While some of the reasons for this have been suggested earlier, it seems well to summarize and go further into an explanation of why this happens to be a phenomenon peculiar to American university students.

To recapitulate some of the ideas presented earlier, we come out of a complex tradition of Calvinism and romantic love, the timing of sexual maturation and tension is quite different between the sexes and varies from individual to individual, and finally, the adolescent at the present is caught in the middle of a sexual revolution with all its attendant tension. However, there may be more profound reasons for the sexual predicament of Americans.

There are essentially four reasons: first, the problem of cross-sexed identity in American society as a consequence of certain changes in family orientation; second, the possibility, as W. R. D. Fairbairn (1952) has suggested, that the typical personality type in the present world has profound schizoid tendencies; third, the tendency of a psychologically oriented group of young people to use intellectualization as a defensive mobilization against the expression of impulse and affect; fourth, the deep conflict that may exist psychically and emotionally in both men and women concerning the opposing values of liberty and commitment. Each of these issues affects the integration of mature sexual relationships into the repertoire of adult living.

The issue of cross-sexed identity is a complex one. It took its point of departure from two quite different lines of attack. The first of these was the work, discussed previously, of John W. M. Whiting and his associates concerning the functional meaning of initiation rites (1958). Stated briefly, these investigators found that harsh initiation rites for males were found in those cultures where because of patterns of marriage, residence, and sleeping arrangements, the possibility of cross-sexed identity was maximized. This was found typically in the mother-child household and mother-child sleeping arrangements that characterized most polygamous societies. Having grown up in a household of women, males had to end this early identification with women dramatically so that they could take their place in the world of men. Other research of great importance is that on lower-class culture by Walter

Miller (1958) and the corollary work of Rohrer and Edmunson (1960). Miller points out that in the mother-child household of the ghetto, where the possibility of feminine identification due to father absence is maximized, highly defensive behavior, particularly masculine protest, is a way in which males compensate for their anxieties concerning their ultimate masculinity. Thus, exploitative sexual behavior, particularly during adolescence, is a group defense against ever being accused of being a faggot or a homosexual. However, it can be argued that both Whiting and Miller are dealing with specialized cases that have little relevance to American society generally. But this is not the case when we broaden our perspective.

Moving from the general and speculative to the particular, we find that it is possible to come to the same conclusions but to a lesser degree about middle-class males. The fact that this can be so is illustrated by a psychological monograph published a few years ago by Lynn K. Carlsmith (1964). Using data derived from records of Harvard undergraduates whose fathers were members of the Armed Forces during World War II, Carlsmith reveals that even in highly integrated middle-class and professional homes the absence of the father can have an effect upon the gender-orientation of males. The implications of these data have never really been properly assessed. While the middle-class male may not be forced to prove his masculinity in the same way as the young man in gang culture, and while he may be permitted to pursue relatively feminine orientations toward the arts and literature, there still remain problems in the interaction between a conformity that demands highly masculine orientation and the psychic structure of one more comfortable with the nonactive role. While Eleanor Maccoby (1966) has summarized in an encyclopedic sense the various studies on sex role and sex-role identity, we are still far away from understanding the implications of gender, its clarification and its meaning, not only to the individual but in the interpersonal context of intimacy.

A summary of these issues is to be found in a series of papers originally published in 1952. Herein W. R. D. Fairbairn attacked certain of the premises of classical libido theory. His attempts at redefining the libido and his revision of Freud's conceptions of ego-structure are beyond the limits of this discussion. What is not beyond it and is highly applicable is Fairbairn's suggestion that in contemporary times, because of what the parent-child relationship has become in technological society, the capacity to love and the anxieties inherent in forming love relationships are probably more difficult and much greater than ever before. Fairbairn's discussion of the so-called "schizoid position" is

highly reminiscent of Sullivan's theoretical insistence that forming
meaningful sexual relationships is far more complex than the gloss
suggested by the word "genitality." Thus, both Sullivan and Fairbairn
in quite different ways are suggesting that in contemporary times,
regardless of value orientation, intimacy is difficult to achieve for
civilized man at any age, but particularly in the midst of the highly
tumultuous era of adolescence.

The third point, namely the issue of intellectualization, is a
close corollary to Fairbairn's general discussion of the schizoid
position, but must be considered in its own right more on the level
of phenomenon than on the level of dynamics (Munter, 1962). The
college generation in matters of sex and intimacy has a high capacity
to verbalize and intellectualize what they think should and should
not be. While open and frank discussion of sexual matters is no
doubt anxiety reducing, the tendency to intellectualize sexual
relationships and to discuss them continually robs them to some
extent of the element of emotional intensity and zest which is the
key to sexual enjoyment. Complex intellectualizations and
rationalizations of why one does or does not do this or that are so
much a part of the college world that even to mention them is to
belabor the obvious. It is not obvious, however, that
intellectualization and rationalization of sexual behavior in a time
when the conformity implied is one of liberality, can cause
individuals to experience profound emotional frustration when they
discover that their expectations are not met as they begin their first
naturally inept reconnaissance.

Finally, our fourth point is closely related to this defense of
intellectualization. This is the profound conflict as a consequence
of these defenses between the desire to be liberal and in a sense
revolutionary about sexual freedom, and admitting to and finding
deep feelings of commitment so much a part of a stable sexual
relationship. This is a subtle conflict. Many individuals find
themselves defending against genuine feelings of love because they
feel that such deep commitments are inappropriate for those who
are "liberated." Others, particularly those with relatively
conventional basic social values, having experienced a sexual
relationship, will form what might be called a pseudo-commitment.
They will insist that they feel an emotional intimacy that in reality
does not exist.*

Without arguing the merits of sexual freedom, we can make
certain general observations about this area of living which, given

---

* For a careful review of the problems of sexual intimacy and commitment
the reader is referred to *Sex and the College Student* published by the Group
for the Advancement of Psychiatry (1965).

the biological destiny of man, are probably inevitable despite protestations to the contrary. There are certain criteria that can be applied to sexual maturity, a form of maturity that is such a central concern to the adolescent. The difference between Erikson's and Sullivan's views of intimacy has already been discussed. In the light of these additional theoretical hypotheses, it would be an exciting intellectual exercise to reconsider whether Erikson's sequence of identity to intimacy is more valid than Sullivan's progression from intimacy to identity. Possibly both are right, possibly both are dealing with a series of factors all of which must be synthesized but which from individual to individual may vary.

It is clear that heterosexual intimacy cannot be successfully accomplished as long as the individual, male or female, has any conflict concerning masculine or feminine gender behavior. Further, sexual relationships that are to be lasting and valid must be, to use Erikson's phrase, "distantiated" and separated from the residual sexual relationships that have existed in the Freudian family romance. Finally, successful integration of heterosexual intimacy demands that it be a motive and behavior in its own right, rather than an arena in which basic hostilities and social and cultural frustrations are fought out with a minimum of intimacy and a maximum of distance and hostility.

A Phenomenological Approach

The literature on humanistic psychology generally reflects a phenomenological approach to human development, and the work of Carl Rogers is one example of this approach. In his chapter "Threads of Permanence, of Enrichment" in *Becoming Partners* (1972), Rogers concludes his study by proposing four threads of permanence and enrichment in any lasting intimate relationship: frank communication of persisting feelings, the dissolution of roles, becoming a separate self, and commitment to a changing relationship.

Rogers illustrates what he means by "frank communication of persisting feelings" by a statement written in the first person:

> I will risk myself by endeavoring to communicate any persisting feeling, positive or negative, to my partner — to the full depth that I understand it in myself — as a living, present part of *me.* Then I will risk further by trying to understand, with all the empathy I can bring to bear, his or her response, whether it is accusatory and critical or sharing and self-revealing. (P. 204.)

Rogers elaborates on "the dissolution of roles" by saying:

> To know one's feelings is not easy or simple. It is in fact a lifetime effort. But to the extent that you can listen to your own organism and move in the directions that "feel right" to it and to you, to that extent you are moving away from behavior guided by role expectations. (P. 206.)

In addition to keeping in touch with and "owning" one's feelings, to communicating any persisting feeling to one's partner, and giving up masks and facades and roles, a person "becomes a separate self" when he or she strives to fulfill self's unique potential *and encourages and appreciates* his or her partner's efforts to fulfill her or his unique potential. Separateness requires and thrives on *some distance and difference* between partners. The joy of having one's partner encourage and appreciate one's self-fulfillment usually is felt by both persons — or neither. This separateness between self and partner is as crucial for intimacy as the separateness between self and parents is crucial for autonomy.

"Commitment to a changing relationship" is summarized by Rogers' statement: "We each commit ourselves to working on the changing process of our present relationship, because that relationship is currently enriching our love and our life and we wish it to grow" (p. 201). Partnership is a continuing process, not a contract. A lasting intimate relationship is a process of renewal and re-creation *lived in the present.* Commitment to a changing relationship is necessarily tentative because it depends on the continuing compatibility of the partners' paths of self-development.

A phenomenological approach to Cases 21 and 22 is to examine these relationships in terms of each partner's self-acceptance and commitment to growth. "Self-acceptance" comprises Rogers' first three threads of permanence and enrichment; "commitment to growth" is synonymous with the fourth.

Topic Eleven

Self-Acceptance and Commitment to Growth

Case 21 / Someone Who Is Willing to Listen

Before meeting Lil: "Any distressing problems I have had in the past were kept to myself, solved by myself, or relegated to the world of fantasy, where Mack emerges supreme."

After meeting Lil: "I am revealing myself to this girl, and I am doing it willingly. . . . Must I tell these secret things because for the first time here is someone who is willing to listen, who can understand what I *mean* and who will not laugh?"

The importance for Mack of this breakthrough with Lil is revealed by his comment, "Meeting you will either be the best or the worst thing that has ever happened to me."

Mack's openness and willingness to get involved are not reciprocated by Lil; however, Mack continues to act as if they were. He makes few attempts to understand what she wants and gets from the relationship. Mack's male friends fill in the holes of his understanding with popular mythology on "the male-female romantic tragedy."

Having been away six weeks from school, I was desperately asking people what had been happening during my absence. I first met

Lil in "philosophy." At first sight she was a fairly attractive girl. Also, she seemed very intelligent in raising and answering many questions in class.

About this time, there was a "philosophy" midterm, and being unprepared, I did not take it. A few days later I noticed Lil in another of my classes and asked her about the exam. The discussion then led to other courses taken and major fields of interest. However, a few friends were waiting for her and the conversation ended.

At the end of the next "philosophy" session, Lil proposed that we have coffee somewhere. Now the topics were work done in the past, limited aspirations for the future, and the fact that neither of us was employed but that we were "borrowing" from our parents. I mentioned a case history I was writing for my psychology seminar and asked if she would read it and give her critical comments.

Next week I saw Lil after the "Freud" class. She suggested that we eat some Chinese food, but I replied that my funds were depleted. "No problem," she said. "My birthday was yesterday and I received some money as gifts. The meal's on me." While we were eating, I asked if she was "sportsman enough" to attend a fight with me next Monday night. "I'd love to," she replied. "I don't know much about boxing but I get very excited at football games and things like that."

That fight was one of the greatest times of my life. Maybe it was because I was taking this girl into a world she had never known. We went into Jack Sharkey's bar, mobbed as usual before Garden events, where old drunks and fight fans meet in good fellowship. The smoke is so thick that it resembles a fog and the talk is coarse. I am drinking a beer, she a ginger ale. Next to Lil is an old drunk.

"Who's fighting tonight?" he asked her.

"I really don't know."

"Probably just a couple of niggers, and you won't be able to tell them apart anyway."

Talk like this could be heard all over the bar, if you listened closely. Yet it was not for me to reprimand the drunk because there was a "lady" present. This, to me, was a part of the boxing game — the lower classes, the vulgar, but at the same time the honest.

On that note, we hit the Boston Garden. Amid that hot stuffiness, I pointed out fighters, managers, the traditional boxing buffs. The bouts themselves were not exceptional, but they showed how sympathetic yet merciless the fight goer is. The boxer whom the crowd felt was not putting forth his best efforts was booed and heckled derisively; the loser who fought his heart out was given a tremendous ovation. Then there was one fighter with the natural physique, the moves, the cat-like quickness, and the superb training. And he was exciting to watch.

When we left the Garden, Lil and I were arm in arm. We walked to Park Square. While I was showing her the Christmas decorations, the attendant shut off all the lights. In the subway we were accosted by a drunk who asked us for money. I gave him a quarter, and out of "gratitude" he told us various historical facts and anecdotes, which were amusing.

We ended the evening at my apartment listening to soft music, relaxing, talking about people and how beautiful they could be. This went on until 1:30 A.M., when she excused herself to leave. "This has been such a great night," she said. "You don't know me well enough yet to realize how much this meant to me." And when I kissed her good night, I believed she was sincere.

Saturday, Lil invited me to dinner at her apartment. There was another couple there also. After a great roast beef dinner with wine and candlelight, Lil and I retired to her room. I was in a pensive mood and began reflecting on time and how much of it I had lost in searching for an identity. Out of high school nearly six years, with but one year of college, so many of my classmates were already working toward Master's degrees. Half of our graduating class is already married. Hence, I considered myself old and traditionally referred to friends as "old" — "Old Dan," "Old Jim," etc. She replied that all of these experiences gave me an edge in living, in interpersonal relationships, above and apart from mere academic learning. This, incidentally, is something I had truly believed for a long time and it formed the backbone of my earlier credo of living: doing the thing in question, experiencing firsthand as many things as possible to form original impressions which are the basis of comparison with later theoretical knowledge. It made me so happy that this girl could understand the value of such a style of life. In fact, Lil's life was not too dissimilar from my own. Although only nineteen, she graduated from high school at sixteen and had spent the succeeding years in "finding herself." She was in the process of applying to various universities as a freshman. Hence, she would begin college at twenty.

We were on her bed and I started making out with her. After a few minutes she stopped me. "I don't want to be a tease," she said. Now this remark puzzled me.

"What do you mean by that?"

"I don't want to be a tease. I want to satisfy you but I am a virgin and want to stay that way."

"Look dear. I don't want you to do anything you don't believe in or feel uncomfortable with."

I proceeded to caress Lil with all the tenderness you might show a newborn infant or someone you deeply love.

We rejoined the other couple and spent the remainder of the evening listening to old 78 rpm records.

At this point I will interject a few related incidents. I got a job as a night watchman, working 11:00 P.M. to 7:00 A.M. Sunday through Thursday.

This year the Bruins have been playing great hockey and will probably make the playoffs. The Garden is sold out nearly every game, and the excitement of the crowd is something to behold. I went to the Garden box office and waited in line for twenty-five minutes to buy tickets for the current big game with the top team. It was sold out. Therefore, I bought two tickets for a game a month in advance, with the same team. The hope, of course, was that the Bruins would still be in contention for first place and the game would have a similar significance. Also, we organized a big social evening in which eight people would attend a Bruins game and hit the town afterwards. Lil was to get a date for a buddy of mine, and two other very close friends would bring their girls. Coming the weekend after exams, and knowing the personalities of the people involved, this night promised to be a great event.

To return to the mainstream of the plot, one morning I returned from work to find a note on my apartment door. It was from Lil:

> *Mack, dear —*
> I realized about 10:00 tonight that my phone was out of order. I tried to call you from a phone down the street (which, incidentally, refused to give my dime back), but you'd already left for work. If you'd gotten that extra key made for the doorsill, I just might've straightened out your kitchen. Oh well!
> Do call if you get a chance. I'll call back if I'm not there. Be happy —
>
> Love,
> *Lil*

I had been contemplating keeping a spare key above the door ledge, as I am in the habit of locking myself out by forgetting the key. The next day I had a few duplicates made and presented one to Lil, who was elated.

Since I was scheduled to work New Year's Eve, Lil and I celebrated the Saturday before. We ate lobster at Ye Olde Oyster House and saw *Gone With the Wind*. Then the evening fell in. That picture is so damn poignant that we came out of the theater emotionally depleted. Lil was crying. There was just nothing to say, no humor to force a smile. I could only console her (and myself) by saying it was but a movie.

We returned to my apartment, put on some records, and talked about the coming year. I gave her a gift, an ashtray, in the hope of a prosperous new year. We began making out, and I suggested she spend the night, since it was late and the roads icy. (It must be noted that she had the car, not me.) Lil readily agreed. As we prepared for bed, she again reiterated that she was a virgin and wished to remain that way for a while. And again, I replied that if that was her desire, I would not try to change her mind.

From here the remainder of the evening is weird. According to the script, the two lovers fall blissfully to sleep, to soft music, in each other's arms. In this case, Lil is wearing my pajama top; both of us are brushing our teeth at the same time. Lil, an insomniac, drinks some medicine which she must take in order to sleep; I throw down a few shots of whiskey. Lil crawls into bed and I shut the lights off before undressing because of a big old hard-on that I don't want her to see. A tiny red light gives the room a seductive appearance. The soft music plays. I get into bed and put my arm around Lil — but she is already asleep. There I am, friends and neighbors, unable to sleep, listening to Sinatra sing songs for the wee small hours of the morning, while the girl beside me is totally unresponsive. This situation is ridiculous, much less frustrating. After fifteen minutes I could stand it no longer. Gropingly I found Lil's sleeping medicine, took three or four gulps, returned to bed, and was in dreamland within two minutes. Potent stuff!

That morning was a bachelor's dream. While I was still sleeping, Lil had bought some delicatessen and fixed me a big Sunday morning breakfast — breakfast in bed. All the while she is running around in my pajama top, which is driving me up a wall, but the effects of the medicine still make me extremely drowsy. Lil leaves and I go back to sleep.

In order to abbreviate this paper, I can say that the next two weeks brought us even closer together. It was not that the things we did were so exciting. There was dinner at my mother's house; her parents visited her for a day and Lil brought them over to my apartment to meet me. We did some shopping and had coffee after classes. The important thing was a sense of complete, utter communication between two people, with conversation frequently entering the realm of "soul talks." It was just that she was *there* that counted. Lil was so wonderful in her way and some of the little things she did were beautiful. For example, I loved to watch her eat. There was no pseudo-femininity and daintiness. When she was hungry, she ate as if this were her last supper, whether it be at a classy restaurant or Joe and Nemo's. One weekend I went to New Hampshire to visit some relatives. Still, I could not get her out of my mind; she was so obsessively fixed and reappearing.

Tuesday I met Lil in Forbes Hall, and she asked if visitors were allowed in the seminar. I seriously doubted it but suggested she ask Dr. Quinn, since she had nothing to lose. As it happened, Lil was a guest that night. For me this was an utterly frustrating two hours. I could feel that there was so much she wanted to say, so much that she could contribute to this group. At various times she would glance in my direction, whispering, "Say something, say something!" I could say nothing. As the discussion unfolded, most of the topics were the very ones that Lil and I had spent hours upon hours talking over. After the seminar ended, over coffee, I poured my heart out to her. This is something I had been doing for the past three weeks — giving her my opinions and conclusions which I could not say to the group. That night I brought my tape recorder to work and, being especially charged up, was able to spontaneously record replies to various issues and their offshoots, brought up in the seminar.

Reflecting on the events of Tuesday night, the whole problem of fear of revealing oneself haunted me like a recurring ugly memory. Lil is so forward, so free. She says what she means and lets the world be damned for their opinions. Lil had several mental breakdowns and is undergoing psychiatric therapy. She told me this as if she was asking for a glass of water. In my childhood, I had a nervous breakdown and for a time visited different social workers and a child psychiatrist. Yet, I told *no one — no one!* My parents are divorced, but when anyone asked what my father did, I would inevitably try to preserve the image of the solid family. When someone asked my age, I would, because of my youthful appearance, give an age younger than I actually was. Why? To save face? To create a better image in others? Who cares about people? I care, for their tactless comments hurt me deeply.

"How old are you?"

"Sixteen."

"God, I could have sworn you were about twelve!"

Remarks like that would cause me to anticipate future recurrences. Hence, I would say "thirteen" so that the person's expectations were somewhat confirmed.

That was seven years ago, but many times I misrepresent and guard myself in the same ways today. Why?

Any distressing problems I have had in the past were kept to myself, solved by myself, or relegated to the world of fantasy, where Mack emerges supreme. In the service the pattern changed a great deal, and I realize that my former isolated life could never be taken up again. Or could it? In the past I could find contentment within myself and enjoy things by myself. I could never do that now. But, some of the crucial problems of living, of identity, of meaning, and of commitment rarely came out in the military atmosphere. They still remain within me. Is it necessary that others know your intimate ideas? I never thought so before. To me one's self is his final individuality. Revealing his ideas and goals prematurely is leaving your world open for others to scrutinize. But who cares if they agree or not? You do, for this future, onward orientation is what makes suffering bearable *now*. It is your final bastion of hope, other than sheer withdrawal and fantasy. It is the idea that my life, my behavior *now* can only be judged as part of a total scheme, which will be shown at some future date. Disclosing this long-range plan now causes the endeavor to lose some of its creativity and surprise. It may be a source of ridicule and skepticism in others. This is to be expected. But *you* have to be ultimately sure; *you* cannot entertain any doubts. Therefore, you must keep these thoughts to yourself to prevent any possible loss of faith.

Now, slowly but surely, I see my inner life fading, just as my external social life has been completely changed. I am revealing myself to this girl, and I am doing it willingly. It is almost like a sponge which, when placed in water, must soak up the water for it has been so depleted for so long. Is this me? Must I tell these secret things because for the first time here is someone who is willing to listen, who can understand what I *mean*, and who will not laugh? Probably so, but there is more. In spilling my guts, with heartfelt emotions, I am causing her to respond similarly, i.e., to reveal *herself!* In the process of creative interchange, facets of our selves which we never had the opportunity to explore are brought to the surface for evaluation. Ideas, formerly considered in one sense only, are infused with dynamic additions and modifications. In short, the self and its ideas, rather than being weakened, in fact are becoming immeasurably strengthened.

Somehow, I had to tell Lil some of these conclusions. I could not "use" her as a means of self-therapy. I had to find out where I stood with her, how she felt toward my interpersonal meditations. The occasion took place the next evening. I invited her up to my apartment for a quick cup of tea. At the time I was so emotionally wrought that my legs quivered and my hand shook as I handed her the tea. Then I began:

"Lil — I might as well lay it on the line to you. Meeting you will either be the best or the worst thing that has ever happened to me. You go along and live in your little world, clearly and carefully differentiating between what is out there, and what is inside. You remain reserved; then suddenly the bubble bursts and your world is no longer safe. This is the way I feel having met you. I'm telling you things I never told anyone before. and it scares me. You're sitting back and listening. Why should you be interested in my problems? Why should I burden you, even though you're kind enough to hear me out? This is so selfish of me!"

"First of all, as I've told you before, I don't do anything I don't want to do. If I was not interested, I would not be here. What you must realize is that PEOPLE NEED PEOPLE, and you can't do everything alone. (Silence) Besides, I might as well tell you — I love you; I LOVE YOU! I don't like to say this because it sounds sentimental, but I am really sentimental at heart. I go out with other guys and I will continue to do so, but I enjoy being with *you* most."

"I love you too. God, this is awful! I never said that to a girl in my life — never thought I could, never thought I'd ever want to. Lil, thank you."

From the apartment I went to work. Before leaving, however, I gave Lil my recorder and the tapes I made the night before. Our conversation had lasted but half an hour, but it had changed my life.

I saw Lil briefly a few more times during the week. She gave no comments on the tapes. On the surface everything remained the same. The feeling, though unexpressed verbally, was nevertheless "love." And as love it must be mutual and selfless. My "problem" was somewhat solved. Now what could I do for her? This does not mean prying into her life, but I must be responsible — committed. As today's popular song goes, if she reaches out, I'll be there. Again, this does not imply any form of "going steady" or possibly marriage in the future. Lil will possibly go to school out of state this fall. Formally this could end the relationship. But for the present, I must care. And if endeavors require us to be separated, I want her to know that she can count on me — anytime!

Next Tuesday, after the seminar, I trudged back to the apartment. My friend Dave had been writing a paper for a course and the place, usually messy, was in complete havoc. When I walked in the revelation was stunning. The apartment had been straightened up! There was a package in an unimposing paper bag. The inscription on the bag read: "Dear Slob — Happy Tuesday. I love you. L" Inside the package was a crimson red pull-over, with a zippered, variable turtle neck. God, I was in orbit. This was about the nicest thing anyone had ever done for me. It was all so unexpected and spontaneous. Happy Tuesday — Tuesday is my good news day!

Friday, Lil and her roommate invited Dave and me to their apartment for dinner. Somehow the evening never got off the ground, despite a good meal. The question was what to do afterwards. Conversation was forced, tense, groping for anything to say just to break the silence. Lil suggested that we smoke some pot. (It should be added that these girls are not habitual smokers, or so they say. The marijuana is just there — available. Neither had smoked the stuff within the last six months, or so they said.) Fine idea, I thought, especially since I had never tried hash before. As it turned out, everyone was getting high but me. At first I could not inhale properly, so they gave me a cigarette to practice with. When I was successful in choking on the smoke, I went back to the pot. Nothing! Then they were convinced that I was too tense; you had to relax for it to be effective. I suggested that a couple of shots of whiskey might serve that purpose. Meanwhile, the other people are exclaiming how at ease and lightheaded they feel. I can sense depression beginning to set in, as they are withdrawing into themselves. Again, there is a lack of communication. They had reached their apex, and no one had "opened up." Where does the show go from here?

We all retired to Lil's room and sat on her oversized bed. A tiny red bulb is the only illumination. I am drinking a half a fifth of Canadian Club. Before each swig of the bottle, I make a toast to an individual member of the group (excluding myself). After three or four toasts, I am damned relaxed in my own way, i.e., half-stiff. The prevailing mood seemed to call for some anecdotes, and I proposed to tell a few service sea stories.

"Do you want to hear when I was at my idealistic best or my lecherous worst?"

Lil and Bonnie were quick to respond: "Oh tell us some of the indecent things you did."

"Okay, fine."

Now I proceeded to relate some of my grossest, most lustful activities — using the same four-letter vocabulary as I would in conversing with my service colleagues in the midst of a big drunk. Somehow, at the time, this talk did not seem out of place and I felt no guilt. After a few stories, I went back to toasting, killed the bottle, and passed out. The other three, now in a normal state, dragged me into the living room and terminated the evening.

After about four hours, I woke up, somehow found my way to Lil's room, and fell asleep beside her. A little later I awoke again. Hung over and sick as I was, everything seemed beautiful to me. Old Lil sleeping — how content and peaceful she looked. I felt such a tenderness toward her; sometimes I would stroke her hair and kiss her lightly on the cheek. At last she awoke and I watched her dress. There was no fooling around. A pair of stockings, cutoff dungarees, her bra, a green blouse, a little make-up, a few brushes of her hair — in eleven minutes she was dressed and looked great. God, she is marvelous! Somehow I think she could sense my feelings. "You know," she said, "I can't see how anyone can love you and you be unable to return that love." Upon leaving I asked if she was still going to the hockey game Sunday night. She replied that she was tired, an exam was coming up Monday, and she could not possibly make it.

That morning I saw Dave. "You were really ridiculous last night," he said. "What a horror show! You were gross and boisterous. If I were you, I'd apologize to the girls for your behavior."

I thought he was exaggerating the situation, but upon his recapitulation I realized that most of my profanity was directed at him.

"Look, Dave — Lil can't make the game. Why don't you go? It will be my treat to make up for Friday."

"Fine. Will pick you up at 7:00 Sunday, after I get back from skiing."

Returning home, I called Lil to apologize. "Oh yes," she said, "about Friday night. I want to speak to you about that. I don't have the time right now, but we'll discuss it Monday."

Now the scene began to bother me. What had I done to offend my two best friends? Did I embarrass Lil in front of her roommate? Why did I insult Dave? That day I walked the streets for hours trying to come to some conclusions. At night I read Freud's *Civilization and Its Discontents* and everything became clear. My greatest offense had been against Dave. Unconsciously I had tried to put him down. This goes back to the years when the boys would sit around and discuss their "conquest" of broads. Any degree of success was elaborated to the minutest detail, to give others the benefit of their "technique." This is all fine if you can counter with stories of your own. Unfortunately, at this time, I was dating no girls, never had, and it was painful to hear these things. Now you certainly do not want your friends to fail with girls or anything else. However, *you* want to feel somewhat on par with them. In other words, you do not want to feel badly inferior. That Friday night the past was completely reversed. Now I had the girl, I had the stories which he could not top, and I was getting drunk and holding my booze. (In past years five cans of beer would cause me to vomit, and the standard joke was to try to predict the exact moment Mack would puke.)

I felt so ashamed and guilty of my actions of Friday night. They were so revengeful. Hence, I resolved to tell these conclusions to Dave at the game. My best friend might be lost but honesty would be upheld. Then I must see Lil on Monday and face her wrath.

Sunday night is here. It is 7:15 and Dave has not yet arrived. The game begins at 7:30. I called Dave at his house. He had just come back from skiing, was exhausted, and was not in the mood for going. Oh God, I thought, he did this on purpose to get back at me. He knew I could not possibly get to the Garden in time by bus. If he could not go, why didn't he call me two hours in advance? This is terrible: I must have hurt him more than I thought. Well, fuck it, I'm going anyway, by myself, no matter how late I get there!

What a hockey game! The Bruins won 6–0 and the crowd was delirious. Yet I could not fully enjoy it. I bought these tickets a month in advance, dreaming of such a game, and when it actually occurred, there was no one to share it with. Nevertheless, I must concentrate on the "Freud" exam, difficult as it may be. On that note I went to work.

I studied for a few hours with only limited success. Then Lil called. I told her about the game, Dave not going, and my interpretation of Friday's incident.

"You may be right," she said, "but again you may be over-analyzing."

"Forgetting Dave – what's your gripe about Friday. Whip it on me now."

"Actually, Friday was one of the best experiences I ever had in turning on with pot – simply because you were there."

"But what about the stories I told. Didn't they offend you? Weren't they out of place?"

"Not at all. They helped make the evening so great. Bonnie and I really pushed you into it; *we* wanted to hear them! As for offending us, you don't know how girls talk when they are alone. It's just as bad!"

"I think you are right, if we can use as a standard of judgment the graffiti in women's bathrooms."

"My criticism was in your getting drunk. You were very loud. It is not that I am against drinking, in feeling good and high. What I object to is having to resort to liquor in order to say 'fuck you' to the world when you can't say it sober."

"Lil you don't realize what a relief it is to hear you say that."

Monday night, after the exam, Lil elaborated further.

"The toasting and the stories seemed a part of a man's world, and I was interested for that reason. In fact, Bonnie and I had been discussing why you never tried to seduce me. She thought maybe you were a virgin, but I said he's been in the service, so how could he be. Then I thought maybe it was because I wasn't attractive, but she rejected that idea. Others have tried to seduce me in the past – unsuccessfully. I've been taking birth control pills in case I met someone who I'd want to go to bed with. Now here is a guy I'm really fond of, and he won't make the move."

"First of all, I have had only two chances to seduce you. In both cases you came on with the 'I'm a virgin and wish to remain so' line – so I respected your feelings."

"Well, as Freud would say, sometimes every 'no' implies a 'yes.'"

I practically floated back to the apartment. Could anything be more obvious? She really was scared of sexual intercourse, but now she had warmed up to me. She trusts me! And, I will not disappoint her.

Wednesday night I sat next to Lil in class. She had just given an astute comment which had caused the professor to modify his view. Suddenly her face became distorted and she ran out of the room. I did not know what to make of this; maybe it was "that time of the month." After a few minutes I left the classroom, and there sat Lil puffing on a cigarette and trying hard to hold back the tears. I put my arm around her in consolation. She took a few pills which calmed her somewhat.

"Are you OK now?"

"Yes, I'm fine."

"Let me ask you about the big weekend. I've got some great plans. What's the situation for this Friday night?"

"Oh, I'm tied up Friday with this Vietnam political meeting. I wasn't particularly interested, but my friends talked me into it."

"All right then — what about Saturday?"

"Saturday I'm doing something with this guy I used to be engaged to. He is involved with this Vietnam thing also, and after the last meeting I spent the night at his place. It was 3:30 in the morning when he asked me. I was very tired and consented although I really didn't care to."

"OK then. I don't suppose you're up for coffee tonight?"

"No, I feel sick and I'm very tired. I'll be going right home."

After class, I had a few beers at Cronin's. The more I thought of it, the angrier I became. What is she doing to me? She's building me up, cutting me down, spinning me round and round, and playing me for a fool. What is happening here? I must find out.

The minute I got into work I called. People were coming and going and I was supposed to check their ID cards, but those people were related to a distant background. Now how do you summarize forty-five minutes of intense emotional interchange? You could practically visualize the sparks flying.

"Lil, you said you didn't want me to say anything drunk that I could not say when sober. Right now, I'm sober. Maybe you care for me less than I thought; maybe I care for you more than I should. I want you to know that you hurt me deeply tonight."

"How did I do that?"

"By the way you approached this weekend — so matter-of-fact, 'Well, this thing came up so I took it even though I wasn't especially interested.' And your former beau — it makes me feel real good to know that you spent the night with him and are going out with him!"

"Do you think I slept with him? Well I didn't!"

"I don't give a shit what you did; just don't tell me about it! I live like a damn dog five days a week. The entire day is in reverse — school nights, work through the night, sleep, and the cycle repeats. Two days I have free, and you can't arrange your schedule so that *one* night of those two we are together. You said that you loved me; I said I loved you. I never said this before meaningfully to anyone. To me this implies some kind of commitment. Doesn't that mean anything to you?"

"I thought I made it quite clear that I would not be tied down. My life is to be free!"

"Free! Not being tied down! Not being hung-up. Who is doing any of these things? One day out of seven? Have I tried to chain you to me, change you, interfere with anything you want to do? Now I'm not going to give you any rinky-dinky ring as a symbol of some sort of bond. God, you say 'love.' What is that to you — when you're in the mood, have nothing better to do, or up for a few laughs at the expense of a possible fool?"

"Do you think I've been laughing at you?"

"I don't know at this point what you are doing? Another thing — you won't be committed to anything; you like to be spontaneous. I bought tickets a month in advance for a hockey game, waiting around at the Garden when I should have been sleeping. At the last moment something came up — you can't make it. I wanted to take you, not Dave; I thought you would enjoy it."

(Crying.) "I'm sorry. I want to do the things you like, to be excited by what excites you."

"Well that did excite me and you were not there! Damn it, stop crying! Is this an omen for the future? Now what happens with the game next week? Will you find some excuse to call that off too?"

"No — I said I would go. Some friends of mine asked me to go mountain climbing, something I really wanted to do, but I said 'no.'"

"Go to your damn mountain climbing if you enjoy that more, if obligations mean nothing to you!"

(Silence — sobbing and sniffling.)

"Lil, I'm living like hell. Seeing you on a weekend makes the week. Going out with you is very meaningful; it's not just a date you'd as soon forget. I look forward to it. But I can't have my weekends vacillating according to your whims. I can't make plans and have them fluctuate according to your moods. This kills me! I've got to know where I stand. (Silence.) Look, we've resolved nothing. Sleep on it and let me know."

Emotionally I was exhausted from the interchange but by no means relieved. I continued to pace the floor for the remainder of the night. Had I done the right thing? Was I too hasty? Had I made a mountain out of a molehill? Was I acting selfishly in thinking of *my* enjoyment, *my* weekends? Was I in fact tying her down?

In the morning I listened to the old records, the words of which I had previously taken for granted. Songs of love – beautiful lyrics and music, the great standards – now had a significance I formerly could not fully comprehend. My gut ached; tears came uncontrollably. Then I heard a song that fully expressed my emotions. Oh, sing it out, Frank, babes:

"All or nothing at all – half a love never appealed to me. If your heart never could yield to me – then I'd rather have nothing at all."

That day I had another exam but was unable to seriously study. I was waiting for Lil's call. Psychologically I was preparing myself for any possible answer she could give me. In my mind I was carrying on two-party conversations of what *might* happen in actuality. God, this was so tough, for anything could happen. I had put my position on the line last night. The decision was up to her, and I could not possibly resolve the problem without speaking to her.

At work, I was walking the floors again. The phone never rang. Finally I could stand it no longer. At 2:30 A.M. I called.

"Lil, I have three exams coming up next week, and I can't concentrate worth a shit. I can tolerate success, and I think I can accept failure. But I can not take indecision. Have you given any thought to what I said last night?"

"You want a simple solution to a complex problem. I could say 'Yes, I'll arrange my life to fit your schedule,' or I could say 'No, it's over.' But if I say 'no' I'm afraid I won't even be able to have coffee with you."

"If you just want to go out occasionally, that can be arranged. But how can we do this when you have the key to my apartment and may, in a spontaneous gesture, do something beautiful like you did two weeks ago?"

"I'll mail your key back tomorrow morning. Can I also enclose a newspaper clipping you may be interested in?"

"Do anything you want."

"Look – it's 2:45 and I'm very tired. Good night." (CLICK!)

Hurt as I was, I nevertheless felt relieved. It's definite; it's over. Still, I could not help recapitulating the events which led to this moment. Oh, how true were the words to that song: "What is this thing called love – this funny thing called love? Just who can solve its mystery? Why should it make a fool of me?"

In the past I would have kept everything inside of me, but I had learned something from this episode. I called Dave, told him briefly what happened, and asked if he would be interested in discussing the situation in detail over a few beers. That night three of us met in good fellowship, amid a glowing fireplace, music and brew. I told Dave of my conclusions to the horror show–hockey incident, which he rejected as ridiculous. To him I *had* overanalyzed. He had been unavoidably detained skiing, a fact corroborated by Eric. Then came the gory details of the breakup.

"Guys," I said. "I feel like such a fool. This has never happened to me before. I told this girl I loved her. I thought it was real, and she responds by hanging up the phone."

"Hanging up," said Eric, "was a bad play and the mark of immaturity. Girls say they love you but they don't really mean it. This has happened to me five or six times. You come to expect it."

"The whole thing is sickening," said Dave. "Broads say 'I love you' like we say 'Let's go eat.' Four and a half years I went with this girl. We were to be married this fall. Our kids were already named. So much of my life was invested in her. And then she ditches me two months ago, and I hear she just got married a few days ago. All that time down the drain and there is nothing I can do about it."

"You see, Mack," responded Eric, "the thing is universal. The best thing to do is try to forget and chalk it up to experience. It happened once and it'll probably happen again."

"Well, does this qualify me to join the club?"

They both agreed that it did.

The next day I felt reassured that what had happened to me certainly was not unique. Still I was not satisfied. Here are three different guys, three different girls, three different circumstances — yet there is a common thread involved. It is an element of betrayal. At first I felt bitter. Then my reasoning became clearer. Maybe girls think differently than guys do. Maybe "I love you" really means "I am quite fond of you generally and at certain moments I can feel love in the traditional sense." If that is the case, an entirely different relationship exists. Now it is not "love" in the sphere of constant, total commitment. Now responsibility has its basis in convenience.

Applying this interpretation specifically to Lil — if we have divergent conceptions of the term "love," then we can go back to our original relationship. If I had something planned that might interest her, I would give her a call. If there was something better to do, the hell with her. Let me drive *me* around at *my* convenience. She talks of seduction. I'll try, damn it, and do it to please myself! I kept thinking about what Dave said, "She's gone and I can't do anything but accept it." Well, Lil is not gone, and I can do something about it.

Almost instantly, I was genuinely relieved and the feeling elated me. Reflecting on my experience with girls, those I cared least about were the most responsive. The one girl I loved treated me like dirt and practically broke my heart. Now she is removed from the pedestal and considered as an ordinary "broad." And as a broad, she can be given her "walking papers" as easily as retained.

A few days later, Dave, my friend Joe, and his girl came up to my apartment. For the benefit of these new people, I briefly reviewed what had occurred up to this point and gave my current battle plan.

"In the light of what has happened, am I wrong? Am I being selfish?"

"Lil is just testing you," said Irene. "I've done the same many times myself. She wants to make you mad. If you call, you're doing what she expects and wants. And if you call, she'll do the same in the future."

"What is the situation about Saturday's hockey game?" inquired Joe.

"I'm not sure," I replied. "I assume it is still on but Lil has not confirmed it."

We then agreed that the future of my relationship with Lil depended on whether or not she upheld her commitment to an affair planned over a month ago. The initial approach was not to ask what her meaning of "love" was. Simply, was she going to the game? If she agrees, we go on from there, one step at a time. If she refuses, it terminates.

I picked up the phone and called her. No answer! At work Dave and I were pulling an all-night study session in preparation for the next day's exams. Periodically I called throughout the night. No answer! In the morning, about 10:00, I finally got through to Bonnie and left a message for Lil to call me. An hour later the phone rang. It was Lil. This is it, boys and girls!

"What's the situation about Saturday night. Is it still on?"

"I don't think so."

"Now Lil — for once in your life, try to transcend your little microcosm and begin to think of others. You realize, of course, how and when this event was planned, who is involved, and who will be the butt if it falls through?"

"I do not realize it. You wanted me to make a decision; I made it!" (CLICK!)

I turned to Dave. "It's all over. The bitch hung up! THE BITCH HUNG UP! C'est fini!"

With that I put a record on the turntable. "That's life! That's what all the people say. You're riding high in April, shot down in May. . . ."

Case 22 / Don't Bring Me Your Hang-ups, I'm Busy with My Own

The idyllic beginning of this love story is followed by a second phase of relating that is glorious at its best and smothering at its worst. Sandy and Bob feel "crowded" when they are together and can't bear the loneliness when apart. Sandy writes, "I toyed with the possibility of finding something (as opposed to someone) to which I could dedicate myself, some interest absorbing enough to balance my relationship with Bob. This was my equivalent to Bob's wanting spatial independence. I wanted something fixed in my life so that my whole happiness wouldn't depend on him . . . and as long as I was absorbed in him, I couldn't even begin to find any such outside stability." The viability of an intimate relationship seems to depend on both persons' maintaining some separate interests and goals and agreeing to a tentative commitment — commitment until the relationship ceases to be mutually growth-enhancing.

Bob was important to me before I really knew him at all. It began when my mother invited him to a dance at the end of my 9th grade year. I didn't see much of him at the dance because I was actively pursuing someone else, and my brother's friends from prep school were being very nice to me as little sister. Afterwards, however, he asked me out a couple of times. We didn't get along particularly well or ill, weren't particularly attracted or repelled; but then I went away to school.

At school I found that everyone else had someone "on the outside" to talk about, and, in most cases, to correspond with or even to visit and have visit them. My problem was that I had never been able to bear any of the boys who had shown a great interest in me, probably because I didn't like myself and thought there had to be something basically wrong with anyone who did. Consequently I had nothing remotely approaching an outside attachment and little hope of forming a spectacular one at school. Still I was determined to keep up with the competition, so I made up a relationship with Bob. This had the advantage of being based in fact. I had gone out with him and he was real. Also he was in school in England, which explained why he never showed up and, to some extent, why he didn't write, since he would have had to ask his parents to find out from my parents where I was. Then too his not having shown much interest in me meant that I didn't despise him. This made it easier for me to represent myself as being madly in love with him.

After a few days I had the other girls convinced, and after a few months I believed it myself. Oddly enough I didn't elaborate on what he was like, didn't make up a dream figure and call it Bob. I didn't even think much about what he was like. Also, at least to myself,

293

I didn't fiddle with what had actually happened – a few pretty uninteresting dates. It was that I found myself expecting to get a letter from him, and that the prospect of getting one was very exciting. I think I loved the idea of having someone I didn't hate care enough to write, and a lot of my fantasies about actually loving someone got attached to the idea of Bob.

During the summer, I went to join my parents in Bob's family's apartment in London. One day I found some photographs of Bob and a girl, and I discovered I was very hurt and jealous. On closer inspection the pictures proved to be of Bob's elder brother, Mat, which really put the lid on it. I couldn't even recognize him, but there I was moaning and hair-tearing with the best of them! It shocked me into realizing that my fantasies about Bob were important and, in some sense, real to me.

I don't know how this fantasy beginning affected our real relationship later, but I think it must have had some effect because I can't get away from the strength of my feelings about it. This has always made me include the fantasy stage in my view of the whole relationship while Bob doesn't. For instance, when we later spoke about the first time we had seen each other I spoke of tearing into my parents' room draped rather inelegantly in a large soggy towel and finding an utter stranger polishing his shoes. Bob spoke of seeing me come down the stairs on the way to the second dance he came to.

During my second year in secondary school I didn't think much about Bob because I was wrapped up in thoughts of Drew, a boy I had met in the summer; but then came the spring dance, our equivalent of a spring weekend. Drew couldn't come and, in trying to find someone, I thought of Bob.

It was a beautiful June night, starlight and moonbeams, and the dance was outside. Bob danced well (I'd forgotten that) and, better still, well with me (Drew didn't and I'd missed it). He touched easily. I remember just walking with his arm around my shoulders feeling very much at home and beautiful. We talked a lot without that awful "making conversation" awkwardness. He seemed at ease with my friends; I was fascinated by and envious of the things he had done, and he wasn't bored by me. When someone cut in he would dance with other girls, but he would come back almost immediately. It was glorious, glamorous, ego-boosting, fun, romantic, all the things a dance is supposed to be and usually isn't. All because Bob made it that way for me, and it seemed I could make it that way for him.

Afterwards we went swimming with a friend, Natalie, and her current love: went diving, splashing, playing tag and water polo, racing, hiding and seeking underwater until, exhausted, Bob and I went to the shallow end to rest and soak up the moon. Then he kissed me. It was a lovely melting feeling, that molten inarticulate wanting of someone that isn't (at least consciously) wanting to make love. I just wanted to flow into and become part of this man with the iron hard, silky smooth body, whose skin all warm and wet felt so good against mine, whose arms folded 'round me holding me close against him, crushing the breath out of me, keeping me safe, and whose mouth moving on mine started a current of pleasure running circles inside me. Eventually it dawned on us that at least part of the reason we were trembling was that we were freezing to death. We parted with hesitant laughs, found Natalie and her friend, and trooped into the friend's house to change. Then we sat in his kitchen talking, laughing, and making breakfast. I remember watching Bob perched on a counter, thinking how beautifully made and how nice he was, thinking of how much I liked being with him. Then he turned and grinned at me. I stopped thinking and felt. Eventually we all went home and collapsed.

The next two days were horrible. I wished and wished that Bob would call so I could see him again before Drew arrived. I don't remember ever wishing as hard for anything since 3rd grade when I wanted to go to Disneyland. Finally he did call, but not until the night before Drew was to come for a visit, and I was furious at having missed our opportunity. I explained that a friend I had invited long before was coming to visit and I couldn't put him off. Bob said he was leaving to go to Europe so it was just too bad. *Giving me back my own huh? Well, I have better things to do.* We both hung up feeling angry and cheated.

I didn't hear from him again until fall when he was starting his first year in college and I was back for my last in secondary school. I was surprised when he called, because I really hadn't expected him to try to get in touch with me again after our last conversation. I'd begun to think of him as part of a brief, if nice, episode. Still, I was pleased at the thought of seeing him again and we arranged to meet on Sunday. The next night Drew called and said he was coming east for the weekend to see me. *And that's supposed to make me happy? Complications and problems.* Things had not gone well between Drew and me. I was continually finding fault with him and nit-picking, then hating myself for doing it. Then I would get mad at him for not noticing what was going on. At the same time I still felt some kind of love and a lot of gratitude, which made everything worse. Altogether an uncomfortable situation which got worse that weekend when Drew did notice what was going on and responded in kind. It was a very tense, painful, fierce, and horribly quiet cat fight while it lasted. Also things were complicated by my unwillingness to tell Drew about Bob.

In the end I resorted to lies which he didn't believe. There is really nothing worse than someone who won't believe you when you are lying.

Finally Sunday arrived and Drew left. Almost relaxing, I set off for Boston to meet Bob, having asked Natalie to find him and tell him I'd be late. When I emerged from the subway I was treated to the sight of Bob and Natalie standing on the corner in deep conversation with (who else) Drew. I turned and ran in the opposite direction. *NO, NO, NO, I can't take it. Why do these things have to happen to me? Well you would pick one of the two people in Boston who knew them both well.*

Later when I worked up my courage and went back, Bob asked me why I had gone tearing off like that. *Neat. I suppose Drew saw me too.* That did it. I poured the whole thing out. Just telling someone was a tremendous relief, but more than that the easiness of being with Bob was very restful and healing after Drew. We spent the day walking beside the river and visiting my brother Ed with whom Bob got along very well. That made me happy too because Drew definitely hadn't, and Ed was, at that point, by far my favorite member of the family.

From here on times tend to run together; I saw Bob for at least part of every weekend. Usually I would come in on Saturday morning and hang around in front of his dorm until I found someone to go tell him I was there. I found that caring so much about him made other people less important, and when I didn't feel I had to consider all the possible consequences of a remark I might make it. I loosened the censorship on my tongue, and found that people actually seemed to enjoy talking to me. Also making friends as a couple, having a large circle of people who thought of me as Bob's and Bob as mine, made me feel good. I think it made our relationship seem solider and more secure. Another nice thing was that we both liked showing each other off. This actually worked quite well, because the knowledge that the other was proud of us made us each happier and more likely to make a good impression, which made the other prouder and so on. Circles within circles of comfort and contentment. All very even-keeled.

The part that wasn't very even or easy was between us. I tended to go overboard in everything, but then, everything about Bob was pretty earth-shaking for me. Being away from him was pure hell. I almost learned to live with it during the week (especially if he called every other night), because that was the way things had to be, but weekends were different.

Sometimes being with him was hell too. Kissing him still excited me, but it wasn't enough. I wanted him to caress and pet me, though I didn't even consider making love to him. Making love was "going all the way" and something that happened to other people. It was probably OK to do it before marriage, but I didn't want to. It was part of the mystique of the wedding night, made precious by the mystique and making precious that night. In the meantime one made do with varying degrees of petting. For Bob, on the other hand, petting was a preliminary to making love, not a substitute for it; and he wasn't about to start the preliminaries if I wasn't ready for the finale. At first I wasn't aware of his attitude and I don't think he was aware of mine.

During Thanksgiving vacation we spent a couple of hours each night lying on the living room couch kissing, aching, and wanting each other. Me wishing he would at least touch my breast, but having an uneasy feeling it wouldn't do much to ease my longing, and fearing I'd only feel dirty later as I had after petting with others. Bob wanted me, but not knowing what to do about it, and fearing he might wreck everything by acting too soon. It was during one of these sessions that he first told me he loved me, but even that didn't help much. It didn't ease the pain of wanting each other; and anyway I had accepted his feeling for me as something pretty big and important, without much caring whether or not he called it love. Sunday night I was wearing a dress that zipped down the front. After a while he unzipped it began kissing the slope of my breast. *Yes, love, please.* Then he jerked back, groaned, and sank his teeth hard into my shoulder. "I'm sorry . . I . . . Christ I didn't mean . . . Sandy, I want you so much, but I won't do anything unless you want me to." *Not anything?*

After that we tended to avoid the breaking point, because it seemed we would only be torturing ourselves. Still it was hard longing for each other, wanting contact and physical closeness, when I couldn't conceive of "going all the way" and he couldn't conceive of anything else. At school we would leave his room when things got tense and go play hearts with the people across the hall or we'd go to a party. At home we'd stay out at discotheques, theaters, or parties and talk to Bob's father or Mat (both of whom tended to be up all night anyway) until we were too tired to do anything but fall into bed. It was much easier to love in the quiet times: riding back and forth on the ferry, sitting by the river, taking his little brother Ethan to the zoo or to play soccer in the park. Easier to be alone and aware of loving in the general gaiety when there were lots of people around.

Christmas was easier but less deliriously happy, because Bob was in the hospital and the nurses even got upset when I sat on his bed. He has a knee which falls apart periodically, the first time in my experience being at Thanksgiving when we had been out dancing (his father said that was probably why, which made me feel just neat). At any rate this was the fifth of a series of operations intended to set it right. After this one they gave up. I turned down a ski trip to stay home and visit Bob, which was frowned upon by my family among whom this kind of minor martyrdom is both prevalent and resisted. Bob himself resented this instance and my giving up skiing in general. He kept telling me I ought to go when I got a chance. The hospital time was also complicated by my wanting to mother him. I liked looking up to him and depending on him; but I didn't want him hurt, and I was so aware of his doing things for me that I wanted to feel I was doing something for him. I enjoyed his preferring me to crutches, enjoyed the obviousness of his need for me in the hospital. I always tried to hide these feelings from him, because it was easy to see he didn't want to feel dependent on me. I also tried, by stressing my need of him, to hide them from myself, because I have a horror of being dominant and aggressive.

We went through the spring loving in calm or crowded times, exploring and fearing some of our growing need for each other, and tying ourselves in tighter and tenser knots sexually. Then during spring vacation I had a strange conversation with my mother.

"Sandy," she said one day as we were driving home from the city, "there's something I've been wanting to talk to you about." A tentative glance at me.

Questions and more questions. I wish she wouldn't watch me when she's driving.

"You know how much we like Bob. I think he's a very fine person, and we're both happy you've found someone so nice."

"Well, I'm glad you feel that way." *Here we go again. Now we start on the think-of-all-you're-missing-by-tying-yourself-to-one-person-when-you're-so-young lecture.*

"But I guess you're in pretty deep water. . . ." another glance at me.

"Uhh!" *Yup, told you so. Here it comes.*

"I . . . well . . . I don't know if I'm behind the times with this but . . . well, when you feel, at least if you do, or if you have. . . . When you and Bob come to making love," a glance at me, and finding me looking rather blank (a result of shock) "having intercourse, I want you to come to us so that Dr. Frankel can fix you up with a diaphragm or something."

"But really . . . I . . . we hadn't even considered it!"

"Still, when you do, I want you to tell us, because we want you to be adequately protected."

"But, Mom. I guess maybe I've never talked to you about this; but I've always wanted that to be part of the excitement of getting married. I suppose that's kind of silly and unrealistic, but it would be nice."

"Well, of course I'm glad you feel that way about it, but still. . . ."

"OK I will, but, you know, I really wouldn't worry about it."

Wow.

When I got over being flabbergasted by the whole thing, I think this conversation had a lot to do with my coming to consider the possibility of making love to Bob. After all if my own mother. . . . Still I did want to keep my dreams about the wedding night. Although I took considerable pleasure in retelling the story around school, I didn't bring it up with Bob.

When school was over I went out to a suburb with Bob's family for a week. They had a house, which they had rented for about twenty years. That first day Bob took me around to all his favorite places. I was reveling in exploring a new part of the countryside and feeling very proud and happy that he wanted me to see places he loved. Also everything was more fun since we'd just finished another year of drudgery (especially for me since I'd managed to get through with, and out of, high school), and the weather was beautiful. Then at night when everyone else had gone to bed we sat downstairs reading, until I looked up to find him studying me from the couch. I got up to join him, and asked what he was thinking.

"How beautiful you are."

"Nut." I grinned and nuzzled his ear. We'd been through that one before and I'd given up arguing about it.

"You are, you know. . . . Actually I've been thinking about today. I realized in a way I've been testing you."

"*How?*"

"I guess just seeing what you're like here. It's funny, people are always talking about finding someone who's like you or unlike you as though there weren't any context, but it's incredible how important it is that they fit in with the places and people you care about."

"Mmm, like me wanting you to come to the country. It's partially because I want to share it with you, but also I want to see if we appreciate each other."

"Yeah. And you know it's great having you here. I like it all much more with you and you . . . Hell, girl, you're so beautiful here; you floor me. Sandy," holding me, "I do love you and," spoken softly into my hair, "I want you so."

I wound up in my usual tense coils. It was worse than ever, wanting him and feeling helpless, trapped, and frustrated. It hurt so much I whimpered, "Please," meaning, I think, "Please, God, won't you do something to keep me from hurting?" but I don't really know that's what I meant. Certainly Bob didn't. "Hell," he said sitting

up, "can't you just relax? Please what?!" That shocked me out of my
circles. I lay back for a minute, then raised one hand and traced down
the side of his face. "Yes, I want you too." His eyes got so glowingly,
blindingly bright and his heart beat so hard against my hand, I was
frightened. It was kind of like lighting a volcano. Then he bent down
and kissed me incredibly tenderly and slowly. Somehow I did relax
and just let all my love and longing float up to the surface without the
hey-help-wait-a-minute-or-stop-it-you-poor-whore business that had
come before. Gently, as though I would break, but with the strength
of his feelings vibrating in his hands, he undressed and caressed me. I,
slowly, in a daze of wonder at what was happening in me, responded.
Then, when he stood up to undress and put on a prophylactic, I began
to be afraid again. When he entered me it hurt and I drew back, but
he kept on and, again slowly, I began to respond and rise to meet him.
He came before I was near it, but I'd gotten a taste of what we could
be together. Even more than that, it was glorious to be rid of that
crippling tension, to be able to touch him and love the feel of him
without terrifying myself. So good not to feel the sick, dirty regret I'd
associated with sexual contact, but to revel in the rightness of our lying
naked together. Bob fell asleep on my chest with this great smile on
his face, and I lay overwhelmed with tenderness and love for him.
Then, thinking of the way he had looked at me, I was filled with awe
that I could make him that happy, that I could move him that deeply.

    After a while he stirred and came part way awake. He smiled
with his eyes still closed, wrapped his arms around me, and rolled us
both over onto the floor. Whereupon we both burst out laughing and
decided to go outside before we woke everyone up. We got dressed
(sort of), stuffing extraneous items behind the sofa cushions, and went
out to a knoll behind the house to watch the sunrise. We sat quite still,
I between his legs leaning back against him, he with his arms around
me, our heads together. Magical dawn, magic around us, in us, between us. When the sun was up and the colors faded into blue, Bob
slipped his hands under my sweater cupping my breasts "Witch, what
am I to do when all I can think of is loving you?" "Silly question."
Wonderfully we found we could laugh in our longing for each other,
no longer finding it a torture, but a gift. Laughing, we ran down to
the beach; laughing, he caught and held me. Then soberly, "Sandy, it's
never been as good for me as this. That's your doing. I know the first
time isn't so good for a woman, but I want to make it good for you,
and it wasn't too bad, was it?" Joy and well-being welling up inside
me, I buried my nose in the hollow above his collarbone laughing.
Seriously, "Christmas with bows on." He nodded, laughing with me,
and we were off again, rolling down the dunes, streaking in and out
of the water, then walking home very close together.

That June was wonderful. We pirated Bob's parents' bed while they were gone and spent whole nights making love — Bob said that somehow having me there next to him put sleep pretty far down on his list of priorities, and I was so enthralled by the sinking, soaring, piercing joy of loving him I didn't regret the sleep. We made up for it on the beach between swims anyway. Then a couple of days after his parents got back, we set off on a round of coming out parties for girls in my class. And back home for a week to recuperate. After that came the bad part. Bob had steadfastly refused to make plans for the summer and, giving up on being able to count on him, I had arranged to drive west with a friend. As the time to leave approached, Bob wavered about coming with us; but one look at my father (who didn't consider a girl my own age adequate chaperonage) decided him against it.

Oddly enough it was easier for us to come together again after that summer than after either of the others. I did blame Bob for the separation, but his letters told me he missed me and, for the first time, that he needed me, both of which encouraged me to believe he had learned his lesson. I was mistaken, but I didn't realize it for a couple of days. Also I think the newness of our physical love helped. At any rate both sets of parents were away when Bob got back from Europe, and we went on another binge of lovemaking (which in some ways got us back to June) before going to join my family in Vermont.

The question of independence kept coming up from then on. I think it had become more pressing for Bob because I would be at school, there and available during the week as well as on weekends. At any rate he and my mother kept urging me to go out with other people. I did (I don't think I could have helped it), but I never really worked up much enthusiasm for it. I simply was not interested in anyone but Bob, except in the role of semi-sexless friend. Also I still felt it was useless, hurtful, and artificial for both of us. Bob might have been all for the *idea* of my seeing other people, but when it came to actually seeing me with someone else it was different.

By the middle of the year I began to wonder if a feeling of independence wasn't Bob's answer to the sort of dilemma I kept running into in myself. I loved him very much and wanted quite simply to share a life with him. To me that meant marriage, but I didn't want the sort of student marriage that includes financial dependence on parents. It seemed to me that you needed to start out as a new and separate unit to have a chance of succeeding. On the other hand, I wouldn't have wanted to make Bob take up something like reporting because he could make money at it, when he didn't know if that was what he wanted to do. Also I had a sneaking suspicion that whatever we might feel about each other, we still had some growing and changing to do before we could make our way in an adult world.

Another thing that came into all of this was Bob's fear of the very idea of marriage. I'm not sure why he felt as strongly as he did about it. I guess he saw it as a trap. Whenever he spoke of specific things that were wrong with marriage they seemed to me to be aspects of going about it unintelligently, but I think that to him they seemed inevitable. I remember once when I was wondering why he should love me, I asked him and he finished up the list by saying, ". . . and you don't want me to marry you." That really floored me. I did want him to marry me; I just didn't see how we could. Then again, maybe he knew that, and this was a warning.

Sometimes I toyed with an idea my mother had given me. She and my father had met first when she was just out of college. She said they had felt they could mean a great deal to each other, but not just then, so they stopped seeing each other. Then, five years later they found each other again, fell in love, and got married. This leaves out the fact that my father had married and divorced someone else in the interval, but still I found myself thinking — wouldn't it be nice if we could skip all this until we could really make a go of being together? One problem with the idea was that I didn't see how I could face a present without Bob, regardless of what that meant for the future.

Another possibility I toyed with was that of finding some thing (as opposed to some one) to which I could dedicate myself, some interest absorbing enough to balance Bob. This was my equivalent to Bob's wish for spatial independence. I wanted something fixed in my life so that my whole happiness (and not only happiness but my ability to feel and to function) wouldn't depend on him. It seemed to be more and more unfair to him that it should. As long, however, as I had Bob, as long as I was absorbed in him, I couldn't even begin to find any such outside stability. For him the situation was somewhat different because he was ambitious. Sometimes this took the form of trying to outdo his brother's record, and in this endeavor I sometimes played a part. "You know," he said once, "I always used to be jealous of Mat's girls, but he was talking in his last letter about how lucky I am to have you." At times, though, his ambition took other more constructive forms; and during that year he was spending a great deal of time and energy on a literary magazine. Admittedly this was partially an attempt to get himself elected editor (an office Mat had just missed), but I think it was also a straight effort to become a really good writer.

Then came summer. I went to Mexico, and he stayed in Boston to work. I wrote for the first part of the summer but then I kept on not getting letters. *OK just see if I don't forget you too! But Bob, Bob, for Christ's sweet sake, where are you? It's glorious here, but without you, forget it.* He wrote for the second half of the summer but he had stopped getting letters. *Hey, girl, please, please come back. I need you in this deep dark drudgery of a Boston summer.* Then I came back and nothing was right. We were somehow out of whack.

Bob introduced me to the people who lived next door to him. They got married because she was pregnant. She has his telegram telling her not to destroy the child, saying he was coming to marry her. She treasures it. *Yep, it's right up there on the bulletin board with her old boyfriend's love letters. Now they have two kids, they fight all the time, and he spends most of his time moving out and moving back in again. He has wasted a real talent for acting, she's turning into a peevish bitch, and the kids are nervous wrecks. Marriage is great, isn't it?*

During the first few months of school I didn't see much of Bob, and then one Saturday I went over to see him. He led me straight into his room and said he didn't think we should see each other anymore.

"What?!"

"I think we should stop seeing each other."

"Any special reason or just on general principles?"

"I've just been thinking a lot, and I can't take this anymore. I think it's bad for you too. We've gotten all ingrown and I think we should stop."

At this point I started crying.

"Sandy, I'm sorry, I don't like hurting you, but it didn't seem fair not to tell you. I mean I could just have gone on seeing you on Saturday and fobbed you off for the rest of the week, but it seemed better for both of us to make a clean break and have done with it.

"I . . . well I guess I've been feeling trapped for a long time. I need to do things and be things without you, if only to prove I can. At least I need to try. Also I want to be able to see other girls without feeling guilty and as though I were betraying you.

"I don't think you're giving yourself a chance either. I mean you said yourself you wished we could be apart; you know that thing about your parents. And . . . well . . . we just need to be free of each other. You know that."

This went on for a couple of hours, mostly just with elaborations of the above. I went home then and cried some more, but after a while I decided that maybe this could be a good thing for me. Maybe I could find my elusive something to be interested in. For starters I could try schoolwork since it was handy. Maybe I could get to know and care about some other people. All of which didn't make me feel any less bereft and alone, but it did give me something to do. For the next month I did try. I tried to be fascinated by schoolwork but, with the exception of one course I didn't find any of my courses very absorbing. I tried, with more success, to get to know and be interested in other people. Also I tried to understand and come to terms with myself (as opposed to myself-with-Bob) and found that it was fun, and sometimes enlightening, to discuss with others the things my attempts to understand had made me wonder about. In some ways it was a good time, but there was always a dull ache nagging at my guts, always something a little wrong, something missing even when I set about proving to myself that I could make love with other men and enjoy it.

One evening Bob came over.

"Well, I said I'd come crawling back. Here I am, hands and knees down, beaten and needing you. Will you take me back?"

"Don't, please don't say it that way. I love you. There's no groveling or 'taking back' about it."

Then, holding me, "Christ girl I've missed you!"

"Me too."

But then I had to go because I was going out with someone else.

In a way things were worse than they had been at the end of the summer. Bob felt he had failed, and I couldn't help feeling like a crutch he wished he could do without. I also felt I'd failed. I still had no balancing interest, and the other people I'd gotten to know turned into a liability. An evening with one of them wasn't much good when I kept thinking I could be with Bob instead; but I found it difficult to say, "Thanks, you've been useful but I don't want you around anymore." Still that was the way I felt. I was grateful to them for helping me when I needed help, but now they were just complicating things and I wished they would disappear. The problem gradually solved itself, because I got to be very bad company; and by exam period there were only two diehards left. Still it was pretty uncomfortable for me while they were disappearing and, in a way, I blamed Bob for having gotten me into such a mess.

Then in February I realized that my period was a few days late and panicked. Actually it is strange that I noticed since I usually had only a vague idea of when it was supposed to be and tended to be irregular anyway. Be that as it may, I did notice and did panic. The summer before, I had finally asked my mother to set up an appointment for me with Dr. Frankel, but we decided it would be better for me to have someone in another city. Dr. Frankel recommended a man, and my mother gave me his name and number, but I didn't go to see him. In the interval I had lost his name so I called Mum to get it. The first test was negative, but Dr. Winfield said that didn't mean much, and sure enough the second was positive. Bob had offered (somewhat less than enthusiastically) to marry me, when I first noticed my period was late, but I knew he would hate it. In the end he might hate me for forcing him into it, and I didn't think I could take that. Abortion was the most reasonable choice all along, and my mother and

Bob both set about trying to find someone good to do it. The problem was that I hated the idea. I couldn't feel it was right to kill our child. Then I would go round in the circles of the alternatives. I could force Bob to marry me, but that would probably be a permanent hell for us and a less than ideal setting in which to grow up. For a long time I thought about going to a home and having the child, but then what would happen to it? It didn't seem fair to turn him (or her) loose in an overcrowded world with nothing but life, with no one who gave a damn about him but me, and I couldn't count. Also it wouldn't be all roses for me either. At least in an abortion he wouldn't know anything about it, wouldn't feel anything. I guess I was reconciled to the necessity of an abortion, but I wasn't happy about it. When we went home Bob's parents kept telling me how brave I was, but I didn't feel brave; I felt helpless. What else could I do?

Bob and Mommy each found someone they thought sounded good, and he turned out to be the same person. My mother and I met the contact (we'd decided it would be better if Bob didn't come) and he took us to the man's office where a nurse asked me a lot of questions. I told her a lot of lies. Then he came in, looked very hard at me, and asked if I was really sure I wanted to have this done. Mom tensed up immediately, but I said, "Yes, I am sure." It was very quick and easy. He said it was a good thing I had come to him so soon. Then he left and the nurse told me what to expect and what I should do. It was over and my child was gone. I didn't say anything on the way home, but then I came inside and Bob was standing in the hall looking even worse than I felt. I ran to him and held on tight bursting into tears.

"Sandy, Jesus, Sandy, are you all right?" A nod. "I've been sitting here imagining. . . . If anything had happened to you, I. . . . You're sure you're all right?"

"Yes. I'm OK. Really." Then I kissed him and went upstairs. It had begun to hurt and I was tired. My father brought me some pills, and I hugged him. He'd been so good about it all that I felt guilty for having been a little afraid of his reaction (Bob hadn't even wanted him to know).

"Poor beloved," he said, "it's hard to have someone living and growing within you and then to lose him."

That opened the floodgates again, "Oh Daddy, I . . . I kept wanting to ask if there were any way of telling if it would have been a boy or a girl. My son or daughter is gone, and I don't even know which!"

Bob said later, "You sacrificed yourself for me," and I suppose I did, but I didn't know that was what I was doing. I had thought of it more as sacrificing the child for both our sakes. Not until it was done did I realize just how much I wanted a child, that child, our child. During the week I spent in bed I kept imagining what he or she would have been like. Sometimes I saw a boy sometimes a girl, always cursed with funny frizzy hair but with Bob's eyes and beautiful.

What with wondering and worrying and hurting, I hadn't done any work at all and, feeling I wasn't in the best possible frame of mind to buckle down and do a semester's work for all my courses in a month or two, I decided to ask my dean if I could drop a course. She said, "No," so I told her what had been happening and that I didn't think I could make it. She said she was sorry this had happened to me, but that she was sure everything would be fine when I settled down to work. I thought about the mountains of undone work, and I guess I just gave up. At any rate I couldn't make myself do it. I ended up a course short and decided to go to summer school. Bob, per usual, didn't know what he would be doing, but then came the Arab-Israeli war and he convinced the *Guardian* to send him to cover it.

That summer was gruesome. The abortion had brought us closer together than we had even been before, and there was again the jolt of sudden loss. At the same time it had knocked us both off balance enough to make it almost impossible for us to cope effectively. This last is probably truer of me, but I think it applies to Bob also.

Letters

Robert, love,

I miss you too much. It's strange that being without you hurts physically. That terrible sickening thud of knowing you have gone, and I won't see you for months. It hurts in a dull dead way to know I can't just call you or come over, to know I won't be able to look at you or touch you, to know you won't make love to me or hold me, to know I won't feel your love. I can't rub my nose on your shoulder when it itches.

It's not fair. I wish there were words or that I could find them. They're all clichés. They sound so fake, but what I feel is very real to me.

This is worse than last summer, I guess because you're away and I'm here. Here isn't here if you aren't, and I'm homesick for wherever you are. For you really. Last summer I was in new places, I was exploring, and it was almost natural for you not to be there. Here it's hell. The whole damn place is haunted. Did you feel that last summer? Which is all a negative way to say I love you, but when you aren't here it's harder to love than just to need you terribly. I need you to be happy. That goes almost without saying, but I need you to be clearly, sharply sad too. I need you to be able to let my feelings be what they like, I need you to be able to be someone I like.

I'm sorry I'm in such a shitty mood. It will get better, I'm just recuperating from three weeks of poor Mom's solicitude. I wish I could be what everyone wants. They all want different things and I can't be any of them. HELL!

I love you, love you, love you. Come back soon please. 'Til you do . . .

Your friendly neighborhood ghost,
Me

Dearest Sandy,

I'm sorry I left so quickly, but I hope you understand. I had to be here as soon as possible. . . .

I do understand and I envy you: the opportunity and the guts, but I needed you and you left.

I don't know what I'll do next. Probably go to Rome. . . . Next time we both have to come to Europe together — this is truly absurd — I already can't wait to get back to you.

I could have told you how absurd it is. I probably did.

Mat and I pulled off one of the most amazing coups today. . . . We are now at the International. . . . I only wish you were here to share my luxury. . . . I would be happy if you were here — as it is all I can do to soak up the sun. Mat is chasing all the girls, but I just don't have the heart. . . .

To think of you, to want you very much, to want to see you smile, to touch and love you.

Me too.

I miss you too much. I will come back to you, because I love you — and don't forget it.

I finally came back to Rome and found a stack of letters from you. I was sitting on the beach thinking about you, and I decided I had to get back here to see how you were.

You now know how I felt last summer, And before I forget let me play jealous long enough to find out *who* is living in that wonderful establishment on Putnam Ave., because I have visions of your nine kept men. . . .

There was a terrible scene today in American Express when I was picking up my mail. A girl started having hysterics because a boy had written her a "Dear Mary," letter — the moral being I don't want to receive the same tidings. Hysterics aren't dignified.

If you are as worried about me as I am about you — don't be. I love you more than ever. I would come home tomorrow except that

I'm basically a miser and feel that once in Europe you have to stay a respectable time.

I needed you today. Not only as a lover but also because I like you. I don't like being alone now, and yet I have been trying to be alone. Often when I'm with people I feel they are the ones who are cluttering up my life. Often they are. But what I forget is the pain of being really alone. Sometimes during the year I even want to get away from you and be alone so that I can confront myself. That is why the summer is good in a way, but I don't seem to have the stamina to stay away. I could say many words of love to you, but they seem meaningless from here — I just know I want you here, now. I love you.

It has been over a week now that I haven't heard from you, and I'm beginning to think my letters aren't reaching you or are falling on deaf ears — which is worse. I go to American Express every day now, hoping you will have written; it means a lot to me to hear from you and know that you are surviving and still love me. Please write. . . .

I miss you very much, but most of all I get worried about you when you don't write.

Fold and cut

I have not written out of (a) laziness (b) perversity (c) anger (d) ignorance (e) general depression (f) no stamps.

I love you passionately but (a) I've run off with another man (b) I've run off with another girl (c) none of the above.

My current occupation is (a) student (b) mistress (c) vegetable.

My current plans are (a) suicide (b) marriage (c) unworthy of mention.

My most drastic move since you left is (a) cut off all my hair (b) gained forty pounds (c) bought a silver back gorilla.

Directions: circle one (and only one) of the choices given. By the end of the exam you should have six (6) answers circled in #2 pencil. Do not be afraid to guess, scores will be computed on the basis of correct answers only. You may begin now. Your results will be mailed to you in less than a week.

I've been thinking about you constantly — I'm worried, as I should be because I haven't heard from you in weeks.

I met a bunch of kids from Whittier. . . . They're wonderful people, and my loneliness left me as I sat in their apartment. . . . They're all hippies.

I'm tired of Rome and of missing you. I want to come home, but have decided I will make every conceivable effort to make it to Austria first.

I do hope my letters are getting to you — I seem to be writing in the dark. I love you, I love you, I love you.

I still haven't heard a peep from you and now I'm really worried — all sorts of horrible thoughts run through my head. . . .

I hope to God you haven't given me up. It would smash the hell out of my insides because . . . well I'll show you when I get back. . . . It's because I love you.

I keep hoping the reason you haven't written is that you haven't received my letters, because I haven't put enough postage on them or something. But then why no reproaches? Even that would be better than 3000 miles of silence.

Bob

Meanwhile, back at the ranch. . . . I had been trying to answer his letters, trying to find something to say that could help, but what can you say? Besides I was even more mixed up than he was. I was trying to grapple with the fact that something in me stopped dead at the thought of schoolwork (even work that I really enjoyed). I could not make myself study. I had run smack up against something in me I couldn't understand or control, a problem in myself I couldn't handle. Eventually I decided to leave summer school, take a year off, and see a psychiatrist. I kept beginning letters in answer to Bob, letters about how I felt, letters about making the above decisions and why. Finally I just stuffed them all into a manila envelope and sent them off to Bob. He never received them.

Then Bob came home and everything was wrong. I told him about what I had decided to do. He disapproved, thought it was a lousy idea. And why on earth hadn't I written?!

Bob, Bob, please love, can't you see I'm on the rocks? I can't handle things in me and I don't know what to do. I'm trying, but don't sit on me. First you abandon me, then you come back to criticize and obstruct, when I need you, need your concern, your love, your support. I realized this summer just how much I do need you, but you don't help, won't help, not at all.

Bitch. You wouldn't even write when I was holed up alone and lonely in Rome. Can't you see I have to come to terms with myself? It's hard. I need you, need your concern, your love, your support. I even told you that. Didn't I? But you wouldn't answer. Now you're running away, running out and leaving me to fight it all through alone. Next you'll dramatize yourself into a crack-up, and then what? The last thing I need is to be burdened with your problems. You could help me, but all you do is weigh me down.

And so through the fall. . . .

Hey! Wait, Bob. Please, can't you see this whole hippie-drug thing is no good? It's silly and pretentious, cowardly, and most of all wasteful. You can't just run out on reality like that. I'm still out here. I can't, won't follow you in. Don't leave me. Love, I know you're having your own hell, but how can I help when I can't reach you? Besides, I need you to help me. Love me, touch me, come to me. Don't bring me your hang-ups, I'm busy with my own. Still, won't you hold me, keep me from these waters? You owe it to me, you took my child, you bastard — NO — Sandy stop it! I don't mean that, I don't, I don't. I love you, but please. . . .

Go away! Can't you see I need my energy for me? What am I to do, what to be? Can I be something, believe something my own? No, miserable punk, coward, liar, worm, you can't. Sandy, help me, love me, make me feel I'm worth something. But do you? No! You hold me back, push me down, hurt me. You with your shrink. Can't you see it's phony, narcissistic, self-defeating? You with your complacence about holding down a job. That's not where life is, certainly not for me. But there you go, leaving me lonely and not letting me be. STOP! GO! GET OUT! COME BACK! STAY! I need you.

Separate circles of silence, lying here. We've made love and what happened? Nothing. Nostalgia. If only I could reach out to you, find you, bring you back to heal and be healed by you. I can't. I'm tired of even trying. Wasteful, wasted, waste, waste, waste, waste. Hell.

This time there wasn't any I'm-afraid-this-has-to-stop scene. I gradually stopped going over. He stopped calling or coming to find me. We petered out. Still when loneliness became too frightening, we came to find each other. It wasn't settled, not finally over, and I felt uneasy. My psychiarist asked if I wanted Bob to come in with me to see him. I thought it might be a good idea, so I called Bob and he agreed to try it.

We went to see my shrink. I kept wanting to defend each of them from the other. We talked kind of generally for a while. Bob and I went over and elaborated on what we had already said to each other. The doctor listened and sometimes asked us questions. Then he said, "To be honest I think you two are not good for each other, and if you go on seeing each other maybe you will end up hating. I think you know that. You have each decided you should part, but how much do you mean it? Do you know that you mean it?" He turned toward Bob.

"Yes, I see what you mean. I don't know if Sandy has told you about this, but she has always had an idea we should do what her parents did — not see each other for a few years and then come back together."

"I know this, but now I am not speaking of Sandy; I am speaking of you. I think you must know that Sandy is a much stronger person than she says. You need not worry about her and make that an excuse for your need. But I don't know you, do you really believe that you can get along without her, or do you think you can come back to her when things become too difficult for you, as you did before?"

That hurt. I could see Bob wince.

"But you know he's right in a way. I do . . ."

"Please, I am asking him."

"No," said Bob, "I won't come back again."

"And you, Sandy, do you wish him to?"

"I can't help wishing sometimes that everything were wonderful in this 'best of all possible worlds,' but it isn't and coming back wouldn't work. So no."

"And you will do well without him?"

"I'll have to, won't I?"

Then our time was up and Bob took me to work. We didn't talk on the way, but when we got there Bob said, "He's right, you know."

"About our coming to hate each other?" I'd been trying to conceive of hating him.

"No, about you. You aren't weak."

"I know. It's just that I give such a good imitation. Even to myself."

"Well, goodbye."

"Adios." I kissed him lightly goodbye, and left.

It hurt being without him, but somehow it wasn't even as devastating as the first time, when I knew he would be back. That made me wonder if I was really taking in the finality of it. I tried saying never, never, never, never will I see him, touch him, love him again. That made me feel a little worse, but it still didn't bring the crash, bang, end-of-the-world feeling I had expected.

He stayed in the back of my mind until the end of the summer, when my sister-in-law kicked me out of the apartment which my brother Ed and I had been sharing all year before he married. I felt very abandoned and alone, and suddenly I wanted Bob terribly. For a few days I clung to the thought of him, longing for him and his love of me. I dreamed about him, dreamed he came back and asked me to marry him. Everything was lovely and I was ecstatic until I got to the point where I had to answer. Even in a dream I couldn't say yes, and I'd wake up.

Sometimes I still long for him when I'm coming home tired and alone, watching other people together, but when I start to think about what I really want, it just isn't Bob. Still, I find myself enforcing a very strict hands-off policy this year. Even when it's just talking, I only open up to other women or men who are married or at least firmly attached. I've been making myself lonely, and I think that is Bob. Maybe I am guarding his memory.

In writing this I have remembered the good things about being with him and it has made me long for him again — a salve to my self-made loneliness. On the other hand I've begun to see more clearly how bad for each other we often were. Especially in rereading his letters I've found him and his needs as well as me and mine coming clearer. Still, if I didn't love him, I cannot admit it.

I just don't know.

An Interpersonal Approach

Harry Stack Sullivan was unusually sensitive to an adolescent's difficulties in integrating sexuality with the rest of his life. Sullivan constantly pointed out the importance of parents' behavior and attitudes toward sexuality which are communicated to their child who eventually becomes an adolescent — no better able to live with his sexuality than were his parents.

Sullivan also was very much concerned with the quality of interpersonal relationships. He considered the stage of preadolescence to mark the onset of gnawing loneliness — which may precipitate one's need for relating intimately to peers. The epitome of preadolescent intimacy Sullivan called *collaboration:* continual and deliberate adjustments of one's behavior to the needs of the other person in order for mutual satisfaction to occur.* Collaborating with a preadolescent chum gives rise to the sense of *we.* Further development in the latter stages, early and late adolescence, contributes other components to a person's matured capacity to relate intimately: a firm sense of self-respect; toleration and appreciation of differences in the other person; and minimal distortion of both the other person and self-while-interacting. To Sullivan, intimacy is the culmination of interpersonal competence.

* Mutual need satisfaction requires a relatively anxiety-free state; thus, the persons involved must have *compatible* security operations, i.e., those actions and mental processes which enable a person to avoid an anxious state. Two examples of security operations are *avoiding* persons or events that may threaten one's security and *selectively inattending* those aspects of one's immediate experience which may induce anxiety if they were attended to.

In early adolescence (typically beginning around age eleven) the increased sense of one's sexuality complicates his or her evolving capacity for relating intimately. It is at this time that the quality of parents' recurring attitudes toward sexuality become vital to the adolescent's heterosexual well-being. Sullivan identified factors in family life that often lead to an adolescent's difficulty with integrating sexuality appropriately with other aspects of his development. Some factors are: parental joking or ridicule when the young adolescent shows interest in cross-sex peers; treating sexuality as an unmentionable or "dirty" topic; denigrating the sexuality of extrafamilial others; telling children that sexuality is the basis for parental conflict; indicating that sexuality is a chore or *the* critical test of one's competence or lovability; equating sexuality with inevitable pregnancy; making sexuality symbolic of all that is mysterious or feared; and banishing sexuality to the world of the adult. Typical symptoms of sexual difficulty are suppressing, flaunting, or being preoccupied with one's sexuality. These symptoms usually are accompanied by inappropriate affect and a lack of awareness of one's actions.* To Sullivan, the key issue in adolescent development is the capacity to feel secure while being sexual and intimate with another person.

Initial endeavors in cross-sex relationships sometimes are prompted by the conviction, "I *ought* to be having a heterosexual relationship." Propelling oneself into such a relationship is followed by ambivalent feelings, immobility, or a sense of not really being there. Case 23 illustrates the lengths a person will go in order to maintain a safe distance when not quite ready for sexual or intimate involvement.

Sullivan devoted considerable attention to the commonly occurring "lust-intimacy conflict," in which a person can be sexual but not intimate with one partner and relatively intimate but not sexual with another partner; this sort of conflict is illustrated in Case 24.

When sexuality becomes intertwined with the developmental issues of autonomy and vocational identity — that is, when sexuality is not a pleasureful end in itself — relationships become strained by confusing multilevels of communication and unfulfilled expectations. Case 25 serves as an illustration. Feeling stuck in a boring, inhibiting, and inconsequential job, and frustrated by a marital relationship in a state of suspension, the case writer pursues an extramarital involvement which awakens the other person's latent

* For a useful summary of "normative and deviant" forms of heterosexuality at various stages of adolescence, refer to Blos's (1962) chapter "The Phases of Adolescence."

sexual life and existential awareness, but leaves the case writer still feeling deeply unappreciated. Sullivan often criticized psychiatrists for "tinkering with their patients' sex lives" when other facets of personality needed more attention. A more contemporary Sullivanian dictum might be: sexuality often is the rug under which issues of autonomy and identity are swept.

An interpersonal approach to Cases 23–25 is to investigate how anxiety interferes with the integration of sexuality and intimacy in a two-person relationship.

Topic Twelve

Anxiety and Intimacy

Case 23 / Love Notes

As a freshman in high school, Denise was "shy, quiet, and passive by nature." When Bob began a ritual of staring at her, she was tongue-tied and immobilized. "How can I, Denise, just approach a boy, become friendly with him, and get close to him? What can I, Denise, possibly say to capture his interest?" Instead of acting directly, Denise began writing "anonymous" love notes to Bob, and much of their relationship from ages 14–16 centered around and was nearly restricted to this interacting-at-a-distance. She wanted a boyfriend — but could tolerate only a limited closeness that she effectively maintained by avoidance, passivity, and conflicting or circuitous messages.

As far back as I can remember, the most troublesome part of my life was between the ages fourteen and sixteen. For me this was a period of rapid transformation and adaptation.

My brother Larry is about two years older than I, my sister Lynn is three years younger. When I was at the age of fourteen, my mother was in her early forties. My father passed away from a heart attack when I was nine years old. Unfortunately, I was the first one to discover my father dead. I found him lying on the kitchen floor when no one was at home. It happened I had just returned home from the market with my aunt who lived on the first floor. My aunt told me to go upstairs and ask my father if he would like a cup of coffee. Obediently, I climbed the stairs and called out to my father. To my disappointment Dad never woke up. This was a very sad time of my life to discover I no longer had a father, but being so young, I eventually got over this unhappy trauma.

Both my parents were not born in this country. My father came to America when he was fourteen, and my mother came when she married. I am of Lebanese and Greek descent and belong to the Catholic religion.

We have always lived at the same address in Somerville. Even though my mother did not work, we were able to live comfortably after my father died. The major money problems we experienced were the expensive upkeep of property. All in all we are about middle-class.

Grammar school years were fairly happy and peaceful. At my school there were about three classrooms for each grade. As a child I was considered quiet, but I did have quite a few close girlfriends. Off and on I had a few crushes on some of the boys in class, but I was shy and kept most of my thoughts to myself. Bob was in my grammar school, but I never thought too much of him or really cared about him in any way. He was in some of my grammar school classes, but it was not until the celebration of our eighth-grade graduation at Canobie Lake that I received a feeling that Bob liked me. It all started on the Canobie bus. Bob would stand and keep staring at me with funny looks in his eyes. Of course, I did not think much of the way he used to stare at me and only smiled back.

In the chartered bus on the way back to Somerville, something rather funny took place. A few of the boys started teasing me. If I recollect correctly, something like a coin went flying in my direction. It looked as though Bob had thrown it, because he came over to pick up the coin. At the same moment, Bob caught my glance. The result of this was that Bob stood where he was and placed both his hands on his waist. Bob kept this strange position and resumed staring at me with funny looks in his eyes. Immediately, a few of the other boys started teasing Bob about liking me. As usual, I let everything go and did not think much about it. I only smiled back at Bob letting him believe I was amused. At last we reached Somerville, and we all went our separate directions until we met again the following fall in high school.

During the summer right before high school, I saw Bob around the neighborhood and public park. Most of the time Bob was either with his one-year-younger brother Bill or his friend Jack and other times with both. Every time Bob would notice me he would go into the same staring episode that he showed me in the bus. Again, I just smiled, but this time with the hope Bob would talk to me. My wish that Bob would talk to me did not come true. One time after Bob stared at me, he just climbed up a tree in order to prove his masculinity. Then his friend Jack ran over to Bob and drew his attention from the tree and me. So this was really all it was; strange staring and showing off which really meant nothing at all unless I wanted to make something out of it. Naturally, I thought nothing about it at the time and let it go while just smiling back.

At last, the first day at Somerville High School started. I will admit that at first it was really frightening. My first week attending classes in high school was just horrible. I felt nervous at everything I discovered about the new school. First of all, I did not take to the school because it was very large compared to the small grammar school I attended. The building itself reflected cold and cruel feelings. At one point I was so nervous that I accidentally dropped all the books I was carrying. Also, to top all that I even ended up in the wrong classroom. Of course, directions were asked and given by a teacher, and I finally reached the right room. Somehow I managed to hold back my tears resulting from disappointment and frustration. Eventually, I got used to finding my way around the building.

The mistake I made was entering high school with the belief I was ready for the world. Fourteen was supposed to be a mature age and the right time to explore the world. The world, people, love, and everything were imagined to be nice and happy at all times. I was looking for a rose garden.

Time and again I ran into Bob, his brother Bill, and other students I attended grammar school with. Also, I made a lot of new acquaintances and became especially fond of a girl named Rosemarie who was in my homeroom. Rosemarie was the nicest girl I met and remained a dedicated friend of mine throughout high school. The nicest boy in my homeroom was named David, because he had a very friendly and warm personality. Outside my homeroom I became friendly with a girl named Maria who was almost as nice as Rosemarie, but Rosemarie was the best. The rest of the girls were rather snobbish and mean. Students formed their own groups, and I was not really a part of any particular group.

Bob's homeroom was not far from mine. Bob's brother Bill was also in his homeroom. Sometimes Bob would stare at me in the halls between classes. I remember one morning right before I entered homeroom, I noticed Bob standing close by and giving the same funny stares as before. This had been going on for quite some time so I felt something had to be done about this situation. It was quickly decided by me that I was now ready for the world, and it is about time I got very friendly with boys by dating. I had an urge to be like the other girls and have a boyfriend as well. Obviously, I was not aware of the demands I may have to meet and believed in being able to date in a real decent manner. Yes, I was naive and innocent. I sure did not know what was really going on. The major problem was that I was shy, quiet, and passive by nature. In other words, how can I, Denise, just approach a boy, become friendly with him, and get close to him? What can I, Denise, possibly say to capture his interest? I get tongue-tied just thinking about what to say. Even though I realized Bob noticed me, I just could not approach him directly. If this situation had occurred now, I know I could be friendly and handle myself properly. Since this happened when I was fourteen, I just could not approach Bob directly and reveal how I felt about him. I forced myself into falling in love with Bob, because I believed he liked me.

This is what I decided to do about Bob. When I arrived at home after school, I went directly to the telephone book. It was easy finding where Bob lived, because I knew the name of the street he lived on. So now I had Bob's address and telephone number at hand. My friend Beverly lived next door to me, and I happened to be doing my homework at her house the next morning. I mentioned to Beverly that I liked Bob and felt that I should let him know. Beverly took everything I said like a funny joke. Then I set my mind on writing love notes to Bob. It was really rather hilarious, and we would both just burst out laughing about the things I used to write. Naturally, I would mention how much I loved him, needed him, could not live without him, and was in a real hurry for him. Somehow, I would also write down my fantasies about how wonderful our love will be. All this went on between my homework. It was exciting, and it gave me something to look forward to. I felt my life was lacking, and I needed some excitement like the other girls in school. Also, I wrote in the note that I planned to call him on the telephone at about 6:30 on Thursday evening and hoped he would be at home to receive my call. To be honest, Beverly did not think I was doing the right thing and was surprised to see me go through the whole plan. Before I forget, I should mention that for some reason in the past our home telephone was removed by my mother. For a few years we did not have a phone until my mother decided to have one put in when I was sixteen. We used the telephone booth nearby and managed to get along without a telephone. This is the reason why I asked Beverly for the use of her phone. Of course, Beverly did not refuse me the use, and I offered to pay her. Beverly was kind enough to allow me to use the telephone without paying, but I forced her to accept some money from me.

Getting back to Thursday evening, I telephoned Bob's home and received no answer at 6:30. Obviously, I assumed no one was at home, but I was persistent and sure of myself. In the notes I kept my identity anonymous and did not wish at this point to let Bob know who I was. In other words, I was still scared even though I was trying to force myself to be brave. About a half an hour later I put through another call and a lady answered stating that Bob was not at home.

You would think that I would give up but, of course, I did not. Instead, I went on writing love notes and kept them anonymous at the same time. On the average, I wrote about one note a week. I tried telephoning a few more times but never got Bob on the line. A few times his mother answered, and the other times it was his sister. Every time Bob was not at home according to his mother or sister. Once Bob's sister got wise and said that Bob did not live there. Eventually, I gave up the fun and game of telephoning and decided to stick to anonymous note-writing. I resumed writing and writing and never signing my name. The writing took place usually between homework in Beverly's house and sometimes in my bedroom.

One time between classes in the corridor I saw Bob and Bill. Bob noticed me, stared, and whispered something to Bill. I thought that Bob might suspect that I may be the anonymous note-writer.

Unfortunately, the note-writing resumed along with my imaginary daydreams about how wonderful life would be for Bob and me together. In my notes I expressed my dreams by writing "just imagine" a few times. It was not until December that I became bold and believed it was the right time to let Bob know who I was. One evening I went to the corner drugstore to buy some school supplies and Christmas cards. To my astonishment, I found an anonymous Christmas card with a picture of a girl sitting down on a chair and holding a telephone in her hand. This card was so perfect for my purpose that I bought it. I mailed the anonymous Christmas card without my name on it. About a week later, I still felt I should go through with the idea of letting Bob know who I was. This would allow Bob to come running to me and treat me right, so I believed. Again I walked over to the drug store and purchased a regular Christmas card with Santa Claus riding his sleigh in the night pictured on it. It was a very pretty card, and I loved the color of it. This time I really made up my mind to give my identity away, although I signed my first name only. I added my address on the envelope so Bob might send me a Christmas card in order to prove his equal love for me. Worriedly, I mailed the card and felt regretful afterwards. It might not be the right thing to do, and I was afraid that all my hopes and dreams may not come true as planned. The question was what do I do if that happened.

One day Bob was walking by across the street and glanced up at me reading in my bedroom. I was close to the window and could see Bob clearly. Naturally, I became curious and resumed looking out of the window. I noticed Bob was carrying a huge envelope in his hand, and he was swinging it happily. Afterwards, Bob dropped the envelope into the mail box and kept looking up towards me. Accordingly, I felt overjoyed and believed I was going to receive a Christmas card from Bob because he liked me.

On Monday and Tuesday of the following week I anxiously waited for the mailman to deliver my card. To my great disappointment I did not receive a card or anything else on Monday, Tuesday, or the rest of the week. Bob just tricked me into thinking I would get a card. Actually, this was the beginning of my great disappointments in love.

After Christmas vacation I saw Bob in front of his locker, and he was about to say something when I immediately felt embarrassed and ran down the corridor away from him. Bob shook his head like he did not understand why I would do such a thing. The truth is that my personality overcame my emotions and proved I was still afraid to get deeply involved. That same evening Bob walked by my house yelling out that I acted just like a little baby that way. Wow! Did I feel embarrassed, and it was all my fault. Guilt feelings and regrets were starting to get into me.

A few days later I again came face to face with Bob after school outside of his homeroom. I was waiting to go in for extra help from Bob's homeroom teacher who was my civics teacher during third period. As I was about to enter the room, Bob, his brother Bill, and their friend Jack walked out of the door. When Bob saw me, he bumped in front of me, stopped, and blew into my face. It looked as though he was waiting for me to say something. The only thing I managed to do was look back at him and could not get myself to breathe a word. All three just gave up and left as I entered the classroom. At this point, I felt ashamed, sick, and regretful. I could not face up to what I had done. Bob was waiting for me to make the first move, and I was waiting for him. How in the world was I going to force my personality to come to terms with what I want? As a result, I became so confused that I really did not know what I wanted.

Sometime after, I attended my high school basketball game with my sister. Once in a while I used to go with my friend Maria to basketball and football games. When Maria could not make it to the game, I would then force Lynn to go with me. This Friday night my sister came along, and we found a place to sit on the lower part of the bench. All of a sudden I heard Bob's voice yelling out to me. Bob's voice was very loud and fresh sounding. First, Bob began teasing me about being plump, and the reason why I brought my sister along. Bob shouted the reason why I brought my sister was because I was so fat that my sister had to get behind me and help push me through the door. Bob resumed laughing loud and hard while he kept yelling out to me. In the meantime I became so embarrassed that I was even too scared to turn around and look at Bob or his friends. After all this, Bob shouted for me to go over and sit beside him. As a result, I could not budge. Next, Bob stated that he could not understand why Denise did not go and sit here. Also Bob threw in another stab by declaring, "You would think that is the least she can do now since she has already done everything else." Oh! That did it, because I was really hurt by this statement and felt nervous. By this time my sister started to become uncomfortable and asked me to move with her to another part of the bench. Quickly I agreed with her and followed her to the other side. Within minutes Bill came over to where we sat and just stood staring at me with a smile on his face. I felt nervous, upset, ashamed, and embarrassed. All Bill did was stand there staring at me with a smile on his face and then return back to where his brother sat. So I went home that evening feeling miserable and heartbroken. The saddest part was that I was more disappointed in myself.

The following day I wrote another love note, but this note was a very depressing one. I wrote how much I regretted what I had started and also insulted myself. Plus I stated how I could not change and how I let myself down. I mentioned how my shyness was going to always hold me back from really expressing myself. It was ridiculous of me to write such a note, but I believed I had to explain myself. As time went by, I felt even worse at what I had done as a freshman in high school. The final note I wrote was in March. In the note I mentioned that it was the last one I will ever write and wish that Bob will forgive me for being so stupid. If I had known any better at the time, I would have quit this silly business while I was still ahead.

Surprisingly, Bob missed receiving my love notes. I suppose to him they were fun. The way I expressed myself in the notes was the manner I would have liked to express myself talking to him in person. Bob returned to teasing me so I might decide to write him more love notes but, of course, I did not write to him anymore. I finally kicked the habit of foolishly writing to someone who lived a few streets away. My friend Gabby told me that Bob enjoyed receiving my notes because of the attention he was getting. It was supposed to help his ego feel good, because he was liked and thought about by someone. In other words, Bob only wanted to receive notes from me, and at this point I was too embarrassed to write anymore. The last note written to Bob was in March. This note-writing lasted about five months.

Socially, my freshman year was a disappointing flop. Academically, my grades were not that good. I started off almost making the honor roll the first quarter, the second quarter I flunked two subjects, and the last two quarters I worked hard to bring up my grades so I could pass the freshman year. Apparently, I passed my first year and was promoted to the sophomore year. I learned that convincing myself that I was in love did not help my grades at all. What I did receive was an exhausted mind from thinking too much about Bob.

Unfortunately, I did not enjoy my sophomore year in high

school. The main reason was because I did not like some of the new students in my homeroom. The boys were very nice, but a few of the girls were very fresh and mean. They would constantly insult and laugh at me for no real reason. They had me almost convinced there was something really the matter with me. Exactly like I mentioned earlier, I am shy and quiet. Plus I looked rather happy. Since they liked to bother people, they picked on me, because it was easy for them to get away with it. It is very sad to think back how I managed to hold back and put up with so much aggravation at such a time in my life.

Once in a while I went to football games with my friend Maria, and sometimes with a group of other girls. I still believed I liked Bob in my sophomore year, especially because I could not think of anyone else to like at the time. I needed something to hold on to and dream about. Actually, I still wanted to feel like the other girls even though I never gave myself a chance to date a boy. One reason why I followed the football games around was in order to see Bob, because he was on the high school team. Bob was more like a substitute player and hardly ever got a chance to go out on the field. There was one game that I recall Bob getting a chance to go out and play. It was very funny, because Bob accidentally started running toward the wrong end of the field. Actually, it looked as though Bob was so excited about getting a chance to play that his attention was mostly directed toward the audience. As a result, there was a lot of booing and yelling so the coach quickly forced Bob to get out of the game.

Before I move on to continue with my sophomore year, I will return to an incident I remember at the end of March of my freshman year. This was the time after my very last love note to Bob. One night I was walking out of the library after I had finished my homework and saw Bob and Bill on their way into the library. We all did not even say hello to each other. After I returned home, I believed it would be a good idea for me to go back and apologize to Bob. Impulsively, I went back to the library and walked over to where Bob was studying. I said, "Hi, Bob, I'm here to say I'm sorry." Bill was considerate enough to get up and leave us both so that we could talk alone. Bob was surprised and looked up at me and asked me what I wanted. Immediately, I apologized to him about the letters I wrote. He pretended at first not to understand what I was talking about. Then Bob almost burst out laughing and replied, "Oh, them." After that I answered that I was sorry and wanted to make everything up to him. Bob commented that the only way I could make everything up to him was by leaving him alone and getting out. He further repeated to me to leave him alone and get out. At the time I was saddened at the way Bob spoke to me. The final reply that I gave Bob was, "But that's not right, I'm sorry, bye." Next I walked away by myself feeling sad, lonely, and rejected. The only thing that was left for me to do was cry on my back porch. I could not understand how Bob could be so cruel and cold toward my feelings, but that is the way some boys are as Gabby would say.

The following day Bob saw Gabby and me walking to her house after school. Bob was riding his bike while following us with constant teasing. Obviously, I was still feeling unhappy regarding the previous evening and was so angry at him that I did not even want to look at him. A few hours later I walked home only to find Bob waiting across the street from my house. As I entered my gate, I slammed it shut and went inside the back door. Through the glass window on the door I saw that Bob crossed the street and walked close by the gate I slammed and walked away. I began to wonder if Bob may have felt guilty about hurting my feelings when I went to apologize. At the time it was difficult to figure out why he would not use the same advice he gave me by leaving me alone also.

During my sophomore year I resumed going to the library in order to do my homework. Sometimes my friend Linda went along with me. Bob and Bill were usually at the library doing their homework with some of their friends. For quite a while Bill had been bothering me whenever he ran into me. Many times Bill disturbed me in school, the library, and once at Revere Beach. Bill swore at me and produced disgusting mean sounds along with bumping into me. In my opinion Bill was going too far in the way he was treating me.

As I was leaving the library one evening, I came upon Bill with some of his friends waiting outside the door. Immediately Bill swore at me and called me a fatso. I replied, "The same to you and if you don't stop, I will get my big brother after you." Bill laughed and answered, "I'll take him too." This remark aggravated me so I went over to where Bill was standing and slapped his arm and then ran. Unfortunately, Bill ran after me and slapped me back. Next I went back and gave Bill a light kick on his foot. Instantly, Bill returned my kick by pressing his shoe hard into my foot. I slapped Bill again on his arm, but he ran after me and slapped me last. After, Bill replied, "I got you last." At that point I gave up and ran on home. What I received was a black and blue mark on my foot from Bill. Thinking back I may have deserved the treatment I received from Bill.

About a week before this incident with Bill, I kicked Bob on his leg when he walked by me in study class. It occurred in sophomore year that Bob and I were in the same study class. As usual I was happy and Bob was surprised that we were in the same class. After I kicked Bob, I demanded that he stop swearing at me. I took out the manner in which Bill was treating me on Bob. Bob stood stunned and then swore at me. At first it looked as though Bob was going to hit me back, but he did not. Instead, Bob returned angrily to his seat after he finished swearing at me.

Unfortunately, Bill continued bothering me until I tried to put a stop to the situation. On an evening the following week Linda and I were at the library studying. Bob was also at the library studying with his friend Tom. Patiently, I waited for a chance to speak to Bob. My chance finally arrived when Bob started walking toward a door leading to the book supply room. Instantly I mentioned how Bill was bothering me and demanded that Bob stop Bill. Bob answered by asking me if Bill was hitting me or anything like that. Remembering what happened last week outside the library, I replied that Bill was hitting me. Bob commented that Bill was acting like that because Bill was in love with me. Next, Tom told me that Bob was in love with me too. This whole situation was getting ridiculous. Later I followed Bob and Tom through the supply door with my friend Linda close behind me. Inside the room I shouted at Bob to make his brother leave me alone. Bob just stood there without saying a word and staring at me. Out of anger I made a fist and was about to punch Bob on the shoulder. Instead I came close to punching and pulled back without touching Bob. In the meantime a boy who works in the library was standing witness to the whole disagreement and stated that there is to be no fighting in this library. This statement added to my embarrassment, and I then ran out of the library with Linda following me. I started crying outside my house, and Linda informed me that after I ran away she asked Bob to please make Bill leave me alone, and Bob shook his head in agreement. A few minutes later Bob crossed the street and walked close by where Linda and I were standing. Then Tom joined Bob, and they both walked away together. I was miserable and upset, but I managed to get over the situation. After all this Bill finally quit bothering me.

Junior year was the big turning point for me. During my first quarter I rarely attended school. After the first quarter I quit going to school at all. My mother returned my books to the principal's office, and I assumed I was a high school dropout. Later on I discovered that there were certain procedures a person has to go through before he is legally labeled as a dropout. As a result, most of the teachers marked me down in their books as absent.

Recollecting the beginning of my third year in high school was very depressing. Obviously, my family was against my decision of quitting school, but they did not force me to go back to the high school. Instead I received help from friends of the family during the second quarter and transferred after nine more weeks to Arlington Catholic High School. Since this school was smaller and friendlier than my previous school along with a happier atmosphere, everything worked out fine, and I graduated the following year with the help of summer school at the end of my junior year.

It was during the second quarter in junior year when I did not show up in school that Bob telephoned my home. Bob was curious as to how I was, why he had not been seeing me, and where I was. My mother told Bob not to call anymore, and there was no reason for him to know what was the matter. The reason why my mother reacted in this manner was because she felt sad at the mean way some of the students treated me. The result was Bob quit telephoning. Later I learned that a note had been mailed to me from Bob stating that he had not been seeing me and had missed me. This note was never given to me. About a year later my sister mentioned the calls and note to me, but, of course, it was too late.

By transferring to Arlington Catholic High School, I ran away from unhappiness and disappointment by leaving behind me Somerville High School and Bob. Of course, memories were not left behind even though I hardly ever recollect. In conclusion, my case history reveals how I managed not to escape from a memory which lives in me and influences my present and future mature decisions regarding the world, people, and love.

Topic Thirteen

Lust and Intimacy

Case 24 / The Magician: To Misdirect His Audience, He Must Misdirect Himself

"I have often noticed that we are inclined to endow our friends with the stability of type that literary characters acquire in the reader's mind. No matter how many times we reopen "King Lear," never shall we find the good king banging his tankard in high revelry, all woes forgotten, at a jolly reunion with all three daughters and their lapdogs. Never will Emma rally, revived by the sympathetic salts in Flaubert's timely tear. Whatever evolution this or that popular character has gone through between the book covers, his fate is fixed in our minds, and, similarly, we expect our friends to follow this or that logical and conventional pattern we have fixed for them. The less often we see a particular person the more satisfying it is to check how obediently he conforms to our notion of him every time we hear of him. We would prefer not to have known at all our neighbor, the retired

hot-dog stand operator, if it turns out he has just produced the greatest book of poetry his age has seen."*
By what processes does L preserve his archaic notion of Ellen?

Among L's effects somewhere is a letter — a letter L considers a Very Important Letter. I say somewhere because L's possessions consist mostly of printed matter — books, magazines (*Partisan Review, New York Review,* a few *Dissents* and *Harpers,* I. F. Stone, five old *Playboys, The Realist* — in case you're interested), newspaper and magazine items clipped out and shoved into a manila envelope, papers for college courses, computer print-outs, also a few . . . but these Salingeresque inventories can be tedious (I almost always skim them; I mean, who cares what color the goddam toothbrushes are and all, for chrissakes). In other words, L is a student — a graduate student in one of the social sciences. Except for the books, these print-items lie strewn about his room in a most unlinear, tactile non-arrangement so that to find the letter to which I referred back in the first sentence, L had to go looking for a few minutes through the cardboard boxes which serve as drawers for his cinderblock-door desk.

When L received this letter, he had recognized the handwriting and postmark immediately; the return address, however, was unfamiliar. Though I cannot reproduce the letter in its entirety here and am not sure exactly where to begin, let us look at the last word of the letter (a single sheet, 8½" × 11": folded once to make four faces, all of them filled with lines of even handwriting in ball-point pen, thus placing this last word in the lower right corner near the fold): "Ellen."

She was also a student, in fact, a very bright one. The fourth paragraph of the letter begins: "Meanwhile, my research is going more slowly than I expected it to." Ellen had planned on getting her doctorate after her third graduate year, after much encouragement from the head of the department — well, that is, what could be interpreted as encouragement, since the professor was notoriously stringent. She had published two or three papers with him — the results of experiments she had designed and carried out with his help. (How nervous and excited she got before preparing delicate tissue samples from mice.) Yet the experiments always posed more questions than they answered, and she felt there was so much that she didn't know, an attitude with which she often faced things academic. For instance, it had always come as a surprise to her whenever she did well on exams and papers. Nor did she bother to think of academic achievements (e.g., graduating fourth in her high school class, finishing third in the

* This introduction, submitted by the case author, and the letter on page 132 are quoted from *Lolita* by Vladimir Nabokov. Copyright © 1958 by G. P. Putnam's Sons. Reprinted by permission.

Talented Youth Exam – given to high school seniors in her city, getting Phi Beta Kappa at school in New York, getting fellowships for research abroad, the early publication, etc.). Anybody else would have thought Ellen quite a success, but she could not think in such terms. And anybody else would also have thought that in the realm of the American Way of Social Life for People Under 25 Ellen was quite unsuccessful.

To begin with – and perhaps to end with – Ellen was not at all pretty. One couldn't really point to any particular flaw in her face – except perhaps her lips, which were overfull in a Charles Laughton sort of way. Certain photographs, such as the one in her yearbook, would not cause a viewer to remark on her unattractiveness; but those were photos. Her figure was far from what it should have been. Her body, if it had to be described in a word, might be said to sag. Though not really fat, Ellen was "thick-waisted" with a slight paunch below the waist; low-slung breasts and flat buttocks. She carried herself in a rather unfeminine manner, and by the time that most girls learn to walk from the hips rather than the waist, Ellen still strode almost as if she were climbing uphill. That natural and socially induced transformation which produces high-school-fuls of Sandra Dees and Annettes and their myriad less attractive, gum-chewing, orthodontured disciples seemed to have passed by dateless Ellen, and while these facts were not lost to her, she remained cheerful and usually happy. She played viola in the orchestra, and she *liked* playing viola in the orchestra. She enjoyed her family (she was the eldest of three sisters) and especially liked their small farm where they spent summers and occasional weekends. Not until her senior year of high school did she do anything that might be called dating; she went out a few times (including the senior prom) with a boy who, for want of any other group to fit into, hung on to the "intellectuals" (those who took advanced courses), a group which included most of Ellen's friends. But somehow, she never took much interest in him.

The tenth paragraph of the Letter starts near the top of page 4, quoted here in its entirety: "I nearly forgot some local news Mother wrote: Pat Michaelson (I can never remember her married name) is moving to New York. And Miss Anders has gone into teacher-training. It's a shame she couldn't stay in Literature."

It is often difficult to say how people met in high school; rather, I think, one "discovers" people who have always been there. Thus neither of our protagonists, Ellen or L, could really remember meeting the other. From tenth grade on they had been in the same English class (advanced English, it was called) and had attended frequently the discussion-parties held after each Friday night football game. The core of these "Friday night philosophers" (the ironic title they used when forced to name the group) consisted of the "intellectuals" among the 11th and 12th grade advanced English sections. Thus, all would have had three years of Miss Anders, a slim woman in her early fifties who taught her classes in a nondidactic way, arranging the chairs in horseshoe pattern (she occupying the sole chair in the opening) and tolerating silences when the discussion lagged. In demeanor, she seemed the embodiment of propriety, reserve, and ladylike-ness. Should it surprise us then that Miss Anders served these Friday groups as absentee mother, totem, pharmakos, and general object of fantasy?

It is 1959. L is in 11th grade. On a Friday night in the fall, he begins to learn how "intellectuals" act. Miss Anders is referred to as the Queen — the Virgin Queen, for her first name is, appropriately, Virginia; and L hears spun out the fantasies which will always evoke giggling speculation: Miss Anders drinking or drunk; Miss Anders taking a lover; Miss Anders having published stories under a pseudonym, and what they must be like (I think she may have truly published such fiction). L learns the game quickly, for not only is he a witty lad, but he enjoys teasing Miss Anders present or *in absentia*. He writes parodies (often slightly risqué) of the poets she makes the class read, and he awaits her red-ink comments with the anxious expectation of a gambler who, having made his irretrievable decision, waits for fate to make hers. But often, L does not turn in assignments at all. Each student in the high school is supposed to write an autobiography; L does not write one. Nor will he next year write a "Vocational Theme" (i.e., a research paper on some occupation — preferably the one the student plans to enter), similarly required of all seniors.

Hold on. This fancy prose exposition was very nice. But don't skip over the tough parts. Why was our bright boy not turning in the papers?

L was a confirmed underachiever, that's all I can say without getting psychoanalytic. He procrastinated, resisted, rebelled. He was forever imagining himself leading students against the school administration. He became president of his homeroom so he could sit in Student Council and make ironic remarks about their conformist flunkeyism (e.g., organizing squads of students to report others who smoked in the lavatories). Five years later, he would learn that he had "a hang-up on the authority issue."

And what about this Pat; is she important?

No. She's just a regular in this Friday group. She was fat and plain and quite nice. She and L used to refer to each other as a twin, as they shared a birthday, and for a couple of years after she graduated, they used to exchange simultaneous birthday cards. Apparently, she got married. One can only guess why Ellen put her in the Letter.

Miss Anders was also the sponsor of the *Review*, the school's literary magazine, and chose its editors. Ellen was quite pleased and surprised to be chosen and of course felt inadequate to the task. She was diffident about her own fiction and verse — and in fact probably would never have written any had it not been required in school. L, on the other hand, had hoped to be chosen editor, and he felt that Miss Anders had made a mistake in overlooking him. Worse, the other co-editor was the girl he was going out with, a prim girl who every few months changed her name from Barbara to Barbie to Barb to Babs, etc., and who had won the national spelling bee in 8th grade. She was the first girl he ever kissed or ever told he loved (an avowal made only once to her), and the first he ever broke up with.

It was late in 11th grade then that L first became acquainted with Ellen, for he used to show up at the *Review* office as companion to Barbara and self-appointed co-editor. They would meet in the small cubicle a few times a week after school, putting together the junior issue; and it was here that L had gotten to know and like Ellen. Of course, L knew the name, and had even, after a year and a half in the same English class, matched it with the proper face. (In 10th grade he could have singled out only a few girls he knew by name.) Ellen though, had known who L was, for there were fewer boys in the class; he was a slightly overweight, not-unhandsome boy, who would speak out — in a class where others were often reticent — sometimes with a quip or a pun. Ellen might even have described him as "neat," a term applied to anything which could hold her interest for more than a few minutes. If Ellen thought something neat, it meant that for the moment it intrigued her and she liked it.

I suppose that somewhere in the high school's archives (and perhaps even in L's or Ellen's desk) that issue of the *Review* is preserved. If we had it here, we might find it merely a dull collection of juvenilia and verse-form exercises: several cinquains, those quaint images — five lines of 2, 4, 6, 8, and 2 syllables; much "free verse," including a long poem of Barbie's which she was rather fond of; and a short poem by Ellen to the effect that "the moon is a golden galleon laden with pirate treasure. . . ." Ellen liked her poem (Miss Anders had returned it marked "Very Good") and would always be slightly embarrassed when L in later years — oh, many years, 6, 7, years later — would recall it almost verbatim and point out the strange similarity the central simile shared with the opening lines of a poem by Alfred Noyes.

In that same small magazine there appeared a short story by L, a somewhat grotesque, surrealistic piece about two young boys who assault a blind beggar outside a ball park. The story was a class assignment, and the day he turned it in, L had "hung around" after school in

Miss Anders' room. He waited while she read from among the stories which had been turned in — waited with that nervous, expectant feeling a gambler has during the split second the dice are in the air. *That's the second time you've used that metaphor. Is that significant?*

I just can't think of anything that fits as well — the expectation of impending doom or glory, putting oneself in the situation, then having no control over the outcome.

When Miss Anders had finished his story and looked up, L tried to feign disinterest, but much to L's delight, she commented that she thought the story quite good. She also explained that there was a problem in the point of view. L was now as overjoyed as he had been nervous. And the same sequence of emotions was repeated later in the week when two or three students were asked to read their stories to the class. Standing in front of the class after his reading, L was inwardly elated at the near-awe he sensed in his classmates. Later, L noticed that when Miss Anders had returned the story, she had neglected to write comment or grade; and all papers were returned with a comment — sometimes brief, more usually ranging upwards of 50 words. Miss Anders looked surprised when after school L mentioned this absence of written approval (he wanted it in writing). She repeated aloud her original thoughts and placed an "A" in the corner of the paper. She also suggested that L revise the story and send it to a national high school literary magazine. L never revised the story.

When they were seniors in high school, L and Ellen were assigned to separate English sections: and it was in their capacities as editor and self-appointed co-editor that their friendship continued. They were among the 3 or 4 people who regularly sat for an hour or more after school in the *Review* office, talking sometimes of manuscripts and art work for the magazine but more often of nothing in particular. Ellen enjoyed L's conversation, laughed quickly at his humor, and listened to his judgments on submitted material. L was suspicious of any piece which did not seem to him at first glance excellent. He would pursue any obvious flaw — meaning sacrificed to rhyme, overworked rhetorical tricks, and especially triteness. Ellen, on the other hand, tended to like anything that had a trace of merit — if only because the author had been kind enough to submit it. "I don't know; I kind of like it," Ellen would say of some poem. Whereupon L would begin to make fun of the rhymes, ideas, or language in the poem; and having formed an opinion, he could not concede a point. If Barbie and Ellen insisted on including a piece he disliked, he would act as if he were making a martyr-like concession in muting his own views. Once during a discussion of poetry or politics, Ellen had laughed after L had made an impassioned point in his argument. What amused her, she said, was to see L get so indignant; it was cute. For some reason, this remark had jarred L, not only because it referred to something completely different from the intellectual content on which he had been concentrating, but because neither Ellen nor L had ever stated directly an opinion of the other's character or feelings about it.

For the magician to misdirect his audience, he must also misdirect himself — he must look at his closed fist as if it really held some object, and he must, with his audience, be astounded when the unfolding of his fingers reveals an empty hand. He polishes the performance until he comes to believe in it and can work his sleight-of-hand (and of eye) without thinking about it. And should some un-misdirected spectator naively point to a concealed card, the magician will regard the palmed ace in his own left hand with chagrin, resentment, and genuine surprise.

What is that supposed to mean?

It means that's how L felt. Ellen had been listening to him, not to what he was saying, and had pointed out the quality of the performance. It meant she saw the relationship as more than intellectual. It was similar to the time when L complained of being depressed and said he was considering suicide. Ellen had been shocked, had tried to buoy L's spirits, and had told him the idea of suicide was unthinkable to her. But L had anticipated her reaction then, and nothing about it had surprised him.

Ellen was the eldest of three sisters. Her father, whom she always called Daddy, was an accountant, an Episcopalian, and a Republican. He had a gentle manner and a quiet humor; he enjoyed Thurber and an occasional sherry before dinner. Her mother, a tall woman with black hair, seemed pleasant and easygoing. One would never have guessed she was a member of a decent literature committee, which had succeeded in keeping *Playboy* and worse out of the town's newsstands and drugstores. That is, she seemed to have some sympathy, understanding, and tolerance for (to use a phrase of TV and magazine psychology) "the problems of young people." Ellen had two sisters: Sallie, who much resembled her mother — they both seemed to have some inner steadiness which allowed them to face daily troubles with relative calm, though of course, in Sallie this sense was less developed; and Terry, eight years younger than Ellen, who was something of a brat. L happened to be visiting Ellen's home one evening when Sallie (then in her early teens) had been very despondent — almost tearful. But L had included her in the conversation and the next day Ellen told him that he had done wonders cheering up Sallie. This in turn had made L feel good, for he was possessed of an urge to protect or comfort children (*Catcher in the Rye* again).

The Letter also contains at one point a little illustration-as-punctuation: a little smiling stick figure at the end of a sentence. This is a gimmick which L started, when in 12th grade he would put a face indicating mood or theme in the loop of his initial (an "L" in handwriting). That summer, after graduation, L worked in New Hampshire and corresponded with Ellen. She soon took to drawing a face in her initial. The plagiarized cuteness irked L slightly, but that is not important. What is important is what L wrote to Ellen. (Unfortunately, none of the letters is preserved, and it is only out of fidelity to Science that I do not here "reconstruct" a few of them and turn this into an epistolary case history.) In any case, L told Ellen of a girl he had met (and there were few girls about), with whom he established some kind of friendship. She was overweight and not attractive, but she was companionship and she loaned L books (*Look Homeward, Angel*) and invited him to dinner with her family, and played piano with him and listened to him play — all of which he had done with Ellen. L didn't know why he told Ellen about this girl, Sue, but when he got back home and went to see Ellen, as he was talking to her, Terry (the brat) piped in, "How's Sue?" Again the broken taboo. It was another of those comments which so destroy the scene that one cannot remember how things were immediately patched up but which themselves stand out in memory years later. L felt the guilt of the *flagrante delicto* adulterer. But how can you be unfaithful when you've never even kissed either girl — and when the flagrancy is not in the least delicious?

When L and Ellen went to college, they corresponded regularly — an average of one letter a month. And when they came home for Christmas, L visited her once, and they saw each other at a party or two. But for L what happened that vacation was that he slept with a girl for the first time — a very pretty girl he had dated in high school, a girl who loved him. I suppose I should not avoid here a brief description of L's relations with girls he did date — relations which, though they had come close before, first reached the crucial stage of actual screwing that December. By the time Ellen's Letter arrives some years hence, L will have slept with far more — upwards of 15. (*Is this cheap bragging part of the syndrome?*) But in all these affairs, L remained "detached," loath to get "involved," and generally in it for the sex and to ward off loneliness. Even when as a senior in college L regularly saw a girl for nearly a year, he was constantly thinking about going out with others; and he frequently incurred the girl's ire because of his un-lover-like attitude. L also, during those years, twice fell in love with girls who rejected him, and at those times he was given to lonely bouts of wretchedness, jealousy, and despair. In fact, the December in question, L was miserably in love with an unreachable girl (whose name also happened to be Ellen). But so caught up was he with the idea of screwing that he left his jealousies hundreds of miles away at the New England campus.

Soon after this enlightening vacation, L received a letter from this girl, then a high school senior, saying that she might be visiting Sarah Lawrence. L wrote back that perhaps he could go to New York and they could spend the night together. The girl left L's letter out; her parents found it and forbade her to communicate with L. Without explaining any of this in detail to Ellen, L asked her to forward his letters to the girl so that they would not bear his condemned handwriting or postmark. The mechanics of this arrangement, which are important, elude memory: did L merely enclose a folded letter in his letters to Ellen — or was there a sealed envelope inside a larger envelope? Probably the former. And did Ellen read those other letters? (probably not) or how curious was she? (moderately) and might she have guessed why L had to send his letters through her? (probably not).

Chronology is crucial here, yet the following incident floats somewhere between five and seven years ago and could have occurred during any school vacation in between. L and Ellen are in Ellen's house. L has taken her out — to dinner or to a movie, but at least he has overcome whatever it was that had kept him from going on anything like a date with her, even if on a just-friends basis. They have talked, L slightly nervous, but Ellen as unselfconscious as ever, quick to laugh, appreciative. Perhaps L has played the piano and tried to explain something about jazz to her. Now sitting beside her on a couch in the den, L turns and kisses Ellen, and awkwardly — oh, so very awkwardly — they embrace. Then L asks if she would — not if she will, but if she would — go to bed with him (given the setting in her home the question must remain hypothetical, for the moment at least). She answers that she would like to but that she cannot because her parents would not want her to, and she could not contravene their will on such an important matter. No, it's not a question of their finding out; it would be the same even if they never found out.

After a while (which is either two minutes or two years) L says, "You know what I wish?" He is thinking that he wishes Ellen were beautiful or at least attractive enough for him to try to love her, to make love to her. He wonders whether he can tell her this explicitly since she will probably not guess, and since it will probably hurt her; but L thinks that honesty is a good thing.

"Yes," says Ellen, "you wish I were ————," naming L's girl-friend, the one he first slept with.

L regrets that he feels no attraction for Ellen, and she suggests the reason is that theirs is a brother-sister relationship. (In high school, L, Ellen, and her best friend–neighbor had all adopted each other as siblings, since in real life Ellen had no brothers, L no sisters.) No, L says, it's just the vagaries of physical attraction.

And Ellen is not insulted? How can she take that sort of remark, whose only virtue is its seeming honesty? I'd sleep with you if you had a trimmer body.

Yes. L is ashamed of himself. But can one will oneself to desire? Besides, Ellen does not seem hurt. She accepts what cannot be changed and makes the best of what is. She is a happy person.

A similar incident occurred a couple of years later in New York. L had stopped off there on his way east for the start of school; Ellen had already started. He walked to her dorm, and she was among the girls sunning themselves. When she saw him, she jumped up, the other girls immediately reminding her of the dorm rule to put up the straps of one's bathing suit when standing. Then she ran to L and gave him a friendly hug.

Ellen went to change, they lunched on the dormitory's skimpy tea-sandwiches, and then they retired to Ellen's room. They talked about dorm regulations (straps up, no locks on doors, visiting hours, etc.), and Ellen mentioned incidents where couples had been surprised by an early-returning roommate. L said he was very tired from travelling and just wished to lie down, so he lay on Ellen's bed while she sat on her roommate's bed. L felt slightly uncomfortable and could not sleep; so they talked quietly, with several long silences, during which they listened to the summer breeze. After an hour or so, L said goodbye and drove on up to Massachusetts.

Then came the year L spent in New York, a last-minute candidate in graduate school after he'd sent off applications — and one acceptance deposit — to law schools. Better a reluctant sociology student than a reluctant law student, he reasoned. Consequently, L had himself a dismal year, academically and otherwise. During the entire year, L had about a half dozen dates, made almost no friends. His roommate was nice enough, though L suspected he was queer. Early in the year, L broke up with the girl he'd been going with — mostly because the 250 miles between Boston and New York gave L a geographical distance to match his emotional detachment. He saw a university psychiatrist, who in the second or third session gave L sets of pictures from which he was to choose those faces he liked and disliked. Seriously disturbed people, the doctor told him, make their choices with much more hesitation than had L. He felt cheered at hearing this. The doctor also told him he was too reserved with his emotions for the university services to be of use. He recommended long-term therapy.

Ellen was still in New York now in her second year of graduate work, and L called her for an occasional long conversation. Once or twice a month, L would call — or Ellen would call him — and they would talk for an hour or more. Often L would not realize he'd spent so much time on the phone till he looked at his watch. About once a month L would drive over to Ellen's for dinner. He sometimes took his recorder and amazed Ellen with his facility, for he had just taken up the instrument. She also tried to learn but was most unsuccessful. They would talk for hours, and often L did not return home till one in the morning.

What did they find so much to talk about?

It's hard to remember conversations like this. At first, Ellen told of her summer and semester in Europe. She had done research there, and, she gradually let on to L, she had had an affair.

What?

Yes. She would speak about her German friend at great length — not about how much they were in love but about things he said or about Germany itself and its university system, vague things she associated with him.

You said an affair. You mean she was sleeping with him?

The question was never asked point blank, and sex was one of the things L and Ellen did not talk about. But she was planning to marry him. They would live in Germany; she had started to learn German from him, and she had a few books with photos of the German countryside. She gave every evidence of being in love with him, and L just assumed she'd slept with him — it was the right thing to do.

One night when L was at Ellen's for dinner, she was telling him about some friends fooling around with a polygraph. Ellen had gotten herself wired up and they were asking her everyday sorts of questions. "Then one of the girls said, 'Oh, Ellen, what's this?'" and Ellen showed L how the girl had indicated the pendant she wore, given her by the German. "And I didn't feel at all different or embarrassed," continued Ellen, "but the needle jumped about a foot." However, more frequently it was L who made sexual allusions — usually in a joking manner, the off-color nuance. For instance, one night in a phone conversation, L was describing one of his professors.

"Is he married?" asked Ellen.

"Yes, he's on his second wife — and considering the hour, I guess that's literal."

Once L even took Ellen to a concert, but only because he knew nobody else he could ask, and he did not want to go alone. But for the most part, L was glad Ellen had a "fiancé," and he hoped she had slept with him. He felt a great deal of pressure because of the nonsexual nature of their relationship. He had often felt as though he ought to be sleeping with her. And as the year wore on, he sensed somehow that Ellen now wanted him to sleep with her. She also spoke less of her German friend. For Ellen, that half year in Europe had been wonderful; she had been in love with someone who had also loved her. And while we cannot know what happened after her return — what their correspondence might have said — the fire of their affair seemed to have faded in Ellen, as if she realized slowly that it was all past.

L began to date Ellen's undergraduate assistant, whom he had met at Ellen's apartment. Amy was a pretty, naive junior, who, in a gentle way, spurned L's advances, thereby spurring his desires. She had a boyfriend and was not at all romantically interested in L. On calling Ellen one evening, he had found her and Amy in the midst of a giggling fit more suited to 15-year-olds, though obviously they enjoyed each other's company, and the feeling L had was jealousy — but he was not sure of whom he was jealous.

One winter Sunday, Ellen invited L to dinner, and L asked if he might watch the football game on her TV. She agreed to give him the key to her apartment, but he would have to meet her at the lab to get it. There L met various people, including his former roommate Bill, now a graduate student. He also saw Amy, who was wearing wheat jeans such that L could not help noticing her shapely figure. He even commented to Ellen à *propos* of nothing and in a very soft voice, "I've never seen her in pants before." But Ellen either did not hear or did not understand. L had never before said anything to her so explicit as to the existence of sexual desire.

L took the key and went to Ellen's apartment, a third-floor walkup, and she returned around 5 or so to cook dinner. She said her parents had been uncomfortably amused when she had told them of this arrangement she'd made; but Ellen had not seen the implications.

Could she really have been as naive as that — the ultimate rationalist: that was the obvious thing to do if he was going to be at the lab and he didn't want to go back across town to watch the game.

Needless to say, L caught all the implications. When you give a guy the key to your apartment and go home to cook dinner for him, you're playing house. And when 22-year-olds from hot-shot sophisticated colleges play house, they screw. And if they don't, something's wrong. And if it's just Platonic, you should get worse problems — what do you think is at the core of the standard bedroom farce, whether it's Beaumarchais or those insipid Doris Day films? So if you don't, it's farce, and if you do, it's incest, the crux of our oldest favorite tragedy — especially since you-know-who's theories were clasped to our intellectual bosom. But Ellen was oblivious to all that.

"Do you believe in Freud?" Ellen asked.

L balked, started a few sentences — "I'm not sure what that means. . . ." — and finally said, "Yes. Do you?"

"No, I don't think so."

The argument over social and physical sciences would go on and off at various times throughout the year, she taking potshots at Freudian excesses, he at rationalist reductionisms. They usually talked about academic matters – the usefulness of language requirements, theory, etc. Or else they talked about movies (L always wondered whom she went with), books, or politics. And in these L practically monopolized the conversation.

One weekend, when L was visiting at Ellen's apartment, she spoke about the chairman of the biology department, one Prof. Benton. All the graduate students except Ellen were terrified of the man. For instance, he had scared them all by asking each to see him individually about some matter which he shrouded in an air of sinister mystery. When Ellen went in, he merely asked her if she'd been using at night a certain room in the building. No, she hadn't. OK. Ellen found out from the other students Benton questioned that someone had been using the room for midnight trysts, visible to a woman across the street.

Then there were all the fantastic tales grad students told about Benton. "One time he was supposed to have gotten so angry at some student," said Ellen, "that he threw a rack of test tubes at him. And they *believe* these stories." L, too, had heard allusions to the temper of this handsome perfectionist. "And there are always rumors that he has affairs with his students," said Ellen, slicing black olives into the tuna casserole.

"Are they true?" L asked.

"Well," said Ellen, "the one about me wasn't."

L laughed a long time at this.

Then came Bill's party. When they were in college, L had always been somewhat envious of Bill's ability not only to "get girls" but to have successful affairs lasting anywhere from a few months to a year or more. When they had roomed together as sophomores, Bill would occasionally speculate on what it would have been like to have married this or that girl in his past, which ones might have been happy marriages. With each successive affair, at college and later in New York City he seemed to approach marriage but never got too close. "I don't know, Buddy, this could be *it* – the big M," Bill would say to L when they happened to meet. and L would be ever so slightly awed inside. The only girl he ever felt he might be compatibly married to was Ellen; she was the only one whom it would not be a chore to talk with at breakfast. Bill's current love was a pretty freshman, whom he was to marry on the spur of the moment next January. L, on hearing the news, suspected pregnancy, but he figured Bill knew better. But I have gotten ahead of my story, and before picking up the plot again, we must go back, for the youth of Bill's mistress had a slightly unsettling effect on L. In high school, he had thought that it was somehow a sign of weakness to date a girl in the grades below him. But obviously L had elaborate ideas about whom he could be seen dating, which along with other imagined taboos kept him from dating very much at all during several periods in his adolescence.

Wait a minute! Don't skip those "other taboos" quite so fast. That's the sort of stuff we're looking for.

Let's put it this way: L was scared of girls. He didn't know why. He supposed it was like that for all high school boys, but the fear persisted in college. If he went to a mixer, he spent most of the time standing alone. His freshman year (you will recall) he fell in love with a girl who would not let him get near her. When he did go out with a girl, he never risked getting personally intimate, being only as charming as he had to be to get the girl into bed (and either L was pretty good at this or it didn't take much charm). Thus, after years of reflection, L decided that those other taboos involved desire for sex and fear of personal intimacy. With his hand halfway through dialing a number, L knew that all he wanted was sex (or so he thought), and my God, what if the girl could see what a dirty guy he was? Or what if she said no? L seldom thought out the real alternatives to these what-ifs. The idea itself was enough to make him put the phone back in its cradle.

At any rate, Bill had been a good friend in college, and had let L use his apartment until L got settled in New York. Bill knew Ellen and was in a graduate program similar to hers. He had also fixed L up with a local girl, whom L went out with twice, in an epitome of his "L-syndrome": He had started to seduce her the first time, finished the job a week later, remained distant throughout, taken her home in the morning, and never called her again.

In the early spring, Bill had a party, and L went hoping to meet girls. But he could see that this was not the place. Not a lot of people came, mostly people from the biology department, and most of them were coupled. Ellen introduced L to Benton, though they had met once at the lab without being introduced. ("Oh, *that's* Benton," L had said on learning who he'd been speaking to — they were talking about recorder-playing and the young man had been referred to only as Jon. He looked like a grad student.) Benton asked L what he did, etc., and when L said he was about to move to Boston and study sociology, Benton said, "Oh yes, I have a friend who interviewed a couple of sociologists for jobs here. None of them really knew what they were talking about."

Ellen chided him for the obvious slur on L, but he replied that he'd said nothing personal against L. L seemed to agree, though he didn't say anything, but inwardly he wondered whether he could hold his ideological ground against this adamant and reputedly brilliant

scientist; and he was grateful for Ellen's support. They did not, however, discuss things directly; instead Benton went on to relate some
scurrilous story about an eminent professor of sociology. Then L
drifted off to some other part of the room.

When he saw that he was not going to be picking up any girls,
L decided just to drink a bit and try to have a good time. He danced
— that exhilarating type of dancing done today — a couple of times
with Bill's girlfriend, who was quite a bouncy thing. Later, as L was
talking with Ellen, she suggested they dance; and she turned out to be
a better dancer than L had expected — not as awkward as he'd feared.
But L felt uncomfortable. When he left, Ellen asked him for a ride
home, and L, of course, obliged. They reached her house, and L
walked to the porch with her. The next thing he knew they were kissing, a passionate (tonguing) kiss, though it was a bit sloppy. How had
it started? Had L gone to hug her or had he meant to kiss her? No
matter; her response was immediate.

"Would you like to come upstairs," she whispered, and this
time L was sure she knew what it meant. She was asking him to sleep
with her, to make love to her.

"No thanks," said L. "I don't know why. I can't explain it now.
I'm too drunk." This last excuse was a lie. "I'll explain later."

Of course, he never explained. He saw her or spoke with her
perhaps two or three times after that, but they never mentioned that
evening. Then school was over, and L left New York.

Ellen's birthday falls on September 1. Usually L forgets to
send even a card; for he is usually not sure where she is any given
summer or whether she is en route to school. Ellen on the other hand
sends L a card each year. But this year L had not heard from Ellen in
quite a while — even though he had sent the last letter in their now-
sparse correspondence. Thus, early in August, L sent Ellen a book
(a clever piece of trans-lingual puns and verse) saying that he was
sending it early so as to make sure the book reached her on time for
her birthday, thinking that she might be back in Europe. But he was
also eager to hear from her.

On the 16th of August, L received The Letter, whose second,
third, and fourth paragraphs read as follows:

> I know I haven't written for a while. I got married last March
> and I've really been busy. I figured Bill or somebody would have
> told you. I'm awful sorry you didn't know.
>
> My husband is Steve Tate, and he works for G.E. as a machin-
> ist. (I met him on a blind date last winter.) We live in the Bronx
> where he grew up, so every one around here knows him. Our apart-
> ment is a really neat one, too; we were lucky to get it.

You might guess what a surprise our marriage was at home. Mother and Daddy took it well after the first shock, and they've been wonderful, though nobody (even Steve's friends and mine) saw much of a future for us.

I think we get along terrifically. I'm learning to clean and cook to his satisfaction, which wasn't as easy as I'd thought. This September or so we'll have a third Tate — a boy we hope.

Ellen goes on in her Letter to tie up a few loose ends of our story: "Bill is at Chicago. . . . Benton left New York and I don't miss him a bit, though I still have to finish a thesis for him." And finally, "If you get to the city, please call. You can come over for dinner and meet Steve. It's been so long since I've talked to you. Yours, Ellen."

After the initial shock, the attempts to set the new Ellen mentally in place of the old, noticing the "Yours" that used to be "Love," L could not help recalling a fictional letter he had read. Here is an abbreviated segment:

Dear Dad:

How's everything? I'm married. I'm going to have a baby. I guess he's going to be a big one. I guess he'll come right for Christmas. . . . Dick is promised a big job in Alaska in his very specialized corner of the mechanical field, that's all I know about it but it's really grand. . . . Write, please. I have gone through much sadness and hardship.

Yours expecting,
Dolly (Mrs. Richard F. Schiller)

Was there really a similarity in the prose? Or was it just the situation? But wait a minute. "Dad" had coveted his Dolly-Lo purely for her very physical nymphetude, had gone "plowing his Molly in every state," ignoring her wishes and her tears, robbing her of her childhood.

Was Steve the machinist really Dick the deaf mechanic? Had L robbed Ellen of anything? Ladies and gentlemen of the jury, I remind you that L seldom even literally touched her.

Why then was L not happy for Ellen — as happy as she herself seemed to be? Of course, he could count the months backward and see that March was less than nine months from "this fall." A card Ellen sent three months later informed L that their daughter was born on September 25, which means by strict count that she was conceived on Dec. 25. So rejoice. Rejoice that on a Christmas Eve blind date, Ellen got knocked up by a machinist.

And now I have failed you again, Ellen. I tried to understand why we never spoke of our love, and again I have left you out of the conversation. I never understood your happiness. Why were you not in frequent despair as I would have been in your position? And you probably never understood my lack of happiness. You had no problem with lust; how could you have known the way it was with me? What has become of us; what shall become of us? Case histories — let alone assigned ones for college courses — fare far poorer than poetry for granting even a speck of immortality (O, Anna O). We come then to a modest end. We have our memories, and as some clever psychoanalyst (who nevertheless let jargon mar his epigrams) once said, "De-cathexis proceeds memory by memory." Most elusive Mnemosyne, mother of all the Muses.

Case 25 / Le Printemps, La Primavera — or La Guérillière et La Crustace

Spiritless marriage, shallow friendships, and vacuous employment as a secretary in a religious institution make up the psychological context for viewing the unlikely relationship between this twenty-three-year-old case author and her forty-four-year-old boss, Brother Arlen. The "musty, beige, and porcine" Brother Arlen becomes an object of conquest — not just sexual, but existential. Mercury, the case author, strives to make a difference in Arlen's life, to shake him up, all the while focusing her attention on *his* actions and *his* unexamined life. Although sparse in phenomenological disclosure, the case is replete with stinging metaphors, diverting ornamentation, and cathartic poems — indirect but rich sources for understanding her inner experience.

To approach this case from a Sullivanian perspective one must consider Mercury's and Arlen's personifications of themselves and each other, their preoccupations with appearance and sexuality, and the "parataxic distortion" that accompanies their anxious efforts to attain a new level of intimacy and self-discovery. To what extent does each person change over the course of this relationship?

"Why do men live in shoals?" persisted Zora.
— Anaïs Nin, *The Four-Chambered Heart*

How heavy this life, the life of men. Is it true they cannot raise one eyebrow without the other? So weighted with their work, eagerly curving their shoulders to the contours of the yoke. A world dry to tears and bleached of colour. One never hears the wind chimes or the music of jewelry. In the mornings they brush away their dreams like flies. There is no carpet and no grass over the rough brown boards of their existence. Perhaps, never owning more than two pairs of shoes, the richness of life has escaped them.

As a child, there was never any doubt in Mercury's mind as to what she would grow up to be but an artist. What remained to be resolved was: what sort? for her talents were scattered, and what would she say and how would she say it? Of course there was always that trite triumvirate of anathema occupations much touted by her mother and step-father — those of the schoolteacher, secretary, and nurse. As fate would have it, Mercury ended up as the worst of the lot.

Five months after being married, Mercury's husband, Pyotr, was drafted into the army and five months after that he was sent to serve in the Heart of Darkness. Mercury accompanied him and, after several grueling and humilitating weeks of hunting, found herself employment in a mazelike office with striped wallpaper, a Ming tree, and several each of etiolated nuns, brothers, spinsters, and priests and an equal number of somewhat healthier-complexioned civilians. "Whew!" said Mercury as she sat down to her typewriter, *"Qui vive ici?"* Mercury tried building a relationship with the Ming tree, her favorite among the plants, but it was difficult since she couldn't take it home with her. For months Mercury's heart lay like a stone at the bottom of a well, Mercury managing to elevate it from lunch hour to lunch hour with the hydraulic fluid of *Ada*. The other office wenches kidded Mercury about her choice of reading matter, insinuating that its cover suggested the colour blue, this being strange stuff to them. Jetting back and forth between the office wasteland and the literary tropics made Mercury dizzy, but dizzy is better than somnambulism.

Shortly after being hired Mercury transcended decorous dress for just about all the law would allow, her favorite being a yellow knit shirt with twin swans closing in for a kiss amidst a spray of cattails. When one feisty old nun asked Mercury whether her pants were sewed together with steel thread, Mercury declared they were sewn with spider webs and maidenhair. It would be inaccurate, though, to attribute Mercury's attire solely to a desire for sabotage, for she had long believed in the legitimacy of display. Nevertheless, she thought, if I have to be their nigger, this'll be one nigger they won't soon forget. She began to sign the drafts she typed with various amusing sobriquets such as "Anne Droid" and "A. Tomaton." Then the files began to reflect her bias with alternate headings such as "Third Rate Ideas" or "Those who can, teach; those who can't become educators," and so forth in that vein. Ho, hum.

As time went on the secretarial stable changed somewhat and, slowly, painfully, Mercury began to develop a stable of her own — you might say a different friend for each day of the week. While none of them were quite what Mercury had ordered, when you put them all together they made a balanced meal. Gradually the gravity of each player made itself felt upon the others and they settled into their various orbits and constellations, ready for the masque to begin. Mercury came to occupy the place of the office *enfante terrible* and when she became embroiled in some office brouhaha, certain staffers drew near to hear what latest *bon mots* she might disgorge. Mercury had always had an affinity for niggers, real niggers, that is, and it was they who became her first friends. Jesse, an affable middle-aged black gentleman who took care of the mailroom would talk about music and swap white man horror stories with Mercury. "Yes, girl, I know just what you mean." When Mercury discovered he was making less money than herself and the other secretaries half his age, she protested to Jim, the office manager, an even more affable and charming Irishman who bore a stunning resemblance to F. Scott Fitzgerald, only finer. But to no avail. Through a blaze of smiles she was informed that the former black mailroom manager had an IQ of 160 and had been paid $10,000 a year because he could really produce. Unfortunately he had had to be put ashore because when he wasn't pouring it on he was pouring it in. Now if Jesse displayed that kind of initiative. . . . The trouble with Jim was that deep down inside he was so damn nice he had difficulty recognizing anything that was not.

First Luvenia and later Di, the only black girls to come to work in the office, albeit temporarily, became Mercury's friends. They were more up front than the white girls and became Mercury's co-conspirators in sensuality. They spent a great deal of their conversations speculating as to whether Brother Paul would know what to do with it if you stuck it in his face, whether Chris and her husband really wore surgical gloves to bed, whether Uncle Ed, priest/president, and Carol, spinster/executive assistant, ever dreamt of . . . , and why the longer you stayed married, the harder it was to get some when you wanted it. Whenever they ate in the office kitchen, people stopped by to tell them to keep it down or to ask what was so funny. Mercury's voice and particularly her laugh were loud and carried apparently phenomenal distances, as she was forever being chastised for these disruptive outbursts — much to her annoyance, for she always suspected her chastisers were a little envious. But more than that, she resented the implication that vitality could somehow overflow the bounds of good taste, convinced it was impossible.

Then there was her friend Jère, a tall, fair, heavy-breasted Anglo-Saxon, daughter of a diplomat, wealthy on both sides of the family, and pretentious because, among other things, she had been born in Egypt. Jère had a Greek boyfriend, Andreas, whose dark good looks and sunny Mediterranean temperament often intrigued Mercury more than waspy Jère. At parties it was Andreas and Mercury who put on the light show. He was a master of the *beau geste*, performing such tricks as plucking the flower from Mercury's hair and tucking it in her *décolletage.* Jère and Mercury had rather intellectual conversations, engaged in amiable argument, and attempted to penetrate, purely for therapeutic purposes, of course, the enigmatic psychologies of Mercury's suicidal/recluse friend, Beryl, and Jère's lonely roommate, Maeva, who, at the ripe old age of twenty-three, had never had a man. To spare the reader idle speculation, we will note here, that physically, Beryl resembled a Beardsley heroine and, secondly, that Mercury's and Beryl's friendship was largely a war of beauty, which they waged when they weren't overwhelmed with other, less ariel concerns.

Then there was Mercury's friend whom we shall call here the Huntress. The Huntress was the closest living thing to a Barbie doll Mercury had ever seen. She was very blond, very blue-eyed, narrow-hipped, with a large high bust, and slender show girls legs. We call her the Huntress, but she was a poor one we're afraid, for on her sorties she always sustained far more wounds than ever did her quarry. Without her make-up she looked like a little shorn lamb, new and vulnerable. Once armored in her twenty layers of paint, however, she was *plus formidable.* Strictly speaking, she was no beauty, but, oh, how she could play Camille! The Huntress *inclined* toward men, like a flower towards a passing ray. No one could incandesce quite so spontaneously as she. She looked at men and women alike with the most intimate expression, conspiratorial, as if she were enlisting you in a secret only you two could share. She was always confiding stories of her life and though you might feel sure she was lying or exaggerating, when she threw you that wistful, ironic look and asked if you knew what she meant, you *had* to say yes, and sincerely. She was, what might even today be described as, the mistress of a married French restauranteur, with whom she was obsessed, but to whom she could never bring herself to say those three little words, "I love you." Most likely because she didn't. She had myriad male friends whom she often lunched off of, and the rest of the girls always wondered whether these gallants ever came to collect the bill. The Huntress and Mercury shared a high appreciation of the still life quality of certain remarkable moments in life, like being drunk on champagne and dancing nude on a balcony in Acapulco, or feeling so much passion for someone that you literally *fell* towards him with a great commotion in your ears. Yes, such things were worth pondering and the rest was, well, so much wasted motion, as they say in typing class.

Then there was Greta, broad of cheekbone and of hip resembling a handsome peasant goosegirl, who had been in the convent for three years but had decided against it, and who one dull afternoon had forever endeared herself to Mercury by regaling her with a song about how to amuse oneself on "Saturdy nite." One of her high school boyfriends had written and recorded this ditty and her friends used to call her up on the phone to listen to it since she possessed the single cut. It covered such time-honored topics as cunnilingus, sixty-nining, and proving your love, and one of its more side-splitting lines went: "Funny, this doesn't taste like tomato juice." Greta was slow, serene, and lazy and what she liked most in the world were long hot baths. Her favorite room was the bathroom where she hung all sorts of pictures and even a sculptured African head, much as other people might decorate their living rooms, an idea Mercury later came to appreciate for its fullness. Greta also used to amuse Mercury by bringing in outlandish pictures of herself in her various nun's prehistoric costumes which reminded Mercury of the stages of an insect. Mercury shared with Greta a feeling for the ambience of things, the propitious atmosphere, and could discuss with her such curious matters as the possible reasons why she had shifted from a preference for earth colours in surroundings to a preference for pale, fragile shades.

After Luvenia's and Di's departures, Mercury found herself in the singular circumstance of being the sole brunette in a place otherwise filled with white-haired ladies, *jolies blondes*, and one *laide rousse*. She took this as a sign of license, grace, or something or other. Mercury came to hold the pivotal position among her friends. Several of them did not care to associate much with each other but would nevertheless confide in Mercury, the liaison, who passed information between them. Greta and Jère looked upon the Huntress as being somewhat tawdry because of her obsession with appearance and her dubious relationships. The Huntress, in turn, regarded the two of them as dull and dulling and, in addition, thought Jère tacky, for though rich on both sides, etc., and personally handsome, resembling the figurehead of a ship in profile, Jère was poor herself, wore dirty underwear, shabby clothes, and was possessed of a singular lack of style.

When Mercury first came to Eunuchland she found her boss, Brother Arlen, musty, beige, and porcine. She thought him rather like a businessman but not a noisy one. She soon took the liberty of calling him Art and, among her friends, christened him with a rhyming sobriquet which the reader can well imagine. Brother Paul likewise resembled a businessman, only more so, as his shoulders were very square and his clothes very proper. He was quite the arrogant prig and his bearing was such that he always looked as though he still had the hanger in his jacket. Father Ed, Mercury's other master and head honcho, resembled nothing so much as a hyperthyroid chicken. When he became excited, which was often, his face took on the colour of the chicken's comb and his voice became high and broke like chicken squawks. Unlike the chicken, however, he flew a lot. He was always off to Africa, Australia, the White House, and thought quite a lot of himself for it. Each mile increased his self-esteem one unit, as he gradually began to feel a sense of presence over the whole earth and its many benighted ants. The priests in general were a noticeably higher caste than the brothers, possessed of greater social graces, more spirit, more money, and better looks. The Church's hierarchy was evident in the office microcosm and, in descending order, went priests, brothers and nuns, with the nuns, of course, being the largest and very much the poorest group. Oh, Charity, thy name is Woman! There was, however, only one nun in an executive position. In fact, there were only a few of them in the office though it was the veiled hordes who supported the organization with their membership dues. Despite a covey of Harvard Ph.D.'s, or perhaps because of them, Mercury found she had enjoyed more stimulating company in sweatshops.

In the beginning Mercury's relationship with these clowns was one of tenuously piquant antagonism. It was difficult to chat with them or make a joke. They were subterranean creatures and it took some spadework to bring them up.

One day, in the throes of despair after having read *Zelda*, Mercury's imagination was triggered by a title on some educational newsletter and, furtively, she wrote the following poem while at her desk.

> I walked a ways into the wood
> My brains they were all stained with blood
> I'd sleep a moment if I could
> Wishes, lies, and dreams
>
> Ferns they have a warm, dark scent
> like you and I when we are bent
> in lifelong tangles dumbly sent
> from hell and heaven
>
> I walked a while along the road
> At every step my rancor showed
> And bloody animals were sowed
> along the asphalt
>
> Blood is dark, now dim, now bright
> Its red gleams through both day and night
> One smear imprints upon your sight
> the eternal colour
>
> I flew a ways into the air
> And everything that I saw there
> was just the same as it is here
> Wishes, lies, and dreams

Yes, thought Mercury, this was something these fucking monks didn't have to wrack their brains over. Perhaps if they were very careful they might slip through life clean without ever having to consider the blastulas, the sutures, and the clefts, the configurations of living things. The worm in its egg and the deaths of myriad minutiae. Though still feeling like some charred piece of cinder or bone, some part of Mercury became lighter than air, for this was the first real poem she had written in years. After having become absorbed with Pyotr at the age of nineteen, she had written little or nothing except for letters and had not begun to do so again until the army had split them apart.

Some time later, cauterized by such duties as typing the same letter a dozen times for those individuals too elevated to receive anything impersonal and sitting in on interminable, vacuous meetings where she was the only woman, the only prole, and half the age of the other attendants, Mercury began to write such poems as the following one.

Acid stay away from me
My memory has gone dirty and coarse
Your invisible stains
Your dreamy scars

Acid stay away
Your burnings have grown insupportable
Soon you will have gone too far
Your hostess will fly up
Your little house will whirl away

Better cut your visits short
This vessel is sick
And death is pastel, mild, and true
to its description

Not like you,
not like you.

One time she fell into a sleep for three or four days, a sort of demicatatonia. She functioned quite well in this state and, though it was difficult to feel anything, she felt some little feather of anxiety that she might be dead, having missed the great event.

Lest the reader be confused on these matters, allow us to point out that, as in all things, there were good times and bad times, but that Mercury's friendships did not come into full flower until many months' time had been served. Likewise it took some doing before the professional staff gave themselves up to the ravages of defrosting.

Mercury amused herself as best she could with books, films, restaurants, and clothes, then later with increased prosperity, the ballet, apartment hunting, and furniture buying and decorating. With the exception of one army couple, an aspiring pianist and opera singer, who soon moved back to New York, the people she and Pyotr occasionally socialized with from the ranks left nearly everything to be desired. Pyotr himself began to lose his sheen, having always had a certain stolid facet to his personality, he became more subdued, withdrawn, lost his rebel, gadfly colouring. Though the separation and grotesque treatment of the army during Pyotr's training period had damaged them both, Mercury was taken aback by how little anger or despair he displayed. He had to play the game. Mercury had wanted him to run away, but it would have ruined his career and probably his life. Mercury tried to dig his feelings out of him, but it was not an easy task. They would both weep and he would promise to be more open but would always soon slide back into his shell. After his release Pyotr told Mercury that the army had destroyed whatever illusions of freedom he had harboured until then. He admitted that the deaths of his parents in the preceding years had affected him more than he had let on (he hadn't seemed to care). In fact, what bothered him the most was that he didn't care more. He confided that a certain revelation about his family by his younger sister had further sobered him. *Roué.*

Mercury's women friends and entertainments were simply not enough. She tried to enroll in a Saturday painting class, but found it prefilled by full-time students. Arlen began to annoy Mercury more and more. He had begun to compliment her on her attire, calling her "Mademoiselle Pieds Rouges." Why doesn't he go eat himself? thought Mercury. He had made his bed; let him lie in it. After dictation he and Mercury began to get into longer and longer chats and engage in extended bouts of *repartée*. Art went on a diet — no breakfast, no lunch — and slimmed down. He bought a new suit or two and decorated his office with art reproductions from the museums. Mercury and Greta liked to go into his office and look at the pictures and make fun of his motley selection and the way he had arranged them, Secretaries were not allowed to decorate their walls. Mercury had already tried and lost amid a flurry of rationalizations. Greta and Mercury also liked to tease Art about what he had concocted on his night to cook for the three brothers he lived with. They would graciously give him recipes and then badger him until he tried them. This sport was made more delicious by the fact that he hated cooking and liked to claim that his taste buds had been atrophied as a child by his mother's boiled turnips and potatoes.

Yes, thought Mercury, blame it on Mama. Can't eat, can't shit, can't screw, can't make a buck? It's Mama. Mama! you jerk! get back up there on the cross. He began to attend the opera, making Mercury order the tickets. "So you're a fan of the opera?" inquired Mercury. "I really don't know anything about it. I've just discovered that I really enjoy it," he replied. I guess you do, thought Mercury — all the mess of life up on the stage.

His little attentions grew. For her birthday he surprised Mercury with a bottle of champagne. For Christmas he presented her with the "Liberated Woman's Calendar" and tickets to a folk ballet. Mercury had not expected a gift, but not to be outdone, she drew a pagan Christmas card and mailed it to him along with Scriabin's *Black Mass/White Mass* and a *Manitas de Plata*. Then later when his birthday came round she drew a little cartoon of them both as a cat and a bear, labelled "*La Belle et La Bête*" and gave him Sylvia Plath's *Ariel*. Arlen didn't care for poor Sylvia's poems, saying that he didn't think they would be much admired a hundred years hence, and complained that the symbols in Sylvia's universe were repeated over and over. "So are the ones in Shakespeare's sonnets," said Mercury. "You just don't want to say what you really think." Mercury was by turns provoked and intrigued with Art. She invited him to her party, but he got called out for the evening on an errand of mercy. He invited her to his party, but she got lost and couldn't find his house.

The convention was approaching and Mercury thought this would be an opportunity to see what fat would render. They would all be together in a strange city for nearly a week in the spring and Pyotr would be out of town for a couple of weekends shortly after their return. Mercury and Chris enlisted Art to take them to see the Phillips Collection since he would have a car and they were going by train, gleefully cornering him into the role of cavalier.

At the convention Arlen agreed to have dinner one evening with Mercury and Jère. They picked the place — a Middle Eastern restaurant with bazouki players and belly dancers, a taste they had acquired through Andreas. As it turned out, Greta, Chicago, Chris, and Bert (a debonair and newly self-defrocked priest) had caught wind of their plans for the evening and decided to join them. Bert flirted with Mercury and Mercury played for both the men. The quips flew under Mercury's orchestration and the girls constructed a huge pyramid of empty grasshopper glasses, which Arlen dismantled. The bazouki players were frenzied, the belly dancers were fat but voluptuous, and the conversation grew more and more *risqué*. They all jumped up and danced and sang for "Hava Nagila" and when they left, Mercury bought a tambourine which she played on the street while Bert did high kicks and tossed his Russian hat in the air while the others yelled encouragements. Then the seven of them piled into a cab and drove to a hotel for another round of drinks. Mercury complained bitterly at the separation of the sexes and protested various conjured lesbian advances from the tangle of feminine bodies in the back seat. Chicago piped up with, "I don't know what we'd do without you sometimes, Mercury." "Sometimes I don't know what I'd do without myself." Everyone thought this hysterical and it became the classic line of the convention, but Mercury thought it was a serious remark.

Gradually the group thinned down to the original threesome of Mercury, Jère, and Arlen. Mercury flirted with Arlen in her poor French so that Jère would not know what she was saying and reminded him of the one sin God would not forgive. He said he had seen the film *Zorba* but didn't remember what sin that was. "*Tu as peur, n'est-ce pas?*" "*Un peu de peur.*" Poor Arlen's French was even worse, so it was difficult to carry on a conversation. Nevertheless, the drift was unmistakable. Finally they parted and Mercury and Jère went to their hotel and Arlen to his. Wild Turkey! thought Mercury. Beyond duplication. She was back in the cauldron of love. From then on Mercury slept in a conscious fevered dream in which her mind whirred like a hummingbird, plumbing the same little flower over and over again. There was nothing that absorbed Mercury so much as peeling back the petals of another soul. She managed to arrange another evening with Arlen, this time with Jère and Walter, a W. C. Fields character *sans* the Fieldsian capacity for sauce. This time they went to a French place in a house in the oldest part of the city. The ambience inspired Mercury though the food did not. Soon Walt was drunk and obnoxious and while he argued with Jère about whether Andreas wanted to marry her for her money, Mercury flirted outrageously with Arlen, employing knee, elbow, and every verbal extravagance. Afterwards Jère and Mercury each took one of Arlen's arms as they searched for a cab while Walter stumbled around the cobblestone streets. Art would occasionally have to leave their company to herd Walt away from an approaching vehicle, but finally they came upon a cab and deposited Walter safely back at his hotel, after many reassurances that they, too, were retiring for the evening. During the cab ride, Art asked Mercury why she didn't become a writer. "Because I'm afraid of being a planarium. When there's nothing else left to sustain it, it begins to feed on itself until nothing remains but the nerve network. Or, there are those artists who suck out the souls of other people like eggs, and then complain about the flavor. You know what I mean?" "Yes," said Arlen, "I know what you mean." The threesome then went to a hotel bar for a nightcap and a few more double *entendres*. Unfortunately Walt had registered their proposed itinerary. Just as they were making their exit, he drove up in a cab and charged up the walk bellowing like a mad bull. It took some time to round the bastard up and get him in a cab again, and while Jère waited in the cab Walt had evacuated, getting the story from the driver, Mercury took advantage of the confusion to drop a few more helpful hints and bestow a good knight kiss upon Friar Tuck. Much to her chagrin, no invitation ensued.

As the convention neared an end, they all began to feel rather strange from the pace and the liquor. Art got sick and left early. Jère and Mercury didn't go to see the Phillips Collection but slept the last morning instead after Jère refused to go. Having dined with Jère's millionairesse grandmother the evening before, Jère and Mercury had had a falling out over the ethical aspects of class. The dinner scene had reminded Mercury of a Genêt play she had once been in called *The Maids*. She declared that the Grandmama had sucked the blood out of her pair of Irish maids and that they resembled two albino mice. Mercury mimicked their Irish accents and minced around the room squeaking in imitation. Jère maintained that it was their own fault they hadn't done any better and that she certainly intended to have help as she was going to maintain her career and a family simultaneously. J. and M. resumed a civilized mien quickly enough, but things were never quite the same after that first frost. At the train station Mercury bought an iris for her buttonhole and gave herself up to chills and reverie all the long way home. The train was crowded and Mercury and Jère had to take separate seats. First a white gentleman and later a black one pressed their stories upon Mercury, intent on making their confessions to passing anonymity. During the journey the train caught fire and they had to be hoisted aboard another. It was all very surreal.

Shortly after Mercury's return from the convention she found the Huntress, whose life was frequently lit by intrigues, dramas, and crises, to be suffering through a particularly painful time. It seemed that Gaston, her restaurateur, had undergone an operation on veins in his legs and was consequently incapacitated for several weeks. The Huntress had always relished the role of the courtesan, what with massages, baby oil rubdowns, and so on, but this time she had gone a little too far. During his convalescence she had taken on the sole responsibility for the sexual and *sine qua non* aspect of their relationship and, now that he was well again, he had become inured of this practice and embraced passivity with a passion. The new pasha charged that Artemis was no longer desirable to him. When he tried and failed it was because she was not desirable enough. Nevertheless he did not object to being serviced. The Huntress began to wax sickly over this dilemma and got so she couldn't keep the tears from coming even between the holy hours of nine and five. She spent half the day crying and the other half in the john trying to repair the damage. She often no longer even bothered with her makeup. All the women tried their damnedest to give the Huntress some solace. They analyzed, advised, exhorted, damned Gaston, and so on. Mercury took the Huntress out to lunch and talked to her at length, advising her to give up on Gaston. Though the advice didn't help, the drinks and sympathy did. The thing that struck Mercury during this episode was the fact that all the men were oblivious to the Huntress's distorted and pathetic face, which stuck out like a sore in the otherwise bland atmosphere of the office.

The exception would have been Bert, the Huntress's boss, who was usually very human but who happened to be on a tour. None of the others asked any questions or dropped any hints. Mercury simply couldn't figure it out. She began the following poem, finishing it several months later when other incidents had coalesced in her mind.

> metal men
> twist and bend
> the nervelike filigree
> throbbing filaments distend
> from wretched eyes and flickering hands
> pain has them in its dance
> the rhythm jerks and jitters
> the rosey childish eyes
> turn up their lids to heaven
> the dullard brain keeps whispering
> unable to catch on
> and lets swim down the dream network
> mercy minnows to feed on
> high bird notes rise to waver and chip
>
> the metal men stride in
> and throw their metal switches
> high voltages whip through the air
> and split and slice the atmosphere
> the robots groan with pleasure
> at their sensational sport
>
> metal men, oh metal men
> go turn to wood
> or stem or leaf or glass
> your metal scrapes our skin
> dull lead and flashing tin
> your banging march dispels our dance
> and cracks the porcelain sky
>
> we once were bright as bubbles
> and glowed like cameos in the night
> we flew along as fast as seeds
> and flowered in the light
> now we exacerbate the air

and make it weep and run
our eyes turn innocent blossoms
garish, stiff, dun

Do you ever wonder
how our voices used to sound
before we learned to wince?
before we were your princesses
and you our graceless prince?

Following the convention, Mercury retrenched somewhat in her advance upon Arlen but nevertheless became incited whenever she saw him going out for a luncheon stroll with the stalwart Paul the Pedant. It galled her to think that only the physical circumstances of the convention enabled them to associate freely as equals; now they must redon the straitjackets of some odd, punitive decorum. Mercury began to write little notes to Art and tear them up. When National Secretaries' Week arrived, by some accident of fate Mercury found out about this convenient vehicle and instigated a rash of retribution throughout the office. When Arlen declared that he, too, would have to do something to honor the occasion, Mercury suggested money or jewels, but he proposed to take her out to lunch instead. The place he chose turned out to be a *pastiche* of styles and cuisines, so he promised to repair the situation by taking her out again the following week to a French place of redoubtable reputation.

At this subsequent luncheon, under the aegis of alcohol, Arlen declared that he liked Mercury a great deal and had come to regard her as his friend, even going so far as to declare his friendship to Chris when she had made some catty remark about Mercury. "I've come to like you, too, Art, although I loathed you at first." Arlen was hard put to understand how such a man as he could inspire hatred and loathing but was flattered all the same. Since she would be leaving soon he wished her luck and offered her his aid if she should ever need it. He went on to say that she had brought a lot of life to the office and that he admired her for being a very honest person. "Yes," laughed Mercury, "my only virtue and my only vice." He added, however, that he hoped she would grow as a person by becoming more tolerant of other people. "Nay," said Mercury, "I cannot be all rounded like a ball, and, furthermore, I don't intend to be." The luncheon ended in a flush as Mercury invited Arlen to dinner informing him that unfortunately he would be deprived of the pleasure of making Pyotr's acquaintance. Arlen remarked on this several times and finally asked, "So Pyotr won't be in town?" "Nope. Just little me. Unless that inhibits your enthusiasm." "I'll be there," he called over his shoulder.

The house was filled with flowers — little yellow tulips with a sweet melting fragrance, blue Japanese iris, and waxy lily-of-the-valley, all exuding their inimitable monocotyledonous odours. If love could not flourish under such a propitious scent, then where indeed? The mirrors, brass, and wine glasses were all shining in their places. Mercury favored mirrors and glass and other transparent ȯr reflective surfaces, feeling they held more truth than opaque objects. All Mercury's dark pictures were like tunnels on the pastel walls. The night before Mercury had decided that the foyers should be mauve and stayed up half the night painting the set. What a go-round of spring colours marked here and there by black and white. The wine was breathing its last as a well-known Pole's nocturnes floated round the rooms, and when the knocker sounded, one might say the stage was set. Mercury staggered to the door laden with perfume and the unanswered question of how she would melt his resistance. He presented her with a bottle of Galliano and they proceeded to make small talk over wine and *hors d'oeuvres*. During the course of the conversation it came to Mercury that to kill herself cooking would ruin the scenario, and so she suggested that they walk a few blocks in the warm spring night to a small, elegant Italian restaurant in a little house, the best Mercury had ever encountered. There the waiters had the wisdom of pasta and *la dolce vita* engraved on their faces. On the way there, Mercury took Arlen's arm and chided him for being so stiff. Every remark was loaded with a heavy cargo and brought forth irrepressible smiles and peals of laughter. At dinner they discussed the people in the office and religion, Mercury playing the dissuader without success. On the way home, Mercury asked Arlen if he had ever had an affair, perhaps before he had entered his religious order at the age of seventeen. He answered that he had had intercourse with neither man, woman, child, nor beast. She then inquired, "Haven't you ever wanted to have a woman friend?" "Oh, God, yes," he answered.

Somewhere along the way home he slipped an arm under Mercury's shawl around her half-bare waist. Mercury remarked on the warmth of his hand, but he quickly withdrew it saying that he shouldn't do things like that. "Why not?" asked Mercury. "Because I've promised," he replied. "You promised ill," she argued. Before they were home his arm was back in place around her. In the elevator he lunged at Mercury. She was annoyed and told him to wait until they were in her apartment.

While Nina Simone and Janis Joplin exuded their musk from the stereo, Arlen and Mercury sipped krupnik and made their way towards Warsaw, or, that is, rather Bethlehem. Arlen confided that the other brothers had razzed him about dining alone with his young secretary, saying they were concerned about his possible loss of chastity. He said he had come prepared to flee at any instant. He had even gone so far as to take care of matters himself beforehand so as to be able to avoid temptation, for all the good it did him. Consequently he was unable to perform or be ministered to but managed to satisfy Mercury nonetheless. This in itself seemed to please him. He confided to Mercury that he had told himself beforehand that he would know whether this was the Last Supper or not by what Mercury wore. And sure enough her attire was not the least ambiguous. Mercury showed him some of her poems, but he claimed he couldn't understand them. This distressed Mercury somewhat, but he protested that he couldn't concentrate under the circumstances. He kept repeating that this was "like a dream" which later gave rise in Mercury's mind to the following jingle.

> I met a man
> who was dead
> who chanced to fall
> into my bed
> where he was gray
> I made him green
> and now am called
> the Dream Queen

Afterward he kept wanting to look at Mercury again and again, saying that this would be the last time he would ever see a woman. He asked what Mercury considered a few prurient questions about sex and made a few self-deprecating remarks which disturbed her later when she thought about them, but for the time being she shrugged off these gnat bites. She was ripe and golden and obligingly opened her robe several times over for Arlen's unending last glimpse, kissed him goodnight, and bid him adieu, for the hour was late, and he must hurry home to his fellow monks before they knew beyond a doubt that the succuba had made way with his soul in the night.

The next day Mercury was sick as a dog from mixing too many juices but jubilant, jubilant, just the same. When she had recovered sufficiently, she threw her protesting cat into the hot car and drove the four hours to her mother's house at the beach to luxuriate in the sun.

Returning to earth the following Monday, Mercury was a little repulsed by Arlen's glazed eyes and proprietal manner. The blatancy of his expression was alarming. Jesus! thought Mercury, he'll give everything away. Mercury thought perhaps he was trying to crow. They all think they're roosters, she thought. Cock-a-doodle-doo! *Die Blaue Engel!* He would call M. into his office and sit and stare at her with what seemed a fixed leer. Mercury didn't like it. She began to feel as pristine as a French mint confronted by grease. After a couple days of this she called him at his home under the pretense of business and told him to cool it. He agreed and toned down his new palette. He then told Mercury that he felt he was in the throes of puppy love and gave her the first of a series of self-revelatory letters. Mercury was touched and humbled by his confidences and shocked because, with the exception of his dead brother, he claimed she was the only person to have ever received them. It was like the binding of the feet, she thought. How could he have lived all these years warmed only by votive candles, Jane Austen, and the half-smiles of other refrigerator men? She wrote him a couple of replies which seemed to affect him a great deal. She began writing the following rough fragments of a poem.

Idée Fixe

She fell in love with a stone
and asked to be turned to same
so that she might draw closer
to that intractable thing
and enter its cold, hard centre
to teach the rock to sing

Fairytales and songs
repeat the same dull story
all tiresome ditties — heavy
with mermaids and swans

Their eyes are filled with feathers
fairy fishtails rent to fringe
their psyches ever thickening
on the swift descent toward love

Their blood has turned the water
as they finger the air

Les anges se rulent
où même les bêtes ont peur d'aller

Filled up on favorite illusions
she never had imagined
that this pale tepid longing
would have to pass for love

Some excerpts from Arlen's letters:

Can't write poetry, prose, but only gobbledegook
No thunder or lightening
No regrets

Memories:
smile
body
generosity
honesty
intimacy
understanding, generous, insightful, but, I think, incomplete
insight
"a good man" you said
seemed content at end
remain friends
would want to talk intimately with you for a week? a month? a year?
Why am I able to talk with you? Say things to you I never said to
others. Not only sex things.
You appear to accept me as a person, not an institution
Made me feel human, likeable
Intimacy more than physical
What about you?
Physical — Mental — Personal — Spiritual (don't laugh, little atheist)

Physical — . . .
Believe it or not my most indelible memory will be of your smile.
You looked happy for a moment. I hope you were. . . .

Mental —
(Is this turning into a memo? a love letter? an outline for a term
paper? an exercise in therapy?)
(Who will read this? When? God knows, and my sweet atheist
[sounds like a phrase from Donne], I do believe in God)

Back to mental —
Your wit, intelligence, quickness
Your naughty little jokes
Your reading of my mind, my perceptions
There are basic things we don't agree on, but I think we recognize
what we don't agree on. (Do we? I wonder. Worlds apart — genera-
tions apart — but, I *think* we communicate). . . .

Personal — I said it above (the outline breaks down and I become
rambling, not stream-of-consciousness, just rambling, sweet little
friend. The term *little* is not condescending; I certainly don't con-
descend to you.) . . . It should involve meeting "every day's most
quiet need." Did you know that you meet some of "my most quiet
needs?")

Spiritual — You have generosity, honesty — all you need is faith
— Some day it may come
When it does, remember me in your prayers (What a thought)
What the world needs is a carnal saint

I don't want to get silly, maudlin, or blasphemous
I don't think you lost belief; I don't think you ever had it.
Did I talk about generosity and intimacy? Let me tell you again.
As I recall that dream (and it becomes a dream) and think about it,
I'm struck, abashed, ashamed by your generosity. What a boorish,
selfish oaf I was most of the time. Just *using* you. Trying to satisfy
my "adolescent" (very apt word, honey) pleasure, curiosity, inquisi-
tiveness. . . . You seemed to do all to help me.

Intimacy — . . . You are adolescent, you say
    I agree
When you grow up (and few people do, but *you* may)
    may you retain all the understanding and kindness you now have
and add wisdom and charity (don't wince, little atheist, it means
love). (This is getting to sound like a business letter or letter of
recommendation.)
    . . . You know, I think, my feelings towards you, I can't say I
love you, but I do like you and hope you like me. You are good (a
term that annoys you. I'm sorry; it seems so appropriate.)
    . . . I must still scribble
I should write (talk) to G as well as to you. I believe in G, but at
the moment you are easier to talk to (Isn't this getting too precious!)
    . . . At the moment my overwhelming feeling is one of peace.
I feel rested . . . but as if something I had to say, to express, to
show, has been said, expressed, shown. I think I remember an
Elizabethan sonnet or miscellany called *A Garden of Delight* —
that's what you are — *you*.
This is starting to sound like a love letter, which I don't mean it to
be — but where does friendship end and love begin?
    . . . M, I wish to be your friend, your true *grade* A friend.

                                                                    AB

    . . . Male chauvinism. I want to overcome that attitude. In a
way I can understand what being the victim of an attitude is — I've
been looked upon as being innately inferior, incomplete for being a
Brother (not a priest), a (putative) virgin, unmarried, a Catholic,
etc.
    . . . The vastness of our differences. I don't want to be differ-
ent or want you to be different. I do want to see that the gulf is
bridged by understanding, kindness, and warmth.
    . . . About "forbidden fruit." You were to me, also.
    . . . Are my defenses down? No, not completely, but more than
they have been with others. Are yours? No. You said something
about always giving help, but never asking. Why? You said that
there were things to be said but they wouldn't rise to the surface. I
agree. They may be very threatening for you, me, either, both.
    . . . My hand was actually trembling. Was this self-induced,
self-indulgence?

I thought of your rapid breathing, almost moments of what?
self-hypnosis? when we had a drink. Is this ordinary? good? . . .

AB

. . . Can people live at the ecstatic level? A few can – poets,
saints, and even they only for short periods. I can't. Does this make
me dull, lifeless? I hope not.

Please, don't laugh. Your ridicule is what I fear most.

AB

Mercury and Arlen would sometimes meet for a drink after
work to discuss their feelings and life in general. Mercury's ardor alternately quickened and waned. A couple of times she felt very passionate towards Arlen, but he demurred saying a hotel tryst would be
demeaning since they couldn't spend the entire night together. He proposed that they meet in New Orleans or New York for a weekend
sometime after her vacation and move from the area. He wanted to
take her to the museums in New York to see the paintings she admired.
"Would the 'The Dream' be there?" she wondered, "and 'The Snake-
charmer?'" He asked if Mercury would object to his discussing the
situation with Carlotta, a nun he had worked with and known for some
time whom he felt was very empathetic, warm, understanding, and
who possibly even liked him. Mercury said by all means and told him
that she had, in fact, confided in her old friend Beryl. The two of
them thrashed through a great many things. Much to her amusement,
Arlen decided to call Mercury a missionary. Mercury laughed, saying
that missionary work was too tedious for her taste. She preferred an
eye for an eye, and a tooth for a tooth. They planned a farewell dinner, but had to abandon the idea as Pyotr had a last minute change of
schedule. Since Mercury's desire was flickering, she confessed relief.
Even though Arlen had said it would be "just dinner, don't worry,"
Mercury saw a little further down the road. Arlen took Mercury out
to lunch one last time to say goodbye. Mercury had more or less decided that after having gambled and won the wager that he was a
human being and now that they were friends in the deepest sense, she
was no longer drawn to him physically. She had gotten what she
wanted. Now when she walked into a room, he looked up and he *saw*.
When she spoke, he listened and he heard. More important, he tried to
understand. But after a couple of "cadillacs" and the seductive soft-
shelled crab, Mercury felt the tide rising again. Arlen's eyes were so
wet they shone like jewels. It was a trying luncheon. Mercury often
wished that restaurants had little antechambers where one could retire
for a nap, a daydream, or a bit of sport, before the spell of mood was
broken. It bothered her somewhat that she couldn't really think of

Arlen as being her equal, nor could she see herself really loving him. But wasn't there room for democracy in love? Couldn't you be friends and have fun without it being the be all/end all? Mercury proposed that Arlen meet her at the beach during her vacation. She promised to call him while she was there and make arrangements. Mercury and Pyotr were staying at Mercury's mother's home.

The day before she was to meet Arlen under the pretext of spending the day with her friend Beryl, Mercury felt the pull of duplicity and felt she must make a clean breast of things with Pyotr. They lay upstairs in their bathing suits across the bed, as Mercury dragged out the tale, piece by piece. She felt no guilt, she had done what she had to do, but now that things were becoming complex, she was afraid of hurting Pyotr. She told him how the cardboard Arlen had driven her to get some spasm of recognition out of him if she had to cut out his gizzard to do it. Then she told him how sad and small Arlen's life had been, how she, transient visitor from another planet, now bore the title of his very best friend. It was a long afternoon and Pyotr and Mercury cried a great number of tears, perhaps hoping to wash away the sadness of the past — his, hers, Arlen's, everyone's. Pyotr said he understood and that what he wanted most was Mercury's happiness. He knew that things had not been right between them, and he had suspected a liaison with Andreas. The next day Mercury had to rise early to get ready to go meet Arlen, as he had arrived late in the night and had spent what remained of it sleeplessly, frantically. Mercury told Pyotr that she had to go, but that she probably would not sleep with Arlen. She told him not to worry, to spend the day visiting his friends, that it didn't matter what she did because nothing would diminish what was between them.

Excerpts from Art's last letter:

> . . . On leaving the Brothers: As you can see, I'm rather cold-blooded about it. No headlong flight. Think, plan, move. Try to line up a job before leaving. Take a "leave of absence." If it doesn't work out, come back. Take a two-year leave. Try to find a girl, woman, friend. Sounds horribly calculated. . . . I'm actually beginning to keep notes on plans to leave the Brothers in that damn little notebook. My code name for it is O.R. — Operation Renaissance. Cornball, n'est-ce pas? About the office — You have made them seem colourless, pale. . . .
>
> Went to a movie tonight with several nuns. The movie was boring; the company bland. So much I wanted to say, I held back.
>
> To see Carlotta this P.M. Probably will tell her why I plan to take a leave of absence. Why tell her? I need to talk to somebody. You have given me a bad habit of wanting to tell the whole truth.

I think/hope C. will accept it without a big deal. On the other hand, I don't want her to be too blasé: that would be a cruel blow to my male ego.

Speaking of male egos, I find myself frequently voicing women's lib viewpoints. . . .

Spent the afternoon with Carlotta. As might be expected, she was wonderful. She was very understanding, kind, thoughtful. Of the many things we talked about, I remember specifically her remark that every attempt at loving makes us more human.

. . . When I walked in this morning and read your note, my heart started beating fast again. Do you mean *"au revoir"*? I hope so. M., I am alive, thanks to you.

I thought talking to C. and spending the day with her would make me think less of you. But it hasn't. All day I think of you.

. . . People at the office keep asking, "Don't you miss M——?" All I can answer is, "Of course," and let it go at that.

. . . Before your call, I was wondering whether I should sit all day in the office awaiting it or go and do some work. Life gets so damn complicated.

Your call: I'm like an adolescent — breathing goes, I heave sighs, I'm at a loss for words (me of the wisecrack).

I'm glad, glad you want me to come. I know it must be temporary. Obviously, it can't be permanent.

M., I *am* honest with you. That's one of the best things about our relationship. I believe we *are* honest. I will try never to lie to you, to hide things from you, to use you. *That* would ruin any possibility of friendship.

I know I'm crude, probably more callow than anything else. I'm sorry.

. . . Again, relatively little sleep. I wake and phantasize . . . Little sleep since your call.

M——, please come. Let's be happy today.

Mercury felt a little dry and numb as she drove to Art's hotel. Not long after she arrived he remarked on how serene she looked. He doesn't recognize anesthesia, thought Mercury. Arlen tried to hustle Mercury; not exactly the direct route to her heart. He smelled very strong, probably because he was extremely nervous and jazzed up. Even though he changed shirts, Mercury could not get the smell out of her nostrils. Mercury tried to contract his fever by making love with him, but she had to say no in midstream — he, in his gaucheries, reminded her too strongly of a blatant, greedy child.

Afterwards, he wanted to know more about her underwear, anatomy, and sexual fantasies, than "her aspirations, joys, or sorrows," — various items on his agenda. Mercury walked gingerly across the water all afternoon, concentrating intently on not leaving a seam or a scar. Above all, she wanted to part friends, to preserve something of the good. Arlen declared that sex was like an itch. If so, said Mercury, it must be like an itch on the inner ear; one you'll never relieve by scratching. At one point he decided it was no wonder that he threw over his past life in an instant, for Mercury was the mythic *femme fatale*. "What a funny phrase," said Mercury. "The *femme fatale. Il y a les hommes qui tuent, pas les femmes.* I'm afraid I would have to add three parts insouciance to my constitution in order to qualify."

Art and Mercury discussed what they might like to be if wishes were horses and beggars could ride. Mercury said she had often wanted to be a singer but didn't think her voice was strong enough. Art declared he would have liked to have been a writer. "Have you ever tried to write anything?" asked Mercury. "Not really. The closest I ever came to writing a story was an occasion when I met a young woman, the wife of a colleague. She was a classic Irish beauty with auburn hair. Her only defect was that her legs were somewhat thick. She was very shy and didn't say much but had such a sad expression on her beautiful face as if to say: 'Love me' – but no one had." Mercury thought Arlen a bit of a coward, whether for not loving the girl or not writing the story, she wasn't sure. Somehow Arlen could not restrain an urge to refine her, a thing which Mercury could not abide. He wanted her to change her hairstyle so as to reveal more of her face, for her to wear less makeup – he didn't like "Egyptian eyes." And wasn't she putting on a little weight? He held forth that Mercury's nose was little and cute, though Mercury was proud of its prominence and *hauteur* in profile. His banal compliments wore on Mercury with the anticipated monotony of a leaking faucet. Mercury sometimes thought that as soon as men looked at you, you disappeared. They continued to scrutinize your image on the screen long after you had left the theatre. Occasionally he grabbed at Mercury which annoyed her greatly. Well, well, she thought, the crab has emerged from his medieval carapace with a new vulgar appetite. She hoped it wasn't virulent. She reminded him that he had managed very nicely to restrain his impulses for forty-five years; he could show a little character and do so for an hour longer. Seeing as the physical side of things had curdled, Mercury was eager to engage in further psychic excavation, mostly his, this being his lodestone, perhaps his principal attraction. Arlen, however, was not up for soul-searching. Mercury did everything she could to disentangle him gently, not to insult him. Unfortunately, his mind took a masculine turn and leapt out for the grossest, crudest solution to his problem.

"Don't worry, I won't rape you," he said. It took a while for the words to draw blood. After the hit, Mercury began to fall, oh God, she could almost hear the air rushing past her. It seemed she fell as fast as a hawk, but still the bottom never came. There was no bottom.

"Well, congratulations, Art, you just said the magic word." Arlen then asked whether Mercury had ever been raped. "What makes you ask a question like that?" inquired Mercury. "Well, I just thought that sometimes young ladies were forced to do things against their wishes." At this last jewel, Mercury did not know which she would suffocate from first — a sob or a fit of laughter. It was too absurd. Gee, she thought, it was really nice of him not to rape her. Perhaps he was making a run for the sainthood. "In heaven your crown will have many jewels." He got upset when Mercury shed a few tears, said he was sorry, etc., etc. Somehow the incident was smoothed over and forgotten.

Arlen talked his life out rather quickly and Mercury wondered why there wasn't more. Where she'd thought to find a jungle, there was mostly desert. A few well-fingered hurts stood out in relief against the monastic gray. *Pas de douleur, pas de joie.* He claimed he didn't like lingering goodbyes and proposed that they part quickly and mercifully. Mercury thought they should break bread together before the final adieu. He stubbornly insisted on the nearby Ho-Jo's because he was extremely afraid of running into a confrère who happened to be visiting his family in the same town. There was nothing Mercury hated worse than a Ho-Jo's, except, perhaps, for fifty million other things.

On the way out the door Arlen made one last grab at Mercury's breast. What a slut he was. They had a tacky little lunch during which Arlen expressed concern over Mercury's black spells of despair. He said he was afraid of her possibly harming herself. "I'm not worried about it," said Mercury. "I'm like an animal. When an animal is sick, it slinks off and lies down to await the verdict. I'm not afraid of death; it's degradation I can't seem to get used to." Then the conversation turned to the so-called liberation of the sexes. Mercury said that in a couple of weak moments she had almost wished she were a man, feeling life would be less painful. "You shouldn't ever wish that," claimed Arlen. "The world would be a sadder place." "Precisely," said Mercury. "But only for you, not for me." They walked along the beach and watched the water. Arlen said he would write to her, but it would be best if she wrote first. He said he would always tell her everything and that if he ever found another woman, she must never, never wear Mercury's perfume. This amused Mercury as she tried to imagine how many people could be induced to alter their most intimate tastes at the beloved's suggestion. All too many, most likely.

As things stood now, he was going to look into a leave of absence from the Brothers, a job on the outside, and attempt to conjure the glimmer of a relationship with Carlotta into a possibility. Mercury decided to seal their *mésalliance* with a kiss, but Arlen stuck half his tongue into Mercury's mouth making her shove him away.

As Mercury drove off, her heart was light. She thought she had crossed the minefield intact. She had not. The happiness of relief lasted only a day or two. That last Sunday was like an encapsuled virus in Mercury's brain which fitfully attacked her as the months went by. It came to Mercury that, despite its name, the nightmare was masculine in gender and she began to write the following unfinished poem.

In the landscape of the dream
gauze pads the brain
but the blood soon seeps through
from without or within?

Ruinous dreams
dredging machines
down in the silty river
poisoned waters
where we dig
as we drown
over and over

Asleep in the chrysallis
I struggled with the dream sickness
I tried to wrench free
from the threads of the night
my black sticky wings
were all matted with tears
as I drowned in the waters —
the sewers of the night

"May your dreams be of roses"
dewlight — jewellight — sunlight — moonlight
May they float upon the water
like a flower or a bubble
and illumine the tent of this night

For a long time she worked on writing Arlen a long and winding bitter, merciless letter. Finally she finished it, insisted that Pyotr read it, but never mailed it. Neither did she call to find out how Art was or whether he had left the Brothers after all. One day after a family of words had formed in her mind, she sat down and, with hardly a pause, wrote the following parable which seemed to rid her spirit once and for all of "Brother" Arlen.

Beggar at the Feast

The Beggar found himself in a room in the midst of a party. He came to himself only to find himself transfixed by the presence of a small Siamese cat. The cat's eyes were luminous and moist and soft — they glowed with liquid light and the blue irises when looked at closely were as though sprinkled and marbled with an iridescent dust like the powder on the scales of butterflies. Yet the eyes were also hard and bright and opaque as smooth-cut jewels. The Beggar strove to think what stone it was that held the complex colours of the cat's eyes. Black opals? No, not quite, he thought. Their pupils were black and deep and bottomless, the lacunae of the soul. Whether they focused outward or inward, one couldn't say. The Beggar addressed all the questions of time over and over again to them, yet they never stopped their ceaseless scrutiny, neither did they blink nor waver with surprise, and they always gave back the same reply, "You tell me, you tell me, you tell me. . . ."

The atmosphere was heavy with gold and autumnal desire. Light arced from one guest to another. Deirdre's eyes, tortoise shell and umber, her rings, topaz, white opals, and tiger's eyes, flashed sparks of spontaneous fire under the golden lamps, giving the sign — they signaled for love to transpire. Each guest held a glass of gold honey liqueur. They sipped the amber slowly, reluctant to put out its light. The room was lacquered with an orange glaze and imbued with the pink and cinnamon tones of a woman's flushed aureole, the sun sign, radial flower, bursting, uncontainable, expanding into the blurred reaches of love, condensing to a red pyracantha center.

For once the Beggar could not contain himself and he cried out, "This must be life. Don't drive me away. Let me stay here at your fire. At your side. I implore you!" he pleaded over and over.

"What have you given?" Deirdre inquired. "Tell me what you have given to add to life's fire? Once I was in your power, in the guise of your inferior, your servant. You would not see who I was but made me serve your guests. You made me serve the other men. You made me hate them and made hatred boil in my heart. You knew I was not born to be a slave. You served me the bitter pill of subservience without a backward glance to see what face I made while swallowing it. You ignored the sinking suns in my eyes. You looked longingly after my undergarments with a glance alternating hot and cold, but you never noticed the suffering in my soul. You saw the flowers on my dress but not the emptiness in my eyes. You saw the whiteness and warmth of my little hands, but you never noticed that my heart had stopped. You tore at me though you never lifted your hand. My soul froze over and over again. You put it to sleep. You never heard it stop breathing. Your ears are not attuned to the comings and goings of little breaths, little lives. You didn't hear the coals bursting in my heart to smolder and die. My breasts captured your imagination. They accelerated your blood and drove you to mad dreams and impetuous actions. They made you thrash in your bed at night. My smile gnawed at your dead flesh. But, tell me, what did you ever do to give my breasts their rosey colour? Whom did you feed that they would form well? What love did you give, and to whom? What juice did you add to the fruit of life that my teeth would grow straight and gleam at you like white shells? What beauty did you bring, what child did you nourish? What salve did you give to those bent over with sadness?"

The Beggar felt a thrust of pain and loss at the knife of each question, but he managed to spit out, "I have given nothing, but I will give anything now. I will open my soul."

Deirdre looked at him with some amusement and some pain. She smiled incredulously and slowly repeated, "Your soul? I don't want your soul."

"What do you mean?" he cried shrilly.

"It's too small," she whispered at him.

The Beggar snatched at her dress to prevent her from fleeing. He felt that if he could only continue to beg and implore her, he would imprint the outline of his pain on her heart and soon shatter her glass facade and reach the soft centre of mercy he knew lay within her. But she filtered through his fingers like mercury and began to melt away. She grew smaller, her gown fluttered, black, gold, and resin-coloured, she seemed to fold into herself like a flower blooming backwards. The guests, the fire, the gold light of the lamps — all went out. He thought he heard the hiss of a snake and whirled around to see where it lay. He peered through the semi-darkness of the room but could not discern the cold, shiny form. Then he saw that it was merely Deirdre's cat, Iris, upon the hearth. It had reared up and suddenly spit at him. Now it was settling back down into its ancient pose. He looked down to see some spittle on his shoes and a few gold flecks on the floor at his feet — they must have crumbled and fallen there when he lay hold of Deirdre's dress. He looked once more into the smooth-cut sapphires of the cat's eyes. They made him numb and cold and he wondered whether he should dare incite its spite with one last riddle. In his heart there formed a silent question. It was just a gesture, a little genuflection to symmetry, he knew better than to ask it aloud and be showered with the ashes of the cat's irony. The words lay within him like a stone: "Is life only a dream of love?" But the cat divined the question. And suddenly the room froze like a horrible tableau in a play and his senses swam miserably and wavered. He drew into himself like an oyster held over the fire as he heard it answer in its throaty, deadpan voice. "Stone on stone," it said. "Metal on metal."

One hopes the reader will not find this account, though larded as it is with poetry and chagrin, overly cavalier. It is difficult to be sincere about the past. *Ecco la primavera.*

An Object Relations Approach

Many sexual relationships are *transitional,* by which we mean: (1) an interlude between a lesser and more advanced state of development, (2) an only partially satisfying relationship, and (3) a relationship which eventually should be terminated or greatly reduced in scope. This definition assumes that people often benefit from involved relationships with each other, but that although both persons may grow, their growth may not be in similar and complementary directions.

Complementation refers to the capacities of two people in a sexual relationship to evoke the best from each other, so that self-definition, mutual satisfaction, and encouragement of the other's potential for self-fulfillment follow. Often the initial thrill of being intimate is a result of *some* complementation; however, the transitional relationship typically allows only limited complementation.

Both people can maintain pseudo-intimacy by overlooking certain aspects of their relationship. Selective inattention and distorted perceptions of self and others (discussed in the introduction to Topics Four and Five) function to keep out of awareness those aspects of a relationship that would disintegrate it. Transitional relationships often require elaborate processes of overlooking in order to perpetuate.

The transitional relationship may continue because each person fears the loneliness that follows break-up or fears the possibility of regressing to what he or she was before the relationship commenced. The partial satisfaction that they have may be seen by them as their best alternative. In contrast, there are factors that encourage discontinuing the relationship, such as: finding an alternate relationship; feeling that one has outgrown the other; recognizing the distortions and limitations inherent in the relationship; or fearing commitment that seems inevitable. Notice how many case authors have mentioned their parents' unhappy marriages; possibly those relationships should have been transitional — should have terminated before marriage.*

Each of the two cases under Topic Fourteen is a history of a transitional relationship which became a marriage that

---

* The preceding comments on transitional relationships should be compared with those of Winnicott (1953), Blos (1962, p. 141), and Modell (1968).

eventually broke up. In both cases people needed to cling to each other as they strived for psychological autonomy, sexual identity, and vocational identity. More specifically, they avoided aloneness, sought in each other an ally when in confrontation with parents, discovered that sex or romance or role playing is not enough to sustain a relationship, received support at times of vocational confusion and emotional instability, and shared a link with the past. An object relations approach to Cases 26 and 27 is to discover how the evolution of a transitional relationship facilitates and hampers personal growth — especially in one's relationships with *significant others* outside the intimate dyad.

Topic Fourteen

Transitional Relationships

Case 26 / What Was Overlooked in Courtship
Was Ever Present in Marriage

Katherine's mother spoke of sexuality as something quite natural, but she often was cold and demeaning to her husband. Katherine's stepfather spoke of sexuality as something quite vulgar, but he often was affectionate and physically expressive to his wife. When Katherine was sexually approached by her older stepbrother and later by her uncle, she rejected them with sympathy and amusement.

Due to lack of funds, Katherine dropped out of college at the end of her sophomore year. Affect accompanying the dropout is not mentioned in her account. Her first sexual relationship ended after several months as abruptly as it began. A second relationship began and was maintained in a whirl of drinking and avid socializing. She offhandedly announced her engagement to her parents. The wedding, preceded by fighting and much overlooking, was followed by a disappointing honeymoon.

Marriage precipitated Larry's frequent impotence. Larry's job dissatisfaction and the death of his father added to their frustration. Two babies and three moves didn't remedy Katherine's boredom or concern with her sexuality. When her parents divorced and remarried, Katherine received funds to return to school. The new situation uplifted her spirit but also led to feelings of sexual attraction at school. Estrangement from Larry was not diminished by marital counseling, and so they separated after seven years.

Is Katherine now better able to carry on a marital relationship, having had these experiences?

The child was born June 1942. The father had been killed in an airplane accident while in Maine on business. Her only recollection of that period is playing peek-a-boo with a man (neighbor) through a hedge. The mother taught school and the girl and her brother (a few years older) were taken care of by a live-in Irish woman, who had been there since the brother's birth.

The mother remarried when the girl was just three. They moved to the stepfather's house in a nearby town. With the stepfather came two new siblings: a girl just a little older than I and a boy five years older — in other words a biological possibility and coherence in the new family. The Irish woman Maude came also but came in by the day.

There exists in recollection the atmosphere of meals, sicknesses (the favorite family story of reporting four children with whooping cough to the honeymooning parents), play, and general scenes. I know I remember some tears and some meanness but not specifically. My new sister and I played together and apparently "loved" each other quite easily. The only outstanding memory is of my defecating in a wading pool and being sent for a spoon and made to clean it out. No one else remembers this.

The war ended and we moved to a huge house and sixteen acres in a "country" suburb. There was a gardener, a cook (live-in), and a cleaning woman. My memories and those of my brothers and sister are of rather complete freedom, around the hours of school and meals. We played together as four in addition to other children in the neighborhood; however, usually in "our" field, pond, or woods.

At this point there are "facts" and there are recollections. The recollections are in fact quite narcissistic and vague. If these are symptoms of happy childhood — what "I" did in vague memories — then it was, as I believe, quite happy. Memories are more of outdoor things and the pleasantness of school and gangs of kids than of any specific things. Of course I know facts which were not the same — but they seemed to have existed outside my personal world. There were sicknesses, there were some remembered parent and brother-sister fights.

An occasion (we were told) was when all of us were taken to Family Court and legally adopted by the stepparent. In fact there was a high degree of objective family solidarity; my father became increasingly hurt and petulant when these "ties" didn't bind. He was quite obvious about his hurt when my sister and I learned to read and didn't want him to read us the funnies any more; all four of us continued to love to have my mother read to us.

My first memory of things sexual was one of mortification and mystification. My sister and I, being typically unbudded ten-year-olds, often wore only shorts in the summer. One evening at the supper table my father suddenly roared at us to "never come to the table again with our titties showing." Not knowing why, we were both reduced to immediate tears and some amount of hatred was conscious and overt. It was the scene of a furious fight between my parents. Were we conscious then of the inappropriate vulgarity (denigration of our femininity) or were we furious because plainly we didn't have any "titties" yet? My father would love to sneak a hand over one of my mother's rather lush breasts when we watched TV *en famille* and her discomfort was evident. The quick opening of their bedroom door on a morning found them sometimes in the same bed "reading" and my father would inevitably get overly mad.

I will insert here my parents' views and attitudes toward sexuality as I formed them. It is consistent throughout that my father reacted either with prudishness or vulgarity to sex. This was observed and not experienced because I must have learned early that it was a taboo personal subject with him. Consistently, my observation of my mother with my father was that she never welcomed his physical demonstrations — he was by observation alone demeaned as a lover. (Much later she told me that for all the physical demonstrativeness my father was just not interested in the sex act but she knew that he masturbated. . . .) Inconsistency marked her attitude toward her body, and, when the subject came up, toward sexuality. She had (has) a lovely body and wore it well; she made me proud of my own, and I cannot recall (during my period of inexperience) any time when a discussion of sex was not somehow enveloped in an atmosphere of reality; i.e., it will happen to you and it is good. It is perhaps easy to see how the latter view came to support a rather elaborate picture of my dead father. He must have been really handsome, really masculine, really a man (to have made you, mother, seem so delighted to be a female when you don't look delighted at all with my stepfather).

My school life was, without exception, uneventfully successful — grades, teachers as "friends," friends. I was also strictly a tomboy. My sister and I were in the same grade as the result of a double promotion in first grade, and she never had an easy time. We shared the same friends until the groups became mixed and we then split off. She was often very unhappy — tears at any frustration (and attempted to slash her wrists when eighteen) — and I guess I may have felt bad (maternal?) but not really concerned. In fact, it was evident that my stepsister and stepbrother had the problems — both academically and socially, my brother as a suburban juvenile delinquent and my sister as a social left-footer. They had the problems as a parental overview, not problems in the sibling view. My two brothers always have been close, but with the younger one dominant, and the same was true in my sister's and my relationship.

My first introduction to physical facts of sex took place when I was about eight. My oldest brother (stepbrother) aged about fourteen came creeping into my bed one night with what later I learned was a hard-on. I was supposed to feel "his" and he to feel "mine." I don't think either of us, or particularly me, received much from the episode except that it was to be repeated some eleven years later. The former episode made me feel, as I remember, quite proud to be "trusted"; the latter one was quite funny in retrospect. My brother, at twenty-six, barged in while I was taking a shower, stared as if transfixed and then left for his room. I dried, dressed for bed and was soon the object of his stuporous romantic intentions. I remember feeling sympathetic and humorous, which I guess was more than he could, as he passed out in the midst of a plea; so we exchanged bedrooms for the night. Of course I was feeling quite sophisticated in my knowledge of sex at the time. It apparently sounded in the house like a French romantic farce because my mother asked me the next morning what all the commotion was upstairs last night. I replied with a smile that "Don just had too much to drink"; the point was made and left. Smugness and sisterly devotion. . . .

At the onset of menstruation (age twelve) I also discovered masturbation ("rediscovered," I suppose, if my early childhood years were normal — I don't remember). It was a pleasant discovery. The next occurrence of it, as autoeroticism, occurred after my marriage, and didn't please me as much.

The summer I was twelve and for six summers thereafter I spent first as paying guest and then as "worker" at a family camp where I found a second family. That is, the parents became parents of affection and their son the object of a very intense friendship which didn't quite survive the change into a male-female relationship. I did, however, learn love in the Sullivanian sense with a chum, albeit of the opposite sex! Later we conventionalized into goodnight necking but somehow the fire was never stoked and was soon engulfed in another relationship my sophomore year in college. Altogether it was a positive introduction to nonsexual intimacy and pleasant memories linger. There were other boys. All relationships were characterized by being broken off by me eventually; whenever the idea of a "pin" or whispered comments came up, it was soon transformed into a death knell. There was a sense of sexual progression (as exploration) and enjoyment in a general way, but I remained relatively mystified as to why boys looked and acted as if urgent and in pain. I don't think I qualified as a "tease"; I just wasn't "with it" yet.

The weekend before I returned to my sophomore year at college was spent with distant relatives who own a farm in Ohio. My "uncle" (in his forties) is a brute of a man — big, handsome, and earthy in a prototypic farmer way. We had a mutual and sudden attraction (built on a mild flirtation the past year) which proved too sudden for me, but he spent some time telling me how I was "ready" and should find "someone" (the cowbarn analogy to being "in season" was a feeling of apt description). It was a first "real" experience of mutuality however. The scene was lovely — we jumped from a tractor and groped around in a freshly plowed field. When it obviously wouldn't work (my physical reaction of fear), we both found ourselves laughing uproariously and then ensued the conversation about "readiness." I received some letters from him during the year checking on my progress and reporting his own (coldness of wife and successes with some local women). A man I remember with warmth and gratitude.

I thus returned to school that fall with a sense of anticipation and restlessness. In one sense all that was lacking was a similarly inclined male. Perhaps what kept it on so long, so intensely, was the very absence of commitment — it was bed, innocent and simple. Dave was a sensualist. Characterized also by bohemianism and nihilism in a social sense, he was, however, committed to the value of sensuality. He was a professional student intellectual (twenty-nine and still after his Master's degree) but all that a girl, or at least me then, could want in bed: ready any time for any mood — a sexual Zorba. Without spending much money, we orgied our way through about eight months — in the water, under a waterfall, on top of a mountain, standing up, sitting down, in bed, in the woods. . . . This erotic scene was externally surrounded with guilt, however. Where is the fine mind applying itself in the library and where, over the telephone and in letters, are the bright newsy letters of sorority-fraternity doings, big weekends, new boys, etc? I don't remember feeling unreal, but I do remember how the interruptions of guilt felt unreal.

I left in June knowing there would be confrontation but still not really worried about it. It was bad, however: no more school funds (for that college at least) and particularly the outrage which occurred when my mother asked me if I wanted to marry Dave and I replied that neither of us had any thoughts of it. So she and I hit a bind, our first big one. Sex was good, but only with marriage in mind. Sex was good, I had learned that well, but marriage with Dave — the idea was ridiculous.

It was a quiet summer. I don't remember much of it. Not actively unhappy, just vague. Dave arrived on his charger (a broken-down '48 Ford) in August and it was dead. I could only see him in the social sense — a good-looking boy-man who looked doomed to wander through life never quite accomplishing anything and not knowing why. This of course may be wrong — I have heard vague reports that he finished his degree and was an instructor or something at the college — but the feeling would be the same I think.

My body must have suffered more open withdrawal symptoms than my psyche showed. I remember starting to smoke quite heavily, being treated for colitis, and beginning treatment for an unknown ovarian disturbance which later that winter turned into a 4 A.M. ambulence case of peritonitis. (I think my parents were convinced it was VD and were only somewhat relieved when the gynecologist assured them such was not the case.)

Home was tense — my mother referred strongly to marital unhappiness (I was initiated and could now therefore be told?) There seemed to be a feeling of debt paid: the four children were raised, her dependency on my father after a major back operation had been met by her helping him through a business reverse and concomitant nervous breakdown. They bickered most of the time — my mother in a huff and my father petulant (somehow I particularly remember him sitting back in a TV lounge chair stuffing himself with Fritos, peanuts and Hershey bars), and yet full of sentimental crap whenever we had any conversation of length. He loved her on a pedestal, and she had no respect for him as a male.

That summer I held a dreadful, dreary job in a women's store in the city and commuted by bus. There was one woman there who was a ray of cheerful reality. She was about to marry a divorced man and kept referring to this man they knew whom I just must meet. With that said several times (the man being in Europe on vacation visiting his brother), the job ended and I started "all over" at Campion Secretarial School for Young Women, which is how it felt, if not like kindergarten. However, they worked you hard although you didn't have to think much — probably very therapeutic. The date with "the man" was organized at a party and he shall hereinafter be referred to as Larry, and later, as my husband.

Both alcohol and the social life of married couples were strangers in my own experience. Most of the people Larry knew or saw were married. He had returned strange from four years of college, and so had I, from the prep school and college mobile friendships. These people for the most part were pleasantly innocuous. They all drank heavily but seemed to accept that as the college social scene.

At any rate the first meeting was positive but in a general way. We went out two or three nights a week — usually dinner at a restaurant which was more club than public, usually with the same cast of characters. Larry made a strong impression but again generally — good-looking, tall and lean, fairly sophisticated, very hard-working, sociable and single-minded. The latter term means not vague, not wandering; i.e., not Dave. He was attending classes at an engineering school for the third year (of a four-year course) and worked as a technical trainee in a Boston firm, where he had started four years before as office boy. Apparently he had returned to Boston for a draft exam after college (4-F due to a knee operation) and had stayed on after being offered the job in conjunction with the schooling. He was twenty-five and I was nineteen. He was living with his parents in a house bought when they were just married. Larry had two older brothers, all three years apart. The oldest brother was working in South America. I heard how brilliant Mark was — the genius of the family — and how generally exotic he was. He had been married briefly and lived a very controlled urbanized existence. He seems neither heterosexual nor homosexual which leaves one concluding that he is, with self-knowledge, a "latent" homosexual. The middle brother was married and living in New Jersey, struggling as a jack-of-all-trades to support his wife and new baby. Although Frank was very loud and predictable, he was a man also of loud and sincere warmth. He seemed to annoy Larry constantly. His wife and I liked each other quickly. The relationship has gotten closer as our marriage progressed. Larry seemed to relax into a more acceptant mood around Frank (although occasionally to the surprise of everyone he would sometimes take incredible offense at some innocuous jibe). The root of his resentment seemed to be based upon a rivalry, or rather defeat, which Larry had experienced in childhood and adolescence. Apparently Frank was the life of the deb party circuit and thrived in this period. Larry, from what I gathered, had had a very lonely childhood — neither making the mark academically (his oldest brother) nor socially (Frank) — and had received little support to change the resultant self-image. At any rate when he returned from college as a grown attractive guy, his brother had tried to introduce him to all his friends. Larry went along but I gather he resented the certain cavalier attitude involved. Indeed, most of the people we saw were people he had met through Frank. This later changed, but at the time Larry definitely seemed to entertain a "leftover" image.

Our sexual relationship progressed in an orderly obvious fashion and in a month or so we were having intercourse as often as we saw each other. Both sets of parents approved of "the match"; our friends were all married and expected that we should do the same. Larry was obviously serious and my reaction, I think, was one of being taken care of in a complete and comfortable fashion. In February the peritonitis hit and I spent three weeks in the hospital. It was close, or so the doctor said later, but the point was that Larry was there — constantly, worriedly, and lovingly. In a sense it "proved" my dependency on him and it "proved" his commitment to me. By the time I had recovered, the relationship had changed into one of equal commitment. Soon thereafter Larry won an award in a project engineering competition which gave him the opportunity for European travel and informal study. A honeymoon thus delineated, he proposed and we were to be married in summer and depart for Europe some three days later, for about two months.

(An irrelevancy? My parents were away when we decided to marry and when they returned some two days later, I casually introduced the fact some three or four hours after their return. They seemed very puzzled [and hurt] by my casual attitude.)

The weeks before the wedding were not all idyllic love. We fought and not terribly well. If this is not unusual, perhaps our way of dealing with it was not either — pretend it isn't happening or laugh self-consciously about it. Our sex stayed the same. In retrospect (which is always suspect), either in rationalization or in honesty, there was a very unlazy quality to it but we were operating either between family homes or "on the road" so that might have been natural. And of course when married, I thought, we'll have time, freedom, and privacy. . . .

Wedding over, we drove to Falmouth to a friend's loaned cottage for the three days before leaving for Europe. Wedding night was a zero, but we both agreed we were pretty tired so what the hell. Next day with sun and privacy on the rocks — still nothing. Second night and day the same. By this time Larry was a nervous wreck and vocal in his shame, and I was upset by his reaction of such complete desolation. I asked him if he'd ever had the problem before, and he said just once or twice. I offered the thought which I'd read somewhere that it wasn't unusual (and not therefore a worry) on a honeymoon and why didn't we just try to forget "it" and "trying" for awhile. This was agreed on, but some rather depressed references were made fairly often by Larry.

We left for Europe. The "agreement" above was renewed on frequent occasions. I think in the two months we were gone we managed intercourse about three times with as many failures in between. The successes then, and throughout the first six years, were characterized by preludes of either quite a bit of alcohol or some strong situation of shared external eroticism. (In Venice no women of course are allowed in the "erotica" room but later when I described some of the collection — a friend had purchased pictures while in the Navy — it seemed to set the only night of really uninhibited sexuality going.)

It was the "normal" nights when nothing worked — when one climbed into bed gently tired, started to caress lazily, and then suddenly there was the presence of almost a third being — the "will it or won't it work" presence. Increasingly this "presence" grew until we almost never even tried unless we'd both had just that more than enough to drink. I withdrew from sometimes actively initiating to always waiting passively for the third presence to resolve itself. This couldn't have helped Larry any, but how many times does a woman get actively hotsy-totsy and then say, "Oh, that's OK, it doesn't really matter," in a light unimportant tone, or, heavily, "Honey, don't worry, just relax. Let's go to sleep." There were some "winners" though – in the elevator of a deserted office building or the Oriental carpet in Washington when we both ended up with bad wool burns. These became part of a humorous reminiscence but made somewhat hollow by lack of a solid core.

Our relationship otherwise was uneven. There seemed to exist a feeling of competition – who works harder, who is more tired. We went in to work together and often weren't speaking halfway in town. We went out a lot and had friends for dinner about twice a week. Larry's father died shortly after our return from Europe, and that seemed to set him off – very sarcastic in the daytime and violent sweating during his sleep at night. Their relationship had been pretty tacky at best: very sarcastic with each other and his father had often made disparaging remarks about him in my presence. (He told my parents, just before we were married, "Larry is doing OK, but you aren't getting any bargain." My parents were really shocked and seemed to write him off as a "mean bastard.") However, his father was dying, knew it, and was taking some rough drugs to prolong his existence, so I tried to pass it off as due to that.

After his father's death and until his mother's remarriage several years later, summers became our worst time. We somehow "managed" to spend every weekend at their summer home with his mother. Larry was edgy, I was bored and growing mad. His mother is a "nice" person, but in the truly conventional sense – I think she sees people as appropriate to the relationship or to the word "friend" and acts accordingly. For me, the kind of person you can't really complain about but in whose presence you find twitchifying boredom setting in. We got along well; in fact she seemed often to take my "side" in a disagreement and to regard Larry as a "nice talented person" but with "a difficult personality." In his presence she laughingly (lovingly?) told me how he had really been a surprise, that they hadn't planned on having any more children. (This was about as close a reference to sex as she ever made, except for embarrassing herself one day by declaring her views on the double–twin bed controversy. Her second marriage really must have brought new breezes in because since she has referred to sex, double beds, etc., with some zest.)

But those summers were bad, and I was close to rebellion. Larry and I talked about it, or rather about doing something else of a weekend or vacation, but the economic argument usually won – where else would the sun, beach, etc., come so cheaply? And soon I didn't mind because in June 1965 we had our first baby, a girl. Pregnancy relieved our sex problem because I didn't care much and that seemed to solve the issue. Being very busy and happy with the baby made the marriage seem much easier going; the "competition" seemed to disappear and although our sex life, with one exception (which resulted in the next baby, a boy, eleven months after the first) was nil, the relationship seemed to have more room to expand and lessen its internal pressure. The second baby was quite a surprise and it took me, I think, about four months after his birth to adjust to and feel reality about his presence. I felt guilty about this (and still do in remembering) and was quite relieved when being the mother of two distinct people became a reality.

We had purchased a house and were enjoying the house and the total family existence. In fact, Larry had felt for too long, in my mind, dissatisfied with his job and seemed to find it a real drag to get to work. He complained about the job situation and the personnel frictions a great deal, and it made me very irritable. Why? First, one of the best things, I felt, about my father was the way he relished his business — glad to go to work and glad to get home. He and my mother talked a lot about his work, and it seemed a very positive kind of communication. Maybe part of my personalized conception of a man is his joy in his work. I don't mean ecstasy or constant ebullience but a solid feeling of doing what you want to do. When I would occasionally explode and ask him why he didn't just quit and get another job (not at all an unusual occurrence in one's early career), there were all sorts of reasons, valid in their way, but it was not the reasons which were unhappy. It took about three years, but he did finally make a move to another firm where in the past two years he has made happy and steady progress. He talked more about the work and not about how bitchy the people were. It made us "better," but by now most attempts at sex had all but disappeared.

A close friend felt compelled to say one day that she and her husband had both remarked on how independent and even cool I seemed around Larry — not difficult or argumentative, just a bit indifferent. That should perhaps not have been a big revelation but it hit me hard, perhaps because it hit something way inside to match. I talked to several "leads," i.e., a highly regarded local minister and my gynecologist, about our getting some help. Two appointments were made which got broken by last-minute business things of Larry's. They were of course real, but was their importance distinct or relative? This is for me a low point, or pivot, because I had some alternatives here, and I took one unwittingly which puts us where we are. I decided that, hell, this wasn't the thing for a woman to nag a man about; I would have to let him initiate the next move. I knew that he knew I wanted to see someone, that I was upset "in the open" and, therefore, next move his, for his pride. Because I cared about his self and his pride, I shut up. What if I had become angry, insisted (my rights)? An insistence involves an "either-or" or "because" statement or at least implication and I didn't feel endangered, just sad, depressed over a kind of "oldness," "sameness" which seemed to have permeated our lives. Larry's deliberateness, common sense, integrity, all seemed to be tied up somehow in an old man's view *back* on life. Where was the forwardness, the feeling of the corner-around-which? Now this may be a description of the so-called "seven year doldrums" (leading to "the seven year itch"): two kids, two cars, suburban house, good job — life seems to appear with clarity for too many years ahead. But it was also the essence of Agnes Gooch's great line in *Auntie Mame:* "I've lived. Now what do I do?" Is perhaps bed the place where a couple accumulate the fragments into the alive whole? Is it in trusting, uninhibited intimacy that the exchange of belief in oneself takes place? These are questions of sex and marriage (entangled like "law and order"). In sexuality there occur more questions. If you are in the place of mutual sexuality and it doesn't occur, how much is the toll of self-beratement and how much the toll of your view of the partner, ever within the hard-won and cultivated confines of respect and companionship? Am I "feminine" without having any femininity to give away? Am I now less of a woman, and therefore more to blame?

Throughout the marriage Larry was always very demonstrative — hugs, kisses, caresses, complimentary about me and my ways — but that was where it stopped. These demonstrations made me increasingly nervous. At times I wanted to scream "I'm a woman, not your baby darling," but that looks as it would have sounded — a little hysterical and very corny. In other words I grew slowly from passive to cold, not unwilling, just never an open invitation: resignation, not welcome. (I had some months after the marriage "rediscovered" masturbation. I was reading a lot as usual but more than ever the vicarious best-seller books and often found these the occasion for proposals of sexual relief. It's a lonesome life. . . . It left me unashamed but feeling more and more isolated. In the midst of the present dirge, it seemed to shock Larry genuinely when I told him of that fairly regular activity and then I had to say, "What the hell did you think I was doing?" and then felt worse because reflected in his face was the fact that that was, true or not, a "vulgarity.")

One of our frequent activities (three times in four years) was moving. The first house was a sinkhole of money, and we loved it as the first is best. But the community, we said, is too expensive for us; for Larry, the town was composed of nice people and snobs, and the snobs were our age group (although friendly enough to us), and for me, why not move, the kids aren't in school yet. A modern house this time which we both liked immediately, bought and moved in. The day of the move Larry said we'd made a mistake and that he hated the house. So while we hung pictures and put down rugs, I heard of all its defects and so did our friends which I thought made us sound like assholes, and if any of them were honest enough, they would have asked him why he bought it. This latter point is not perhaps important except that it removed some of the fretwork glue. No sex life, strange town, unliked house. Again, as usual, and forever, we have two great kids. But when you count down to one item of living cohesion and it's your children, the modern mother goes, "Gulp, isn't that bad for children? I'll smother them, etc." What seems living too is the companionable habits, routines, and friends of seven years, but they don't live inside of you; they form the pathways outside which you can travel blindfolded.

My parents were very messily divorced in the midst of the second move. There had been infrequent talk by my mother of divorce for some years (the last I'd heard she'd decided to forget it and "stick with her lot"). At my brother's wedding (I shall report this as a fascinated on-the-scene observer), my mother and her now husband fell in love over the fruit cocktail while my father looked on frantically from the other end of the table. It helped, not in the financial sense so much as the dynamic competitive sense, that this man is many times a millionaire, a devotee of everything and a 19th-century gentleman (after he gets!) to boot. It really was a surrealistic feeling though to watch the mother of your childhood come alive for one man as you'd thought it might have been in the past and here it is in living color. He proposed the next day and after getting through two divorces and an archaic but pride-saving (my father) alienation-of-affection suit, they were duly married. My father got remarried long before they did and has spent most of the time recovering with the aid of a rather marvelous woman. All four of their children are agreed upon the intelligence of their choices, after having survived in neutrality the process in between. My mother's got a man who can match her dominant spirits, spirit for spirit, and my father a woman who loves not a home but The Home as much as he seems to.

(Did the remarriages, as positive ends, also bring the possibility, or the potential, of admitting a mistake and trying some action instead of drifting passively? Is the societal danger of divorce not dissolution of the individual family but the cumulative danger of the contagion it radiates into other troubled marriages?) What the remarriages did, in a factual sense, is to make some money available in the form of an offer to pay my tuition if I wanted to go back to school. (Larry and I had discussed it agreeably and positively before but couldn't manage it financially.) Offer accepted, I was accepted, and also an apartment in Cambridge for the first year — to try city living for a change and make the transition earlier (no commuting hours). I also liked the idea of the children having a chance to try out some time free of my presence. They were to go to nursery school (Lucy's second year at age four and Greg's first at age three) five mornings a week and to have a sitter three afternoons a week. Greg took to the new schedule very easily and seemed to thrive on nursery school friendships and the busyness of the city — building construction, subways, boats on the river, playgrounds, lots of police and firehouse activity, "hippies," etc. Lucy has had a struggle all year. She turned from a very outgoing child to being quite withdrawn and often depressed and often spoke of wishing she was still living in the "country." Always more temperamental, she and I had had a closer relationship and perhaps she has resented my absence and particularly my enthusiasm for something in which she felt little part. The bonus, however, seemed to be the fact that they were seeing far more of their father. Larry's relationship with them as babies and more had been loving but distant. Greg had developed more recently a distinct non-interest in his father and very rarely seemed to initiate contact with him. He had remarked to me on several occasions that "he didn't like grown-up men." This year Larry walked them to school every morning and could see them in the evening. On weekends, usually Saturdays, he took them on outings while I either cleaned or caught up on some schoolwork.

He and I were busy being cooperative — meshing schedules, who's to walk the dog, move the car, run an errand. His willingness to make sacrifices to make my life easier was very open. His own work was proving very satisfactory, and he had been made an associate in the firm. We were the recipients of many verbal compliments from friends — our "courage" to try such a drastic change and surprise at the way in which we both accepted the change as "fun." Larry didn't like the city at all however, and except for seeing friends in their homes we hardly ever went out.

My own emotions were in upgear. I really felt cheerful and positive, especially on the days I went to class, hearing the babble of many people seemingly intent on projects of personal importance. My original small fear that as an undergraduate I would not really "fit" was quickly ameliorated. People were interested, interesting, and friendly. The work was stimulating and not as difficult as I had anticipated. My sister-in-law of two years remarked that she had never heard me sound so happy and enthusiastic about everything. True, life did seem distinctly alive in a very personal (me) sense.

The experience of sexual attraction, the process of feeling increasingly an inner tightness and sensitized awareness to the presence of a specific person — perhaps there is the excuse of some years passed for not recognizing its appearance. Perhaps unknowingly the recognition was suppressed. However, the inner experience was made aware by the fact of acquaintanceship. Once having established the concreteness of friendly contact, however, my sexual feelings quickly became far too conscious. I actually felt tormented and degraded by the irrational waves of physical desire and mental frustration. To be carrying on a light casual conversation over a cup of coffee and to have one's hand shaking so that the trip from saucer to lip became a feat of concentration. The feeling of degradation stemmed from sharing that common feature of "first" sexual feelings in described "puppy love" or "crush" — the sense of unreality due to the lack of reciprocity by fact not by choice. After a couple of months of this, it became obvious that this situation, and any more to come, were symptomatic of sexual drift, or "vulnerability" as I put it. I spoke to my husband about it and of corollary feelings of fear (marriage) and restlessness (sexual and personal).

An irony, meaningful and disturbing to me (and perhaps it has a deeper implication) is that when I received a telephone call one evening in February from this man to pursue a conversational question unresolved, there occurred the only incident of sexual initiative by my husband in over a year. Its quality was different, however; I felt not only "away" but objective to the point of revulsion. He did not offer the usual *tendresse* but made a rather business-like affair of it — there was a quality of property rights rather than affective rights to it all. A fews days later the kids and I went to Washington to visit my mother and stepfather during the semester break. Larry and I were to see a marriage counselor (at last) when I returned. The time away was filled with thinking and none of it bringing rational clarification. The conclusive feeling was one of recognition of the death of sexual feeling for Larry and the personal search of a definition of marriage in future years. Pandora's box was opened.

In conversation soon after my return (he asked why I seemed so nervous), I told "the man" of the situation. (Rationale #1: to defuse my attraction to him [brother not lover], or rationale #2: to force a statement from him about presence or lack of some reciprocity?) Instead I received #3: a blunt statement of a personal view that I should obviously get a divorce — was I trying to rebuild a marriage with ashes. Three inner reactions were evinced in me: first, that "sex aside" it's a pretty good marriage; second, that divorce as fact is a shocker; and third, I still don't know where you are, my friend. However, he was there, not to match the intensity of my inner turmoil, but with warmth and care and still as friend. Sexually I felt nowhere but at least this wasn't someone to run when informed of his unwitting implication in my personal life.

The marriage counseling sessions were total zero. The doctor was hitting it from an angle of sublimatory development — why didn't we develop separate interests and not try to force the intimacy. It was weird being told to do just what I felt we had done perhaps too much of — a dead-end development via an ostrich attitude. Larry also felt we were getting nowhere or at least not touching home base. After a few weeks, as our relationship fast deteriorated, we started with separate psychiatrists (in professional communication); Larry ostensibly to work on the impotence problem and me, well, to try to separate fact from fiction, justified self-blame from unjustified, rationalization from sexual facts, and some idea of the future — a past, present, and future sorting. My "sessions" thus far are strange — nonpsychiatric in the sense that there never seem to be very personal questions asked (unless I offer the information) and in the main supportive of my emotions versus doubts of a "moral" nature. In some ways it is a grasshopper-ant situation. There is a resurgence of an ego-libido partnership in me; I Will Not (Can Not) cut off this new feeling of emotional aliveness.

However, with this feeling is the element of fidelity (supposedly the natural characteristic of marriage). The latter element, coupled with increasing affective reciprocity (not commitment) in the extramarital relationship, made me feel very strange with Larry. A heightened objectivity toward him created a different man: stranger with many good features but unconnected to me. Larry, however, was reacting to the stress by emotional pressure. An habitual hand on the shoulder in passing became interpreted as a move *toward* him, an invitation. He wanted to hold me constantly, and I wanted to back away (an "I don't know you" feeling). The kids were getting obnoxious in a natural bid for attention in the midst of this atmosphere. The quintessential description is the following verbal exchange, repeated often by Larry: "What can I do to make you love me?" I would reply, "That's just it, you can't do anything. I have to do it and I need room." However, he was really coming apart and kept pressuring me to leap to him. I couldn't and that kind of exchange was doing what we did have — respect — no good. We separated in early April. The kids act at home (and at school too we are told) more open and secure. Although on occasion they question the new "arrangement," they seem to accept it most of the time. In a sad way it has improved Larry's relationship with them. Prior to the separation his love for them was strongly characterized by a possessive "love of one's family"; now it is more sharply delineated into love of them as *his* children (not more possessive, just more personal) where his being their father has a more distinctive importance. This, I think, has been good; for him to stop defining them in a family unit but as his children — people.

Larry and I see each other alone about one evening a week. I find myself quite exhausted after two or three hours. I am not sure why. When the conversation gets forced into discussions of the future, which Larry cannot seem to help doing, it gets very bad as I am "forced" to say that I can't make any plan or commitment to a future yet. He is recently getting more and more intent on asking about the future in openly hostile references to my "friend" at school. I have to remain mute or noncommittal. To the psychiatrist I only can say that I have to see this other relationship "through," that in my own mind I regard it as 50–50 that Larry may "win" by default, that some of my feeling is of eventual defeat. The rest of the time I am really quite happy with a positive feeling: I am an attractive woman who is lucky to have two active healthy children, that "life is what you make it" and I'm in action, that the future has good in it because there has been tapped (developed, let go?) an inner aura of optimism and activity.

The major source of any present unhappiness is living with *awareness* of the torrent of emotional, sexual feeling held in check. It is with me constantly, but I can't let it out — I feel in fact that it might, in its present state, terrify any man; it is legally (my vulnerability in potential legal arrangement for child custody) dangerous and perhaps most important, I'm not sure it would resolve any basic issues. Sex may be expressed in specific sexual situations but sexuality, as psychological necessity, is not a big drink of water when thirsty, but a constant way of being able to love, especially "within" the freedom of reciprocity.

Case 27 / The Convergence of Two Autobiographies

The two autobiographical accounts that follow are unique with respect to the rest of the cases in three ways: first, the reader has the opportunity to become familiar with both partners' views of their ongoing intimate relationship; second, the data are extensive and rich enough for discussing simultaneously the issue of autonomy, identity, and sexual intimacy; third, the behavior of the case authors is more "deviant" than that of most of the people in the preceding cases.

Having rich data and two persons' points of view on the same relationship, the reader is able to identify subtle distinctions in point of view and then speculate on their origin and implications. Knowing something about the case author's family lives, peer relations, career paths, and intimate experiences, the student of human development has the opportunity to view each person's experience as it arises in a variety of situations over time.

It is up to the student to formulate his own view on the issue of what is normal versus pathological adolescent experience, e.g., asceticism, sexual promiscuity, militancy, role playing, "sanctioned" violent behavior, alienation, drug use, drug selling, depression, suicide threats, inevitably unsuccessful suicide attempts, ephemeral breakdowns, and what-the-hell risks and thrills. Some of these behaviors are illustrated in the accounts that follow. Is the mere occurrence of any of these behaviors indicative of pathology, or is the extent or circumstance of the occurrence the basis for distinguishing the "normal" from the pathological?

Separate introductions to Dawn's and Stephen's lives before meeting each other are presented below and then followed by prefatory remarks on their relationship.

Never Saying the Wrong Thing

The constant tension between Dawn's parents precipitated their living on different floors at opposite ends of the house. "Refusal to talk to someone was the most characteristic method of punishment in our family, and since someone always felt that someone needed punishing, family dynamics turned out to be the dynamics of silences." Divorce never was mentioned, "because of the children," yet Mother constantly threatened to leave. Mother felt herself "wasting away" at home while Dawn continued "to live off us and give nothing back."

Dawn was expected to respond empathically to her mother's moods. Often Mrs. McLaren's hostility toward her husband and self was displaced to Dawn, who under attack did not want to hurt her mother back. Dawn has had ambivalent feelings for her mother, who is debilitated by excessive drinking, an unhappy marriage, and inadvertent distortions of everyone. Could Dawn recall her mother's ever averring an *unqualified* statement of Dawn's competence or lovability?

Being quite studious, Dawn did well in advanced courses and was accepted by every college of her choice. She had no friends and remembers "staring emptily and hungrily" at the lit-up bedroom window of the girl next door. Later in college she sought heterosexual experience with multiple partners as a palliative for her "hunger."

In early adolescence Dawn began to feel manipulated from within by an evil spirit which took the form of an older woman and intensified when the solitary and socialized Dawn was feeling beaten or tired. Release, often sexually gratifying, could be obtained from self-mutilation, an ad hoc compromise of punishing and pleasing the inner self. Her self-eroticism culminated while at college when she ingested thirty aspirin tablets; this act prompted a short confinement and then periodic visits to the University Psychiatric Services. For a while life became a whir of short-term relationships and self-indulgence.

Always Overcoming Odds

Stephen considered his parents to be fine community members but inadequate family members. Dad seemed to love Mom and to try to please her on his own terms. Mom seemed to barely tolerate Dad and at times to persecute him. She made several suicide attempts, each time recovering and returning home. She felt that her marriage and abrupt donning of the role of "the school superintendent's wife" had pre-empted her opportunity to pursue her interests in drama. Stephen constantly fought with Mother because she always told him what to do, told him things he already knew, and had unreasonable restrictions, e.g., wearing galoshes when there was no snow. He was said to be more like his mother, but he did not feel close to her and saw himself as rebellious. He wanted to tell Dad about how badly Mother treated her sons, but Stephen feared being a traitor. Stephen felt competitive with his brothers, seven and eleven years older, but didn't strive to match their efforts directly; he gleefully indulged in comic book reading and television watching. When alone, he devised elaborate fantasy games involving his television experiences.

Always the youngest in his class and proud of it, Stephen learned easily and gained his peers' respect. He was criticized for being outspoken and rebellious at school, lazy and messy at home. The family moved to Baltimore against his mother's wishes; there Stephen was the only Jew in class. "Violent conflicts with some peers gave way to a more peaceful atmosphere of mutual hatred which I came to enjoy."

At age fifteen, while he was away for the summer, Stephen was jolted with the news that his parents would separate: his father staying in Baltimore and his mother returning to Boston. Against his mother's wishes Stephen chose to live with his father. Dr. Silbiger's busy schedule left him little time to see his son. Stephen lived in daydreams and fantasies, emerging when he spent time with a girlfriend, Lynn.

Shortly after his parents divorced, he wrote integration editorials for the school paper and intensified his advocacy of causes. Stephen experienced a complex of affect when his father hinted that Stephen's genealogical father might be Mother's former professor.

Uplifted somewhat by his high school successes and acceptance at the college of his choice, Stephen shortly thereafter learned that Lynn was pregnant.

Three Years Later

When Dawn and Stephen met, they were both unattached; Dawn had terminated her first steady relationship and Stephen had separated from Lynn after her abortion.

What was missing in each of their lives was sought and found in each other. Dawn sought someone to care for her and about her, while Stephen sought someone who would accept him as he was. Stephen paid Dawn's bills and opened himself to her life.

This two-person relationship was more like a foursome: Stephen, Dawn, the "Old Woman," and Mrs. McLaren. Dawn's emotional breakdowns were especially likely after returning from home visits where she received parental rejection. Stephen's vehement declaration of wanting her to live combated the potency of the "Old Woman."

Satisfactorily resolving the question of sexual fidelity, Dawn and Stephen wed. Stephen regards his getting married as "the most constant, single-minded effort I have been able to put forth."

Their more salient problems seem to be Dawn's frigidity and distantiation from others, Stephen's inveterate use of drugs and career crisis, and the vagaries of Mrs. McLaren.

What are the key events in each person's development? What affect accompanied those key events? Was the affect "appropriate"?

Why did they marry rather than separate, get together off-and-on, or just live together? What are the strains and strengths of their relationship?

Never Saying the Wrong Thing

I wake up in my bed late at night. It may be ten or two, but the sky is black, and by my seven o'clock bedtime standards, it is a very adult hour of the night. I can hear loud noises, a shuffling of feet, a confusion of movement. Children in their limited familiar territories are experts at recognizing what is disruptive to the odd balance of that small world; and the sounds in their randomness frightened me. There was nothing I could relate them to: someone getting a midnight drink of water or preparing for bed would make more purposeful patterns of noise. But these sounds made no sense to me, and at an age when I dealt with my fears by finding sensible words for them or by concocting elaborate definitions, the noises were the worst thing I could imagine. I lay frozen in bed, hardly breathing, begging God to keep the sounds at a distance from my room.

Suddenly, though, there was a voice in the middle of the shuffling. It was my mother's voice, talking to herself; I imagined that she was calling for me. I wiggled out of bed and opened the door to the bedroom with a trace of apprehension. I could then hear my mother more plainly, but the words were a jumble, incoherent. I could see her vaguely from my vantage point; she had her back to me through the kitchen door and was leaning on a counter in the bright uncanny fluorescence. For a moment she was dead silent and I could hear the buzz of the refrigerator and various clocks and electricities, to which these hours normally belonged.

When I stepped into the hall my mother heard me. Turning to face me, she was the embodiment of something wrong. I stood dumbly in the dark hallway and saw her framed in the brilliant doorway; her red hair wisping wildly from her head, her eyes half-lidded and mournful, and her teeth biting the thin lower lip. Neither of us knew what to say. As children, my sister and brother and I had never seen our parents undressed, or spoken to them in any but the most supervised expressions. Acting in a scene far more revealing than any nakedness of body, and called upon for the most sophisticated verbal diplomacy, I was prepared to handle neither.

I had no conception that mothers were such changeable, vulnerable things, or that they would ever admit their pain or humiliation in such a shouting way as my mother's face did now; it had always been expected of me that I would respond empathically to her moods and somehow mirror them, but never was anything of the sort directly verbalized. Now I felt at the mercy of uncontrollable forces, because my mother appeared to be. It was a raw scene: a drunken miserable mother and a rather tongue-tied child. From that moment nothing could be trusted entirely again, because nobody was really in control: nothing could be counted on as dependable. Twelve years later my sister was to begin to act strangely, having her pet dog killed and seeming unresponsive in the most charged situations; and the same mistrust ate into my acceptance of things.

But the moment of recognition was only a moment, and I broke the silence with a tentative "Mummie?" and went to her.

I don't recall what she said to me, or whether she was indeed weeping. But she put her arm around my shoulders and leaned on me; I led her through the doorway, down the back hall and into their bedroom. In the immediacy of my new role, I neglected to wonder why my father wasn't there in bed, or anywhere in the house. I got her to the edge of the bed and she collapsed on it. Vaguely offended that she should fall so abruptly into her own dreams, I managed to slip her shoes off; but undressing her proved to be too weighty a problem and I compromised by unbuttoning her blouse and covering her with a blanket from the closet. Before turning the light off, I got one of those vivid visions of things *as they actually are:* my mother sprawled under the blanket the one arm dangling, her head tilted strangely, and the sound of her breathing, as I always imagined a dying man would, in long, deep, convulsive grabs.

When I was back in my own bed, there was nothing but numbness in my thinking. I had never had to explain something so eminently unquestionable as my mother, and although I couldn't fall asleep again, there was no particular localized fear. But there were new possibilities for fear in every corner of my hitherto perfectly dependable room, and when I remembered with great discomfiture that I had left the kitchen light on, I couldn't move. An hour later I fell into a sleep which was more like a paralysis.

When I got up the next morning the kitchen light was off, nobody said anything, and an absurd cluster of new shadows hung over the ordinary breakfast table. I saw shadows, very plainly and painfully occupying the air, and I remember thinking that they were grape leaves. But I had no idea what grape leaves must look like.

We moved to Atlanta when I was twelve. The huge modern schools rather awed me. My mother, in her most embellished manner, told us how exciting living near the city would be, but she was also afraid. She didn't even attempt driving downtown until six months after we had arrived, and then when she finally ventured out it was with such caution and infrequency that my aunt declared that she was tired of chauffering my mother all over looking at rug samples and house-hunting. I remember the night we arrived in Atlanta, a tired rather unsophisticated family drinking warm drinks in a sort of fuzzy wonder at the Woolworth's which was part of a tremendous shopping complex outside of Atlanta. It was about eleven P.M.; very late for all of us (my father still gets up at 6 A.M. every day), and there were so many fluorescent lights and so many sounds of traffic that I was dazzled. My mother and father argued about directions the whole way. We ended up at about midnight at the apartment buildings where we were to live for several months until a house was found. It looked like an old redevelopment project, nothing but dull brick rectangles three floors high hugged in by parking lot. But I loved it. I loved the City already. I loved the sense of countless people. Ever since, the sound of heavy traffic all night long through an open window evokes in me real feeling: and it is the feeling of being surrounded, and comforted.

After a hot three summer months in the apartments (during which time my brother was living with some friends or something, I can't really recall anything about that except his absence) we moved in with a very strange woman named Mrs. Lang. My mother was grateful to the woman for giving us rooms in her large house, but her ready mistrust was called up when she found out that the woman had a son who came home from school on vacations, who was psychotic or something; anyway I remember my mother whispering things to me all the time like "Watch out for your purse" and "Just don't be alone in an empty room with that Richard when he comes." I was a good audience; my imagination was fired, and I trembled at the sight of Richard Lang every time I saw him. He never did anything that was really strange; it was just that my mother and then I both reacted to our preconceived image of him rather than any real qualities of Richard Lang — we misinterpreted everything he said and did to fit the scheme. My mother has a tremendous capacity for this kind of distortion, and I caught it young. Although being conscious of it is half the battle, it is not always easy to want to work against it, since its imaginative source also distorts in very pleasant directions — it romanticizes and it creates.

After that nervous period we finally moved into our new house, which my mother (unable to find any available used house to suit her) had had built on an acre of wooded property in a rather exclusive part of Atlanta. The house was terribly modern to me: it had sliding glass doors, a patio, dishwasher, disposal, two porches and we had our own bathroom (the children were to inhabit the lower level, while the parental bedroom and the other rooms were on street level). I describe the house this way because I want to emphasize the importance of Our House; it was home territory, it was privacies and secret understandings; and later, when my mother began to work and was out a lot, it became Jenny's and my realized dream – our personal idea home. Jenny would go into the kitchen and cook something and I would read a book with an apple or a finger keeping my mouth occupied, and we were immensely happy at those times. Occasions when the family was all together were situations which I learned to anticipate as dangerous; there was always a battle – beginning perhaps over my brother's behavior (he was the "problem" in the family until he left, after which time he became its hero and perpetuator) but always getting back to the bitterness between my parents. They disputed insurance and tax payments, money, my father's responsibilities as a father in my mother's romanticized sense of the word; like Stephen's father mine was rather passive in the face of attack, becoming enraged only after a tremendous amount of restraint (my mother would not give up her verbal persecutions until he made some sort of action to resolve the argument; usually the resolution was in the form of his walking out). The situation was always much more frightening when we were all going somewhere together in the car: usually the atmosphere was stiff and prickly, we were all dressed up to present ourselves at some necessary wedding or dinner, and underneath we all were full of the tension between my parents which couldn't be ended by my father's walking out – although sometimes in his fury he stopped the car short with a screech of brakes and threatened to. My mother capitalized upon the inevitable outburst from my father by calling him childish and getting in the old jabs about his being less than a man. I could never understand why they didn't get a divorce; they lived in separate ends of the house on different floors and, except for rare periods of mutual tolerance such as around Christmas, they never spoke any unnecessary word to one another. Refusal to talk to someone was the most characteristic method of punishment in our family, and since someone always felt that someone needed punishing, family dynamics turned out to be the dynamics of silences. But there was a determined self-destructive quality to my mother's devotion to the family; the divorce was never considered "because of the children," work was done "for your sake," and when I went to college every letter was full of "we're having a hard time of it because of your tuition – but of course we're glad to as long as . . ." some kind of repayment was made, in the form of winnings or overflowing verbal appreciativeness.

Junior high school was the most excruciating period I lived through until my sophomore and junior years at college. I was impossibly silent in classes, by far the shyest and most afraid student in the school. It was attributed by my mother to the change of atmosphere, but neither Don nor Jenny had any such obvious social reactions to the move. Although I was very conscientious about my work, it was in junior high school that I first had difficulties in any academic subject — I got C's in Science. After having won the scholarship at school it was hard to take, but the A's in English and my success in writing poetry was compensation. What could not be compensated for was the fact that I had no friends. The closest thing I ever had to a "chum" was the girl next door, an attractive and rather snobbish girl whose father worked for the State Department and had just moved from Switzerland. But I was not in any way intimate with her; we were in the same grade and went to school together, but shared neither friends, nor confidences. I do recall staring emptily and somehow hungrily at her bedroom window lit up at nights, hoping to catch a glimpse of her.

If I was afraid with people in a situation where I was expected to communicate with them, such as in classes, I was even more afraid of being alone. I was terrorized by noises and shadows when left alone in the house at night. And after bedtime I lay in bed for hours paralyzed by my imagination; I had many nightmares and often sleepwalked, as did Jenny; and we put bells on the doorhandle to our bedroom to alert each other if one of us should start wandering. The house was new, and there were centipedes on the ground floor for the first three years; this too was a source of terror for me, and even when in high school Don left for college and I got his room, I used to have nightmares from which I would awaken to see the wall next to my bed crawling with every kind of bug. I'm not sure how often there actually were bugs and how often I invented them, but certainly there was a real basis for some of my fears, since I was always having to drop books on centipedes. But I still think I see spiders or bugs on my sheets and the wall next to my bed sometimes in the middle of the night; often I am certain enough of it to rush from bed and not return for half-an-hour, until I can convince myself of the impossibility of it.

Jenny had many more friends and was always far more charming in social situations than I was. My edge on her in age was a prized possession to me, although at times it caused me some anguish. I was particularly afraid, when I began to menstruate the first year in Atlanta, that she would discover evidence of my new functioning and ask questions; it was an invasion of privacy which I feared disproportionately; I guarded my secret knowledge like a miser, and for some reason even discouraged my mother from telling my sister any details on the facts of life when she asked me about it. But on the whole the relationship between my sister and me was the most empathic and most understanding of the interactions that went on in the family, and by the time I was in high school I already treasured it.

In junior high school, however, I had much difficulty in establishing a cooperative or affectionate relationship with my brother. Although he was certainly the underdog in most family arguments at that time, constantly criticized by my mother for his low grades, absence of ambition and motivation, and untidiness at home, my sympathies were overcome by my hostilities when he began to direct his frustration at the most obvious target — his younger sister. I remember scenes in which he would pound on the wall and shout at me for being in the bathroom in the morning when he wanted to use it; and he even picked the lock and forced his way in, throwing me out on many occasions. I was not a tattle-tale, and I knew that he was in enough trouble from my parents without my adding to it; and so when on one particularly exasperating occasion he began to force his way in when I was trying to guard my little bit of growing-up privacy in the bathroom, and as I resisted, pushed me against the wall with the door with such force and such an expression of hatred on his face and I felt as though I were going to die, I could only collapse on the floor crying in an unmanageable mixture of confusion, unbearable frustration, humiliation and pain. It is perhaps the scene which I remember with the most clarity about my brother. My attitude toward him was always a combination of scorn, fear, and sympathy; and I felt as though I lacked an Older Brother in the same way that I felt I lacked a Father, since neither of them ever really permitted real communication. Trying to fight my mother with words was always a failure, she misinterpreted and distorted logic so easily; and the result was that all of us developed interpersonal styles which avoided the dangers of saying the wrong thing by saying little or nothing at all. For the most part Don ignored my sister. He was quite popular as a class joker at school and was affable in his relationships with most of his teachers. He had an IQ of 140 and flunked out of Beloit College after one year there. He then entered the Air Force and was in Vietnam until this year, when he and his wife (a thin, pleasant, uninspiring nurse whom my mother disliked) went to Canada. He is rather conventional in thinking, but stubbornly righteous about it. On the whole he has emerged from the family difficulties with a desire not to make mistakes on that scale in his own life and is now a reasonably fair if somewhat domineering husband and father.

My high school years were much better. I had my own bedroom, and I began to excel in my courses. I found that I could get into advanced placement courses in not only English but also math and French; and I began to acquire extracurricular credits in art at an institute in Atlanta and in human kindness by teaching retarded children to swim at the YMCA. Out of an atmosphere of emotional frustration, I was able to use my talent in writing and in the arts to convince myself of the existence of creative possibility, of hope. I began to believe I could do everything. In one respect this was hopelessly untrue: I never made friends. I had numbers of acquaintances at school, and I was the favorite of most of my teachers; but I never invited anyone home, nor was I invited to anyone else's house. It was not for nothing that when I was awarded the Most Studious award at a school dance in my senior year, I was not there to accept it; I heard later that after announcing my name a number of times they decided I was studying and were confirmed in their choice. The times of greatest joy were notably (a) when I received both first place and honorable mention in different categories of a national writing contest, and was given a beautifully headswelling introduction at a school assembly, where I was also awarded prizes in the state French and Spanish contests and various other awards, and (b) when I got acceptances from all the colleges of my choice on the same day in my senior year. It was a time when all things could be done, and I looked forward to college as the arena for the accomplishment of all things.

I began masturbating in my sophomore year in high school, sometimes with the aid of neighborhood pets; but I never went out on a date until my junior year, when I met a strange broody melancholic character who decided he was in love with me after an evening discussing Camus, and then with a bull-doggish looking boy from my high school who invited me to the senior prom. It was most uncomfortable, and I hated kissing him because he was uncommunicative and nervous and awkward, and because I felt nothing toward him; whereas the other suitor had rather mystified and intrigued me, and I was elated when he rather gently and meaningfully kissed me one day behind the front door. But after my senior year in high school my mother, as a combination reward and educational experiment, decided I should travel to Europe. I went to Belgium for a session at a sterile Protestant school and a visit with the wealthy family of a prefect of one of the provinces. My first real sexual experiments took place at the hands of the son in this family, a handsome huge boy with a talent for sexual diversity; and there at the age of 16 had intercourse for the first time. There was no pain, and the pleasure was immense; but I think throughout it, as has been true ever since, I was more concerned with being a successful partner and evoking the most pleasure in the man than with "forgetting" myself and slipping into orgasm unconsciously. When I arrived at college, I felt tremendously experienced and excited, and during my first year there I had only the mildest case of freshman doldrums. I kept in touch with my family but was relieved to experience the self-determination that my separation from them had brought. Now at a distance from the turmoil, I began to actively wish that my parents would get a divorce, that my mother would find someone in whom to confide (I was no longer so selfishly cruel as I had been in junior high school, condemning my mother silently for an affair that she had with a rather slick married man whom I detested) and realize her fantasies, and that my father would be spared the contention which sent him off to work at 6:30 A.M. and kept him away until 8 or 9 at night at his office. I myself felt that my fantasies were being realized; I basked in the sensations of scholarliness: the books and wood-panelled reading rooms, the tolerance of diversity, high teas and jolly-ups. My roommate was a rather stuffy masculinely energetic girl from Baltimore with whom I had long wishful discussions revealing her narrow-mindedness and inordinate stinginess with her possessions. (She used to tell me that if she were to lend out her hair-dryer or scales to hallmates, as she was occasionally asked to do, they would be returned broken or late or not at all; and she used to suspect that people had been in her drawers if anything looked out of place.) In spite of her surface liberalism her tremendous capacity for gossip ended up revealing her rather strong prejudices. She once told me that she had been asked out by a Jewish boy from Baltimore who seemed very nice but she had just never been out with a JEW before and she wasn't sure she could bring herself to do it. I recall being quite vehement in the defense of the unknown gentleman, which was to be quite amusing in light of the fact that he was Stephen Silbiger, whom I would one day marry. I did not meet him that year, though, and was anyway very involved with a senior whom I met at a jolly-up near the end of my freshman year. In my anxiousness to get tangible evidences of being liked, I came on very hard at mixers and even in classes; and this particular boy was quick to respond in kind. We seldom talked, and anyway he was sick of school and glad to be graduating. He was what I should have recognized as a jock. But he was out to make me and I was out to be made, and it happened that way. There was a rather painful episode about a girl in Beverly, Mass., whom he loved; he told me that on his last night in town, after calling me up at two in the morning (which infuriated my roommate) and telling me to come to the Gotham Hotel, where we went through the whole Mr. and Mrs. Smith cliché as I tried to be cheerful. But it was a cold night and I had been ordered out of bed a little too brusquely to be told that there was nothing between us but that he needed to fuck someone and he loved this chick in Beverly. I remember he had cut himself shaving over his remarkably bad complexion, and when I awoke the next morning I found blood all over my face. The next morning he didn't talk to me and we left, by plan, pretending not to know each other.

That summer I spent working full-time in Atlanta and studying Russian on a scholarship at night. I kept up the pace stoically for three months and was glad to see Cambridge again when I returned.

I was remarkably erratic in my attempts to find my major; I had always had difficulty making decisions, since so many pros and cons seemed incumbent upon the choice. As it turned out English was not the chance for creativity that I had expected it to be, and I transferred to architectural sciences, then switched back to English, and finally plunged into social sciences in my junior year. Meanwhile, my sophomore year was dominated by my relationship with a sophomore at school, whom I met through an architecture course, and who needed me in many of the same ways that I needed him. For five months we were delightfully in love; we saw each other frequently and I became the mascot of his dormitory suite. It was for me the first time I had felt genuinely loved by someone outside my family, and I invested everything I had emotionally in returning that love. He was very handsome to me at that time, and everything we did I saw as if through the eyes of a third person: what-a-lovely-couple-we-are was the golden light in which I saw the relationship. I went to his home in Vermont for Thanksgiving, where his family was very kind to me and had all the semblances of family unity and trust and celebration which I had always dreamed of in my own. When he visited Atlanta for Christmas, everyone agreed tactfully that he was very handsome, but my mother told me he wasn't "good enough for me," a phrase which was re-iterated a month later by the girl who had introduced him to me. He was one of the most remarkably passive people I've ever known; even his posture in chairs was virtually horizontal. He was not scholastically outstanding, was very much concerned with appearances and modishness, and (except in his relationship with me as I perceived it) was unusually lacking in affectual response. He had been an adopted child, his parents were unknown, and he had no real desire to know them (a discovery which perplexed me). His family in Vermont not only was very outspoken and frank about his adoptedness, but even told me quite matter-of-factly that this was probably the reason for his "indifference." His sister said she had never seen him cry. His mother became very fond of me and even asked me to call her Mom. I had absolutely no desire to think of marrying him and the notion was even amusing. The relationship began to get shaky as the romantic color wore off and he, Warren, became more and more preoccupied with his affective dilemma. He had been reluctant to have intercourse at the beginning (I suspect he was virginal), but I encouraged him in the best older-woman style, and we had been having lukewarm intercourse ever since. In order to encourage him as well as to ensure that he would want to continue the sexual aspect of the relationship, I got into the habit of faking orgasm; and it seemed to work, although his own contentment never came across and I always had to ask if he had really "come" or not. It was with Warren that I first began smoking grass; and it was with him that I first got really stoned. The relationship was not an easy enough one to make being stoned a relaxing experience, both of us were primarily concerned with the impression we were making on each other and the world, and there was all the embarrassment and uncomfortableness that first intimacies imply in terms of self-exposure. After one episode in which Warren was so stoned that he became convulsive, and in which I could not help him since whenever I touched him it became worse (a reaction which I am quite certain was an effect of my having expected intercourse so regularly and hungrily, despite his disinclinations), the relationship steadily deteriorated until one night in the spring of my sophomore year, when after an evening of dead silence and unresponsiveness, he told me it was over.

I might have been able to take the letdown if it had not happened just after spring break, during which I had had a catastrophic visit home. My mother and father had gotten entangled in a more-heated-than-usual dinner table argument during which my father walked out of the house, leaving a lot of my mother's complaints still unspoken. I had sat at the dinner table in silence, fidgeting with the camera I had been allowed to bring home from my film course, and relieved to find that by focusing my attention on its mechanical calm I could avoid even being aroused by the shouting and insults; for the first time in my life I felt unattached to either of them, equally understanding of both parents' positions, and much older. After dinner I calmly washed the dishes without being asked to and went downstairs. Moments later my mother rushed through my bedroom door, her face red and her eyes half-lidded, on the verge of tears and rage, and accused me of soaking up their money while turning my back on their difficulties. The root of her accusations was the fact that I had not taken her side (she failed to see that I hadn't taken anybody's side) in the argument. I saw in a sort of flash of sympathy that what she was lashing out against was the tremendous loneliness that having lost her husband and slowly losing her children implied. I felt her terror and I wanted to cry. That was my first feeling. The second feeling took over as I started to really hear the words she was screaming at me: "What makes you think you can just sit up there on your ass all the time living off us and giving nothing back? You certainly have changed since you went to college: you're hard and cold, Dawn, and I don't think there's a grain of the goodness that you used to have left in you. Tell me one thing you've done for this family — one thing! It's hard enough to bear your father's unconcern for what happens to the family, but you're getting more and more callous every day too. I don't know why I didn't leave a long time ago (a common threat). God knows I've wasted my life here." Etc., etc. At first I tried to respond, but everything I said was turned around to further her argument; if I pointed out that I had gotten good grades at school and was not therefore wasting their money, and that I phoned home all the time, and sent surprise packages (as examples of my concern for them), she would reply, "You think that such material gestures constitute love? Do you think that that is enough?" I soon learned, as my father had long ago, that it was impossible to argue on any reasonable level with my mother. Her distortion of what she perceived was her reality, as is anybody's; only her distortions were grosser than most people's, and always went in the direction of mistrust and self-pity. On the other hand, it is impossible to ignore my mother. Her interpersonal problems so clearly cry of pain — her drunkenness is always so clearly tortured — that even under attack you cannot want to hurt her any more than she has been hurt (even if it has been by herself). And it is characteristic of my mother that two days after the most violent attack she will make a gratuitous lovely gesture (such as buying gifts or planning a theater outing, or, as was to be the case with our honeymoon, giving the tickets for escape). At any rate, on this particular occasion during spring break, her attack did not end; it grew on itself, every word she said reminded her of things which made her even more miserable and enraged, and finally, when holding my hands over my ears would no longer keep out her voice and when I was crying and trembling uncontrollably, I could not stand it and rushed out of the room into the bathroom, where I locked the door. I spent most of my unhappy times in the bathroom, since it was the only room in the house with a lock; and on this occasion, as I leaned on the window ledge trying to get my mind out of that house and that frustration by staring at the trees and sky, my mother began banging on the door. I don't remember what preceded or followed her last words to me in that interaction, but the words hit me like a fist. "I don't know how anyone could love the kind of person you've become. I certainly can't."

I do know that my sister was crying in her bedroom and that my mother in a panic of loneliness and misery asked her to get out of the house with her and go shopping; I remember hearing my sister say, "Not until you say you love Dawn," and my mother begging and begging for Jenny to come with her. Finally my mother saw it all as an alliance against her and ran up the stairs crying, out of the house, and drove away. That night (my mother still gone) I wrote a miserable loving letter to Warren telling him he was all I had now and I would die without him. I never sent it, perhaps thinking that things like that didn't have to be said in our relationship.

And then there was his rejection of me when I returned to Cambridge. I drove back to the dorm after hearing his words, almost hitting two cars because I couldn't see through my tears. That night was like a horrible dream, as I wandered about the dormitory corridors, afraid of my room which was full of scissors and aspirin and glass and afraid of being alone with my thoughts. I tried to watch a movie being shown downstairs but almost couldn't restrain myself from screaming out loud, so I left in the middle of it. As I recall there were a lot of people hanging around the dorm that night, and I waded through them as though I were walking through a mist, staring each one pleadingly in the face and getting no response. I couldn't talk and I wasn't talked to. Finally I went up to my room to sleep and found that not only couldn't I relax but part of me was telling myself rather maliciously that I would be up all night. These were the thoughts I had wanted to avoid.

Perhaps here I should introduce the other side of Dawn which had been developing since I was in high school (in its most blatant forms) and probably started long before that in my imaginings. By this I mean that early in my high school years I found that there was a temporary release from the tensions of living with my family in setting up in myself another person who watched me. I suppose that in its most primitive form this was also the source of my angel when I was seven. But when I was in high school this other personage became the observer and the ultimate controller of my victimized self; it was power and cruelty and invulnerability in contrast to the Dawn who was timid and anxious to please and easily hurt. I began to be seduced by this other side, always when I was by myself, giving myself over to its whims and manipulations and deriving immense pleasure and relief from them. Often its control was sexual; the scenes were frequently masturbatory. The behavior it produced was self-destructive; I began to discover the releases of self-flagellation and mutilation, and in my imagination there were all kinds of embellishments, in which I was the powerless victim of men who conjured up exquisite tortures for me. These periods of fantasy and self-destructive indulgence were not overly frequent then. My life was largely oriented in the real world of achievement and advancement, in which I was very certainly an agent, and not an acted-upon. In college, again in the privacy of my single room during sophomore year, I discovered that I could lie on the bed and burn myself very effectively on the radiator; but cigarettes and razor blades were at various times also instruments of the Controller in me. Gradually this aspect of Dawn became personalized: it assumed the form of an older woman, a rather mysterious, dark, emphatically communicative evil spirit who could manipulate me at her whim as long as we were in private, and particularly when the socialized Dawn was feeling beaten or tired. (I just remembered, in a stream of association flash, my agonies when at various times when I was young the other children called me a witch — I even played a witch in a school production once. The recurrence of that singsong accusation "Witch!

Witch!" was something that at first frightened and confused me, because I could not understand what about me made them choose that label, and may later have been incorporated into my self-image. In describing the Woman who played such an active role in my self-mutilation episodes, it occurred to me that how I visualized her was rather identical with my conception of a witch, that is, someone who although possessed of evil powers, is also strangely supernatural, a positive attraction.)

After returning to my room that night I stood for a long time in front of the mirror, until I was practically entranced and my face in the mirror became rather viscous and strange, a new person. Another of my high school habits was a tendency to find a sort of escape while taking a bath by allowing myself to hypnotize myself by concentrating on the reflections in the water; once entranced, I would direct myself to turn on the hot water and hold my hand or leg under the scalding stream. This mirror self-hypnosis was much the same process. After having successfully and rather easily (under the circumstances) gotten myself to give up the Woman I was "told" by her to begin taking aspirin ("You will go to sleep," she said. "I want to help you, I want you to go to sleep in my arms and under my watchfulness. Do it. I shall take care of you.") I began to take aspirin one by one, each time feeling a distinctly sexual pleasure at having forced myself to make the irretrievable step. There was an exultation in the dual sensations of control and victimization. Then something began to happen which neither she nor I had counted on. My ears began to ring. The entrancement was shattered. An external effect had broken the communicative link. I was left alone in my room, suddenly miserable and afraid again, with my ears ringing and making impossible noise in my head. Now there was no chance of my going to sleep, or escaping the loneliness.

I called up the Health Services to ask them how to get the ringing out of my ears, hoping perhaps to get a sleeping pill or something. The lady asked me to come down to the Center immediately. It was one o'clock in the morning by this time. I didn't care what happened now. I drove to the Health Center and was put through a grilling examination on why I swallowed the pills; my response was most inadequate ("I wanted to sleep.") since an honest answer would have taken too much time and energy, but I emphasized that I was not thinking of killing myself. I had only ingested about thirty tablets, but I was put in the infirmary for the night and the next morning began my association with Dr. Roberts, a psychiatrist. He saw me twice a day for my first week in the infirmary, and at one point I was introduced to a woman psychiatrist whom I couldn't stand and said so with such vehemence that Dr. Roberts agreed not to make me see her. Rob-

erts was quite effective in de-emphasizing the seriousness of my behavior and encouraged the competitive socialized Dawn to keep on
top – which she began to do. After two weeks I was released from the
infirmary, much to my chagrin since I had never been so happy as in
the second week at the Health Center, when I was allowed to go to
classes and slept at the infirmary; I was in the center of town (could
hear traffic through the window, an old appeal) and no longer felt isolated. My return to my cramped single at the dorm was a lugubrious
one for me, and I only got through the rest of the year there by living
with as many men as I could in their apartments, often not spending
one night a week in my room. It was at this point that I began to
approach all relationships from a decidedly promiscuous standpoint. I
would fuck the first person who seemed inclined, out to prove that
people could (and would) want and love and touch me. Of course it
was something that never could be proven in such a way; thus, the
attitude became habitual; I began to need to be fucked every other
night in order to feel confident in any social way; it became the
orientation for my whole interpersonal style. It was also at this time
that I began telling myself that I dislike women in general, I had never
had female friends. This new attitude somehow legitimized that failure. There was also some relation between this professed "woman-
hating" and my sexualized relationship with the Other Woman in me,
that is, the sexuality was all the more intense because I was being
sexually manipulated by someone I thought I hated. Later this confusing tangle of attitudes was to make me look for a homosexual relationship, but at this point I directed all my sexual energies into finding
one-night fucking mates. (Sorry to lay it on you so bluntly, but at least
it's honest, and it may help someone somehow – if only myself.)

    At the end of my sophomore year I met a tall striking-looking
black party-goer who talked about the economic bases of black power
and took me to his apartment. I was rather afraid of him because I
could not seem to control (whether by understanding or categorizing)
him and his gestures were strangely hypnotic. He gave me a vase of
plain flowers from his apartment and told me he wanted to take care
of me. He had long beautiful fingers and was incredibly gentle. He
cooked me dinner and we went to bed and I came the closest to
orgasm that I ever have in that relationship. I lived with Will for the
rest of the year, and was indeed treasured by him and taken care of. I
was as responsive (in a sort of passive accepting way) as I dared to be.
He would take me to parties which were attended only by black
militants and their chicks and made them accept me. I felt swept up,
involved, involuntary. But the involvement was too passive to be a
real giving on my part, and Will really loved me in the most emotional
way. Eventually I was to do to him what Warren had done to me, but

until that time he helped me more than anything else in developing my self-confidence and trust.

That summer I was the winner of a guest editor contest. I disentangled myself from Will, arrived at a horrible hotel to discover that I was the fiction and poetry editor and that it was a whole new world. For a month I was further away from my problems than ever before: there was a trip to France and all the glamor of being the center of attention. But I disliked most of the girls, was more or less the intellectual in the group, and found myself throwing myself at the available men again. In France I was spending nights with the photographer who traveled with us, and feeling nothing. I met two young English moviemakers who were traveling through Europe, toward whom I felt every possible romantic attachment. One of them, Ian, followed us throughout Europe and back up to Paris (turning up by surprise in the seat next to mine in various airplanes and trains, like a magical elf). He was a delightfully kind and comical friend whom I almost started to love. Then I had to return to school.

I had been receiving calls at work from Will, who now began to knock at my door and call at all hours of the night. I did everything I could to discourage him, but never did learn how to terminate a relationship, being afraid of the consequences for both the other person and for myself in their eyes. He even appeared with a plate of food he cooked for me on several occasions, and his haunting, frightening quality was reminiscent of my Woman who had also promised to "take care of me." Will frightened me most of all, I suppose, because I thought I saw a tremendous capacity for violence in him if he were wronged; and I did feel that I was wronging him. On the other hand to continue the relationship when I felt repulsed by his presence, even though he came in a sort of devotion, would have been unfair as well. At the time I had a small dark apartment in a gloomy building. At nights I was afraid to go to sleep because either Will or this other character who claimed to have a mystical attachment to me would call or try to get in. One particularly horrible night Will tried to force his way into the apartment (so like my brother who forced his way into the bathroom) and he was drunk and talked to me in slow mournful words for over two hours at two o'clock in the morning. When I finally talked him into leaving, trying to assure him both that I appreciated and liked him and that I never wanted to see him again, it was four A.M. When I got up to go to work at eight, there was this other tormentor sitting on the steps to the apartment building waiting for me. He became rather abusive when I desperately told him I didn't have the time or the energy to talk. It was in that same week (which was more nightmarish than I can describe — there was no one of whom I wasn't afraid, and Dr. Roberts was not around) that my mother became suspicious of my tired tone on the telephone and flew up to spend a week "seeing how I was doing." She came up on the first plane (like a fourth evil spirit) and bedded down in my little living room. She brought a suitcase full of kitchen gadgets for me, but I was so exhausted and apprehensive that I must not have seemed very appreciative. By the time she left she was more disquieted than when she arrived, and she later sent me a letter saying she knew that I had been smoking grass and that this was causing serious damage in my "character." This was perfectly false, because the cigarette butts in the ashtrays were not roaches and indeed I hadn't smoked in over three months; but because I had told her that I didn't even smoke cigarettes (afraid of her fury over that) and that the butts were those of a friend who visited occasionally, she sensed that I was lying and assumed what to her was the worst possible thing — that I was some kind of drug addict. She had accused me of being a liar before (and was not entirely wrong, since I had always been given to evasion and exaggeration and understatement, depending on the situation with her, in order to avoid arguments), but now her new line of attack was drugs. I promised her quite truthfully that I had not and would not smoke grass that summer, but she said it meant nothing since I could not be depended on to tell the truth. "What does your word mean? Nothing."

Late in the summer I met a girl by the name of Anna, who invited me to share an apartment with her that fall. I was delighted; not only was Anna troubled by emotional difficulties also but she seemed to want privacy, to dislike intimate friendships with girls, and to be a good writer with many of my ambitions in the literary field. We got a lovely apartment with a fireplace right in the Square (something I had always dreamed of since living at the Health Center) and furnished it rather elegantly and simply. We developed an easy symbiotic style of living together, going our own ways and politely asking each other to share food and give judgments on each other's poetry. I think her sense of delicacy was slightly offended by my having various male friends over for the night so often, but she was perhaps more hurt by the fact that she had no one than by my apparent promiscuity. She knew that essentially I was as lonely as she. During the summer I had gotten to know a group of seniors living together who were very kind to me and who invited me over to cook dinner for them during the latter part of the summer practically every night. Although I started off fucking the one of them I had originally met (he was the first case of real impotence I had ever run into and in fact we never really actually fucked at all, he was very tormented by his inability to actually carry out intercourse), he left for Denmark and became engaged there to a girl with whom he had no sexual relations. After he left I became intimate with one of his roommates, a gentle energetic life-loving boy who was very fair and kind to me and who seemed to enjoy fucking as much as I did (and I did most certainly love it).

When Anna and I early in the fall decided to have a party to reacquaint ourselves with the outside world, he was one of the people I invited, although by that time the relationship was very painlessly and gently tapering off. One of Anna's invited guests was a tall rather handsome junior by the name of Stephen Silbiger, and I saw him for the first time that night through the door to Anna's bedroom where he was sitting with Anna and her most sympathetic friends listening to her troubles. I didn't have time in my hostessing fervor to stop and think about it, or even to really register who he was; I was too busy flitting around trying to satisfy everybody as both hostess and as a person and feeling a little annoyed when the drinking started and people began coming in hordes most of whom we didn't know. Anna (in an agony of nerves and nervousness) split without saying anything to me. I felt as though I had been left to handle a party which had gotten out of control. I had grass in my bedroom and didn't want the place to be busted. The noise was getting louder and people were bringing in yards of ale. In my general anxiety, I forgot completely about the dark appealing face I had glimpsed through the bedroom door, and it was not until the next day, when he knocked on the door after the debris of the party had been cleaned up, that I really met Stephen.

Stephen and Dick knocked on the door to our apartment when I was there with the brother of the boy I had been fucking over the summer. I was turning this boy on and generally leading up to having him stay the night. He was very gentle and sweet and I wanted (as his brother had once said he wished) for him to have "a good woman" the first time. When I answered the door I expected that they were there to see Anna, but they said that they had heard that I had some grass and they were having a hard time getting through the "dry" spell before harvest and would like to buy a little. I was really disappointed not to be able to ask them to stay and smoke with me, particularly since both of them looked very strange and interesting to me and I was dying to talk to someone who had run the gamut at school and would provide some feedback, rather than the awkward and reticent boy in the other room. I asked them into my bedroom and poured out some grass into an envelope to lay it on them, by which gesture they seemed rather surprised and very grateful. I told them I could get unlimited amounts through Will and could probably arrange a deal.

Later that week Stephen called to see if the deal could go through and he picked me up in his Volvo and we went over to cop. Will was out and we returned to Cambridge. In the car Stephen asked

me if I would come over and have a smoke at his apartment, but I was
reluctant since I had a paper due the next day. But as usual I was easily talked into going, and I discovered that he was into soul music
(which I loved) and Dylan (which I hated). Smoking the first time with
him was very stiff and unrelaxed for me; but he rolled over on the bed
and we could really feel each other, and I felt immediately more at
ease. I remember I got as excited as I ever had with all my clothes on,
and Stephen said he came a couple of times before we even fucked. It
was a very successful evening for me, but had no real emotional content. That I was looking for a deeper relationship must have been true,
because I remember thinking as I told him of my studies toward con-
version to Judaism that since he was Jewish he would understand what
I saw in Buber and what I strove for in myself. As it turned out he was
something of an alienated Jew, but he must have been interested anyway, because the next day he called to invite me to go to Marblehead
with him. We loaded my alpaca rug and fur coat into the car and
spent a wonderful day staring at the sea which I had always loved so
much. All of this fit very easily into romantic moulds for me, and I was
truly happy for the first time in many months. Not only was it the
source of relief from loneliness, but Stephen took over from the beginning and insisted on paying off my bills, which amounted to a good
$500 and were causing me all kinds of agony and nightmares, since
creditors kept phoning and threatening. At the time I was considering
doing a few weekend lays for a pimp I had met during the summer,
but couldn't quite carry it out, more out of fear than any revulsion; the
idea itself rather appealed to me. At any rate Stephen's entrance into
my life was heralded by a joy and an elimination of fears that quite
surprised me. And yet I never quite gave myself to him any more than
I had given myself to anyone else. It was to take many months before
I knew him well enough to reveal things to him that no one else knew;
it took Stephen a long time and a lot of painful discussion to make me
trust him that much.

On October 21 we drove to Washington to attend the march.
We were speeding on meth as we drove and the sunset and sunrise
were only long instants apart. In those intervening instants we shared
wonderful optimistic fantasies about Stephen resuming his writing in
a dedicated way, about our going to Japan together the following summer, and about having three weddings. It was during that trip that
Stephen asked me to marry him. I said I couldn't decide so quickly
and he was glad to wait; then a half-hour later I just said "Yes." It was
delightful to have made the decision so quickly and so happily. And
by the time we arrived in Washington I was ready to learn how to be
in love all over again.

When we arrived in Washington I called my father in Atlanta, who said he hoped my travelling companion was not "one of those long-haired students" (I had to disappoint him in that respect); then we went on to the march. As it turned out the whole thing was very disillusioning to me, the marchers were heckling and at some points harassing the guards outside the Pentagon; and if I couldn't stand violence and brutality in Vietnam I couldn't stand it there either. I began to cry and begged Stephen to take me away, which he seemed glad to do. We continued on to Atlanta. When we arrived my mother was already drunk (she could get stone-drunk from one drink before dinner, which often explained why dinner was such a dangerous time of the evening). Stephen, who had driven all night, was very tired and I let him rest downstairs while I talked to my mother and a friend of hers from Florida, Mrs. Manor, who was visiting. As the grievances of my mother began to come out (as soon as we started talking she began to accuse Stephen of being lazy and rude by needing to rest a while) I could see that Mrs. Manor saw things in the same perspective I did, which for the first time suggested to me that my mother's reality was not the ordinary one. Mrs. Manor became more and more sympathetic as the evening went on and my mother got drunker and more insinuating, trying to moderate my mother's views (whereupon my mother turned on Mrs. Manor, saying that she knew nothing of these matters and should keep out of them). I felt terribly humiliated not only for myself but for Mrs. Manor's sake. Finally I went down to awake Stephen and explained that my mother was in a rather belligerent drunken state; I hardly know whether he could have expected what he came up against, a barrage of questions which went on for two hours. My mother's form of interrogation is always hinting at underlying evil motives, and she applied it in full force to Stephen. He remained very strong and polite as long as he could, and finally began to get a little exasperated, as he saw that I was about to cry under the strain. Realizing that we had to drive back that same night and were already tired, we announced after two hours of such discussion that we had to get going, whereupon my mother accused me of only dropping in whenever I felt like it, at my own convenience, and not having the decency to stay and talk a while, etc. We left her in a very annoyed and upset state of mind. She sat absolutely still and cold as I kissed her goodbye; while Mrs. Manor very warmly and sympathetically kissed us both and wished us all the good things she could think of. Getting back into the car to return to Boston was the most relieving feeling of the whole day, and I was beginning to feel the strength in Stephen, and to take him as my strength.

When we had finally returned to Boston it was to Stephen's apartment, since I had been living there for a week. There were no few complications in that matter, either. At first Stephen had refused to sleep with me at my place because Anna's bedroom was next door. I couldn't understand his reluctance, explaining that I had had people there before. I didn't find out until months later that Stephen had slept with Anna at one time; then suddenly Anna's apparently unprovoked hostility toward me after Stephen and I began to be together fell into place. She had never told me of any intimacy with Stephen and I guess he assumed that I knew. Not only was Anna antagonistic after I began to be only an occasional visitor at the apartment, but my mother (thoroughly aroused by our visit to Atlanta) began to phone Anna's apartment at all hours asking for me. Anna gave her Stephen's phone number, and she called me there to give me a tongue-lashing about living with someone unless I intended to marry him. At that point, although I was very unwilling to be forced into any such position by her suspicions and attacks, I finally made public my agreement to marry Stephen; I replied to all her insistences by saying, "Don't worry, we will get married," which as it turned out was the last thing she wanted. She hung up on me (it was the first time she had done this, but it was to be repeated in the months ahead).

As for my scholastic work at this time, I was way behind in my courses. Most days were spent cuddled next to Stephen on his unmade bed while he wrote papers; for the first time in my life I felt really protected and really comforted by a PERSON and not simply a haystack or a dream. In the end it became clear that I could not organize myself enough to save my courses, and I applied for a leave of absence, which I received. Free to love and write, I finished up a manuscript and got poems accepted by several magazines (this was the last time for a year that I got any writing accepted anywhere) and received tentative encouragement toward publication of a collection. Stephen fucked me every day and loved me as well (two aspects of relationship which were not really at all related in my mind) and I was very happy, except for the occasional rupture of my new world by a phone call from my mother.

It was arranged that we would spend Thanksgiving in Boston with Stephen's mother so that the "family" and friends which gathered would get a chance to meet me. I suspect that when Stephen informed his mother over the phone of his intentions to marry me, it came so abruptly that she was inclined to think it would blow over. She was not too enthusiastic and readily pointed out the dangers of marrying so young (we were both nineteen, a year younger than even our classmates). But her reaction was one of normal parental concern, and in the end she was overflowing in her wishes for our happiness. Stephen had appeared to me to be rather hostile toward his mother until she turned out to be so encouraging after her former quarrels over Lynn; from the time of that conversation with her I think that their relationship was improving again, and since then (although Stephen's mother can be very annoying in her concern) he has spoken more and more appreciatively of her very generous gestures to us in the months between November and now. Certainly in contrast to the ungenerous and untrusting attitude of my parents, his mother was even more outstanding. Stephen's coolness toward his father, however, has not changed. His father frowned on the marriage of his son to a convert with so obviously Christian a name as Dawn McLaren; his father was rather distant in his few talks with me and was more concerned with the technicalities of my confirmation than with my conception of Judaism or what I believed in. In fact to me it was an organization of my belief in mystical levels of existence and communication and was oriented around what I knew of Buber and the reform view of the world introduced to me. But more significant than Dr. Silbiger's attitude toward me was the tension between him and his son; it was at this point that Stephen informed me of his relationship with his father since its turn for the worse in Baltimore, and I realized how intense and deep-seated his hostility toward his father and all that he represented was.

By Thanksgiving, we had exchanged all of the basic intimacies about our former "love" relationships (I could not fairly be said to have had any clear love relationships), about our families, and some of our own secrets. But I was still faking orgasms with Stephen, and it disturbed me, since it seemed to me that complete honesty was the only real way of giving oneself entirely to another person, and since secretiveness had always been my weapon against people. Somehow there was no time that seemed appropriate for such a revelation: certainly not just before or after intercourse, and yet at any other time I convinced myself that it wasn't that important a secret. We did discuss at great lengths, though, my growing apprehensions about marriage; I put up every kind of resistance to it, and whatever resistance I actually showed on the surface was prompted by a far larger pool of fear than I ever told Stephen. I could not remember having ever seen a successful marriage, that is, one in which a working, cooperative, loving relationship had persisted for very long. I had promised myself since I was in high school that I would marry someone who would find me socially convenient (I saw myself as a well-mannered and elegant runner-of-a-house and giver-of-parties) in return for his quite certain economic means. Moreover, in my conception of realistic marriage, each partner would have an understanding with the other by which each could fuck whomever he chose to, as long as his obligations to and respect for the other were not infringed upon. This was totally at odds with Stephen's conception of marriage, as he had imagined it with Lynn (who certainly seemed to me to be the Ideal Wife type) and as he had seen it happen with both of his brothers. He had only happy visions of companionship and sharing, and eventually of children; and slowly he allowed my imprisoned fantasies to emerge into possibility by his words. I was not convinced until after we were married that it could be the source of such happiness, and I'm sure I caused him much suffering and anxiety by being so resistant. As for my dissociation of sexuality and love, it still has not been overcome. It was one of the most painful things to me that Stephen had had a relationship in which sexuality had been nothing more or less than a beautiful extension of love and trust, while I saw sexuality as a route toward that love and trust. I felt as though I could never offer him what Lynn had, and indeed as the relationship progressed it became clear that anything I had with Stephen he had already felt with Lynn in its original and first-love form, while for me everything we did was new and nothing was to be taken for granted.

Meeting Stephen's mother at Thanksgiving was a tense and difficult experience complicated by the fact that there were twelve or so inspectors in attendance at the huge dinner. In my anxiousness to be helpful to Ruth (Stephen's mother insisted that I call her by her first name) I hardly saw Stephen and felt tormented when the girl he had been "destined" to marry by his mother's expectations and by virtue of the close relationship between her family and Ruth, sat talking to Stephen about me and even running her hands through his hair, and saying how lucky I was. I felt somehow trapped and used and frustrated; but the overall impression that I made was good and when we left I felt that Stephen's mother liked me for my honesty and my attempts at forthright amicability. We even had a chance to talk about our respective emotional difficulties, and I think I made her feel at ease by virtue of my similar bouts with analysis and hospitalization. From that time on Ruth was almost always encouraging and kind to us.

We decided to get our own apartment. The difficulties with Anna and the cramped quarters in Stephen's apartment made it not only desirable but practical to look for our own place. We found a lovely apartment which we fell in love with, leased, and spent a week painting. It was as though the most tangible parts of our dreamings were being realized. I had been delighted to find that Stephen loved cars and driving, since I always had been given to great speeds and skillful steering; we were both excited about getting an Alfa after the Volvo was sold. We both loved soul music, and I had a good collection (which Stephen was to jokingly refer to as one of the reasons he married me); our tastes in most things generally coincided. The only source of real disturbance to me in Stephen's habits was his daily grass habit; he began to deal on a fairly large scale that winter in order to earn money, and for many months I was fearful of a bust, particularly since we lived so close to a head shop. But gradually I began to see that not only could he do anything he chose to while stoned (which I still cannot) but that it was a source of great pleasure and relaxation to him. On those terms, I learned to accept it. Now I am still a much less frequent user than he, but haven't had a thought in months about being busted, other than a sort of pioneerish conviction that it should be legalized and that the social effects of grass are not only not dangerous, but can even be very useful in a person's mode of dealing with the world. I am convinced that it will, by force of logic, eventually be legalized, and I now take the position that to be busted would help the cause, since it will be the number of supposedly "respectable" people who are discovered smoking that will tip the balance of opinion in favor of the drug, since reports by commissions obviously have had no effect. I do however still strongly object to dealing speed or acid, because I know that they can get out of hand. Stephen has no real convictions on this point, feeling that people for whom a drug is harmful are not likely to buy it — yet this is not true of speed freaks, who get their eight-hour highs at the expense of their lives eventually. But for the most part we don't deal speed, and never acid, so that that point of contention is avoided.

Christmas was to be spent at my home, and my parents in typical style sent just enough money for my fare home. We both went, however, as they knew we would. And the spectacle of pre-Christmas manipulation and maneuvering was quite horrifying; my father and mother never knew what each other were doing, and by mistake ended up getting Jenny the same gift, so that one of them had to be given to Stephen (it was a knife), who already knew about it. Somehow the whole thing was so unspontaneous and so preplanned that by Christmas morning we were all rather embarrassed and uncomfortable. I don't remember much about the trip except things about my father: his falling asleep in the middle of a conversation in a living room chair, having had one drink too many; and a scene with him (father-daughter talk ostensibly) in which he told me that he didn't approve of my getting married and I said I was sorry but it was going to happen. He said since he was paying for it he didn't understand my attitude, at which point I began to think that BOTH of my parents were out to use their levers on me. Daddy's putting my real and loving attachment to Stephen in terms of his paying for it disgusted me, although I had come to expect his penny-pinching and my mother's in daily life; but somehow it shouldn't have applied to love as easily as it applied to college. As I tried to ask him these questions, I realized that the point wasn't getting through and finally he said what coming from my father was tantamount to a rejection: "I am disappointed in you." I knew that my mother had been badgering him about my "atti-

tudes" and "degeneration" and that this was partially behind his
suspicions, but I couldn't battle my mother in two people. I ran out of
the room crying quite hysterically to Stephen in the living room; he
couldn't tell whether I was laughing or crying, but either one was
uncontrollable and he knew that as a bad sign. When my mother came
into the living room, wondering what the noise was I couldn't stand it
and ran out into her bedroom; she followed close behind me and
slammed the bedroom door in Stephen's face who was following her.
He came in anyway and knelt beside the bed I was screaming on, and
I tried to explain to him what had happened. My mother was on the
other side of the bed trying to get me to talk to her, and both of them
were consoling me in their different ways: Stephen very effectively by
saying we would leave and go home and he would take care of me
forever and I didn't need people who didn't seem to need me; and my
mother by saying that my father hadn't meant any harm and that she
too had worries and they were only being concerned and I mustn't
condemn them. I was trying to answer both of them — to tell Stephen
that I couldn't walk out without making my father love me again, and
to tell my mother that they were going about it the wrong way, asking
them why they didn't express their concern and then discuss it ra-
tionally with me instead of using their peculiar holds on me to keep
me from what I wanted and needed so much. I finally went with
Stephen downstairs to the bedroom he was sleeping in and lay there
with him for an hour. Then my mother came down and suggested that
I go to the room where I had been sleeping with Jenny, to which I replied something vague and exhausted (fearing another argument) and
she left. Stephen begged me to stay with him and it is one of my retro-
spective regrets that I did not, but felt compelled (as though I were a
dog being dragged by the leash) to sleep in the other room as I had
led my mother to believe I would. In their house I was still their sub-
ordinate.

When we returned to Cambridge I prepared to resume school.
But that term was interrupted by a series of attacks which I now believe to have been psychotic episodes, in which I would feel totally
commanded by my former guardian, the Other Woman in me. She
would come over me like an electrical current and force me to act in
very strange and unfortunate ways. This was a terrible period for
Stephen, because I knew that it was a battle of strengths, his against
hers, whoever she was; I somehow no longer could do any more. Exhausted, I was taken over. Usually when I felt that it was going to
happen (and I could feel it in a very physical way, trembling and
apprehension and excitement from the inside), I would tell Stephen
and he would pin me on the bed and hold me down until the violence
passed. The attacks were directed against him, and I was told by my

alter ego that she, not Stephen, possessed me and that one of them had to be killed, or failing that, that I had to be. And so I told Stephen to please fight her when she took over, and he did. I will never admire anybody more than I do him for his courage and compassion and endurance during those days. When I was "taken over" and began to fight him, he would pin me down and hit me, often until my face bled; and then when it passed and I came out of it, crying and confused, he covered me with kisses. He would alternately swear and strike out at the "bitch" when she appeared (and Stephen told me that my face changed drastically when this transference took place although I had no sense of anything except intense apprehension) and then chant Hebrew prayers to me when I asked him after the fit until I fell asleep. I remember that on the third or fourth night of these "attacks" he was so exhausted from fighting me and from making the violent changes of emotion that were required, that he began to cry as he was holding me down, and I couldn't stand it: I just felt as though I were going under a drug or something and couldn't stay with him and comfort him and hold him and thank him. It was the most wonderful thing anyone has ever done for me. And after that week the Woman never reappeared in such strength, preferring to catch me when I was alone and never again challenging Stephen. I was tremendously disappointed in Dr. Roberts during this period; I had been seeing him since the spring before every week and was very indebted to him for helping me to move off-campus; but when Stephen called him at the worst of these episodes, afraid of hitting me any harder for fear of breaking bones and sick of the blood coming out of my face and tired of having to be strong under unpredictable attack, to ask for help or advice, Dr. Roberts responded by making my appointment a day earlier, at which time he asked me why Stephen was giving up on me and couldn't stand up under a few attacks. He told me that the whole thing could have been avoided if I hadn't cancelled my last appointment. So I give full credit to Stephen with his love and determination for pulling me out of that very bad and very delusional time. Although the attacks ended, I was still terrified of being left alone in the apartment and became very afraid at night when the telephone rang, thinking that it would be my mother. After every telephone call from her (which always ended up in a yelling session) I collapsed in tears and became quite unmanageable for an hour or more. Gradually though, under the influence of Stephen's amazing love, my distress at these phone calls decreased until by early spring I felt quite able and controlled again. During the month of March, as a token gesture to my mother (who sent me clippings and wrote little notations in the margins about how my children would be deformed if I continued to use contraceptive pills or to smoke pot) I went off pills, assuming that rhythm would be contraceptive enough if I were careful. Six days before my period was due (one day before what is normally considered the infertile period) I began to feel creepy again (if you will forgive the expression) and felt full-force the power of the old other voice urging me to get Stephen to fuck me; but the voice expressed itself mainly in the strongest sexual desire I ever felt, and I convinced Stephen that it would be all right, believing that myself.

In April I made an appointment with a physician; the pregnancy test was positive. I was both elated and afraid, and I remembered with a kind of bitter amusement that this would be the second time around for Stephen and that the pattern was repeating himself. What was such a source of joy and love for me would be a repeat experience for him. I felt rather acutely that Lynn's pregnancy had outdone mine and that Stephen's joy in hers must have been enhanced since it was the first time he had made a baby in anyone. Lynn had given him support instead of problems as I had. But when I told Stephen, it was with positive joy; and he responded with smiling.

As it turned out, that same afternoon I had an appointment with Dr. Roberts, and he immediately had me put in the infirmary, afraid of the disturbances that he felt the new condition would create in me after the initial numb disbelief. The next week was a very depressing one: I didn't want to kill that peculiar combination of Stephen and me that was growing in me, and yet from all sides I was told that to have the child would be disastrous. Stephen took me to a metropolitan hospital where I was given a battery of tests and several interviews by two psychiatrists. I was classified as an hysteric and was eligible for a therapeutic interruption under state law. The only remaining hitch was the anaesthetic consent which had to be signed by a parent. It was plain that I could not tell my mother; I was quite certain that she would fly up immediately and worsen everything. I knew that my father would be jolted, but the chances were better. I tried to reassure him over the phone after writing him a letter, and although he was hit hard in his Puritan core (as he had been by our living together before we were married, refusing even to come into the apartment), he came through with the signature and agreed not to tell my mother. I made a number of phone calls to my mother to prevent her calling home at night not to find me there; but as if by instinct she called anyway on the night before the abortion was to be performed; Stephen immediately called me and said she had demanded that I call her back "when I got in"; and so from my bed at the hospital having asked the nurses to keep out for a few minutes so there would be no telltale noises, I called her up and went through an agonizing half-hour being lectured about parking tickets and not writing letters.

The operation was incredibly smooth and painless and I was out the next day. I felt emptier but relieved.

There are two areas which in this stream of associations I have failed to touch. One is that of work. It has always been characteristic of me that I was healthiest when I was busiest, and during the first few months with Stephen, I was working full time in the emergency ward of a hospital, until I was too exhausted to go on. Stephen would drop me off and pick me up every night, and his dependability and calm was wonderful. But one of the unfortunate trends in my association with Stephen has been a gradual loss of drives and concentrated energies toward working; I get my schoolwork done in spurts, and haven't held a job since that spring. At the beginning of the relationship I was particularly worried about my inability to write poetry as I lived with him longer and longer; and it was only during the summer months when he was working that I got any real writing done. I am still battling with myself for the poetic inspiration that used to come so easily. On the other hand, this form of expression has been supplanted gradually by my interest in psychodynamics and their social implications. I have been doing my best work since I came to school in my social science courses. Although I have neglected my artwork, I feel capable of turning it out if I had the time, so that the loss of inspiration seems to be limited to my long-time poetic talent.

The other topic I should touch briefly on is drugs. As I have already described, I have come not to scorn Stephen's dependence on a smoke in the evenings and even sometimes before starting the day off, but to see it as a part of his psychodynamic relation to the world. And I myself have learned to overcome the tendency to become suspicious and fearful when smoking grass, having replaced it with a very healthy relaxation and general rosiness which usually puts me to sleep.

Our experiments with other drugs together include only one acid trip, which was very strange and came too early in our relationship for me to be entirely relaxed during it. I remember the distortion of Stephen's face which made his forehead concave and the horror of looking in a mirror and seeing the swimming putty which was my own face. I had a much more visual experience than Stephen, which may be partially because I am used to imagining things when I think of them and partially because I am slightly nearsighted and distortions when I'm not stoned are relatively common. Stephen kept repeating that he was not feeling anything (an echo of his central complaint about his experience of life in general). Stephen tells me that at one point I retreated into the closet out of some embarrassment or desire to hide, and although I remember the interpersonal experience on acid as one of extreme self-consciousness about the very things I could not change — my figure and physiognomy — although certainly not about nudity since I was sitting around in a bra and skirt when Stephen's roommates came dropping in — although I remember these sensations, I have completely forgotten the reasons for my closet hiding and the act itself.

Months later a friend shot heroin with us, but the sensation was unpleasant in the main to both of us, and we have absolutely no desire to get hooked on smack or speed anyway.

The only really bad experiences with drugs that I had after meeting Stephen occurred when I was the most disturbed. At the height of the period of being afraid to be left alone, I was stoned one night when Stephen had to go out for something, and I remember huddling on the bed afraid of noises. Someone knocked on the door, and I answered it to find what appeared to me to be a terrible figment of my imagination — a young man with only one arm. He went into the usual magazine selling spiel, with the added dimension that he was a Vietnam veteran, but my mind was racing in all kinds of unholy paranoid directions; and even after I got him to leave (after convincing him, I'm sure, that I was thoroughly mad) I thought for two days that he was following me around and would catch up with me eventually. Fortunately in Stephen's company those feelings can be relatively short-lived. I used to find myself falling into that kind of misinterpretation of the attitudes of others toward me quite frequently when I was stoned, but that has completely disappeared now.

One other momentous event which I left out was the confession which I finally made to Stephen that I had never had an orgasm with any man, and not even with him. I was afraid to tell him because then I could be accused of having lied every time we had had intercourse by my exaggerated ecstasies, and also because I sensed that an integral part of his joy in intercourse came from the sensation of giving me such joy and release. His reaction was initially one of disbelief and a passing disappointment, followed immediately by eloquent reassurances that he loved me, that we would be married anyway OF COURSE, and that with a lot of love and persistence he would bring me around. Since then I have held rather desperately on to that dream — that this relationship will join my dissociated concepts of sexuality and love in eventual orgasm, and I have cried in frustration after intercourse many times, wanting so much to give him the gift of my unconscious and complete surrender, but unable to make it happen.

The marriage date was June 5. In late April invitations were to be sent out. I made a brief visit home (ostensibly to make arrangements with my mother for the wedding) sometime in March which had the usual dramatics and confrontations, in one of which I ended up on the bed in my room crying and trying to block out my mother's words with my hands over my ears. I moved so close to the wall to get away from her that the bed slipped out and I ended up on the floor, which was good occasion for my mother to call me childish and to capitalize beautifully on my humiliating position behind the bed. But the arrangements were somehow made, with every eye toward economy in order to give them little to complain about (my wedding gown was a simple evening dress which costs less than that of the attendants!). I had written a girl I had met the summer before and known for only two months to ask her to be my bridesmaid. Somehow no one I knew, not even Mimi who had shared my propensities for self-torture and self-examination when I was in my black period at college, was friend enough to be an obvious choice for bridesmaid, and I had felt that this girl and I had had an affinity which convinced me that she would accept. She did, but with the condition that she couldn't pay for the dress and her transportation (she had her problems too), and although I wrote offering to pay for one or the other, she never wrote back and, in the end, my only bridesmaid was Jenny. There were no other attendants. Stephen's best man was to be the charming bum, Dick, and his ushers were his freshman year roommate and another friend. Stephen's father had arranged to fly into town just for the day with his new wife and children. Stephen thought of this, as he did the whole ceremonious affair, as a concession to his parents; it was only our concern and love for each other that got us through those harried preparations. Somehow my mother was remarkably inept in arranging things for her first daughter's wedding; she sent out half invitations without any RSVP printed on them and then complained when people didn't RSVP, and she somehow miscalculated the punch proportions and there wasn't enough to go around even after she complied with my suggestion to get more spiking (which for economy they had brought with them in the car). Stephen's mother was very sweet, giving me a treasured and very old lace handkerchief and sending us gifts in a continuous and cheering stream from March through June, something she could not really afford to do on her allowance from Stephen's father.

In the middle of April, afraid that Lynn would get her invitation before he had been able to tell her himself, Stephen wrote a letter to her, which I was not permitted to read and which therefore my fantasies made into something of a love letter. I knew that he had received a letter from Lynn months before when she had first read in a Baltimore newspaper that he was to marry. I also knew that she had said in it that she still loved him. This letter had disturbed me

immensely, although it was one subject on which I was as contained
as I could be with Stephen; but it broke out of me one day and he
tried to explain their relationship to me in terms of its ongoing mutual
affection and said that since Lynn hadn't changed, he still loved her.
It was a point on which my whole belief in his conception of love
and marriage pivoted; for weeks I thought that I would fall apart, that
if his love wasn't exclusive why must my sexuality be? At this point
there appeared a third voice (another woman, but much younger, very
attractive and confident and impatient with the pre-marital stretch of
fidelity) which encouraged me to walk the streets in hopes of being
picked up and fucked by any anonymous passerby. I used to go out
after Stephen was asleep and do just that, feeling myself at those times
to BE that other person (whose name for some reason was Giselle);
but my walks ended up at the river in lonely contrition, and I walked
back half afraid that what I had originally come out for might happen.
As the months with Stephen went on, his desire to have intercourse
had lessened, until after the wedding we fucked only once a week or
even more seldom. It was a point of great delicacy and great uneasiness between us that I was so hungry for sexual expressions of his love,
but I had at least partially learned my lesson from Warren and tried to
keep myself from demanding it of him more than he cared to give it.
Sometimes it was impossible, and on occasions my advances were even
turned down; and yet the last thing I wanted or needed was for
Stephen to fuck me because I had pressured him into it. I wanted to
learn how to come, I had dreams of somehow giving my orgasm to
him as a gift, but I couldn't see how that could be achieved if intercourse were so infrequent as to make me feel that each one must be
taken fullest advantage of — precisely the wrong emotional predis-
position for that kind of abandon. And so the drive to be unfaithful
was stronger than any force I had ever fought against except the
older woman in me; since I conceived of intercourse as in no way limited to people for whom it was an expression of love, since I could
without any emotional contradictions which I was conscious of fuck
someone I was not emotionally intimate with, I could not see mere
physical unfaithfulness as any infringement on my love for Stephen (as
I felt that his continued love for Lynn was keeping some of his love
from me), since the whole of my spiritual and emotional giving (which
I treasured most of all, and seldom had given freely) was to him. My
logic and my emotions both fought my promise to remain faithful,
which was such an important aspect of Stephen's conception of a relationship (evidenced by his declaration that he found it impossible to
try to perpetuate his relationship with Wendy Cass after she had
fucked other men); and somehow through those months and the suc-

ceeding summer, when conditions made it even more difficult, my promise won out. I was, at least, determined to be honest.

I thought that the wedding day was something of a fiasco. Not only did I ruin my lines in Hebrew (we had forgotten to memorize them until the morning of the ceremony, and I have a memory that is adversely affected by any self-consciousness and had to be prompted), but the punch ran out at the reception, and the whole day was weatherly uncooperative, with the heaviest rain we had had all spring. The chapel, however, was quite lovely, and to see Stephen in his Nehru suit waiting to be my husband was the best of all superlative feelings for me. Although I was trembling and forgot to pass my three big gardenias to Jenny, I held his hand tightly and we kissed earlier than we were supposed to. The spectators however seemed to like it; the rabbi gave an eloquent talk about us and brought tears to a number of eyes, and no one was as conscious of my memory problem as I. The reception dwindled early, partly I suppose because as our only concession to ourselves we turned on soul music halfway through it, and I put on a rather too flippy minidress for most of the guests to stand; but we couldn't fail to be happy. My mother had paid for us to accompany a women's club vacation to the Bahamas, and we left the next morning.

The following week was lovely for me for several reasons. One was that we fucked every night to the sound of the ocean. Another was the fact that Stephen finally met a member of the family (other than Jenny) whom he really could like and enjoy the company of — my mother's sister who had moved to the Bahamas with her husband. She was the one who had been able to arrange our inclusion in the group outing, and her lusty colorful style as well as her inclinations to abandon the socialized world of the States appealed very much to Stephen. And the beaches, after all, were lovely. The only unpleasant part was the company of the middle-aged women who were intent on getting their full bar privileges between 12 and 12 (when free drinks were part of the package). Neither of us can stand drunkenness or the tinges of condescension which the group's acceptance of us as the Honeymoon Couple implied.

We returned to Cambridge for exams and job hunting, and much to our amazement did better academically than we ever had; Stephen for the first time did very well, and I got my first A's in courses outside of the English department.

That summer Stephen spent working as manager of a hip record shop, and for some reason I found his regular absence during the day and the promise of his return in the evening a very liberating routine.

The liberation came in the form of a returned ability to organize my time and to get things done, a very important dynamic in my mode of dealing with the world. It still distresses me that in Stephen's presence I feel able only to think of him and to react to him, and not to creatively structure or handle the number of activities I had always been used to before. It was a phenomenon I could not understand in any way, except that I knew that when he was there I had to give everything to him, and this to me must have implied not dividing my attention. I did some writing, but was relieved when August came and my one-month job at a local library began. It was tedious work, but rewarding in that I was finally earning money and contributing to the financial pool. It was around this time that I first made quite plain to my mother that there were priorities in my life which put Stephen at the top of everything; as I said it over the phone to a stunned silence on the other end, "I have my own family now." But the major emotional complication in the relationship consisted of my unmanageable and totally unreasonable jealousy, even of girls on television. Since I had been forbidden by Stephen to continue working as a go-go dancer as I had been when he met me, and since I felt unsatisfied in the sexual aspect of our relationship, it seemed immensely unfair and very frustrating to me that he should be able to study someone else's sexuality on television or on the streets. Most of these feelings were highly unfounded and irrational, in light of Stephen's personality, which simply didn't see things in a sexually arousing way in general, while I saw sexual implications in everything. The other problem which first became evident to me at this time was Stephen's returning sense of his inability to handle his life in a socially acceptable way; he saw indications of this inability in his lack of career or specialization directedness, in his resorting to grass to take the corners off of the bad days as well as to round out the good ones, and I was instrumental in making these "shortcomings" plain to him by being so achievement-oriented, so directional and able to activate my talents, and so demanding of sexual constancy. Part of the problem was that I couldn't get Stephen to tell me straight what the roots of his difficulties were, although I knew that they were in the area of competence, and that part of his difficulty was that he had reacted to his self-image by withdrawing and found it nearly impossible to give so much — in sex or confidences — to yet another person (after having been buffeted around by his parents and his emotional attachments to girls). But on the other hand I worsened the situation by not extending that unquestioning trust which he needed for once to get out of the morass on his own (his sense of his own incompetence would have invalidated any solutions based on my provocations or insistences). I had to learn to lose control, in short, which was something which had always appeared to me to be a dangerous condition. It is something which I am still working on in the relationship, and when I am not feeling too down under my own head problems, my central aim is to be a background but available supportive figure in Stephen's life, until he can resolve the uncertainties which somehow characterize his sense of himself in the world. From the bitterness of his attitude toward his father and Laurence, his "real" father, I am inclined to think of the roots of his difficulty lying in formulating a clear, positive self-image in terms of his struggle to both understand and please both fathers and in his subsequent realization that in effect they were manipulating him in his readiness to bring a deep emotional involvement to bear on situations involving his life, a readiness he has (almost in defense of himself) suspended from his current perception of the world.

At the end of the summer, Stephen ran up against some strong inner resistance to returning to school, which had proven so unhelpful in his struggle to achieve a sense of his own competence; while I was too obviously anxious to get to work again, to return to the structured schedule and the directioning of clearly-laid-down expectations. Stephen had fulfilled his obligations and was free to experiment with courses. He took two behavioral science courses, both of which I too enrolled in, and found that he did quite well in them and found them less tiresome than his dryly structured English regime had been. Forced by parental expectations and questioning to indicate a preference for some field, for some career direction, he began to give out the answer that he wanted to make money and that he thought he could best do so in business; advertising seemed particularly appropriate. But it was more of a token preference than a real one, and the decision was not yet ready to be made, as it still is not. In his desire to have some sort of efficacy in his control of his environment, he began to have rather violent fits when he felt particularly incompetent or disoriented; he would strike out at walls or any available hard piece of furniture in a surge of violent frustration, and told me in no uncertain terms to get out or he might hit me too. I usually was able to see this as a generalized violent reaction, not as hostility toward me. But it was difficult to have to leave the house when he seemed most disturbed and all my inclinations were toward comforting and helping him. And, too, I myself was not (and still am not completely) assured in my image of myself and was hanging on the reactions of others toward me as a barometer of my acceptability, so that occasionally these fits would reactivate the old uncertainties about myself and what I had done, leading to my wandering the streets crying for two hours, feeling I had nowhere to go, until I felt it was "safe" to come home again. Stephen always apologized afterwards, and there was no question that it was not a matter of our love for each other, which re-

mained unchanged, but only of each of our problems in orienting ourselves to the internalized and external expectations of us.

Stephen has now decided to see a psychiatrist whom he had
heard lecture and particularly admired. I, having quite effectively
asserted my emancipation from my family with the help of Stephen's
continuous and unselfish support, am now cementing my career ambitions in the direction of clinical psychology, although my love for
creative writing and for art could very possibly preempt these newer
ambitions. What happens to us in the future is largely dependent upon
whether Stephen is able (by hook or by crook) to obtain a deferment
when he graduates, since he is quite certain of his disinclinations to
go on to graduate school. Once that point is decided, we will have to
find a way in which to allow ourselves to grow away from the past
which still influences each of us in its indirect ways, and to find our
own modes for dealing with a social world. Such a development will
have to take place somewhere away from the strain of social expectations and acceleration, in a place where we shall be able to postpone
meeting those external demands until internal organization can be
completed. On the whole I am immensely optimistic: I have already
managed to separate myself emotionally as well as physically from my
mother's turmoil in order to begin to straighten out my own in some
effective way (I was hardly upset at all by a recent telephone conversation with my mother in which she revealed that SOMEHOW she had
discovered that I had had the abortion and had, moreover, provided
my sister with grass and explicit guides to its use when she asked it of
me this year, even though she called me a "murderer" in effect and
was very abusive); my misinterpretations of the attitudes of others
toward me is diminishing noticeably, and moreover I am less concerned now than I used to be about what they think, which appears
to me to be a healthy trend; I haven't seen Dr. Roberts in months, or
had a recurrence of "psychotic" delusions (such as the bleeding broom-
handles I had seen when I was at my worst); and Stephen is very
much aware of his difficulties and their nature, which is the first step
toward dealing with them when he gets a chance. Our avoidance of
parties and visiting is largely functional in allowing us to get holds on
ourselves before we try to deal with the complications of social interaction; I can see only love, promise and mutual trust in the future.
Remembering the trend of things, from my petrified silence being
driven home in the car by my mother when she was drunk, along the
lines of my conviction that I was ugly (which lasted in its most unrealistic forms until only a few months ago), to the fear I felt when
Stephen was considering seeing Lynn with me over our spring vacation just before we were married — all reflecting the undependability
of other people with respect to myself, and my reaction of mistrust —

remembering these things in the light of my present sense of fullness, of solidity, of essential trust, makes me feel very lucky. And if it didn't have such dangerous implications, I would say that my angel was right: I have been looked after. Things are on the way up.

Appendix: Excerpts from a Letter from My Mother

Dawn Dear,

I can't avoid any longer speaking out frankly about the subject of marijuana and its deleterious effects on you or on Stephen, and indirectly on your future family. Your emphatic and negative reactions to discussing it at all leads me to think that you have serious misconceptions about it. If you believe, as you have said, that "one's reactions to its use are a function of one's own personality" and that therefore in the hands of a healthy person its effects are innocuous, then apparently you are unable to relate to it the sequence of events that it has precipitated since you started using it [I might interject here that she had no idea when I started using it, which was in fact two years before; so that how she can date events or characteristics which it "precipitated" is beyond me.] Perhaps you do not know all the facts relating to the subject, nor wish to face the reality of them for a reason unknown even to yourself. . . . [For facts, she sent *The Marijuana Papers* (edited by D. Solomon) in which she underlined all the mentions of possible hazards, and ignored such statements as the editor's statement of purpose: "*The Marijuana Papers*, then, have been compiled with the express purpose of supplying the accurate and authoritative information needed to perform the belated last rites for the marijuana myths. In addition to changing people's minds about marijuana, it is further hoped that this anthology will serve as a basic factual manual for that growing number of concerned, courageous Americans who, in recognition of the plant's many virtues, risk official disapproval by openly arguing and campaigning for its legality."]

I am not sitting in judgment on your present opinion of marijuana use. The conclusions you must come to yourself. . . . I am hopeful that you are not developing a psychic dependency on it or a tolerance for it that my instincts tell me Stephen has, or that you are not prostituting your writing by using it as a crutch.

A sufficient amount of marijuana can produce (p. 403) effects exactly like those of LSD, so I presume that lesser amounts for susceptible persons (like yourself) can have a like reaction.

Can you honestly not relate the following effects — which by your own admittance or my observation you have experienced — to when you have been using pot: anxiety, depression, dizziness, loss of drive, drowsiness, fatigability, fantasies and grandiose ideas, hostility, irritability, negativism, antagonism, suggestibility, impaired judgment, nervousness, ringing in the ears, time distortion, diarrhea, visual illusions, emotionability, seeing faces as grotesque, sexual dysfunction, tremors, black-outs [the interesting thing about this list is that parts of it are alphabetized, and also that I never experienced any of the conditions she mentions in periods when I was smoking and never at all suggested to her that I saw faces as grotesque, had black-outs or ringing in the ears (except from the overdose of aspirin, a physiological response)].

Each one of these effects is mentioned separately in the book: see p. 144, index. How do you weight the pleasures of pot against all these factors? Is it really worth it, Dawn? Surely disorientation from the real world is not what you want; I can't believe that you could ever be, for long, satisfied with a life of escapism and chemically induced pleasures that risk health and success in work and marriage. Moreover, an untenable disability in marriage can occur from long use: sexual impotence (p. 405), and I think Stephen should keep this in mind. . . .

Referring to the classical Freudian interpretation of the Ego as a balance between the Id (the animal self with desires, lust, etc.) and the Superego (the legislative self, or control factor, conscience), it appears that pot feeds the Id, overstimulating all senses and sexual drives while at the same time suppressing the efficiency of the Superego by eliminating conscience, inhibitions, anxiety and the sense of time. In diminishing the Superego factor, drug users are vulnerable to he hazards of the external world and unprotected in danger by nature's warning devices. The prognosis for survival, then, in either a competitive world or in the raw jungle, is not optimum. . . .

Intellectual capacity may not be greatly affected by marijuana use, it is true, except for the user's inability to concentrate and the tendency to daydream and be distracted — in other words, achievement, performance, and judgment are affected even if the skills are not. And what good then is intellectuality without its proper use? Intelligence is a highly overrated commodity when abused or misused, as history confirms. Certainly the drug user's intellectuality can dissipate itself to the point of ineffectuality.

Dear Dawn, I have seen you when you were high and also when recovering from the effects of pot and I cannot tell you how the sight and sound of it saddened me. [This is absolutely untrue; I would never get stoned if I had to confront my mother; she assumes from her visit to me during the summer when she thought that the butts in the ashtrays were roaches, that my truly near-psychotic behavior was caused by smoking and not by the combined anxieties I was acting under; I can only guess that this is her reference; I do not remember such exaggerated scenes however as she describes.] The picture of yourself in August recovering that day from drug use [????] is still in my mind — eyes red-rimmed and shifting [from crying and embarrassment], body tense and swaying as you walked, half-doped, a mute and distant expression on your face and such anxiety and fear looking out at me; and you, disorganized in routine and the room full of butts and dust. And at Cambridge even then you flaunted the visible evidences of it in great hilarity, shrieking with mirth at my concern, flaying your legs and arms in abandon on the bed as though you were indeed a child again, and saying things with such callousness and ridicule it was hard for me not to cry.

This is not the kind of happiness for you, and I somehow think you know it too. [Compare with her previous statement that the conclusions are mine to draw.] I ask you only to consider all sides of this question which will affect your entire life and your relationship to everyone — apart, if you insist, from the legality of it, which your conscience cannot ignore forever. If you and Stephen truly love one another, you will find no need for drugs to stimulate or to give you a sense of well-being or happiness, and you may find that the use of marijuana to establish communion between you is artificial and superficial and not consistent with your true goals in life.

My intent in sending this book and in passing on these opinions and observations is only to bring to your attention the possible insidious and long-range effects. It is an expression of my love and concern for you, and an extension of my trust in you that you and Stephen will seek together a way of life that denies neither the laws of nature nor of God [not only history but God is called up against me], for this is where your happiness lies. . . . Living is a series of infinitely varied decisions bearing on judgment and evaluations, each with a cause and effect. I trust that the decisions you make and the judgments you form will never be drug-distorted or drug-induced.

Be moderate, dear, in your aspirations, and patient with yourself and those who love you. And grant at least my wish that you read this book carefully with serious intent and an open mind.

Lovingly always
(*no signature*)

Always Overcoming Odds

At first, I shared a room with Richard, who was seven years older, and I slept in a low convertible chair. I fought with Richard because he always thought he knew what was right and always assumed when he wanted me to be quiet that I should be quiet.

My brother Barry was four years older than Richard and had his own room and everyone in the family knew that Richard suffered from trying to do everything Barry did, but that was only cosmic justice to me and an amusing family tradition to my parents. It was understood that I would suffer too when I was old enough. I was ready to suffer ahead of time though, and it infuriated me not to be treated like a responsible adult with true ideals. I certainly knew what was right, never did anything wrong without knowing it was wrong. My brothers had a lot of things — little knives, old stamp collections of my grandfather's. Most especially, they had grown up together, only four years apart, and they were funny together and full of each other. They were adults and they did things that proved it to themselves and made them illustrious characters to their parents. I stole from them. I took their best little things when I was alone in the house and hid them in a stash behind the books in the maid's room, but somebody found it and Richard thought it was very funny and later threatened to tell my teacher Miss Martin about my "old stealing days."

I was different from my brothers, I knew that. It was assumed that I was different. They were fair and blue-eyed like my father, but wittier than he was, like my mother. I was like my mother as she always said to people, but I had dark brown eyes and hair and nobody in my family had those. And I was so thin, Richard said I was like Mother and said I was closer to her. I knew he was wrong. I was obviously not closer to her, I fought with her all the time, I was no more dependent than they were and more rebellious. If anything, my mother may have held on to me more as a baby because I was the last, but that was when I was very young and did not know what was being done to me. It was foolish to give Richard more respect when I knew everything that he did, and I would be more practical than he was. And more of an individual.

My parents were right about many things, like being intellectuals and knowing how to stand as a person in the world, but they were always wrong about how they treated each other and how they managed the family. Mom was always wrong for the way she bitched at Dad and got angry at him and slammed the door on him and made him sleep in the other room. Dad never got angry or did anything to hurt Mom; he only tried to do things to please her. But he had the habit of being "able to do only one thing at a time," so that he always drifted away reading something or thinking and fooling with his nose, and he had a hearing loss in one ear so that Mom always had to say things to him three times before he paid any attention and then a few times more before he heard. Mom got furious every time she said something and Dad's hand went up to his ear and he bent forward saying "Eh?" with a big smile to cover up his inattention.

But Dad always loved Mom and did the things she told him and did things for her, and Mom never loved him and only tolerated him or treated him like a child when she was being nice to him and only said how good he was when she was telling me. It was obvious because Dad was always nice to Mom, and Mom always wanted to be unhappy and she persecuted him. I never understood why Dad let her get away with it. He could have told her to shut up and it would have made her happy to find out that Dad was a strong man and could make everyone happy. He knew that my mother was bad to me and told me what to do the same way she was bad to him, but he didn't do anything about it. He could have done it, there was no reason he couldn't because I could do it but not all by myself. He only needed someone to tell him, to make him realize what was happening, and he would stand up for himself at last and deliver me. Barry and Richard knew how bad Mom was but they were not going to tell Dad. I had to tell him, but I couldn't, I couldn't think how to tell him, I was afraid of looking in his fat, loving face and telling him. He might think I was a traitor and hate me for it or he might not be able to do anything when I told him and I couldn't believe this, so I could never tell him. And the years went by the same way with Mom always, and I always wanted my father to know the things I could have said to Mom in anger, but never to Dad.

I always fought with Mom because she told me what to do, and I knew everything that was right for me to do. Either she told me to do things that I already knew to do and annoyed me because she wanted me to feel that she was making me do it, or she told me to do things that weren't right or wrong but just things that she wanted me to do that I didn't want to do. There was no reason to wear galoshes on a day when it wasn't snowing and they were ugly to walk into school with, but if she insisted that I wouldn't leave the house without them, I would have to sneak out of the house and shut the door quietly before she could know I was gone. There was no reason to tell me what to wear except that Mom was a sick woman who needed someone to treat her as if her orders meant nothing to anybody. I knew perfectly well how to dress myself without dying of exposure on the bus.

I went to nursery school for two years in the steeple of a church and climbed there on the jungle jim every day until my mother came to take me home. The jungle jim was next to the window and the kids used the ledge to reach up to the third bar. One day, I lost my footing on the ledge and slipped out of the window halfway with my hands holding onto the bar. The other kids did not think I was in trouble because I was afraid to yell for help and the old women were not watching. They had never said anything about climbing on the ledge but I knew that it was dangerous and wrong and I was afraid that if they saw me half out the window high over the street, they would reprimand the whole class for climbing on the ledge, so I kept quiet and tried to pull myself up while the kids just clambered up next to me as if they were used to seeing me hang there. When I realized that I was too weak to pull myself up, I really got scared and started scrambling with my knees and feet against the stone outer ledge, scuffing up my shoes, which I would have to explain later, and at last I felt the center of my body go over the inside and I fell back into the room. No one had noticed. I told everyone in the family about it later, although I had not meant to, but no one would believe it.

I learned the alphabet when I was three from the back of a newspaper my mother was reading. In the same year, I learned to read with Richard's patient tutoring. Richard was a good teacher and I really loved him when he taught me how to read. But he was a big reader, like Barry, spending hours and hours each day reading *Moby Dick* in the sixth grade. I would never do a lot of reading although I would often become intensely excited by a story or a book that yielded new knowledge immediately. But I would be just as excited by television, a toy that Barry and Richard had missed as children. They lived totally without it while I watched it constantly, because for me TV was a fantastic other to involve in my games. After Barry left for college and Richard moved into his own room, I was left almost completely alone with plenty of warning whenever someone started down the hallway to my room. It was a room with great possibilities for games and one-character fantasies, and I think I was almost never bored because there were so many games to invent and then to follow. I was able to involve the TV in my games in the same way that Dawn involved her sister in her fantasies, but with clearly different results. Only later in my life when I found that the number of possible games had decreased to only a few, did TV begin to smother my imagination. But it was essential to have all this to myself just as it was essential to be alone, to be left alone.

I began school early at a liberal, creative private school. Richard said later that I did not go to public school where Barry and Richard had both gone because Mom now thought that the neighborhood was getting too tough. I had been told that I was too young to get into public school first grade and that only a private school would take me so soon. I was always the youngest in the class and it made me proud because it made me feel that I was overcoming odds and that I was being even better for that. The school stressed the importance of environment and each kindergarten class was assigned to a single teacher who stayed with the class all the way through to the eighth grade. I usually felt confident in this atmosphere and enjoyed myself greatly, staying with a select group of friends at the top of the class, joking secretly in the back of the room, and getting them all in trouble for laughing. I was a disciplinary problem because easy or uninteresting classes always wound up for me in laughter, and I could never control it when I was called on or reprimanded. But I learned almost every-

thing easily and both my parents and teachers were more pleased with my way of taking things than strict about my behavior.

At home, I was more of a problem, especially to my mother's sensibilities to control and proper behavior. She was upset by my laziness and messiness. She couldn't stand to see me waste time with comic books or TV, my two great pleasures. She was all the more anxious to know what I did in secret because she knew that I was trying to keep my life as independent and secret from her as possible. She never stopped me from watching TV because she found that suspending this privilege when I had defied her was the only way to make me recant. We fought and did not speak to each other for weeks at a time. One fantastic afternoon, I discovered the fun of dropping things from my thirteenth story window. On her way home from work, my mother suddenly realized that the parked cars, the entire street was covered with dried hunks of yellow toilet paper like plaster. She was uncontrollably angry and embarrassed that someone would discover whose child had misbehaved.

At age ten, I was forced to leave my friends and school when my father's career included a move from Boston to Baltimore — my father was an influential superintendent of schools and consultant to school systems. He began as the only child of an anti-Zionist storekeeper in Boston but he grew up with the ambition to become a school administrator. He went to an Eastern college and did everything. He played on varsity teams, organized a catering business, edited the yearbook, met my mother and married her at graduation. After graduate school my father's early career took them to a series of towns where my mother was forced to play the school administrator's wife to thousands of dull, stupid parents in crass suburbia. The path led eventually back to Boston, but by this time my mother was sick of the life her husband gave her and in her words, she simply got tired of following him around.

My mother came to college from a different background. She was the oldest of three daughters born in a Jewish ghetto to poor immigrant parents. Her father, a gentle little man, was completely dominated by her strong, hard-working mother who never did a thing in her life that she did not know was right. My mother was brought up to recite poetry for audiences and posed in costumes for pictures while her mother filled her with her vivid memory of the old country and her own childhood. My mother grew up with the qualities of intellectual curiosity and artistic appreciation, but her notions of right and wrong were so completely and rigidly predetermined that she was never able to feel sure of them. Her mother only did what was right and so made it difficult for my mother to say exactly what these things were that she kept secret from her mother. Her main interests at college were drama and acting which quickly made her the belle of a lively social and intellectual set. She was advised by older men to continue her acting and she was asked to go to New York to try for a part in a Broadway play, but her impending marriage put it all out of the question. In later years, she came to feel that she had given up a lot for my father and received little in return. The marriage broke apart many times over my mother's dissatisfaction with my father's basic selfishness, his lack of real concern, and his failure to give her the sort of love she could believe in. She would torture him until she could stand it no more, then she would run away from him and try to commit suicide. She tried several times during their years of marriage and each time, she recovered to return home to confront the same dissatisfaction and loneliness.

When my father found his job with a school system in Baltimore, my mother went along reluctantly. The move meant uprooting herself from all her ties in Boston for the sake of being the administrator's wife again. But the job offered more money and they found an old mansion on the river for rent, so she went along. Baltimore fully measured up to her worst expectations and for me it was a totally new and alien environment.

For sixth grade, I was sent to the small, backward public school where I encountered the stiff virginal principal Miss Parks, who made me stay after school to work on, of all things, my handwriting. Everything about the place surprised me. The kids stood up when called upon and recited their answers like boy scouts. In my first week, Miss Parks called on me with some stupid quiz questions that I couldn't answer, so rather than bend my head down in the few moments of silence that she always allowed for soul-searching, I began to whistle the familiar concentration jingle for the Sixty-four Thousand Dollar Question. Miss Parks's upper plate slipped in surprise and the kids looked shocked. She made me leave the room and later lectured me and sent me home with a note. My parents thought it was very funny and so did I. No one ever whistled in school.

The kids came from lower-middle-class families and seemed to have almost no sympathy for each other. They had never laid eyes on a Jew before and this increased the distance between us. I soon became friends with a group of older boys in the neighborhood, the community's budding juvenile delinquents. I began smoking and running around with the group who went looking for general trouble and who committed generally harmless acts of vandalism. At last, I got in trouble for hitting a passing car with a pellet gun. I was apprehended for my crime and given a series of stern lectures from my parents and the police. After that, I went straight and spent the rest of the year by myself.

My parents sent me to a private prep school starting with seventh grade, but here too I found difficult problems. I think that my first three days of school came as such a shock to me that I couldn't face it again for three months. In any case, the official diagnosis was bronchitis and I had to spend a couple of weeks in the hospital and then a couple of weeks in Florida to shake it out of wherever it was. When I returned to school, I was stranger than ever to my classmates. They too had never seen a Jew. Capitalizing on my family name, Silbiger, they soon invented for me the name of Sillyjew which I then heard everywhere I went for the next two or three years. I had a long string of fights and jokes played on me, and finally I was called in to the office of the headmaster because he had found that my conflict was a disruptive influence in the class. He said that he knew who the people were who were persecuting me and, asking me to tell him if he wasn't absolutely right, he read off a list of names from his gradebook. He did this, he said, to show me that he knew all about it, but he was very sorry to have to say that the situation was very delicate and there was nothing he could do to change it. He gave me some advice that implied that perhaps I would be better off at some other school. My parents were shocked over the situation, but they really didn't know what to do about it either, so I decided that I would rather stay in the school to see what would happen. As the years passed, the violent conflicts gave way to a more peaceful atmosphere of mutual hatred which I came to enjoy. They could have forgiven me anything but being unathletic, so they simply gave up on me.

My parents' arguments over "geography" came to a head during the summer when I was fifteen. It was arranged that I should spend the summer in New Mexico, working on an Indian reservation with a youth service organization, the farthest possible point from the scene of the conflict. The experience, starting with a forty-hour bus trip across the country, was entirely new to me. The crowding of forty Jewish adolescents into a bus immediately produced an atmosphere of freedom that was never intended by the troubled adults left waving in the Bus Terminal. A boy and girl in the front seat, who had never seen each other an hour before, began to make out violently with each other and carried on vigorously until she suddenly got up angrily at the rest stop and announced to the group that she was simply not that sort of girl. But things in the back of the bus were looking better.

The only other person in the group from Baltimore was the daughter of a school principal whom my father knew. Lynn was a kind, red-haired, slightly heavy girl, two years older than myself, with a healthy, open, warm-hearted outlook that easily contracted friendships. Our long hours of talking on the bus and afterwards quickly established common lines of humor and sympathy and, astonishingly, there seemed to be no topic on which we disagreed. After that, it took me about a week to realize that I was in love and that Lynn was the most important person in my world. She had the qualities of kindness and openness that I needed to allow me to pursue my sexual desires despite my embarrassment.

These rewarding explorations, however, soon suffered the intrusion of other problems. A letter from my brother announced that my parents were separating with the eventual object of a divorce. It was the old argument over "geography." At the end of the summer, my father would simply stay in Baltimore without my mother, who was already apartment-hunting in Boston. I would have, I was informed, my choice of residence and school or, more simply, my choice of parent. The letter also implied that my parents' decision had been put off some time due to my tender years and that now they felt that I would be able to handle my responsibility maturely. I remember receiving and reading the letter in the dining room where I sat eating with Lynn. I finished it, handed it over to her, and walked out of the dining room and away into an empty field crying. I felt nothing definable and I remember thinking that it must be for the best since, as far back as I can remember, I had wanted my parents to break up. I only felt clutched inside as if a string had been pulled. Lynn followed soon after to comfort me and I remember lying with her in the field thinking about my brother's apologetic admonition to love and support both my parents no matter how difficult it seemed. From that point on and for the next three years, Lynn became the only person who understood what I felt and who accepted it without the distortion of self-interest.

My decision to remain in Baltimore with my father was a simple one. Life with my mother meant constriction, conflict, and head-bending. With my father, I was promised freedom, certainly seclusion, and perhaps even some realization of my childhood dream of my father free from his wife. But when I arrived home, feeling now much older than when I left, I found that my mother had relied heavily in making her decision on my stated preference for Boston. By my decision, it seems, I made a clean break between my parents impossible. As she later phrased it, my mother needed moral support for her stand. For the next year in Baltimore then, my father and I received intermittent visits of no expressed purpose or duration from my mother. During this year, my junior year of high school, my relationship with Lynn continued in intensity if not consistency. Lynn was troubled by her parents' opposition to me and my family on "moral grounds," and she found it difficult to remain in my isolated world at the cost of losing contact with her friends and the approval of her parents.

Although we now shared an apartment, I saw little of my father at this time. He visited out-of-town school systems two and three times a week now, and many weeks passed with no more than a few words between us. But the words were friendly, if few. At least, no one wasted my time with instructions or tried to keep me from making my own life. At the age of sixteen, no matter what anguish I found in Lynn's inconsistencies or in loneliness, I enjoyed myself when I was by myself. I indulged in daydreams and fantasies constantly. I managed to get out of my hated gym class (it was the headmaster's idea) for the project of writing "a novel" which was the story of my relationship with Lynn and morbid fantasy. I had now developed a shell of isolation, a buffer of special treatment that separated me from my classmates who allowed me a certain amount of respect for my "secret life." The news of my parents' impending divorce became a scandal which gave a veneer of romance to my habitual strangeness at school. My tormentors learned at least to stay away from me and some of them even gave out the myth among the new Jewish boys in the school that I had been the first Jew to get in. I was certainly not the first; many had slipped through unidentified and unnoticed. Given the chance to be an oddball without the danger of actual physical attack, I became as annoying as possible to my waspish classmates. I wrote integration editorials for the paper, gave speeches in chapel, and joined relatively radical organizations such as student CORE. Also at this time, I gained a driver's license and the use of my mother's car, which she had left behind, and with these the freedom to go out with other girls when Lynn wouldn't see me and the chance to get into accidents. Cars had always been favorite objects of my childhood fantasy, and I remember trying to make off in cars when I was a little boy, either by releasing the emergency brake and rolling, pulling the starter in gear, or stealing the keys, depending on my age and understanding at the time. Nothing frees my mind like fast driving, and at first I got into a few accidents and ran a few radar traps. It was also in this year that I began drinking for entertainment when I was alone in the apartment. My parents had always allowed me moderate, and often immoderate, exposure to liquor, but now I frequently drank hard liquor, which I disliked, to get stoned and to enjoy the sensation.

As part of my parents' peculiar arrangement (we were as yet a family in separation), I was given the opportunity to travel between Baltimore and Boston. I went to see my mother during every vacation, occasionally over weekends, at first with my father, later alone. As my father's life in Baltimore began to develop, I took on the martyrish view that my dutiful, excruciating visits to my mother served to keep both my parents above water as they sailed off in opposite directions. In these visits to Boston, I began to see more and more of a man who held a certain amount of influence in my parents' conflicts. L had been my mother's teacher at college and, over the years, he and his style of

life came to represent everything desirable to my mother and everything that she had missed in marrying my father. L started out as a
Catholic, turned atheist as a boy, and became an architect before he
decided on teaching. He was, then, a man of culture with a firm,
masculine grasp on his environment. He speaks foul language with the
best stage-English accent and drawing room manner. He strives for
the appellation of Renaissance Man, which is to say, he is concerned
with nothing so much as presenting the image of infallibility to the
world. In his interactions with individuals, his biting aloofness an-
nounces that he is not one with whom to take liberties although he
rarely extends the same measure of respect to anyone else. Through
the stock market and the sales of his books, he takes in large amounts
of money which he uses only to augment his comfort and vanity.

About two or three years after I was born, L moved his domi-
cile to our building, bringing with him his new wife K, a kind offbeat
Scottish lady, a commercial artist, who had never learned to cook or
buy clothes. From what I have been able to gather, L was involved in
a previous marriage and divorce to some sort of artist, while my
mother carried on in her precarious relationship with my father just
after finishing a year of confinement in a mental hospital. These events,
and more that I do not know, all took place about a year before my
birth. Later, at the time of the divorce, my father revealed to me his
intense jealousy of L, his arrogance, and his long-standing "intimacy"
with my mother. He declined to say exactly what he meant by "intimacy," but went on to say that in that year before my birth, my
mother turned away from him to L with whom she took daily "long
walks." He said that he had only survived the ten years of close association with L by carrying on a parallel closeness of spirit with L's
wife K. His statement astonished me, and not only for its obvious implication about my genealogy. When L and K moved into our family's
apartment building, they moved into both my parents' lives and
changed them profoundly. They visited nightly, went out together
frequently, played games together, developed "family" traditions, took
their vacations together, broke all the limits of social reserve. Ten years
later, my father's story of his jealousy and the tension of their relations
added a new dimension of hopelessness. My father lived those years
of interaction and activity only as an adolescent torture. And on the
other side of the coffee table, L played his role smoothly against my
father, stealing the lines, the self-respect, and his wife's affections.

My father made his revelation in vague terms, signifying that
he would not be pinned down, even if someone had been alert enough
to ask. His utterances are only as vague as his thoughts. But this is
evidence only important to me. There is much more (not to mention
the problem of family resemblance) which only leads to the same

conclusions. At any rate, it is only really important because L was presented to me throughout my childhood as an important man and was pushed upon me by my mother after the divorce as one who "loves" me, one whom I could not "simply discard." In my last real fight with my mother during Christmas vacation of my freshman year of college, she tried desperately to keep me from living on the other side of town with Lynn by saying that I would never get any more presents from L because L did not approve. An hour later, she denied that she had said such a thing. He emasculated my image of my father, just as he emasculated my mother's image of him, and, of course, my father himself, laughing too heartily over his sherry on the other side of the coffee table. L held out gifts, gruff advice, endless scrutiny and evaluation, and a consciously fabricated role-model for my benefit while my father, through his own stupidity, wasted the faith I had had in him. My mother sat on the couch watching, or buzzed around in the kitchen, managing my exposure to the role she had chosen for me. L would sit me down at, say, the age of seventeen, look critically into my face and at my pimples, seeing me flinch, pulling back and saying, "Aha. I thought so," and asking me if I shaved with an electric razor. He would then proceed to the merits of the electric razor that he was about to bestow on me (someone had given it to him and he had only used it a few times) and it would clear up my "skin problems," followed by innuendoes that I would never use it, that I was generally a stubborn, foolish upstart, and that this act was a stroke of benevolence that I could hardly deny I needed. Every attitude, opinion, or unconscious mannerism at table was subjected to the same scrutiny. To be right was to be clever; to be wrong was to be simply "schmalz." L's selfish interest in the character of my future soon displaced my father's disinterest, and as he seemed to sense the increasing effect of his judgment on me, L stepped up his "good-natured" attacks on my sensitivity. This was perhaps, as my mother always tried to convince me, only his way of showing affection and concern for me. But he never gave me anything of himself, never sacrificed any bit of his comfort or pride to spare me discomfort or degradation. He admitted openly that he had never been interested in my father's friendship and hinted that my mother had denied her husband over a period of years that spanned my birth date.

Eventually my father announced to me that he was not made to live alone (a fact that I had already discerned from the hours he kept), and suddenly it seemed that my dream for him had come true. I was introduced to the lady in question, a young divorcee, mother of three, and former nightclub singer. ("She was always interested in music," her parents said.) For a few months, thanks to the rosiness of my dream, we all got along beautifully in a new atmosphere of honesty and freedom. My mother, of course, was shocked and shaken; she felt betrayed, tricked, and morally outraged. I was required to expend my best efforts in comforting her and assuring her of my support and sympathy. But my sympathies were with my father in his new situation, and when he approached me on the subject of the divorce deal he had made, I was all sacrifice and martyrdom. My mother refused to grant the divorce until assured that I would not live in the same house with my father.

The question of my sacrifice, put to me by my father in terms of adult responsibility, was precluded before I opened my adolescent mouth. It was clear that my father had sacrificed my comfort for his own, but after years of waiting for his liberation, I could hardly deny him this. The infuriating part was that he had weighed all the motives and effects of the matter beforehand, and after making sure the deck was stacked, he played out his hand with a perfect poker-face. Early that winter, I served as best man for the small private wedding ceremony and afterwards took up residence with one of my teachers and his family, twenty-five miles removed from the new house. My father gave me a key and the privilege of visiting on weekends, which I used at first until I bumped into a few obstacles in the vague new atmosphere of freedom. F, the new lady of the house, had some definite ideas about spending money, and my father, saddled with alimony and deeper in debt than ever before, fell instant prey to every ugly extravagance that his new wife could dream up. She complained constantly of the great strains on my father's income, as if my mother still owned a bigger piece of the pie than she did. In a sense, she had a right to be dissatisfied. My father was a boob with money. Despite his large income, he always spent more than he made and never saved a cent for investment or return. Taking for granted the expenses of his wife's hospital bills and the education of his children, money seemed to leak through his fingers because he was helpless, out of touch with his surroundings like an hysterical only child, unable to say no to the women who dominated him. The result of F's sexuality and greed and my father's weakness was a new definition of limits in the house which my father proved helpless even to recognize. At first, F raised objection to my sitting in the living room on her new plastic slipcovers, then she did not like my smoking in the house, and finally, after a string of encounters and mutual avowals of dislike, I found the lock on the front door changed.

In all this, I have no doubt that I made myself as objectionable to the newlyweds as they were to me. With my graduation from high school, I began to act with much more concern for my own wants. My small group of social outcasts in the senior class celebrated their survival with a long silly party which developed into my first and last binge. I suddenly had a lot to celebrate; I was on my way to an outstanding university, I had won all the awards I could get close to, I made good publicity for my parents in the paper, I managed to bring them together without incident for the graduation ceremony, but best of all, I broke the long silence between me and Lynn, now at Swarthmore, by an invitation to the graduation. From this day on, the relationship became more frankly intimate, though of course it was still a secret from everyone else. I drove to Boston to take a summer job with a distant relative, but within two weeks I ran into my first stroke of bad luck, a kidney and liver infection, probably the result of all my celebrating. On the way to the hospital, I was handed a special delivery letter from Lynn, telling me what I already feared, that she was pregnant.

Three Years Later

I have gone to a party with Dick, but I am extremely down in the corner getting drunk and angry. I have met on the stairs with Anna, the hostess, who says to come see her over the weekend because she is going to be sick, but I beg off saying that I am going to be sick too. Dawn is her roommate and she too looks sick. She dances around the room modishly in Anna's absence, trying to make the party swing for the beer-drinkers. She is working her way across the room, performing a use for each one, jiggling now in front of me, now sitting silently near me, waiting — for a break in the clouds. But I am not in the mood for giving breaks, because I am feeling sick too.

She, like her roommate, inspires scorn in men. Clearly, she has slept with a lot of men, and equally clearly, they have all used her without her knowing it. This is all I have gathered from seeing her dance around the room. But a few days later, Dick and I go looking to get turned on and we hear that Dawn knows where to get a pound. She is very sorry but she can't turn us on because in the next room she's turning on some other guy, and I see that she really is sorry, and reaching for her little bottle of grass, she pours out a big nickle and lays it on us. We are all immensely grateful to each other and I make a date with her to go see her connection in Boston. It is very good grass and lasts for two days and Dick speculates that I am the more likely one to get to sleep with her.

Dawn's friend in Boston did not show up, so we turn around and drive back toward Cambridge. I take the opportunity to invite her to my apartment for a smoke. She replies that it is Yom Kippur, that she has been fasting all day, that it would hardly seem consistent. I stare at her in a moment of dread. Can she be a Jew? I try to construct the new, elusive face in my mind but nothing comes yet. I put the question aside and tell her that the Hasidim were always stoned. She accepts.

Later at Dick's, sitting and playing cards with the group, I can feel the change that has started. I am not in love because I cannot isolate it yet, but I am certainly going to be in love. Dawn is a puzzle of secrets and the first secret is how beautiful she can be. As a sex-object, she is just another sex-object, and no one thinks any more about her. But as a person, Dawn is exciting, suddenly beautiful in her sexuality. She is frank and open in what she wants and what she will give, even before she has said it, and her smiling, which she has not shown before, makes me feel like giving myself to her. I have expected to find only a dull sickness, but Dawn gives away her secret when I give away mine. The wants that struggled for a while beneath the surface suddenly break out between us in a big, wise smile. She intuitively knows about giving and taking, feels the giving that will take place easily. I am now a newer person; I feel myself glowing to the people around the dark room. I have turned a corner and do not quite know where I am. But it is so easy, I will wake up the next morning and find out.

Our first weeks together were spent in finding out who we were to each other. We already felt so many things happening between us that it seemed strange to know so little. I woke up in Dawn's room and suddenly I wanted to know everything about her. She said she would answer any three questions I asked, but that was no help because I didn't know where to begin. I asked her how a blonde with a waspish name could come to be fasting on Yom Kippur. She told me that she was a convert, or a would-be convert, because she felt that Judaism was her religion. I could not help feeling a bit cynical, but really I did not know what to think about this girl. She said she was a poet. With all the people in Cambridge who call themselves poets, I took it that she was only claiming solidarity with the group, and so I said that I was a poet too. "No, no," she said, "I'm really a poet, a good poet." She showed me a few things out of drawers full of writing, and she was a real honest to goodness poet. I was amazed.

I found out hundreds of things about her. She was born in Texas and brought up in rural and suburban Georgia, the middle child and older daughter of a metallurgist.

Mrs. M. met Dr. M. at college and soon dropped out of school to marry him. The early years of marriage were very difficult and Mrs. M. learned to scrimp on everything so that Dr. M. could complete his schooling. Mrs. M.'s renegade sister Irma tells the story of a visit to her sister's home during these years and the fight that ensued between them over a tea bag. When Irma threw the bag away after making her cup of tea, Mrs. M. exploded with anger, calling her wasteful and inconsiderate because she always made several cups out of the same tea bag. Dawn remembers only fighting or silence between her parents and especially her father's fits of temper in trying to deal with his wife. Only the force of inertia now keeps the marriage together.

Dawn thought of herself as having been an ugly child with few friends and no one who understood her feelings except her younger sister. With her younger sister as her audience and confidant, Dawn created elaborate scenes of fantasy and escape. Fantasy made up an important part of Dawn's existence because here she was able to build on the hopes that seemed so futile in real life. She became shy when people looked at her and afraid to make contact with anyone at school except among her teachers, who valued and rewarded her openly. She took on an attitude of superiority to her classmates in her isolation from them. Dawn developed the identity of being a special person, singled out by the gift of talent for a blessed future. She had seen, she said, the vision of an angel who had told her this. As Dawn grew out of childhood, the dreamworld continued to be her special sphere where her talents for poetry, painting, sculpture and music all received energy. She did very well in her schoolwork in general, but her competence in artistic fields won the awards and recognition that was really important to her. Dawn's achievements in this early part of her life still seem amazing to me. At the age of fifteen, a year before I began my abortive attempt at a novel, Dawn was pouring out her talent and insight in so many different shapes that her productivity seemed endless. When we visited her family over Christmas, I found the works of these teen-age years all over the house. A terra cotta figure of a praying peasant woman displayed a startling unity of conception. The kneeling figure swept up in an arc from the knees to the upturned face, contrasting without a trace of sentimentality the body of coarseness with its striving for grace. She was at once a huge, worn pack-animal and an inspired priestess. Behind, her massive calves and feet seemed the most expressive part of the piece, fallen against each other in stubby repose, forgotten in this moment despite the heavy duty of their service. I had never seen anything like it, the technique suited so well to the subject, it seemed a perfect idea, the product of birth rather than effort. Dawn did this and much more at fifteen. The walls were covered with drawings and paintings, simply executed faces of sad-eyed girls surrounded by other faces or figures crumpled in on themselves in different perspectives. She never drew a man. Dawn had a freshness of outlook, an unhesitating attack on her material which never paused to think how someone else might do it. She accomplished her works in great confidence and pride in her ability which allowed maximum concentration and freedom. When I first met her, Dawn

wrote her poetry in the same way. She could simply sit down and produce her highly structured poems one after another until someone
broke in from the outside and interrupted her concentration.

Also around the age of fifteen, Dawn began to pick up sexual
experience. She still thought of herself as unattractive and had few
social contacts with boys. She found them, for the most part, unattractive also and almost invariably stupid. She first had intercourse with a
boy whom she described only as an ugly football player. The experience was the result of a simple arrangement between them rather than
any sort of romance with intermediate stages. Dawn found it unpleasant, but soon she had procured a supply of pills and went searching for more experience. This is difficult to understand except in the
light of Sullivan's statement that loneliness is more terrible than
anxiety. In the social world of high school that felt so alien to Dawn,
this idea would have been expressed only as the proverbial "Ugly girls
go down." In any case, when Dawn graduated from high school at the
precocious age of sixteen with all the awards and honors that could be
given her, the different realms of her life and personality were dissociated as widely and as forcefully as possible. On the conscious level,
Dawn earned her way through the control of her energies. She was
tense and alert to her tasks. She bit her nails and clenched her fingers
together, whether in concentration or simple anxiety. She worked on
her assignments, both in school and home surroundings, until they
were neat and clean. Like her father, she could not live with filth or
disorder. Like her mother, she had little sense of "practicality" and,
unlike her, no sense of waste. Dawn's creative productions were the
results of applying controlled effort to the world of fantasy she had
known since childhood. Her teachers often showered her with love
for her talents, but her mother pushed the values of accomplishment
and industry ahead of the value of Dawn as a person. When the color
of adolescent loneliness and sexuality began to show itself in Dawn's
poetry, Mrs. M.'s appreciation dipped slightly. She wondered if this
new kind of stuff wasn't just wandering away from the good things
that Dawn had done before; she asked if Dawn didn't feel that she
was getting lost. And behind these questions always lay Mrs. M.'s
judgments against getting lost and against people who got lost. During
our Christmas visit to Atlanta last year, Dawn discovered in her mother's room a collection of all the poems she had sent home for her.
Mrs. M. had annotated and labelled it with marginalia such as "Summer eroticism," and so forth. By the summer of her graduation, when
she went off to Europe and further points in the worlds of competence
and sex, Dawn had learned the freedom of living in secrets along with
the style of being watched.

Dawn's freshman year at college passed with very little in the way of human contact. She was not likely to be popular among the freshman boys or happy with her familiarly well-bred, upper-middle-class roommate. The practice of dating could never pretend to supply a social life, but even intercourse yielded nothing more than a few hours with someone who meant nothing. In sophomore year, Dawn got away from her roommate into a small single room which gave her the freedom of not being watched with almost total isolation. She later described it to me as her torture chamber. It was in this room that Dawn's depression developed into masochism. She began to take active steps against loneliness and moved toward the local hippie scene, walking through the streets as blatantly as possible, picking up as many men as she could get. It seems strange that we didn't run into each other. Although Dawn was never able to believe that she was attractive, she met with a high degree of success in the streets. She succeeded in making dozens of short-term acquaintances with men and boys of almost any description. She found that once out on the street, a man always led to a party where she could meet a boy from school who would turn out to have three or four roommates and one might have a younger brother in the freshman class and there would be no reason to stop. A man can only use up women at a certain rate, but a woman who thinks she is worthless and who, for that reason, doesn't mind being used, she can devour men without limit. I remember Dawn telling me in the first week I knew her that she had gotten pills when she was sixteen after sleeping with the ugly football player. I asked her why she wanted to get pills when she was sixteen because it then seemed strange to me that she should go as far out of her way to do something she didn't like. She replied simply that she could not stand contraceptive devices. The increase in Dawn's sexual activity was parallelled by the growth of masochistic tendencies, and when they started to work in her, once again, there seemed no reason to stop. In sophomore year, Dawn met and fell in love with Warren, a small, handsome boy whom I had known from the freshman dorm. Dawn enjoyed herself with Warren, who was not only handsome and a nice person to be seen walking with but who always had an unassumed air of understanding that made him interesting. The relationship was successful enough so that Dawn went home with Warren for part of Christmas vacation and even took him to her house for a few days afterwards. Mrs. M. took a dislike to Dawn's boyfriend because she suspected that they were sleeping together. After he went back to Cambridge, leaving Dawn with her family, Mrs. M. attacked Dawn's taste in boys, accusing Warren of sleeping too much and paying too little attention to his hosts. Mrs. M. evidently said a lot of other things because she had become greatly worked up over Dawn's immorality, and finally when Dawn felt she could stand it no more, her mother yelled at her that she could never love such a bad person. Dawn left the house very shaken up and flew back to Cambridge to find Warren. She went straight to his room and found him there, but unfortunately Warren had picked this night to tell Dawn something he had been thinking about for a little while. He said he was confused and couldn't decide whether or not he felt anything for her. He wanted to stop seeing her at least until he could decide. That evening, Dawn went back to her room and spent the rest of the night swallowing large quantities of aspirin. She was taken to the infirmary to have her stomach pumped, and she stayed there for a few weeks until it was thought safe for her to return to school. But the infirmary could not change what had happened, and soon Dawn took up her life on the streets.

Dawn's doctor, recognizing her great capacity for productivity, emphasized the importance of keeping busy. He introduced her to a publisher who took an interest in her poetry. Dawn wrote incessantly this year and especially during her stay in the hospital. In addition, she took on a series of part-time jobs to keep her mind off herself and to earn the money that she spent so easily. She soon found that she could handle several of these jobs at once and, since it always relieved her depression to buy clothes, she came to depend on the money they brought in. But no matter how much she spent and worked, she could do little to relieve the effects of loneliness. She found nobody who was willing for anything but sex, and it seemed that the more people she saw, the further she got away from them. During the summer, she worked at a number of jobs, including a college guest-editorship at a tasteless fashion magazine, but none of the people she met worked any sort of change in her. She now presented to the world the image of a "sicky" and she soon found that no female image could be more attractive to men.

The traffic converged on Washington in the morning and by three o'clock the pile-up of hippies, soldiers, and police had pushed each other into senselessness on the steps of the Pentagon. We were stopped on the line of scrimmage against the pointed muzzles and fresh faces, and for a sickening moment, we saw that only another stupid order was lacking to kill us all. Silence dropped; the soldiers were scared. The crowd broke back and around and rushed in closer to the building to take over the steps. Small sorties of tightly packed soldiers cleared the way and backed us against a wall. The crowd struck back and separated a few soldiers from the company; helmets and guns were snatched off and pitched into the air, the kid in uniform could not get away. Dawn screamed at them to stop and hid her face and cried against my shoulder, and soon we were threading through the soldiers and police and at last back across the long bridge with the quiet crowds of people who had given up.

When we finally arrived at Dawn's large suburban house near Atlanta, I was too knocked out to be social and I was quickly put away in a downstairs bedroom. I woke up as if after a long drunk and Dawn was telling me that her mother was upstairs with company and I should be prepared, that she was very drunk. Dawn was upset and afraid that any moment her mother would come downstairs. She was both afraid of her mother finding us together and ashamed that I would see she was drunk. Before I could get up, she came in and sat down on the sheets, started talking with warmth and hospitality done up on top of a tense nervousness, formal and stiff, a busy, moral maliciousness full of insinuations. She was near fifty with a face which, according to Dawn, had only recently collapsed into wrinkles. Her eyes were pale and frightened, but they were either closed or looking away as she spoke to me now. Her presence made Dawn extremely nervous and had the same effect on me. Mrs. McLaren put me on my guard and demanded my attention every moment she was in the room.

Upstairs, Mrs. McLaren interrogated me at length in front of Dawn and her dinner guests. She ranged in broad generalities over all the things that I was supposed to represent; youth, hip, sex, sports cars, activism and, at greatest length, integrity. She asked me what I thought it was; I told her. Her nose and chin were turned up and her eyes were closed, as if she could see horrible things about me in her head. She asked me what I really thought it was; I told her again. She asked me if I thought I had integrity; I said I had always thought so up till now. She asked me again as if she really wanted to know if I had slept with her daughter. She was taunting now and although I wanted to throw a punch at her, I told her as discreetly as possible that I was sick of being questioned. Mrs. McLaren's friends took the hint and intervened, trying to joke her out of it, but she was adamant in asking me her question, as closely as she could put it into words. I used my pretense of anger to get us out of the house as quickly as possible, and we were soon heading north again in the drafty but private old car.

Dawn was intensely apologetic about her mother as she was about all things on her side that she felt put a strain on our relationship. She thought that perhaps after meeting her mother, I might want to retract my proposal. It was less than a month later that I met Dawn's father, a friendless, fatherly sort of man whose wife had raised his children to believe that he was inferior, dull, and mistrustful of people. He had been sent up to Boston on the strength of his wife's innuendoes to check on us in our new pre-marital apartment. He spent two days in town without calling us and when he finally invited us to his hotel for dinner, we found him stoned out of his mind. He seemed to be a kind, simple man with little to say or do outside his job. He lived at the opposite end of the house from his wife, convinced after many years that she conspired to make herself unhappy; he had given up on her and on everybody. But on his vulnerable side, he was still open to the terrors brought on by shockline words like "dope" and "draft-dodger" which Mrs. McLaren planted carefully in his mind while suggesting that he drive up and check on us. Dawn told stories of his extreme neatness and said that the sight of her eating from my plate would have sickened him because it was unsanitary. At the threshold of our house, he refused to come in because he had caught sight of both our names on the mailbox and it had thrown him.

The month of November was one of doubt and worry for Dawn. We were still living together in my small room, and with cramming for hour exams night after night, the carefree atmosphere quickly became depressing. Dawn's mother often resorted to the long-distance telephone, seemingly for the purpose of throwing her daughter into fits. Once, she even demanded that Dawn pay for a phone call from home, the third of the evening, because, after all, it was Dawn's own fault that her mother had to badger her. At the point of greatest illogicality, Mrs. McLaren firmly believed that she was the most reasonable person in the world. She would have denied ever telling Dawn that she could not love her, and it would have been useless to confront her with it. She seemed to have no continuity of consciousness in what she said or any idea of what she was doing to Dawn. Her life was a series of aphorisms, undeniable maxims about health, wealth, and morality, from which she could move no higher or deeper. Caught in the double-bind of half believing everything her mother accused her of, Dawn found it difficult to share my optimism about the future. She said she had always thought of marriage in terms of finding or being found by a rich man whose money would free her to go after the men she really wanted to be with. She was just beginning to see the possibility of a marriage with love, but she did not think that she was fit for such an existence and, although she had been attracted to no one else since meeting me, she as yet felt no reason to believe that she could be "faithful" to one man for any length of time. Nor did she believe that I would remain faithful — she simply could not see why I would.

My part in all this was to play the image of strength, and I take this point in the narrative to officially slap myself on the back. Getting married was my idea, and it took a lot of fast argument to make it sound even halfway convincing to Dawn. I suddenly found myself saying that marriage is a positive, constructive social value, but that was about as close as I was able to put it. What I meant to say was that we needed each other, not just to use up and throw away, but to take care of each other. It was implicit in our relationship from the beginning, from the time I bailed Dawn out of her debts, from the moment that I met her mother, that I was supposed to take care of her. I had no questions to ask myself about marriage or what I was doing, because for once everything felt perfectly right and fitting. The role, the sacrifices made me happy, and in twenty years I will probably still see getting married as the most constant, single-minded effort I have been able to put forth.

Our decision to move into our own apartment in December brought more troubles. Dawn became the victim not only of her parents' criticisms but also those of her roommate, my old acquaintance, who felt threatened by the suddenness of Dawn's new romance. Dawn was, and is still to a lesser extent, a perfect target for anyone's anger or vengefulness, because she could never escape feeling guilty when someone blamed her for something. She has the habit of apologizing for herself in normal discourse, either where no apology is called for or where no accusation of fault seems appropriate. As a result, I think, she carries her vulnerability and self-deprecation written all over her face. When people become angry with me, I am more likely to yell back or throw a punch, even though I may get beaten up for my efforts. Most people sense this when they see me, and after hesitating for a moment, reserve their anger for someone else. Dawn, however, is easy prey for secretaries, telephone operators, men on the street, anyone who is looking for the opportunity to get himself off on another person. At this time then, Dawn was more or less constantly upset by her interactions with other people, while I reached for a degree of self-assurance that now seems to me amazing. We were never out of each other's sight for more than an hour at a time.

Dawn's parents worried about their daughter for more reasons than just the new apartment. Dawn had decided to take a leave of absence from school, partly because she was far behind in work and felt little motivation and partly because she felt she had more important things to do. Both a publishing company and magazines expressed interest in her writing, and schoolwork became dross by comparison. Dawn thought a leave of absence to do a few months of writing was a brilliant idea and I thought so too. It was a simple matter of interest and disinterest. But Dawn's doctor did not agree, although in the face of her enthusiasm he consented to writing the necessary letter. Dawn's parents, however, were convinced that she had suddenly become corrupted and had lost sight of her goals. They were not disposed to accept possible success in writing as a substitute for grade-card performance. They were all for bringing Dawn home for the duration of the absence and shaking her upside down to see what was wrong with her. I was more or less helpless to keep their hands off her, and at this point, Dawn's doctor stepped in with a strong recommendation to Mrs. McLaren not to keep her daughter at home for more than a brief visit. To Dawn, he merely said I told you so. Dawn was forced to fly home alone for a week to be subjected to the sort of ceaseless maternal torture which no longer seems even imaginable. Dawn was made to feel worthless and ungrateful, spiteful of the love she had been given. There was no way for her to get through to her mother, to make her understand how she was torturing her. She could only keep quiet and cry during the tirade, keep quiet and get her head bent out of shape. When Dawn finally got back to Cambridge, she was full of nightmares and violence.

Our new apartment was wonderful for us. It gave us all the freedom of privacy we had dreamed of, but the place was a mess for a long time. Dawn's old place had been neat and organized, but my place was disorganized and filthy. Dawn worked on things in the apartment until they were neat, colorful, and attractive while I aimed mostly for subdued browns and blacks and kicked my papers into the closet. We talked often about the potential problems that Dawn's efficiency and ease of accomplishment would make for my eternal underachievement. She was afraid that my resentment against my talented older brothers and the rest of my family would soon be directed at her. I tried to reassure her and show her how little it all meant to me, but the real reason I was not concerned was that I was sure of Dawn's continuing troubles and of my own temporary superiority in dealing with them. Dawn's need for me to comfort her when she was upset, to keep her from swallowing pills, or simply to love her was enough to give me the upper hand in all my own problems, at least the ones that concerned me.

Dawn's nightmares were leading up to a crisis, an unavoidable collision of worlds in Dawn's mind. She was ashamed of losing control and afraid that her sickness would drive me away to someone else. She felt guiltiest at the moment of greatest outside persecution and she fed herself on feelings of self-recrimination and worthlessness. Each time the depression started, it became harder and harder to stop. Dawn was entirely cheerful and carefree when things were going well, but when the depression fell, it took hours and hours to stop the crying. Unlike me, when Dawn is hurt, she closes her eyes and goes off into her dreamworld where endless self-torture is possible. In this world, depression led to masochism in a matter of minutes, and my task of comforting and consoling became far more crucial for both of us than simple role-playing. If left alone in a state of depression, Dawn would try to cut or burn herself and she often succeeded. She obtained thorazine and nembutol from her doctor, but it soon became more of a problem to keep them hidden from her to make sure that she took only small doses. The crisis was building to a revelation, a secret that she hinted would destroy our relationship and drive me away. I told her whatever it was it would make no difference, and after a long while, she slowly began to spell it out with her eyes shut tight, saying that it was a secret that she had never told anyone. In a word, she was frigid, but the word disgusted her and it seemed to me impossible. I could feel my mind gaping to take it all in, but I had promised that I would not be surprised. Because when you turn a corner, there is never an actual moment of surprise, only recognition, refocusing. Dawn had never had orgasm with a man. At first, I could not understand how in over two solid months of living and thinking Dawn I had failed to find it out. The sex between us was so good, so warm in taking and giving, that I might have gone on for years without finding it out. Only now, I see what a secret it was, how important for Dawn to hide, how self-centered of me not to see. And, of course, it turned the tables completely around; Dawn had been secretly allowing me to live my life of happy sexuality at her expense. She had fooled all those men with her sexuality so that she could get close to them, and then go far, far away into that autistic world where poetry, visions, and masochism all had free course.

Dawn lay on the bed crying with her arm pressing against her eyes. She told about her masturbation, how her attempt to commit suicide had been part of a masturbation fantasy. She said that the voice of an old woman directed her in elaborate scenes of masochism which always ended in orgasm. The old woman could take possession whenever she wanted, she said, and she gave rewards, like poetry prizes, when she obeyed well. I could not stop to question any of this; I knew very well that Dawn was not in control and I had seen and understood that she was dangerous to herself. The old woman was a devious and clever personality, blown up with energy and power. Dawn's description of her brought to mind the eyeless, taunting image of her mother from the first night I had seen her. It was this woman who took over and enjoyed herself with men and who filled in the lonely spaces with fantasy. And now, Dawn told me, the old woman felt dissatisfied with her because she was spending too much time with me. She wanted her to go out and find other men on the street, and she vowed, Dawn said, that if she did not belong to her, she would not belong to anyone. She would kill me, she said, or failing that she would kill Dawn or do anything to separate us. I was in no position to think of the reality of Dawn's vision; the old woman was real or the personification of something real and equally dangerous. Dawn was telling me that she was about to be taken over, that she was about to have a fit of suicide or murder, that I must stop her, even beat the old woman out of her to keep her from getting her way. It was two in the morning, impossible to reach a doctor or to make him understand. Dawn guessed what I was thinking and begged me not to let her be taken to a hospital where they would think she was insane and lock her up. I promised. She was begging to stay alive with me.

When it started, Dawn said she could feel the old woman coming over her like a chemical. Her eyes began to close and she seemed to be going off into a trance. She told me to sit on top of her and hold her arms when she got violent, and I was braced now and ready to hold her down. I tried to keep her eyes open, shouting at her as she floated off, trying to keep her awake, telling her that she could fight it in her mind if she could keep her eyes open. This worked for a short while, but then the fit came anyway, passing over her eyes in a heavy glaze. For a moment, Dawn stared up at nothing and seemed to be no one. Suddenly, she was screaming and flinging herself about, trying to get away from me. I held her down against the bed for several minutes, but she would not stop fighting and the strain increased her frenzy. I hit her with an open hand behind the ear and she roared out in a large bawl, because with her eyes closed she did not see it coming, and then struck back with her knees, trying to push me off. She got away and flew blindly across the room. I caught her and hit her until she stopped fighting and lay once more on the bed, bawling like a new baby while I said her name over and over again in her ear. The fits went on all through the night, and when the sun came up, Dawn was sore from bruises and I was shaking like a leaf. Dawn said that the old woman had been beaten but she was not finished. She would come back but at least not for a little while.

Dawn consented to seeing her doctor but she wanted me to talk to him first. She was still more afraid of being locked up than of what she might do to herself when I wasn't watching. I called the doctor who was busy as usual, but the moment I got him on the phone and heard the sound of his voice, I realized my problem in communicating to him what had happened. I tried to tell the story in the most naive terms possible to avoid the impression that I was telling him his business. I said that Dawn was possessed by something like a "dybbuk," that I was afraid that she would hurt herself, and I thought that she ought to see him as soon as possible. I could hear him taking it the wrong way on the other end, but there was no way of getting around his professional pride. I suddenly saw what sort of frustration Dawn was up against in her personal relations. The doctor asked to talk to Dawn. He wanted to know who this young man was who seemed to be so afraid for himself and said that perhaps if Dawn had not cancelled her last appointment with him, none of this would have happened. It made me furious to see Dawn's complexity and needs once more underestimated and misinterpreted by male pride. The doctor saw Dawn that morning, but concluded that hospitalization was unnecessary. He asked her if she had ever read *The Dybbuk* by Ansky, and when she replied, "No," he muttered "Strange . . . ," as if she were shamming. The next weeks were full of upsets, visitations, and masochistic episodes as the old woman developed subtler methods of attack. She refused to show herself now in my presence, but came out all the more irresistibly for Dawn when I slept or went out. Perhaps with all the wounds that she inflicted on herself, Dawn would have been safer in the hospital. I know that many times I was lucky enough to snatch the pills or broken glass out of Dawn's hand just in time to put off the fatal step. During those weeks when I felt her slipping away from me, I felt that I was keeping Dawn alive only by watching twenty hours a day and sleeping four. I was terrified by the idea that Dawn might be dead and I might be left alone to make sense of it. I tried to construct in my mind a life alone again, but I could not see beyond the grief. My story seems to lay itself open to the interpretation that Dawn's sickness became worse the more it was watched, or more dramatically reckless as Dawn became surer that someone cared what she did. But, Dawn's earlier attempt had arisen from feelings of worthlessness, the torture of a schizoid superego, and these episodes can only be logically traced to the same source. There was no sham. Dawn's behavior revealed the coexistence of a will to live and a will to die, but Dawn's attempts on herself, unlike mine, are never resisted by the will to live. As she told me again and again, she was not in control of her downhill progress toward suicide, and I believe this, in the same way that I am not in control of external events that change my life. In these dangerous weeks, the will to live presented itself in Dawn only intermittently, and when Dawn at last went in for hospitalization, it came as a great relief to me because I had by this time run out of ways to keep Dawn alive.

All through this period, we were subject to phone calls, even a visit, from Dawn's mother who deeply resented my getting in the way. Dawn was barraged with fears, orders, newspaper clippings all about "pills and pot," the two great threats to her daughter's well-being in her purist mind. She gave up her arguments against me and her efforts to make Dawn understand, as she put it, that the girl was always the one to be left and hurt in love because of male irresponsibility. She now focused all her attention on getting Dawn to give up these two things, "pills and pot," saying that this was all she wanted, that it was not too much to ask. The unreality of it all astounded me. Mrs. McLaren had no idea that Dawn had been taking pills since the age of fifteen, that she had slept with perhaps fifty boys, that she had tried to commit suicide the year before as the result of her mother's torture and rejection, that she knew more about the problems between them than her mother would ever be able to comprehend. There could be no enlightenment. Mrs. McLaren was a childlike bundle of nervous fears, and the truth would have killed her. At last, Dawn gave in and went off pills, despite all her loathing for the rhythm method. We followed all the rules exactly and soon became extremely frustrated over the inconvenience, but Dawn wanted to keep her promise and we did. In a month, the consequences became clear to us. Her gynecologist was amazed and Dawn was pregnant.

Dawn went into the infirmary on the day we received the news. Her attempts on herself became more frequent and dangerous as her vision of the future became further complicated by the desire to have a baby. She understood why it was impossible, the medical certainties of stress and collapse, but she could not help imagining the baby and drawing me into repeating the reasons for abortion. I felt sure that Dawn would never make it through nine months of pregnancy. This certainty made it impossible, as far as I was concerned, to have the baby. At the age of seventeen, I had wanted to preserve Lynn's baby because I felt there was a chance for all three of us. But here there was no chance. I arranged for Dawn to be interviewed and tested at a city hospital where there was the possibility for a legal abortion. We ran into the problem of parental consent for the surgery which meant a confrontation with at least one of Dawn's parents. We agreed that the news should be kept from her mother at all costs. Dawn called her from the infirmary to keep her from calling us at home and becoming suspicious, but her constant prying and ordering instantly destroyed Dawn's composure and brought on the worst effects of her sickness. It was always after these phone calls, and often just in anticipation of them, that Dawn became most upset and violent. She broke the news to her father first by letter and then by phone, confident that he would not break his habitual silence to tell his wife. The tidy old veteran was shocked and could not help moralizing a little, but he was concerned most for the welfare of his daughter, of whose problems, it seems, he had never been informed. With his consent, we set the earliest possible date for the operation, but it was a month before a bed became available at the hospital and my hopes dropped for seeing Dawn out of the infirmary before then. At first, Dawn enjoyed staying in the hospital. She didn't have to worry about the bed being unmade and she didn't have to feel guilty about freaking out. But I could not stand to see Dawn in the hospital. She seemed to be drifting away from me into her dreamworld, and the old woman now found many more opportunities for her attacks than she had at home. Dawn was upset by the things that happened to her but not by the things she did to herself. She was repelled when she thought about them, but the person who cut herself up with broken glass was to Dawn entirely separate from her true character and behavior. She had no will to stop hurting herself and she often talked spitefully to me about the pills and pieces of silverware that she had hidden from me and the stupid nurses for when she would need them. Only after I begged her to fight the old woman for my sake did Dawn take any interest in staying alive. She talked of dying with a hard, determined manner that made me feel as if I were standing on nothing, as if I were standing in a graveyard in the future, watching Dawn being lowered in a box and feeling my feet sinking into the ground. I pleaded with her to stop, not to leave me alone and after a while, Dawn began to understand how important it was to me that she should live. She could not believe it herself, but she was willing to believe what I told her because I loved her, because she could understand the terror of being left alone, and because she now realized that she had been thinking only in terms of hurting herself, thinking that, whether I knew it or not, I would be better off without her. Perhaps she only wanted to be convinced that I still loved her, but it was characteristic of the relationship that I was able to talk Dawn into the decisions about herself that affected our future together. More than anything else, we wanted to love and hold onto each other, so that our individual needs became common goals very easily, almost naturally.

After the operation, Dawn was soon able to return to the frustration of school, home, and her mother's program of wedding preparations. The burden of deceiving her mother had fallen off at last, but it seemed that the meddling and badgering would never stop. Dawn's parents had now fully accepted the idea of the wedding but they were very nervous and illogical over the proper way to do everything and, of course, the cost. With our goal in sight, we were able to tell ourselves that they were making their final difficult adjustments, that they were only working themselves up to an ultimate sweetness for the wedding. Mrs. McLaren's uncertain generosity, now giving and now reconsidering and taking back, seemed calculated to torture, but there could be no doubt that real generosity lay behind the distortion somewhere. If we could only reach that day without getting angry or breaking down, we would all come out heroes. With the added problems of re-entering school late in the semester and switching majors from English to social sciences, Dawn often fell into long periods of depression which usually started with feeling imprisoned and frustrated. But Dawn now suffered much less dangerously from masochistic distortion, and our problems, although as numerous as ever, now seemed easier to relate to the approaching day of denouement. When Dawn was forced by her mother to make a last visit home alone before the wedding, she continued to be helplessly upset by her mother's illogical scoldings but in the long run she was able to grit her teeth and bear the parental generosity. We knew that the months of preparation were all for the parents who loved ceremonies, but we also knew that somehow at the end we would be able to sneak out under the cover of organ music and be free from them forever.

The day came at last and bestowed heroism on us all. A rabbi performed the ceremony, Dick played best man in his best double-breasted barracuda style, and Dawn and I kissed too soon. My mother passed the test of seeing father's new wife, Mrs. McLaren spent large sums of money to send us on a honeymoon to the Bahamas, and Dr. McLaren dropped his silent passivity long enough to turn on to some of the crafty Jewish businessmen who were friends of my family. For each one, the day seemed a turning point. Dr. McLaren became delighted with his new family connections and said that he had suddenly discovered the sterility of his life; Mrs. McLaren now believed in the marriage as firmly and illogically as she had opposed it; and my mother at last saw her baby son and problem-child go down the ways. For us, it was graduation day. No one held us up for scrutiny or asked us if we planned to behave ourselves; obviously, we did not and everyone now thought of it as wonderful.

Mrs. McLaren had only arranged to pay for our trip by booking us with a group, a national women's club, and we dreaded the idea of spending two weeks with a bunch of middle-aged women and their husbands, for whom a vacation meant bar privileges. But here too, we felt the effects of our changed status; they accepted us as fellow-seekers of fun and irresponsibility, while we were almost shocked to find them so drunken and childish. But there was certainly enough that was beautiful in the Bahamas to make it a real honeymoon for us. The pressures of what we remembered vanished into the sky, and soon our marriage, which had actually begun seven months before, began to heal up between us in the atmosphere of dreamworld. This was actually a second honeymoon, after our first weeks of happiness fell away into sickness, a reward for having made it. Our sexual relations, put off over the long period of Dawn's hospitalization and post-operative, suddenly became easy, expressive, and enjoyable again. The things I had said about marriage being socially constructive seemed to be coming true.

Two middle-aged couples that we met in the islands convinced us of this. The first was Elaine and John, Dawn's aunt and her second husband, a sweet, witty former lawyer who was never without a joke or a perceptive comment to make. They got married five years ago and escaped from their traps to the islands where they slowly worked their way up from debt to a comfortable business. They were the perfect couple and they treated and understood each other perfectly. Elaine is a vigorous, youthful woman, bold and sure in everything that scares her sister Mrs. McLaren. Her assertiveness, spark, and need to be entertained are balanced perfectly by John, who manages the responsiveness of the relationship so perfectly, it seems as if he consciously carries in front of him a formula for happiness. We admired Elaine and John because they combined their love for each other with a fresh, open-minded rebelliousness against age that also allowed them to appreciate our relationship. The second couple that sold us on marriage were the Murphys, Ralph and Jane, who at first seemed extremely nice but plain and middle-western. Ralph had come close to dying from some internal disorder and the many subsequent operations, and, forced to retire from work, he was now spending the rest of his life taking it easy. His large, jolly wife Jane took care of him out of love in the sort of way that could never be emasculating to him. They both enjoyed themselves drinking tremendously and Jane had a laugh that cut through walls and made people laugh at the other end of the hotel, for no reason other than the thought that Jane must be enjoying herself tremendously. As we got to know the Murphys, we found that they too, like Elaine and John, had a responsiveness and open-mindedness that understood us perfectly, a freedom of taking and giving between them that they created constantly for themselves and easily extended into their relations with other people. When we got back to Boston, we were full of our honeymoon and what it had told us.

With the coming of summer, a new set of postmarital problems presented itself. I found it difficult to get any sort of respectable job for the summer, so I turned my sights toward the less respectable. I made a deal to work as manager of a hip record shop in return for seven per cent of the gross. At first, I saw great possibilities for the job and the business, and things went well as long as I kept up my enthusiasm. A great part of my income was made up from drug dealing, the business that I had now practiced safely for about a year, because the music shop was a major outlet for drugs in the area. Success in this field is totally dependent on "customer-relations," and I soon found out that making money is a function of the image that one presents, so I made money. On the other hand, Van, my employer, was often so aggressive, moody, and irresponsible that he often frightened away customers. For the first month, I got along well with Van and after a while the shop gross had doubled. We began to run ads on radio and we were doing quite well. As long as we were feeling good about it, we could both increase sales volume through demonstrations and gimmicks. But Van was a case of arrested development and he had to louse things up. One day, he called up Dawn while I was out and asked her to go out with him. When I found out, I told him that it was stupid of him to think because I was taking his money that I would take his shit too, that if he tried to burn me, I would burn him. He showed that he understood me, but we never got along very well after that. I soon ceased to care about Van's business and found working with him a chore. He started taking a daily dose of speed to perk up his efforts, but after the first week, the speed just took him on one long crush. He was peevish with his customers and sales people. Soon, Van was losing customers and deals, but between drugs and my percentage, I kept on making money long after I had given up on Van.

I quit the job in September and went back to school for my senior year. Dawn was depressed about not having escaped the area all summer, but the beginning of school excited her as always. It was her first semester in two years that was not disrupted by serious problems, but now there were other problems. We found out that we were both domestic types who preferred staying home to going out. This is mostly due to the influence of my laziness, which has a bad effect on Dawn. Before she met me, Dawn's life had been a matter of control and channeling of her energy. She felt happiest and most efficient when she was holding down several jobs at once, and her greatest problem in our relationship is learning how to relax. Unfortunately, my way of life doesn't help Dawn either to relax or to work. Since we spend so much time at home doing nothing, Dawn always feels guilty about housework. She hates to wash dishes and clean the house but it upsets her to see things left undone because she knows that she will have to do them eventually. She feels best when she washes the dishes without hesitating and gets them done, but she has become far more relaxed about the amount of messiness and laziness that she can tolerate perhaps because now she feels that she can relax without falling back into the pit of troubles and emotions. But my image of relaxation and underachievement hardly provides the proper model. Since we got married, Dawn has lost the routine of writing that used to produce so much good poetry. It is frustrating to her now to try to get back into her discipline and then find that she still has dishes to wash. If her style of life is tense, she cannot be happy when she is supposed to relax, and she cannot relax for very long without feeling degenerate. We have the sort of relationship that demands that we be together all the time, but since I usually spend so little of my time working, Dawn feels she cannot work off her energy without neglecting me or making me feel lazy. Dawn's normal day then is a series of jagged ups and downs, situations which she handles according to the conflicts of control, relaxation, and guilt. Fortunately, I have reached some success in learning how to reverse Dawn's depressions, and Dawn has developed certain kinds of strength, for example, in dealing with her mother and avoiding upset, but it may be a long time before she can find the sort of adaptability to handle the various situations that demand different kinds of response from her.

Although Dawn has made compromises in her behavior to suit me, it appears that I have made very few compromises in my own behavior. I have done nothing to get myself together or to control my laziness. My fixation with drugs and my withdrawal from the world have only become more pronounced. I use drugs as tranquilizers because I find that as soon as I get straight, I get angry or just completely hopeless. I am sick of drugs and everything about them. I have tried to stop smoking time and time again, but each time I have found the consequences of being stoned far superior to those of being straight. It used to be when I was a child that I would get frustrated or angry and would throw things around until I broke something, and then it would all be over, released. But now, destructiveness is never a release unless it is continual destructiveness and, since there can be little room in my life for this, only smoking works to cool me down. Then, I can laugh again and it all seems foolish.

Because laughing is what makes us happy. We are incredibly foolish with each other, and it even makes people on the street start laughing. We spend so much time together because we make each other happy and we depend on each other for happiness. With such a healthy dyad, I can still have some hope for the monads.

Epilogue

Before concluding, some general comments about the field of study and where it seems to be going are in order. We will talk about some of the difficulties involved in referring to the study of the transition to adulthood as the psychology of adolescence.

The very phrase *psychology of adolescence* implies a separate and isolated part of human life. Yet attempts to define what adolescence is become extremely shaky once one gets beyond the profound and deeply complex psychological effects which accompany the physiological changes of puberty. The psychology of adolescence implies something that is preadult, yet begs the question of when a person becomes an adult in the psychological sense. Furthermore, attempts to establish criteria of adulthood, such as holding a job, getting married, driving a car, graduating from high school or college, entering the armed services — the list is endless — reveal that while all of these clearly have something to do with a change from the status of being a child, they are far from being definitive criteria of adulthood. A person can fulfill several of these criteria and yet be called by those who know him or her a "perpetual adolescent." Hollingshead (1949) has said that there is a period of time when society refuses to call an individual an adult and yet ceases to call him a child. Our own solution to this problem is to suggest that it may be more fruitful in the future to speak of the psychology of transition; that the transition involved is probably multiple rather than merely physiological; and that as diffuse and difficult to define as the field of study is, some important work has been done which can set some guidelines.

One of the major changes in the study of the development of personality since the end of the Second World War has been the profound effect on psychological thinking of the work of Anna Freud (1946) and of Erik Erikson (1950). Sigmund Freud (1933), in his great final essay on human personality (Lecture 31 of the *New Introductory Lectures in Psychoanalysis*), makes the point that the human experience depends on two facts, one biological and one psychological. The biological fact is the long period of human dependency brought about by our primate status; the psychological fact, the Oedipus complex. While Freud acknowledged what he called the transformations of puberty, he had little in a formal sense to say about the psychology of transition, although his work is replete with valuable statements about it. What Anna Freud did, first in the 1940s and subsequently in 1958, was to illuminate the fact that after puberty there must come a restructuring of personality so that the emerging adult can live in the adult world which surrounds him. Her essays on the defenses and their reorganization preceding adulthood are important reading for any serious student in this field. An equally important contribution, discussed in the Overview to this book, was made by Erikson. Erikson revolutionized psychology by systematically reviewing the psychology of the life cycle as a whole. Whether one agrees or disagrees with Erikson's theoretical formulations is beside the point. The point is that Erikson sees in his eight stages of man a way to relate all the experiences of life to a chain of several transitions, of which what we call adolescence happens to be but one. Both Anna Freud and Erikson may be called stage theorists, which is a far step from Freud, who saw personality as a consequence of the more or less successful solution of early trauma.

Erikson, in his Preface to *Childhood and Society*, acknowledges the work of Harry Stack Sullivan (1953) and his profoundly important conceptualization of "the significant other." Sullivan, quite independently, deals with the life cycle theory, which depends not so much on biological factors, although of course those are included, but rather the way in which a person's total life is of necessity structured around critical interpersonal relationships. One's life is spent, as Sullivan sees it, in broadening and deepening collaborative relationships with others. W. R. D. Fairbairn (1962), in his provocative book on Object Relations Theory, suggests that the whole of the human life cycle evolves in three stages: first, infantile dependency; second, a transitional stage, which may take many years; and finally "mature dependency." In the last stage, a person acknowledges that one cannot exist in isolated autonomy, but must instead depend to some degree on others for psychological and emotional support, in order to remain not only sane but human. Lawrence Kohlberg (1968), in a series of brilliant papers, has attempted to deal with the development of personality using the theoretical hypotheses of Piaget. His own work and his work with Carol Gilligan (1971) on moral development and its stages, as well as the work of William G. Perry, Jr. (1970), on ethical development, are contributions not only to the psychology of cognition, but to stage theory as well. The point that must be emphasized is that all these theorists, whether like Kohlberg they embrace the point of view of cognition or whether like Fairbairn they take an orthodox psychoanalytic position, insist that life consists of several stages, and that the critical points, psychologically, are the transitions between stages. Thus they all see adolescence as part of a life rather than as an isolated turbulent episode.

Robert White's work (1966) exemplifies a different approach to the study of lives. White does not subscribe to stage theory in the way most theorists do. Instead, he takes the position that as important as overall development is, the critical issue is the key incidents that facilitate or prevent growth and fulfillment of an individual's potential. His brilliant case studies of Hartley Hale, Joyce Kingsley, and Joseph Kidd all reveal turning points at which critical incidents shape the lives of the protagonists. In Hale's case, his later aggressiveness and assurance as a surgeon was contributed to markedly by his sister's forcing him to stand up and fight during a childhood quarrel. In contrast, Joseph Kidd had to wait until his forties until the social disruption caused by the double promotion forced on him by his socially mobile parents could be ameliorated. And Joyce Kingsley had to expend tremendous effort to adjust to the extremely high ideals and standards set by her ministerial father.

Research by Stanley King (1973), Norma Haan (1963), and Jane Loevinger and her colleagues (1970) is beginning to suggest that critical incidents may or may not affect people, depending on the strength of their egos, or their coping mechanisms, and on the degree of distortion in their defensive processes. What future research is going to have to show is, other things being equal, why some people can cope and defend better than others.

Probably the most significant work recently published on the life cycle is by George Vaillant (1971, 1974) and by Vaillant in collaboration with Charles McArthur (1972). As sometimes happens, these extremely important contributions have come to light in relatively obscure journals. Vaillant, in addition to being a professor of psychiatry at Harvard Medical School, is curator of the Cambridge-Somerville study and the Grant study archives. The Cambridge-Somerville study was a sample of both delinquent and nondelinquent youths in Cambridge and Somerville, Massachusetts — young people largely from blue-collar backgrounds — originally undertaken by Gordon Allport and first published by McCord and McCord (1959). The Grant study was done on the Harvard classes of 1942 and 1943. For decades these people were followed, particularly those in the Grant study, and in the last five years Vaillant has begun to analyze the material gathered. His findings are astonishing. In essence, what Vaillant and McArthur discovered is that stage theories which suggest a linearity of life or personality, while they are useful, may oversimplify the problem. What comes out in an examination of the data is that in the course of their life cycles, males at least seem to fluctuate between times which appear very much like what are called in psychology latent stages, and periods of storm, stress, and new experience very much like adolescence. The data imply that *psychology of transition* is indeed a legitimate term, and furthermore that personality development is probably neither a linear function, related to age, nor a curvilinear function, ascending and then descending in later life. Instead, the life cycle may indeed be much more like James D. Watson's famous double helix model of the DNA molecule.

Thus the field itself could be entering a period of exciting transition.

References

Erikson, E. H. *Childhood and Society.* New York: W. W. Norton, 1950.

Fairbairn, W. R. D. (1952). *An Object-Relations Theory of the Personality.* New York: Basic Books, 1962.

Freud, A. *The Ego and the Mechanisms of Defense.* Translated by Cecil Baines. New York: International Universities Press, 1946.

———. "Adolescence," in *Psychoanalytic Study of the Child.* Vol. 13. New York: International Universities Press, 1958.

Freud, S. *New Introductory Lectures on Psychoanalysis.* Translated by W. J. H. Sprott. New York: W. W. Norton, 1933.

Haan, N. "Proposed Model of Ego Functioning: Coping and Defense Mechanisms in Relationship to IQ Changes." *Psychology Monograph* 77 (1963): 1–23.

Hollingshead, A. B. *Elmtown's Youth: The Impact of Social Classes on Youth.* New York: Wiley, 1949.

King, S. H. *Five Lives at Harvard: Personality Change During College.* Cambridge: Harvard University Press, 1973.

Kohlberg, L. "Stage and Sequence: The Cognitive-Developmental Approach to Socialization," in D. Goslin (ed.), *Handbook of Socialization.* Chicago: Rand McNally, 1968.

Kohlberg, L., and Gilligan, C. "The Adolescent as a Philosopher: The Discovery of the Self in a Postconventional World." *Daedalus* 100, no. 4 (1971).

Loevinger, J.; Wessler, R.; and Redmore, C. *Measuring Ego Development.* Vols. 1 and 2. San Francisco: Jossey-Bass, 1970.

McCord, W., and McCord, J. (with I. K. Zola). *Origins of Crime: a New Evaluation of the Cambridge-Somerville Youth Study.* New York: Columbia University Press, 1959.

Perry, W. G., Jr. *Forms of Intellectual and Ethical Development in the College Years.* New York: Holt, Rinehart and Winston, 1970.

Sullivan, H. S. *The Interpersonal Theory of Psychiatry.* New York: W. W. Norton, 1953.

Vaillant, G. E. "Theoretical Hierarchy of Adaptive Ego Mechanisms." *Archives General Psychiatry* 24 (1971): 107–18.

———. "Natural History of Male Psychological Health, II: Some Antecedents of Healthy Adult Adjustment." *Archives General Psychiatry* 31 (July 1974).

Vaillant, G. E., and McArthur, C. C. "Natural History of Male Psychological Health, I: The Adult Life Cycle from 18–50." *Seminars in Psychiatry* 4, no. 4 (1972): 415–17.

Watson, J. D. *The Double Helix, a Personal Account of the Discovery of the Structure of DNA.* New York: Atheneum, 1968.

White, R. W. *Lives in Progress.* 2d ed. New York: Holt, Rinehart and Winston, 1966.

Selected Bibliography

Adler, A. *The Individual Psychology of Alfred Adler.* Edited by H. Ansbacher and R. Ansbacher. New York: Basic Books, 1956.

Aichhorn, A. (1925) *Wayward Youth.* New York: Viking Press, 1948.

Alexander, F. "From Adolescence to Adulthood." *Mental Health Bulletin* (Illinois Society for Mental Hygiene), 1948.

Allport, G. *Pattern and Growth in Personality.* New York: Holt, Rinehart and Winston, 1937; 1961.

————. *The Person in Psychology.* Boston: Beacon Press, 1968.

Ausubel, D. P. *Theory and Problems of Adolescent Development.* New York: Grune and Stratton, 1954.

Bach, G. R., and Deutsch, R. M. *Pairing.* New York: Avon Books, 1970.

Bandura, A., and Walters, R. H. *Adolescent Aggression.* New York: Ronald Press, 1959.

Bazeley, P., and Viney, L. L. "Women Coping With Crisis: A Preliminary Community Study." *Journal of Community Psychology* 2, no. 4 (October 1974).

Beach, F., ed. *Sex and Behavior.* New York: Wiley, 1965.

Bell, H. M. *Youth Tell Their Story.* Washington, D.C.: American Council on Education, 1938.

Bell, R. R., and Buerkle, J. V. "Mother-Daughter Attitudes to Premarital Sexual Behavior." *Journal of Marriage and Family Living* 23 (1961).

Bene, E. "Suppression of Heterosexual Interest and of Aggression by Middle Class and Working Class Grammar School Boys." *British Journal of Educational Psychology* 28 (1958).

Benedict, R. "Continuities and Discontinuities in Cultural Conditioning," in W. E. Martin and C. B. Stendler (eds.), *Readings in Child Development.* New York: Harcourt, Brace and World, 1954.

————. *Patterns of Culture.* Boston: Houghton Mifflin, 1934.

Bernard, J. *The Sex Game.* Englewood Cliffs, N.J.: Prentice-Hall, 1968.

Bernfeld, S. "*Über eine typische Form der Männlichen Pubertät.*" *Imago* 9 (1923).

Bettelheim, B. *Symbolic Wounds, Puberty Rites and the Envious Circle.* Chicago: Free Press, 1954.

Bion, W. *Learning From Experience.* New York: Basic Books, 1962.

Blaine, G., and McArthur, C. *Emotional Problems of the Student.* New York: Appleton Press, 1961.

Block, J., and Turula, E. "Identification, Ego Control and Adjustment." *Child Development* 34 (1963).

Blos, P. *On Adolescence: A Psychoanalytic Interpretation.* New York: Free Press, 1962.

Blum, R. *Utopiates: The Use and Users of LSD-25.* New York: Atherton Press, 1964.

Bowen, M. "The Family Concept of Schizophrenia," in Donald Jackson (ed.), *The Etiology of Schizophrenia*. New York: Basic Books, 1962.

Brim, O. G., and Wheeler, S. *Socialization After Childhood*. New York: Wiley, 1966.

Bronfenbrenner, U. "Freudian Theories of Identification and Their Derivatives." *Child Development* 31 (1960).

————. "The Changing American Child," in E. Ginzberg (ed.),*Values and Ideals of American Youth*. New York: Columbia University Press, 1961.

Brown, D. G. "Sex-Role Development in Changing Culture." *Psychological Bulletin* 55 (1958).

Brown, D. G., and Philblad, C. T. "Aspirations and Expectations: A Reexamination of the Bases for Social Class Differences in the Occupational Orientations of Male High School Students." *Sociological Social Research* 49 (1965).

Bugental, J. *The Search For Authenticity*. New York: Holt, Rinehart and Winston, 1965.

Buhler, C. "The Curve of Life as Studied in Biographies." *Journal of Applied Psychology* 19 (1955): 405–09.

Burton, A., and Harris, R. E. *Clinical Studies in Personality*. Vol. 2. New York: Harper, 1955.

Burton, R. V., and Whiting, J. W. M. "The Absent Father and Cross-Sex Identity." *Merrill-Palmer Quarterly of Behavior and Development* 7, no. 2 (1961). Also in Grinder, R. E. (ed.), *Studies in Adolescence*. New York: Macmillan, 1963.

Carlsmith, L. "Effect of Early Father Absence on Scholastic Aptitude." *Harvard Educational Review* 34, no. 1 (Winter 1964).

Carol, F. G. "Social Class and Attitudes of Youth Relevant for the Realization of Adult Goals." *Social Forces* 44 (1966).

Cervantes, L. F. "Family Background, Primary Relationships, and the High School Dropout." *Journal of Marriage and the Family* 5 (1965).

Christensen, H. T. "Cultural Relativism and Pre-marital Sex Norms." *American Sociological Review* 25 (1960).

————. *Handbook of Marriage and the Family*. Chicago: Rand McNally, 1964.

Christensen, H. T., and Carpenter, G. R. "Value Behavior Discrepancies Regarding Premarital Coitus in Three Western Cultures." *American Sociological Review* 27 (1962).

Cloward, R. A., and Ohlin, L. E. *Delinquency and Opportunity: a Theory of Delinquent Gangs*. Glencoe: Free Press, 1960.

Coleman, J. S. *The Adolescent Society*. Glencoe: Free Press, 1961.

Committee on the College Student, Group for the Advancement of Psychiatry, J. B. Wheelright, Chrm. *Sex and the College Student* 6, no. 60. New York: Mental Health Materials Center, Inc., November 1965.

Committee on Adolescence, Group for the Advancement of Psychiatry, C. F. Settlage, Chrm. *Normal Adolescence: Its Dynamics and Impact*. New York: Scribner's, 1968.

Conger, J. J. "A World They Never Knew: The Family and Social Change." *Daedalus,* Fall 1971.

Conger, J. J., and Miller, W. C. *Personality, Social Class, and Delinquency.* New York: Wiley, 1966.

Conger, J. J.; Miller, W. C.; and Walsmith, C. R. "Antecedents of Delinquency, Personality, Social Class and Intelligence," in P. H. Mussen, J. J. Conger, and J. Kagan (eds.), *Readings in Child Development and Personality.* New York: Harper and Row, 1965.

Cuber, J. F., and Harroff, P. *The Significant Americans.* New York: Appleton-Century-Crofts, 1965.

Dahlstrom, E. "Analysis of the Debate on Sex Roles." *The Changing Roles of Men and Women.* Boston: Beacon Press, 1967.

Davis, A., and Dollard, J. *Children of Bondage.* Washington, D.C.: American Council on Education, 1941.

Douvan, E. A., and Adelson, J. *The Adolescent Experience.* New York: Wiley, 1966.

Douvan, E. A., and Kaye, C. *Adolescent Girls.* Ann Arbor: Publication of Survey Research Center, University of Michigan, 1957.

Dunphy, D. C. "The Social Structure of Urban Adolescent Peer Groups." *Sociometry* 26 (1963).

Ehrmann, W. "Some Knowns and Unknowns in Research into Human Sex Behavior. *Marriage and Family Living* 19 (1957).

————. *Premarital Dating Behavior.* New York: Holt, Rinehart and Winston, 1959.

Eisenstadt, S. N. *From Generation to Generation: Age Groups and Social Structure.* Glencoe: Free Press, 1956.

Elkind, D. "Egocentrism in Adolescence." *Child Development* 38 (1967).

English, O. S., and Pearson, G. H. J. *Emotional Problems of Living.* New York: Norton, 1955.

Erikson, E. H. *Childhood and Society.* New York: W. W. Norton, 1950.

————. *Identity and the Life Cycle: Psychological Issues.* New York: International Universities Press, Vol. 1, no. 1 (1959).

————. *The Challenge of Youth.* New York: Anchor Paperback, 1966.

————. *Identity: Youth and Crisis.* New York: Norton, 1968.

Eshleman, J. R. "Mental Health and Marital Integration in Young Marriages." *Journal of Marriage and the Family* 27 (1965).

Evans, R. I. *Dialogue with Erik Erikson.* New York: Harper and Row, 1967.

Fairbairn, W. R. D. (1952). *An Object-Relations Theory of the Personality.* New York: Basic Books, 1962.

Farnsworth, D. *Mental Health in College and University.* Cambridge: Harvard University Press, 1957.

Fitzgerald, M. P. "Sex Differences in the Perception of the Parental Role for Middle and Working Class Adolescents." *Journal of Clinical Psychology* 22 (1966).

Fletcher, J. *Situation Ethics.* New York: Westminster Press, 1966.

Ford, C. S., and Beach, F. A. *Patterns of Sexual Behavior.* New York: Harper and Row, 1951.

Freud, A. *The Ego and the Mechanisms of Defense*. Translated by Cecil Baines. New York: International Universities Press, 1946.
————. "Adolescence," in *Psychoanalytic Study of the Child*. Vol. 13. New York: International Universities Press, 1958.
Freud, S. (1905). "The Transformations of Puberty," in *Three Contributions to the Theory of Sex*. Translated by Joan Riviere. Vol. 7. London: The Hogarth Press, 1953.
———— (1905). "Fragment of an Analysis of a Case of Hysteria," in *Collected Papers*. Translated by Alix and James Strachey. Vol. 3. London: The Hogarth Press, 1950.
———— (1914). "On Narcissism: An Introduction," in *Collected Papers* (trans. by Joan Riviere). Vol. 4. London: The Hogarth Press, 1950.
———— (1917). "Mourning and Melancholia," in *Collected Papers*. Translated by Joan Riviere. Vol. 4. London: The Hogarth Press, 1950.
———— (1924). "The Passing of the Oedipus-Complex," in *Collected Papers* (trans. by Joan Riviere). Vol. 2. London: The Hogarth Press, 1950.
———— (1930). *Civilization and Its Discontents*. Translated by Joan Riviere. London: The Hogarth Press, 1957.
————. *New Introductory Lectures on Psychoanalysis*. Translated by W. J. H. Sprott. New York: W. W. Norton, 1933.
Friedenberg, F. Z. *The Vanishing Adolescent*. Boston: Beacon Press, 1959.
————. *Coming of Age in America*. New York: Random House, 1963.
Fullerton, G. F. *Survival in Marriage*. New York: Holt, Rinehart and Winston, 1972.
Gershon, S., and Angrist, B. "Drug-Induced Psychoses: II." *Hospital Practice* 2 (1967).
Gesell, A.; Ilg, F. L.; and Ames, L. V. *Youth: The Years from Ten to Sixteen*. New York: Harper and Row, 1956.
Goethals, G. "The Sexual Revolution: Cross-Cultural Perspectives," in *A Report of the Twentieth Annual Conference, National Association of College and University Chaplains and Directors of Religious Life*. Boston University, April 1967.
————. "Factors Affecting Permissive and Nonpermissive Rules Regarding Premarital Sex," in J. M. Henslin (ed.), *The Sociology of Sex: A Book of Readings*. New York: Appleton-Century-Crofts, 1971.
————. "Symbiosis and the Life Cycle," *British Journal of Medical Psychology* 46, no. 91 (1973).
————. "Adolescence: Variations on a Theme," *Youth 1975* (Chicago: The National Society for the Study of Education, 1975), Seventy-fourth Yearbook, pp. 46–60.
Goffman, E. *The Presentation of Self in Everyday Life*. Garden City, N.Y.: Doubleday Anchor Books, 1959.
Grinder, R. E., ed. *Studies in Adolescence*. New York: Macmillan, 1963.
Grinder, R. E., and Schmitt, S. S. "Coeds and Contraceptive Information." *Journal of Marriage and the Family* 28 (1966).
Grinder, R. E., and Strickland, C. E. "G. Stanley Hall and the Social Significance of Adolescence." *Teachers College Record* 64 (1963).

Guntrip, H. *Schizoid Phenomena, Object-Relations and the Self.* New York: International Universities Press, 1968.

Haan, N. "Proposed Model of Ego Functioning: Coping and Defense Mechanisms in Relationship to IQ Changes." *Psychology Monographs* 77 (1963):1–23.

Hall, G. S. *Adolescence: Its Psychology and Its Relation to Physiology, Anthropology, Sociology, Sex, Crime, Religion and Education* (2 vols.). New York: D. Appleton, 1904.

Hamilton, G. V. *A Research in Marriage.* New York: Boni, 1929.

Havighurst, F. J., ed. *Youth: The Seventy-fourth Yearbook of the National Society for the Study of Education.* Part I. Chicago: University of Chicago Press, 1975.

Heath, R. *The Reasonable Adventurer.* Pittsburgh: University of Pittsburgh Press, 1964.

Henry, G. W. *Sex Variants: A Study of Homosexual Patterns.* New York: Paul B. Hoeber, 1941.

Heron, A., ed. *Towards a Quaker View of Sex.* London: Friends Home Service Committee, 1963.

Hollingshead, A. B. *Elmtown's Youth: The Impact of Social Classes on Youth.* New York: Wiley, 1949.

Horrocks, J. E. *The Psychology of Adolescence.* Boston: Houghton Mifflin, 1962.

Hurlock, E. B. *Adolescent Development.* 3d ed. New York: McGraw-Hill, 1962.

Huyck, E. E., ed. *White-Nonwhite Differentials in Health, Education, and Welfare.* Washington, D.C.: Department of Health, Education, and Welfare, 1965.

Inhelder, B., and Piaget, J. *The Growth of Logical Thinking from Childhood through Adolescence.* New York: Basic Books, 1958.

Jaques, E. "Death and the Mid-Life Crisis." *International Journal of Psycho-Analysis* 46 (1965): 502–14.

Jersild, A. T. *In Search of Self.* New York: Columbia University Press, 1952.

———. *The Psychology of Adolescence.* 2d ed. New York: Macmillan, 1963.

Jones, E. (1922) *Some Problems of Adolescence: Papers on Psycho-Analysis.* 5th ed. London: Bailliere, Tindall and Cox, 1948.

Jourard, S. *The Transparent Self.* New York: Van Nostrand, 1971.

Kagan, J. *Psychological Review* 65 (1958): 296–305.

———. "The Stability of Passive and Dependent Behavior from Childhood through Adulthood." *Child Development* 31 (1960).

———. "Acquisition and Significance of Sex Typing and Sex Role Identity," in M. L. Hoffman and L. W. Hoffman, *Review of Child Development Research.* Vol. 1. New York: Russell Sage Foundation, 1964.

Kagan, J., and Freeman, M. "Relation of Childhood Intelligence, Maternal Behaviors, and Social Class Behavior During Adolescence." *Child Development* 34 (1963).

Kagan, J., and Moss, H. A. *Birth to Maturity.* New York: Wiley, 1962.

Kahl, J. A. "Educational and Occupational Aspirations of Common-man Boys." *Harvard Education Review* 23 (1953).

Kallen, D. J. "Inner Direction, Other Direction, and Social Integration Setting." *Human Relations* 16 (1963).

Katz, J., ed. *No Time For Youth*. San Francisco: Jossey-Bass, 1968.

Keniston, K. "Alienation and the Decline of Utopia." *American Scholar* 25 no. 2 (Spring 1960).

————. "Inburn: An American Ishmael," in R. White (ed.), *The Study of Lives*. New York: Atherton, 1963.

————. *The Uncommitted: Alienated Youth in American Society*. New York: Dell, 1960.

————. *The Young Radicals: Notes on Committed Youth*. New York: Harcourt, Brace and World, 1968.

————. "Youth: A New Stage in Life." *The American Scholar* 39 (Autumn 1970).

————. *Youth and Dissent: The Rise of a New Opposition*. New York: Harcourt Brace Jovanovich, 1971.

Kenyatta, J. *Facing Mount Kenya*. New York: Vintage Paperback, 1962.

King, S. H. *Five Lives at Harvard: Personality Change During College*. Cambridge: Harvard University Press, 1973.

Kinsey, A. C.; Pomeroy, W. B.; and Martin, C. E. *Sexual Behavior in the Human Male*. Philadelphia: Saunders, 1948.

————. *Sexual Behavior in the Human Female*. Philadelphia: Saunders, 1953.

Kirkendall, L. A. "Sex Concerns of Adolescent Boys." *Marriage Hygiene*, 1948.

Klassen, D.; Roth, A.; and Hornstra, R. K. "Perception of Life Events as Gains or Losses in a Community Survey." *Journal of Community Psychology* 2, no. 4 (October 1974).

Klein, M. *Envy and Gratitude: A Study of Unconsicous Sources*. London: Tavistock, 1957.

Kohlberg, L. "Development of Moral Character and Moral Ideology," in W. L. Hoffman and L. W. Hoffman, *Review of Child Development Research*. Vol. 1. New York: Russell Sage Foundation, 1964.

————. "Stage and Sequence: The Cognitive-Developmental Approach to Socialization," in D. Goslin (ed.), *Handbook of Socialization*. Chicago: Rand McNally, 1968.

Kohlberg, L., and Gilligan, C. "The Adolescent as a Philosopher: The Discovery of the Self in a Postconventional World." *Daedalus* 100, no. 4 (1971).

Kretschmer, E. *Physique and Character*. New York: Harcourt, Brace and World, 1925.

Kroeber, T. C. "The Coping Functions of the Ego Mechanisms," in R. White (ed.), *The Study of Lives*. New York: Atherton Press, 1963.

Kvaraceus, W. C. *Juvenile Delinquency and the School*. New York: Harcourt, Brace and World, 1945.

Kvaraceus, W. C., et. al. *Delinquent Behavior: Culture and the Individual*. Washington, D.C.: National Education Association, 1959.

Laing, R. D. *The Divided Self*. Baltimore: Penguin Books, 1965.

Langer, J. *Theories of Development.* New York: Holt, Rinehart and Winston, 1969.

Lansky, L. M.; Crandall, V. J.; Kagan, J.; and Baker, C. T. "Sex Differences in Aggression and Its Correlates in Middle-class Adolescents." *Child Development* 32 (1961).

Lessing, D. *The Golden Note-book.* New York: Ballantine Books, 1968.

Levinson, D. J., et al. "The Psychosocial Development of Men in Early Adulthood and the Mid-Life Transition." *Life History Research in Psychopathology.* Vol. 3. Minneapolis: University of Minnesota Press, 1974.

Lifton, R. J. "Protean Man." *Partisan Review,* Winter 1968.

Lipset, S. M., and Bendix, R. *Social Mobility in Industrial Society.* Berkeley: University of California Press, 1959.

Loevinger, J. "The Meaning and Measurements of Ego Development." *American Psychologist* 21 (1966):195–206.

Loevinger, J.; Wessler, R.; and Redmore, C. *Measuring Ego Development.* Vols. 1 and 2. San Francisco: Jossey-Bass, 1970.

Louria, D. *Nightmare Drugs.* New York: Pocket Books, 1966.

Lowrie, S. H. "Early and Late Dating: Some Conditions Associated with Them." *Marriage and Family Living* 23 (1961).

———. "Early Marriage: Premarital Pregnancy and Associated Factors." *Journal of Marriage and Family* 27 (1965)

Lozoff, M. "The Development of Autonomy in the Female," in R. Kundsin (ed.), *Women and the Professions.* New York: New York Academy of Sciences, 1973.

Lynn, D. B. A. "A Note on Sex Differences in the Development of Masculine and Feminine Identification." *Psychology Bulletin* 66 (1959).

Lynn, D. B. A., and Sawrey, W. L. "The Effects of Father-Absence on Norwegian Boys and Girls." *Journal of Abnormal Psychology* 59 (1959).

Maccoby, E. E., ed. *The Development of Sex Differences.* Stanford: Stanford University Press, 1966.

Maccoby, E. E.; Newcomb, T.; and Hartley, L. *Readings in Social Psychology.* New York: Henry Holt, 1958.

Madison, P. *Personal Development in College.* Reading, Mass.: Addison-Wesley, 1969.

Maslow, A. H. *Motivation and Personality.* New York: Harper, 1954.

McCammon, R. W. "Are Boys and Girls Maturing Physically at Earlier Ages?" *American Journal of Public Health* 55 (1965).

McClelland, D. C.; Rindlisbacher, A.; and deCharms, R. "Religious and Other Sources of Parental Attitudes Toward Independence Training." In D. C. McClelland (ed.), *Studies in Motivation.* New York: Appleton-Century-Crofts, 1955.

McCord, W., and McCord, J. (with I. K. Zola). *Origins of Crime: a New Evaluation of the Cambridge-Somerville Youth Study.* New York: Columbia University Press, 1959.

Mead, M. "From the South Seas: Part III," in *Sex and Temperament in Three Primitive Societies.* New York: Morrow, 1939.

———. "Adolescence in Primitive and Modern Society," in Maccoby, Newcomb, and Hartley (eds.), *Readings in Social Psychology.* New York: Henry Holt, 1958.

———. *Male and Female.* New York: Morrow, 1939.

Miller, D. R., and Swanson, G. E. *The Changing American Parent: A Study in the Detroit Area.* New York: Wiley, 1958.

Miller, W. B. "Lower Class Culture as a Generating Milieu of Gang Delinquency." *Journal of Social Issues* 14, no. 3 (1958).

Modell, A. H. *Object Love and Reality.* New York: International University Press, 1968.

Munter, P. "Intellectualization of Sexual Experience." Unpublished paper, University Health Services, 1962.

Murdock, G. P. *Social Structure.* New York: Macmillan, 1949.

Murphy, G. *Historical Introduction to Modern Psychology.* New York: Harcourt, Brace and World, 1950.

Muuss, R. E. *Theories of Adolescence.* New York: Random House, 1962.

Mussen, P. H.; Conger, J. J.; and Kagan, J. *Child Development and Personality.* 3d ed. New York: Harper and Row, 1956.

Mussen, P. H., and Jones, M. C. "The Behavior Inferred Motivations of Late and Early Maturing Boys." *Child Development* 29 (1958).

———. "Self Conceptions, Motivations, and Interpersonal Attitudes of Late and Early Maturing Boys." *Child Development* 28 (1957).

———. "Some Antecedents and Consequences of Masculine Sex-typing in Adolescent Boys." *Psychological Monograph* 75 (1961).

———. "Long Term Consequences of Masculinity of Interests in Adolescence." *Journal of Consulting Psychology* 26 (1962).

Murray, H. A. "American Icarus," in A. Burton and R. E. Harrie (eds.), *Clinical Studies in Personality.* Vol. 2. New York: Harper, 1955, pp. 615–41.

Neugarten, B. L., ed. "Middle Age and Aging," in *A Reader in Social Psychology.* Chicago: University of Chicago Press, 1968.

Parsons, T. (1942) "Age and Sex in the Social Structure in the United States," in Martin and Stendler (eds.), *Readings in Child Development.* New York: Harcourt, Brace, 1954. Also in Kluckhohn, Murry, and Schneider (eds.), *Personality in Nature and Society and Culture.* 2d ed. New York: Alfred A. Knopf, 1967.

Parsons, T., and Bales, R. F. *Family, Socialization and Interaction Process.* Glencoe: The Free Press, 1955.

Parsons, T., and Platt, G. *A Sociology of Age.* New Brunswick, N.J.: Rutgers University Press, 1969.

Perry, W. G., Jr. *Forms of Intellectual and Ethical Development in the College Years.* New York: Holt, Rinehart and Winston, 1970.

Peterson, R. E. *The Scope of Organized Student Protest in 1964–65.* Princeton: Educational Testing Service, 1966.

Pleck, J., and Sawyer, J. *Men and Masculinity.* Los Angeles: Spectrum Productions, 1974.

Poppleton, P. K., and Brown, P. E. "The Secular Trend in Puberty: Has Stability Been Achieved?" *British Journal of Educational Psychology* 36 (1966).

Powers, E., and Witmer, H. *Prevention of Delinquency: The Cambridge-*

Somerville Youth Study. New York: Columbia University Press, 1951.

Putney, S., and Putney, G. *The Adjusted American: Normal Neurosis in the Individual and Society.* New York: Harper Colophon Books, 1964.

Reckless, W. C.; Dintz, S.; and Murray, E. "Self-Concept as an Insulator against Delinquency." *American Sociological Review* 21 (1956).

Reevy, W. R. "Adolescent Sexuality," in A. Ellis and A. Abarband (eds.), *The Encyclopedia of Sexual Behavior.* Vol. I. Englewood Cliffs, N.J.: Hawthorn, 1961.

Reiss, I. L. *Premarital Sexual Standards in America.* New York: Free Press of Glencoe, 1960.

―――. "The Sexual Renaissance in America." *The Journal of Social Issues* 22, no. 2 (April 1966).

Remmers, H. H. "Cross Cultural Studies of Teenagers' Problems." *The Journal of Educational Psychology* 53 (1962).

Ricks, D. F.; Thomas, A.; and Roff, M., eds. *Life History Research in Psychotherapy.* Vol. 3. Minneapolis: University of Minnesota Press, 1974.

Riesman, D. *The Lonely Crowd.* New Haven: Yale University Press, 1950.

―――. *Individualism Reconsidered.* New York: Free Press of Glencoe, 1954.

Rogers, C. "Toward a Modern Approach to Values." *Journal of Abnormal and Social Psychology* 68 (1964): 160–67.

―――. *On Becoming a Person.* Boston: Houghton Mifflin, 1961.

―――. *Becoming Partners.* New York: Dell Books, 1972.

Rohrer, J. H., and Edmonson, M. S. *The Eighth Generation.* New York: Harper and Row, 1960.

Rosenblith, J. F., and Allensmith, W. *The Causes of Behavior,* 2d ed. Boston: Allyn and Bacon, 1966.

Salisbury, H. E. *The Shook-Up Generation.* New York: Harper and Row, 1959.

Sanford, N. "The Developmental Status of the Entering Freshman," in *The American College.* New York: Wiley, 1962.

Scarpitti, F. R.; Murray, E.; Sintz, S.; and Reckless, W. C. "The 'Good' Boy in a High Delinquency Area: Four Years Later." *American Sociological Review* 25 (1960).

Schonfeld, W. A. "Primary and Secondary Sexual Characteristics: Study of Their Development in Males from Birth through Maturity, with Biometric Study of Penis and Testes." *American Journal on Diseases of Children* 65 (1943).

Sears, P. S. "Doll Play Aggression in Normal Young Children: Influence of Sex, Age, Sibling Status, Father's Absence." *Psychological Monograph* 6 (whole No. 32), 1951.

Sears, R. *Patterns of Child Rearing.* Evanston, Ill.: Row, Peterson, 1957.

Seeley, J. R., et al. *Crestwood Heights: A Study of the Culture of Suburban Life.* New York: Basic Books, 1956.

Seidman, J., ed. *The Adolescent: A Book of Readings.* Rev. ed. New York: Holt, Rinehart and Winston, 1960.

Sex and the College Student. Report Number 60 Group for the Advancement of Psychiatry. New York: Group for the Advancement of Psychiatry, 1965.

Sheldon, W. H. (with the collaboration of S. S. Stevens and W. B. Tucker). *The Varieties of Human Physique: An Introduction to Constitutional Psychology.* New York: Harper, 1940.

Silverstein, M. "The Development of Identity: Power and Sex Roles in Academia," in W. Bennis (ed.), *Interpersonal Dynamics.* Homewood, Ill.: The Dorsey Press, 1973.

Simmons, K. "The Brush Foundation Study of Child Growth and Development, II: Physical Growth and Development." *Monograph of Social Res. Child Development* 9, no. 1 (1944).

Slater, P. *The Pursuit of Loneliness.* Boston: Beacon Press, 1970.

Stolz, L. M. *Father Relations of Warborn Children.* Palo Alto: Stanford University Press, 1954.

Stone, L. J., and Church, J. *Childhood and Adolescence: A Psychology of the Growing Person.* New York: Random House, 1957.

Sullivan, H. S. *Conceptions of Modern Psychiatry.* New York: W. W. Norton, 1940.

———. *The Interpersonal Theory of Psychiatry.* New York: W. W. Norton, 1953.

———. *The Psychiatric Interview.* New York: W. W. Norton, 1954.

———. "The Dynamisms of Emotion." *Clinical Studies in Psychiatry.* New York: W. W. Norton, 1956.

———. *Schizophrenia as a Human Process.* New York: W. W. Norton, 1962.

Super, D. S.; Starishevsky, R.; Matlin, N.; and Jordann, J. P. *Career Development: Self Concept Theory.* New York: College Entrance Examination Board, 1963.

Tanner, J. M. *Education and Physical Growth.* London: University of London Press, 1961.

———. *Growth at Adolescence.* 2d ed. Oxford: Blackwell, 1962.

Terman, L. M., with P. Buttenwieser, L. W. Ferguson, W. B. Johnson, and D. P. Wilson. *Psychological Factors in Marital Happiness.* New York: McGraw-Hill, 1938.

Terman, L. M., and Tyler, L. E. "Psychological Sex Differences," in L. Carmichael (ed.), *Manual of Child Psychology.* 2d ed. New York: Wiley, 1954.

Tuller, P. O. "Father Absence and Personality Development of Children in Sailor Families: A Preliminary Research Report." Part II in N. Anderson (ed.), *Studies of the Family.* Vol. 2. Göttingen: Vandenhoeck and Ruprecht, 1957.

Vaillant, G. E. "Theoretical Hierarchy of Adaptive Ego Mechanisms." *Archives General Psychiatry* 24 (1971): 107–18.

———. "Natural History of Male Psychological Health, II: Some Antecedents of Healthy Adult Adjustment." *Archives General Psychiatry* 31 (July 1974).

Vaillant, G. E., and McArthur, C. "Natural History of Male Psychological

Health, I: The Adult Life Cycle from 18–50." *Seminars in Psychiatry* 4, no. 4 (1972): 415–17.

Van Gennep, A. *The Rites of Passage.* Chicago: University of Chicago Press, 1960.

Walters, P. "Student Apathy," in G. B. Blaine and C. McArthur, *Emotional Problems of the Student.* New York: Appleton-Century-Crofts, 1961.

————. "Promiscuity in Adolescence." *American Journal of Orthopsychiatry* 35, no. 4 (1965).

Washburn, W. C. "The Effects of Physique and Intrafamily Tension on Self Concepts in Adolescent Males." *Journal of Consulting Psychology* 26 (1962).

Watson, J. D. *The Double Helix, a Personal Account of the Discovery of the Structure of DNA.* New York: Atheneum, 1968.

Wattenberg, W. W. *The Adolescent Years.* New York: Harcourt, Brace and World, 1955.

Weakland, John H. "The Double-Bind: Hypothesis of Schizophrenia and Three-Party Interaction," in D. Jackson (ed.), *The Etiology of Schizophrenia.* New York: Basic Books, 1962.

Wedge, B., ed. *Psychosocial Problems of College Men.* New Haven: Yale University Press, 1958.

Weinberg, G. *Society and the Healthy Homosexual.* New York: Doubleday Anchor Books, 1972.

West, J. *Plainville, U.S.A.* New York: Columbia University Press, 1945.

Wheelis, A. *Quest for Identity.* New York: W. W. Norton, 1958.

White, R. W. "Motivation Reconsidered: The Concept of Competence." *Psychological Review* 66 (1959).

————. "Competence and the Psychosexual Stages of Development," in *Nebraska Symposium on Motivation.* Lincoln: University of Nebraska Press, 1960.

————. "Ego and Reality in Psychoanalytic Theory." *Psychological Issues* 3, no. 3, Monograph II (1963a).

————, ed. *The Study of Lives.* New York: Atherton Press, 1963b.

————. *Lives in Progress.* 2d ed. New York: Holt, Rinehart and Winston, 1966.

White, R. W. *The Enterprise of Living: Growth and Organization in Personality.* New York: Holt, Rinehart and Winston, 1972.

Whiting, B. B., ed. *Six Cultures: Studies of Child Rearing.* New York: Wiley, 1963.

Whiting, J. W. M. *Becoming a Kwoma.* New Haven: Yale University Press, 1941.

Whiting, J. W. M., and Child, I. L. *Child Training and Personality: a Cross-Cultural Study.* New Haven: Yale University Press, 1953.

Whiting, J. W. M.; Kluckhohn, R.; and Anthony, A. "The Function of Male Initiation Ceremonies at Puberty," in E. Maccoby, T. Newcomb, and E. Hartley (eds.), *Readings in Social Psychology.* New York: Henry Holt, 1958.

Winch, F. R. *Mate Selection.* New York: Harper and Row, 1958.

Winnicott, D. W. *Collected Papers Through Pediatrics to Psychoanalysis.* London: Tavistock, 1953.

Wolfenstein, M. "Trends in Infant Care." *American Journal of Orthopsychiatry* 33 (1953).

Worchel, P., and Byrne, O. *Personality Change.* New York: Wiley, 1964.

Yankelovich, D. *The New Morality.* New York: McGraw-Hill, 1974.

Young, R. *Initiation Ceremonies.* New York: Bobbs-Merrill, 1965.

Zuk, G. H. "The Plasticity of the Physique from Early Adolescence Through Adulthood." *Journal of Genetic Psychology* 92 (1958).